TCP/IP ARCHITECTURE, DESIGN, AND IMPLEMENTATION IN LINUX

IEEE

TCP/IP ARCHITECTURE, DESIGN, AND IMPLEMENTATION IN LINUX

Sameer Seth
M. Ajaykumar Venkatesulu

A JOHN WILEY & SONS, INC., PUBLICATION

Library of Congress Cataloging-in-Publication Data is available.

ISBN 978-0470-14773-3

CONTENTS

For more than a decade, Linux has been the most popular choice for server technology, embedded systems, or research work in the networking domain. It slowly gained momentum beginning with the student community and slowly reaching researchers and the corporate world. Networking, when combined with Linux, gives birth to an innovative product line, be it in the high-end telecom sector, data centers, or embedded systems, and so on.

In 1996, I was introduced to Linux while doing my first assignment on TCP/IP socket programming. At that time, I had a very little knowledge about a server program using a unique port number to register itself with the system or a client program using the same port number to communicate with the server. I also had little knowledge of an IP address that is fed to the client program to identify the host. I then set myself to learn about how all that was made possible.

Much information needed to be explored at that time, such as system calls, protocols, Linux kernel, drivers, and kernel framework that supports the stack, and so on. Slowly, I explored the Linux kernel and user–land program interaction with that kernel by writing new system calls and kernel modules.

This learning process began with the *TCP/IP Illustrated, Volume 1* by the honorable Richard Stevens. But it continued to be really difficult to map the protocol with the implementation on Linux because there was so little documentation, and available books provided hardly any information. So, I decided to dive deep into the jungle of the huge source base to find out how the stack is implemented. Finally, I got hooked to the socket and VFS layer to understand how socket layer is linked to the VFS layer. Then slowly I was pointed to the TCP layer and the first routine that interfaces TCP protocol to send out data. Then the journey of documenting and experimenting with the TCP/IP stack began. When the documentation had grown big enough, the idea of making it available to the Linux community emerged. But writing a book was beyond my strength and it was too much work, requiring a lot of time and dedication. But I was determined to expose the complex topic to the Linux community to whatever extent I could even if it demanded many requirements. The absence of detailed, leveled documentation or a book that would have made the subject easier to understand, forced me to think about the topic. The idea of writing a book was supported when I received acceptance on the subject from IEEE Computer Society Press and John Wiley & Sons.

Working on the book along with office work became difficult so I searched for a co-author who would help cover some of the topics. After a long struggle, I convinced M. Ajaykumar Venkatesulu to be my co-author and work on a giant and most complex routing subsystem and QOS.

This text tries to cover almost all the aspects of TCP/IP stack and supporting kernel framework. The idea is to present the topic in a way that dilutes its complexity so that it can be easily understood. To understand TCP/IP implementation on any OS, we need to understand the kernel frameworks that support the stack. On Linux, these frameworks include VFS layer, socket framework, protocol layer, timers, memory management, interrupt handling, softIRQ, kernel threads, kernel synchronization mechanism, and so on. This is the kernel perspective of the stack. Apart from this, we also need to know the basics of the communication protocol and application interfaces (system calls) to open TCP communication sockets and the client–server program. This knowledge is helpful as a reference for experienced professionals and for students willing to learn the complex subject and contribute to the Linux community.

This book is written for the Linux kernel 2.4.20. The newest kernel version 2.6 does not have much variation as far as the TCP/IP stack is considered. Kernel version 2.4 is the most widely accepted kernel in the Linux world. Version 2.6 specific changes will be discussed in subsequent revisions of the book.

AUDIENCE

The book is targeted for large cross section of audience:

Researchers at Worldwide Premier Institutes. Researchers who work on various aspects of the TCP/IP stack find BSD the most suitable networking OS. But BSD is not a popular choice in the corporate world. So, the next most popular choice of researchers is the Linux OS and improvement of the TCP/IP stack performance on this OS. Networking is currently the most popular field for research because of growing usage and popularity of the Internet. Mostly, researchers prefer an OS with commercial viability that can run on cheap hardware.

Academia. Advanced academic degree projects, such as MS, M. Tech., B. Tech. and PG, are mostly done on Linux because it was the first UNIX-like OS available with fairly good documentation and stability. In the networking area, students usually choose Linux over TCP/IP for their project work. The project may require modifying the router or TCP performance, implementing some new TCP/IP RFC, network drivers, implementing secured IP layer, or improving scalability factor to handle network traffic.

Corporations. For the most part, the corporate world has widely accepted Linux as the base OS for networking products. Many companies are developing network products, such as IP security, QOS (class-based routing), developing routers, bandwidth management products, cluster servers and many more, which require modifying the TCP/IP stack or writing a new module altogether that fits into Linux TCP/IP stack somewhere. Linux is not only popular as an open system but is also a major choice for embedded products or real-time OS. These embedded products are mostly developed for networking domains such as routers, embedded web servers, web browsers, and so on.

Entrepreneurs. New ideas keep popping up which need to be turned into products. With the Internet gaining popularity, many ideas have been born to develop networking products. Linux is once again the most popular choice for development among entrepreneurs.

The Open Source Community. Because of the growing popularity of Linux and Internet technologies, many fresh college graduates or even software professionals want to contribute to Linux networking capabilities. Their goal is to make Linux more powerful, stable, secure, and full of network capabilities in order to meet corporate requirements in every possible way. Many professionals want to contribute to Linux networking capabilities but don't find enough time to get acquainted with its networking stack and the kernel framework.

Defense Organizations. There is a growing popularity of Linux as network OS in defense organizations with increasing military adoption of Linux IP security with some modifications for secured military network transactions.

All these audiences require a thorough knowledge of Linux TCP/IP stack and kernel framework for networking stacks. To understand TCP, IP, BSD sockets, firewall, IP security, IP forwarding, router network driver, complete knowledge of how networking stack implementation and design work is needed. If IP security or firewall implementation is wanted, then knowledge of how the packet is implemented in Linux, how and where packet is passed to the IP layer, how the IP processes the packets and adds headers, and finally how the IP passes the packet to the device driver for final transmission is needed. Similarly, implementation of the QOS or some modifications in the existing implementation is needed, knowledge of Linux routing table implementation, packet structure, packet scheduling and all related kernel frame work including network soft IRQs is required. So, anything and everything that requires modifying the Linux network stack or adding a new feature to the stack, requires complete knowledge of the design and implementation of Linux TCP/IP stack.

ORGANIZATION OF THIS BOOK

This book completely explains TCP/IP protocol, its design, and implementation in Linux. Basically, the book begins with simple client–server socket programs and ends with complex design and implementation of TCP/IP protocol in Linux. In between, we gradually explain the different aspects of socket programming and major TCP/IP-related algorithms. These are:

Linux Kernel and TCP/IP Application Interfaces: Chapter 1 covers the Linux kernel basics and we kick start with kernel interfaces (system calls) to use TCP/IP protocol stack for communication.

Protocols: Chapter 2 covers TCP/IP protocols and supporting protocols such as ARP and ICMP. We cover some of the major RFCs with illustrations to acquaint the reader with the protocols so that it will be easy to map Linux implementation on Linux in further chapters.

Sockets: Chapter 3 explains the implementation of BSD socket implementation in the Linux kernel. Here we discuss in detail how socket layer is hooked to VFS layer and how various protocols are hooked to BSD socket.

Kernel Implementation of Connection Setup: Chapter 4 explains the client–server application with the help of the C program. We explain the complete process of connection setup with the help of tcp dump output in different chapters. We cover kernel implementation of system calls used by application program to implement client–server interaction. We see how connections are accepted on the server side and at the same time, learn how the server program registers with the kernel to bind to a specific listening port.

Linux Implementation of Network Packet: Chapter 5 explains sk_buff which represents network packet on Linux. We explain important routines that manipulate sk_buff.

Movement of Packet Across the Layers: Chapter 6 covers the complete TCP/IP stack framework, showing how the packet is generated and trickles down the network stack until it is out of the system. Similarly we explain the complete path taken by a packet received from the device to reach the owning socket, covering complete kernel framework that implements TCP/IP stack on Linux.

TCP recv/send: Chapters 7 and 8 address TCP receive/send implementation and cover all the aspects related to TCP receiving and sending data. We also explain the TCP segmentation unit when an ICMP error (mss change for the route) is received by the TCP. There is a small description of how urgent data are processed.

TCP Socket Timers and Memory Management: The kernel keeps track of memory consumed by a connection at the socket layer so that a single-socket connection is not able to hog all the system memory because of a misbehaving application. We also try to collapse sequential buffers in the receive queue when the application is not reading enough fast and socket has exhausted its quota. This aspect of memory management is covered in Chapter 9. TCP is an event-driven protocol. TCP implements timers to track loss of data, to send delayed ACKs, to send out zero window probes, and so on. Chapter 10 addresses all these aspects.

TCP State Machine: Chapter 11 covers TCP core processing, such as reception of packets, sending ACKs, sliding window protocol, Nagle's algorithms, scheduling of delayed ACK's, processing of out-of-order segments, processing SACK, D-SACK, and so on. The tcp_opt object represents state machine implementation on Linux. Chapter 12 covers TCP congestion control algorithms implementation.

Netlink Sockets: User–land applications, such as netstat and iproute, and routing protocol daemons use special netlink sockets to update/read routes and configure QOS in the kernel. We cover netlink sockets in Chapter 13.

IP Layer and Routing Table Implementation: Chapter 14 covers implementation of routing table (FIB) on Linux. We also explain different aspects associated with routing, such as multipathing, policy routing, and so on. This chapter also explains the different kernel control paths that update kernel routing tables and route cache management.

IP QOS: IP in today's network is an advanced topic and is used for different services in the public network. Linux implements QOS very cleanly and we discuss PFIFO and CBQ queuing discipline implementation in Chapter 15.

Netfilter Framework: Linux provides extensions to the TCP/IP stack by way of the netfilter framework. These extensions can be firewall, masquerading, IP security, and so on. Chapter 16 covers netfilter hooks at different layers in the stack and also netfilter implementation.

SoftIRQ Implementation for Scalability: Network frames are received in the kernel memory in the interrupt handler code but complete processing of the packets can't be done in the interrupt handler. Linux associates softIRQ, one each for reception and transmission of packets for processing of packets. Chapter 17 explains net softIRQ framework with the help of illustrations. This chapter completely explains the high scalability of Linux on SMP architecture in handling network traffic.

Link Layer and DMA Ring Buffers: Chapter 18 covers link layer(device driver) processing of packets. Design and working of DMA ring buffer for reception and transmission are also addressed and are explained with the help of a device driver and interrupt routines for a real device.

Debug TCP/IP Stack: Debugging the TCP/IP stack is discussed in Chapter 19. The lkcd (linux kernel crash dump) debugger is used to illustrate the debugging technique, peeking into different kernel data-structures associated with TCP/IP stack.

LEVEL OF DISCRIPTION

As outlined here, we have touched upon critical portions of the implementation that are required to understand core TCP/IP stack and kernel framework. Each chapter begins with a chapter outline and ends with a summary that highlights important points. Source-level explanations with diagrams are provided where ever required. Important routines are explained line-by-line. Code snippets are provided for all those routines with line numbers and files of code snippet. Sometimes routines are so big that they are split into different code snippets. Routines that are called from the main routines are explained in different sections. If the called routine is a couple of lines long, there is no separate section for those routines. Line number and code-snippet number (cs-) are provided with the explanation to assist understanding. When the routines are very big in size, notification is provided at the beginning of the section stating, *see cs ••.••, unless mentioned*; this means that where ever line numbers are mentioned, we need to see the code snippet mentioned at the start of the section.

In the explanation if we encounter some concept that is already explained in some other section, a cross reference to that section is provided, as *see Section ••. ••*. Cross references are provided because the subject is interrelated, for example while explaining queuing of incoming TCP packet, we refer to sockets receive buffer. If we have exhausted the receive socket buffer, we need to call routines to collapse receive queue to make space for the new TCP data segment. For this we may need to refer to a section from the TCP memory management chapter. We have explained major data structures with significance separately. Where ever that has not been done, fields of those data-structures are explained as and when they appear in the routines.

Examples and illustrations are provided where ever it is required to make subject easier to understand. For example, diagrams to link various kernel data structures are drawn to illustrate connection requests in the SYN queue. Then we illustrate shifting of connection requests from SYN queue to accept queue when a three-way handshake is over with the help of diagrams. All these illustrations assist in visualizing the complex data structures and scenarios.

SAMEER SETH

Bangalore, India
September 2008

ACKNOWLEDGMENTS

For me, this is the heaviest section of the book that carries the most weight. First of all, I'm very thankful to my family for being so supportive and patient when I was working on the title, with little time left for them. My wife, Sumam, provided selfless support to the work right from day one. She provided me with confidence to convert my hard work into a book on the day she provided me with the list of publishers. When submitting my book proposal, only 20% of the work was done and that too was not organized.

I thank my co-author, M. Ajaykumar Venkatesulu, who agreed to join hands with me at the much-needed hour. His commitment eased the load on my shoulders and he worked very hard with all dedication to make this possible. He had a really tough time setting up QOS on Linux, with a couple of Linux boxes, and modifying the kernel for his illustrations.

I'd like to thank the very first person at the IEEE Computer Society with whom I interfaced, Deborah Plummer, who worked on the proposal until it was finished. She helped me in many ways to understand the publication process and was very patient all through, clarifying my doubts. IEEE Staffers, Janet Wilson and Dante David, were so nice and prompt throughout the review process. Even a small communication gap caused serious concerns because this was the first time I was working on such a big project. But Janet and Dante were patient and always prompt in their replies to make sure that all my concerns were addressed. I was introduced to Lisa Van Horn from Wiley much later, when the book had entered the production phase. It is a great experience working with her because she spent time educating me at every point. At times I would be very irritating to her by asking silly doubts but she tackled them all with grace. She has worked very hard editing the book because there were grammatical corrections in almost every line. Through the production process, she was very helpful, cooperative, and prompt in the same way.

There are a few names without which this book would look incomplete. I thank Richard McDougall, the respectable author of *Solaris Internals,* for time spent educating me on the publication process. His inputs helped me achieve the most from my hard work. The respectable senior engineer from SGI and owner of the dwarf extract utility for lkcd, Cliff Wickman, is owed thanks for without him this book would have looked quite dry. He provided a tool to generate a kernel-type database (kerntypes) because the basic lkcd utility does not come with all the stubs for kernel data-structures in kerntypes. Without this tool, the debug chapter would not have been possible. He not only provided the tool but also helped get the kernel-type database built for the kernel 2.4 when the tool was compatible only with kernel 2.6.

S. S.

Writing or co-authoring a book was never even in my wildest dreams. The opportunity came by chance and then it became my choice. God has been kind enough to give me such an amazing opportunity. I have a couple of people to thank with whom my words fall short. First of all I would like to thank the author of the book who had faith in me that I could write on this subject. He gave me a lot of trust when he gave me an opportunity to work on this book. It was solely his brainchild which he shared with me selflessly. He gave me guidance whenever I faced any difficulty in any subject matter. His valuable suggestions and most importantly his inspirations have made it possible for me to finish this assignment.

I thank my family for all their support: My father who stood beside me through all the odds and evens of life so that I could concentrate on this project; my newly wedded wife, Priyanka, who never complained when I had less or sometimes no time left for her; and lastly, my brother-in-law Balaji who has been a great source of inspiration in my life.

Last but not least, I thank Deborah Plummer, Janet Wilson, and Dante David from IEEE for being so cooperative and nice.

The book is not a result of any inspiration but the need of the day. When you have the strong desire to achieve something, then the whole of creation conspires to accomplish your goal.

M. A. V.

1

INTRODUCTION

Internetworking with Linux has been the most popular choice of developers. Not only in the server world where Linux has made its mark but also in the small embedded network OS market, Linux is the most popular choice. All this requires an understanding of the TCP/IP code base. Some products require implementation of firewall, and others require implementation of IPSec. There are products that require modifications in the TCP connection code for load balancing in a clustered environment. Some products require improving scalability on SMP machines. Most talked about is the embedded world, where networking is most popular. Real-time embedded products have very specific requirements and need huge modifications to the stack as far as buffer management is concerned or for performance reasons. All these require a complete understanding of stack implementation and the supporting framework.

As mentioned above, some of the embedded networking products require a minimum of the code to be complied because of the memory requirements. This requirement involves knowledge of source code organization in the Linux source distribution. Once we know how the code is distributed, it becomes easier to find out the relevant code in which we are interested.

Mostly all the networking application work on very basic client–server technology. The server is listening on a well-known port for connection requests while the client is sending out connection request to the server. Many complex arrangements are made for security reasons or sometimes for load balancing to the client–server technology. But the basic implementation is a simple client–server program in which the client and server talk to each other. For example, telnet or

TCP/IP Architecture, Design, and Implementation in Linux. By S. Seth and M. A. Venkatesulu
Copyright © 2008 the IEEE Computer Society

ftp services are accessed through the inet program which hides all the details of services. There are many tunable parameters available to tune your TCP/IP connections. These can be used to best tune the connection without disturbing overall system wide tuning.

Most of the network applications are written to exchange data. Once a connection is established, either (a) the client sends data to the server or (b) data flow in the opposite direction or may flow in both directions. There are different ways to send and receive data over the connection. These different techniques may differ in the way that application blocks once the socket connection either receive or send data.

In the entire book we discuss only TCP and no other transport protocol. So, we need to understand the TCP connection process. TCP is a connection-oriented protocol that has a set process for initializing connections, and similarly it has a set process for closing connection cleanly. TCP maintains state for the connection because of handshakes during connection initiation and closure processes. We need to understand the TCP states to completely understand the TCP connection process.

In this chapter we will present an overview of how the TCP/IP protocol stack is implemented on Linux. We need to understand the Linux operating system, including the process, the threads, the system call, and the kernel synchronization mechanism. All these topics are covered though not in great detail. We also need to understand the application programming interface that uses a TCP/IP protocol stack for data transmission, which is discussed. We discuss socket options with kernel implementation. Finally, we discuss the TCP state, which covers a three-way handshake for opening connection and a four-way handshake for connection closure.

1.1   OVERVIEW OF TCP/IP STACK

Let's see how the TCP/IP stack is implemented on Linux. First we just need to understand the network buffer that represents the packet on Linux. *sk_buff* represents the packet structure on Linux (see Fig. 1.1). *sk_buff* carries all the required information related to the packet along with a pointer to the route for the packet. *head*, *data*, *tail*, and *end* point to the start of the data block, actual start of data, end

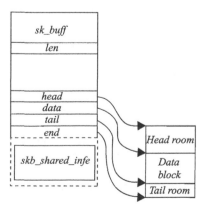

Figure 1.1. Network buffer, *sk_buff*.

of data, and end of data block, respectively. *skb_shared_info* object is attached at the end of the *sk_buff* header which keeps additional information about paged data area. The actual packet is contained in the data block and is manipulated by data & tail pointers. This buffer is used everywhere in the networking code as well as network drivers. Details are discussed in Chapter 5.

Now we will have a look at how the stack is implemented in Linux. We will first start with down-the-stack processing of the packet from the socket layer to the driver layer and then move up the stack. We will take an example of sending TCP data down the stack. In general, more or less the same stack is used for other transport protocols also, but we will restrict our discussion to TCP only.

1.1.1 Moving Down the Stack

When an application wants to write data over the TCP socket, the kernel reaches the socket through VFS (see Fig. 1.2). *inode* for the file of the type socket contains a socket object, which is the starting point for the networking stack (see Section 3.2 for more details). The *socket* object has a pointer to a set of operations specific to the socket type pointed to by field *ops*. Object *proto_ops* has a pointer to socket-specific operations. In our case, the socket is of type INET, so *send* systemcall ends up calling *inet_sendmsg()* inside kernel via VFS. The next step is to call a protocol-specific send routine because there may be different protocols registered under INET socket (see Section 3.1). In our case, transport later is TCP, so *inet_sendmsg()* calls a protocol-specific send operation. The protocol-specific socket is represented by a sock object pointed to by the *sk* field of the *socket* object. A protocol-specific set of operation is maintained by a *proto* object pointed to by *prot* field of *sock* object. *inet_sendmsg()* calls a protocol-specific send routine, which is *tcp_sendmsg()*.

In *tcp_sendmsg()*, user data are given to a TCP segmentation unit. The segmentation unit breaks big chunks of user data into small blocks and copies each small block to *sk_buff*. These sk_buffs are copied to the socket's send buffer, and then the TCP state machine is consulted to transmit data from socket send buffer. If the TCP state machine does not allow sending new data because of any reasons, we return. In such a case, data will be transmitted later by a TCP machine on some event which is discussed in Section 11.3.11.

If the TCP state machine is able to transmit *sk_buff*, it sends a segment to the IP layer for further processing. In the case of TCP, *sk→tp→af_specific→queue_xmit* is called, which points to *ip_queue_xmit()*. This routine builds an IP header and takes an IP datagram through the firewall policy. If the policy allows, an IP layer checks if NAT/Masquerading needs to be applied to the outgoing packet. If so, a packet is processed and is finally given to the device for final transmission by a call to *dev_queue_xmit()*. Device refers to a network interface, which is represented by *net_device* object. At this point, the Linux stack implements QOS. Queuing disciplines are implemented at the device level.

Packet (*sk_buff*) is queued to the device according to their priority levels and queuing discipline. Next is to dequeue the packet from the device queue, which is done just after queuing *sk_buff*. The queued packet may be transmitted here, depending on the bandwidth for the packet's priority. If so, the link layer header is prepended to the packet, and the device-specific hard transmit routine is called to transmit the frame. If we are unable to transmit the frame, the packet is requeued

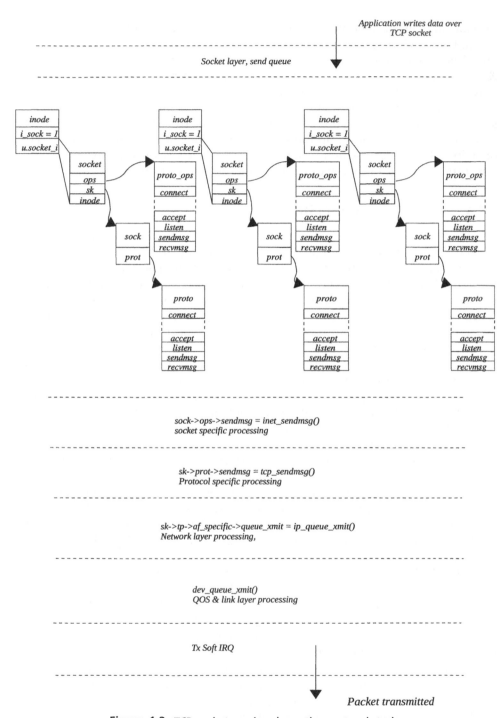

Figure 1.2. TCP packet moving down the protocol stack.

on the device queue and Tx softIRQ is raised on the CPU adding device to the CPU's transmit queue. Later on when the TX interrupt is processed, frames are dequeued from the device queue and transmitted.

1.1.2 Moving Up the Stack

Refer to Fig. 1.3 for the flow of packet up the stack. We start with the reception of packets at the network interface. Interrupt is generated once the packet is completely DMAed on driver's Rx ring buffer (for details see Section 18.5). In the interrupt handler, we just remove the frame from the ring buffer and queue it on CPU's input queue. By CPU I we mean the CPU that is interrupted. It is clear at this point that there is per CPU input queue. Once the packet is queued on the CPU's input queue, Rx NET softIRQ is raised for the CPU by call to *netif_rx()*. Once again, softIRQ's are raised and processed per CPU.

Later when Rx softIRQ is processed, packets are de-queued from CPU's receive queue and processed one-by-one. The packet is processed completely until its destination here, which means that the TCP data packet is processed until the TCP data segment is queued on the socket's receive queue. Let's see how is this processing done at various protocol layers.

netif_receive_skb() is called to process each packet in Rx softIRQ. The first step is to determine the Internet protocol family to which a packet belongs. This is also known as packet protocol switching. We send the packet to the raw socket in case any raw socket is opened for the device. Once the protocol family is identified, which in our case is IP, we call the protocol handler routine. For IP, this is the *ip_rcv()* routine. *ip_rcv()* tries to de-NAT or de-masquerade the packet at this point, if required. The routing decisions are made on the packet. If it needs to be delivered locally, the packet is passed through firewall policies configured for the locally acceptable IP packets. If everything is OK, *ip_local_deliver_finish()* is called to find the next protocol layer for the packet.

ip_local_deliver_finish() implements INET protocol switching code. Once we identify the INET protocol, its handler is called to further process the IP datagram. The IP datagram may belong to ICMP, UDP, and TCP.

Since our discussion is limited to TCP, the protocol handler is *tcp_v4_rcv()*. The very first job of the TCP handler is to find out socket for the TCP packet. This may be a new open request for the listening socket or may be another packet for the established socket. So here, various hash tables are looked into. If the packet belongs to the established socket, the TCP engine processes the TCP segment. If the TCP segment contains in-sequence data, it is queued on the socket's receive queue. If there are any data to be sent, they is sent along with the the ACK for the data arrived here. Finally, when application issues read over the TCP socket, the kernel processes the request by providing data from the socket's receive queue.

The Linux stack maps to the OSI networking model (see Fig. 1.4).

1.2 SOURCE CODE ORGANIZATION FOR LINUX 2.4.20

Figure 1.5 shows the kernel source tree.

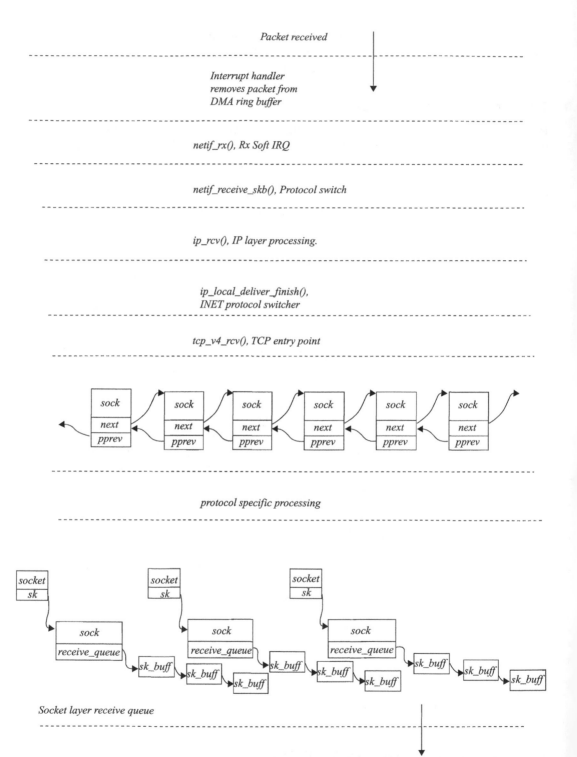

Figure 1.3. TCP packet moving up the stack.

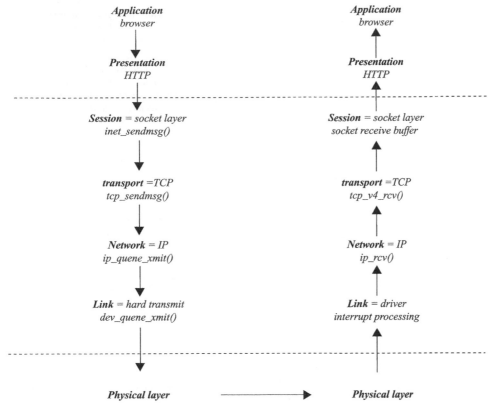

Figure 1.4. Linux network stack and OSI model.

1.2.1 Source Code Organization for Networking Code

Figure 1.6 shows the kernel networking source tree.

1.3 TCP/IP STACK AND KERNEL CONTROL PATHS

In this section we will see how TCP data are being processed by the Linux kernel. In totality, we will see different *kernel control paths* and *processor context* that are involved in packet processing through the kernel. When the process writes data over the TCP socket, it issues write/send system calls (see Fig. 1.7). The system call takes the process from the user land to the kernel, and now the kernel executes on behalf of the process as shown by the solid gray line. Let's determine the different points in the kernel where the kernel thread sending TCP data on behalf of the process preempts itself.

Kernel Control Path 1. In this kernel control path, the kernel thread processes TCP data through the complete TCP/IP stack and returns only after transmitting data from the physical interface.

Kernel Control Path 2. This kernel control path processes data through TCP/IP stack but fails to transmit data because the device lock could not be obtained. In

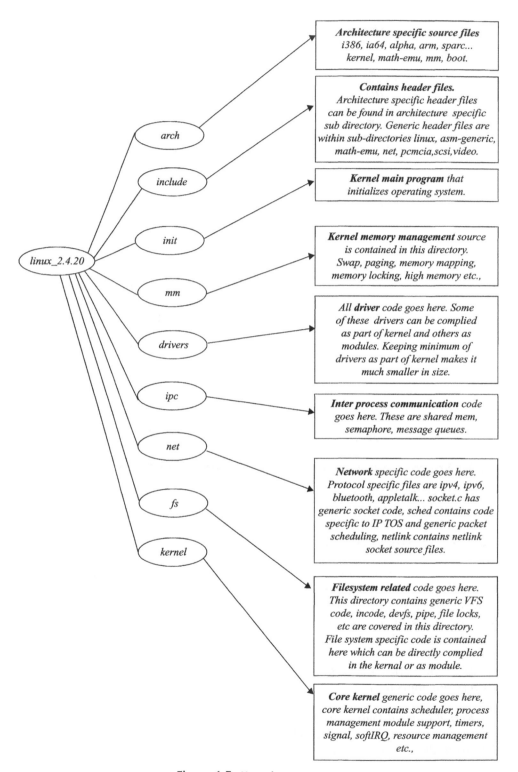

Figure 1.5. Kernel source tree.

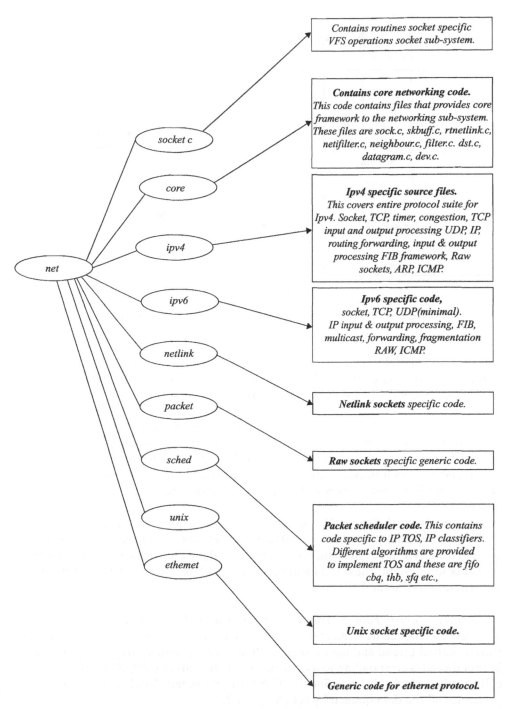

Figure 1.6. Kernel networking source tree.

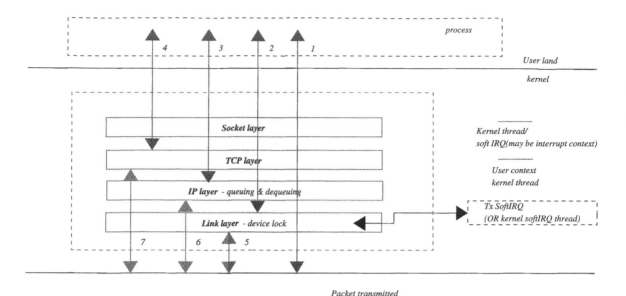

Figure 1.7 Packet transmission via different kernel control paths.

this case, the kernel thread returns after raising Tx softIRQ. SoftIRQ processing is deferred to some later point of time which will transmit data queued up on the device. See Section 17.1 for details on softIRQ processing.

Kernel Control Path 3. This kernel control path processes data through the TCP layer but is not able to take it further because the QOS policy is not allowing further transmission of data. It may happen that either someone else is processing the queue on which packet is queued or the quota for queue is over. In the later case, a timer is installed which will process the queue later.

Kernel Control Path 4. This kernel control path processes data through the TCP layer but cannot proceed any further and returns from here. The reason may be that the TCP state machine or congestion algorithm does not allow further transmission of data. These data will be processed later by the TCP state machine on generation of some TCP event.

Kernel Control Path 5. This kernel control path may execute in interrupt context or kernel context. Kernel context may come from softIRQ daemon, which runs as kernel thread and has no user context. Kernel context may also come from kernel thread corresponding to user process which enables softIRQ on the CPU by call to *spin_unlock_bh()*. See Section 17.6 for more detail. This kernel control path processes all the data queued by control path 2.

Kernel Control Path 6. This kernel control path executes as a high-priority tasklet that is part of softIRQ. This may also be executed in interrupt context or kernel context as discussed above. This processes data queued by control path 3.

Kernel Control Path 7. This kernel control path executes as softIRQ when incoming TCP packet is being processed. When a packet is received, it is processed

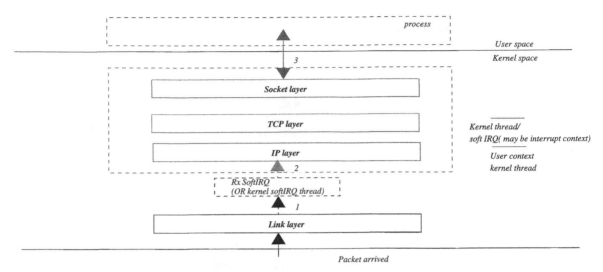

Figure 1.8. Packet reception and different kernel control paths.

by Rx softIRQ. When a TCP packet is processed in softIRQ, it may generate an event causing transmission of pending data in the send queue. This kernel control path transmits data that are queued by control path 4.

On the reception side, the packet is processed in two steps (see Fig. 1.8). An interrupt handler plucks received a packet from the DMA ring buffer and queues it on the CPU-specific input queue and raises Rx softIRQ. Rx softIRQ is processed at some later point of time in interrupt context or by softIRQ daemon. The TCP data packet is processed completely by Rx softIRQ until it is queued on the socket's receive queue or is eaten up by the application. The TCP ACK packet is processed by a TCP state machine, and softIRQ returns only after action is taken on the events generated by the incoming ACK.

1.4 LINUX KERNEL UNTIL VERSION 2.4 IS NON-PREEMPTIBLE

Let's define the term *preemptive* first and then we will move ahead with its effect on the Linux kernel. Preemption in general means that the current execution context can be forced to give away CPU for some other execution context under certain conditions. Now we will say that what is so great about it is that it is happening on any multitasking OS. On a multitasking OS, many user land processes run on the CPU one at a time. These processes are assigned quota and continue to occupy CPU until they have exhausted their quota. Once the quota for the currently running process is over, it is replaced by some other runnable process on the CPU even if the former was already executing by the kernel scheduler. So, we can say that the process was preempted here. Very true, the user land process is preempted to fairly give other processes a chance to run on the CPU. We are not discussing scheduling with respect to real-time processes and are discussing only normal priority processes that are scheduled based on a round-robin scheduling policy. This way kernel preempts the user land process.

What we would like to know in this section is very different from what has been discussed so far. We want to know how a kernel can be preemptive. Let's suppose

```
arch/i386/kernel/entry.S

256 ENTRY(ret_from_intr)
257     GET_CURRENT(%ebx)
258 ret_from_exception:
259     movl EFLAGS(%esp),%eax        # mix EFLAGS and CS
260     movb CS(%esp),%al
261     testl $(VM_MASK | 3),%eax     # return to VM86 mode or non-supervisor?
262     jne ret_from_sys_call
263     jmp restore_all
264
265     ALIGN
266 reschedule:
267     call SYMBOL_NAME(schedule)    # test
268     jmp ret_from_sys_call
```

cs 1.1. Return from interrupt.

that some kernel control path is being executed on the CPU and it is looping into infinite loop by mistake. Can a kernel preempt itself to get out of the infinite loop and give a CPU to some other runnable process. (*Note:* I'm taking an example of infinite loop inside the kernel just to explain the term preemption, but the intent here is very different. Normally, a kernel code does not end up in this situation). Kernel control path gives away CPU to other burnable process by calling scheduler. We must first know what event causes a running process to preempt. This is done by the timer interrupt which is raised on the CPU at some definite time interval and is nonmaskable. This interrupt does all the necessary calculation determine the duration of the current execution context on the CPU. If it has expired its quota, it sets a 'scheduling needed' flag for the process. While returning from the interrupt, this flag is checked but only if we were interrupted in the user mode (which essentially means that the CPU was executing user land code when the timer interrupt occurred).

Control is passed to an assembly code at line 256 in cs 1.1 when we are returning from the interrupt. Line 257 first gets the pointer to a current process (kernel thread corresponding to the user land process) in ebx%. At line 259, we get EFLAGS for the current process from the stack pointer (%esp) and save this to eax%. At line 260, we get a code segment byte from the stack pointer and save it as a byte in eax%. At line 261, we check if the execution mode was within the kernel or user land at the time when the CPU was interrupted. This can be verified from the code segment that is copied to eax% at line 260. If the CPU was executing in the kernel, we jump to *restore_all* at line 263. restore_all will switch to the execution context within the kernel by loading register values saved at the stack and will start executing from where it was interrupted. If we were interrupted in the user land, control is passed to *ret_from_sys_call. re_from_sys_call* does lots of checks; for example, if there is a pending signal for the current process, reschedule is needed, and so on, and takes appropriate action. If the current process has not consumed its time slice, it will continue to execute in the user land; otherwise, some other runnable process will be given the CPU.

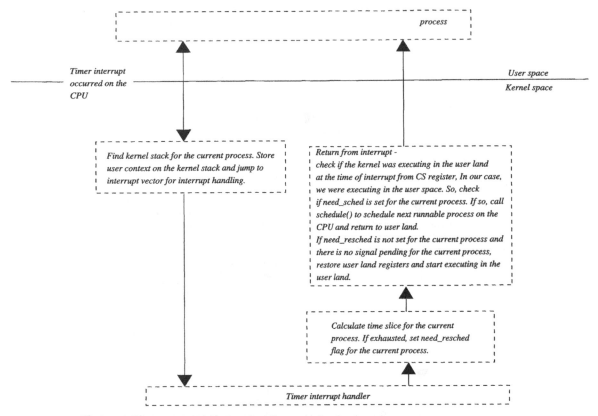

Figure 1.9a. Interrupt happened while executing in the user space.

As shown in Fig. 1.9a, we switch to kernel mode to handle interrupts. We have shown timer interrupt in particular, but it may also happen that some other interrupt may also cause the current user process to give away CPU to some other process. For example, network interrupt may cause some process to wake up that is waiting for data over the connection. Since I/O intensive processes always have a higher priority over the CPU intensive processes, network interrupt carrying data may cause current process to give CPU to the process waiting for I/O over this connection. In the case where the current process has not consumed its time slice, it will continue to run on the CPU in case it has not received any kill signal.

Figure 1.9b shows that when a timer interrupt happens with CPU executing in the kernel, control is passed to the interrupted kernel path that was being executed at the time of interrupt. This allows the kernel to complete its execution before it can return to the user space. This design makes sure that the kernel will continue to run unless it kernel gives away CPU (by calling schedule()). Nothing can force kernel to give way CPU for any thing else other than interrupts/exceptions. The simple reason for this is data consistency, and this causes the Linux kernel to be non-preemptible. For example, if by mistake any buggy driver causes a kernel to execute an infinite loop, the single CPU system will be frozen forever.

In short, the Linux kernel 2.4 and below are not designed for real-time requirements as there may be huge latencies introduced because of a non-preemptive

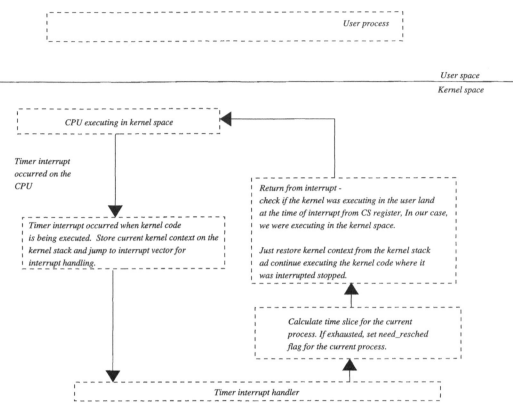

Figure 1.9b. Interrupt happened while executing in the kernel space.

kernel. An attempt is made to make Linux kernel 2.6 onwards preemptible, though not completely. We will see this in the next revision of the book.

1.4.1 System Call on Linux

In this section we will learn implementation of system call on Linux system running on Intel X86 architecture. Any Unix system implements a system call so that user-level application programs can request kernel services. Let's take the simple example of an open system call. When an application wants to open a file for read and write, the very first step is to issue an open system call. Just like regular files, Pipe, fifo, socket, device, and so on, are also treated as special files on the Unix systems and will use an open system call for further I/O.

Why do we need kernel services to open a file? This is required because file-system-specific information is maintained in the kernel. File-system-specific data structures are maintained in the kernel and is accessed only in the processor privileged mode; the reason for this is consistency and uninterrupted execution. Every care is taken inside the kernel to maintain data consistency by very careful programming where an execution of code can be made uninterrupted by blocking maskable interrupts. Also, kernel is non-preemptive. So we are assured that even if the kernel is interrupted by some high-priority interrupt, the processor returns its control to the point in the kernel where it left. The kernel control path can itself give away

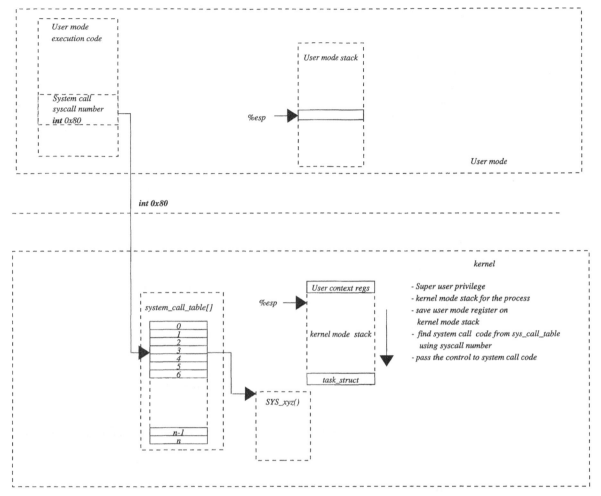

Figure 1.10. System call implementation on Linux.

CPU, and no one can force it to preempt. One of the most important reasons for a file system to be inside the kernel is that it is not an independent subsystem. The file system code has to interact with other subsystems such as virtual memory, network, device controllers, paging, and scheduling; all these subsystems cannot afford to run in the user land because of the reason mentioned above.

So, for execution of the system, a call takes place inside the kernel (see Fig. 1.10). The processor has to switch from user mode to privileged mode to access kernel code and data structure. This is done by software interrupt 0x80, which is generated by the open library routine. The system call number is loaded in *eax*, and arguments are loaded on *ebx*, *ecx*, *edx*, registers. The processor determines kernel stack for the process from by loading ss and eps registers. The user context is saved on the stack by the processor control unit. Once this is done, control is passed to the system call handler.

The system call handler looks into the system call table *sys_call_table*, which indexes system call handling routine vectors based on system call number. Control

```
include/asm-i386/unistd.h

 8 #define __NR_exit          1
 9 #define __NR_fork          2
10 #define __NR_read          3
11 #define __NR_write         4
12 #define __NR_open          5
13 #define __NR_close         6
14 #define __NR_waitpid       7
15 #define __NR_creat         8
.....
```

Figure 1.11 . System-call-associated number.

```
arch/i386/kernel/entry.S
.data
ENTRY(sys_call_table)
    .long SYMBOL_NAME(sys_ni_syscall)    /* 0 - old "setup()" system ca     .long SYMBOL_NAME(sys_exit)
    .long SYMBOL_NAME(sys_fork)
    .long SYMBOL_NAME(sys_read)
    .long SYMBOL_NAME(sys_write)
    .long SYMBOL_NAME(sys_open)          /* 5 */
.....
```

Figure 1.12. System call table in the kernel.

is passed to the system-call-specific routine; and after execution of system call, the return value is stored in *eax*.

1.4.2 Adding New System Call

Let's see how we can we add a new system call to the system. To add a new system call, a new number is associated with the system call, and the system-call-specific handler should register with the system. System call numbers are listed in *include/ asm-i386/unistd.h* file as macro __NR_*sys*, where *sys* is the name of the system call (see Fig. 1.11). In this file we need to add one more line for the new system call.

The next step is to write system call routine in appropriate file in the available in kernel source tree. For example if the system call is specific to scheduling, it should be added to *kernel/sys.c*. Conventionally, the name of the routine should start with sys_. Once a system call number and system-call-specific routine are added to a kernel source, we need to add the system call routine to the system call table by using macro SYMBOL_NAME(). A new line should be added to file *arch/ i386/kernel/entry.S* (see Fig. 1.12). The line for the new system call should be added exactly to the sys_call_table at the line number matching the system call number. So, it is always better that a system call number for the new system call should be the next available number, and the entry for this system call should come at the end of the *sys_call_table* table. The kernel is compiled and a new kernel is placed in the correct location.

How do we access the new system call from application program. So, we can use syscall() or syscall*() system calls to invoke our system call. To syscall(), we

```
/usr/include/asm/unistd.h

289 #define _syscall1(type,name,type1,arg1) \
290 type name(type1 arg1) \
291 { \
292 long __res; \
293 __asm__ volatile ("int $0x80" \
294     : "=a" (__res) \
295     : "0" (__NR_##name),"b" ((long)(arg1))); \
296 __syscall_return(type,__res); \
297 }
```

Figure 1.13. Implementation of syscall1.

need to pass the system call number corresponding to the new system call registered. If we use syscall() interface, we can't pass any arguments to our system call. If our system call takes one argument, we can use syscall1(), for two arguments we can use syscall2(), and so on; we can pass four arguments using these interfaces.

Let's see how syscall1 is implemented (see Fig. 1.13). This is implemented as a macro in */usr/include/asm/unistd.h*. It can take one argument arg1. The macro breaks into an inline assembly code that generates software interrupt int 0x80 at line 293. Line 294 indicates that the result needs to be stored in *eax*%. There are two inputs: eax% contains a system call number that is combined as (__NR_##name) at line 294, and ebx% contains the value of the first argument for the systemcall.

1.5 LINUX PROCESS AND THREAD

Each user land process has an associated task_struct object associated with it in the kernel. The process has two modes, *user* and *kernel*. The user land context is different from the kernel context, where each one has different code, data, and stack segment registers. Each process has user mode and kernel mode stack. The kernel mode stack is an 8 K memory block, which has *task_struct* object at the end of the stack (see Fig. 1.14). The application runs in user mode and uses a user mode stack until it makes a system call when it switches from user mode to kernel mode where it starts using kernel mode. See Section 1.4.1 for more details.

Each process has a unique process ID by which it is identified in the system. *task_struct* object contains the entire information about the process, including hardware context. Some of this process-specific information is file system information, file table, signal handling, memory management, and so on. Each process has a kernel level thread associated with it which is seen by the scheduler as scheduling entity. This thread is represented by *task_struct* object. The kernel maintains a doubly linked link list of *task_object* corresponding to all runable processes in the system.

1.5.1 *fork()*

New processes can be created by calling *fork()*. It inherits all the property of the parent process and shares VM, open files, and so on. Initially, user stacks for child and parent are shared; but as the stack grows for the child, it gets its own copy of

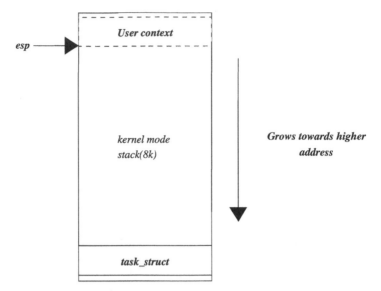

Figure 1.14. Kernel mode stack for the process.

the stack via a COW (copy-on-write) mechanism. Child created by fork has separate *task_struct* object and different kernel mode stack. Fork internally uses a clone to create a new process. The exec*() family of system calls is used to replace an existing process with a new process.

1.5.2 Thread

A thread on Linux can be user level or kernel level. User level threads are ones that are scheduled in the user land by libraries. The kernel has no idea about these threads, and there is only one kernel thread for all the threads which corresponds to the process which has created these threads. Kernel level threads are much like Linux processes. These are also called lightweight processes (LWPs). Each thread created by the process has a corresponding kernel level thread and is treated as a scheduling identity by the kernel (see Fig. 1.15). Each thread is scheduled irrespective of every other thread for the process. So, there is much better control as far as a blocking system call is concerned. The only thing that differentiates it from a normal process is its lightweight.

Threads share virtual memory, signals, and open files with its parent. But each of them has separate process IDs. A clone system call can be used to create LWPs for the process. Clone flags to create LWPs are

- CLONE_VM
- CLONE_FS
- CLONE_FILES
- CLONE_SIGHAND
- CLONE_THREAD

The pthread library creates kernel threads for the process. LWPs created by using a clone systemcall with the above flags have separate process IDs. The option

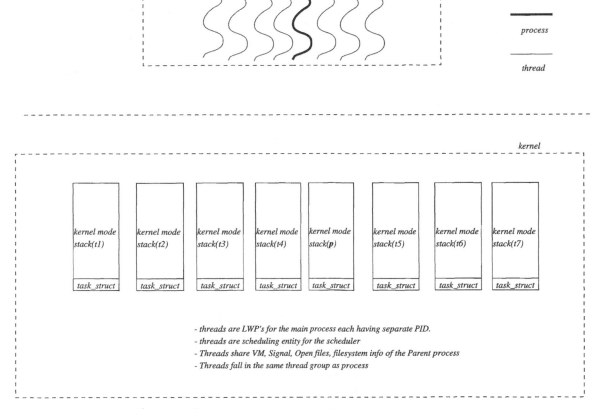

Figure 1.15. Process, LWPs, and kernel thread.

m of *ps* command can show all the threads corresponding to the process. In one example, I creates a program to spawn kernel level threads using *pthread_create()*. The ps command is used to display all the threads for the process as shown in Fig. 1.16.

1.5.3 Kernel Threads

In this section we will discuss the threads that are created inside the kernel and not by user land processes. Kernel threads are the same as the one created by the user land applications in the way they both use a clone kernel interface and both have a separate kernel mode stack. Kernel threads are created by making a call to *kernel_thread()*. Kernel threads have no user context because they are not associated with any user process. A kernel thread executes in a user kernel address space and does not have an address space of its own, unlike a user process. A kernel thread is not interrupted by any one once it starts executing. It can yield CPU by itself by going to sleep. These threads are very much visible using a *ps* command and can be recognized by the name because they start with a *k*—for example, *ksoftirqd*, *kflushd*, and so on. These threads either wake up on expiry of the timer by

```
[root@moksha root]$ ps -aejlcm | grep thread

F S  UID  PID  PPID PGID  SID  CLS  PRI  ADDR   SZ   WCHAN   TTY    TIME      CMD
0 S   0   3028 2708 3028  2708   -   24     -   12639  schedu  pts/1  00:00:00  thread-p
1 S   0   3029 3028 3028  2708   -   24     -   12639  schedu  pts/1  00:00:00  thread-p
1 S   0   3030 3028 3028  2708   -   24     -   12639  schedu  pts/1  00:00:00  thread-p
1 S   0   3062 3028 3028  2708   -   24     -   12639  schedu  pts/1  00:00:00  thread-p
1 S   0   3072 3028 3028  2708   -   24     -   12639  schedu  pts/1  00:00:00  thread-p
1 S   0   3073 3028 3028  2708   -   24     -   12639  schedu  pts/1  00:00:00  thread-p
1 S   0   3076 3028 3028  2708   -   24     -   12639  schedu  pts/1  00:00:00  thread-p
```

Figure 1.16. ps output showing process and associated threads (LWPs) created using a clone interface.

```
kernel/softirq.c

398 static __init int spawn_ksoftirqd(void)
399 {
400     int cpu;
401
402     for (cpu = 0; cpu < smp_num_cpus; cpu++) {
403         if (kernel_thread(ksoftirqd, (void *) (long) cpu,
404                 CLONE_FS | CLONE_FILES | CLONE_SIGNAL) < 0)
405             printk("spawn_ksoftirqd() failed for cpu %d\n", cpu);
406         else {
407             while (!ksoftirqd_task(cpu_logical_map(cpu)))
408                 yield();
409         }
410     }
411
412     return 0;
413 }
```

cs 1.2. spwan_ksoftirqd().

themselves or are woken up by some other thread inside the kernel and are scheduled by the kernel as usual.

Let's take an example of *ksoftirqd* kernel thread to illustrate kernel threads. Soft IRQ are also processed by kernel daemons in case there is a lot to be processed by softIRQs; this is mostly true in the case of network packet processing. Softirq daemons are created per CPU in routine *spwan_ksoftirqd()* (see cs 1.2).

kernel_thread() is called in a loop 402–410 to create one kernel thread per CPU. The routine that needs to be executed as a kernel thread is passed as a first argument to *kernel_thread()*; that is, *ksoftirqd* and second argument is CPU ID. Let's see why we pass CPU ID when we are creating a kernel thread. The name of the kernel thread is stored in current→comm. Since softirq daemons are per CPU, the name of each daemon contains a CPU number (see cs 1.3, line 375). This name of

FS	LTD	PID	PPID	PGID	SID	CLS	PRI	ADDR	SZ	WCHAN	TTY	TIME	CMD
1S	0	4	1	1	1	-	5	-	0	ksofti	?	00:00:00	ksoftirqd_CPU0

Figure 1.17. ps output shows kernel thread as *ksoftirqd_CPU0*.

```
kernel/softirq.c

361 static int ksoftirqd(void * __bind_cpu)
362 {
363     int bind_cpu = (int) (long) __bind_cpu;
        .....
375     sprintf(current->comm, "ksoftirqd_CPU%d", bind_cpu);
        ....
396 }
```

cs 1.3. *ksoftirqd()*.

```
include/linux/irq_cpustat.h

33 #define ksoftirqd_task(cpu)   __IRQ_STAT((cpu), __ksoftirqd_task)
```

cs 1.4. *ksoftirqd_task()*.

```
kernel/softirq.c

53 static inline void wakeup_softirqd(unsigned cpu)
54 {
55     struct task_struct * tsk = ksoftirqd_task(cpu);
56
57     if (tsk && tsk->state != TASK_RUNNING)
58         wake_up_process(tsk);
59 }
```

cs 1.5. *wakeup_softiqd()*.

kernel softirq daemon appears with the name *ksoftirqd_CPU0* on running *ps* command as shown in Fig. 1.17.

softIRQ daemon is awakened by using interface *wakeup_softirqd()*. This routine gets access to softIRQ thread for the CPU by calling *ksoftirqd_task()* at line 55. *ksoftirqd_task()* is a macro that accesses thread information from CPU-specific structure by using another macro *__IRQ_STAT* (see cs 1.4).

Once *ksoftirqd_task()* gets softIRQ thread for the CPU, it checks if it is not already in running state (cs 1.5, line 57). If not already scheduled, it is woken up by a call to *wake_up_process()* at line 58. This routine changes the state to *TASK_RUNNING* and puts the thread on the kernel run queue.

1.6 KERNEL SYNCHRONIZATION MECHANISM

The Linux kernel implements many synchronization mechanisms that are applicable in different situations on different kernel control paths. Some of these synchronization mechanisms are

- Semaphore
- Atomic operations
- Disabling interrupts locally or globally
- Spin locks

The above synchronization mechanisms work on different principles, but the aim is to synchronize access to kernel global data structures across different kernel control paths and also across CPUs. Different kernel control paths are discussed in Section 1.3, but let us summarize here:

- Kernel path executing system call on behalf of process
- Kernel path executing interrupt routine
- Kernel path executing softIRQ.

Let's see what synchronization mechanism could be best used for different kernel control paths. Spin lock is the most commonly used synchronization mechanism in different flavors. We will discuss this in more detail in shortly. Let's see how semaphore is implemented, and let's discuss its usage.

1.6.1 Semaphore

A semaphore is used to synchronize access to global data structure in an asynchronous way. When many kernel control paths want to acquire a kernel resource, only one gets the lock and the rest are put to sleep until the lock is released by the one that is acquired. *down()* and *up()* are the two routines that manipulate semaphores. When the kernel control path wants to acquire a semaphore, it calls *down()*. If we are the first one to acquire semaphore, we change the state of the semaphore and get access to the shared resource. If somebody has already acquired the semaphore, the caller has to wait on a semaphore wait queue until it is woken up by the control path that has acquired it. *up()* routine is called by the kernel control path to release the semaphore, and it also wakes up all the processes waiting on a semaphore wait queue.

The best example that explains the usage of a semaphore is page fault. Process address space may be shared by many threads (LWPs) or a child process. It may happen that page fault occurs while executing for the code area or stack area. In this case, a page fault handling routine takes a semaphore for its kernel address space (*current→mm→mmap_sem*). Then it starts to find the cause of fault and tries to get the missing page and map it to the process page table. In the meantime, some other thread which is sharing the address space of the process which is already in the process of finding page for the faulting address also faults. In this case, the thread that has faulted later will go to sleep on *mm→mmap_sem* and will be woken up once the page fault handler returns for the process that faulted first.

1.6.2 Atomic Operations

This is mainly used to synchronously access a memory region when two or more kernel control paths are trying to access them simultaneously. There are instructions that may require us to test and modify a bit atomically (without being interrupted by interrupts) on the CPU. On SMP machines, such instructions appear to be non-atomic as both the CPU's read the same value in a given memory location in two simultaneous read cycles. If the 0 value in the memory location means acquire the lock, both will acquire the lock and will wait for the big blast. On an SMP machine, these instructions should be preceded by lock instruction to lock the memory bus by any CPU until atomic instruction is executed completely.

1.6.3 Spin Lock

The third and most commonly used synchronization technique used everywhere inside the kernel is *spin locks*. It is used to synchronize data access when kernel control paths on two or more CPUs try to access the same memory region simultaneously. It differs from a semaphore in the way that the semaphore freezes the process that wants to acquire the semaphore when it is already acquired. Spin lock, on the other hand, does not put the process to sleep that wants to acquire the spin lock when it is already acquired. Instead, it executes a tight loop spinning around the lock each time atomically testing the lock, also called busy-wait loop. If it finds that the lock is released, it tries to acquire it atomically. Spin lock makes use of atomic instructions. Whichever CPU succeeds in acquiring the lock first gets it, and others continue to move in a tight loop and this continues.

Spin locks have an edge over semaphores because we save a lot of time in context switching when the process trying to acquire a lock is put to sleep by the semaphore. Critical section in the kernel is refereed to code that modifies/accesses global data-structures accessed from a different kernel control path. Critical sections should be protected by locks. Locks held for a longer time cause other kernel control paths to paths to wait for a longer time causing a performance hit. A critical section of the kernel code is executed for a much shorter period of time. If the time required in context switching is much more than the time spent in executing a critical region, semaphores penalize the performance extensively. In such cases, waiting on a busy loop to acquire the lock gives a much better performance. Not only this, there are other reasons to use spin lock on SMP machine instead of semaphores for serialized access of global data. For example, data that are shared between a kernel control path and an interrupt cannot be protected by a semaphore because it could freeze the system by calling a schedule in interrupt routine (hypothetical case). In the same way, a spin lock cannot be used for serialized access of data shared between interrupt and kernel control path on a single CPU machine. This would cause the machine to freeze because the tight loop in the interrupt routine would never let us come out of it when a spin lock is already acquired by the other kernel control path. For this reason, we acquire a spin lock with local interrupts disabled when data are shared between kernel control path and the interrupt routine. This doesn't stop interrupts from occurring on other CPUs, which is OK because they will wait in a tight loop until we release the lock. Maskable interrupts are disabled locally by using the macro *local_irq_disable()* and are enabled by using *local_irq_enable()*.

```
include/linux/spinlock.h

10 #define spin_lock_irqsave(lock, flags)    do { local_irq_save(flags);    spin_lock(lock); } while (0)
11 #define spin_lock_irq(lock)               do { local_irq_disable();      spin_lock(lock); } while (0)
12 #define spin_lock_bh(lock)                do { local_bh_disable();       spin_lock(lock); } while (0)
```

Figure 1.18. Interface to acquire spin lock.

```
include/linux/spinlock.h

22 #define spin_unlock_irqrestore(lock, flags)   do { spin_unlock(lock);  local_irq_restore(flags); } while (0)
23 #define spin_unlock_irq(lock)                 do { spin_unlock(lock);  local_irq_enable();       } while (0)
24 #define spin_unlock_bh(lock)                  do { spin_unlock(lock);  local_bh_enable();        } while (0)
```

Figure 1.19. Interface to release spin lock.

A spin lock can also be used to serialize data shared between the kernel control path, softIRQ also. In such cases, two macros can be used to disable and enable soft IRQ; these are *local_bh_disable* and *local_bh_enable*, respectively. Check Section 17.2 for details.

Different flavors of spin_locks are shown in Figs. 1.18 and 1.19. In some cases we need to store EFLAGS for the CPU before disabling interrupts locally to restore it once we enable interrupts once again as interrupts are handled in nested fashion. Nested interrupt handling means that an interrupt is raised when another low-priority interrupt is already being handled on the CPU. We do this because we are not sure whether interrupts were enabled at the time we disabled them. This means that IRQs may already have been disabled by an upper layer before we are going to disable them.

In such cases, *spin_lock_irqsave()* and *spin_unlock_irqrestore()* are used to serialize data access between kernel control path and interrupt. *spin_lock_irq()* and *spin_unlock_irq()* are used simply when we want to serialize access of data shared between kernel and interrupt. *spin_lock_bh()* and *spin_unlock_bh* are used to serialize access of data shared between kernel and softIRQ.

Similarly, we have the same flavors of spin locks for reader and writer locks, which we won't discuss here in much detail. Read spin lock allows multiple readers to get access to the shared data, whereas writer lock exclusively allows only a single writer to access the resource. When writer lock is acquired, no one including the reader is allowed access to the resource.

1.7 APPLICATION INTERFACES FOR TCP/IP PROGRAMMING

In this section we will see various interfaces that are provided to the user application to write a client–server program. All networking applications are based on client–server technology other than multicasting and broadcasting applications. There may be variants to the outlook of these applications, but basically the underlying functionality remains the same. Normally, a server is a program that provides a known service to the client program. The example is telnet, FTP, http, and so on. Client and server are in some kind of understanding with each other for all such services. But there is one thing in common in all the programs: client–server technology. In all the cases, a server has established its identity, which is known to the client. The client sends out a request to the server for the service, which in turn offers its services once they are connected to each other. We first discuss simple server application and then client application and see how they use TCP protocol over IP to communicate with each other.

1.7.1 Server Application

A server program has to provide its identity to the client programs by way of listening on a specific port. Port is a unique number that identifies a connection or specific services on a given host. When we say identifying specific connection on specific port it means that the server application needs to register its service with the kernel by way of port number. When we request a kernel to register our service, a unique port number is provided by server application to the kernel to associate its services with this number.

This port number should be known to the client application so that it can send its request to the host machine running this service. Let's see what all interfaces are providing to hook its services with specific port number and register its service with the kernel.

We want to start service using TCP transport protocol (see Fig. 1.20). The first step is to make a *socket()* system call at line 25. The socket is a framework to communicate with the network protocol within the kernel. This call opens a socket in the kernel. The arguments to the socket call are AF_INET and SOCK_STREAM. This means that we want to open an internet family socket of type STREAM referring to TCP. The socket initializes INET socket-specific data structures and also TCP protocol-specific data structures and a set of operations. It links the socket with the VFS, which is then associated with the file descriptor and returned to the application. Now using this file descriptor, the server can request to kernel any operation on the socket.

The next step is to bind the socket with a specific port number by making the *bind()* system call at line 33. This is the way we are requesting a kernel to allocate a specific port number to its service. Here comes the concept of socket address whose C equivalent is *sockaddr_in*. This has two fields: port number and IP address. If the host machine has more than one interface, an application can request a kernel to bind the socket with a given interface or with all the available interfaces. This means that application may want to accept connection requests from only one interface or from all the available interfaces. In the former case, the *sin_addr* field of the socket address is initialized to the specific IP address and the same field needs to be initialized to INADDR_ANY in the latter case, line 31. Since this is INET address family, the *sin_family* field of the socket address is initialized to AF_INET. The port number to which we want to glue the services is initialized at line 32. The socket address is now ready for registration as object *sockaddr_in*.

The socket address is passed to *bind()* call. If the return value is less than zero, the socket could not be bound to the given port number because there may be any reason, including the fact that a port number may already be allocated to some other services. Otherwise, we got the port number that was requested.

```
----------------server-------------------------------------

 1 #include <stdio.h>
 2 #include <sys/types.h>
 3 #include <sys/socket.h>
 4 #include <netinet/in.h>
 5 #include <signal.h>


.....
11
12 #define READ_BUFFER 50000
13
14 int main(int argc, char *argv[]) {
15
16    int sockfd, newsockfd, portno, clilen, childpid;
17    char buffer[READ_BUFFER];
18    struct sockaddr_in serv_addr, cli_addr;
19    int n;
20    signal(SIGCHLD, SIG_IGN);
21    if (argc < 2) {
22       fprintf(stderr,"ERROR, no port provided\n");
23       exit(1);
24    }
25    sockfd = socket(AF_INET, SOCK_STREAM, 0);
26    if (sockfd < 0)
27       error("ERROR opening socket");
28    bzero((char *) &serv_addr, sizeof(serv_addr));
29    portno = atoi(argv[1]);
30    serv_addr.sin_family = AF_INET;
31    serv_addr.sin_addr.s_addr = INADDR_ANY;
32    serv_addr.sin_port = htons(portno);
33    if (bind(sockfd, (struct sockaddr *) &serv_addr, sizeof(serv_addr)) < 0) {
34       perror("ERROR on binding");
35       exit(2);
36    }
37    listen(sockfd,5);
38    while (1) {
39       clilen = sizeof(cli_addr);
40       newsockfd = accept(sockfd, (struct sockaddr *) &cli_addr, &clilen);
41       if (newsockfd < 0) {
42          perror("ERROR on accept");
43       if ( (childpid = fork()) < 0) {
44          error("server: fork error");
45          exit(3);
46       }
47       else if (childpid == 0) {
48          close(sockfd);
49          while (1) {

51             bzero(buffer,READ_BUFFER);

53             n = read(sockfd,buffer,READ_BUFFER-1);
54             if (n < 0)
55                perror("ERROR reading from socket");
56             n = write(sockfd,buffer,READ_BUFFER-1);
57             if (n < 0)
58                perror("ERROR writing to socket");
59          }
60          exit(0);
61       }
62       close(newsockfd);
63    }
64 }
```

Figure 1.20. Server program.

Next is to request the kernel to start the accepting the connection, which is done by making a call to *listen()* at line 37. A listen call will actually start the services for the server application. Now the kernel will start accepting connection a request for the socket. A second argument to *listen()* call is to accept a queue length for the listening socket. All the established connections for the socket sit in this queue to be accepted. Connection requests can come faster than they can be accepted by the application. For this reason we need a queuing mechanism to buffer a pending connection on the busy server.

The final step is a call to *accept()* systemcall at line 40. *accept()* call is made in an infinite loop. This call blocks until a new connection is available from the accept queue. As soon as a new connection is available, application is awakened and new connection is returned to the application associated with the file descriptor associated with the new socket connection.

The returned value of the accept call is associated with a new connection and can be used for communication between two ends. This opens a new channel between the two ends and is differentiated from all other connections for the same service using a remote port and an IP address. For each connection, a remote port number or a remote IP address will be unique.

Our serve program forks a new process for the newly accepted connection by a call to *fork()* at line 43. *fork()* syscall returns with value zero in the child process. In the parent process, it returns childs PID. This way we start services in the child thread in while loop 47–61. We are blocked to read data over the socket by a call to *read()* at line 53. Once it has read data over the socket, it writes received data back to the sender at line 56 by a call to *write()*. A child thread closes a listening socket at line 48 because additional reference was held on the listening socket when we were waiting on accept in parent. Parent thread closes a new socket at line 62. In the next section we will see what the client program does.

1.7.2 Client Application

A client program has to be sure of the server it needs to contact. To contact the server, it has to know two things about the server:

- Port number of the server at which it is listening
- IP address of the host machine where this server is running

Refer to Fig. 1.21 for a client program. The socket address consisting of these two information C equivalent of socket address is *struct sockaddr_in*, as discussed in Section 4.2. First we make *socket()* call at line 27 to open TCP socket. *sin_addr* field is initialized to the IP address of the server and *sin_port* field is initialized to port number of the listening server at lines 39 and 42, respectively. Next we make a call to *connect()* at line 43, to which we pass the socket address of the server. We pass the socket descriptor to the *connect()* on which the connection is to be established. The kernel finds route for the destination (server) and then initializes the connection process. Once the connection is established, the connect returns.

Once *connect()* returns, we are ready to communicate with the server using *read & write* calls using a socket descriptor. In the while loop 47–56, we are reading one line from the standard input (keyboard) at line 49 and writing it over the socket by a call to write at line 51. Just after writing data over the socket, we are waiting to

```
------------------------------client------------------------------

1 #include <stdio.h>
 2 #include <sys/types.h>
 3 #include <sys/socket.h>
 4 #include <netinet/in.h>
 5 #include <netdb.h>
    ...
13 #define READ_BUFFER 50000
14
15 int main(int argc, char *argv[])
16 {
17     int sockfd, portno, n;
18     struct sockaddr_in serv_addr;
19     in_addr_t addr;
20     struct hostent *server;
21     char buffer[READ_BUFFER];
22     if (argc < 3) {
23         fprintf(stderr,"usage %s hostname port\n", argv[0]);
24         exit(0);
25     }
26     portno = atoi(argv[2]);
27     sockfd = socket(AF_INET, SOCK_STREAM, 0);
28     if (sockfd < 0) {
29         perror("ERROR opening socket");
30         exit(2);
31     }
32     server = gethostbyname(argv[1]);
33     if (server == NULL) {
34         fprintf(stderr,"ERROR, no such host\n");
35         exit(0);
36     }
37     bzero((char *) &serv_addr, sizeof(serv_addr));
38     serv_addr.sin_family = AF_INET;
39     bcopy(&addr,
40       (char *)&serv_addr.sin_addr.s_addr,
41       sizeof(addr));
42     serv_addr.sin_port = htons(portno);
43     if (connect(sockfd,(struct sockaddr *)&serv_addr,sizeof(serv_addr)) < 0) {
44         perror("ERROR connecting");
45         exit(3);
46     }
47     while(1) {
48         printf("Please enter the message: ");

49         fgets(buffer,READ_BUFFER-1,stdin);
50         bzero(buffer,READ_BUFFER);
51         n = write(sockfd,buffer,READ_BUFFER-1);
52         if (n < 0)
53             perror("ERROR writing to socket");
54         n = read(sockfd,buffer,READ_BUFFER-1);
55         if (n < 0)
56             perror("ERROR reading from socket");
57         else {
58             buffer[n] = '\0';
59             printf("%s\n", buffer);
60         }
61     }
62     return 0;
63 }
```

Figure 1.21. Client program.

read data over the socket by a call to read at line 54. Data received are printed at line 59. The server returns whatever it has read over the socket, which is read by the client and displayed at standard output. This makes an echo server.

1.7.3 Socket Options

Sockets can be tuned as per the requirements by an applications. This facility can save us from tuning the entire system where different applications have different requirements. For example, telnet connection requires setting a KEEP_ALIVE timer for the TCP connection between telnet server and client. This facility is required because telnet connection can be open for months without any activity. With *KEEP_ALIVE* socket option, the server can probe client to find out if it is alive. On the other hand, FTP doesn't need this option.

setsockopt(). There are many socket options that can be used to tune different TCP connections. *setsockopt()* is an interface that is provided to the application to set socket options for a given connection without disturbing global settings (see Fig. 1.22). Arguments to the system call are as follows:

s: This is the socket descriptor as returned by the socket.

optname: This is the name of the socket option that needs to be tuned.

optval: This is the value of the socket option to be set.

optlen: This is the length of the optional value that is passed to the kernel to mark the end of option length. The reason is that optlen is a pointer to void.

getsockopt(). *getsockopt()* is an interface provided to get the value of socket option (see Fig. 1.23). The arguments are the same as they are for *setsockopt()*, with the difference being that they are used to fetch the value of the socket options.

1.7.4 Option Values

SO_DEBUG. This turns on debugging at various protocol layers. This may be useful when we want to track allocation of buffers, traversal of packets on the stack, behavior of TCP algorithms, and so on. If the socket debug option is enabled, the *SOCK_DEBUG* macro prints messages on reception of bogus ACK for the byte that is not yet sent (line 1908, cs 1.6).

```
int setsockopt(int s, int level, int optname, const void *optval, int optlen);
```

Figure 1.22. *setsockopt().*

```
int getsockopt(int s, int level, int optname, void *optval, socklen_t *optlen);
```

Figure 1.23. *getsockopt().*

```
net/ipv4/tcp_input.c

1896 static int tcp_ack(struct sock *sk, struct sk_buff *skb, int flag)
1897 {

            ....
1908        if (after(ack, tp->snd_nxt))
1909            goto uninteresting_ack;
            ....
1983 uninteresting_ack:
1984        SOCK_DEBUG(sk, "Ack %u out of %u:%u\n", ack, tp->snd_una, tp->snd_nxt);
1985        return 0;
1986 }
```

cs 1.6. tcp_ack().

```
include/net/sock.h

467 #ifdef SOCK_DEBUGGING
468 #define SOCK_DEBUG(sk, msg...) do { if((sk) && ((sk)->debug)) printk(KERN_DEBUG msg); } while (0)
```

cs 1.7. SOCK_DEBUG().

```
net/ipv4/udp.c

416 int udp_sendmsg(struct sock *sk, struct msghdr *msg, int len)
417 {
            .....
525            if (rt->rt_flags&RTCF_BROADCAST && !sk->broadcast)
526                goto out;
527            if (connected)
528                sk_dst_set(sk, dst_clone(&rt->u.dst));
            .....
569 }
```

cs 1.8. udp_sendmsg().

The *SOCK_DEBUG* macro uses the kernel *printk()* interface to write debug messages. These messages can be seen through *dmsg* command or from file */var/log/messages*. We can see that *SOCK_DEBUG* first checks if debug option is on for the socket (*sk→debug*) at line 468 (cs 1.7). *sk→debug* is set by the application using *setsockopt()* interface.

SO_BROADCAST. This enables sending of broadcast messages, if this is supported by the protocol. Broadcast is not supported by TCP. Only UDP and raw socket support broadcast. In *udp_sendmsg()*, if the route is of type broadcast (*RTCF_BROADCAST*), it can send broadcast messages only if socket option enables (*sk→broadcast*) is set (line 525, cs 1.8).

```
net/ipv4/tcp_ipv4.c

202 static int tcp_v4_get_port(struct sock *sk, unsigned short snum)
203 {
    ....
249     if (tb != NULL && tb->owners != NULL) {
250         if (sk->reuse > 1)
251             goto success;
252         if (tb->fastreuse > 0 && sk->reuse != 0 && sk->state != TCP_LISTEN) {
253             goto success;
254         } else {
    ....
283 }
```

cs 1.9. tcp_v4_get_port().

SO_REUSEADDR. Whenever any server application wants to bind to a port which is already in use by some other application on the same machine, this option may allow us to use the same port number under certain conditions. This option sets the *reuse* field of the *sock* object.

tcp_v4_get_port() is called inside the kernel through a bind path when application wants to bind to a specific port. We traverse through the bind hash list; and if we find port already occupied and *sk→reuse* is set more than 1 (line 250, cs 1.9), we can directly use the port. Otherwise, if the value of *sk→reuse* is set to 1 (line 252, cs 1.9), it has to go through some additional checks before getting the port.

SO_KEEPALIVE. This option enables a heartbeat mechanism for TCP connection. An application like telnet may be active for months, where one end never knows about the other end when connections are ideal. It may happen that the one end has gone down, in which case the other end will never know. Half-connection will unnecessarily be open, thereby occupying resources. This option keeps sending messages to the other end once connection is idle for some time. In return, the sending end expects acknowledgment. If acknowledgments are not received, the connection is closed after a certain number of retries.

When the option is enabled, *tcp_set_keepalive()* is called to set the keepalive timer for TCP, and *sk→keepopen* is set to 1. *tcp_set_keepalive()* resets the keepalive timer in case it is not already set; this is done by calling *tcp_reset_keepalive_timer()* (see cs 1.10, line 568).

SO_LINGER. The linger option is to enable a TCP socket to provide enough time to send unsent data in the send queue when a socket is closed by an application. We provide a timeout value with this option so that the kernel hangs on for this much time before closing the socket. In this time, the TCP gets enough time to flush all the data to the receiver. If timeout is not provided, the kernel waits until all the data are flushed out.

This option sets *sk→*linger to 1, and sk→lingertime is set to a timeout value provided by user application. When an application issues a *close()* syscall an INET socket, *inet_release()* is called. If a linger option is set, a linger timeout value is taken

```
net/ipv4/tcp_timer.c

562 void tcp_set_keepalive(struct sock *sk, int val)
563 {
564     if ((1<<sk->state)&(TCPF_CLOSE|TCPF_LISTEN))
565         return;
566
567     if (val && !sk->keepopen)
568         tcp_reset_keepalive_timer(sk, keepalive_time_when(&sk->tp_pinfo.af_tcp));
569     else if (!val)
570         tcp_delete_keepalive_timer(sk);
571 }
```

cs 1.10. *tcp_set_keepalive()*.

```
net/ipv4/af_inet.c

444 int inet_release(struct socket *sock)
445 {
446     struct sock *sk = sock->sk;
447
448     if (sk) {
449         long timeout;
            ....
461         timeout = 0;
462         if (sk->linger && !(current->flags & PF_EXITING))
463             timeout = sk->lingertime;
464         sock->sk = NULL;
465         sk->prot->close(sk, timeout);
466     }
467     return(0);
468 }
```

cs 1.11. *inet_release()*.

from *sk→lingertime* (cs 1.11, line 463). Finally, a protocol-specific close routine is called with a linger timeout value at line 465 (see cs 1.11).

In *tcp_close()*, we check the timeout value passed as an argument to the routine. If set, the kernel puts the process to sleep before by calling *add_wait_queue()* at line 1978 (see cs 1.12). By the time we request a timeout, all data would have been flushed. Once we have performed the timeout, the socket is closed.

SO_OOBINLINE. This option is related to a TCP urgent byte. If the option is set, the TCP urgent byte is received inline; otherwise, it is received on different channel as out-of-band data. The option sets *sk→urginline* to 1. *sk→urginline* is discussed in much detail in Section 8.3.2.

SO_SNDBUF. This option sets send buffer size for the socket, *sk→sndbuf*. This value puts a limit on the total amount of memory allocated for the send buffer. In

```
net/ipv4/tcp.c

1900 void tcp_close(struct sock *sk, long timeout)
1901 {
1902     struct sk_buff *skb;
         ....
1976     if (timeout) {
1977         struct task_struct *tsk = current;
1978         DECLARE_WAITQUEUE(wait, current);
1979
1980         add_wait_queue(sk->sleep, &wait);
         ....
2064 }
```

cs 1.12. *tcp_close().*

```
net/ipv4/tcp.c

680 static inline int tcp_memory_free(struct sock *sk)
681 {
682     return sk->wmem_queued < sk->sndbuf;
683 }
```

cs 1.13. *tcp_memory_free().*

case the segments get acknowledged, they stay in the send buffer and account for the send buffer consumption.

tcp_memory_free() is called when application data are written over the TCP socket to check if we have enough space in the send buffer for application data. If this returns TRUE, we can queue new data to socket's send buffer, otherwise not (see cs 1.13).

SO_RCVBUF. The option is the same as *SO_SNDBUF* with the difference that this option sets an upper limit on the receive buffer, *sk→rcvbuf*. In *tcp_data_queue()*, we check if allocated memory for receive socket buffer is more than socket send buffer limit at line 2571 (cs 1.14). If the condition is true, we try to squeeze some memory from the receive queue by calling *tcp_prune_queue()* at line 2573.

SO_DONTROUTE. This option is mainly used by RAW sockets or UDP sockets and sets *sk→localroute* to 1. If this option is enabled, the normal routing policy is disabled for the outgoing packet. The packet will be routed only if the destination is directly connected to the network.

SO_RCVTIMEO. This sets the timeout value for the socket that specifies the maximum amount of time the process should be blocked for an incoming event such as the following:

- Accept blocked for new connection on listening socket.
- Read is blocked to receive data on the connected socket.

```
net/ipv4/tcp.c

2522 static void tcp_data_queue(struct sock *sk, struct sk_buff *skb)
2523 {
       .....
2570            if (eaten < 0 &&
2571              (atomic_read(&sk->rmem_alloc) > sk->rcvbuf ||
2572              !tcp_rmem_schedule(sk, skb))) {
2573                 if (tcp_prune_queue(sk) < 0 || !tcp_rmem_schedule(sk, skb))
2574                      goto drop;
2575            }

2726 }
```

cs 1.14. tcp_data_queue().

```
include/net/sock.h

1238 static inline long sock_rcvtimeo(struct sock *sk, int noblock)
1239 {
1240      return noblock ? 0 : sk->rcvtimeo;
1241 }
```

cs 1.15. sock_revtimeo().

```
include/net/sock.h

1467 int tcp_recvmsg(struct sock *sk, struct msghdr *msg,
1468            int len, int nonblock, int flags, int *addr_len)
1469 {
       .....
1488      timeo = sock_rcvtimeo(sk, nonblock);
       .....
1638           } else {
1639                 timeo = tcp_data_wait(sk, timeo);
1640           }
       ....
1770 }
```

cs 1.16. tcp_recvmsg().

sock_rcvtimeo() returns a value of timeout for blocking sockets, (see cs 1.15).

tcp_recvmsg() calls *sock_rcvtimeo()* at line 1488 (cs 1.16) to get a timeout value for the socket. Once requested data are not available, *tcp_data_wait()* is called at line 1639 (cs 1.16) with a timeout value returned by *sock_rcvtimeo()*. This puts the process to sleep until timeout occurs or until data are received, whichever happens first.

SO_SNDTIMEO. This option is similar to *SO_RCVTIMEO* except that this sets a timeout for receiving events on the socket. This sets a value of *sk→sndtimeo*.

```
include/net/sock.h

1243 static inline long sock_sndtimeo(struct sock *sk, int noblock)
1244 {
1245     return noblock ? 0 : sk->sndtimeo;
1246 }
```

cs 1.17. sock_sndtimeo().

```
net/ipv4/tcp.c

1009 int tcp_sendmsg(struct sock *sk, struct msghdr *msg, int size)
1010 {
         ....
1025     timeo = sock_sndtimeo(sk, flags&MSG_DONTWAIT);
         .....
1067             skb = tcp_alloc_pskb(sk, select_size(sk, tp), 0, sk->allocation);
1068             if (skb == NULL)
1069                 goto wait_for_memory;
         .....
1176 wait_for_memory:
         .....
1180             if ((err = wait_for_tcp_memory(sk, &timeo)) != 0)
1181                 goto do_error;
         .....
1210 }
```

cs 1.18. tcp_sendmsg().

sock_sendtimeo() returns a timeout value as sk→sndtimeo for blocking sockets (see cs 1.17).

tcp_sendmsg() calculates records timeout value at line 1025 (cs 1.18) by call to sock_sndtimeo(). If it fails to allocate memory for copying new data into a network buffer (line 1068, cs 1.18), it has to wait for memory by calling wait_for_tcp_memory() until it times out or memory is available, whichever happens first.

1.8 SHUTDOWN

The client–server program may be sending and receiving data from both the ends because TCP is a fully duplex stream protocol. It may happen that one end doesn't want to send or receive any more data because it is already done. In such a case, it will close that end of the socket. If any activity happens on that end further, the socket will throw an error saying that operation is not permitted. The shutdown() function shall cause all or part of a full-duplex connection on the socket to be shut down.

The shutdown() function takes the following arguments (Fig. 1.24).

```
int shutdown(int socket, int how);
```

Figure 1.24. *shutdown()*.

socket. This is a file descriptor associated with the socket.

how. This specifies what action needs to be taken. The values are as follows:

SHUT_RD. This disables reading of any more data over the socket. TCP
may be accepting data, but the application is not allowed to read data over
the socket.
SHUT_WR. This disables writing of data over the socket. When application
wants to send data over the socket after write side is shut down, the socket
throws an error to the application, indicating that a pipe is broken.
SHUT_RDWR. This disables further send and receive operations.

1.8.1 Kernel Shutdown Implementation

Let's see how shutdown is implemented in the kernel. *sk→shutdown* flags shutdown
events. There are two flags here:

- *SEND_SHUTDOWN*, set to disable send events.
- *RCV_SHUTDOWN*, set to disable receive events.

1.8.2 Send Shutdown

When an application wants to send a message after the send side of the socket
is shut down, *tcp_sendmsg()* handles the situation. *sk→*shutdown has *SEND_
SHUTDOWN* bit set for the socket in this case. An error is initialized to *E_PIPE*
at line 1042, cs 1.19. At line 1043 we check the shutdown flag. If the *SEND_SHUT-
DOWN* bit is set, we go to error handling at line 1202. It is rare that any data are
copied to the application buffer. I mean that it is rare that shutdown is called from
application when the kernel is in the process of reading data from the socket buffer.
So, we move to error handling at line 1205. Here we do some cleanup operation
and then return error number which is set to E_PIPE.

1.8.3 Receive Shutdown

When an application wants to receive data over a TCP socket, a kernel calls *tcp_
recvmsg()*. Error number is initialized to *ENOTCONN*. We read data in do-while
loop 1502–1703, cs 1.20. In the process, we check if a shutdown bit is set for the
socket at line 1568. If so, we break. We do a cleanup operation and then return the
value of copied, which may be a positive value if there was any data copied from a
receive buffer or 0 if there was nothing copied from the receive buffer. It doesn't
return an *E_PIPE* error instead 0. Zero return value to the application means that
nothing was there to be read from the socket.

```
net/ipv4/tcp.c

1009 int tcp_sendmsg(struct sock *sk, struct msghdr *msg, int size)
1010 {
        ....
1042     err = -EPIPE;
1043     if (sk->err || (sk->shutdown&SEND_SHUTDOWN))
1044         goto do_error;
        ....
1202 do_error:
1203     if (copied)
1204         goto out;
1205 out_err:
1206     err = tcp_error(sk, flags, err);
1207     TCP_CHECK_TIMER(sk);
1208     release_sock(sk);
1209     return err;
1210 }
```

cs 1.19. *tcp_sendmsg()*.

```
net/ipv4/tcp.c

1467 int tcp_recvmsg(struct sock *sk, struct msghdr *msg,
1468         int len, int nonblock, int flags, int *addr_len)
1469 {
1470     struct tcp_opt *tp = &(sk->tp_pinfo.af_tcp);
        ....
1484     err = -ENOTCONN;
        ....
1502     do {
            ....
1568         if (sk->shutdown & RCV_SHUTDOWN)
1569             break;
            ....
1730     } while (len > 0);
        ....
1758     TCP_CHECK_TIMER(sk);
1759     release_sock(sk);
1760     return copied;
        ....
1770 }
```

cs 1.20. *tcp_recvmsg()*.

1.9   I/O

In this section we discuss different system calls on Unix systems that deal with I/O. Our discussion will be more focused on the feature that system call adds to I/O activities. These system calls can be used to receive or send normal- or high-priority data over the socket.

1.9.1   *read()*

This is the simplest system call to read data over the socket. We specify a socket descriptor as a first argument, address of the location where data should go as a second argument, and number of bytes to be read in the buffer as a third argument (see Fig. 1.25). The system call can a block or return immediately, depending on whether the socket is blocking or nonblocking. By default, it is blocking. If the socket is blocking, read blocks in case its request is not satisfied completely.

1.9.2   *write()*

This is simplest system call to send data over the socket (see Fig. 1.26). Arguments are same as that for the read; the difference is that instead of reading, this will write data. The blocking and non-blocking nature is the same as that for read.

1.9.3   *recv()*

This system call would receive data over the socket with some added control (Fig. 1.27). The first three arguments are the same as that for read, with an additional fourth argument as control *flags*. With the additional flag, we can just peek for the data or can receive TCP urgent data as out-of-band data. In the latter case, the process will never block even if the socket is blocking.

```
ssize_t read(int fildes, void *buf, size_t count);
```

Figure 1.25. *read()*.

```
ssize_t write(int fildes, const void *buf, size_t count);
```

Figure 1.26. *write()*.

```
ssize_t recv(int s, void *buf, size_t len, int flags);
```

Figure 1.27. *recv()*.

```
ssize_t send(int s, const void *msg, size_t len, int flags);
```

Figure 1.28. *send()*.

```
int select(int nfds, fd_set *readfds, fd_set *writefds, fd_set *exceptfds, struct timeval *timeout);

void FD_CLR(int fd, fd_set *set);

int FD_ISSET(int fd, fd_set *set);

void FD_SET(int fd, fd_set *set);

void FD_ZERO(fd_set *set);
```

Figure 1.29. *select()*.

1.9.4 *send()*

This system call would send data over the socket with some added control (Fig. 1.28). This is the same as recv, with the difference being that this is used for sending data instead of receiving data. The flags argument has the same meaning as it is for recv.

1.9.5 *select()*

The select system call offers more features with added complexity (Fig. 1.29). The added feature is to do I/O multiplexing demultiplexing. With the system calls discussed so far, we can do I/O only on a single socket descriptor or file descriptor. With select, we can block on multiple events for different descriptors. The events are read, write, and exception. For each event, we have pointer to *fd_set* object. We can mark the bit corresponding to the file/socket descriptor in *fd_set* object. We do this by using macro *FD_SET()*. We pass pointers to *fd_set* for each event to select. The first argument to select is a maximum file descriptor number that will be one more than the highest number received as the file/socket descriptor for the process. We can also provide a timeout value as the fifth argument. Once select returns, the return value indicates the number of events that has occurred. We need to check each event by using macro *FD_ISSET* on each descriptor to check which event has occurred. For example, if there are data to be read on the socket and we want this event to be notified, select returns with bit set for read event. *FD_ISSET()* for readfs event will return 1 for the descriptor that received data.

1.10 TCP STATE

TCP is a state-oriented protocol. Each TCP session maintains a state of its own. The state of the TCP connection is a kind of marker for the protocol which decides the behavior of the protocol at any given point of time. Each state will have a pre-decided set of rules that need to be followed strictly. Specific events can change the

1 10:07:35.210908 192.168.1.4.32966 > moksha.isakmp: S [tcp sum ok] 552231777:552231777(0) win 49640
<mss 1460,nop,wscale 0,nop,nop,sackOK> (DF)

2 10:07:35.210974 moksha.isakmp > 192.168.1.4.32966: S [tcp sum ok] 1163300465:1163300465(0) ack 552231778
win 5840 <mss 1460,nop,nop,sackOK,nop,wscale 0> (DF)

3 10:07:35.211186 192.168.1.4.32966 > moksha.isakmp: . [tcp sum ok] ack 1 win 49640 (DF)

Figure 1.30. TCP three-way handshake.

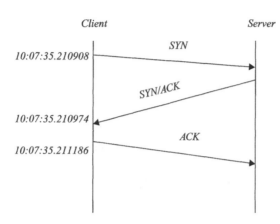

Figure 1.31. Time-line diagram for three-way handshake.

state of the protocol, which in turn changes the next course of action. Any diversion from the current course of action may lead to major failures caused from breaking protocol. As we see later in the discussion, there is a way in which a connection needs to be established initially between two TCP peers. If the protocol is not followed as expected, the two ends keep on exchanging the connection-specific packets forever, thereby causing a lot of damage to the system as well as to network resources.

Let's see what these TCP states are. We divide the discussion into three different categories, depending on the stage of the TCP connection:

1. Connection initiation (active and passive)
2. Established connection
3. Connection closure (active and passive)

Connection initiation (*three-way handshake*) is illustrated in Fig. 1.30. We have already discussed the client-server program in Section 1.7. We take the same example and see what happens when a client is trying to send a connection request to the server.

On a time-line diagram, the connection initiation would be as shown in Fig. 1.31. Connection initiation is started by the client, which invokes connect system call. So, a client sends SYN packet to the server at time *10:07:35.210908*. The server responds to the connection request by ACKing (acknowledging) the SYN. Finally, the client acknowledges the SYN/ACK by sending the final ACK. From Fig. 1.30,

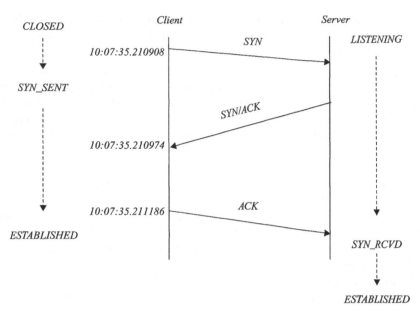

Figure 1.32. TCP states during three-way handshake.

it is worth noting that some information is exchanged between the peers in initial SYN and SYN/ACK packets. The information contains TCP options. Please refer to Section 2.2 for detailed information about protocol headers. Let's see how the client and server side TCP state changes with each event.

Figure 1.32 shows the transition of TCP states at client and server when some event triggers. First look at client side states:

- Initially, the client's TCP is in a CLOSED state when it sends out SYN packet to the server. This SYN packet is a connection request to the server from client. Here the client is supposed to be doing active open.
- After the client has sent out the SYN packet (connection request), its state changes from CLOSED to SYN_SENT.
- Now the client waits for the server to send ACK for the SYN sent. Once the client receives ACK for the connection request, its TCP state changes from SYN_SENT to ESTABLISHED.

Handling error at client end. If the client receives an RST (reset) packet in reply for the initial SYN sent, its state changes to CLOSED.

Let's look at the server side TCP state transition:

- At the server side, we have a listening socket. So, the initial TCP state at the server side is LISTENING.
- The server receives connection request for the LISTENING socket—that is, the first SYN packet from the client. The server sends out an SYN/ACK packet in response to the client's connection request. The server side TCP state doesn't change because the connection request is still pending to be completed until the server receives the final ACK from the client. This

connection request remains open until the final ACK is received from the client and is queued in the SYN queue for the listening socket. No new socket is created at this point in time.

- The final ACK is received from the client. So the three-way handshake is completed here. A new socket is created for the connection request, which is in the SYN_RECV state. Before any event occurs, the socket is further processed and its state is changed to ESTABLISHED because both sides have agreed completely for this connection and negotiation is completed between client and server.

Once the connection is in an established state, both ends can exchange data until one of the ends decides to close the connection. Let's see what happens when one of the ends does an active close. The client is 192.168.1.4 and the server is moksha. The client sends 100 bytes of data to the server and then does an active close to the connection. Figure 1.33 shows the tcpdump output of the life cycle of the TCP connection.

We have already discussed three-way handshake, so we won't discuss packets 1, 2, and 3. Packet 4 is 100 bytes of data from a client which is ACKed (acknowledged) by a server in packet 5. Thereafter, the client closes the connection and hence sends FIN packet (packet 6) with 1 byte of data. The server acknowledges byte 101 in packet 7 and then sends out an FIN packet with 1 byte (packet 8). Finally, the client that did the active close gets a final FIN with ACK from the server. The client sends the final ACK to the server. Now we see how the state of TCP connection changes with each event during close.

Let's see how the state transition happens at the two ends of the TCP connections. We take the same example where the client is writing data to the server; and after the write of 100 bytes is over, the client closes the connection (Fig. 1.34). From Fig. 1.35 we can see that once the client does an active close, it sends out a FIN segment to the other end and its state changes from ESTABLISHED to FIN_WAIT1. So, the FIN_WAIT1 state indicates that FIN still needs to be acknowledged. At the server side, FIN is received so it knows that that the client wants to close the connection in a normal way. On reception of FIN for the connection, the state of server side TCP changes from ESTABLISHED to CLOSE_WAIT. In response to the FIN received, the server can do two things here:

```
1   09:46:52.920305 192.168.1.4.33002 > moksha.5000:S 2135112431:2135112431(0) win 49640
<mss 1460,nop,wscale 0,nop,nop,sock OK> (DF)
2   09:46:52.920364 moksha.5000 > 192.168.1.4.33002:S 4191973139:4191973139(0) ack 213511243 2 win 5840
< mss 1460,nop,sock OK,nop,wscale 0> (DF)
3   09:46:52.920556 192.168.1.4.33002 > moksha.5000: ack 1 win 49640 (DF)
4   09:46:52.920774 192.168.1.4.33002 > moksha.5000: P 1:101(100) ack 1 win 49640(DF)
5   09:46:52.920802 moksha.5000 > 192.168.1.4.33002: ack 101 win 5840(DF)
6   09:46:52.920840 192.168.1.4.33002 > moksha.5000: F 101:101(0) ack 1 win 49640(DF)
7   09:46:52.956438 moksha.5000 > 192.168.1.4.33002: ack 102 win 5840(DF)
8   09:46:52.768805 moksha.5000 > 192.168.1.4.33002: F 1:1(0) ack 102 win 5840(DF)
9   09:46:52.769001 192.168.1.4.33002 > moksha.5000: ack 2 win 49640(DF)
```

Figure 1.33. Complete life cycle of TCP connection.

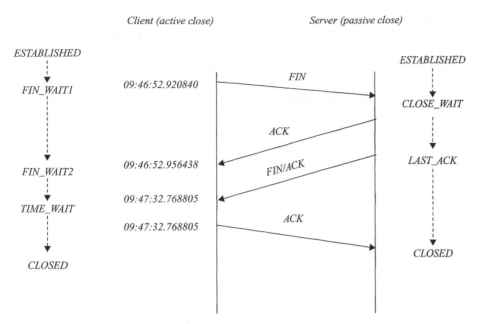

Figure 1.34. Four-way connection closure process.

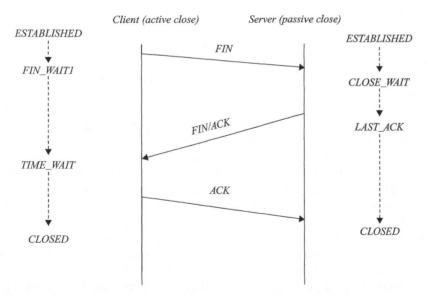

Figure 1.35. TIME_WAIT2 state is skipped as ACK is piggybacked with FIN segment.

1. It sends out ACK in reply to the FIN received from the client & send out FIN segment as another packet (Fig. 1.34).
2. It sends out FIN with ACK (Fig. 1.35).

In the former case, the state of the server side TCP doesn't change after it has sent out ACK. But the client is actually waiting to receive a FIN segment from the server.

The client receives ACK from the server in response to its FIN. This event changes the client side TCP state from FIN_WAIT1 to FIN_WAIT2. So, the FIN_WAIT2 state indicates that FIN has been acknowledged but is waiting for the FIN segment from the peer. In the latter case, the FIN_WAIT2 state is skipped at the side that has done an active close. Finally, the server sends out a FIN segment to the client so that the server side TCP state changes from CLOSE_WAIT to LAST_ACK, which means that now the server is waiting for the final ACK from the client that would be acknowledgment for the server side of FIN. On reception of FIN from the server, the client sends out a final ACK to the server and the server goes to the TIME_WAIT state. The server receives the final ACK form the client and goes to the CLOSED state. Now when does the client close the connection that is in the TIME_WAIT state?

TIME_WAIT. The TCP side that has done an active close goes to the TIME_ WAIT state finally before going to the CLOSED state. It remains in the TIME_ WAIT state for some definite time which we discuss later before it goes to the CLOSED state. It is primarily because this side of the TCP connection is the last to send out the ACK segment to the peer. After sending out the final ACK, it has to wait to make sure that the final ACK is received by the peer. It might happen that the final ACK is lost and the peer retransmits the FIN once again, thinking that its FIN is lost because it has not received the final ACK. So, someone has to be there at the active close end to respond to such retransmissions. If the TIME_ WAIT state does not exist and the active close end does not bother to wait any longer for the final ACK segment status, it might mess up the closing process because a response to the retransmitted final FIN from the passive close end will be an RST segment.

This is one of the reasons that we need to have the TIME_WAIT state for the TCP that did the active close.

Other reasons are more obvious which might happen rarely but nevertheless cannot be ignored. Suppose the server does an active close and does not go into the TIME_WAIT state. In the meantime, the client crashes and reboots. Immediately after reboot, the client tries to connect to the server using the same port number that it used for the previous connection. It gets the connection. The two ends start communicating with each other. The sequence number used by the client in the current connection overlaps with the previous connection by coincidence. If there is some TCP segment from the previous connection held with some router and it reaches the server (delayed segment), that this is surely to cause a mess up with the data integrity. If we wait here in the TIME_WAIT state, the server refuses the connection request from the client because it finds a TCP connection for the qua- druplet (local IP, local port, remote IP, and remote port) which is in the TIME_ WAIT state. Make sure that no connection is established with the client using a port number for which the TCP connection exists in the TIME_WAIT state, thus avoiding any unforeseen disaster.

Consider another case where a client does an active close and does not go into the TIME_WAIT state. In this case, it might reuse the same port as used by the previous connection to connect to the server. This may again cause the same problem. This problem may be curbed if the client has entered the TIME_WAIT state. Some of the implementations may allow reuse of the port that is already in use by a TCP that has entered TIME_WAIT state by deciding on the sequence number for the new connection. Here we need to make sure that the new connection gets the sequence that will never overlap with the sequence number from the previous connection. So, in case the new sequence number obtained is overlapping with the previous connection that has gone into the TIME_WAIT state, we add a number to the current selected sequence number that makes it greater than the maximum sequence used by the previous connection and reuse the port (RFC 1185). This makes the connection unique, and delayed segment if any from the previous connection can be taken care of. Please refer to Section 4.6.7 for implementation of the logic in Linux.

Now we should be wondering for how long the connection should go into the TIME_WAIT state? RFC 793 states some of the fixed values for the TIME_WAIT state duration. Any fixed values for this may cause overestimating or underestimating the values. For example, if we are in a local subnet and we go into the TIME_WAIT state for a fixed duration of 1 minute, this causes an unnecessary wait period because any delayed segment from the last connection will not get held up for so long. On the other hand, if we keep the TIME_WAIT duration on the lower side (few seconds), and the destinations are many routers away (say internet), we might end up waiting for the disaster to happen. So, we need to decide upon TIME_WAIT duration dynamically for each connection, depending on how many routers a packet has to pass to reach to the destination. This is decided by the number of hops. So, *msl* (maximum segment lifetime) is the correct parameter to decide upon the TIME_WAIT duration. *msl* is the maximum lifetime of the segment in the internet after which it should be discarded. So, this is updated at equal intervals and averaged out each time because for the same destination, routes may differ at different times. The msl for the packet is a function of the hops field in the IP header. For more details refer to Section 2.11.

1.10.1 Partial Close

Until now we have seen the case where data flow is in one direction and the end that is sending data initiates the close when it has sent all the required data. Now we will look at the case where the connected TCP ends are sending data whereby each end can notify its peer that the data transfer is over from their side. This means that application can do partial close from its end when it thinks that it is done with sending all the data it had and we will see how the other end is notified in such case.

We take an example where both client and server are sending data to each other. The TCP end that is done first with sending all its data will close the write end of the socket. It means that it won't send any more data to its peer. At the same time it can still continue to receive data from its peer until the peer closes its write side. We take client and server programs that will use shutdown.

A client issues a connect to the server; and after getting connected, it enters a loop where it issues three writes of 1024 block of data over the TCP connection to the server and then does a partial close to close its write end. At the same time it continues to receive data from the server until the server is done. Finally, the client doesn't issue any close on the socket. The client does close the write end of its side by issuing shutdown() with the *SHUT_WR* option.

The server accepts the connection request from the client by issuing *accept()* and gets a new socket for this connection. It then enters a loop for five iterations of data transfer. At each iteration it reads data; and if the read returns 0, it knows that the client will send no more data. So, it doesn't issue any additional reads. At the same time it continues to send data in a block of 1024 bytes. After issuing 5 writes of 1024 bytes each, the server issues a close from its side, which is an indication for the client that the server is done with sending data. After this close, both ends are done and finally the sockets at both client and sever close the connection fully.

Let's study the whole phenomenon of data transfer and TCP signaling with the help of the tcpdump output when the client and the server are transacting data. Figure 1.37 is the tcpdump output for the entire transaction until both the ends are finally closed. The client is 192.168.1.4 and the server is moksha. The first three packets are nothing but a three-way handshake when the connection is initiated. Packets 4 and 5 are a first write of 1024 bytes issued by client and acknowledgment for this write from server. Packets 6 and 7 are a repeat of packets 4 and 5; but this time, write is issued from the server side, and this write is acknowledged by the client. This continues to happen from both the ends until the client and server have issued three writes and received acknowledgment for all the writes (until packet 12). Packet 13 can be seen as a client sending FIN to the server. This means that after the third write is over, the client has closed its write end by issuing shutdown. This shutdown generates FIN from the client's side TCP. Packets 14 and 15, each consisting of a 1024-byte block, are writes issued by the server. After these two writes, the server decides to close the connection. So, FIN is combined with the final TCP data segment; that's why FIN appears in packet 15. The client acknowledges the FIN segment, and the connection is closed at both ends.

Let's map the transaction to the time-line diagram (Fig. 1.36).

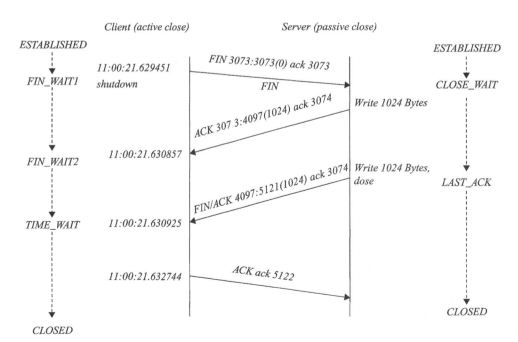

Figure 1.36. Time-line diagram for client that issues shutdown on write.

1.10.2   tcpdump Output for Partial Close

1. 11:00:21.622198 192.168.1.434289 > moksha.5000: S 960507178:960507178(0) win 49640<mss1460, nop, wscale 0, nop, nop, sack OK > (DF)

2. 11:00:21.622255 moksha.5000 > 192.168.1.4.34289: S 1884652429:1884652429(0) ack 960507179 win 5840 < mss 1460, nop, nop, sack OK, nop, wscale 0 > (DF)

3. 11:00:21.622448 192.168.1.4.34289 > moksha.5000: ack 1 win 49640 (DF)

4. 11:00:21.623359 192.168.1.4.34289 > moksha.5000: P 1:1025(1024) ack 1 win 49640 (DF)

5. 11:00:21.623414 moksha.5000 > 192.168.1.4.34289: ack 1025 win 8192 (DF)

6. 11:00:21.623443 moksha.5000 > 192.168.1.4.34289: P 1:1025(1024) ack 1025 win 8192 (DF)

7. 11:00:21.624478 192.168.1.4.34289 > moksha.5000: ack 1025 win 49640 (DF)

8. 11:00:21.625369 192.168.4.34289 > moksha.5000: P 1025:2049(1024) ack 1025 win 49640 (DF)

9. 11:00:21.625390 moksha.5000 > 192.168.1.4.34289: P 1025:2049(1024) ack 2049 win 11264 (DF)

10. 11:00:21.626389 192.168.1.4.34289 > moksha.5000: ack 2049 win 49640 (DF)

11. 11:00:21.627284 192.168.1.4.34289 > moksha.5000: P 2049:3073(1024) ack win 49640 (DF)

12. 11:00:21.628420 moksha.5000 > 192.168.1.4.34289: P 2049:3073(1024) ack 3073 win 14336 (DF)

13. 11:00:21.629451 192.168.1.4.34289 > moksha.5000: F 3073:3073(0) ack 3073 win 49640 (DF)

14. 11:00:21.630857 moksha.5000 > 192.168.1.4.34289: P 3073:4097(1024) ack 3074 win 14336 (DF)

15. 11:00:21.630925 moksha.5000 > 192.168.1.4.34289:FP 4097:5121(1024) ack 3074 win 14336 (DF)

16. 11:00:21.632744 192.168.1.4.34289 > moksha.5000: ack 5122 win 49640 (DF)

Figure 1.37. tcpdump output to illustrate TCP shutdown process.

1.11 SUMMARY

When an application sends out TCP data, the application's associated kernel thread may return after transmitting data completely. TCP data may be queued at different levels such as socket's send queue, device queue (TOS), and CPU output queue. This data are transmitted asynchronously by kernel timers or Tx softIRQ.

TCP data are processed in two steps: The packet is queued to CPU's input queue and is processed completely later on by Rx softIRQ. SoftIRQ may execute in interrupt context or may also be executed by a kernel thread.

A network-specific kernel code can be found under *net* directory of the kernel source tree. An IPv4-specific code can be found under *ipv4* subdirectory of *net*. A packet-scheduling-specific code can be found under *sched* subdirectory of *net* directory.

Linux kernel 2.4 and below are non-preemptive kernels; as a result, they are not suitable for real-time applications that require low latencies and timeliness for execution.

A system call is implemented by raising soft interrupt *int 0x80*. This interrupt switches from user to kernel mode and switches processor privilege to super-user mode where kernel code and data structure can be accessed on behalf of application. A kernel searches *sys_call_table* to execute systemcall. *sys_call_table* maps a system call number to systemcall callback routines.

Each Linux process has a kernel thread and kernel mode stack. A processor switches to kernel mode stack when the process enters a kernel via systemcall. The kernel thread is a scheduling entity for the kernel. The pthread library on Linux creates an LWP for the process. These LWPs share resources with the parent process including process address space. All the lightweight processes (LWP) as scheduling entities inside the kernel.

Threads created in the kernel cannot be preempted unless they yield on their own. Kernel threads can be seen with ps command and usually start with the letter k, like *kflushd*.

Linux implements atomic operations, semaphores, and spin locks as a synchronization mechanism. Spin locks are the most extensively used synchronization mechanism to synchronize data access between two CPUs, kernel control path and softIRQs, kernels, and interrupts and have a performance edge over semaphores.

Applications communicate over the TCP/IP protocol by way of client–server technique. These programs use a socket interface to open connection and communicate over the socket using different I/O interfaces provided to the application programs.

TCP is a connection-oriented protocol that maintains state. To start a connection, TCP completes a three-way handshake and attains an established state. TCP closes connection cleanly by way of a four-way handshake. It maintains state at each step of connection initiation and connection closure stages and defines action for each state.

2

PROTOCOL FUNDAMENTALS

The TCP/IP protocol suite works on an OSI networking model. Each layer has its own functionality defined very clearly. TCP is a transport layer protocol, and IP is a network layer. TCP manages connection and data integrity, whereas IP is responsible for delivery of data to the correct destination. The link layer manages the transmission and reception of frames by converting digital data into signals and converting signals into digital data. The physical medium actually carries all the data and control signals in the form of voltage or waves.

Irrespective of physical medium or the link layer, TCP and IP core functionality remain unchanged even though TCP may tweak around with congestion algorithms for wireless mediums. TCP functionality can be divided into two parts: connection management and reliable data transfer. TCP connection management is discussed in detail in Section 4.4. TCP is a heavyweight protocol that requires acknowledgment of each byte it has transmitted for reliability. This may overload the network in case a huge number of small packets are generated. Then there are situations where loads of data need to be transmitted with maximum throughput utilizing maximum network bandwidth. There may be situations where packets get lost because of network congestion. In all these different situations, TCP is adaptive and alert and takes corrective action to minimize losses and maximize throughput. TCP also uses extensions to normal protocol for enhanced performance and reliability.

IP, on the other hand, carries TCP data over the internet. IP has many functionalities such as routing, sending back error message to the originator, packet encryption decreption, NAT, masquerading, and so on. Routing is the most basic

TCP/IP Architecture, Design, and Implementation in Linux. By S. Seth and M. A. Venkatesulu
Copyright © 2008 the IEEE Computer Society

functionality that IP offers. There are thousands of routers that make up the internet. Routing information is maintained by each router and is updated regularly with the help of routing daemons implementing routing protocols. IP also needs to take care of the erroneous situations such as packets never reaching the destination and living in the internet forever. The frame size that can be transmitted over a link is limited by the physical capability of the medium and is called MTU. This limit may vary over the internet. Packets bigger than the MTU for the link are fragmented by IP which are reassembled at the final destination. Errors are inevitable is such a vast internet, and ICMP is widely used in the internet to report common errors.

In this chapter we learn all about TCP/IP protocols in much detail.

2.1 TCP

TCP is a connection-oriented communication protocol. It maintains the state of the connection at any given point of time. The behavior of TCP protocol changes with change in the state. There is a well-defined set of actions for each TCP state which is followed to maintain the integrity of the connection between the two ends. The connection is initiated by exchanging a set of messages between the two ends, and the same way connection is closed. We learn more about it in the later chapters. TCP is considered as a reliable protocol because it keeps account of each byte of sent data received by the other end. Any loss of data is detected and is dealt with care by TCP. Since TCP is a connection-oriented protocol, each end needs to take care of the other end to better understand each other's problem. Any shortage of resources in terms of memory/CPU at one end is communicated to the other end so that the other end takes corrective action to slowdown the rate of data transaction. This avoids the duplication of efforts and unnecessary network traffic. For doing this, TCP implements the sliding-window algorithm, which we will study in this chapter. TCP not only sends/receives data reliably but also works out the best way to avoid any duplication of efforts because of loss of data. So, it works in conjunction with the network layer to find out the network traffic situation. Depending on the traffic conditions, TCP makes a decision on whether to send data in smaller or bigger chunks. This is known as the congestion control mechanism. Without this provision, TCP would end up increasing network congestion in the case of heavy network traffic and at the same time reduce the throughput when network has high bandwidth to accommodate high data transfer rate. There are many algorithms designed for congestion control which we discover in this chapter. All this makes TCP a more reliable, more stable, and more controlled protocol to be used most extensively in the internet technology.

2.1.1 TCP Header

The TCP segment contains a TCP header and the TCP data (payload). The header contains protocol control information, connection-specific information and field to validate integrity of the TCP header. Normally, the TCP header is 20 bytes long (Fig. 2.1), but there are TCP options in the header which makes TCP header length variable. We will discuss fields of the TCP header in the first 20 bytes, and then we will discuss TCP options.

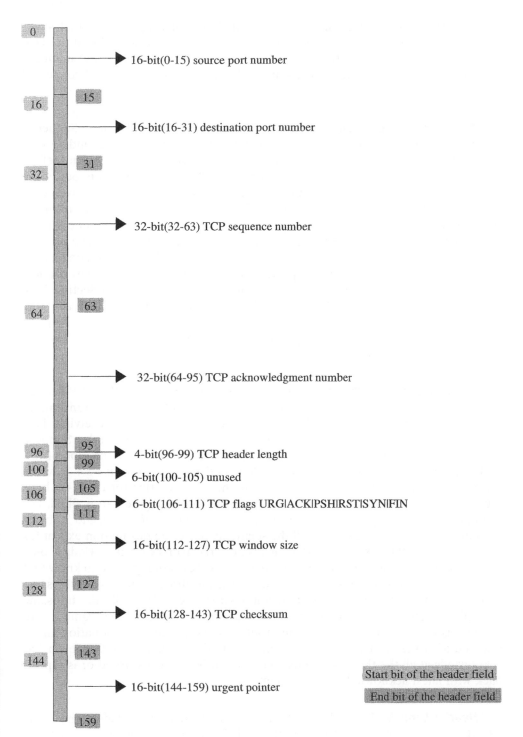

Figure 2.1. TCP header.

Port Numbers. TCP connection is identified by a quadruplet—that is, destination IP, destination port, source port, and source port. The first two fields of the TCP header contain source port (0–15 bits) and destination port (16–31 bits) numbers, each of 16 bits. These port numbers uniquely identify sockets at each TCP-connected end.

Sequence Number. This is a 32-bit (32–63) field in the TCP header. Sequence number indicates the offset of the first byte in the byte stream that the sending TCP intends to send in the current TCP segment to the receiving TCP. This doesn't reflect the number of bytes transmitted by the sending TCP. The sequence number in the header field is an offset from the initial sequence number selected for a given connection. So, offset is the actual indication of the number of bytes already transmitted by the sending TCP +1. The initial sequence number, ISN, is generated at each end of the connecting TCP ends. The ISN is unique for a given connection. The primary reason to keep it unique for a given connection is to avoid any misunderstanding any delayed TCP segment from the previous connection as part of the new connection that is reincarnated of the previous connection. Please refer to Section 2.8.4 (TCP close) for more details. SYN and FIN segments are considered to carry one byte. This field gets rolled over after reaching $2^{32} - 1$. Sequence number helps in maintaining TCP data integrity and identifying the retransmissions that will be discussed later in this chapter.

Acknowledgment Number. This is a 32-bit (64–95) field in the TCP header. TCP is a reliable protocol, so it needs to keep track of each byte transmitted/received. Acknowledgment number helps TCP doing this. The receiving TCP acknowledges the last byte in the stream of bytes received from the sender. Suppose the sender sends n bytes of data with the sequence number s. On reception of this TCP segment, TCP acknowledges with acknowledgment number $n + s + 1$, which means that it has received n bytes of data and now it is waiting for the $n + 1$ byte. Out-of-sequence TCP segments are not acknowledged until the gap is filled. For example, if the sending TCP sends out three TCP segments of 10, 20, and 30 bytes of data in the same sequence and all the segments reach the destination except for a segment with 20 bytes of data which is lost, the receiver TCP acknowledges only 10 bytes of data. Because of this, the sending TCP will eventually come to know that one of the segments is lost and thus it will retransmit those segments. At the same time, duplicate TCP segments are also not acknowledged. We will take the same example to explain the phenomenon. If, because of some reason, the segment with 20 bytes is not lost but is stuck at some router on its way to the destination and is released after the sender has already retransmitted this segment and receiver has acknowledged all the three segments, the segment is either discarded or is replied back with latest acknowledgment number.

Header Length. This is 4-bit field in the TCP header. TCP header is normally 20 bytes without any TCP options. With the TCP options in place we never know the exact length of the TCP header. For the same reason we have the field. The field indicates the number of words that comprise of TCP header. So, the maximum TCP header length that we can have is restricted to 60 bytes.

Unused Field. A 6-bit field (100–105) is still unused and is saved for future use.

TCP Flags. This is a 6-bit field in the TCP header. Each bit in this field represents a TCP flag. These flags are in the order URG|ACK|PSH|RST|SYN|FIN.

URG: This indicates that there is an urgent pointer set and we need to check urgent pointer field to find the address of the urgent pointer.

ACK: This indicates that this TCP segment is acknowledgment by the sender. If this field is set, we check the acknowledgment number field of the TCP header. Except for the first SYN segment, all the TCP segments have this field set because we are losing nothing by doing this.

PSH: This indicates that the sender wants these data to be consumed on priority basis.

RST: This indicates that the sender wants to close the connection without any formal handshake. This bit is set by the TCP when it wants to inform the other end that the TCP segment is no more valid. For example, if the host receives a connection request for which it doesn't have any listening socket, it generates an RST TCP segment in response.

SYN: This indicates that the TCP segment is being exchanged between the two ends trying to synchronize at the time of connection initiation.

FIN: This indicates that one of the TCP wants to close the connection.

Window Size. This is a 16-bit field in the TCP header. TCP detects resource crunch of its peer with the help of this field and acts accordingly. The field indicates the receive buffer size available at any point of time. The receive buffer is consumed when data are received and is vacated as these data are processed and are consumed by the application. If the application is not able to consume the data from the receive buffer as fast as it is received, the receive buffer gets full and eventually the window size also reduces to 0. When the sender gets this information, it stops sending any more data until further notice of window size is advertised by the receiving end. Each TCP peer declares its window size at the time of synchronisation (connection initiation). We take this up in Section 2.6 (sliding window).

Checksum. This is a 16-bit (128–143) field in the TCP header. This is the field used by the receiver to verify that the TCP segment it has received is exactly the one sent by the valid sender. This covers the TCP header and the payload. This way we make sure that the correct TCP segment is being received. This is calculated with the following algorithm: Take TCP header + payload as a stream of a 16-bit word. Sum up all 16-bit words and take 1's complement of this number. This is the final TCP checksum. At the receiving end, the same thing is repeated. The final value obtained at the receiving end should be all 1's in 16-bit number $2^{16} - 1$.

Urgent Pointer. This is a 16-bit (144–159) field in the TCP header. This is the offset from the sequence number in the current TCP segment where the urgent data reside and need to be processed at the earliest. This field is set only if the URG flag is set in the TCP header. This is discussed in Section 11.7.

2.2 TCP OPTIONS (RFC 1323)

At the time when TCP was first designed, future requirements were not very well defined. So, TCP was designed in a very flexible way by introducing options in addition to the basic functionality in order to keep the basic functionality untouched when additions are made to it. Basic TCP works fine with first 20 bytes of information provided in the TCP header. There are continuous efforts to enhance the performance and reliability of TCP with time. RFC 1323 and 793 provide specifications and need for the TCP options in detail. In this section we will cover only the description of the TCP options, and details will be covered in the later sections. Extended TCP header with options would be more than 20 bytes and less than 60 bytes as shown in Fig. 2.2. Four-bit length field in the TCP header indicates the total length of the TCP header. So, if the value of the field is greater than 20, it means we need to check for additional TCP options.

There is a standard format for TCP optional header to properly identify the options. The basic format of the TCP options header contains three fields (Fig. 2.3):

- Kind
- Length
- Value

Kind: This field identifies the TCP option. Each option is assigned a specific number.
Length: This indicates the length of the TCP optional header.
Value: This contains the actual TCP option value.

There are two special formats for TCP options:

- *End of Option List.* This is a 1-byte field with value 0. It indicates that there are no more options.

kind = 0

20 Bytes | <= 40 Bytes

Figure 2.2. TCP header with options.

kind = 1 Byte | length= 1 Byte | Value =Variable length

Figure 2.3. TCP option format.

• *No Operation.* This is a 1-byte field with value 1. It indicates that there is no option here. It is used to pad the fields for memory alignment purposes.

kind = 1

2.2.1 mss Option

Maximum segment size (mss) is a mere reflection of maximum size of the TCP payload that can be accepted by the remote host. mss is a function of the maximum transmission unit (MTU), which is a property of the link layer. So, TCP has to work in coordination with the IP layer to arrive at this value. It is the IP layer which finds out the lowest MTU for the internet path (MTU discovery, RFC 1191). RFC 793 specifies that standards to arrive at the send and receive mss for TCP. The mss option is always exchanged with the TCP SYN segment at the time of connection initialization. The idea of exchanging mss information is to improve the performance of TCP. In the case where sending TCP can send more than the receiving end can accept, the IP datagram will be fragmented at the IP layer. Each fragment is now transmitted with the header overhead consuming the bandwidth. If any of the fragment is not received or lost, the entire TCP segment needs to be retransmitted hitting the throughput. On the other hand, if the sender TCP is generating smaller TCP segments with default mss (536 bytes) where it is capable of sending bigger segments and the other end is also capable of receiving bigger TCP segments, TCP will be operating at lower throughput and hence low performance. Format for the mss option is shown in Fig. 2.4.

2.2.2 Window-Scaling Option

RFC 1323 provides specification for the Window scaling option. Window size is exchanged between connected TCP peers at the time of synchronization. It indicates the receive buffer size of the receiving TCP end. The window size in the TCP header is a 16-bit field. Any TCP can advertise a maximum of 2^{16} bytes (i.e., 65,536), even though it has more resources. In Section 2.7 we will study how window size plays role in deciding throughput of the TCP. In short, lower window sizes will restrict TCP throughput to lower value with high rtt and high bandwidth networks. With the window-scaling option, TCP can advertise window sizes as high as 30 bits in size. The format for the option is shown in Fig. 2.5. It is a 3-byte header identified by kind with value 3. The value in the window-scaling header is a shift count by which the actual window size in the TCP header should be left shifted to get the final window size. For example, if the shift count is 2 and the actual window size from the TCP header is 2^{16}, the final window size will be calculated as

Figure 2.4. mss option format.

Figure 2.5. Window scaling option format.

Figure 2.6. Timestamp option format.

$$\text{Final window size} = \left(2^{16} << 2\right) | \left(\left(2^{16}\right) >> (16-2)\right)$$

which makes the new window size as 2^{18}. Now that the window size cannot exceed 2^{31}, the value of the shift count in the window-scaling option should not exceed 14.

2.2.3   Timestamp Option

TCP needs to accommodate more changes with fast changing network speeds to maintain high performance and reliability as well. Timestamp option is used for both improving the reliability and performance. RFC 1323 provides specification for the timestamp TCP options. TCP uses this option to average out rtt for the entire life cycle of the TCP connection. At the same time, this option is used to implement the PAWS algorithm for reliability. PAWS stands for *protection against wrapped sequence numbers*. TCP data corruption may occur if the delayed TCP segment is confused with the in-sequence segment when the sequence number has wrapped in the case of high speed of networks. The timestamp option is helpful in detecting such delayed TCP segments. Figure 2.6 shows the format of the timestamp optional header.

The timestamp option is identified by kind as 8, and the total length of the timestamp option is 10. There are two timestamp fields, each of size 4 bytes. The TS value contains the sender TCP's timestamp, and the TS echo reply contains the value of the sender's timestamp (TS value field) copied by the receiver in the ACK segment.

The timestamp option is agreed upon at the time of connection initialization. The first SYN packet must contain this option, if the connection initiator wants timestamp option. SYN/ACK should contain this option if:

1. It has received the timestamp option in the SYN segment and it supports the timestamp option.
2. It has not received any timestamp option from the connection initiator but it wants the timestamp option to be active for the connection.

The calculation is simple: The sender sends out its timestamp in the TS value field, and the receiver copies this value in the TS echo reply field while ACKing this segment. The original sender calculates tss by taking the difference of the current timestamp and the timestamp in the TS echo reply field of the ACK segment.

2.2.4 Selective Acknowledgment Option

Receiver TCP acknowledges every in-sequence data segment in a normal way as explained in Section 2.3.1. There is a provision in the TCP to identify any out-of-sequence data segment (RFC 793). On reception of any out-of-sequence data, the receiving TCP gets an indication of a lost segment probably due to the network congestion. In that case, it acknowledges the last in-sequence segment arrived. On reception of such a sender, the TCP gets an indication of data loss and it knows that data segments beyond acknowledged sequence number are lost; then it retransmits the entire data from the sequence number identifier in the acknowledgment field of the receiver, even though unacknowledged data segments are queued up at the receivers end. This causes a drop in the TCP's performance because it has to retransmit entire data beyond the last acknowledged sequence number. RFC 1072 specifies standards to selectively acknowledge the lost data with selective acknowledgment TCP option. The option supplements the existing acknowledgment field in the TCP header. If the receiver finds a hole in the received TCP segments, it sends the last in-sequence TCP segment received in the acknowledgment field in the TCP header and then sends the first offset of the first byte received as out-of-sequence TCP data segment with length of the data segment received as TCP-selective acknowledgment option. So, sender TCP knows which data segment is lost and it retransmits only those segments. For example, receiver TCP received in-sequence data segments until sequence number X and then received the next data segment starting at sequence number $X + n$ of length m bytes. So, there is a hole of n bytes in the stream of data received starting from sequence number X. This is reported to the sender by the way of selective acknowledgment option. The receiver sends ACK for last in-sequence data $X + 1$, and in the selective acknowledgment header it sends $X + n$ with block length of m. So, the sender knows that it has to retransmit the blocks of data of length m bytes that start from sequence number $X + n$. The selective acknowledgment TCP option should be exchanged at the time of connection synchronization (in SYN packets). If either of the peers doesn't support this option, the SACK-permit option is discarded for the connection. The SACK-permit option has a format shown in Fig. 2.7.

Once both the sides agree for the selective acknowledgment option, the receiving TCP can send SACK whenever it receives out-of-sequence data in the format shown in Fig. 2.8. The kind for the SACK option is 5 and its length is variable, which means it can hold information about more than one hole in the stream of bytes received. There are two fields for each SACK block that will have information about one out-of-sequence segment.

kind = 4	length= 2

Figure 2.7. SACK option type 8 length.

kind = 5	length= variable	Start sequence= 32-bits	End sequence= 32-bits	

Figure 2.8. SACK option format.

Figure 2.9. Segments received out-of-order.

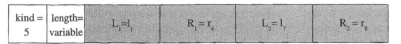

Figure 2.10. SACK block generated for out-of-order segments in the example.

Start Sequence: This is the start sequence number of the contiguous blocks of data segment received (SACK block).

End Sequence: This is the end sequence of the contiguous block of data segment received (SACK block).

There may be many such TCP SACK blocks selectively acknowledging noncontiguous data blocks, with each block having in-sequence data. For a better understanding of the SACK option, lets take small example where sender TCP has sent 12 data segments each of length 1 k. Figure 2.9 shows the queuing of the segments at the receiving end with some of the intermittent segments missing.

s1, s2, s3, and s4 are the only segments that have arrived in sequence. After segments s5 and s6 are missing, then we have segments s7 and s8 contiguous segments; later on, we have s9, s10, and s11 segments missing so that we have segment 12. With this scenario we have SACK enabled, and the receiver will send the TCP segment with the SACK header option as shown in Fig. 2.10. *L* and *R* are the left and right end of the SACK blocks. *l* and *r* are the left and right edge of each segment.

This way the sender will come to know about the missing TCP segments and will retransmit blocks s5, s6, s9, s10, and s11. If the SACK option was not there, the sender would probably retransmit all the TCP segments starting from s5 through s12.

2.3 TCP DATA FLOW

TCP is a reliable transport protocol whose main functionality is to make sure that the data integrity is maintained and also that it is sending data to the correct recipient. There are different algorithms that TCP uses in different situations to ensure high throughput, but data integrity is maintained by one basic algorithm. A very basic algorithm used by TCP to ensure data integrity is *acknowledgment for every Byte of data.* In this section we will discuss (a) the acknowledgment scheme used by the TCP and (b) other algorithms used for improved efficiency. Discussion is based on the assumption that there is no data loss and network congestion.

2.3.1 ACKing of Data Segments

The sender TCP expects acknowledgment for each byte of data it has sent to the receiving TCP. Even the SYN/FIN TCP segments carry one byte of data. The TCP

1st write

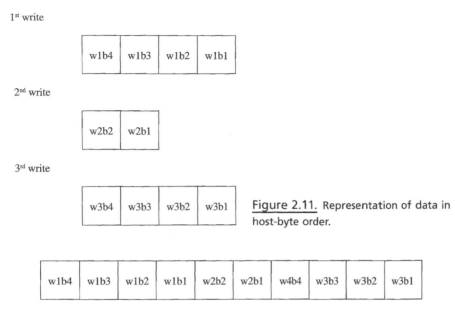

2nd write

3rd write

Figure 2.11. Representation of data in host-byte order.

| w1b4 | w1b3 | w1b2 | w1b1 | w2b2 | w2b1 | w4b4 | w3b3 | w3b2 | w3b1 |

Figure 2.12. Data organized in TCP stream of bytes.

header has two fields—*sequence number and acknowledgment number*—which are used by the acknowledgment scheme to maintain data integrity. The TCP treats user data as a *stream of bytes* and associates a number with each data byte, known as *sequence number*. By *stream of Bytes*, we mean that no matter how and in what format user application writes data over the TCP socket, the TCP arranges them in the stream of bytes in the same sequence as they were written by the user application. For example, an application sends 10 bytes of data in three consecutive writes of 4 bytes, 2 bytes, and 4 bytes, respectively, as shown in Fig. 2.11. Each byte is represented as wxby where x represents write number and y represents the order number of each byte in which they are written by the application on each write. After three writes by the application, the TCP write buffer will have all these data as a stream of 10 bytes as shown in Fig. 2.12. These bytes may be transmitted by the TCP as blocks of contiguous bytes, which means that this stream of bytes can be transmitted as blocks of 2 bytes, 3 bytes, 2 bytes, and 3 bytes, respectively, as shown in Fig. 2.13.

Thus, the application may have written a 4-byte integer or a 2-byte short or a character, but it makes no difference for the TCP. Ultimately, all the user data are arranged as a stream of bytes and are transmitted by the TCP in the same order in which they are arranged in the stream of bytes but in different chunks. The TCP makes sure that each and every byte of data in the stream of bytes reaches the peer in the same sequence as they are arranged at its end. If an application is writing an integer or a short, it should not forget to convert them into network byte order because byte ordering matters here. So also the other side of the TCP socket must read those integers after converting them into the host byte order. Essentially, the TCP has two buffers: send buffer and receive buffer. Data written by an application is first copied to the TCP send buffer, and then the TCP makes a decision on how to transmit that data. Similarly, data received by the TCP are copied to the receive

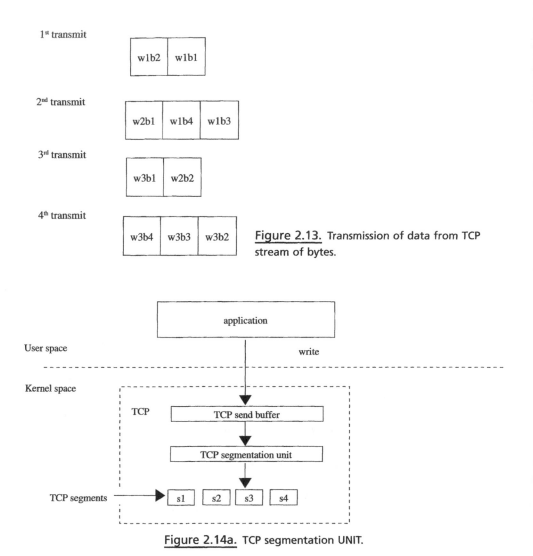

Figure 2.13. Transmission of data from TCP stream of bytes.

Figure 2.14a. TCP segmentation UNIT.

buffer, and the application reads data in whatever chunks of bytes from TCP's receive buffer. Figure 2.14a shows how data written by user application are buffered into TCP send buffer before transmitting it. The segmentation unit then takes some bytes from the send buffer, and then it generates TCP segments and sends them to the next layer for processing. The length of each segment depends on different parameters which we discuss later. The TCP data are received in a similar way. TCP segments are received by the lower layers and then sent to the TCP segmentation unit, which will extract payload from the segments and place it in the TCP's receive buffer. Now it is up to the application to read the data from TCP's receive buffer as a different block of data (see Fig. 2.14b). So, essentially there is TCP send and receive buffer per connection.

Thus, we have learned how a TCP treats user data as a stream of bytes. Now we will see how a TCP sequence number is associated with each byte in the stream of bytes to be transmitted. At the time of connection initialization, each TCP end

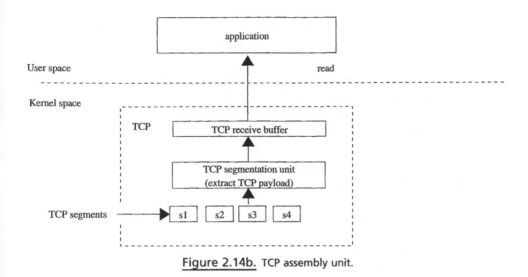

Figure 2.14b. TCP assembly unit.

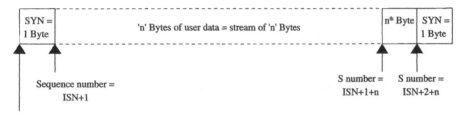

Figure 2.15. TCP sequence number association with stream of bytes.

gets the sequence number called the initial sequence number. The very first byte (sent as a SYN TCP segment) is associated with the Initial sequence number. In Fig. 2.15, we can see an association between the sequence number and the stream of user data bytes. Since the SYN segment is always considered to carry one byte of data (different from user data), the first byte of the user data is associated with the sequence number ISN (initial sequence number) + 1. According to this association, the nth byte of the user data is associated with the sequence number ISN + n + 1 as shown in Fig. 2.15. We will see this phenomenon with the help of client–server program. The client *parikrama* sends a connection request to the server *moksha* and waits to read data from the server. The server sends 8 bytes of data in one chunk and then closes the connection. tcpdump output is captured to study the sequence number associated with the user data and acknowledgments. Figure 2.16 shows *tcpdump* output of data transaction. *tcpdump* uses the S option to print absolute sequence numbers rather than relative sequence numbers. So, the sequence number output format will be *first_byte:last_byte(number_of_bytes)*, where *first_byte* is the sequence number associated with the byte in the stream of bytes which the sender intends to send, *last_byte* is the sequence number associated with the last byte in the sequence of bytes that sender intends to send (excluding last_byte), and

```
1.  09:45:57.483412 parikrama.33015 > moksha.5000: S 2020749023:2020749023(0)
win 49640 <mss 1460,nop,wscale 0,nop,nop,sackOK> (DF)

2.  09:45:57.483485 moksha.5000 > parikrama.33015: S 738652172:738652172(0)
ack 2020749024 win 5840 <mss 1460,nop,nop,sackOK,nop,wscale 0> (DF)

3.  09:45:57.483675 parikrama.33015 > moksha.5000: . ack 738652173 win 49640 (DF)

4.  09:45:57.518037 moksha.5000 > parikrama.33015: P 738652173:738652181(8)
ack 2020749024 win 5840 (DF)

5.  09:45:57.518250 parikrama.33015 > moksha.5000: . ack 738652181 win 49640 (DF)

6.  09:45:57.518314 moksha.5000 > parikrama.33015: F 738652181:738652181(0)
ack 2020749024 win 5840 (DF)

7.  09:45:57.518483 parikrama.33015 > moksha.5000: . ack 738652182 win 49640 (DF)

8.  09:45:57.518549 parikrama.33015 > moksha.5000: F 2020749024:2020749024(0)
ack 738652182 win 49640 (DF)

9.  09:45:57.518570 moksha.5000 > parikrama.33015: . ack 2020749025 win 5840 (DF)
```

Figure 2.16. Sequence of packets exchanged when TCP sends 8 bytes of data over the connection.

number_of_bytes is the number of bytes of user data that the sender intends to send in the current TCP segment. The first three packets are three-way handshake synchronization packets exchanged between client and server at the time of connection initialization. In the first packet, the client sends a SYN segment with ISN as 2020749023 and 0 bytes of user data, as is obvious from the format 2020749023:2 020749023(0). In the second packet, the server responds with an acknowledgment to the client's SYN segment with its ISN as 738652172 (0 bytes user data) and its acknowledgment number as 2020749024 (ACK 2020749024). Even though the client sent 0 bytes of user data, the server responds with acknowledgment of clients ISN + 1. Acknowledgment number, as explained earlier, is the next byte in the stream of bytes that receiver is expecting, which means that the SYN segment is supposed to carry one byte of data and is well agreed upon between the two connected TCP ends. Similarly, the third packet from the client acknowledges the server's SYN segment with acknowledgment number 738652173.

In the fourth packet, we can see that the server sends out the first eight bytes of user data where the first byte is associated with sequence number 738652173 and not 738652172 (ISN for the server). So the client acknowledges 8 bytes of user data in the fifth packet with acknowledgment number 738652181, which means that the client is expecting the 9th byte associated with sequence number 738652181. The sixth packet is a FIN segment from the server because it has no more data to send to the client. Once again we can see that sequence number is 1+ sequence number associated with the last byte of the user data (738652180) with 0 bytes of user data. 738652181 is the acknowledgment number from the client in packet 5, which the server sends in the FIN segment, which means that the client is expecting a byte associated with sequence number 738652180. If the server doesn't send a FIN segment with sequence number 738652180, the client would consider this as a bogus packet and reject it because it is expecting a byte with sequence number 738652181. So, now it is self-explanatory why the FIN segment is considered to carry one byte of data. The acknowledgment number is the same as it was in the last segment from the server because the client has not sent any data. The seventh packet from the client is an acknowledgment for the FIN segment from the server with acknowledgment number as 738652182, which means that the client is expecting the next byte with sequence number 738652181 from the server. The eighth packet is the FIN segment from the client to the server when it closes the connection from its side. We can see that the client's sequence number is 2020749024, which is ISN + 1; this is acknowledgment from the server to the client so far and 0 bytes of user data (2020749024:2020749024(0)). At the same time, it acknowledges the byte associated with sequence number 738652182 because the server has not sent any data after the FIN segment. The final and ninth packet is an acknowledgment for the FIN segment from the client to the server with acknowledgment 2020749025. This means that the server has received the byte associated with sequence number 2020749024 and is expecting the next byte associated with sequence number 2020749025, indicating that the FIN segment from the client to the server is considered to contain one byte of data.

From the above discussion, we have seen how the sequence number is associated with the user data (stream of bytes for TCP) with the relationship between the TCP sequence numbers and the acknowledgment numbers. We have also learned that there is an acknowledgment for each byte of data sent to maintain data integrity at each TCP connected ends. We will view the acknowledgment scheme from a different angle to have better insight into it. We will see how TCP data are buffered at the receiving and the sending TCP ends with the help of the same example and how sequence number and acknowledgment numbers are advanced when data are sent or received (see Figs. 2.17a–17i).

1. Client has sent the SYN segment to the server:

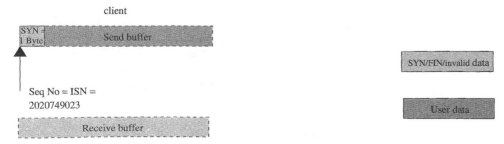

Figure 2.17a. SYN sent by client.

2. Server ACKs client's SYN with the SYN segment:

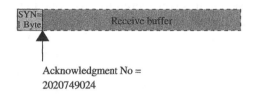

Figure 2.17b. SYN ACK'ed by server.

3. Client acknowledges server's SYN segment:

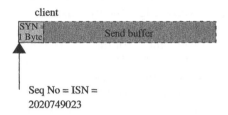

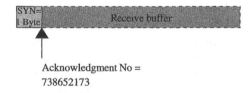

Figure 2.17c. SYN ACK'ed by client.

4. Server sends 8 bytes of user data:

Figure 2.17d. 8-bytes transmitted by server.

5. Client acknowledges 8 bytes of data from the server:

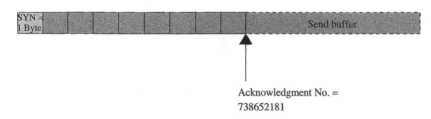

Acknowledgment No. =
738652181

Figure 2.17e. 8-bytes ACK'ed
by the client.

6. Server sends the FIN segment because it is over with sending data and is closing its end:

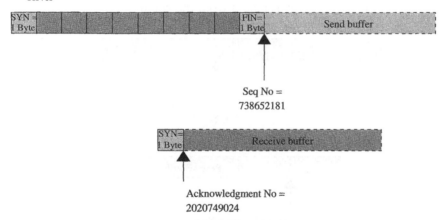

Seq No =
738652181

Acknowledgment No =
2020749024

Figure 2.17f. FIN sent by
the server.

7. Client ACK's the FIN segment from the server and one additional byte associated with the FIN segment:

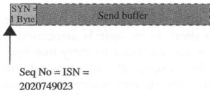

Seq No = ISN =
2020749023

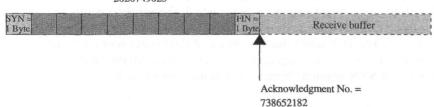

Acknowledgment No. =
738652182

Figure 2.17g. FIN
ACK'ed by the client.

8. Client sends the FIN segment when it closes its end:

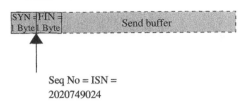
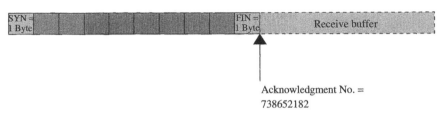

Figure 2.17h. Client send's FIN.

9. Server acknowledges the FIN segment from the client:

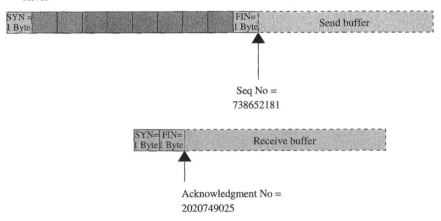

Figure 2.17i. Server ACK's final FIN.

We have seen the sequence number–ACKnowledgment scheme used by the TCP to ensure data integrity. In short, every byte is associated with a sequence number. Even SYN/FIN segments are supposed to carry one byte of data that is not mixed up with the user data. Every segment sent needs acknowledgment from the receiver, with an acknowledgment number indicating the sequence number associated with the byte in the stream-of-bytes which the receiver wants to receive next. This model ensures complete data integrity between the sender and the receiver TCP ends. The TCP sends the next block of data (data segment) only when it receives ACK for the last data segment. Each segment contains an ACK field set other than the first SYN segment because it has nothing to ACK.

This was the very basic TCP functionality. Until now, we have considered only one end sending data to the receiver. We will see in the next section how TCP can enhance its performance when both ends are sending data.

2.4 DELAYED ACKNOWLEDGMENT

Until now, we have seen a very basic ACKing scheme that TCP implements to maintain data integrity. Now let's look at the case where we need to maintain data integrity along with the improved efficiency. Here we will consider data flow in both the directions. The best example would be an interactive TCP session where each byte of data typed needs to be echoed like telnet, rlogin, and so on. If we use the same ACKing scheme as discussed for such interactive sessions, let's see what happens.

Figure 2.18 shows the condition where character 'e' is typed at the command line telnet client. The TCP segment is generated to transmit character 'e' to the server. Segment 2 is acknowledgment from server for reception of character 'e'. Segment 3 carries character 'e', which is an echo of the last byte sent by the client. Segment 4 is an acknowledgment for segment 3. So, we see that there is an acknowledgment for every data segment that TCP receives. With this kind of acknowledgment scheme, we know that we are ensuring data integrity but at the same time we also know that for each byte of data typed in at the client, we are generating four segments. Each segment carries at least 50 bytes of header (20 bytes TCP, 20 bytes IP, 10 bytes MAC). So, there is overhead of network traffic and resource utilization associated with each segment at each TCP end. If we can reduce the number of segments generated for each byte typed in by the telnet client, we can make the TCP work more efficiently. The TCP makes this possible by introducing the *delayed acknowledgment* scheme. With this scheme, the TCP waits for some time to acknowledge the received data segment so that it can send some data along with the acknowledgment if any data are available by that time. Let's look at the same example when delayed acknowledgment is implemented by TCP. The TCP registers a delayed acknowledgment timer with the system after it receives any data segment from the other end. By registering timer, I mean to say that every OS implements timer interrupts that are generated after every fixed time interval (mainly implemented for time-slicing the runable processes). There is a list of tasks that need to

Telnet client   server

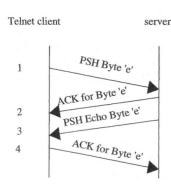

Figure 2.18. Four TCP segments generated to echo a character.

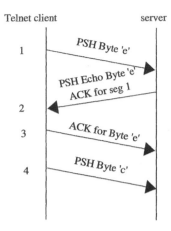

<u>Figure 2.19.</u> Delayed ACK is piggybacked with data segment.

be performed by the system when this timer interrupt comes. So, we register our task with the timer interrupt and we specify the delay in multiples of time interval at which the timer interrupt occurs. Every time a timer interrupt occurs, it checks every registered task if its time has expired. So, all those tasks are executed whose time has expired. Thus, the delayed acknowledgment timer is registered such that it is performed whenever the next timer interrupt comes. So, the acknowledgment timer may expire any time between 0 and t time units, where t is the time interval at which the timer interrupt comes. In short, delayed acknowledgment can be generated anytime between 0 and t time units after it is registered. Suppose that t is 200 ms; the TCP can generate acknowledgment for the received data segment any time between 0 and 200 ms with the delayed acknowledgment in action.

Now we must be thinking as to why we need this delayed acknowledgment scheme as we are delaying the ACK which slows down the entire process. But it is the other way around. With the delayed acknowledgment, the TCP tries to send the data ready to be sent along with the ACK for the last data segment received. In our example, the TCP receives data and puts it in the receive buffer. Telnet application reads the data and writes it back to the TCP's send buffer (see Fig. 2.19). This happens very fast, in case the server is not heavily loaded. So, by the time the server's delayed acknowledgment timer expires, the echoed data is there in the TCP's send buffer. Like this, the ACK is piggybacked along with the data to be sent. Here, we can see that the echo of character 'e' generates only three segments, which is less by 1. To continue with this, we can see that the client has generated a data segment for character 'c' after sending ACK for the data segment 2, which means that client side TCP did not have any data in its send buffer by the time the delayed acknowledgment timer expired. This may be because there was no input from the keyboard by the time the timer expired. This scheme works fine as long as we limit ourselves to high-speed networks such as LAN. We are sending out data when they are available. It is just that we are delaying ACK for any data received so that we can piggyback the ACK along with any data to be sent. If any data are available even when there is time for TCP's delayed ACK timer to expire, we send it. So, essentially this scheme will generate a large amount of segments carrying one byte of data in the interactive sessions such as telnet, rlogin, and so on. In the case of WANs or slow networks, a large number of data segments carrying small payloads might cause problems of network congestion. For this reason, we slightly refine the scheme for slow WANs, which we discuss in the next section.

2.5 NAGLE'S ALGORITHM (RFC 896)

A delayed acknowledgment scheme helps in reducing the number of small packets by piggybacking the ACKs along with the data to be sent in the same direction, delaying the acknowledgments. This scheme still doesn't prevent a large number of segments to be generated carrying one byte of payload in the case of interactive sessions. This would surely cause problems in slow networks. To overcome this issue, Nagle's algorithm was introduced; it says that no data would be sent out until we have an unacknowledged data, which means that all the data that need to be sent out are collected until the time we receive an ACK for the last sent data. So, all the data are now sent out in one data segment. This makes the entire process self-clocking. In the slow networks where the ACKs are received after a long delays, we collect a lot of data and send them all in one segment. On the other hand, in fast networks we receive ACKs very fast and hence we can send large number of packets with smaller payloads very fast. This algorithm is self-adjusting in the sense that it adjusts itself according to the network conditions and automates the data transfer rates. From Fig. 2.20 we can see that when ACK for data segment is received, we have collected three characters and hence send all of them in one data segment. With Nagle's algorithm in action, we still have delayed ACK timer applicable. Consider a case where ACK is received for the last data segment in Fig. 2.21 and there are no data to be sent out. So, the client waits for some data input before it acknowledges the echoed data (segment 2).

At the client's end, there was no data to be sent when the delayed ACK timer expired, which generated ACK segment (segment 3). We then send the next character 'c' because TCP sends out data (segment 4) when they are there in the send buffer because there is no unacknowledged data. We receive acknowledgment for segment 4 (character 'c') in segment 5. We send out characters 'h' and 'o' together in segment 6 which are collected in the TCP's send buffer by the time the ACK for character 'c' is received in segment 5 following Nagle's algorithm.

We will compare the behavior of TCP with Nagle's algorithm in place over LAN and WAN. Tcpdump output shown in Fig(2.22) is taken from the telnet session over

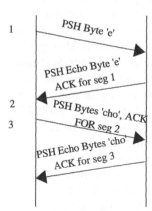

Figure 2.20. Fewer number of small segments generated with Nagle's algorithm.

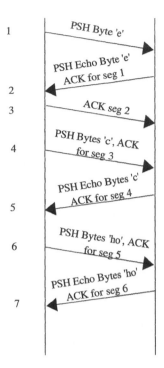

Figure 2.21. Packets exchanged on slow WAN with Nagle's algorithm enabled.

LAN(*moksha = client, parikrama = server*). We are doing nothing but typing some characters at the telnet prompt which are echoed back from the server. We can see that TCP is following Nagle's algorithm completely because data are sent only when we get back ACK for unacknowledged data. We can see one more thing here that delayed acknowledgment timer expiring at the client end. Segments 3, 6, 9, 12, and 19 are simply ACKs from the client moksha to the server parikrama because the delayed acknowledgment timer has expired before any data are available to be sent (there is no input from the keyboard when the delayed acknowledgment timer expired). Let's look at Fig. 2.22, which shows the tcpdump output taken from telnet session over WAN. The telnet client and the server are 9 hops apart.

We see here how Nagle's algorithms work effectively with slow networks. The tcpdump data are collected at the server, and we can see an average RTT of 350 ms (see Fig. 2.23). We type in a character at the telnet client, and packet 1 is generated. Packet 2 is an ACK for 1 and also contains an echo of character contained in segment 1. Then we proceed with the subsequent characters until segment 5, which is an ACK for character echoed by the server in segment 4, is generated. Most probably segment 5 is generated because of the delayed acknowledgment timer. Segment 5 doesn't contain any data, which means that no data were available by the time the delayed ACK timer expired. We proceed once again by typing in a character and generating a packet for each character (segments 6, 7, 8, and 9) probably because only one character is typed in by the time the ACK for the last unacknowledged byte appears. But here onwards we increased our typing speed and see that instead of 1, we are sending 2, 3, 5, and 7 characters in segments 10, 12, 14, and 16, respectively. So, by the time our ACK are received, we have collected more data to be transmitted and we transmit them as one segment instead of generating one segment per character. So Nagle's algorithm is helpful in slow networks where we

1. *19:30:59.901376 moksha.1305 > parikrama.telnet: P 1765803975:1765803976(1)*
ack 431576686 win 5840
2. *19:30:59.901672 parikrama.telnet > moksha.1305: P 1:2(1) ack 1 win 49232*
3. *19:30:59.901705 moksha.1305 > parikrama.telnet: . ack 2 win 5840*
4. *19:30:59.904281 moksha.1305 > parikrama.telnet: P 1:2(1) ack 2 win 5840*
5. *19:30:59.904490 parikrama.telnet > moksha.1305: P 2:3(1) ack 2 win 49232*
6. *19:30:59.942200 moksha.1305 > parikrama.telnet: . ack 3 win 5840*
7. *19:31:00.068928 moksha.1305 > parikrama.telnet: P 2:3(1) ack 3 win 5840*
8. *19:31:00.069206 parikrama.telnet > moksha.1305: P 3:4(1) ack 3 win 49232*
9. *19:31:00.069237 moksha.1305 > parikrama.telnet: . ack 4 win 5840*
10. *19:31:00.181595 moksha.1305 > parikrama.telnet: P 3:4(1) ack 4 win 5840*
11. *19:31:00.181884 parikrama.telnet > moksha.1305: P 4:5(1) ack 4 win 49232*
12. *19:31:00.181936 moksha.1305 > parikrama.telnet: . ack 5 win 5840*
13. *19:31:00.184557 moksha.1305 > parikrama.telnet: P 4:5(1) ack 5 win 5840*
14. *19:31:00.184767 parikrama.telnet > moksha.1305: P 5:6(1) ack 5 win 49232*
15. *19:31:00.187568 moksha.1305 > parikrama.telnet: P 5:6(1) ack 6 win 5840*
16. *19:31:00.187780 parikrama.telnet > moksha.1305: P 6:7(1) ack 6 win 49232*
17. *19:31:00.195539 moksha.1305 > parikrama.telnet: P 6:7(1) ack 7 win 5840*
18. *19:31:00.195748 parikrama.telnet > moksha.1305: P 7:8(1) ack 7 win 49232*
19. *19:31:00.232208 moksha.1305 > parikrama.telnet: . ack 8 win 5840*

Figure 2.22. TCP dump output for telnet session on slow WAN.

1. *15:28:56.855969 eth0 < client.1081 > server.telnet: P 2366787223:2366787224(1)*
ack 3196104816 win 6642
2. *15:28:56.856129 eth0 > server.telnet > client.1081: P 1:2(1) ack 1 win 5792*
3. *15:28:57.195473 eth0 < client.1081 > server.telnet: P 1:2(1) ack 2 win 6642*
4. *15:28:57.195529 eth0 > server.telnet > client.1081: P 2:3(1) ack 2 win 5792*
5. *15:28:57.575488 eth0 < client.1081 > server.telnet: . 2:2(0) ack 3 win 6642*
6. *15:28:57.601943 eth0 < client.1081 > server.telnet: P 2:3(1) ack 3 win 6642*
7. *15:28:57.601989 eth0 > server.telnet > client.1081: P 3:4(1) ack 3 win 5792*
8. *15:28:57.955909 eth0 < client.1081 > server.telnet: P 3:4(1) ack 4 win 6642*
9. *15:28:57.955955 eth0 > server.telnet > client.1081: P 4:5(1) ack 4 win 5792*
10. *15:28:58.296227 eth0 < client.1081 > server.telnet: P 4:6(2) ack 5 win 6642*
11. *15:28:58.296280 eth0 > server.telnet > client.1081: P 5:7(2) ack 6 win 5792*
12. *15:28:58.636017 eth0 < client.1081 > server.telnet: P 6:9(3) ack 7 win 6642*
13. *15:28:58.636080 eth0 > server.telnet > client.1081: P 7:10(3) ack 9 win 5792*
14. *15:28:58.977773 eth0 < client.1081 > server.telnet: P 9:14(5) ack 10 win 6642*
15. *15:28:58.977840 eth0 > server.telnet > client.1081: P 10:15(5) ack 14 win 5792*
16. *15:28:59.319531 eth0 < client.1081 > server.telnet: P 14:21(7) ack 15 win 6642*
17. *15:28:59.319609 eth0 > server.telnet > client.1081: P 15:22(7) ack 21 win 5792*
18. *15:28:59.695524 eth0 < client.1081 > server.telnet: . 21:21(0) ack 22 win 6642*

Figure 2.23. TCP dump output for telnet session on slow WAN.

are automatically controlling the traffic depending on the network characteristics. In this example, we didn't get to see the network characteristics changing like congestion because RTT is more or less the same. But have tried to explain how a large number of small segments containing one character can be avoided with the help of Nagle's algorithm.

2.6 TCP SLIDING WINDOW PROTOCOL

As of now, we have seen the TCP algorithms associated with the interactive sessions such as telnet and rlogin in fast and slow networks. We were concerned with a small amount of data transfer per segment in our discussions until now. Let's see how a TCP behaves when an application wants to send bigger chunks of data. When an application is sending bulk data, TCP has to take into account some additional TCP header fields to decide upon the data transmission rate. We will see how ACKs are generated in a different way and how TCP controls data transmission rates in our current discussion in the case of bulk data transfer. We introduce here one more TCP parameter, *window size*, which is a part of the TCP header, and see how it helps the sender TCP to understand the receiver's resource constraints based on which sender controls the data transmission rate. If we just recall from the previous discussion regarding window size, we know that it is the indication of resource available at the receiver TCP end. First we will see how window size and TCP's receive buffer are associated and then move along with the actual discussion.

Consider a situation where bulk data are flowing in one direction in a high-speed network. Now from Figs. 2.14a and 2.14b we know that when application writes data over TCP socket it is not directly transmitted to the receiver. The TCP first copies the data to the send buffer for various reasons—for example, waiting for an ACK (Nagle's algorithm). In the same way, receiver TCP gets data from the TCP segments and puts it in its receive buffer. Further application reads the data from TCP's receive buffer when it has chance. If we don't have send and receive TCP buffer arrangements, there are great chances of a TCP connection hogging resources such as memory, CPU, and network bandwidth starving other connections from using the resources. With the TCP buffers in place, it is clear that the sender can send data in two cases (given that other conditions are favorable for data transmission)—

1. There are data ready to be sent in sender TCP's send buffer.
2. There is space in the receiver's TCP receive buffer.

As discussed earlier, receiver TCP puts data in its receive buffer before application can read it. Once an application has read data from TCP's receive buffer, space is created to accommodate more data. In short, at any given point in time, receiver TCP can receive maximum data bytes restricted to the space in its receive buffer. On the other hand, space in the receiver buffer is created only when the application reads the data from the receive buffer. If the receiver's receive buffer is full, no more data will be accepted from the sender, and the sender has to wait until the space is available in the receiver's receive buffer. The question is, How does the sender know about the availability of space in the receiver's receive buffer? The TCP exchanges this information using TCP's header field *window size*. Each TCP segment carries this information irrespective of whether it is a data segment or not. Let's look at this example with the help of an example where the server is sending bulk data in a chunk of 1 kB to the client continuously. Client application is programmed not to read any data sent by the server. This is done deliberately to explain the concept of the TCP's window size and also the flow control imposed by the TCP's window size. As we have already learned, the application writes data over a TCP socket that goes into the TCP's send buffer. The TCP reads the data from the send buffer and sends it in small segments. At the other end, the TCP gets these data segments, extracts data from the segments, and puts them in the receiver's TCP receive buffer. Finally, an application reads in data from the TCP's receive buffer and makes space for more data to be stored in the TCP's receive buffer. We will see how the receiver TCP's receive buffer information is passed on to the sender TCP and then how the sender TCP reacts to the changing receiver buffer size.

Network activity for bulk data transfer from server to client is captured using tcpdump. The captured data are shown in Figs. 2.24a and 2.24b. Packet's 1–3 are the initial SYN segments exchanged between client and server as part of the TCP connection initiation handshake. The client sends *mss* as a TCP option (1460) and also the initial window size (5840). Similarly, segment 2 is again a SYN segment from the server with *mss* (1316) TCP option and the initial window size (5216). Window size advertised by the client in the SYN segment is nothing but the size of its receive buffer (5840 bytes) and similarly for the server. We will concentrate only on the client's window size because it is at the receiving end and the server is only sending data and not receiving any data from the client.

Server application writes 1024 bytes of data at a time, but we can see that TCP is generating a TCP data segment of 1304 bytes. This is because it waits until we have data equal to maximum segment size from the application in its send buffer. Server side TCP has an *mss* from the client which is less than its own *mss*, but still the TCP data segment is never found to have data more than 1304 bytes (<1316, client's *mss*) in the entire session. This is because the IP would have found out some intermediate router whose MTU (maximum transmission unit) is such that an *mss* of 1304 comes into picture. So, we can see that the server can send 5840 bytes of data without receiving any acknowledgment from the receiver at this point in time. The server keeps on sending data segments of 1304 bytes and receives acknowledgment for each data segment. We can see that the client is advertising increased window size each time with the reception of data, and this seems to be slightly confusing. When the client has advertised its window as 5840, how can it advertise window size 7842 after the reception of 1304 bytes of data which remains in its receive buffer (because the application is not reading data). This is because TCP can receive data more than the initially advertised window size. But by advertising small window size initially, it is imposing control on the rate of data flow from the sender. When the receiving TCP senses no congestion in the network, it gradually increases the window size until it finally reaches the actual window size. Actually, this is congestion control mechanism. The client continues to increase its window size until the client has sent 19,560 bytes of data (packet 32). At this point in time, the client's window size has increased to 45,640. It means that the client has 19,560 bytes of data in its receive buffer and still it can receive 45,640 bytes of data, which means that total receive buffer size of the client is 45,640 + 19,560 = 65,201 bytes. Thereafter (packet no. ≥34) we can see the window size decreasing on reception of each data segment. The decrease in window size is exactly equal to the number of bytes received. This is because client application is not reading any data from TCP's

```
 1  16:42:01.077677 eth0 > client.33496 > server.5000: S 3803112996:3803112996(0) win 5840
      <mss 1460,sackOK,timestamp 5903892 0,nop,wscale 0> (DF)
 2  16:42:01.418479 eth0 < server.5000 > client.33496: S 2982028701:2982028701(0) ack 3803112997 win 5216
      <mss 1316,sackOK,timestamp 592429 5903892,nop,wscale 0> (DF) [tos 0x20]
 3  16:42:01.418507 eth0 > client.33496 > server.5000: . 1:1(0) ack 1 win 5840
 4  16:42:01.796991 eth0 < server.5000 > client.33496: . 1:1305(1304) ack 1 win 5216
 5  16:42:01.797083 eth0 > client.33496 > server.5000: . 1:1(0) ack 1305 win 7824
 6  16:42:01.815506 eth0 < server.5000 > client.33496: . 1305:2609(1304) ack 1 win 5216
 7  16:42:01.815579 eth0 > client.33496 > server.5000: . 1:1(0) ack 2609 win 10432
 8  16:42:02.168928 eth0 < server.5000 > client.33496: P 2609:3913(1304) ack 1 win 5216
 9  16:42:02.168953 eth0 > client.33496 > server.5000: . 1:1(0) ack 3913 win 14344
10  16:42:02.192321 eth0 < server.5000 > client.33496: . 3913:5217(1304) ack 1 win 5216
11  16:42:02.192338 eth0 > client.33496 > server.5000: . 1:1(0) ack 5217 win 16952
12  16:42:02.213164 eth0 < server.5000 > client.33496: . 5217:6521(1304) ack 1 win 5216
13  16:42:02.213182 eth0 > client.33496 > server.5000: . 1:1(0) ack 6521 win 19560
14  16:42:02.235281 eth0 < server.5000 > client.33496: P 6521:7825(1304) ack 1 win 5216
15  16:42:02.235298 eth0 > client.33496 > server.5000: . 1:1(0) ack 7825 win 22168
16  16:42:02.543288 eth0 < server.5000 > client.33496: . 7825:9129(1304) ack 1 win 5216
17  16:42:02.543305 eth0 > client.33496 > server.5000: . 1:1(0) ack 9129 win 26080
18  16:42:02.565528 eth0 < server.5000 > client.33496: . 9129:10433(1304) ack 1 win 5216
19  16:42:02.565546 eth0 > client.33496 > server.5000: . 1:1(0) ack 10433 win 28688
20  16:42:02.588800 eth0 < server.5000 > client.33496: P 10433:11737(1304) ack 1 win 5216
21  16:42:02.588817 eth0 > client.33496 > server.5000: . 1:1(0) ack 11737 win 31296
22  16:42:02.609151 eth0 < server.5000 > client.33496: . 11737:13041(1304) ack 1 win 5216
23  16:42:02.609175 eth0 > client.33496 > server.5000: . 1:1(0) ack 13041 win 33904
24  16:42:02.631592 eth0 < server.5000 > client.33496: . 13041:14345(1304) ack 1 win 5216
25  16:42:02.631609 eth0 > client.33496 > server.5000: . 1:1(0) ack 14345 win 36512
26  16:42:02.653178 eth0 < server.5000 > client.33496: . 14345:15649(1304) ack 1 win 5216
27  16:42:02.653196 eth0 > client.33496 > server.5000: . 1:1(0) ack 15649 win 40424
28  16:42:02.674845 eth0 < server.5000 > client.33496: . 15649:16953(1304) ack 1 win 5216
29  16:42:02.674861 eth0 > client.33496 > server.5000: . 1:1(0) ack 16953 win 43032
30  16:42:02.698110 eth0 < server.5000 > client.33496: . 16953:18257(1304) ack 1 win 5216
31  16:42:02.698127 eth0 > client.33496 > server.5000: . 1:1(0) ack 18257 win 45640
32  16:42:02.968926 eth0 < server.5000 > client.33496: . 18257:19561(1304) ack 1 win 5216
33  16:42:02.968944 eth0 > client.33496 > server.5000: . 1:1(0) ack 19561 win 45640
34  16:42:02.991001 eth0 < server.5000 > client.33496: P 19561:20865(1304) ack 1 win 5216
35  16:42:02.991018 eth0 > client.33496 > server.5000: . 1:1(0) ack 20865 win 44336
36  16:42:03.013938 eth0 < server.5000 > client.33496: P 20865:22169(1304) ack 1 win 5216
37  16:42:03.034950 eth0 < server.5000 > client.33496: . 22169:23473(1304) ack 1 win 5216
38  16:42:03.047034 eth0 > client.33496 > server.5000: . 1:1(0) ack 23473 win 41728
39  16:42:03.057852 eth0 < server.5000 > client.33496: . 23473:24777(1304) ack 1 win 5216
40  16:42:03.080130 eth0 < server.5000 > client.33496: . 24777:26081(1304) ack 1 win 5216
41  16:42:03.101919 eth0 < server.5000 > client.33496: . 26081:27385(1304) ack 1 win 5216
42  16:42:03.123747 eth0 < server.5000 > client.33496: . 27385:28689(1304) ack 1 win 5216
43  16:42:03.123766 eth0 > client.33496 > server.5000: . 1:1(0) ack 28689 win 36512
44  16:42:03.145864 eth0 < server.5000 > client.33496: . 28689:29993(1304) ack 1 win 5216
45  16:42:03.167820 eth0 < server.5000 > client.33496: . 29993:31297(1304) ack 1 win 5216
46  16:42:03.167837 eth0 > client.33496 > server.5000: . 1:1(0) ack 31297 win 33904
47  16:42:03.189569 eth0 < server.5000 > client.33496: . 31297:32601(1304) ack 1 win 5216
```

Figure 2.24a. TCP dump output for bulk data transfer (application not reading data from socket buffer).

```
48  16:42:03.212878 eth0 < server.5000 > client.33496: . 32601:33905(1304) ack 1 win 5216
49  16:42:03.227033 eth0 > client.33496 > server.5000: . 1:1(0) ack 33905 win 31296
50  16:42:03.234130 eth0 < server.5000 > client.33496: . 33905:35209(1304) ack 1 win 5216
51  16:42:03.255142 eth0 < server.5000 > client.33496: . 35209:36513(1304) ack 1 win 5216
52  16:42:03.279184 eth0 < server.5000 > client.33496: P 36513:37817(1304) ack 1 win 5216
53  16:42:03.279201 eth0 > client.33496 > server.5000: . 1:1(0) ack 37817 win 27384
54  16:42:03.302496 eth0 < server.5000 > client.33496: . 37817:39121(1304) ack 1 win 5216
55  16:42:03.337033 eth0 > client.33496 > server.5000: . 1:1(0) ack 39121 win 26080
56  16:42:03.340008 eth0 < server.5000 > client.33496: . 39121:40425(1304) ack 1 win 5216
57  16:42:03.361761 eth0 < server.5000 > client.33496: . 40425:41729(1304) ack 1 win 5216
58  16:42:03.383427 eth0 < server.5000 > client.33496: . 41729:43033(1304) ack 1 win 5216
59  16:42:03.405308 eth0 < server.5000 > client.33496: . 43033:44337(1304) ack 1 win 5216
60  16:42:03.417040 eth0 > client.33496 > server.5000: . 1:1(0) ack 44337 win 20864
61  16:42:03.427127 eth0 < server.5000 > client.33496: . 44337:45641(1304) ack 1 win 5216
62  16:42:03.452362 eth0 < server.5000 > client.33496: . 45641:46945(1304) ack 1 win 5216
63  16:42:03.472835 eth0 < server.5000 > client.33496: . 46945:48249(1304) ack 1 win 5216
64  16:42:03.496098 eth0 < server.5000 > client.33496: . 48249:49553(1304) ack 1 win 5216
65  16:42:03.496116 eth0 > client.33496 > server.5000: . 1:1(0) ack 49553 win 15648
66  16:42:03.519736 eth0 < server.5000 > client.33496: . 49553:50857(1304) ack 1 win 5216
67  16:42:03.539842 eth0 < server.5000 > client.33496: . 50857:52161(1304) ack 1 win 5216
68  16:42:03.561673 eth0 < server.5000 > client.33496: . 52161:53465(1304) ack 1 win 5216
69  16:42:03.561691 eth0 > client.33496 > server.5000: . 1:1(0) ack 53465 win 11736
70  16:42:03.585063 eth0 < server.5000 > client.33496: . 53465:54769(1304) ack 1 win 5216
71  16:42:03.608658 eth0 < server.5000 > client.33496: . 54769:56073(1304) ack 1 win 5216
72  16:42:03.608675 eth0 > client.33496 > server.5000: . 1:1(0) ack 56073 win 9128
73  16:42:03.628680 eth0 < server.5000 > client.33496: . 56073:57377(1304) ack 1 win 5216
74  16:42:03.650798 eth0 < server.5000 > client.33496: . 57377:58681(1304) ack 1 win 5216
75  16:42:03.667039 eth0 > client.33496 > server.5000: . 1:1(0) ack 58681 win 6520
76  16:42:03.677136 eth0 < server.5000 > client.33496: . 58681:59985(1304) ack 1 win 5216
77  16:42:03.695689 eth0 < server.5000 > client.33496: P 59985:61289(1304) ack 1 win 5216
78  16:42:03.717273 eth0 < server.5000 > client.33496: P 61289:62593(1304) ack 1 win 5216
79  16:42:03.737033 eth0 > client.33496 > server.5000: . 1:1(0) ack 62593 win 2608
80  16:42:03.739105 eth0 < server.5000 > client.33496: . 62593:63897(1304) ack 1 win 5216
81  16:42:03.762166 eth0 < server.5000 > client.33496: . 63897:65201(1304) ack 1 win 5216
82  16:42:03.807033 eth0 > client.33496 > server.5000: . 1:1(0) ack 65201 win 0
83  16:42:05.123565 eth0 < server.5000 > client.33496: . 65200:65200(0) ack 1 win 5216
84  16:42:05.123610 eth0 > client.33496 > server.5000: . 1:1(0) ack 65201 win 0
85  16:42:07.434423 eth0 < server.5000 > client.33496: . 65200:65200(0) ack 1 win 5216
```

Figure 2.24b. Receive buffer is full, zero-window is advertised (segment 82).

receive buffer. The client continues to accept data until it has space in its receive buffer. We can see the client's window size diminishing as follows: 15,648 (seg 65), 11,736 (seg 69), 9128 (seg 72), 6520 (seg 75), 2608 (seg 79), and 0 (seg 82). Segment 82 is an ACK from the client for reception of 65,200th byte with window size of 0. After this we can see that the server is not able to send any data to the client because the window size advertised by the client is 0, which means that there is no space in the client's receive buffer. The server cannot send anymore data until the client advertises a positive window size.

So, we have seen from the above example how sender TCP uses window size information from the other end (receiver TCP) to adjust its data transmission rate.

Let's now see the TCP sliding window protocol in completeness. Window size is the indication of the available space in the receiver TCP's receive buffer to the sender TCP. Sender TCP can always send data equal to the last advertised window size by the receiver TCP. The ACK for the reception of the data segment from the receiver TCP will have a new window size, and the sender will use this new value of window size to transmit more data. We will learn that it is not only the window size but also the acknowledged sequence number from the receiver that will finally decide the rate at which the sender can transmit data.

The sliding window protocol is demonstrated in Fig. 2.25. We will learn how the window slides when data are transmitted by the sender TCP and it receives acknowledgment for the sent data. Each block represents 1 Kbyte of data. We consider here that the receiver TCP has provided maximum receive buffer size because window size and sender TCP is transmitting 1 Kbyte of data per segment. Gray-colored blocks shows the window size at any given point in time. The sender TCP maps the receiver's window size to a stream of bytes ready to be sent in its send buffer as shown in Fig. 2.25a. In Fig. 2.25a the window size advertised by the receiver is 12 Kbytes, which means that the receiver TCP's receive buffer is 12 Kbytes long. The arrow always points to first unacknowledged byte in the senders stream of bytes. We take the absolute byte number with respect to the ISN (initial sequence number) to map each byte. So, the first byte is mapped to ISN + 1. From Fig. 2.25a it is clear that at this point in time the sender TCP has not sent any data and the send window starts from ISN + 1. We know that sender TCP can send 12 Kbytes of data at this point of time. Let's see what happens when sender TCP transmits the first segment. Figure 2.25b shows that gray blocks cover only the 11-Kbyte portion of the send buffer. The left end of the send window is shifted by 1 Kbyte toward the right, which means that after sending the first segment, sender TCP can only send 11 Kbytes of data. The arrow still points to ISN + 1 because the sent data are still unacknowledged. Next we receive acknowledgment for the first data segment. The receiver sends an acknowledgment for the first data segment with a window size of 12 K, which means that the application at the receiver's end has read all 1 Kbyte of data

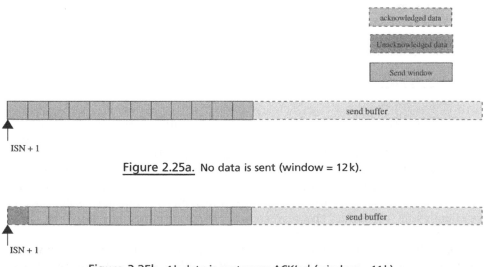

Figure 2.25a. No data is sent (window = 12 k).

Figure 2.25b. 1 k data is sent none ACK'ed (window = 11 k).

ISN + 1+1k

Figure 2.25c. All (1k) data is ACK'ed (window = 12k).

ISN + 1+1k

Figure 2.25d. 4k data is rent, only 1k ACK'ed (window = 9k).

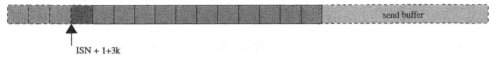

ISN + 1+3k

Figure 2.25e. 4k data Sent, only 5k ACK'ed (window = 11k).

ISN + 1+3k

Figure 2.25f. 6k data Sent, only 3k ACK'ed (window = 9k).

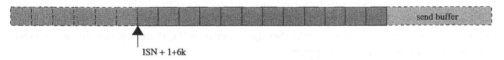

ISN + 1+6k

Figure 2.25g. All 6k data ACK'ed (window = 12k).

from the receiver's buffer before it sends the acknowledgment. So, the right end of the send window is shifted by 1 Kbyte toward the right (Fig. 2.25c). Once again the sender knows that it can send 12 Kbytes of data and the sender sends next three consecutive data segments; the situation is shown in Fig. 2.25d. Next, the sender receives acknowledgment for the second and third data segments sent a the window size of 11 K (see Fig. 2.25e), which means that the sender still can send 11 Kbytes of data. But this time the right end of the window is shifted toward the right by 2 Kbyte because the fourth data segment is still unacknowledged. The arrow is now pointing to ISN + 1 + 3 K. Next, the sender transmits another consecutive fifth and sixth data segments. The left end of the window is shifted to the right by 2 Kbyte (see Fig. 2.25f). Finally, the sender receives acknowledgment for fourth, fifth, and sixth data segments with window size of 12 K. At this point in time, we have no unacknowledged data, so the right end of the window is shifted by 3 Kbyte towards the right while the left end remains unchanged with the arrow now pointing to ISN + 1 + 6 K (see Fig. 2.25g).

Let's see, in different situations, how the left and right ends of the window move in different situations. Window size may increase or decrease in different situation.

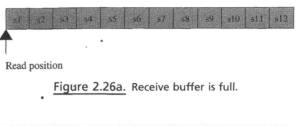

Read position

Figure 2.26a. Receive buffer is full.

Read position   Write position

Figure 2.26b. Application needs 2 k bytes from socket receive buffer.

The window size may increase because the right end of the window moves toward the right side while the left end remains intact. There is no chance that the left end moves toward the left because the position of the left end is pointing to the location in the stream of bytes, which is either acknowledged or unacknowledged. If left end moves toward the left, it means that the TCP is by some means deleting the existing data, which is highly impossible.

The TCP send window can increase because the right side of the send window can move toward the right while the left end remains intact. This may happen because the receiver TCP can increase the receive buffer size at any point in time because of two reasons. First, application can increase the receive buffer size at any point of time using socket options. Second, the application has read some data from TCP's receive buffer which has created some space in the receiver TCP's receive buffer to accommodate more data. So, the receiver TCP advertises its increased window size whenever it so happens.

Figure 2.26a shows the situation where the receiver TCP's receive buffer is full because the application is not able to read data. The receive buffer is seen to be 12 Kbytes long (each block shown is 1 Kbyte long). Furthermore, application is scheduled and starts reading data. It reads 2 Kbyte of data so that it creates 2 Kbyte of space in the receive buffer (see Fig. 2.26b). When this space is created, TCP advertises a new window size to the sender. This is just an example, but there are RFC defined to decide the condition when the new window size should be advertised.

Let's consider a case for decreasing window sizes. The window size may decrease in a normal way when the rate at which data transmission is greater than the rate at which data is read by the application. In such cases the receiver TCP's receive buffer keeps filling and available space in the receive buffer goes down. In such cases the right end of the sender's window will remain intact but the left end will keep moving toward the right.

As shown in Fig. 2.27a, the receiver TCP has received two segments each of 1 Kbyte but application has not read the data. So, the window size advertised at this point of time is 10 Kbytes along with the ACK. Figure 2.27b shows that two more data segments each of 1 Kbyte have arrived and the data are collected in the receive buffer. So, total space occupied by the data in the receive buffer is 4 Kbyte, which application has not read yet. Thus, the TCP advertises window size of 8 Kbyte along

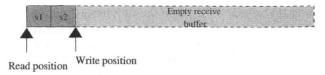

Read position Write position

Figure 2.27a. 2k data in socket receive buffer.

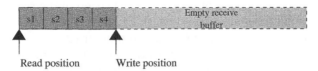

Read position Write position

Figure 2.27b. 4k data in socket receive buffer.

with the ACK. Another way that the sender's window size decreases is that the left end remains intact and the right end moves toward the left. This may happen in the case where the receiving TCP shrinks its receive buffer because of scarcity of the available resources.

2.7 MAXIMIZING TCP THROUGHPUT

Until now we discussed the effect of window size on the bulk data transfer, and we have seen that the TCP's throughput depends on (a) the rate at which the application sends data, (b) the receiver's window size, and (c) the rate at which the application reads data from the receiver TCP's receive buffer. We have not considered the network characteristics on TCP's throughput. We will introduce two more parameters that will have an effect on the TCP's throughput. These parameters are *bandwidth* offered by the physical layer and the *rtt* (round trip time).

Life is not that easy when it comes to packets traveling over the internet. We never know what path the TCP segment is taking, and this is not under our control. We may reach the router, which is heavily loaded where the queue is full and there is no space for the new packet which might result in dropping the packet. On the other hand, it may so happen that we may reach the network, which is operating at a very high speeds. In short, the packet might pass through high-speed or low-speed network segments, which is not predictable in advance to the TCP before it injects the next packet in the network. With the existing sliding window protocol scheme which we just covered in our previous section, we know that once the sender has knowledge of the receiver's window size, it will start transmitting data without caring for acknowledgments for those segments until it knows that the window size of the receiver's window size is a positive nonzero number. All this occurs without the knowledge of the network characteristics. If the receiver's window size is too big but the network is slow, the sender continues to transmit data segments that might get lost on the way leading to retransmissions of lost segments and hence might introduce performance issues. Keeping this in mind, some modifications are made to the existing sliding window protocol which would impose restriction on the rate at which data should be transmitted from the sender TCP initially. This restriction is gradually relaxed with the reception of acknowledgments for the transmitted segments. This way the sender TCP takes the defensive side initially and gradually reaches the data transmission rates that would utilize full network capacity. A self-clocking mechanism is introduced which says that the rate at which data are to be transmitted should depend on the rate at which acknowledgments are received. The rate at which acknowledgment for a segment is received makes a sender guess the network characteristics or the processing speed of the receiver. The slowest node in the path of the packet decides the speed at which it travels. It may be some intermediate router, network speeds, or the processing speed of the receiver. But for the sender it does not matter which is the slowest. The time taken to receive an acknowledgment for a segment is known as round-trip time or rtt.

This algorithm is implemented by introducing a new parameter at the sender side, namely, the congestion window. The congestion window is initialized to 1 mss (maximum segment size) received from the receiver when the connection is initialized. The sender at any point in time can send data which is minimum of the congestion window and the window size advertised by the receiver. The sender sends first a TCP data segment of size 1 mss. Once it receives acknowledgment for this segment, it increases the congestion window by 1 mss. So, the congestion window size at the sender now becomes 2 mss. When it receives acknowledgment for the subsequent segments, the congestion window is incremented by 1 mss. This way the sender increases its congestion window size exponentially as follows: Initially, the sender can send only 1 mss byte of data. After reception of acknowledgment for the first segment, it increases its congestion window by 2 mss. On reception of acknowledgment for these two segments (second and third segments), it increases the congestion window size to 4 mss. It can now send 4 mss bytes of data. It can now send four segments, each carrying 1 mss bytes of data. On reception of acknowledgment for these four segments, it can increase its congestion window size to 8 mss. So, the congestion window is increasing exponentially as 1, 2, 4, 8, 16, … times until it saturates the network. Let's see how it actually happens with the help of an example.

In Fig. 2.28a–e, we illustrate the relation between send congestion window, window advertised by the sender, and segments acknowledged. When the connection is just established, we can see that the congestion window is 1 mss and the receiver window is 12 mss as shown in Fig. 2.28a. So, one segment s1 is transmitted; and until it is acknowledged, the situation will remain the same as shown in Fig. 2.28a. Once s1 is acknowledged, the congestion window is incremented by 1 but the receiver's window remains unchanged. So, we can transmit two more segments as shown in Fig. 2.28b. s2 and s3 are transmitted and the situation remains unchanged

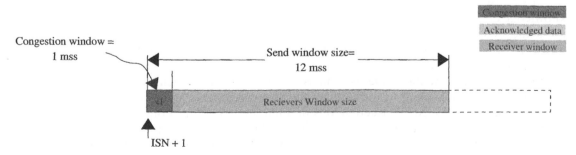

Figure 2.28a. Congestion window when no data is sent.

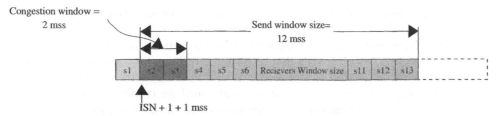

Figure 2.28b. Congestion window when 1 segment is ACK'ed.

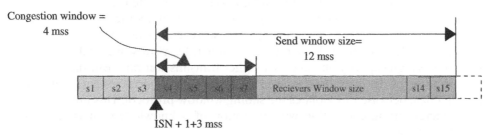

Figure 2.28c. Congestion window incremented to four when three segments are ACK'ed.

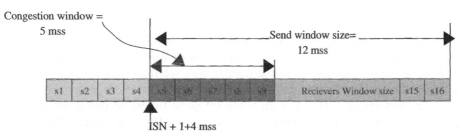

Figure 2.28d. Congestion window incremented to five after four segments are ACK'ed.

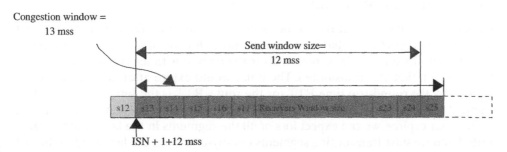

Figure 2.28e. Congestion window is more than the send window (saturation point).

until they are acknowledged. Figure 2.28c shows the situation where both segments are acknowledged and the congestion window is incremented to 4. Segments are transmitted when the congestion window allows them. For example, when acknowledgment for s2 is received, congestion window is incremented by 1 and becomes 3, which means that we can send two more segments at that point in time since s3 is still unacknowledged. Figure 2.28c is the snapshot at the time when s2 and s3 are acknowledged; and by the time the acknowledgment for s3 arrives, s4 and s5 may have been transmitted.

In this way, when the acknowledgment for s4 has arrived, the congestion window is incremented to 5, which means that segments s5–s9 can be transmitted, whereas the send window advertised allows segments up to s16 to be transmitted as shown in Fig. 2.28d. We keep on transmitting segments until we receive acknowledgment for s12. The congestion window is incremented to 13 in this situation whereas the send window advertised by the receiver is still 12 as shown in Fig. 2.28e. In this situation, we can transmit only 12 segments because the receiver's buffer has taken over the congestion window here and transmission is limited by the receiver's buffer size at this stage. This way initially the congestion window limits the transmission rate because in this period we are accessing a network congestion state whereas the receiver's window allows a higher transmission rate. Slowly we realize that the network has high capacity and allows a higher transmission rate. But the receiver's window becomes the limitation because we can't transmit more than a receiver can accommodate because this violates the sliding window protocol. This initial stage of slowly incrementing congestion with reception of acknowledgment is called the slow-start phase.

2.8 TCP TIMERS

A TCP generates asynchronous events, which is the reason we need timers to detect the faults. For example, we send out data and wait for data to be acknowledged. This is an asynchronous event. In the similar way, we may wait for the receiver to open a window, which is again an asynchronous event. There are many other events that are generated by a TCP. For all these we need timers to detect timeouts. We don't discuss these timers much in detail here because they are discussed in Chapter 10.

2.8.1 Retransmission Timer

Whenever a TCP sends out data, it needs to make sure that the data have reached the receiver properly. For that it has to set a timer for the first data segment that is transmitted. Once the ACK is received for the data, this timer is reset for the next data segment that was transmitted. The timer would expire after an interval that is decided by the round-trip time RTT for the route. RTT is the time taken by a data segment to be acknowledged, which is calculated using the TCP timestamp option. If the timer expires, we can expect loss of all the segments in the last window transmitted and we start transmitting segments one-by-one from the last window. In this case we enter the loss state and slowdown rate of data transmission as we can sense network congestion. Sometimes the RTT changes due to change in route or change in transmission medium; in this case, packets may get delayed and timeout may occur spuriously (check RFC 3522). RFC 2988 specifies how effective RTO calculation can be done.

Just to illustrate the retransmit timeout example, *tcpdump* output is taken from a connection that was made to experience timeout in Fig. 2.29. The receiver (parikrama) was unplugged from the network and the sender (moksha) continued to send data. We have skipped the three-way handshake from the output. It is clear

```
1   07:10:26.978338 moksha.1520 > parikrama.5001: P 1013601:1015049(1448) ack 1 win 5840
2   07:10:26.978369 moksha.1520 > parikrama.5001: P 1015049:1016497(1448) ack 1 win 5840
3   07:10:27.198258 moksha.1520 > parikrama.5001: P 1013601:1015049(1448) ack 1 win 5840
4   07:10:27.638270 moksha.1520 > parikrama.5001: P 1013601:1015049(1448) ack 1 win 5840
5   07:10:28.518259 moksha.1520 > parikrama.5001: P 1013601:1015049(1448) ack 1 win 5840
6   07:10:30.278273 moksha.1520 > parikrama.5001: P 1013601:1015049(1448) ack 1 win 5840
7   07:10:33.798261 moksha.1520 > parikrama.5001: P 1013601:1015049(1448) ack 1 win 5840
```

Figure 2.29. Retransmission of TCP segments for TCP dump output.

that segment 1 containing 1448 bytes of TCP payload is transmitted with sequence space [1013601, 1015049]. Segment 2 containing 1448 bytes is transmitted with sequence space [1015049, 1016497]. Segment 3 is retransmission of segment 1 since this segment is not yet acknowledged and retransmit timer expired (check the sequence space of segment 3). In the same way, segments 4, 5, 6, and 7 are retransmissions of segment 1, which is not acknowledged. If we look at the time stamp of retransmissions, it is more or less exponentially increasing. The time interval for retransmissions are 219,920, 440,012, 879,989, 1,760,014, and 3,519,988 ms, respectively. This does not go exactly with an exponential increment of RTO because timers are high-priority tasklets and are executed when timer interrupt occurs. Timer interrupt happens at fixed frequency. So, the timer boundaries won't match exactly with the RTOs.

2.8.2 Persistent Timer

The TCP has its own flow control mechanism which is controlled by the buffer size at the receiving end. The sender TCP gets an idea of the amount of data to be transmitted from the window size advertised by the receiver. At the receiving end the data gets queued on the receive buffer, until it is consumed by the application. If the sender is sending data at a much faster rate than it can be read by the application, data will keep on queuing on the receiving TCP's receive socket buffer. It may also happen that there is no space left out in the receiving TCP's socket buffer. At this point in time, the receiving TCP advertises a zero window. When the sender gets zero window indication, it applies flow control on data and stops sending any more data until the receiver opens a window.

In this situation, whenever the application reads data from the receiving TCP's socket buffer, it generates space in the receive buffer for more data. In this process, the receiving TCP sends an ACK with a nonzero window. There is a probability that this ACK gets lost and the sender never gets the window open indication. In this case there would be a deadlock between the two TCP ends because the receiver thinks that it has already sent a window open segment and the receiver will send data whenever it has something, whereas the sender is waiting for a window open advertisement from the receiver, which it never gets.

To tackle this situation, the sender TCP sends out a zero-window probe that is exponentially backed off by way of the persistent timer. This timer sends out the next sequence number with no data. Linux sends out one sequence number smaller than what it has transmitted last. This timer is explained with the help of an example. The sender TCP sends out data in a chunk of 1448 bytes (mss for the connection).

1	*22:16:55.146010 moksha.1210 > parikrama.5004: P 95569:97017(1448) ack 1 win 5840*
2	*22:16:55.199083 parikrama.5004 > moksha.1210: . ack 97017 win 0*
3	*22:16:57.405951 moksha.1210 > parikrama.5004: . ack 1 win 5840*
4	*22:16:57.406189 parikrama.5004 > moksha.1210: . ack 97017 win 0*
5	*22:16:57.905952 moksha.1210 > parikrama.5004: . ack 1 win 5840*
6	*22:16:57.906176 parikrama.5004 > moksha.1210: . ack 97017 win 0*
7	*22:16:58.905952 moksha.1210 > parikrama.5004: . ack 1 win 5840*
8	*22:16:58.906185 parikrama.5004 > moksha.1210: . ack 97017 win 0*
9	*22:17:00.905952 moksha.1210 > parikrama.5004: . ack 1 win 5840*
10	*22:17:00.906190 parikrama.5004 > moksha.1210: . ack 97017 win 0*
11	*22:17:04.905961 moksha.1210 > parikrama.5004: . ack 1 win 5840*
12	*22:17:04.906194 parikrama.5004 > moksha.1210: . ack 97017 win 0*
13	*22:17:12.905953 moksha.1210 > parikrama.5004: . ack 1 win 5840*
14	*22:17:12.906186 parikrama.5004 > moksha.1210: . ack 97017 win 0*
15	*22:17:28.905951 moksha.1210 > parikrama.5004: . ack 1 win 5840*

Figure 2.30. Zero-window probe timer for TCP dump output.

The application at the receiving end does not issue any read on the socket. So, all the data gets queued on the receiving TCP's socket buffer. *tcpdump* output is taken for this connection as shown in Fig. 2.30. Stage comes when the receiver's buffer is full; it advertises zero window (packet 2). Packet 3 is the first zero-window probe, and the sequence number it sends is not shown in the output. The first probe is immediately acknowledged by the receiver (i.e., packet 4). The next probe is sent after 500 ms as packet 5. Subsequent probes are sent at an interval of 1000 ms (packet 7), 2000 ms (packet 9), 4000 ms (packet 11), 8000 ms (packet 13), and 16,000 ms (packet 15), respectively. This shows that the window probe timer fires with timeout value exponentially backed off.

2.8.3 Keepalive Timer

There are many situations where the connection is alive for ages without either ends communicating. For example, there may be a telnet session open for many days without a client issuing any command to the server. In this situation, how will either end know that the connection at the other end is alive because the connection at one end may remain open even when the other end has crashed or rebooted? The server sends out the first pure ACK segment after the connection is in an idle state for a certain fixed time. This is implemented with the help of keepalive timer.

Once the connection is in an idle state, a timer is fired and a pure ACK segment is sent out to the peer. If we get a response for the ACK, the other end is still alive and in this case we rest the keepalive timer to fire after a connection is found in an idle state for a certain duration. In case the we don't get a response for the ACK segment sent by the keepalive timer, the timer is reset with timeout exponentially increased. This continues until we have exhausted maximum re-tries. There are different system-wide configurables related to the timer that can be tuned to get the most optimum results.

Socket option SO_KEEPALIVE can be used to enable keepalive timer for the connection. This can be tried as an exercise.

2.8.4 TIME_WAIT Timer

When the TCP does an active close on the socket, it does a four-way hand shake to cleanly close the connection. It sends the FIN and receives ACK for the FIN. Then the peer (doing passive close) sends a FIN segment that is acknowledged by this end. Once a final FIN is acknowledged by the TCP doing active close, it remains in the TIME_WAIT state to deal with the following situations:

- The final ACK may get lost.
- There may be reincarnation of the connection in case the peer crashes and reboots very fast.

The socket remains in this situation until the TIME_WAIT period has elapsed which is usually 2*MSL (maximum segment lifetime). Each implementation has its own way of calculating the MSL value. As soon as the socket enters the TIME_WAIT state, the TCP sets the TIME_WAIT timer for the socket that expires after given time and finally closes the socket. Until then, the connection remains locked from both ends, meaning that the tuple source/destination IP address and port numbers are locked for this duration. Both TCP ends can't use these port numbers for a new connection until the timer expires and the socket is removed from the TIME_WAIT state.

2.9 TCP CONGESTION CONTROL

The TCP is a reliable protocol that keeps track of data that have reached the other end with the help of acknowledgment for every byte of data received by the peer. The TCP can sense network congestion by way of retransmit timer timing out and reception of duplicate acknowledgments. There are different ways of handling these situations. If the retransmit timer expires, it is an indication of complete loss of data transmitted in the last window because a timer is set when the first data segment from the last window is transmitted (given that we have not timed out spuriously). In this case we need to transmit all the data from the last window and we start with retransmitting the first segment in the retransmit timer. If we receive duplicate acknowledgments, it is an indication that some packet is lost and we transmit a lost segment (given that there is no reordering of segments in the network). This is also called an early detection of loss, and the corrective action is fast retransmit and fast recovery. There are two TCP congestion state variables:

1. Congestion window
2. Slow-start threshold

When the TCP enters the loss state, we revert to slow start where the congestion window is initialized to 1 and slow-start threshold is initialized to half of the congestion window or 2 (whichever is greater). In the slow start phase, the rate of data transmission depends on the rate at which acknowledgments are received. We continue to send out lost segments at an exponentially increasing rate starting with one segment. This continues until the congestion window reaches the slow-start threshold. Thereafter, congestion avoidance takes over. In the congestion avoidance phase, the congestion window is incremented per RTT and does not depend on the rate at which acknowledgments arrive. We do this because it is the last congestion window that got us into a loss state by saturating the network. Considering that we were doing a slow start at the time we entered the loss state, the congestion avoidance should take over from the window prior to one that caused loss of data (half of the congestion window that got us into loss state). That is the reason we set the slow-start threshold to half of the congestion window at the time we encountered loss.

In case we detect loss because of reception of three duplicate ACKs, initialize the slow-start threshold to half of the congestion window at that point in time and initialize the congestion window to slow-start threshold plus 3 (for three duplicate ACKs). The reason is that we know that data are still flowing between the two ends and it is just that one segment is lost. So, we don't touch the transmission rate, but the rate at which congestion window is incremented further will be function of RTT (linear with respect to RTT). This will help control the rate of data transmission further. Specification is provided in RFC 2581 and RFC 2001.

2.10 TCP PERFORMANCE AND RELIABILITY

Extensions to the TCP is introduced to give it better reliability and for high performance. At the time when the TCP was in the development phase, the internet was not all that powerful. But room was left for any extensions required for the TCP in the future, depending on the requirement. These extensions are implemented with the help of options in TCP header. These are already discussed in Section 2.2; in this section we will see how they enhance TCP features.

2.10.1 RTTD

rtt (*round-trip time*) is one of the very critical parameters that decides the performance of TCP. Sending TCP needs an acknowledgment for each byte of data transmitted. If it doesn't get an acknowledgment for the sent TCP within a specific time, it needs to retransmit that segment, assuming that the segment is lost. The time to retransmit the TCP segment is based on rtt. If rtt is underestimated for slow networks, we may end up retransmitting TCP segments even when the original TCP segment or its ACK is on the flight. This is wastage of bandwidth and additional overhead of generating a packet and transmitting it. Moreover, entering into a congestion state involves lowering of data transmission. If we are falsely entering into a loss state, TCP throughput is hampered severely, whereas if the rtt is over estimated for high-speed networks, we end up retransmitting TCP segments after a long delay even if the data are lost, resulting in slow recovery form losses, thus hitting the performance.

2.10.2 SACK/DSACK

SACK is selective acknowledgment and DSACK is duplicate SACK. SACK gives useful information in the case of reordering or loss of one or more segments. Without SACK enabled, we get to know that segments have reached out-of-order with the help of duplicate acknowledgments. But this information is incomplete to predict the network congestion state. We don't know which TCP segments have reached the other end. This is important information as far as reordering of segments is concerned. Based on reordering length, we start fast retransmit fast recovery on the connection. By default, reordering length is three. With SACK information available we can exactly calculate reordering length from the lowest and highest sequence spaces that have been selectively acknowledged (FACK). Based on this information, we can avoid false retransmissions by starting the fast retransmit and fast recovery phase. With the SACK information available, we know exactly what to retransmit in the fast retransmit and fast recovery phase. Because we already know which segments have reached the other end safely, we transmit only the holes. DSACK is just an extension of SACK where DSACK is generated when both the original and retransmission reach the receiver. This gives us an indication that we have falsely entered into the fast retransmission and fast recovery phase because the packet got delayed in the network or because of excessive reordering. With the DSACK options available, we may be able to detect false entry into the congestion state and may recover fast.

2.10.3 Window Scaling

The receiving TCP advertises window size, which is the size of the receive buffer; this is limited to a 16-bit value in the TCP header. The sender transmits at the rate which is determined by two factors: congestion window and the receiver's buffer space. A 16-bit window becomes a bottleneck for TCP throughput in two cases:

1. With high-speed networks and Long Fat Networks where bandwidth is huge, we can transmit data at the speed of few gigabytes per second.
2. The receiver has a huge buffer space for the incoming data.

In the above two cases, even though network capacity is too much and resources available with the receiver is too high, the sender can't do much because the window advertised by the receiver is limited.

A new extension to the TCP allows the receiver to increase the limit on the allowable window. This way the sender can have the maximum advantage of the above two conditions and transmit data at a maximum rate improving TCP throughput.

2.11 IP (INTERNET PROTOCOL)

This protocol carries the entire Internet traffic. IP is a stateless and connectionless protocol, which means that neither end maintains any state for the IP datagram sent and received. The IP datagram may take any path to reach the destination. The IP datagram hops from router to router to reach its final destination. Each router will have entry for the next hop for the IP datagram. The datagram is queued on the routers outgoing interface queue in case there is traffic for the link. It may also happen that the router crashes or the queue for the outgoing interface is full. In both the cases, the packets are dropped.

Other than IP carrying internet traffic, it has many roles to play such as routing, quality of service, congestion reporting using an IP ECN flag, and soon. In this section we will have a brief overview of the protocol with some examples illustrating routing table, network interface, and *traceroute*.

2.11.1 IP Header

The IP header has fixed as well as optional fields. The fixed header is 20 bytes long and the rest is optional (see Fig. 2.31). Later in the discussion, we will determine the total header length. We will discuss these fields one by one.

ver. This is a 4-bit field indicating the version of IP. As of now we have only two versions, 4 and 6.

hlen. This is a 4-bit field indicating the header length of IP datagram including IP options. The number in the field is the count of 32-bit words that make an IP header. For example, if the length of the IP header is 20 bytes, this field will have value of 5. This limits the length of the IP header to 15 32-bit words, that is, 60 bytes.

TOS. This is an 8-bit field indicating the class to which an IP datagram belongs. There are different type of applications using internet resources. Each application has different requirements as far as network resource usage is concerned. Some applications require reliability more than speed, whereas others would like to minimize delay. All this is controlled per packet and queuing discipline at each router. In the internet IP packet hop from router to router. Depending on the packet type, router needs to queue the packet in such a way that the required target is achieved. Each packet should contain information about the queuing discipline based on which router will queue it on different queues. This information is available in TOS field of the IP header and details are mentioned in RFC 1349.

total len. This is a 16-bit field and indicates total length of the IP datagram in bytes. This is required for may reasons like data integrity and marks the end of the IP datagram. If the total length is included in the IP checksum, we are sure what we have received is complete. Because the packets are fragmented by any intermediate router, this field is also modified and so also IP checksum. The Ethernet frame

0   31

ver=4-bit	hlen=4-bit	TOS=8-bits	total len= 16-bits
ID = 16-bits		Flg=3-bts	frag offset = 13-bits
TTL=8-bits	prot=8-bits		checksum=16-bits
src addr=32-bits			
dst addr=32-bits			
options			
data			

Figure 2.31. IPV4 header format.

has a lower limit on the size. If the length of an IP datagram falls below this minimum frame length, the Ethernet will pad the frame to make minimum frame length. If we don't have this field, the IP payload will be misinterpreted because of extended padding.

ID. This is a 16-bit field that uniquely identifies a packet on the destination host. The ID field has a role to play in fragmentation and reassembly. When IP datagram is fragmented, this field uniquely identifies each fragment.

flg. This is a 3-bit flag field in the IP header. As of now, these flags are used mostly for fragmentation and reassembly units.

- The zeroth bit is not yet used.
- The first bit indicates whether the packet should be fragmented. If set, the IP datagram won't be fragmented by any router.
- The second bit indicates whether we have more fragments for the IP datagram. When an IP datagram is fragmented by any intermediate router, this bit is set for all the fragments except for the last fragment.

frag offset. This is a 13-bit field and is used by the fragmentation and assembly unit to mark the offset in the original IP datagram for the fragment. With the help of this field, the assembling unit places all the fragments in order.

TTL. This is an 8-bit field keeping *time-to-live* information. *time-to-live* is a maximum number of hops (routers) that a packet is supposed to take before it should be dropped. This field is decremented by 1 by each router. We never know what route a packet takes. It may happen that the broken route causes a packet to hop in a loop. In such cases, this field avoids the packet to hang out in the internet forever. The maximum number of hops that an IP datagram can have is 254.

prot. This is an 8-bit field indicating protocol number. As such, an IP datagram is just a traffic carrier over the internet. It may carry TCP, UDP, ICMP, and IGMP data. At the receiving end, this field is used to multiplex packet to the next protocol layer.

checksum. This is a 16-bit field containing checksum for the IP header including optional field. This checksum is calculated as follows:

- Dividing the entire IP header as 16-bit words.
- Sum up these 16-bit words.
- Calculate the 16-bit 2's complement of the sum.

At the receiving end, the entire IP header is once again divided as 16-bit words and summed up. The result of the sum should have all the bits set. If not, the IP header is considered corrupted. Since the IP header is modified at each hop as the TTL field is modified, the IP checksum is recalculated. RFC 1071 illustrates better ways to calculate the IP checksum.

src addr. This is a 32-bit field containing an IP address of the generator of the IP datagram. This field is modified by masquerading/NAT software when a packet from a private network is forwarded to the internet by the gateway.

dst addr. This is a 32-bit field containing an IP address of the host for which packet is destined. Once again this field is modified by the gateway when packet coming from public network is destined for the host in the private network (de-masquerading/de-NAT).

2.12 ROUTING

An IP datagram reaches its destination by hopping through a series of routers in the internet, which means that each router needs to have information about the next hop router and the outgoing interface for the packet. Each router maintains a table of all the possible routes through all the available links. This table is called routing table. A route can be added manually by using a *route* command. In the complex internet, a router may go down and come up and there is nothing certain. So, having static routing entries will not help much. Thus, there is a provision for modifying a routing table dynamically. This can be done by routing daemons that implement various routing protocols. The neighboring routers may broadcast their routing tables to all others in the domain or the router may query a routing table from the neighboring routers. Whichever way it is, routing information is made available to the routers and then the best route for a given destination is added to the routing table. The following routing protocols are most widely used:

- Routing Information Protocol (RIP)
- Open Shortest Path First (OSPF)
- Border Gateway Protocol (BGP)

The Routing decision is done in three steps:

- Compare the IP address of the packet with the destination field of the routing table. If an entry exists in the routing table, we use that route.
- If the first test fails, we compare the subnet ID of the packet with the destination field using a subnet field in the routing entry. If the subnet ID matches, we use this route.
- If both tests fail, we simply use the default route for the packet for the routing decision.

2.13 *netstat*

On Unix systems, the *netstat* command is used to display a kernel routing table. Figure 2.32 shows the kernel routing table from *netstat* command. The output of the

```
23   [root@moksha sameer]# netstat -nr
24   Kernel IP routing table
25   Destination    Gateway      Genmask       Flags   MSS Window   irtt   Iface
26   192.168.1.0    0.0.0.0      255.255.255.0  U       0 0           0      eth0
27   127.0.0.1      0.0.0.0      255.0.0.0      U       0 0           0      lo
28   0.0.0.0        192.168.1.1  0.0.0.0        UG      0 0           0      eth0
```

Figure 2.32. Netstat output for host pointing to default Gateway.

netstat command is taken on Linux, where we have default static kernel routing entries. It shows three entries:

- 192.168.1 network, line 26
- Loopback 127.0.0.1, line 27
- Default gateway, line 28

We will see how we can differentiate between three types of routes from the route flag. Following are the routing flags as shown in the *netstat* output:

U Indicates route is 'up'.
G Route is to a gateway.
H Route is to a host and not a network.
M Table entry is modified by ICMP redirect message.
D Route was created dynamically or by ICMP redirect.

There are three rows for each routing table entry in the *netstat* output. There is much more associated with each routing entry, but seven main entries are displayed here. The first entry at line 26 is for subnet 192.168.1.0, which means that any packet destined for subnet 192.168.1.0 should use interface eth0. Only subnet ID will be compared for this entry, which can be obtained by ANDing IP address with the *Genmask* entry (255.255.255.0). If the subnet ID of the packet matches the *Destination* entry (192.168.1.0), why do we say that we need to compare the subnet ID of the packet for this entry? The reason is that the routing flag is set to *U*. *U* means that the route is up and nothing more.

The next entry is for a loopback entry (127.0.0.1), which is a special case. Any packet that is destined for 127.0.0.1 is sent to a loopback interface (*lo*). Here only subnet ID is compared because the *U* flag is set for the route. The third entry is for a default route. *Destination* and *Genmask* are set to all 0's here because it is a default route and will unconditionally route any packet that comes to this stage. We can see that Gateway is set to 192.168.1.1, meaning that packets should be sent to this machine for the next routing decision using eth0 as an outgoing interface. We can also see that the flag is set to *UG*, meaning that the route is UP and *G* indicates that the route for gateway. When the *G* flag is set, the packets need to be sent to the gateway machine for routing decisions. So, the destination hardware address in the link layer header is set to that of the router instead of the hardware address of the destination IP.

2.14 *traceroute*

In this section we will see how packets hop in the internet to reach a final destination. We will use a network utility *traceroute* to see how a packet is traversing through the internet. We will discuss the mechanism used by *traceroute* in the next section. *traceroute* reports three round trip times for each router. I have an internet connection at home connected through a DSL router with IP address 192.168.1.1.

The First line of *traceroute* output shows that a route is being traced for *mail.yahoo.com* with IP address 209.191.92.114 (see Fig. 2.33). The maximum number of hops for this destination is set to 30. Every line shows three round trip times from each router. We can see that as we are moving away from the host machine toward a destination, rtt is incrementing. Everything is ok until we reach the 19th entry. We can see that each time three different routers are being reported. This happens because the 19th hop packet ends up at three different routers. This may happen because the routing table at the 18th hop may have an updated entry at three different times. Once again we can see something different at line 23, which is three stars. This means that the traceroute has timed out and didn't get a response

```
traceroute to mail.yahoo.com (209.191.92.114), 30 hops max, 40 byte packets

1  router (192.168.1.1)  0.716 ms  0.663 ms  0.652 ms
2  ABTS-KK-Dynamic-001.96.167.122.airtelbroadband.in (122.167.96.1)  44.216 ms  26.430 ms  26.394 ms
3  dsl-KK-static-158.63.101.203.airtelbroadband.in (203.101.63.158)  25.733 ms  29.952 ms  34.780 ms
4  59.145.6.85 (59.145.6.85)  28.489 ms  27.925 ms  26.395 ms
5  125.17.12.229 (125.17.12.229)  43.597 ms  34.404 ms  33.826 ms
6  59.145.7.133 (59.145.7.133)  308.078 ms  302.166 ms  302.364 ms
7  59.145.6.161 (59.145.6.161)  62.751 ms  36.647 ms  34.523 ms
8  sl-st21-pa-6-0.sprintlink.net (144.223.243.1)  303.914 ms  308.952 ms  306.304 ms
9  sl-bb22-sj-11-0-0.sprintlink.net (144.232.8.240)  304.678 ms  304.786 ms  304.681 ms
10  sl-bb25-sj-12-0.sprintlink.net (144.232.3.210)  300.984 ms  296.637 ms  306.816 ms
11  sl-st21-sj-12-0.sprintlink.net (144.232.9.240)  296.765 ms  297.804 ms  296.818 ms
12  144.232.18.26 (144.232.18.26)  292.153 ms  290.710 ms  290.554 ms
13  vlan69.csw1.SanJose1.Level3.net (4.68.18.62)  314.398 ms  303.852 ms  308.401 ms
14  ae-63-63.ebr3.SanJose1.Level3.net (4.69.134.225)  310.011 ms  308.251 ms  304.915 ms
15  ae-2.ebr3.LosAngeles1.Level3.net (4.69.132.10)  320.267 ms  309.593 ms  321.626 ms
16  ae-78.ebr2.LosAngeles1.Level3.net (4.69.135.13)  312.771 ms  309.665 ms  321.885 ms
17  ae-3.ebr3.Dallas1.Level3.net (4.69.132.78)  310.680 ms  309.624 ms  307.697 ms
18  ae-68.ebr1.Dallas1.Level3.net (4.69.135.1)  311.886 ms  306.835 ms  307.703 ms
19  ae-11-55.car1.Dallas1.Level3.net (4.68.122.141)  308.625 ms ae-11-51.car1.Dallas1.Level3.net
   (4.68.122.13)  303.655 ms ae-11-55.car1.Dallas1.Level3.net (4.68.122.141)  319.407 ms
20  4.79.180.2 (4.79.180.2)  345.385 ms  340.821 ms  339.936 ms
21  ge-0-1-0-p130.msr2.mud.yahoo.com (216.115.104.85)  351.986 ms ge-1-1-0-p120.msr1.mud.yahoo.com
   (216.115.104.89)  353.937 msge-1-1-0-p130.msr2.mud.yahoo.com (216.115.104.93)  345.542 ms
22  te-9-1.bas-c2.mud.yahoo.com (68.142.193.11)  345.123 ms te-9-1.bas-c1.mud.yahoo.com (68.142.193.9)
   358.573 ms te-8-1.bas-c1.mud.yahoo.com (68.142.193.5)  355.124 ms
23  * * *
```

Figure 2.33. *Traceroute* output.

from the router. The router may not respond or the response is blocked by a router.

2.14.1 *traceroute* Mechanism

traceroute uses the ttl (time-to-live) field of IP to get this wonder done. In Section 2.11.1 we discussed that there is maximum number of hops that an IP datagram can take before being dropped, which is decided by a *ttl* field. *traceroute* starts with ttl value of 1 and increments this value by 1 for each hop. This field is decremented by one at each router and if the value reduces to zero, the router sends back a 'time exceeded in transit' ICMP message to the originator of the IP datagram.

We collected *tcpdump* of the *traceroute* program discussed in Section 2.14 (see Fig. 2.34). First line shows that a UDP packet destined for *login.mud.yahoo.com* of length 40 bytes with ttl set to 1 is transmitted. The second line is the return of ICMP message from the very first router (DSL router). Similarly, lines 3–6 are repeated. Similarly, for the next hop the ttl field is set to 2 at line 7. We get an ICMP message from the second router *ABTS-KK-Dynamic-001.96.167.122.airtelbroadband.in*. We need not mention that the same thing is repeated until we get to the final destination.

2.15   ICMP

ICMP stands for as internet control messages protocol. This is a general-purpose protocol carrying control messages. These control messages can be an error message from a router, such as 'network unreachable' or 'fragmentation not allowed,' or TCP/UDP error messages such as 'port unreachable' and many other messages. There are numerous utilities like *ping* that also use ICMP.

An IP datagram carries an ICMP message. Whenever an ICMP message is generated to report some error, an IP header is built for the return path of the IP datagram from the IP datagram. An ICMP header is added to this IP datagram, and this datagram is transmitted. Figure 2.35a shows an ICMP message that contains 20 bytes of IP header built from the original IP datagram that caused ICMP message generation followed by ICMP message. The ICMP message format is shown in Fig. 2.35b. It has three fields:

> *type.* this is 8-bit number which classifies the ICMP messages.
> *code.* this is 8-bit number which differentiates ICMP messages in each class.
> *checksum.* this is a 16-bit field that covers ICMP message. Algorithm is same as discussed in Section 2.11.1.

Type and code are specified in RFC 792.

The contents of an ICMP message in a data field varies with type and code field. For example, when an ICMP error message is generated for a TCP/UDP port that is unreachable, the data field contains 8 bytes from the IP datagram payload that generated an ICMP message. So, the originator finds out that the TCP/UDP socket for which the ICMP message is generated as the first 8 bytes includes destination and source port numbers for these two protocols.

```
 1   20:11:40.529629 parikrama.33553 > l2.login.vip.mud.yahoo.com.traceroute: [udp sum ok] udp 12 [ttl 1] (id 38845, len 40)
 2   20:11:40.530175 router > parikrama: icmp: time exceeded in-transit (ttl 254, id 148, len 56)
 3   20:11:40.530537 parikrama.33553 > l2.login.vip.mud.yahoo.com.33435: [udp sum ok] udp 12 [ttl 1] (id 38846, len 40)
 4   20:11:40.531078 router > parikrama: icmp: time exceeded in-transit (ttl 254, id 149, len 56)
 5   20:11:40.531201 parikrama.33553 > l2.login.vip.mud.yahoo.com.33436: [udp sum ok] udp 12 [ttl 1] (id 38847, len 40)
 6   20:11:40.531741 router > parikrama: icmp: time exceeded in-transit (ttl 254, id 150, len 56)
 7   20:11:40.531873 parikrama.33553 > l2.login.vip.mud.yahoo.com.33437: [udp sum ok] udp 12 (ttl 2, id 38848, len 40)
 8   20:11:40.557584 ABTS-KK-Dynamic-001.96.167.122.airtelbroadband.in > parikrama: icmp: time exceeded in-transit
     (ttl 126, id 0, len 56)
 9   20:11:40.576298 parikrama.33553 > l2.login.vip.mud.yahoo.com.33438: [udp sum ok] udp 12 (ttl 2, id 38849, len 40)
10   20:11:40.602563 ABTS-KK-Dynamic-001.96.167.122.airtelbroadband.in > parikrama: icmp: time exceeded in-transit
     (ttl 126, id 0, len 56)
11   20:11:40.602742 parikrama.33553 > l2.login.vip.mud.yahoo.com.33439: [udp sum ok] udp 12 (ttl 2, id 38850, len 40)
12   20:11:40.628999 ABTS-KK-Dynamic-001.96.167.122.airtelbroadband.in > parikrama: icmp: time exceeded in-transit
     (ttl 126, id 0, len 56)
13   20:11:40.629169 parikrama.33553 > l2.login.vip.mud.yahoo.com.33440: [udp sum ok] udp 12 (ttl 3, id 38851, len 40)
14   20:11:40.654732 dsl-KK-static-158.63.101.203.airtelbroadband.in > parikrama: icmp: time exceeded in-transit [tos 0xc0]
     (ttl 253, id 57300, len 56)
15   20:11:40.655075 parikrama.33553 > l2.login.vip.mud.yahoo.com.33441: [udp sum ok] udp 12 (ttl 3, id 38852, len 40)
16   20:11:40.684888 dsl-KK-static-158.63.101.203.airtelbroadband.in > parikrama: icmp: time exceeded in-transit [tos 0xc0]
     (ttl 253, id 57313, len 56)
17   20:11:40.685043 parikrama.33553 > l2.login.vip.mud.yahoo.com.33442: [udp sum ok] udp 12 (ttl 3, id 38853, len 40)
18   20:11:40.719667 dsl-KK-static-158.63.101.203.airtelbroadband.in > parikrama: icmp: time exceeded in-transit [tos 0xc0]
     (ttl 253, id 57336, len 56)
19   20:11:40.719863 parikrama.33553 > l2.login.vip.mud.yahoo.com.33443: [udp sum ok] udp 12 (ttl 4, id 38854, len 40)
20   20:11:40.748187 59.145.6.85 > parikrama: icmp: time exceeded in-transit [tos 0xc0]  (ttl 252, id 38854, len 56)
     ....
23   20:11:40.780698 parikrama.33553 > l2.login.vip.mud.yahoo.com.33444: [udp sum ok] udp 12 (ttl 4, id 38855, len 40)
24   20:11:40.808485 59.145.6.85 > parikrama: icmp: time exceeded in-transit [tos 0xc0]  (ttl 252, id 38855, len 56)
25   20:11:40.808641 parikrama.33553 > l2.login.vip.mud.yahoo.com.33445: [udp sum ok] udp 12 (ttl 4, id 38856, len 40)
26   20:11:40.834908 59.145.6.85 > parikrama: icmp: time exceeded in-transit [tos 0xc0]  (ttl 252, id 38856, len 56)
27   20:11:40.835058 parikrama.33553 > l2.login.vip.mud.yahoo.com.33446: [udp sum ok] udp 12 (ttl 5, id 38857, len 40)
28   20:11:40.878502 125.17.12.229 > parikrama: icmp: time exceeded in-transit (ttl 251, id 0, len 56)
     ....
31   20:11:40.917744 parikrama.33553 > l2.login.vip.mud.yahoo.com.33447: [udp sum ok] udp 12 (ttl 5, id 38858, len 40)
32   20:11:40.952010 125.17.12.229 > parikrama: icmp: time exceeded in-transit (ttl 251, id 0, len 56)
33   20:11:40.952162 parikrama.33553 > l2.login.vip.mud.yahoo.com.33448: [udp sum ok] udp 12 (ttl 5, id 38859, len 40)
34   20:11:40.985869 125.17.12.229 > parikrama: icmp: time exceeded in-transit (ttl 251, id 0, len 56)
35   20:11:40.986013 parikrama.33553 > l2.login.vip.mud.yahoo.com.33449: [udp sum ok] udp 12 (ttl 6, id 38860, len 40)
36   20:11:41.293920 59.145.7.133 > parikrama: icmp: time exceeded in-transit [tos 0xc0]  (ttl 240, id 54584, len 168)
     ......
```

Figure 2.34. TCP dump ouput for *traceroute*.

20 bytes IP header	ICMP message

Figure 2.35a. ICMP packet.

2.16 *ping*

ping is a general network utility that is used to check the network connectivity of any host. It uses echo ICMP messages for request and reply. The ICMP echo message format is shown in Fig. 2.36.

type is set to 8 for an ICMP echo request and 0 for an ICMP echo response.

code is set to 0.

checksum is computed as mentioned in Section 2.11.1.

identifier is 16-bit field that identifies each echo reply uniquely. We may run many *ping* programs in parallel, in which case a reply for each ICMP request is identified by this field.

sequence number is incremented for each ICMP echo request; on reception of ICMP, an echo reply sequence number is checked. If they match with the current sequence number, *timestamp* is used to calculate rtt.

Figure 2.37 shows typical output of the *ping* program. We send 56 bytes of ICMP data to *parikrama*. Each line of output is displayed once we get a reply for the ICMP echo request. Each ICMP echo reply is 64 bytes of length, and each line of output shows sequence number (*icmp_seq*), ttl is set to 255 (infinite life time), and time is rtt calculated from *timestamp* echoed in ICMP reply. At the end of the output is the total statistics for the ICMP echo program. It shows that packets were transmitted and received, there was no packet loss, total time spent is 5055 ms, and finally rtt observed as minimum, maximum, average, and mean deviation over the entire *ping* program is printed.

Figure 2.38 shows snoop output of the *ping* program. Moksha is pinging parikrama and ID is unique for each ICMP packet (i.e., 950). The sequence number for which snoop output is shown is 4. The first ICMP echo request is sent with type 8, and finally we get a response for the ICMP request with type 0. Code is 0 for both request and reply. An ICMP message is encapsulated in the IP datagram with a protocol field of IP datagram set to 1.

0		31
8-bit type	8-bit code	16-bit checksum
data		

Figure 2.35b. ICMP message format.

0		31
8-bit type	8-bit code	16-bit checksum
16-bit identifier		16-bit sequence number
data		

Figure 2.36. ICMP header format for echo request-reply message.

```
[root@moksha sameer]# ping parikrama
PING parikrama (192.168.1.4) 56(84) bytes of data.
64 bytes from parikrama (192.168.1.4): icmp_seq=1 ttl=255 time=0.297 ms
64 bytes from parikrama (192.168.1.4): icmp_seq=2 ttl=255 time=0.299 ms
64 bytes from parikrama (192.168.1.4): icmp_seq=3 ttl=255 time=0.293 ms
64 bytes from parikrama (192.168.1.4): icmp_seq=4 ttl=255 time=0.296 ms
64 bytes from parikrama (192.168.1.4): icmp_seq=5 ttl=255 time=0.297 ms
64 bytes from parikrama (192.168.1.4): icmp_seq=6 ttl=255 time=0.292 ms

--- parikrama ping statistics ---
6 packets transmitted, 6 received, 0% packet loss, time 5055ms
rtt min/avg/max/mdev = 0.292/0.295/0.299/0.020 ms
```

Figure 2.37. TCP dump output for output of ping program.

```
Snoop output of ping command -

IP:  ----- IP Header -----
IP:
IP:  Version = 4
    ....
IP:  Protocol = 1 (ICMP)
IP:  Header checksum = 2c51
IP:  Source address = 192.168.1.4, parikrama
IP:  Destination address = 192.168.1.3, moksha
IP:  No options
IP:
ICMP:  ----- ICMP Header -----
ICMP:
ICMP:  Type = 8 (Echo request)
ICMP:  Code = 0 (ID: 950 Sequence number: 4)
ICMP:  Checksum = 47ea
ICMP:

IP:  ----- IP Header -----
IP:
IP:  Version = 4
    .....
IP:  Protocol = 1 (ICMP)
IP:  Header checksum = bc22
IP:  Source address = 192.168.1.3, moksha
IP:  Destination address = 192.168.1.4, parikrama
IP:  No options
IP:
ICMP:  ----- ICMP Header -----
ICMP:
ICMP:  Type = 0 (Echo reply)
ICMP:  Code = 0 (ID: 950 Sequence number: 4)
ICMP:  Checksum = 4fea
ICMP:
```

Figure 2.38. Snoop output for ping request.

2.17   ARP/RARP

ARP is an address resolution protocol that is designed for link layer addressing. RFC 2176 defines specifics about the protocol in detail. In this section we will discuss specifically about Ethernet technology and IP. In an IP over an Ethernet link, there are one or more IP addresses associated with one Ethernet network interface. Each Ethernet interface has a specific address.

In the Ethernet network, when we need to send a packet to a specific host whose IP address is known, ARP is generated to know the hardware address associated with the IP. ARP is hardware broadcast to the network and is replied by the host whose IP address matches the IP address in the ARP packet. An ARP packet is encapsulated in the link layer frame and is then broadcast, which means that the destination hardware address of ARP frame should be set to all f. The destination protocol address in the ARP header is set to a known IP address.

RARP is the reverse of ARP, where we want to know the IP address corresponding to the Ethernet address. In this case, a destination hardware address in the ARP header is set to a known hardware address. The RARP server replies the query. The RARP may be generated by a host to know its own IP address and is mostly used by network booting clients. Note that the RARP server should be within the same subnet as the requesting host because the RARP request is a broadcast that doesn't go over the router.

The packet format for ARP and RARP is shown in Fig. 2.39.

hardware type. This is a 16-bit field that indicates the link layer identity for which ARP/RARP is generated. For Ethernet, this field is set to 1. For RARP, this field is set to 0x8035.

protocol type. This is a 16-bit value that is the identity for the network layer protocol that is associated with the hardware address. For IP, this value is 0x0800.

hardware addr len. This is an 8-bit field containing the length of the hardware address. For Ethernet, the hardware address length is 6 bytes.

proto addr len. This is an 8-bit field that contains the length of the protocol address associated with the hardware. In the case of Ipv4, this value is 4 bytes.

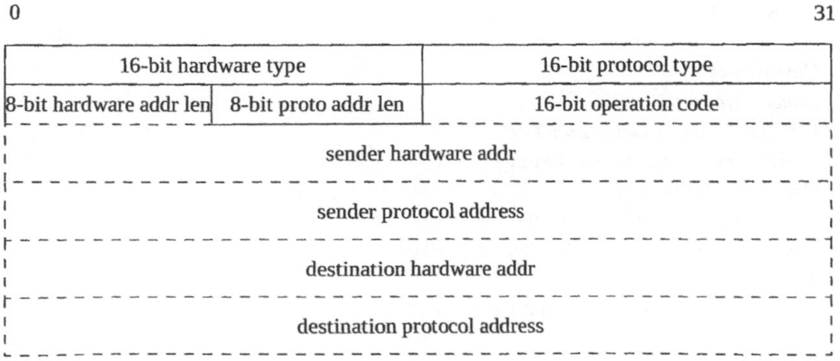

Figure 2.39. ARP header format.

operation code. This is a 16-bit value that indicates the operation to be performed on the ARP packet. Since the same packet format is used for request and replies, this field identifies whether this is an ARP request or reply. For an ARP request and replies the values are 1 and 2, respectively. For an RARP request and replies the values are 3 and 4, respectively.

sender hardware addr. This is the hardware address of the originator of the request/response. This will be 6 bytes long in the case of the Ethernet.

sender protocol addr. This is the address of the protocol address of the sender. This will be 4 bytes long in the case of Ipv4.

destination hardware addr. This is the hardware address of the destination host. This will be 6 bytes long in the case of the Ethernet. Thus will be set to the hardware address of the host for which IP is not known in the case of RARP. This field is filled by the replier of the ARP request.

destination protocol addr. This is the protocol address associated with the destination hardware address. In the case of ARP, this field is set to the protocol address (IPv4 address) for which the hardware address is not known. This field is filled by the replier of the RARP request.

Fig. 2.40 shows a snoop output of ARP request. The destination address in the Ethernet header is set to all *f's*. The Ethernet type in the Ethernet header is set to 0x806, which is ARP. The ARP header HARDWARE type is set to 1, which is Ethernet. The protocol for which ARP is generated is set to 0x0800 for IP. The hardware address length is 6 bytes (Ethernet address), and protocol address length is set to 4 bytes (IP address). Opcode is 1, which is an ARP request. The last four lines are the hardware address and the IP address of the sender; the target hardware address is null because this needs to be found out for target protocol address 192.168.1.8.

```
ETHER:  ----- Ether Header -----
ETHER:
ETHER:  Packet 48 arrived at 22:08:22.13004
ETHER:  Packet size = 42 bytes
ETHER:  Destination = ff:ff:ff:ff:ff:ff, (broadcast)
ETHER:  Source      = 0:c0:9f:61:8a:43,
ETHER:  Ethertype = 0806 (ARP)
ETHER:
ARP:  ----- ARP/RARP Frame -----
ARP:
ARP:  Hardware type = 1
ARP:  Protocol type = 0800 (IP)
ARP:  Length of hardware address = 6 bytes
ARP:  Length of protocol address = 4 bytes
ARP:  Opcode 1 (ARP Request)
ARP:  Sender's hardware address = 0:c0:9f:61:8a:43
ARP:  Sender's protocol address = 192.168.1.4, parikrama
ARP:  Target hardware address = ?
ARP:  Target protocol address = 192.168.1.8, 192.168.1.8
ARP:
```

Figure 2.40. Snoop output for ARP request.

2.18   SUMMARY

TCP is a connection-oriented stream protocol. It makes sure that every byte sent is received at the other end by means of an ACKing mechanism.

TCP implements Nagle's algorithm for small packets.

A delayed acknowledgment scheme reduces load on the network by piggyback-ing data along with the ACK segment.

The TCP sliding window protocol is implemented for bulk data transfer. It takes an advertised window and a congestion window in consideration for rate of data transmission at any point in time.

TCP extensions like SACK, timestamp, mss, and window scaling provide enhanced performance as well as reliability.

TCP congestion control algorithms use two TCP state variables to control the rate of data transmission: send congestion window (*cwnd*) and slow-start threshold (*ssthresh*).

The IP is a stateless protocol that carries most of the internet traffic.

An IP datagram is routed through the internet by hopping one router at a time.

Every router maintains a routing table that keeps all the information about the next route for a given destination.

The *netstat* command is used to display a kernel routing table.

traceroute is a powerful utility to trace the route that a packet is taking to reach a destination.

The internet uses ICMP messages to report errors.

ARP/RARP are protocols designed to resolve a hardware address from a pro-tocol address and vice versa.

3

KERNEL IMPLEMENTATION OF SOCKETS

Linux supports different communication protocols that fit into the OSI model. The BSD socket is an interface to different protocol families. The BSD-compatible sockets have a uniform socket interface between the user process and the network protocol stacks in the kernel. The BSD socket is a framework to the different families of socket that Linux supports. The BSD socket concept is very similar to the VFS (virtual file system) layer, which is just a framework that provides a common interface to various different file systems/pipe/devices/sockets to the user without user knowing how things are organized inside the kernel. This way different protocol families are supported by Linux, and their services are accessible to the user using a common socket interface. For example, the protocol modules are grouped into protocol families such as PF_INET, PF_IPX, PF_PACKET and socket types such as SOCK_STREAM or SOCK_DGRAM, as shown in Fig. 3.1.

There are some standards laid out by the BSD socket framework which need to be followed by each protocol family. These standards are nothing but a set of functions such as create, bind, listen, accept, connect, read, write, ioctl, setsockopts, getsockopts, and so on, and are data-structure-specific to the protocol family/type. Each protocol family and their types need to register with the kernel BSD socket framework to provide its service to the user.

The *socket()* systemcall is the common interface to the BSD socket. User application lets the BSD socket framework know which protocol family/type/protocol it is interested in by way of passing arguments to the *socket()* systemcall. These parameters will be used by the BSD socket layer to set up the appropriate protocol stack, which suits user requirement, inside the kernel without the user knowing how it is happening. In this chapter we get to know about the BSD socket interface, the VFS layer, and how sockets of different protocol families are plugged into the BSD

TCP/IP Architecture, Design, and Implementation in Linux. By S. Seth and M. A. Venkatesulu
Copyright © 2008 the IEEE Computer Society

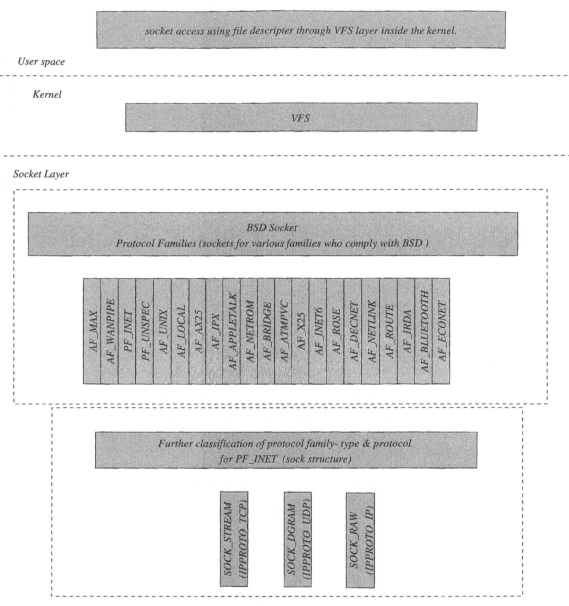

Figure 3.1. Socket architecture.

socket within the kernel. The discussion will be based mainly on PF_INET (specific to ipv4) protocol family sockets here. Various important functions and data structures related to the PF_INET protocol family are explained.

3.1 SOCKET LAYER

The BSD socket is associated with sock structure, which contains fields specific to the protocol family and type. Fields in the sock data structure point to protocol-family-specific data. These are a protocol-specific set of functions (struct inet_ protosw contains the set of functions), control flags, and pointers to data containing protocol-specific information. There are some standard interfaces provided to the user to set up the protocol stack and initialize the connection for the client/server.

The *socket()* systemcall just identifies the set of functions for each protocol family and type and accordingly initializes the socket and sock data structures. There are set of functions that need to be called to set up the complete stack for the given protocol family and initialize the connection. These functions are *bind()*, *listen()*, *accept()*, *connect()*, and so on. These functions are very specific to the protocol family and type. These functions are registered at system initialization time using sock_register() function.

3.2 VFS AND SOCKET

Let's examine the kernel data structures and functions related to the socket layer. *sys_socket()* is the function called in the kernel when user application makes a call to *socket()* systemcall. The arguments to the *socket()* systemcall (to *sys_socket()*) is protocol, family, and type. These arguments passed to *socket()* systemcall is used by the socket framework to decide the protocol stack to setup. *sys_socket()* does nothing more than calling *sock_create()* to initialize the socket and sock structure for the protocol family and links the socket with the VFS by calling *sock_map_fd()*.

For association of VFS and socket, refer to Fig. 3.2. Each process has a file table that can be accessed from an *fd* field of object *files_struct*. *fd* is a double pointer of type *file*. Each open file for the process has an associated *file* object linked with file descriptor. *file* objects are indexed into a file table with an associated file descriptor.

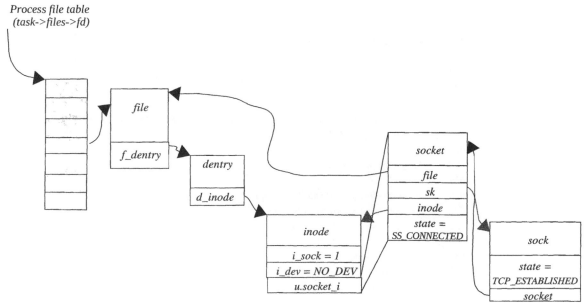

Figure 3.2. Socket accessed through process file table.

The *files* field of *task_struct* objects for the process is a pointer to an object of type *files_struct*. The *f_dentry* field of *file* object is a pointer to a *dentry* object. The *d_inode* field of *dentry* object is a pointer to an inode object associated with the file. An *inode* object is a common for any file type. A socket is also considered as a special kind of file that is identified by an *i_sock* field of *inode* object. *u* is union for all types of file supported by VFS subsystem. A *socket* object can be accessed from a *socket_i* field of union *u*.

From here our job is very easy because socket- and protocol-specific information is available once we have access to a *socket* object. A socket has a pointer to a sock object that has a pointer to a protocol-specific set of operations pointed to by a *prot* field.

sock_create() finds the *create()* function specific to the protocol family and calls it to initialize the sock structure associated with the BSD socket. *net_families[]* is the array of type struct *net_proto_family* that is indexed by a protocol family. This structure contains two main fields:

    int   *family*
    int   (*create)(struct socket *sock, int protocol)

The 'family' field contains the protocol family, and the 'create' field is a function pointer that points to the socket create function specific to the protocol. *net_families[]* contains *net_proto_family* data for the registered protocol family. The *sock_register()* function gets the registration of *net_proto_family* done for the protocol family as shown in cs 3.1. For the INET family, the *inet_family_ops* is registered.

From now onward, everything will be very much specific to the protocol family. So, I'll take the *PF_INET* socket type to explain the socket layer everywhere until it is mentioned. Thus, *sock_create()* finds the entry of the *PF_INET* protocol family

```
net/socket.c
1620 int sock_register(struct net_proto_family *ops)
1621 {
1622     int err;
1623
1624     if(ops->family >= NPROTO) {
1625         printk(KERN_CRIT "protocol %d >= NPROTO(%d)\n", ops->family, NPROTO);
1626         return -ENOBUFS;
1627     }
1628     net_family_write_lock();
1629     err = -EEXIST;
1630     if (net_families[ops->family] == NULL) {
1631         net_families[ops->family]=ops;
1632         err = 0;
1633     }
1634     net_family_write_unlock();
1635     return err;
1636 }
```

cs 3.1. *sock_register()*.

in *net_families[]*. If *net_families[family]* is not NULL, call the 'create' function specific to this protocol family *net_families[family]→create*(sock, protocol). We need to allocate a new socket structure and set its '*sock→type*' field to the protocol family type 'type' passed as an argument to the *socket()* systemcall. For PF_INET protocol family, the 'create' function pointer is pointing to *inet_create()*. This function initializes the sock structure, which keeps information very specific to the IP protocol.

3.3 PROTOCOL SOCKET REGISTRATION

We first need to find out the element in list head array *inetsw[SOCK_MAX]* containing entry for *sock→type* (initialized in *sys_socket()*). *inetsw* is the array initialized at the time of system initialization and is indexed by socket type. *inet_register_protosw()* is the function called to register inet sockets. There is a static array of type *inet_protosw* (Fig. 3.3) *inetsw_array[]* which contains information about all the inet socket types as shown in Fig. 3.5. The *Inetsw[]* array is populated at the system initialization time reading information for inet sockets from *inetsw_array[]* (see cs 3.2). So, finally all the inet socket types that are registered with the system have their entries in *inetsw[]*, which can be done by calling *inet_register_protosw()* (see cs 3.3). The following code samples in cs 3.2 and cs 3.3 show the registration of sockets.

(Here we check if we want to register the already registered socket type. In the case where a socket is already registered, we can't override the entry if the socket is marked as permanent answer→flags is set to INET_PROTOSW_PERMANENT. In the case where this flag is not set, we can have multiple entries for the same socket type and only the one which is at the beginning of the list will be considered for this socket type, which

```
include/net/protocol.h

67  struct inet_protosw {
68       struct list_head list;
69
70       /* These two fields form the lookup key. */
71       unsigned short   type;    /* This is the 2nd argument to socket(2). */
72       int              protocol; /* This is the L4 protocol number. */
73
74       struct proto     *prot;
75       struct proto_ops *ops;
76
77       int              capability; /* Which (if any) capability do
78                            * we need to use this socket
79                            * interface?
80                            */
81       char             no_check;  /* checksum on rcv/xmit/none? */
82       unsigned char    flags;     /* See INET_PROTOSW_* below. */
83  };
```

Figure 3.3. *struct inet_protosw.*

net/ipv4/af_inet.c

```
1102  static int __init inet_init(void)
1103  {
              ...
1138      for(q = inetsw_array; q < &inetsw_array[INETSW_ARRAY_LEN]; ++q)
1139          inet_register_protosw(q);
1140
              ....
1194  }
```

cs 3.2. *inet_init().*

net/ipv4/af_inet.c

```
1035  void
1036  inet_register_protosw(struct inet_protosw *p)
1037  {
              ....
1040      int protocol = p->protocol;
1041
1042      br_write_lock_bh(BR_NETPROTO_LOCK);
              ....
1049      list_for_each(lh, &inetsw[p->type]) {
1050          answer = list_entry(lh, struct inet_protosw, list);
1051
1052          /* Check only the non-wild match. */
1053          if (protocol == answer->protocol &&
1054              (INET_PROTOSW_PERMANENT & answer->flags))
1055              break;
1056
1057          answer = NULL;
1058      }
1059      if (answer)
1060          goto out_permanent;
              ....
1066      list_add(&p->list, &inetsw[p->type]);
1067  out:
1068      br_write_unlock_bh(BR_NETPROTO_LOCK);
1069      return;
1070
1071  out_permanent:
1072      printk(KERN_ERR "Attempt to override permanent protocol %d.\n",
1073          protocol);
1074      goto out;
1075
              ....
1081  }
```

cs 3.3. *inet_register_protosw().*

means that the overriding entry will be in effect until this entry is removed so that the original behavior of the socket comes into effect.)

One thing worth noting here is that so far.there is only one protocol per socket type at the system initialization time. Since all the entries in *inetsw_array[]* have a flag set to *INET_PROTOSW_PERMANENT*, we cannot override the behavior of any of the inet sockets in the current implementation.

We have seen how the *inet_protosw* structure for each socket type is registered with the system and they can be accessed while opening a socket by the socket layer. Let's see how the sock structure is initialized using the information in the *inetsw[]* array element for this socket type and how sock is linked to socket structure.

3.4 *struct inet_protosw*

list: This is a pointer to the next node in the list.

type: This is the socket type and is a key to search entry for a given socket and type in *inetsw[]* array.

protocol: This is again a key to find an entry for the socket type in the *inetsw[]* array. This is an L4 protocol number (L4→Transport layer protocol).

prot: This is a pointer to struct proto. This structure contains a set of functions that are very specific to the IP protocol (like TCP/UDP). These functions are *close(), connect(), accept(), bind(), setsockopts(), getsockopts(), recvmsg(), sendmsg()*, and so on. For example, tcp_prot corresponds to *SOCK_STREAM* and *udp_prot* corresponds to *SOCK_DGRAM*. This way we are interfacing an IP protocol block with the socket layer with the help of struct proto, which will be discussed later.

ops: This is a pointer to the structure of type '*proto_ops*'. This structure contains a set of functions very specific to a protocol family. This structure contains a similar set of functions as '*struct proto*' but it operates at the socket level. For example, *inet_stream_ops* corresponds to *SOCK_STREAM* and *inet_dgram_ops* corresponds to *SOCK_DGRAM*. The sequence goes like this: Once any socket-related systemcall is made, first it has to make a corresponding function call from a '*proto_ops*' structure, and the then corresponding IP-protocol-specific function is called from a '*proto*' structure.

3.5 SOCKET ORGANIZATION IN THE KERNEL

As shown in Fig 3.4. when user application makes a systemcall on socket, kernel first invokes a corresponding function from socket-layer-specific operations for the protocol family from *sock→ops*, and subsequently it calls a corresponding function from IP-protocol-specific operations from *sk→prot*. There may always not be one-to-one correspondence for each systemcall between *sock→ops* and *sk→prot*. For example, there is no corresponding *tcp_listen()/tcp_bind()* when there is *inet_listen()/inet_bind()*. This is because bind and listen is managed by a BSD socket layer and is not very specific to the IP protocol layer. The *inet_protosw* structures initialized for different socket TYPE for *PF_INET* family are shown in Fig. 3.5.

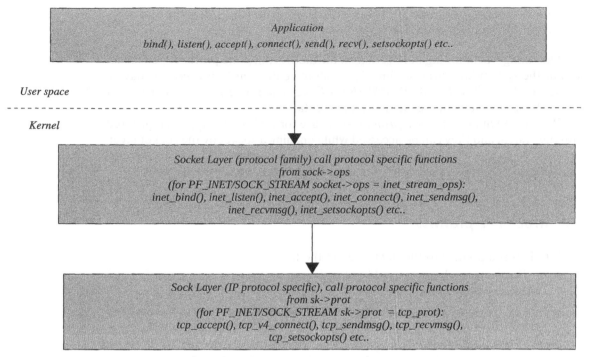

Figure 3.4. Accessing a protocol-specific socket through a BSD socket.

At this point in time, we are in *inet_create()*, where we are able to find out the appropriate entry for protocol type in the inetsw[] array. The structure *inet_protosw* contains all the information for a specific IP protocol. For ease of further socket operations, we won't always refer to the *net_protosw* entry in inetsw; instead we store all this information in the sock and socket structure for the current socket. Now we go about initializing the sock structure fields for this IP protocol under consideration.

3.6 SOCKET

We will be discussing the fields of the socket structure every now and then. So, they are brought together here, as shown in Fig. 3.6.

state: This flied describes the connection status of the socket.

There are five states for the BSD socket:

SS_FREE	(sock is not yet allocated)
SS_UNCONNECTED	(sock is allocated but is not yet connected)
SS_CONNECTING	(sock is in the process of connecting)
SS_CONNECTED	(already connected to sock)
SS_DISCONNECTING	(in the process of disconnecting)

```
net/ipv4/af_inet.c

 999  static struct inet_protosw inetsw_array[] =
1000  {
1001      {
1002            type:       SOCK_STREAM,
1003            protocol:   IPPROTO_TCP,
1004            prot:       &tcp_prot,
1005            ops:        &inet_stream_ops,
1006            capability: -1,
1007            no_check:   0,
1008            flags:      INET_PROTOSW_PERMANENT,
1009      },
1010
1011      {
1012            type:       SOCK_DGRAM,
1013            protocol:   IPPROTO_UDP,
1014            prot:       &udp_prot,
1015            ops:        &inet_dgram_ops,
1016            capability: -1,
1017            no_check:   UDP_CSUM_DEFAULT,
1018            flags:      INET_PROTOSW_PERMANENT,
1019      },
1020
1021
1022      {
1023            type:       SOCK_RAW,
1024            protocol:   IPPROTO_IP, /* wild card */
1025            prot:       &raw_prot,
1026            ops:        &inet_dgram_ops,
1027            capability: CAP_NET_RAW,
1028            no_check:   UDP_CSUM_DEFAULT,
1029            flags:      INET_PROTOSW_REUSE,
1030      }
1031  };
```

Figure 3.5. Inet protocol family base.

flags: These flags reflect the resource status for a given socket and is associated with the receive and send buffer (space availability).

These flags are:

SOCK_ASYNC_NOSPACE. This is the set when there is no space available to write data on the socket because the send buffer is full. This is also used with asynchronous operations.

SOCK_ASYNC_WAITDATA. This is set when the recv buffer is full for a given socket and there is no space to accommodate anymore data in the receive queue. This is used with asynchronous operations.

```
include/linux/net.h

65  struct socket
66  {
67       socket_state         state;
68
69       unsigned long        flags;
70       struct proto_ops     *ops;
71       struct inode         *inode;
72       struct fasync_struct *fasync_list;  /* Asynchronous wake up list  */
73       struct file          *file;        /* File back pointer for gc   */
74       struct sock          *sk;
75       wait_queue_head_t     wait;
76
77       short                type;
78       unsigned char        passcred;
79  };
```

Figure 3.6. struct socket, representing the BSD socket on Linux.

SOCK_NOSPACE. This flag is set when there is no space available to write data over the socket synchronously; sendbuf is full here.

ops: This is the pointer to the proto_ops structure containing the set of functions specific to protocol family as explained earlier.

inode: This is the pointer to the inode associated with this socket. Hook to VFS.

fasync_list: This is the pointer to 'struct fasync_struct,' which is a list of all those async threads waiting for resources to be available on the socket. Basically, threads wait for send and recv buffers to make space available for the new data.

file: This is the back pointer to the file structure associated with the socket. Figure 3.2 explains the link between socket and VFS.

sk: This is a pointer to the sock struct associated with the BSD socket very specific to the IP protocol. We will be discussing the sock structure very shortly.

wait: This is the pointer to the wait 'Q' for any asynchronous threads waiting for some event on the socket.

type: This is the number that is associated with the IP protocol. This was explained earlier.

3.7 *inet_create* (see cs 3.4)

Initialize the BSD socket state to indicate that it is still unconnected (*sock→state = SS_UNCONNECTED*). BSD socket (on Linux represented by struct socket, Fig. 3.6) maintains its own state which corresponds to the actual state of the connection and will be discussed later.

net/ipv4/af_inet.c

```
319  static int inet_create(struct socket *sock, int protocol)
320  {
321       struct sock *sk;
322       struct list_head *p;
323       struct inet_protosw *answer;
324
325       sock->state = SS_UNCONNECTED;
326       sk = sk_alloc(PF_INET, GFP_KERNEL, 1);

332       br_read_lock_bh(BR_NETPROTO_LOCK);
333       list_for_each(p, &inetsw[sock->type]) {
334            answer = list_entry(p, struct inet_protosw, list);
335
336            /* Check the non-wild match. */
337            if (protocol == answer->protocol) {
338                 if (protocol != IPPROTO_IP)
339                      break;
            ....
350       }
351       br_read_unlock_bh(BR_NETPROTO_LOCK);
352
353       if (!answer)
354            goto free_and_badtype;

        ....

360       sock->ops = answer->ops;
361       sk->prot = answer->prot;
362       sk->no_check = answer->no_check;
363       if (INET_PROTOSW_REUSE & answer->flags)
364            sk->reuse = 1;
365
366       if (SOCK_RAW == sock->type) {
367            sk->num = protocol;
368            if (IPPROTO_RAW == protocol)
369                 sk->protinfo.af_inet.hdrincl = 1;
370       }
        ....
379       sock_init_data(sock,sk);
380
381       sk->destruct = inet_sock_destruct;
382
383       sk->zapped      = 0;
384       sk->family      = PF_INET;
385       sk->protocol    = protocol;
386
387       sk->backlog_rcv = sk->prot->backlog_rcv;
388
389       sk->protinfo.af_inet.ttl      = sysctl_ip_default_ttl;
390
391       sk->protinfo.af_inet.mc_loop   = 1;
392       sk->protinfo.af_inet.mc_ttl    = 1;
393       sk->protinfo.af_inet.mc_index  = 0;
394       sk->protinfo.af_inet.mc_list   = NULL;
        ....
400       if (sk->num) {
            ....
406            sk->sport = htons(sk->num);
            ....
410       }
411
412       if (sk->prot->init) {
413            int err = sk->prot->init(sk);
            ....
418       }
419       return 0;
        ....
435  }
```

cs 3.4. *inet_create()*.

3.7.1 Sock

Memory for 'sk' (sock structure) is allocated initially and then the fields are initialized. We discuss some of the main fields of sock structure which are initialized here and will carry the discussion of sock structure further.

ops: The field of socket structure 'sock' is initialized to 'ops' field of 'answer'. As discussed earlier, this contains a set of functions that are specific to the *PF_INET* protocol family.

prot: The field of sock structure 'sk' is initialized to IP-protocol-specific operations from answer→prot as discussed earlier.

reuse: This field is initialized to 1, in the case where the flag field of *inet_protosw* for this IP protocol is set to *INET_PROTOSW_REUSE*. This field indicates whether the local port associated with the socket can be shared in certain conditions. These conditions are mentioned in *include/net/tcp.h file*.

num: If *sock→type* is set to *SOCK_RAW*, we initialize num field to protocol number (which is nothing but the protocol field in *inet_protosw*; in the case of *SOCK_RAW*, this is set to *IPPROTO_IP*).

destruct: This field contains the pointer to the function *inet_sock_destruct()*, which is called for cleanup operations on the socket when it is destroyed.

family: This is the protocol family associated with the socket. For the inet family, it is initialized to *PF_INET*.

protocol: This is the IP protocol number associated with the socket. This is passed as an argument to the *inet_create()*. The field also corresponds to the protocol field of the *inet_protosw* structure for this IP protocol type.

backlog_recv: This field is initialized to the '*backlog_recv*' function from the '*prot*' field of this sock structure initialized earlier, depending on the IP protocol type. At this point in time, it looks like this function processes the backlog list of the socket; let's see later.

sport: Source port for this socket. This file is initialized to 'num' in the case where 'num' is already initialized (only in case or raw sockets). Finally it is linked to the protocol hash chain *sk→prot→hash()*.

protinfo: This is a field that contains information specific to the protocol. Some of these fields are initialized here, which will be discussed later.

Discuss the other fields in the sock structure. Also discuss *sock_init_data()* and *sk→prot→init()*, though not in detail.

sock_init_data() initializes the rest of the fields of sock structure associated with the IP protocol. We will get to know the significance of these fields shortly.

Let's see what fields *sock_init_data()* initializes.

Initialize the queues for sock structure: *receive_queue, write_queue*, and *error_queue*. These are queue heads of type sk_buff_head (Fig. 3.7), called *skb_queue_head_init()*. This function will initialize prev & next field to point to queue head, initialize qlen to 0, and initialize the spinlock for the queue.

prev & next: These fields point to the previous and next elements of the queue (of type *sk_buff*).

qlen: This field indicates the number of elements in the queue.

```
include/linux/skbuff.h


 97  struct sk_buff_head {
 98        /* These two members must be first. */
 99        struct sk_buff  * next;
100        struct sk_buff  * prev;
101
102        __u32         qlen;
103        spinlock_t    lock;
104  };
```

Figure 3.7. *sk_buff list head.*

lock: This is a spinlock lock to protect the members of *sk_buff_head*. We need to hold the lock before inserting/deleting the node from the queue and updating the 'qlen' field.

Now let's look at what receive_queue, write_queue, and error_quque point to.

receive_queue: This field points to the queue of incoming packets (received packets sk_buff).

write_queue: This field points to the queue of the outgoing packets (packets to be sent out).

error_queue: This field is rarely used to point to the queue of defective packets.

Call *init_timer()* to initialize '*timer*' field (of type *timer_list*) of *sock* structure. This field points to *timer_list*, which contains a list of timers to be fired at different times specific to this socket.

allocation: This field contains the policy using which memory for *sk_buff* for this socket needs to be allocated. For this case, this field is initialized to *GFP_KERNEL*.

rcvbuf: This fields contains the number indicating a maximum limit for the receive buffer at any point in time. This is initialized to *sysctl_rmem_default* and can be changed using *setsockopts()*. This value is checked whenever we are want to allocate memory for an incoming packet. If the limit has been reached, a new buffer is not allocated until the receive_queue is consumed. This restricts the socket from consuming the entire system memory when the packets are flooding in for a given socket.

sndbuf: Same as *recvbuf*, but it is used to limit the send buffer size. The value is initialized to *sysctl_wmem_default*, which can be changed using *setsockopts()*.

state: This is the state of the socket for a protocol—in this case the socket state for the TCP connection. This is initialized to *TCP_CLOSE* since there is no connection on this socket at this point in time. The rest of the states for TCP socket are shown in Fig. 3.8.

```
include/linux/tcp.h


59  enum {
60    TCP_ESTABLISHED = 1,
61    TCP_SYN_SENT,
62    TCP_SYN_RECV,
63    TCP_FIN_WAIT1,
64    TCP_FIN_WAIT2,
65    TCP_TIME_WAIT,
66    TCP_CLOSE,
67    TCP_CLOSE_WAIT,
68    TCP_LAST_ACK,
69    TCP_LISTEN,
70    TCP_CLOSING,   /* now a valid state */
71
72    TCP_MAX_STATES /* Leave at the end! */
73  };
```

Figure 3.8. TCP state.

These states of TCP socket define the stages in which the current TCP connection is involved. Some of the states are clients and the others are servers. It will be discussed later when we explain the connection initiation and closure.

sock: This field points to the socket stucture for this sock structure.

If there is a BSD socket associated with this sock structure, we also initialize the following fields:

type: This is same as the type of field for the BSD socket structure initialized earlier (IP protocol type).

sleep: This is the same as the wait queue field (*sock→wait*) of the BSD socket structure for this sock.

sk: This is a pointer to the sock structure for the BSD socket structure corresponding to this sock, which is just initialized in *inet_create()*.

dst_lock: This is the lock to protect the destination cache (*sk→dst_cache of type dst_entry*) for this socket. It is initialized here.

callback_lock: This is the lock to protect (socket, sleep, dfead field of sock structure, and sk field of the associated BSD socket structure). It is initialized here. Basically, these fields are used to attach/detach an IP protocol socket with the process context. So, using the lock we can synchronize the attachment/detachment of the IP protocol socket with the process (socket structure). If the socket structure is delinked with the sock structure and vice versa, the process context is lost for further protocol communicationn from and to the process but the IP protocol is still alive.

state_change: This is a callback function which is initialised to *sock_def_wakeup*. This function is called whenever some event occurs on the IP protocol socket which changes the state of the socket.

data_ready: This is a callback function called whenever data are available on the socket. This function wakes up all the processes waiting for the data on sockets wait 'Q' *sk→sleep* & also sends appropriate signals to the processes waiting on the async list of the parent BSD socket (*sk→sock→fasync_list*).

write_space: This is the callback function called when somehow write space is available on the socket, which means that space is available on the write 'Q'. This function pointer is initialized to *sock_def_write_space*. This callback function should wake up all the processes waiting on the socket's wait 'Q' for the space to be available on the send 'Q' and also sends appropriate signals to the processes waiting on the async list of the parent BSD socket (*sk→sock→fasync_list*).

error_report: This is a function pointer to the callback function that is called whenever some error is reported on the socket to report the socket state to all the processes waiting on sockets wait 'Q' (sleep) and sends appropriate signal to all the processes in the parent socket's 'fasync_list' list. This is initialized to the *sock_def_error_report*.

destruct: This is a function pointer to the callback function whenever socket is being destroyed. This is initialized to sock_def_destruct. Finally, this can point to a protocol-specific destruct function (*inet_sock_destruct()* in case *PF_INET* protocol family).

peercred: This structure is used to identify the ownership of the socket. This field is mainly used in the case of UNIX domain sockets. In general the fields of peercred structure are initialized to 0, 1, and –1; but in the case of UNIX domain sockets, the fields of peercred structure are initialized to *current→pid, current→euid*, and *current→egid*.

rcvlowat: This field is just an indication that the receive buffer has reached the low water mark. This helps in making decisions when to process the receive queue and stuff. The rest will be explained later.

rcvtimeo: This field keeps the value of the maximum timeout for any blocking event on the IP protocol socket. It may be a timeout value when we are blocked to receiving TCP data or when we are blocked to accept TCP connections. Initialized to *MAX_SCHEDULE_TIMEOUT*.

sndtimeo: The same as rcvtimeo, but in the opposite direction. It may be a timeout value when we are blocked to send TCP data (waiting for memory to be available for sending data when send 'Q' is full and there is no memory available to accommodate more send data) or when we are blocked to make TCP connections (client is waiting for acknowledgment of connect request). Initialized to *MAX_SCHEDULE_TIMEOUT*.

The rest of the fields of the sock structure are initialized at later-stage connection setup steps. We will discuss them as they come.

Finally, *sk→prot→init* is called to initialize some more fields of sock structure and also protocol-specific fields. In the case of TCP, this is *tcp_v4_init_sock()*. We will discuss this function in detail here; the sock structure contains transport-protocol-specific information in the field *tp_pinfo* (Fig. 3.9).

Get an IP-protocol-specific information field from a sock structure (in case of *PF_INET, SOCK_STREAMS*, it will be *sk→tp_pinfo.af_tcp*). We initialize some of the fields of *tcp_opt* structure for this socket. Initialize '*out_of_order_queue*' (*tp→out_of_order*) member for the *tcp_opt*. This is the queue of *sk_buff* containing out-

```
include/net/sock.h


576      union {
577          struct tcp_opt        af_tcp;
578 #if defined(CONFIG_INET) || defined (CONFIG_INET_MODULE)
579          struct raw_opt        tp_raw4;
580 #endif
581 #if defined(CONFIG_IPV6) || defined (CONFIG_IPV6_MODULE)
582          struct raw6_opt       tp_raw;
583 #endif /* CONFIG_IPV6 */
584 #if defined(CONFIG_SPX) || defined (CONFIG_SPX_MODULE)
585          struct spx_opt        af_spx;
586 #endif /* CONFIG_SPX */
587
588      } tp_pinfo;
```

Figure 3.9. Union for transport layer specifics.

of-segment data for the tcp connection. Initialize tcp timers for the socket, call *tcp_init_xmit_timers()*. Let's see what it does. There are a minimum of three events associated with any TCP connection for which a timer needs to be fired:

- Retransmit event.
- Delayed acknowledgment (in case we are waiting for any data to be sent to the other end). This timer will be fired at a specified time after a packet is received from the other end.
- Keep event alive. (This timer is fired if the KEEPALIVE option is set for the socket. This end of the connection will keep on sending probe packets to the other end when the connection is idle for some time. The timer that does the probe is fired.)

tp→retransmit_timer.function is initialized to *tcp_write_timer()*.

tp→delack_timer.function is initialized to *tcp_delack_timer()*.

tp→timer.function is initialized to *tcp_keepalive_timer()*.

The data field for all the timers (*struct timer_list*) is initialized to a pointer to sock for this socket.

tp→pending and tp→ack.pending are initialized to 0.

tp→pending indiates that one of the timers is pending.

tp→ack.pending field indicates the state of *ACK* packet. There are three states for the *ACK* packet:

TCP_ACK_SCHED = ack is scheduled.

TCP_ACK_TIMER = timeout for delayed ack timer is scheduled.

TCP_ACK_PUSHED = ack is forced in emergency case.

Call *tcp_prequeue_init()* to initialize fields of the ucopy member of the *tcp_opt* structure. (Discussed in Chapter 8)

Initialize retransmit timeout (*tp→rto*) for the TCP socket to *TCP_TIMEOUT_INIT*.

Initialize fields related to (mean deviation) rtt measurement in *tcp_opt* structure (*tp→mdev*) to *TCP_TIMEOUT_INIT*.

Initialize fields of *tcp_opt* structure related to congestion control and slow start algorithms. Some of these fields are:

tp→snd_cwnd = 2 (sending congestion window size)

tp→snd_ssthresh = 0x7fffffff (slow start threshold; this should be half of congestion window size but not less than two segments)

tp→snd_cwnd_clamp = ~0 (upper limit for congestion window, tp→ snd_cwnd)

tp→mss_cache = 536 (cached effective maximum segment size for he connection).

tp→reordering = *sysctl_tcp_reordering* (3). This field is used in detecting false retransmits. This value indicates maximum number of duplicate 'ACKS' received before fast retransmit can start.

sk→state is set to *TCP_CLOSE* as there is still no connection open for this socket.

sk→write_space is set to *tcp_write_space()*. This is a callback function used by TCP to wake up the processes waiting for write space to be available on the send queue, when 'ACKS' are received and they can free the *sk_buffs* on the send queue.

sk→use_write_queue. This field indicates that someone needs to write to the queue. More will be explained later.

tp→af_specific is initialized to *ipv4_specific* containing set of functions specific to TCP. Will discuss more about it later.

sk→sndbuf is initialized to *sysctl_tcp_wmem[1]* (16K). This is the maximum memory that can be allocated for the send buffer at any point of time, and this value can be changed by *setsockopts()*.

sk→rcvbuf is initialized to *sysctl_tcp_rmem[1]* (87,380 bytes). This is the maximum memory that can be allocated for the receive buffer at any point of time, and this value can be changed by *setsockopts()*.

tcp_sockets_allocated increment this global variable by 1. This variable keeps the count of the number of sockets open in the system at any point in time.

End of ***tcp_v4_init_sock()***.
End of ***inet_create()***

Until now, we have seen that various fields of structures socket, sock, and tcp_ opt are initialized in *inet_create()*. We have an IP-protocol-specific set of operation set for the PF_INET socket and have also initialized some of the protocol-specific fields in sock structure and tcp_opt structure. We will now see the steps involved at the server and client end to set up a TCP connection. Thereafter, we move to a discussion on *bind(), listen()*, and *accept()* systemcalls on the server side and

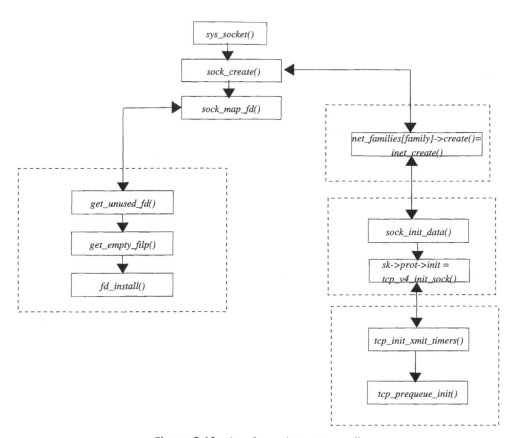

Figure 3.10. Flow for socket system call.

connect() on the client side. For PF_INET sockets, this will be *inet_bind(), inet_listen(), inet_accept()*, and *inet_connect()* functions inside the kernel.

3.8 FLOW DIAGRAM FOR SOCKET CALL

Figure 3.10 shows flow of control for socket implementation in the kernel. We have shown major routines called by sys-socket().

3.9 SUMMARY

There are two levels of socket abstraction. At the top is the BSD socket layer defined as *struct socket* and then protocol-specific socket defined as *struct sock*.

  sock_register() is an interface to register BSD sockets for different net families. For INET family, *inet_family_ops* of type *net_proto_family* is registered.
  net_families is a global array to indexed on net family number. Net family sockets are registered with this table.

inet_register_protosw() is an interface to register protocols supported by the
     INET family. These protocols are TCP, UDP, and RAW.

inetsw_array is a global table that registers the INET family protocols, object
     of type *inet_protosw*.

inet_stream_ops is set of operations for INET stream BSD socket, and *tcp_prot*
     is a protocol-specific set of operations TCP socket.

Init routine for inet family type registered using *sock_register()* initialises BSD
socket and also protocol specific socket when application makes *socket()* call. We
pass to *socket()*, protocol family as well as protocol type e.g., to create TCP socket
net family is PF_INET and type is SOCK_STREAM.

A socket is accessed by application using descriptors the same way that files are
accessed. *Socket()* call creates a socket and links it with VFS. The inode for the
socket has a socket object embedded in it, and the socket object also has a back-
pointer to the inode it belongs to. An entry is created in a processes file table for
the socket's inode.

4

KERNEL IMPLEMENTATION OF TCP CONNECTION SETUP

TCP connection involves a client and server side setup for the two ends to communicate. In Chapter 2 we have seen how we make two ends communicate over TCP using a client–server model. So, just to recapitulate, the client has to make two systemcalls, *socket()* and *connect()*, to connect to the server. The server has to make arrangements to create a listening socket so that the client can generate request to connect to this socket. To make such an arrangement, the server has to make four systemcalls: *socket()*, *bind()*, *listen()*, and *accept()*. We also saw the significance of each systemcall. From an application point of view, it is all very simple but in this chapter we will see what these systemcalls do inside the kernel. In this chapter, we will study the implementation of each systemcall in the kernel. This covers the major data structures associated with the TCP connection in the Linux kernel.

In Chapter 3, we saw what happens when we make a socket systemcall. We pass *protocol family* and *type* to *socket()*, and this does all the initial setup that involves initializing BSD and protocol socket operations. This involves initializing *socket* and *sock* structures. Now we need to do the rest of the work on the socket, which is already initialized by a call to *socket()* for client and server in different ways.

In this chapter we will study the details of the kernel data structures associated with TCP connection setup on both client and server side. The chapter covers the details of port allocation by the server when we call *bind()*. This also details how the conflicts are resolved when the server generates a request for specific port allocation. We will study the SYN queue design where the open connection request for the listening socket first sits until the connection is completely established (three-

TCP/IP Architecture, Design, and Implementation in Linux. By S. Seth and M. A. Venkatesulu
Copyright © 2008 the IEEE Computer Society

way handshake is over). We will also see how the open connection request is moved from the SYN queue to the accept queue when the TCP connection is established. Finally, we will see how the established connections are taken off the accept queue by making *accept()* call. Similarly, we will see how the client generates a connection request to the server (sends SYN segment to the listening server). In this chapter we will not cover the IP and link layer details (which will be discussed in later chapters) but will surely cover everything that is associated with the client–server connection setup in the kernel.

4.1 CONNECTION SETUP

Before two ends start communicating using TCP/IP protocol stack, each end needs to do some initial setup which requires the following:

- Asking the kernel to allocate some resources to setup this connection.
- Informing the kernel regarding existence of this connection.

Until now we have been discussing some initial setup inside the kernel to initialize BSD socket & IP-protocol-specific data structures. This initial setup is done when user application invokes socket() systemcall. This is the very first step involved to setup socket connection on both the server and client side. As discussed before, socket() systemcall requires arguments that are used to identify the protocol family and IP protocol type so that kernel can initialize a set of operations and data structures corresponding to the protocol. Finally, the kernel returns a file descriptor associated with the socket to the user application. This file descriptor is used further to identify this BSD socket by the kernel when application sends further requests to the kernel to do some more initialization for the connection. The initial setup done inside the kernel (linking of various kernel and socket data structures) after issuing socket() systemcall from the user application is shown in Chapter 3. All the TCP client and server discussions make use of 'C' programs and are defined in Chapter 2, unless specified.

4.1.1 Server Side Setup

Server application has to seek a series of kernel services to let the kernel apprise the existence of the socket. This is done with the help of invoking systemcalls from the application in the same sequence (see Fig. 4.1):

- Socket
- Bind
- Listen
- Accept

We have already seen how the socket() systemcall acts inside the kernel to initialize socket and sock data structures and a socket/protocol-specific set of operations based on the protocol-family-type argument passed to the systemcall. After this systemcall returns to the application, only socket-specific data structures are initial-

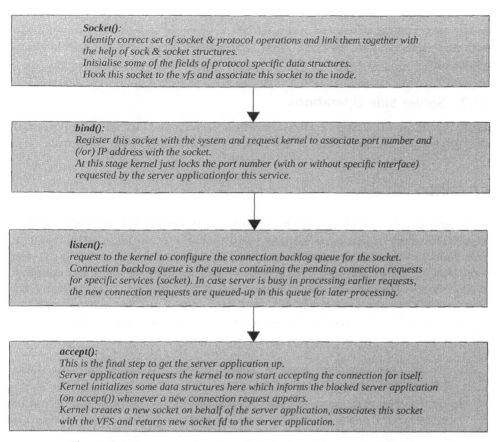

Figure 4.1. Sequence of systemcalls to be issued by server application.

ized. The server needs to do something more than this because it has not yet registered its identity with the system.

A server application is recognized on the system based on the port number (sometimes IP address also) associated with the server. So the server application by some means needs to request the kernel that it needs to associate itself with specific port (IP address in some cases). Application does this by invoking *bind()* systemcall. After *bind()* returns to the application, we are still not ready as a server. We have just gotten ourselves registered with the kernel but can't serve any client request. At this point in time, we need to do some basic configuration for the socket, which means that we need to tell the kernel how many connection requests a kernel should keep in the backlog queue for this socket if the server is not able to handle that many requests at any given point in time. This is done by invoking *listen()* systemcall. After *listen()* returns to the server application, we are still not ready to serve any client request because the server application still needs to request the kernel that now kernel should start accepting the client request. For this server invokes *accept()* systemcall. By doing this, kernel initializes some socket- and protocol-specific data structures and actually registers the services of the application with the system. *accept()* systemcall blocks forever until it gets a request for a new connection from the client. Once the connection request is received, *accept()* systemcall returns with a new file descriptor associated with the new connection. The server uses the file descriptor returned by *accept()* systemcall to communicate with the client. We will now see what the kernel does when we invoke these systemcalls.

4.1.2 Server Side Operations

Figure 4.1 shows the sequence of systemcalls to implement TCP server program. If also provides short description on functionality provided by each systemcall.

4.2 BIND

As discussed before, *socket()* systemcall only creates space for the socket in the kernel. This socket still has no identity and is capable of nothing at this point in time. *bind()* systemcall creates an identity for the socket and is the next step to create the server application. Each open socket needs to be identified uniquely in the system. For that we have concept of socket address. *Bind()* takes this socket address as one of its argument and kernel associates this address with the socket. 'C' structure that represents this socket address is 'struct sockaddr' (see Fig. 4.2).

sa_family: This stores the protocol family number associated with the socket that we have already discussed earlier.

sa_data[]: This array contains data very specific to the protocol. In the case of the PF_INET protocol family, this array contains {port number, IP address (*struct in_addr*)}.

Since we have been discussing mainly the IP protocol, the 'C' structure that represents the socket address for IP protocol (*PF_INET* family) is 'struct sockaddr_in' (see Fig. 4.3). A socket address is defined by a combination of three things:

sin_family: This is an address family (*PF_INET* for IP protocol).

sin_port: This is a 16-bit number that is used to distinguish between sockets for same protocol family.

sin_addr: This is a 32-bit number that represents an IP address. In the case of server application, this is generally set to *INADDR_ANY*, which means that if the server has many interfaces (physical/virtual), it can accept connections from any of those. Server applications can restrict connections from any

```
include/linux/socket.h

17  struct sockaddr {
18      sa_family_t   sa_family;    /* address family, AF_xxx*/
19      char          sa_data[14];  /* 14 bytes of protocol address*/
20  };
```

Figure 4.2. 'C' structure representing socket address.

```
include/linux/in.h

113 struct sockaddr_in {
114   sa_family_t        sin_family;   /* Address family*/
115   unsigned short int sin_port;     /* Port number*/
116   struct in_addr     sin_addr;     /* Internet address*/
117
118   /* Pad to size of `struct sockaddr'. */
119   unsigned char      __pad[__SOCK_SIZE__ - sizeof(short int) -
120                      sizeof(unsigned short int) - sizeof(struct in_addr)];
121 };
```

Figure 4.3. Socket address for IP.

specific interface by specifying an IP address corresponding to that interface in the *sockaddr_in* structure while binding the socket. This way the kernel allows a single port number to be used by different server applications accepting connections from mutually exclusive interfaces (having different IP addresses).

4.2.1 Data Structures Related to Socket BIND

tcp_hashinfo
tcp_bind_hashbucket
tcp_bind_bucket

4.2.2 Hash Buckets for tcp Bind

- *tcp_ehash = tcp_hashinfo.__tcp_ehash* (Fig. 4.4)
- *tcp_bhash = tcp_hashinfo.__tcp_bhash* (Fig. 4.5)
- *tcp_listening_hash = tcp_hashinfo.__tcp_listening_hash* (Fig. 4.6)

4.2.3 tcp_ehash

Figure 4.4 illustrates snapshot of hash table for sockets in established state. First half of the hash table is reserved for established sockets and rest for sockets in TIME_WAIT State. This hash table is discussed later in the chapter.

4.2.4 tcp_listening_hash

Figure 4.5 illustrates snapshot of hash table hashing all the sockets in TCP_LISTEN STATE in the system. Listen hash table is discussed later in the chapter.

4.2.5 tcp_bhash

Figure 4.6 illustrates snapshot of hash table hashing sockets based on the post to which they are bound bind hash table is discussed later in the chapter.

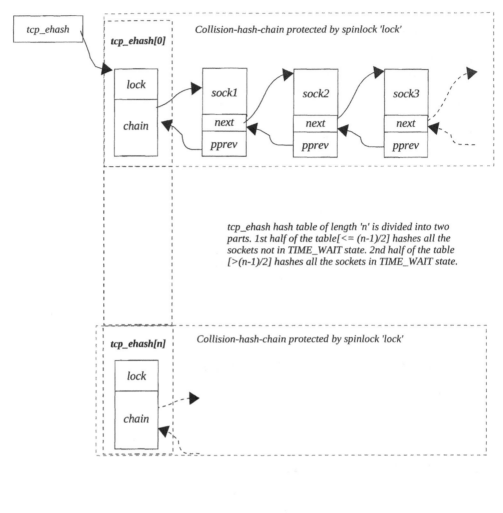

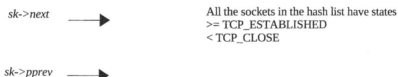

Figure 4.4. System-wide hash chain for sockets having states >= TCP_ESTABLISHED && < TCP_CLOSE.

4.2.6 *tcp_hashinfo*

This structure manages the tcp bind hash bucket. The members of *tcp_hashinfo* are as follows:

struct tcp_ehash_bucket *__tcp_ehash: This is a list of all the sockets with complete identity. With a complete identity, it means that the socket state should be

1. >= *TCP_ESTABLISHED*
2. < *TCP_CLOSE*

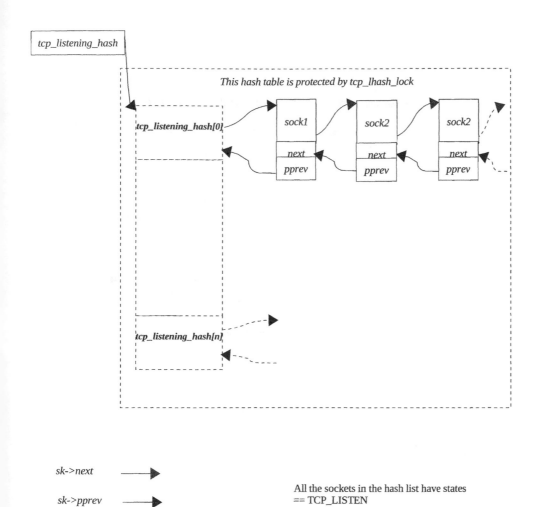

Figure 4.5. System-wide hash chain for all listening sockets having states == TCP_LISTEN.

The first half of the table is for sockets not in *TIME_WAIT*, and the second half is for *TIME_WAIT* sockets only within the socket state boundary mentioned above. The collision hash chain is linked by next and pprev fields of sock structure.

struct tcp_bind_hashbucket *__tcp_bhash: This is the hash bucket that hashes entities containing information about all the port numbers that are already in use. The elements in the hash table are hashed based on the local port number.

int __tcp_ehash_size: This is the size of the *tcp_ehash* table.

int __tcp_bhash_size: This is the size of the *tcp_bhash* table.

struct sock *__tcp_listening_hash[TCP_LHTABLE_SIZE]: This is hash table containing all the sockets in *TCP_LISTEN* state. Sockets are hashed in the table based on local port number. The collision hash chain is linked by next and pprev fields of sock structure.

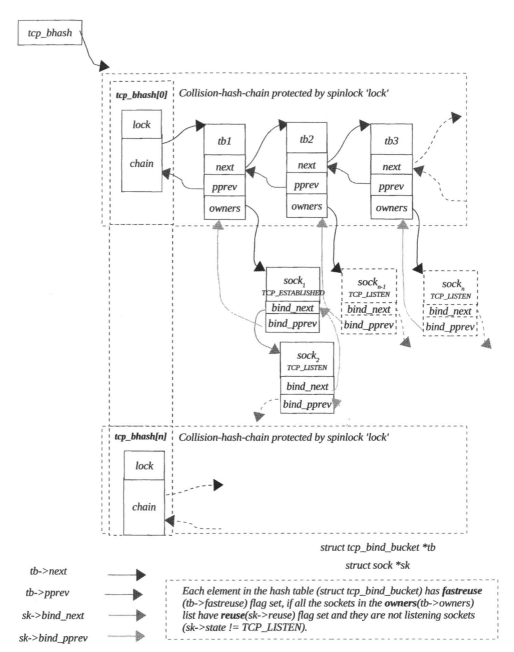

Figure 4.6. System-wide hash table that links all the sockets which are bound tot one or the other port.

rwlock_t __tcp_lhash_lock: This lock protects *__tcp_lhash_users* and also the *__tcp_ehash* table.

atomic_t __tcp_lhash_users: This variable is used to synchronize the readers/ writers of *__tcp_listening_hash*. This member is incremented every time the process wants to acquire reader/writer lock for the *tcp_listen_hash* list. This is decremented when we release the lock; and if the value comes down to 0, we wake up all the processes waiting to acquire the lock.

wait_queue_head_t __tcp_lhash_wait: This is a wait Queue for the readers/writers of *__tcp_listening_hash*.

spinlock_t __tcp_portalloc_lock: This is lock used to synchronize access of global variable *tcp_port_rover* and *tcp_bhash* hash table. This lock should be held when we are requesting a local port to bind a socket.

4.2.7 *tcp_bind_hashbucket* (See Figure 4.6)

This describes the hash bucket and consists of two members:

spinlock_t lock: This is a lock to protect the collision hash chain *chain*.

*tcp_bind_bucket *chain:* This is the element of the collision hash chain for the bind hash bucket.

4.2.8 *tcp_bind_bucket*

This structure keeps information about the port number usage by sockets and the way the port number is being used. The information is useful enough to tell the new binding socket whether it can bind itself to a particular port number that is already in use. The data structure also keeps track of all the socket's that are associated with this port number.

unsigned short port: This is the port number associated with *tcp_bind_bucket*. Whenever a socket wants to bind itself to some port which is not in use, we allocate a new tcp_bind_bucket structure, assign the port number in question to *port*, and hash it in the *tcp_bind_hashbucket*.

signed short fastreuse: This is the flag that indicates whether the port number that is already in use can be reused by a new socket. Whenever a new socket requests to allocate a port number to it, we check if the port number is already in use by some other socket. So, we check *tcp_bind_hashbucket* for the entry associated with a port number. Now if we have requested to bind the socket with the port number for which hash entry exists, we check for the *fastreuse* flag. If this flag is set, we are sure that we can bind the socket with the associated port number and add the socket to the *owner's* list. In short, if the *fastreuse* flag is set, we have all the sockets in the *owners* list, which are as follows:

1. These sockets are bound to the same TCP port but on different network interfaces. We can have server applications listening on the same post but different IP address configured on different interfaces.
2. Or all the sockets have a *reuse* flag set and are not listening sockets, which means that for all the sockets in the owners list the following conditions should be met:

$$sk \rightarrow reuse \ \&\& \ sk \rightarrow state \ != TCP\_LISTEN$$

3. Or all the sockets are bound to the same port using same interface, but the *recv_saddr* for all the sockets is different.

sys_bind(int fd,struct sockaddr *umyaddr, int addrlen)

Figure 4.7. Entry point for bind sys call in the kernel.

struct tcp_bind_bucket *next: This is the next node in the tcp-hash-bucket collision chain, for which associated port numbers hash to the same values.

struct sock *owners: This is the list of the sockets that are using same port
number. These are linked by the following members of the sock structure:

1. sk→bind_next
2. sk→bind_pprev
3. sk→prev

struct tcp_bind_bucket **pprev: This is the address of the location that contains
address of current tcp_bind_bucket node.

4.2.9   bind()

Systemcall accepts three arguments returned by socket() systemcall:

socket descriptor (file descriptor)
socket address (struct sockaddr_in)
address length

Since socket() systemcall has already associated the file descriptor with the socket,
this descriptor will be used by the application further to identify this socket. When
bind() systemcall is invoked, the kernel calls the sys_bind() function. Let's see what
this function does.

4.2.10   sys_bind()

sys_bind() is the function called inside the kernel with three arguments
(Fig. 4.7).

fd: This is the socket file descriptor returned by socket call.
umyaddr: This is the socket address to which we want to bind the socket.
addrlen: This is the socket address length.

First, we do a lookup for the socket associated with the socket descriptor. This socket
descriptor is nothing but the file descriptor, and it links a socket with the VFS as
shown in Fig. 4.2. So, we call sockfd_lookup() with the socket descriptor.

4.2.11   sockfd_lookup()

First the kernel needs to get the file structure from the current process's file table.
We call fget() to do this.

4.2.12   fget()

Get hold of *files* member for the *current* process (current→files). Now the file descriptor (socket descriptor here) is indexed into the *fd* array, member of the files_struct structure, for the current process. Before accessing an element of the array *fd* (*current→files→fd[fd]*) corresponding to the socket descriptor, we need to make sure that the socket descriptor is well below the maximum number allocated to the file descriptor; until now, we did it by calling *fcheck()*:

$$if\ (fd < file{\rightarrow}max\_fds)$$

If the *above* condition is true, we return the file structure corresponding to the socket descriptor from the file table:

$$current{\rightarrow}files{\rightarrow}fd[fd].$$

Now, increment the reference count (*file→f_count*) of the file structure returned by *fcheck()*. Return the file structure.

    End of fget(). Get hold of the inode associated with the socket descriptor, *file→f_dentry→d_inode*. Now we need to check if the inode represents a socket. This can be confirmed if *inode→i_sock* is set. If the above is true, get the socket structure associated with this inode, call *socki_lookup()*. *socki_lookup()* returns socket structure, which is part of the *union u* of the *inode structure*

$$inode{\rightarrow}u.socket\_i.$$

Return socket structure (*inode→u.socket_i*).

    End of sockfd_lookup(). Once we get the socket associated with the socket descriptor from s*ockfd_lookup()*, we copy-in the socket address from user space to kernel space and finally call the bind function specific to the protocol family: *sock→ ops→bind()*. In the case of *PF_INET* protocol family, this function corresponds to *inet_bind()*.

4.2.13   inet_bind()

This internally calls a bind function specific to IP protocol with *fd* replaced with corresponding *socket*. This is protocol-specific:

$$sock{\rightarrow}sk{\rightarrow}prot{\rightarrow}bind().$$

As we have already seen in our earlier discussion for *SOCK_STREAM*, *sock→sk→ prot* is initialized to *tcp_prot*. We don't have any bind function specific to *SOCK_ STREAM (in tcp_prot)*. So we move ahead with some sanity check on the socket address passed as an argument to the function. Then we need to check the IP address type in the socket address. To get the IP address type (to which application has requested to bind the socket), we call *inet_addr_type()*. Based on that, we see how decisions are made. *sysctl_ip_nonlocal_bind* is a control parameter that controls the 'binding behavior' of the sockets. If the control parameter is set, it means that we can bind our socket to any IP address, which includes *nonlocal* types also.

Nonlocal IP addresses are those that are external. This means that it can be a gateway address or a direct route. Any interface that gets IP addresses dynamically, is directly connected to the gateways of different networks, and acts as gateway for the host is considered as a nonlocal IP. For example, PPP, PLIP, SLIP, and so on, interfaces get IP addresses that are nonlocal because they get an IP addresses dynamically only when the link between the two ends is up and the IP address assigned to the interface belongs to the network between the two ends. In the case where *sysctl_ip_nonlocal_bind* is not set, we can allow the socket to bind to only those IP addresses that fall in the following categories:

INADDR_ANY = address to accept any incoming message
RTN_LOCAL = accept locally
RTN_MULTICAST = multicast route.
RTN_BROADCAST = accept locally as broadcast and send as broadcast.

Now we are left with one class of IP address to which a socket is not allowed bind if *sysctl_ip_nonlocal_bind* is not set. This is *RTN_UNICAST* indicating that the IP is a gateway or a direct route. Once we have checked the validity of the IP address to which socket needs to be bound, we go ahead with some more checks. Get the port number from the socket address (*addr→sin_port*). Here we check if the port number requested is reserved for privileged applications. Ports 0–1023 are reserved for applications running as a super-user. The following conditions does the check:

$$snum < PROT\_SOCK \ \&\& \ !capable(CAP\_NET\_BIND\_SERVICE)$$

Now the nonprivileged application can also have permissions to avail some of the super-user facilities. We can check this capability of the current process by calling *capable()* and passing capability number to it. The process structure has a capability-related field, current→cap_effective, which keeps information about the capabilities that a current process possesses. We are capable of binding the socket to the privileged port. So, we move ahead with some more sanity checks. We check if we are binding the same socket once again. The following check does the same:

$$(sk→state \ != TCP\_CLOSE) \ || \ (sk→num \ != 0)$$

Until now, the socket state is unchanged because we don't have any activity on it (we see this in later discussions when the socket state changes from TCP_CLOSE to something else). If the socket state shows that it is in any state, it means that we have already bound the socket before and are trying to bind it once again (by mistake). At this point of time, *sk→num* is set to a value greater than 0 only in case of *SOCK_RAW*. We are discussing *SOCK_STREAM*, for which we have not yet allocated *sk→num*. So if the value is set, we have entered the wrong code path. Now we assign values to source address for this socket. There are two fields in *sock structure* associated with the source address. These are:

sk→rcv_saddr

sk→saddr

sk→rcv_saddr. This is a source address used by hash lookups, and *sk→saddr* is used to transmit (source address for IP headers). These are initialized to an IP address specified in socket address (*addr→sin_addr.s_addr*). In the case where the socket's IP address is of type multicast or broadcast, we set *sk→saddr* to 0 (which means that the sending device address is used in such cases).

The next step is to find out whether we are allowed to bind to specified port (address already being used by another socket). Call *get_port()* specific to the protocol *sk→prot→get_port()*. This is *tcp_v4_get_port()* from *tcp_prot* (set of protocol operations specific to *SOCK_STREAM*).

1. >= *TCP_ESTABLISHED*
2. < *TCP_CLOSE*

4.2.14 *tcp_v4_get_port()*

Arguments passed to this function is *sock structure* associated with the socket and the *port number* to which a socket needs to be bound. If the port number specified is 0 in the socket address, we are asking the kernel to find a free port number and allocate it to the socket. Here we need to select a free local port within the range specified by *sysctl_local_port_range[2]* (1024–4999). This range can be changed by using *sysctl*. *tcp_portalloc_lock* is a global lock that serializes the port allocation. So, we need to hold the lock here before accessing any of these global variables associated with port allocation. These are

cp_port_rover

tcp_bhash

tcp_port_rover: This is another variable that keeps the last port number allocated to the socket.

tcp_bhash: This is a global hash bucket containing information about all the allocated port numbers and related information. This is a macro that accesses *__tcp_bhash* member of global variable *tcp_hashinfo* (of type *struct tcp_hashinfo*), *tcp_hashinfo.__tcp_bhash*.

Starting from *tcp_port_rover*, we check for all the available free ports within the max local port value stored in *sysctl_local_port_range[1]*.

$$rover = tcp\_port\_rover;$$

We access the hash chain head corresponding to each port number from *tcp_bhash* hash table (see cs 4.1).

Before accessing the collision hash chain, we need to hold the chain lock (*head→lock*).

$$spin\_lock(\&head\rightarrow lock);$$

```
net/ipv4/tcp_ipv4.c

220                    head = &tcp_bhash[tcp_bhashfn(rover)];
```

cs 4.1. *tcp_v4_get_port()*.

Now we traverse each element of the collision hash chain using the *next* member of the chain element (*struct tcp_bind_bucket*). For each element we try to match the current port number with the port number corresponding to the hash chain element.

if (tb→port == rover)

If we find that none of the elements (*tb*) corresponds to the selected port number (*rover*) in the current hash collision chain, we move on to the next port number (*++rover*) and start over again. Otherwise, we get out of the loop and release the global lock *tcp_portalloc_lock*. We are here because of two reasons:

1. Either we have exhausted the entire port numbers (all are in use)
2. Or we have found one unused port number.

In the former case we return the error, whereas in the latter case we need to create an entry in the hash table *tcp_bhash* for the new port number allocation. Here we store the allocated port number in the global variable *tcp_port_rover* and initialize *tb* (element of the collision hash list) to NULL because we need to create a new entry later.

In the case where the application has specified the port number to which it wants to bind the socket, we get hold of the collision hash-chain element corresponding to the port number from the *tcp_bhash[]* hash table. We traverse through each element of the collision hash chain and try to match each element's port number with the port number in question. If we are able to find the matching entry, we know that the port is already in use. Nevertheless, we don't give up here because if we are able to satisfy certain conditions, we can reuse the ports. If we are here, we know that

1. either we have gotten an available free port number
2. or gotten the requested port number which is not in use
3. or gotten the requested port number which is already in use.

For cases 1 and 2, we need to create a new hash entry in the *tcp_bhash* table. We allocate new *struct tcp_bind_hashbucket*, initialize all the fields of the allocated structure. We link the current hash-chain element to the head of the list using *next* and *pprev* members of the *tcp_bind_bucket* structure. Now we need to initialize the *fastreuse* member of the the element. We have already discussed this flag in detail, and now we see how to initialize. In the following case, we set this flag (*tb→ fastreuse*):

1. *reuse* flag is set for the current socket (*sk→reuse == 1*)
2. and current socket is not in listen state (*sk→state != TCP_LISTEN*)

Otherwise, this flag remains 0. This means that the socket can only be allowed to be reused if the owning socket allows it to be reused ($sk \rightarrow reuse == 1$) and it is not in the listening state ($sk \rightarrow state \; != \; TCP\_LISTTEN$).

We have not yet updated the *owners* field of the new element and so also the *num* field of the socket (associate the port number with the socket). For this we call *tcp_bind_hash()*. This function links the current socket with the owner's field of the hash bucket element with the help of the $sk \rightarrow bind\_pprev$ and $sk \rightarrow bind\_next$ fields. For case 3, we have already found *tb* corresponding to the port number which is requested by the application, in which case we have reached here with *tb != NULL*. In this case we need to make some checks before proceeding further. We need to check whether

1. the current socket allows sharing of port number
2. the current socket qualifies for binding to the port already in use.

The former can be verified by checking the *reuse* field of the socket ($sk \rightarrow reuse$). If this is set to 1, we are sure that it is passed. For the latter case, we need to check two things:

1. $tb \rightarrow fastreuse$ for *tb* found from the tcp collision-hash chain.
2. state of the current socket ($sk \rightarrow state$).

If $tb \rightarrow fastreuse$ is set to 1, it means that all the sockets (in the $tb \rightarrow owners$ list) still allow some others to use it for binding. $sk \rightarrow state$ for the current socket should not be set to *TCP_LISTEN*, which means that the current socket is not in the listening state.

If case 3 passes, we go ahead and bind the port with the current socket and link the socket with the tcp bind hash bucket, we call *tcp_bind_hash()*. In case we fail, we still have a chance to bind the socket with the port already in use. We can still bind this socket to the given port if *tcp_bind_conflict()* finds it appropriate.

4.2.15 *tcp_bind_conflict()*

This function traverses through the entire list of sockets in the $tb \rightarrow owners$ and do the following checks:

$$sk2 = tb \rightarrow owners$$

1. First we check whether the current owner socket is bound to a different interface (IP address) from the interface to which new socket wants to bind (see cs 4.2). If this they are different, we move on to the next socket ($sk2 = sk2 \rightarrow bind\_next$) in the list and repeat the same step.
2. If the above condition passes, we check whether the current owning socket is a listening socket (see cs 4.3). If it is not so, we move on to the next socket ($sk2 = sk2 \rightarrow bind\_next$) in the owner's list and start over from the step 1.
3. If the above condition passes, we check whether the IP address to which new socket wants to bind to is different from the IP address to which the current owning socket is bound on the same physical interface and also the two IP

```
net/ipv4/tcp_ipv4.c

183          if (sk != sk2 &&
184              sk2->reuse <= 1 &&
185              sk->bound_dev_if == sk2->bound_dev_if) {
```

cs 4.2. *tcp_bind_conflict().*

```
net/ipv4/tcp_ipv4.c

186          if (!sk_reuse ||
187              !sk2->reuse ||
188              sk2->state == TCP_LISTEN) {
```

cs 4.3. *tcp_bind_confilict().*

```
net/ipv4/tcp_ipv4.c

189              if (!sk2->rcv_saddr   ||
190                  !sk->rcv_saddr    ||
191                  (sk2->rcv_saddr == sk->rcv_saddr))
192                  break;
```

cs 4.4. *tcp_bind_confilict().*

addresses are not INADDR_ANY (see cs 4.4). If the condition is true, we come out of the loop. Otherwise, we move on to the next owning socket (*sk2 = sk2→bind_next*) and start over all again from step 1.

If we have come out of the loop, it may be because of the two reasons:

1. We have exhausted all the owning sockets (*sk2 == NULL*)
2. We have found at least one owning socket that is bound to (*sk→state == TCP_LISTEN*) the same port number, IP address (*sk→rcv_saddr*), and interface to which the new socket wants to bind.

In the former case, there won't be any conflicts and we can bind the new socket to the requested port number and thus we link the new socket in the owner's list; call *tcp_bind_hash()*. In the latter case, we have conflicts because of which we cannot bind the socket to the requested port.

We return from *tcp_bind_conflict()* with the indication that we can reuse the port number because the conflicts are resolved. Now we need to modify the *fastreuse* flag for the bind hash bucket (*tb→fastreuse*). If the current socket doesn't allow us to reuse the port (*sk→reuse == 0*) and tb→fastreuse is nonzero (possible values are –1 or 1), we reset *tb→fastreuse*, which means that neither the listening nor the connecting socket can use this port number. We carry out all the activities in the function with local bottom-half disabled, because some new connection request may also access the tcp bind hash table as we will see later.

End of tcp_v4_get_port(). We return to *inet_bind()* with the error code. If we check that the error has occurred, we return with the error code *EADDRI-NUSE*. If we have come until this point, it means that the socket is successfully bound to the requested port. We need to update certain fields of the socket structure.

3. If the new socket is not binding to *INADDR_ANY(sk→rcv_saddr != NULL)*, we need to set *SOCK_BINDADDR_LOCK* bit of *sk→userlocks* flag. This indicates that that we are bound to a specific IP address and are not receiving connections from any IP address.

- If the new socket has gotten the valid port number to bind to without any conflicts, we set the *SOCK_BINDPORT_LOCK* of *sk→userlocks* flag.
- We update the source port of the socket (*sk→sport*) of the socket with the requested port number. *sk→sport = htons(sk→num), sk→num* is assigned value in the function *tcp_bind_hash()* called from *tcp_v4_get_port()→ inet_bind()*.
- As of now we don't know the destination port (*sk→dport*) and IP address (*sk→daddr*), which is known only when we get a request for new connection for this bound socket. So we initialize them to 0.
- Initialize *sk→dst_cache* to *NULL*. This field is related to the destination route cache and we will discuss it later.

End of inet_bind(). If this passes, we are successful in getting the requested port number which is already in use; otherwise we fail. The complete flow of bind() is shown in Fig. 4.8.

4.3 LISTEN

Here we need to tell the kernel that we are willing to accept the connections. At the same time we need to configure the socket as to how many socket connections the kernel should keep in the backlog queue before it starts rejecting the new connection request. The backlog queue for listening sockets may fill up for two reasons:

- In case the kernel is not able to process the request.
- In case the application has not invoked *accept()* systemcall.

Once the backlog queue is full for the socket, the kernel rejects/drops the request. In the latter case, it sends a message to the client with error code *ECONNREFUSED*.

listen() systemcall accepts two arguments:

1. Socket descriptor (ret urned by *socket()* systemcall).
2. Number and length of the backlog queue.

Let's see what happens inside tke kernel when we invoke *listen()* systemcall.

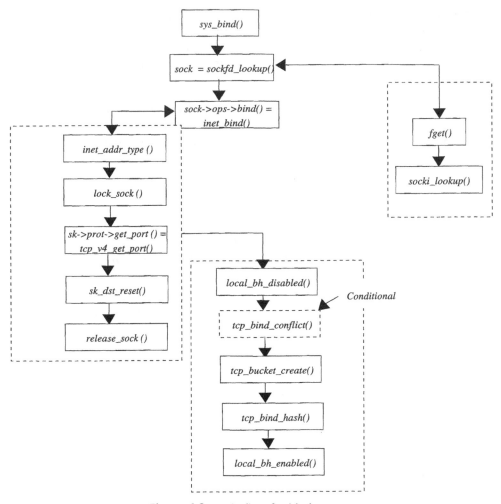

Figure 4.8. Code flow for bind process.

sys_listen(int fd, int backlog)

Figure 4.9. Kernel interface for listen systemcall.

4.3.1 *sys_listen()*

sys_listen() is called inside the kernel with the following arguments (Fig. 4.9):

fd: This is the socket file descriptor on which listen operates.
backlog: This is the length of the backlog queue to handle accepted connection
requests for the listening socket.

First we try to get the sock entry corresponding to the socket descriptor, *sockfd_
lookup()*. This function was explained earlier. Do some sanity check for length of
the backlog queue (should not be more than *SOMAXCONN*). We are now ready

to put this socket to listening state for which we need to initialize some of the members of the *sock structure* and protocol-specific data structures, which informs the kernel that we are willing to accept the connections and have configured the connection backlog queue. We call the protocol-specific listen function finally. This is *sock→ops→listen()*. For the *PF_INET* protocol family, *sock→ops* is set to *inet_stream_ops*. So, we are calling *listen()* function from *inet_stream_ops*, *inet_listen()*.

4.3.2 inet_listen()

We carry out some sanity checks here like the socket should be in close or listen state, *TCP_CLOSE* or *TCP_LISTEN*. In the latter case, we should be allowed only to adjust the connection backlog Queue length (*sk→max_ack_backlog*). Otherwise we do something more to put the socket to listening state. In the case where the socket is currently in *TCP_CLOSE* state, we call *tcp_listen_start()*.

4.3.3 tcp_listen_start()

Here we initialize some of the fields of following structures:

a. *sock*
b. *tcp_opt*
c. *tcp_listen_opts*

sk→max_ack_backlog: This is the maximum length of the connection backlog queue. This is initialized to 0.

sk→ack_backlog: This indicates the number of connection requests currently in the connection backlog queue. This value is incremented whenever a new connection is accepted. A check is made with *sk→max_ack_backlog* before the new connection is accepted. Initialize accept queue for the socket, (see cs 4.5).

An open connection backlog Queue or accept Queue is maintained by *tcp_opt* structure *sk→tp_pinfo.af_tcp*, with the help of two different members *accept_queue* and *accept_queue_tail*. Queue points to struct *open_request* which we discuss little later. Allocate space for struct *tcp_listen_opt* and initialize the members.

Initialize syn queue access lock, (see cs 4.6). This lock protects sockets SYN QUEUE which contains list of connection requests.

```
net/ipv4/tcp.c

533     tp->accept_queue = tp->accept_queue_tail = NULL;
```

cs 4.5. *tcp_listen_start()*.

```
net/ipv4/tcp.c

534     tp->syn_wait_lock = RW_LOCK_UNLOCKED;
```

cs 4.6. *tcp_listen_start()*.

```
include/net/tcp.h

1592  struct tcp_listen_opt
1593  {
1594        u8                 max_qlen_log;   /* log_2 of maximal queued SYNs */
1595        int                qlen;
1596        int                qlen_young;
1597        int                clock_hand;
1598        struct open_request    *syn_table[TCP_SYNQ_HSIZE];
1599  };
```

Figure 4.10. Structure used by listening socket.

SYN QUEUE. Precisely speaking, this is the new request created by the kernel when the SYN packet arrives for the listening socket. This list is maintained by socket's $sk \rightarrow tp\_pinfo.af\_tcp \rightarrow listen\_opt$ member of type struct tcp_listen_opt. Let's discuss tcp_listen_opt structure.

max_qlen_log. This keeps the number that indicates the maximum number of SYN connection requests for a listening socket. Whenever, the kernel receives a SYN packet for a listening socket, the $qlen$ field is checked against the max_queue_len field of this structure. If the former is greater than the latter, we drop the current connection request. Otherwise we increment $qlen$ by 1 and add this open connection request to the SYN queue hash table.

qlen. This is the counter that keeps track of the number of open connection requests in the SYN queue. This field is incremented whenever we add a new connection request to the listening sockets SYN queue.

qlen_young. This is the counter that keeps track of the number of number of open connection requests in the SYN queue, which are still young. The field is incremented by 1, whenever a new open connection request is added to the SYN queue. It is decremented by 1, whenever TCP needs to retransmit the SYN/ACK packet for any of the open connection requests in the SYN queue because it has not received the ACK for the SYN/ACK packet already sent for any reason. Basically, the policy is to still drop any new connection request based on the young connection requests in the following case:

- SYN queue can accommodate more open connection requests in the SYN queue ($tcp\_synq\_is\_full() == 0$), **and**
- Accept queue is full ($tcp\_acceptq\_is\_full() != 0$) and SYN queue still contains more than one young connection request ($tcp\_synq\_young() > 1$).

syn_table. This is the SYN queue hash table that hashes all the open connection requests (of type $struct\ open\_requests$) for the listening socket. These requests are hashed based on destination port and destination IP (client's port and IP which generated the connection request). The SYN queue hash collision chain for syn_table is linked by dl_next field of $open\_request$ struct. Call $tcp\_delack\_init()$.

Now we need to set the max_queue_len for the tcp_listen_opt structure just allocated for this listening socket. This value is set based on the global variable $sysctl\_max\_syn\_backlog$ (which is system configurable and is initialized to 256 for

```
net/ipv4/tcp.c

542     for (lopt->max_qlen_log = 6; ; lopt->max_qlen_log++)
543         if ((1<<lopt->max_qlen_log) >= sysctl_max_syn_backlog)
544             break;
```

cs 4.7. *tcp_listen_start()*.

```
net/ipv4/tcp.c

555     sk->state = TCP_LISTEN;
```

cs 4.8. *tcp_listen_start()*.

```
net/ipv4/tcp.c

556     if (sk->prot->get_port(sk, sk->num) == 0) {
557         sk->sport = htons(sk->num);
558
559         sk_dst_reset(sk);
560         sk->prot->hash(sk);
561
562         return 0;
563     }
```

cs 4.9. *tcp_listen_start()*.

machines >= 256 MB). The value of the field should not exceed $\log_2$ of the value stored in global variable *sysctl_max_syn_backlog* (see cs 4.7).

Initialize listen_opt member of socket's sk→tp_pinfo.af_tcp with the tcp_listen_ opts structure just allocated and initialized with the SYNQ lock just initialized *tp→ syn_wait_lock*.

We have already made all the required changes to the socket to get it to the listen state. We are still not in the listen hash table, *tcp_listening_hash*, because we are still not in the *TCP_LISTEN* state. We set the socket state to *TCP_LISTEN* state (see cs 4.8).

Now we need to check if we are still eligible to use the same port to which we earlier bound this socket. There is a window between the *bind()* and *listen()* calls form an application when two threads can race to bind two sockets to the same port. After both the threads are bound to the same port (both the sockets are in the bind hash list, *tcp_bhash*), one of the sockets makes the socket port not reusable (resets sk→reuse for itself) and gets into the *TCP_LISTEN* state. The other thread now enters the *listen()* systemcall and gets into this part of the code. So, once again it needs to make sure whether it can use the same port that it requested earlier. So, it checks this by calling *sk→prot→get_port()* (tcp_v4_get_port()), which returns 0 if still this socket can use the same port (*sk→num*) to which it was bound. If we can't use the port, return 1. Otherwise if that is the case, we set sport for the socket (*sk→sport*) and hash this socket to the listen hash table *sk→prot→hash()*. This function points to *tcp_v4_hash()* in the case of *TCP* (see cs 4.9). *tcp_v4_hash()* hashes the socket to the listen hash table, *tcp_listening_hash* (Fig. 4.5), with the local bottom half-disabled. The socket is linked in the listen hash collision chain using

```
net/ipv4/tcp.c

307       sk->max_ack_backlog = backlog;
```

<u>cs 4.10.</u> *inet_listen().*

$sk{\rightarrow}next$ and $sk{\rightarrow}pprev$ pointers. The hash function, *tcp_sk_listen_hashfn()*, uses $sk{\rightarrow}num$ to calculate the hash value.

END of tcp_listen_start(). we return from *tcp_listen_start()*, either with error code set or successfully putting the socket in the listening state. In the case where the socket is successfully put to the listening state, we need to set *max_ack_backlog* field of the socket to the value passed as an argument to the *listen()* (see cs 4.10).

END of inet_listen(). The complete flow of listen() is shown in Fig. 4.11.

4.3.4   Listen Flow

Figure 4.11 shows flow of control for listen implementation of TCP/INET socket in the kernel. Here we show maps routines that are called from sys_listen() for details, see Section 4.3.3.

4.3.5   *struct open_request*

The structure keeps account of all the open connection requests which are not yet accepted by the application (see Fig. 4.12). There is one open_request for each connection request for a listening socket. When the connection request arrives, a new structure is allocated and various fields of this structure are initialized. Most of the fields are initialized from tcp and ip header fields of the SYN connection request and are very specific to the connection. These are explained ahead. The structure is hashed in the listening sockets syn Queue $sk{\rightarrow}tp\_pinfo.af\_tcp{\rightarrow}listen\_opt{\rightarrow}syn\_table$ according to the port number of the connection requester (see Fig. 4.17). The SYN/ACK packet is sent to the connection originator (client). When the final ACK is received for the SYN/ACK packet associated with this connection request, a new socket is created which is marked to be in the TCP_ESTABLISHED state because a three-way handshake is over for this connection. Most of the fields of the new socket are duplicated from the parent socket except for the fields that are very specific to the connection. Now the *open_request* node is moved from Syn queue to the listening sockets (parent) accept queue (see Fig. 4.18). Since the new connection is not yet accepted, it remains in the accept queue and no I/O occurs over the connection from our end. Now let us discuss struct open_request.

   dl_next: This is the pointer to the next link in the *SYN* queue collision hash table for the listening socket.
   rcv_isn: This is the initial sequence number taken from the SYN packet received as connection request.
   snt_isn: This is the initial sequence number calculated at the listening socket end. This is calculated each time a new connection request is received. The

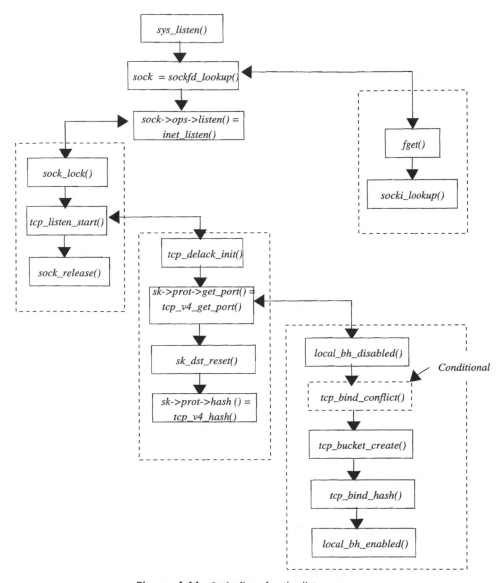

Figure 4.11. Code flow for the listen process.

value is sent in SYN/ACK reply as part of the TCP header's sequence number field.

rmt_port: This is the port number of the other end of the TCP connection, which has generated the connection request. The value is taken from the TCP header of the SYN packet received as connection request.

mss: This is the maximum segment size used for the TCP connection. The value is taken from either the TCP mss options (of SYN packet received) or the *tcp_opt* structure (*tp→user_mss*), whichever is smaller.

retrans: This field is incremented whenever the SYN/ACK packet is retransmitted for the received SYN connection request. It keeps track of the number

```
include/net/tcp.h

494  struct open_request {
495         struct open_request   *dl_next; /* Must be first member! */
496         __u32              rcv_isn;
497         __u32              snt_isn;
498         __u16              rmt_port;
499         __u16              mss;
500         __u8               retrans;
501         __u8               __pad;
502         __u16  snd_wscale : 4,
503              rcv_wscale : 4,
504              tstamp_ok : 1,
505              sack_ok : 1,
506              wscale_ok : 1,
507              ecn_ok : 1,
508              acked : 1;
509         /* The following two fields can be easily recomputed I think -AK */
510         __u32              window_clamp; /* window clamp at creation time */
511         __u32              rcv_wnd;     /* rcv_wnd offered first time */
512         __u32              ts_recent;
513         unsigned long        expires;
514         struct or_calltable   *class;
515         struct sock         *sk;
516         union {
517              struct tcp_v4_open_req v4_req;
518  #if defined(CONFIG_IPV6) || defined (CONFIG_IPV6_MODULE)
519              struct tcp_v6_open_req v6_req;
520  #endif
521         } af;
522  };
```

Figure 4.12. Linux representation of open connection request.

of retries attempted to get ACK for the SYN/ACK packets sent. When maximum attempts are tried, the connection request is dropped.

snd_wscale: This 4-bit field is the window scaling value received from the sender. It is taken from TCP options for the SYN packet received as a connection request. Stored in *tp→snd_wscale*. All this if window scaling option is set in TCP header options.

rcv_wscale: This 4-bit field is the window scaling value to be sent to the other end of the TCP connection, which has generated the connection request. This is done only if the window scaling option is set in TCP header options.

wscale_ok: This 1-bit field is set if the window scale option is set for the SYN TCP header (packet received as a connection request).

tstamp_ok: This 1-bit field is set if the timestamp option is set for the SYN TCP header (packet received as a connection request).

sack_ok: This 1-bit field is set if the SYN bit is set in the TCP header for the packet received as a connection request.

ecn_ok: This 1-bit field is set if the ECN option is set for the SYN TCP header (packet received as a connection request) and our side of the TCP is configured to use this option.

acked: This 1-bit field is set if the SYN/ACK packet is sent for the received connection request SYN packet.

rcv_wnd: This is the receive window size offered first time in the SYN/ACK packet.

ts_recent: This is set to the timestamp received in the SYN connection request packet, in the case where the timestamp option is set in the TCP header option.

expires: This is the timeout value for the TCP when it should attempt retransmit if it doesn't receive any ACK for the SYN/ACK sent to the connection originator.

sk: This is the pointer to the newly created socket for the new connection request (struct open_request is created for this socket). The field is initialized to NULL when open_request is created for the new connection request and the request is in the syn queue. When the new socket is created and the open_request is transferred to the accpet queue, the filed is initialized to the newly created socket.

af: This is a union of two pointers for IPv4/v6-specific information. In the case of Ipv4, this is a pointer to *struct tcp_v4_open_req*. There are three fields for this structure.

loc_addr: This is the IP address for which connection request has arrived. It is taken from the destination IP address (field) of the IP header for the packet received as a connection request.

rmt_addr: This is the IP address of the originator of the connection request. It is taken from the source (IP address) field of the IP header for the packet received as a connection request.

opt: This is the IP header options obtained from the IP header of the SYN connection request packet.

This way we have seen that when the *listen()* systemcall returns to the application, the socket is in a TCP_LISTEN state and all required settings are done by the kernel to accept connections for this listening socket, though still not fully functional. For doing this, the kernel has to associate and initialize tcp_listen_opt and open_request structures with the socket. Since this is a listening socket and is recognized as accepting connection requests by the kernel, any new connection for this socket is queued up in the syn queue (sk→tp_pinfo.af_tcp→listen_opt→*syn_table*) until a three-way hand shake is not completed as shown in Fig. 4.17. Once the TCP three-way handshake is over, we remove the open_request node from the syn queue and place it in the socket's accept queue (*sk→tp_pinfo.af_tcp→accept_queue*) as shown in Fig. 4.18. All the open requests in the accept queue are associated with a new socket (*req→sk != NULL*) and are in a TCP_ESTABLISHED state. The socket associated with the open requests in the accept queue are detached from the parent socket and inherit most of the properties of the parent except for the one's very specific to the connection. TCP-related information (sk→*tp_pinfo.af_tcp, tcp_opts*) is also initialized for this socket, with most of the fields inherited from the parent socket except for the new connection-specific field. Since this is not a listening socket, the listen-specific field of the tcp_opt structure for the new socket (sk→tp_pinfo.af_tcp→listen_opt) is set to NULL and at the same time accept queue (*sk→tp_pinfo.af_tcp→accept_queue*) is also intialized to NULL. The new socket is hashed in the tcp_ehash table. At the same time the new socket is associated with the owner's list of the bind hash bucket that is hashed according to the port number(sk→num). There will be many such entries in the owner's list of the tcp-bind-hash bucket, but a socket for a specific connection is identified by a quadruplet (dst IP, dst port, local IP, local port). This way, a child socket gets its separate identity and can operate as a separate communication channel irrespective of its parent socket. Let's see how this new socket in the TCP_ESTABLISHED state, associated with the open request that is still in the accept queue, is not fully functional. We know that the all the initial handshakes for the TCP connection are done between the client and the server, and the client here knows that it has reached the correct destination and a communication channel is set up between the two peers.

We see the behavior of the server side socket toward the new connection request when it arrives for the socket that is not completely accepting the connections. Here we see how the connection requests are accepted when

- The socket is bound to a port but is not yet in a 'listening' state.
- The socket is in a 'listening' state but are not yet accepted.

We explain this with the help of 'tcpdump' output for the connection requests initiated by the client for the server that is not yet completely accepting the connections. We use same client and server application program examples defined in Chapter 2.

- *The socket is bound to a port but is not yet in a 'listening' state*: This means that the server application has invoked *bind()* but has not yet invoked *listen()* systemcall (see Fig. 4.13a). *tcpdump* for the above setup is shown in Fig. 4.13b. Client (192.168.1.3) sends a connection request to the server (SYN packet # 3). The server side TCP replies with an RST packet (#4).
- *The socket is in a 'listening' state but is not yet accepting the connection*: This means that the server application has invoked *bind()*, *listen()* but has not yet invoked *accept()* systemcall as shown in Fig. 4.14a. Let's see how server side TCP responds to this connection request. To study this, a small experiment was conducted where a client tries to connect to the server that has done listen on the socket but has not yet invoked *accept()*. From the tcpdump output (see Fig. 4.14b) for this connection request, we can see that the three-way handshake takes place between the two ends, packets 1, 2, and 3. The client writes data over the socket in blocks of 50 k at a time. The client side TCP splits these data in small chunks of 1460 bytes (limited by MTU), packets 4 and 7. The server acknowledges those and the client keeps on sending data until the server acknowledges the last sent data (packet 73, 73,360 bytes) with the window size of 0 (packet 74). The client gets an indication that it doesn't need to send anymore data to the server until the server advertises nonzero positive window size.

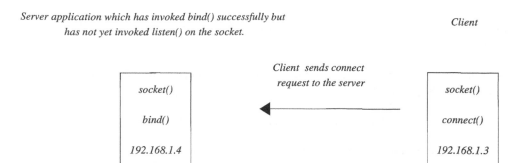

Figure 4.13a. Client initiated connection request for a nonlistening socket.

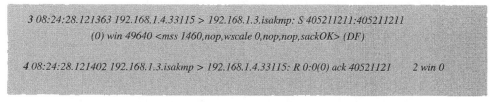

Figure 4.13b. Client–server interaction for Fig. 4.13a.

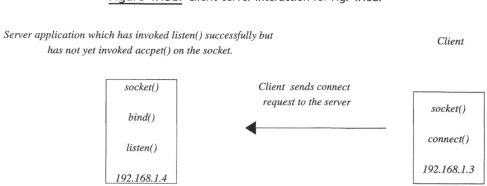

Figure 4.14a. Client generates connection request for nonaccepting listening sockets.

This indicates that the serve side receive buffer has gotten full and that it cannot accommodate any more data. All this is happening because there is no one to consume the data in the server's receive buffer. The only way these data are consumed is when it is read by an application. Since the server application has not yet accepted the connection fully by issuing accept(), the client can get connected to the server and do very limited one-way data transfer from client to server. But this study tells that the even though the connection request is in the accept queue in the established state, the TCP connection is fully functional between the two ends, but the absence of read/write at the server end makes this socket connection a very limited one-way channel from client to server.

4.3.6 Accept Queue Is Full

When there is no space in the accept queue to accommodate the new connection request, we can still accommodate the request in the SYN queue which has no

```
1  10:07:35.210908 192.168.1.4.32966 > moksha.isakmp: S [tcp sum ok] 552231777:552231777(0) win 49640
<mss 1460,nop,wscale 0,nop,nop,sackOK> (DF)

2  10:07:35.210974 moksha.isakmp > 192.168.1.4.32966: S [tcp sum ok] 1163300465:1163300465(0) ack 552231778
win 5840 <mss 1460,nop,nop,sackOK,nop,wscale 0> (DF)

3  10:07:35.211186 192.168.1.4.32966 > moksha.isakmp: . [tcp sum ok] ack 1 win 49640 (DF)

4  10:07:37.681869 192.168.1.4.32966 > moksha.isakmp: . 1:1461(1460) ack 1 win 49640 (DF)

5  10:07:37.681944 moksha.isakmp > 192.168.1.4.32966: . [tcp sum ok] ack 1461 win 8760 (DF)

6  10:07:37.683098 192.168.1.4.32966 > moksha.isakmp: . 1461:2921(1460) ack 1 win 49640 (DF)

7  10:07:37.683148 moksha.isakmp > 192.168.1.4.32966: . [tcp sum ok] ack 2921 win 11680 (DF)

....
...

70  10:07:45.398495 192.168.1.4.32966 > moksha.isakmp: P 68980:70440(1460) ack 1 win 49640 (DF)

71  10:07:45.403419 192.168.1.4.32966 > moksha.isakmp: P 70440:71900(1460) ack 1 win 49640 (DF)

72  10:07:45.421935 moksha.isakmp > 192.168.1.4.32966: . [tcp sum ok] ack 71900 win 1460 (DF)

73  10:07:45.423338 192.168.1.4.32966 > moksha.isakmp: P 71900:73360(1460) ack 1 win 49640 (DF)

74  10:07:45.481940 moksha.isakmp > 192.168.1.4.32966: . [tcp sum ok] ack 73360 win 0 (DF)

75  10:07:49.441471 192.168.1.4.32966 > moksha.isakmp: P [tcp sum ok] 73360:73361(1) ack 1 win 49640 (DF)

76  10:07:49.441521 moksha.isakmp > 192.168.1.4.32966: . [tcp sum ok] ack 73360 win 0 (DF)
```

Figure 4.14b. One-way communication from client→server is possible for nonaccepting listening sockets.

limitation on the queue length because of the conditions (see cs 4.11) that need to be satisfied in *tcp_v4_conn_request()*. Even if the accept queue is full, we can accept the new connection request and queue it in the SYN queue, in case there are no young connections not yet ACKed (see cs 4.12).

tcp_synq_young() gets the value of *sk→tp_pinfo.af_tcp.listen_opt→qlen_young*, which indicates the number of requests in the SYN queue that are not yet ACKed. If there is congestion, this would be more than 1, otherwise no problem. We can still have an entry for a new connection request in the SYN queue even if the SYN queue and accept queues are full. Now the SYN queue keeps on growing because the accept queue is full; and when the ACK for any new connection request in the SYN queue is received, we cannot unlink this request from the SYN queue and link

```
net/ipv4/tcp_ipv4.c

1406        if (tcp_synq_is_full(sk) && !isn) {
1407 #ifdef CONFIG_SYN_COOKIES
1408            if (sysctl_tcp_syncookies) {
1409                want_cookie = 1;
1410            } else
1411 #endif
1412            goto drop;
1413        }
```

cs 4.11. tcp_v4_conn_request().

```
net/ipv4/tcp_ipv4.c

1420        if (tcp_acceptq_is_full(sk) && tcp_synq_young(sk) > 1)
1421            goto drop;
```

cs 4.12. tcp_v4_conn_request().

it with the accept queue. In such cases, *tcp_v4_syn_recv_sock()* returns NULL to *tcp_check_req()*. *tcp_check_req()* finds that the return value is NULL, and it sets *req→acked* to 1 and returns NULL. Nothing happens now. It is the job of the SYN/ACK timer to take care of all such open requests in the SYN queue of the listening socket which cannot be processed further at this point of time. The SYN/ACK timer is implemented as *tcp_synack_timer()*. It is fired after some time interval and checks if any connection request is old enough to be removed from the SYN queue (see cs 4.13).

From cs 4.13 (line #515) it is clear that SYN/ACK is sent to the peer by calling *req→class→rtx_syn_ack()*, untill we have exhausted the *max_retries* number of tries. Since we have already received ACK for the given connection request, *req→acked* is always set. By default, *max_retries* is initialized by the *sysctl_tcp_synack_retries* control parameter which is set to TCP_SYNACK_RETRIES (5). So, the server sends 5 SYN/ACK to the peer (connection initiater) before it removes the connection request from the SYN queue.

The *tcpdump* output in Fig. 4.15 shows how the server generates SYN/ACK packets for a connection request which cannot be accommodated in the accept queue. This was all about the role of *listen()* systemcall. We have seen how the connection request is generated and new sockets are created for the connection requests and associated with the same. There are various queues for connection requests depending on the state of the three-way handshake. We have also seen the behavior of TCP at the stage when the *listen()* is called, but the established socket is not yet accepted by the server application. We now move on to *accept()* system-call, which is the last step to complete the server application. We have not yet discussed the way connections requests are dealt by TCP at the functional level inside the kernel. We will discuss it later.

We need to explain TCP socket multiplexing. This explains how sockets are finally identified by the TCP subsystem when a packet is received by the TCP layer.

```
net/ipv4/tcp_timer.c
 509        do {
 510              reqp=&lopt->syn_table[i];
 511          while ((req = *reqp) != NULL) {
 512              if ((long)(now - req->expires) >= 0) {
 513                  if ((req->retrans < thresh ||
 514                      (req->acked && req->retrans < max_retries))
 515                      && !req->class->rtx_syn_ack(sk, req, NULL)) {
 516                      unsigned long timeo;
 517
 518                      if (req->retrans++ == 0)
 519                          lopt->qlen_young--;
                            ...
 523                      reqp = &req->dl_next;
 524                      continue;
 525                  }
 526
 527                  /* Drop this request */
 528                  write_lock(&tp->syn_wait_lock);
 529                  *reqp = req->dl_next;
 530                  write_unlock(&tp->syn_wait_lock);
 531                  lopt->qlen--;
 532                  if (req->retrans == 0)
 533                      lopt->qlen_young--;
 534                  tcp_openreq_free(req);
 535                  continue;
 536              }
 537              reqp = &req->dl_next;
 538          }
```

cs 4.13. tcp_synack_timer().

__tcp_v4_lookup_established() does a lookup for all the established socket connections in the tcp_ehash table. The Quadruplet destination port, destination address, local port, and local address are used to identify the socket for each packet (Fig. 4.16).

4.3.7　Established Sockets Linked in tcp_ehash hash Table

Figure 4.16, illustrates the snapshot of tcp_ehash table which hashes system wide sockets in TCP_ESTABLISHED and TIME_WAIT state.

4.3.8　State of the Connection Request when the Three-Way Handshake Is Still Pending

Figure 4.17 illustrates snap shot of a listening socket. It shows how accept queue and SYN queue are implemented for the listening socket. Open requests in SYN queue (Syn_table) in the SYN-RECU state are discussed in Section 4.4.

1 11:27:01.322057 192.168.1.4.33325 > moksha.5000: S 592090401:592090401(0) win 49640
<mss 1460,nop,wscale 0,nop,nop,sackOK> (DF)

2 11:27:01.322102 moksha.5000 > 192.168.1.4.33325: S 1329484814:1329484814(0) ack 592090402 win 5840
<mss 1460,nop,nop,sackOK,nop,wscale 0> (DF)

3 11:27:01.322317 192.168.1.4.33325 > moksha.5000: . ack 1 win 49640 (DF)

4 11:27:04.920795 moksha.5000 > 192.168.1.4.33325: S 1329484814:1329484814(0) ack 592090402 win 5840
<mss 1460,nop,nop,sackOK,nop,wscale 0> (DF)

5 11:27:04.921028 192.168.1.4.33325 > moksha.5000: . ack 1 win 49640 (DF)

6 11:27:10.920783 moksha.5000 > 192.168.1.4.33325: S 1329484814:1329484814(0) ack 592090402 win 5840
<mss 1460,nop,nop,sackOK,nop,wscale 0> (DF)

7 11:27:10.921020 192.168.1.4.33325 > moksha.5000: . ack 1 win 49640 (DF)

8 11:27:22.920792 moksha.5000 > 192.168.1.4.33325: S 1329484814:1329484814(0) ack 592090402 win 5840
<mss 1460,nop,nop,sackOK,nop,wscale 0> (DF)

9 11:27:22.921032 192.168.1.4.33325 > moksha.5000: . ack 1 win 49640 (DF)

10 11:27:46.920792 moksha.5000 > 192.168.1.4.33325: S 1329484814:1329484814(0) ack 592090402 win 5840
<mss 1460,nop,nop,sackOK,nop,wscale 0> (DF)

11 11:27:46.921032 192.168.1.4.33325 > moksha.5000: . ack 1 win 49640 (DF)

12 11:28:35.120806 moksha.5000 > 192.168.1.4.33325: S 1329484814:1329484814(0) ack 592090402 win 5840
<mss 1460,nop,nop,sackOK,nop,wscale 0> (DF)

13 11:28:35.121043 192.168.1.4.33325 > moksha.5000: . ack 1 win 49640 (DF)

Figure 4.15. Server sends out 5 SYN/ACK segments before it assumes that the connection-request should be dropped.

4.3.9   State of the Connection Request when the Three-Way Handshake Is Completed

Figure 4.18 shows a snapshot of listening sockets SYN queue and accept queue when three-way handshake is completed for open requests. Req. 1 is moved from SYN queue to accept queue when three way hand shake is completed for open request req. 1. (Compare with Fig. 4.17; see in Section 4.4).

4.4.   CONNECTION REQUEST HANDLING BY KERNEL

Here we discuss how the connection requests for the listening sockets are handled by the kernel. We only discuss the functional details and not the TCP-protocol-

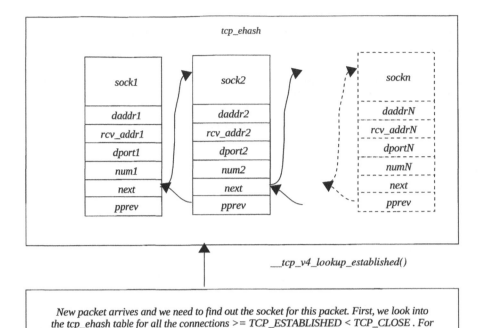

Figure 4.16. System-wide hash list for established sockets.

specific details. Any connection request is handled by the kernel in two steps because of the nature of the TCP protocol.

- SYN Queue Processing: In first step, the connection request is received by the kernel which is put in the SYN queue of the listening socket. The kernel sends SYN/ACK for this connection request and waits for ACK to last SYN/ACK for the connection in the SYN queue.
- Accept Queue Processing: In the second step, once the ACK for the SYN/ACK is received by the kernel for the connection in the SYN queue, a new socket is created for the connection request and the connection request is removed from the SYN queue of the listening socket. The connection request is put into the accept queue for the listening socket.

Let's see how the first SYN packet for the connection request is handled by the kernel. Refer to function *tcp_v4_conn_request()*. *tcp_v4_rcv()* is the interfacing function that processes the packets for TCP. *sk-buff* represents a packet on Linux which is passed to the routine for TCP Processing. *sk_buff* contains header and data information for the packet. We discuss more about it later, but for now we should stick with the fact that *sk_buff* represents the IP packet. Pull down the TCP/IP header from *sk_buff* and extract four fields from the header: destination port, destination IP, source port, source IP. This quadruplet is required to identify the socket for the packet, if any. Now we call *__tcp_v4_lookup()* to identify the socket. This function looks into the various hash tables for the socket. The hash tables that are

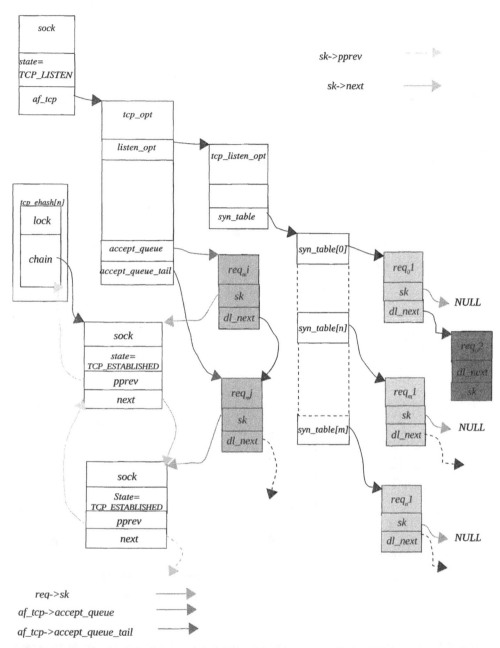

Figure 4.17. Open connection request waiting in SYNQ until the three-way handshake is over.

searched are *tcp_ehash* and *tcp_listening_hash* in the same order by calling functions *__tcp_v4_lookup_established()* and *tcp_v4_lookup_listener()*, respectively. As we have already discussed, these two hash tables are in Section 4.2.2, so we move ahead. Assuming that we already have a listening socket for this (application has invoked *listen()* successfully), we find the listening socket in the *tcp_listening_hash* table. We move on to the *tcp_v4_do_rcv()* for further processing of the connection request.

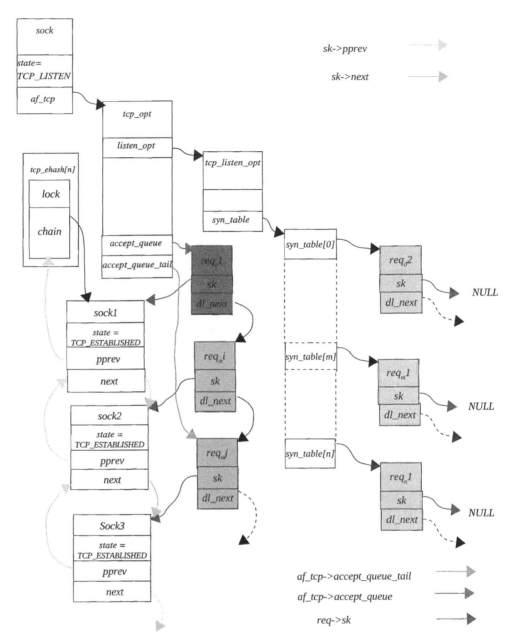

Figure 4.18. Connection request converted into established socket and placed in to accept queue after the three-way handshake is over.

Here we do some sanity checks on the TCP header and first check the socket state. Since we are concerned with the listening socket, we enter into the block to process the socket with the *TCP_LISTEN* state. We call *tcp_v4_hnd_req()* for further processing. *tcp_v4_hnd_req()* looks for any connection connection request in the SYN queue of the listening socket (*sk→tp_pinfo.af_tcp→listen_opt→syn_table*). If the connection request is found, we create a new socket for this connection and return the pointer to the new socket in case this is not a duplicate SYN packet and is proper

SYN/ACK for the connection request identified. Otherwise, if any connection request for this SYN packet is not found in the SYN queue, we search the *tcp_ehash* table (see Fig. 4.16) for any possibility of established socket for the current connection request. This is done because the packet may be a duplicate of the original connection request that is already in the established state now. If nothing is found, we return the same socket pointer that was identified for the packet. From here we can separate the two steps discussed above.

4.4.1 SYN Queue Processing

If this is the original SYN packet (connection request), *tcp_v4_hnd_req()* returns socket pointer which was identified. So we move on to further process the connection request and call *tcp_rcv_state_process()*. This does various sanity checks on the TCP headers; and if it finds that things are OK and we are processing a listening socket, we call a connection request function specific to the protocol, *tp→af_specific→conn_request()*, for further processing. This function is part of '*struct tcp_func*' registered with *tp→af_specific* at the time of *socket()* call for the TCP protocol in *tcp_v4_init_sock()* to *ipv4_specific*. This function *tp→af_specific→conn_request()* in our case points to *tcp_v4_conn_request()*. *tcp_v4_conn_request()* checks if the SYN queue is full for the listening socket by calling *tcp_synq_is_full()*. If it is full, it drops the request and returns error; otherwise, it goes ahead and checks the accept queue for the listening socket by calling *tcp_acceptq_is_full()*. If the accept queue is full, we can still accept the new connection, in case we don't have a large number of connection requests for which the final SYN is not yet received for the SYN/ACK it last sent because of which TCP is firing SYN/AC retransmissions for the listening socket. We check the SYN/ACK retransmissions by calling *tcp_synq_young()*. If everything is OK, we go ahead and create an open connection request for the new request, initialize open_request structure for the new open request, send SYN/ACK response for the connection request, and add the new connection request in SYN queue of the listening socket by calling *tcp_v4_synq_add()*. Now we are waiting in the SYN queue of the listening socket for the final ACK to complete the TCP connection process and return to *tcp_v4_do_rcv()*.

4.4.2 Accept Queue Processing

Let's consider a situation where we have already queued up a connection request in the SYN queue and already transmitted a SYN/ACK response for this connection request. We are waiting to get the final ACK for the connection request. We receive the final ACK for the connection request and we enter the same code path *tcp_v4_rcv()→tcp_v4_do_rcv()→tcp_v4_hnd_req()*. In this case we have a connection request queued up in the SYN queue of the listening socket. So we move on to finally process the connection request for which the final ACK is received call *tcp_check_req()*. *tcp_check_req()* does a lot of sanity checks on the packet headers received because we don't know the flags set in the TCP header until now. If we get the retransmitted SYN packet for the same connection, we once again generate the SYN/ACK packet. We also make checks for any malicious third-party involvement as the originator of the packet. So, we do window size comparison from the original packet and current packet; if there is a great difference, we drop the request but send the ACK. If the sequence number for the ACK received is not 1 more than the sequence number of the first SYN packet, just mark an indication to the calling function that the RST needs to be sent. Similarly, make checks on the TCP header flags. If they are not ACK but are RST or SYN, we make a decision appropriately. Finally, we have passed all the tests and the ACK is proper, so we need to process the connection request further. We call the *syn_rcv_sock()* function specific to the protocol. As mentioned earlier, this function is part of *'struct tcp_func'* registered with *tp→af_specific* at the time of *socket()* call for the TCP protocol in *tcp_v4_init_sock()* to *ipv4_specific*. This function *tp→af_specific→syn_rcv_sock()* in our case points to *tcp_v4_syn_recv_sock()*. *tcp_v4_syn_recv_sock()* creates a new socket for the connection request as the three-way handshake is over and both the ends of the connection have verified their identities. The new socket is created only if accept queue is not full. Status f the accept queue is checked by calling *tcp_acceptq_is_full()*. In case the accept queue is full, we still have the connection request in the SYN Queue so that later when the final ACK is once again received for this connection and the accept Queue is not full we can accept the connection. If the accept queue for the socket is not full we go ahead with initialising the new socket. Most of properties are inherited to the socket from the listening socket and rest of the fields specific to the connection are initialised from the tcp/ip header. We call *_tcp_v4_hash()* to hash the newly created socket on *tcp_ehash* table (see Fig. 4.4). So we return to *tcp_check_req()* where the connection request is unlinked from the SYN queue and is added to listening accept queue. New socket just created is in *TCP_SYN_RECV* state. We return from with new socket pointer form *tcp_v4_hnd_req()* to *tcp_v4_do_rcv()*. Form *tcp_v4_do_rcv()* we call *tcp_child_process()* to do some more processing on the newly created socket. *tcp_child_process()* calls *tcp_rcv_state_process()* in case we have no user for the socket (*child→lock.users == 0*). In *tcp_rcv_state_process()* we once again do some sanity checks on the TCP flags and initialise TCP options for socket's tcp_opt structure (*sk→tp_pinfo.af_tcp*) extracted from TCP header options field by calling *tcp_fast_parse_options()*.

Finally change the state of the socket to *TCP_ESTABLISHED* state. We queue the *sk_buff* to sockets receive queue by calling *tcp_data_queue()* so that process can be notified of the reception of the data. Finally we return to the *tcp_child_process()*. We did the entire processing for the socket with the socket lock held and bottom half disabled as bottom half may change the state of the process while processing. Complete flow of the connection request handling by kernel is shown in Fig. 4.19.

4.4.3   Flow Control for Handling a New Connection Request

Figures 4.19a and 4.19b show flow control for TCP connection request handling implementation in the kernel. Here we show major routines that implement connection handling which is discussed in Sections 4.4.1 and 4.4.2.

4.5   ACCEPT

As we have already learned from our previous discussion, *listen()* systemcall makes the TCP socket accept connections, but the socket is not yet fully functional. The listening socket accepts connections and puts it in the accept queue once the three-way handshake is completed between the two ends of TCP. The sockets in the accept queue are in the established state. Now the server application has to pick up

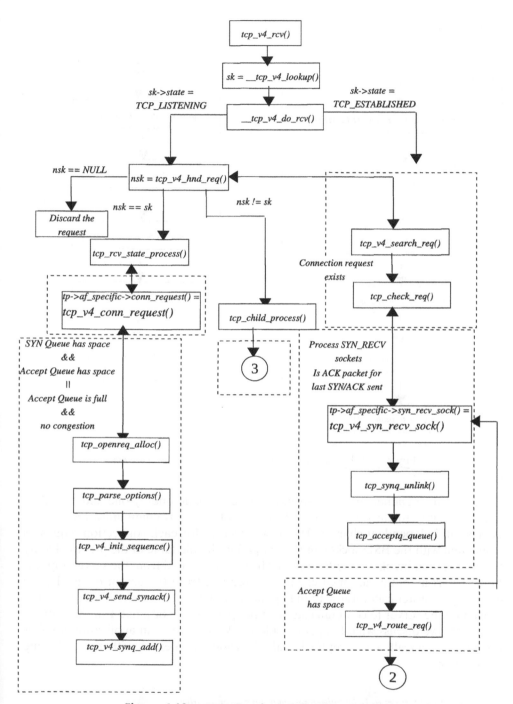

Figure 4.19a. Code flow for handling a connection.

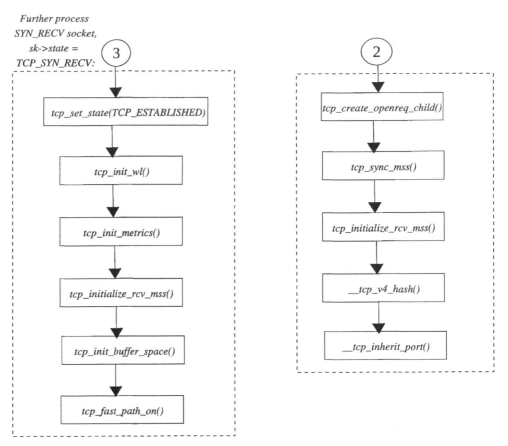

Figure 4.19b. Code flow for handing a connection request.

the established connection requests in the accept queue one-by-one and provide a unique identity to each socket so that the socket can start communication with its peer as an independent channel. The *sock* structure for each connection request is associated with the BSD socket and is mapped in the file table of the process. Doing this application invokes *accept()* systemcall. *accept* is issued from the server application to start accepting an open connection request from the accept queue, Figure 4.1. *accept()* systemcall returns to the application with a new socket descriptor that is used by the server to communicate with the peer or the originator of the connection. Here we discuss what happens inside the kernel when an application invokes *accept()* systemcall. sys_accept() is called inside the kernel with the following arguments:

```
sys_accept(int fd, struct sockaddr *upeer_sockaddr, int *upeer_addrlen)
```

Kernel interface for accept.

fd: file descriptor of the listening socket.

upeer: socket address (s *truct sockaddr *) of the remote end of the connection which needs to be filled by the kernel and send back to the application.

upeer_addrlen: address length of the socket address.

sys_accept(). This identifies the bsd socket associated with the parent socket (listening socket) using the socket file descriptor (fd) passed as an argument to the *accept()* by calling sock *fd_lookup()*. Let's see how *fd_lookup()* works: It gets a *struct files_structure* table for the *current* process, which maintains the account of all the open files for the current process; this is *current→files*. max_fds field of the file table, *files→max_fds*, indicates the maximum number allocated as a file descriptor to the current process's open files at any point of time. It makes a sanity check on the listener socket file descriptor to make sure that it doesn't exceed *files→max_fds*. If *fd* is well below *files→max_fds*, we get the file structure, which is fd'th element of the file array *fd, files→ fd[fd]*, which is the file structure for the listener socket file descriptor in question here. The process file table, *current→files*, is accessed with file table lock (*current→files→file_lock*) acquired. The BSD socket associated with the socket file descriptor can be obtained from the file structure just gotten from the *inode* associated with the *file* structure, *file→f_dentry→d_inode*. We also need to make sure that the inode is associated with the socket. This can be done by checking *i_sock* field of the *inode, inode→i_sock*. If the field is set, the *inode* represents *socket*. Now socket is part of the this *inode* and can gotten from *inode→u.socket_i*. Links between file, inode, and socket are shown in Fig. 4.21.

So. we return to *sys_socket()* and we have the gotten the *socket* structure associated with the listening socket. We need to create a new socket for the new connection request and associate the socket with the VFS in the similar way as it was done for the listening socket (see Fig. 4.20). Allocate new socket structure for the new connection by calling *sock_alloc()*. This function allocates a new socket inode and initializes inode and socket fields associated with the socket inode with default values as shown in cs 4.14.

The *socki_lookup()* function returns the socket fields associated with the *inode, inode→u.socket_i*. This inode is marked to be associated with no device *NO_DEV;* *i_sock* field of the *inode* is also set to represent a socket *inode*. The socket's inode is made to point to the inode, and the socket state is set to *SS_UNCONNECTED* as the socket is in the process of being connected. The new socket should inherit some of the properties of the parent (listening) socket. So the *type* and *ops* fields are duplicated from the parent socket to the new socket. Call the inet-specific accept (sock→ops→accept), inet_accept(), which puts up the connection request in the parent sockets accept queue and associates it with the new socket just created in the following way.

4.5.1 *inet_accept()*

This calls a protocol-specific *accept* function (*sk→prot→accept*), *tcp_accept()*. Let's see what *tcp_accept()* does. It holds the socket lock and does the entire operation; before returning, it releases the lock. It checks for the state of the parent (listening) socket. It should be in the *TCP_LISTEN* state. If not so, it returns with error. Now get hold of the *tcp_opt* structure for the parent socket, *sk→tp_pinfo.af_tcp*. This structure keeps a pointer to the accept queue (pending connection request queue; see Fig. 4.18). Check if there is any pending connection request in the accept

```
net/socket.c

434  struct socket *sock_alloc(void)
435  {
436       struct inode * inode;
437       struct socket * sock;
438
439       inode = get_empty_inode();
440       if (!inode)
441            return NULL;
442
443       inode->i_sb = sock_mnt->mnt_sb;
444       sock = socki_lookup(inode);
445
446       inode->i_mode = S_IFSOCK|S_IRWXUGO;
447       inode->i_sock = 1;
448       inode->i_uid = current->fsuid;
449       inode->i_gid = current->fsgid;
450
451       sock->inode = inode;
452       init_waitqueue_head(&sock->wait);
453       sock->fasync_list = NULL;
454       sock->state = SS_UNCONNECTED;
455       sock->flags = 0;
456       sock->ops = NULL;
457       sock->sk = NULL;
458       sock->file = NULL;
459
460       sockets_in_use[smp_processor_id()].counter++;
461       return sock;
462  }
```

cs 4.14. sock_alloc().

queue, *tp→accept_queue*. If *tp→accept_queue* is NULL, there is no pending connection request. So we need to wait on parent sockets wait-queue(*sk→sleep*) by calling *wait_for_connect()* until we have at least one new connection request in the accept queue, or we timeout if the socket is blocking; otherwise we return. If we are here, we have at least one pending connection request in the accept queue so we process it. Access first element from the queue, *tp→accept_queue*. Remove the request from the accept queue and decrement the counter of the parent socket, which indicates the number of pending connection requests in the accept queue, *sk→ack_backlog*. Get the connection *sock* structure from the connection request structure, *req→sk*, and free the connection request structure (struct open_request req). The new tcp socket should not be in the syn receive state (*sk→state != TCP_SYN_RECV*). Return the new tcp socket to *inet_accept()*. We are back in inet_accept() with either error or pointer to a new socket. If error is encountered, we return the same; otherwise we further process the new tcp socket and associate the *TCP* socket with the BSD socket. Hold lock on the new *TCP* socket and associate the new *TCP* and *BSD* sockets by calling *sock_graft()* (see cs 4.15). It initializes the *sleep* field of the TCP

```
include/net/sock.h

1011  static inline void sock_graft(struct sock *sk, struct socket *parent)
1012  {
1013      write_lock_bh(&sk->callback_lock);
1014      sk->sleep = &parent->wait;
1015      parent->sk = sk;
1016      sk->socket = parent;
1017      write_unlock_bh(&sk->callback_lock);
1018  }
```

<u>cs 4.15.</u> sock_graft().

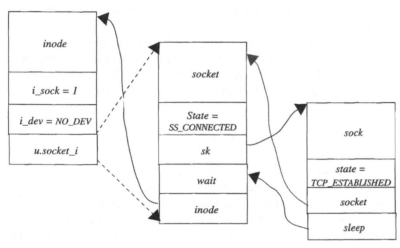

Figure 4.20. New socket is created (but not linked in process file table) for the connection that has just a completed three-way handshake.

socket with the *wait* field of the BSD socket, which means that the wait queue for both the BSD and TCP sockets is the same for a connection. Initialize the *sk* field of the BSD socket to point to the TCP socket and initialize the socket field of the TCP socket to point to the BSD socket, as shown in cs 4.15. In the process, we hold the bottom half lock during the entire process because the socket structure is accessible from the bottom half.

Change the state of the BSD socket to connected, *newsock→state = SS_CONNECTED*.

4.5.2 Linking of Inode and Socket Data Structures when the Three-Way Handshake Has Completed and Is Accepted by Application

Return to *sys_socket()* with pointer to the new BSD socket in the connected state.

Untill now we have linked socket inode, BSD socket, and TCP socket as shown in Fig. 4.20. Now we need to associate file structure with the socket inode and index it into the process file table, *current→files→fd[]*. We call s*ock_map_fd()* to get this done. The function first finds out the unused file descriptor by the process by calling *get_unused_fd()*. This makes use of three fields of the *current→files* file table *open_fds, max_fdset, and next_fd*, where *open_fds* is the bitmap for the file descriptors which are allocated, *max_fdset* is the maximum number that can be allocated as file descriptors at any point in time, and *next_fd* is the next number that is to be allocated as file descriptor, and this field is incremented by 1 whenever a new file descriptor is allocated. The logic is to start searching from the *next_fd* bit in the memory region starting from the address pointed by *open_fds* and find the bit number which is not set. That bit number is the next fd to be allocated. The bit is then set. This fd is returned by *get_unused_fd()*. We return to s*ock_map_fd()* with the allocated file descriptor fd. Now we need to allocate the file structure and link it with the socket inode. This is done by calling *sock_map_fd()*. The function allocates file structure and dentry structure, initializes fields of the file and dentry structures, links dentry structure with the file and socket inode, and returns file structure, as shown in cs 4.16.

We have done most of the work until here by linking the socket with the VFS. The last step is to index the file structure for the socket inode in the process file table, *current→files→fd[]*, at *fd*'th element. This is done by calling *fd_install()*. This function is passed the *fd & file* structure just allocated, and it does the indexing of the file in the process file table:

$$current \rightarrow files \rightarrow fd[fd] = file;$$

The file table lock, *current→files→file_lock*, was held while doing this. *sock_map_fd()* returns with the file descriptor allocated to *sys_accept()*, and *sys_accept()* returns from kernel to user application which had invoked *accept()* systemcall with the fd for the new connection. After return from *accept()*, we have the process file table as shown in Fig. 4.22. So, server application can use the new *fd* returned by *accept()* to communicate with the client and things continue like this.

4.5.3 Linking of VFS and Socket Data Structures in the Kernel when a New Connection is Established

Figure 4.21 illustrates snapshot of the kernel data-structures that link socket layer with VFS. New socket is linked with VFS only when application has accepted the socket connection.

Flow control for accept() is shown in Fig. 4.23.

4.5.4 File Table Entry of a New Accepted Connected Socket

Figure 4.22 shows snap shot of the process file table when a new socket connection is accepted by the application. Since socket is considered as a special file by unix, it can be accessed using socket descriptor in the same way regular files are accessed. This is possible because socket is also linked to process file table.

4.5.5 Flow Control for Accepting New Established Connections

Figure 4.23 show flow of control for TCP/INET accept implementation in the kernel. It shows major routines called from sys-accpt().

```
net/socket.c

328  static int sock_map_fd(struct socket *sock)
329  {
330      int fd;
331      struct qstr this;
332      char name[32];
         ....
338      fd = get_unused_fd();
339      if (fd >= 0) {
340          struct file *file = get_empty_filp();
341
342          if (!file) {
343              put_unused_fd(fd);
344              fd = -ENFILE;
345              goto out;
346          }
             ....
353          file->f_dentry = d_alloc(sock_mnt->mnt_sb->s_root, &this);
354          if (!file->f_dentry) {
             ....
358              goto out;
359          }
360          file->f_dentry->d_op = &sockfs_dentry_operations;
361          d_add(file->f_dentry, sock->inode);
362          file->f_vfsmnt = mntget(sock_mnt);
363
364          sock->file = file;
365          file->f_op = sock->inode->i_fop = &socket_file_ops;
366          file->f_mode = 3;
367          file->f_flags = O_RDWR;
368          file->f_pos = 0;
369          fd_install(fd, file);
370      }
371
372  out:
373      return fd;
374  }
```

cs 4.16. sock_map_fd().

4.6 CLIENT SIDE SETUP

At the client end we need to do a little work to get connected to the server (see Fig. 4.24). The client should only have information about the server's IP and the service port number to get connected to the server. The client can do this by invoking the following systemcalls in sequence:

Socket
Connect

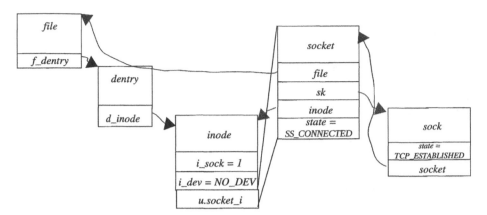

Figure 4.21. Connection is accepted by the listening socket from the accept queue and is linked to process file table.

We have seen how a socket systemcall works in our earlier discussions. We pass on port number and IP address information about the server as an argument to the connect systemcall. By default, connect() is blocking. So if the connection is established with the server successfully, connect() returns with proper error code and we can use the file descriptor returned by socket() systemcall to communicate with the server. In the clients case, the kernel doesn't need an application to specify any port number for client application. Instead, the kernel assigns any unprivileged free port to the client by which the client socket will be recognized by the system. In our further discussions we see how all this happens inside the kernel. First we discuss the server and client steps involved for connection setup and then explain in detail the arrangements done by the kernel at each step of connection setup.

4.6.1   Client Side Operations

Figure 4.24 shows sequence of systemcalls to implement client program. It also describes functionality of each system call in short.

4.6.2   Connect

We need not worry about the socket systemcall here because it has already been discussed. We look at how connect works. *connect()* systemcall is invoked from the application and is called within the kernel as *sys_connect()*. Connect has to do a lot of work before it sends out a connection request to the server.

sys_connect() accepts three arguments:

```
sys_connect(int fd, struct sockaddr *upeer_sockaddr, int *upeer_addrlen)
```

Kernel interface for connect.

fd: This is the socket file descriptor returned by the socket call.
umyaddr: This is the socket address to which we want to bind the socket.
addrlen: This is the socket address length.

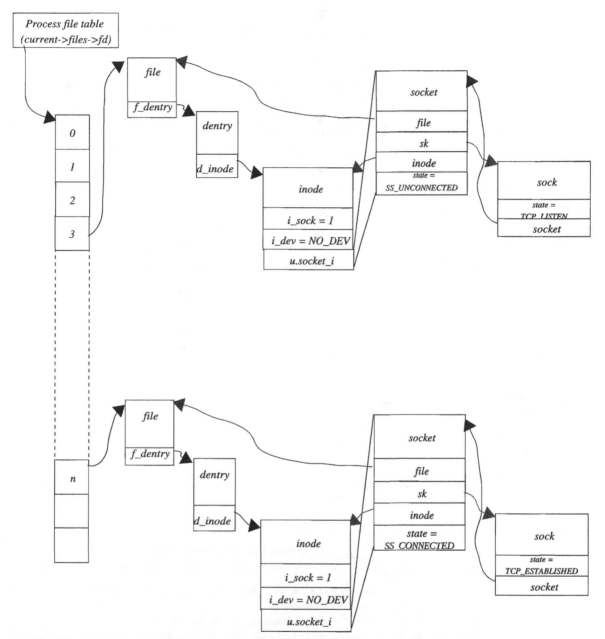

Figure 4.22. Linking of various data structures when a connection request is accepted by a listening socket.

sys_connect(). This first finds out the socket associated with the socket file descriptor *fd* by calling *sockfd_lookup()*. This function was explained earlier in Section 4.2.11. Once we have a socket from *sockfd_lookup()*, we need to copy the socket address from user space to kernel space by calling *move_addr_to_kernel()*. We now call a connect function specific to the *inet* address family, *sock→ops→ connect()*. This is *inet_stream_connect()*.

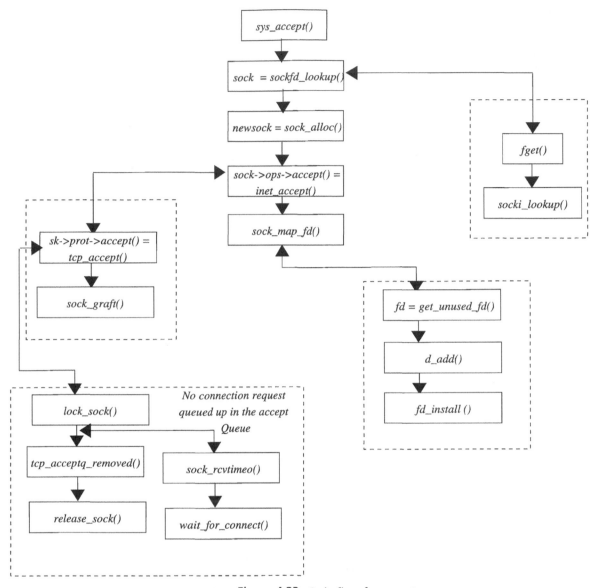

Figure 4.23. Code flow for accept process.

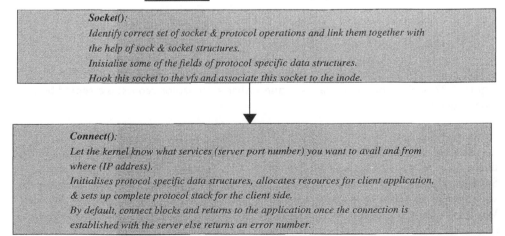

Socket():
Identify correct set of socket & protocol operations and link them together with
the help of sock & socket structures.
Inisialise some of the fields of protocol specific data structures.
Hook this socket to the vfs and associate this socket to the inode.

Connect():
Let the kernel know what services (server port number) you want to avail and from
where (IP address).
Initialises protocol specific data structures, allocates resources for client application,
& sets up complete protocol stack for the client side.
By default, connect blocks and returns to the application once the connection is
established with the server else returns an error number.

Figure 4.24. Client side sequence of systemcall made to generate a connection request.

inet_stream_connect(). It does some sanity check on the address family of the socket address. If things are OK, we move ahead and check the state of the socket (*sock→state*). Any state other than *SS_UNCONNECTED* is unacceptable for processing. Socket states *SS_CONNECTED* or *SS_CONNECTING* means that connect is called twice on the socket. If the socket state is *SS_CONNECTED*, we make some more checks on the state of the TCP specific socket associated with the BSD socket (*sock→sk→state*). It should not be *TCP_CLOSE*. We call TCP-specific connect now, pointed to by *sk→prot→connect()*. This function is *tcp_v4_connect()*.

4.6.3   tcp_v4_connect()

This first gets the pointer to the TCP-specific data structure (*tcp_opt*) associated with the socket (*sk→tp_pinfo.af_tcp*). Do some sanity checks on the socket address family and the address length. One of the many things that the connect needs to do is to define the route and get the available port for the connecting socket. We will see how this is done.

Getting Route Information. We get the routing information from two parameters:

1. Source address
2. Next hop address

The default next hop is set to the destination address provided in the socket address. If the *ip_options* structure (*sk→protinfo.af_inet.opt*) is initialized for the socket and *srr* field of this structure is set, the next hop is taken from *sk→protinfo.af_inet.opt→ faddr*. We call *ip_route_connect()* to get the route for the destination address. The function returns routing information in the *struct rtable*.

4.6.4   ip_route_connect()

This fills in the '*struct rtable*' for the destination route, depending on the source address and the interface being used for the destination. It calls *ip_route_output()*, which calls *ip_route_output_key()*. *ip_route_output()* initializes '*struct rt_key*' for the routing table search. It finally passes the key to.

4.6.5   Flow Control for Generating a Connection Request

Figures 4.25a and 4.25b show the flow of control for INET/TCP connect implementation in the kernel and major routines called from sys_connect.

ip_route_output_key(). *struct rt_key* has four fields: destination IP, source IP, TOI (type of service), and outgoing interface number. All routing entries for the system are hashed in the global table *rt_hash_table[]*. This is an array of '*struct rt_hash_ bucket*' (see Fig. 4.26).

The member *chain* of '*struct rt_hash_bucket*' points to the hash collision chain, and *lock* is the lock to protect the hash collision chain *chain*. If we find the entry for a given destination in the routing hash bucket, we use that or else we try to

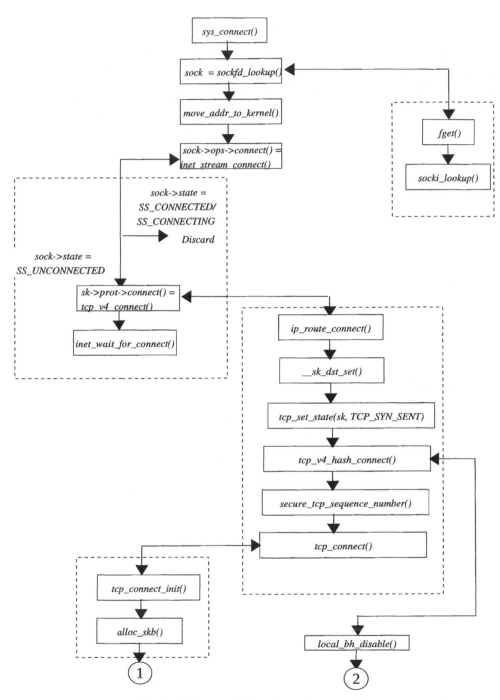

Figure 4.25a. Code flow for connect process.

make a new entry for the routing hash bucket by calling *ip_route_output_slow()*.
We return to *tcp_v4_connect()*.

End of ip_route_connect(). If *ip_route_connect()* returns < 0, it means that
we could not get a route for the destination and hence we return from here. We

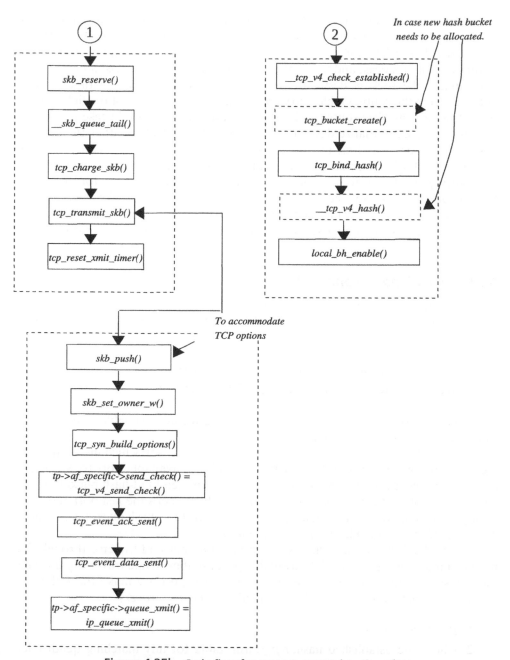

Figure 4.25b. Code flow for connect process (*continued*).

```
net/ipv4/route.c

189  struct rt_hash_bucket {
190      struct rtable   *chain;
191      rwlock_t        lock;
192  } __attribute__(( __aligned__(8)));
```

Figure 4.26. Routing table hash bucket.

have gotten the routing entry for the destination, and we still need to do some sanity checks on the routing flag. If the routing flag ($rt{\rightarrow}rt\_flags$) is set to *RTCF_MULTI-CAST* or *RTCF_BROADCAST*, we return error, which means that our destination is multicast or broadcast and we want to connect only to such unicast addresses. We now update the sockets destination cache field ($sk{\rightarrow}dst\_cache$) with the value obtained from the routing table entry ($rt{\rightarrow}u.dst$). Initialize some of the fields of the sock structure. Initislize source address ($sk{\rightarrow}saddr$) to $rt{\rightarrow}rt\_src$ in case the source address is not set. Initialize destination address ($sk{\rightarrow}daddr$) to either the address passed in the socket address or from the routing table entry just found ($rt{\rightarrow}rt\_dst$). Initialize the destination port ($sk{\rightarrow}dport$) to the port number in the socket address ($usin{\rightarrow}sin\_port$). Initialize some of the fields of the tcp_opt structure for the socket ($sk{\rightarrow}tp\_pinfo.af\_tcp$). Set the socket state to *TCP_SYN_SENT*. We have not yet allocated the local port for the socket, so call *tcp_v4_hash_connect()* to allocate the free port for the socket and associate the socket with the appropriate hash list.

4.6.6   *tcp_v4_hash_connect()*

This functions more or less like *tcp_v4_get_port()*, which is called to bind a socket to a specific port when *bind()* systemcall is invoked. A couple of things change here:

1. We are not requesting for a particular port number.
2. We have different view for reusage of port numbers.

If $sk{\rightarrow}num$ is not set, it means that we are looking for any available free port that can be used or reused. $sk{\rightarrow}num$ is not set.

Most of the time *connect()* is called without $sk{\rightarrow}num$ set, which means that we are not looking for any specific port but instead any available port to which the connecting socket can bind. So, we need to search the tcp-bind-hash bucket list for each port number starting from *tcp_port_rover*, which keeps the last port allocated to anyone on the system. The logic to traverse the tcp-bind-hash bucket is the same as discussed in Section 4.2.14: *tcp_v4_get_port()*.

We get hold of a hash bucket for each port number and traverse through the hash chain until we get hold of the available port number. While traversing through the collision chain of tcp-bind-hash bucket for each port, we make the following checks, if the matching port number is found ($tb{\rightarrow}port == rover$):

1. $tb{\rightarrow}fastreuse >= 0$.
2. Check the established hash, *tcp_ehash*, table for any matching quadruplet (source IP, destination IP, source port, destination port).

If a matching port number is not found ($tb{\rightarrow}port\ != rover$), we move on to the next element in the hash collision chain. We repeat this until we have traversed the entire list. If we don't find any entry with matching port number, we come out of the collision chain travers loop and create a new bucket for this port number by calling *tcp_bucket_create()*, and we set fastreuse flag ($tb\text{-}fastreuse$) to −1 and come out of the main loop. We are able to find the hash bucket with a matching port number.

We go to the next port number in case we find condition 1 satisfied. This way we are ensuring that we are not allocating any port number to the connecting socket, which is already in use by the listening socket whether or not the listening socket wants to share the port number. If the only connecting socket is already using the port number, it would set the *tb→fastreuse* to −1. If condition 1 fails, we can still consider the reuse of the port number, if one or more connecting sockets are associated with it. If condition 1 is false, we move ahead to check whether we are qualified to reuse this port number to check condition 2. For that we call *__tcp_v4_check_established()*.

4.6.7 *__tcp_v4_check_established()*

This function is called with the local bottom half disabled, because the bottom halves may get scheduled on different CPU and modify the *tcp_ehash* table. We first get the hash number from the combination of *sk→rcv_saddr, sk→daddr, sk→ dport*, and selected local ports by calling *tcp_hashfn()*. Sockets are hashed in the *tcp_ehash* table using the above quadruplet where source IP is *sk→rcv_addr* and not the *sk→saddr*. We try to find the hash bucket from the hash number obtained (see cs 4.17). First try to search all the sockets in TIME_WAIT state. This is the second half of the tcp_ehash table and can be accessed as shown in cs 4.18.

We actually need to check each socket in the chain pointed to by skp and find out any possibility of reusing the port. The first check is to match the quadruplet and the interface used by the two sockets. For doing this, we call use macro *TCP_IPV4_MATCH()*. If they match, *TCP_IPV4_MATCH() returns TRUE and* we move ahead to check if still we can reuse the port. The next step is to check the timestamp when the FIN was received from the peer. We consider the case, only if the FIN segment reception time is more than 1 second old (we need to justify this). We know that the socket that does an active close (sends first FIN) gets into the TIME_WAIT state after receiving FIN from the other end and after it has sent the final ACK. Please refer to Section 2.8.4 for TIME_WAIT state. If we have already received the FIN from the peer, *tw→ts_recent_stamp* is set to the system time at the time when FIN tcp segment was received. If timestamp is more than 1 seconds old, we can consider the socket to use the port number. Otherwise we return with failure code. Suppose we pass here, we need to initialize the sequence number which is such that it should never overlap with the sequence number from the last connection (see cs 4.19). The reason for this is that the reception of any packet hanging in the net from the last connection should not cause any damage to the new connection

```
net/ipv4/tcp_ipv4.c

553    struct tcp_ehash_bucket *head = &tcp_ehash[hash];
```

cs 4.17. *__tcp_v4_check_established()*.

```
net/ipv4/tcp_ipv4.c

560    skp = &(head + tcp_ehash_size)->chain
```

cs 4.18. *__tcp_v4_check_established()*.

```
net/ipv4/tcp_ipv4.c

584        if ((tp->write_seq = tw->snd_nxt+65535+2) == 0)
584        tp->write_seq = 1;
```

cs 4.19. __tcp_v4_check_established().


```
net/ipv4/tcp_ipv4.c

606        sk->num = lport;
607        sk->sport = htons(lport);
```

cs 4.20. __tcp_v4_check_established().


```
net/ipv4/tcp_ipv4.c

609        if ((sk->next = *skp) != NULL)
610            (*skp)->pprev = &sk->next;
611
612        *skp = sk;
613        sk->pprev = skp;
614        sk->hashent = hash;
```

cs 4.21. __tcp_v4_check_established().


```
net/ipv4/tcp_ipv4.c

623            tcp_tw_deschedule(tw);
```

cs 4.22. __tcp_v4_check_established().

(like data integration problem or resetting of connection). Now we break from the loop and go ahead with other initializations.

Considering that we could not get the requested port number after completely searching TIME_WAIT socket list, we search *tcp_ehash* table for all the sockets in TCP_ESTABLISHED state using the port in question. We traverse through the list of sockets in the chain (*head→chain*), where *head* is pointer to tcp_ehash bucket. Once again, in each iteration we compare the quadruplet and the interfaces which are associated with the sockets by calling *TCP_IPV4_MATCH()*. If the function returns FALSE, we are not eligible to use the port number and hence return.

If we get here, the socket is qualified to use the port number. Hence we need to initialize some of the socket fields and also need to do some cleanup stuff. We obtained the port, so initialize the socket fields (see cs 4.20).

Add the socket to the head of the *tcp_ehash* table (see cs 4.21).

If we obtained the hash bucket from TIME_WAIT socket list, we need to cleanup time-wait related links (see cs 4.22). Now remove the TIME_WAIT socket from the TIME_WAIT bucket, and finally remove this socket from the *tcp_ehash* and *tcp_bhash* tables (see cs 4.23). We have obtained the requested port and done, so return from **__tcp_v4_check_established()**.

```
net/ipv4/tcp_ipv4.c

624            tcp_timewait_kill(tw);
```

cs 4.23. __tcp_v4_check_established().

```
net/ipv4/tcp_ipv4.c

716            tcp_bind_hash()
```

cs 4.24. tcp_v4_hash_connect().

```
net/ipv4/tcp_ipv4.c

718            sk->sport = htons(rover);
719            __tcp_v4_hash(sk, 0);
```

cs 4.25. tcp_v4_hash_connect().

We need to explain the relation between sock and tcp_tw_bucket structures. Also explain the linking of TIME_WAIT sockets (sk→next_death and sk→pprev_death). We return to *tcp_v4_hash_connect()*. If we obtain the port for the socket, we come out of the main loop; otherwise we iterate the loop once again with next port number.

We have come out of the loop, which means that either we obtained the available free port number or shared port number. We carry out searching process with lock for the hash bucket held and bottom half disabled. We need to link the socket to the hash bucket owners' list (see cs 4.24).

We need to assign the selected port number to the socket (*sk→sport*) and hash the socket in the *tcp_ehash* table in case the new hash bucket is created; otherwise this field is assigned value in __*tcp_v4_check_established()* (see cs 4.25). Condition cs 4.26 should be true if new hash bucket is allocated for the socket, because this is the only socket in the owners' list of the hash bucket, and we return from here.

Let's see the case where the port number was specified (*sk→num != 0*) get the pointer to the hash bucket for the port number (see cs 4.27). Hold the lock for the tcp hash bucket (*head→lock*) and now check if the socket is the alone socket in the hash bucket pointed to by *sk-prev* (see cs 4.28).

```
net/ipv4/tcp_ipv4.c

717            !sk->pprev
```

cs 4.26. tcp_v4_hash_connect().

```
net/ipv4/tcp_ipv4.c

733            struct tcp_ehash_bucket *head = &tcp_ehash[tcp_bhashfn(snum)];
```

cs 4.27. tcp_v4_hash_connect().

net/ipv4/tcp_ipv4.c

736   if (tb->owners == sk && sk->bind_next == NULL)

cs 4.28. *tcp_v4_hash_connect().*

net/ipv4/tcp_ipv4.c

839   sk->protinfo.af_inet.id = tp->write_seq^jiffies;

cs 4.29. *tcp_v4_hash_connect().*

If that is the case, we can safely allocate the port to us and then return. Now we wonder how *sk→prev* has the *tcp_ehash_bucket* allocated to it. This is possible because the application has already set the *sk→num* by calling *setsockopts()* if it wants the connecting socket to bind to a specific port. We just need to call *__tcp_v4_hash()* to associate the socket with the *ehash_list* table. If we are not able to satisfy the above condition, we need to walk through the tcp_ehash table to resolve any conflicts for the port sharing *__tcp_v4_check_established()*. If we get the requested port number, then *__tcp_v4_check_established()* returns success, which is returned to *tcp_v4_connect()*.

END OF *tcp_v4_hash_connect()*

We return to *tcp_v4_connect()* with either success or failure. If we fail to get the port number, then we return; otherwise we continue with connecting process. Until now we got the route to destination, and obtained the local port number, and we have initialized remote address, remote port, local address, and local address fields of the socket. We have already initialized most of the fields of the socket and tcp_opts for the socket with default values. The rest of the fields will be initialized when we a receive a response from the peer. We need to get the initial sequence for our end of the TCP connection; call *secure_tcp_sequence_number()*. The function calculates sequence number based on quadruplet, system time, and some random number. Linux implementation follows RFC 793 as close as possible for system time issues. Get the packet ID counter based on the initial sequence number and the jiffies (see cs 4.29).

Now since the initial setup is done, we need to generate a SYN packet and give it to the IP layer for further processing. We call *tcp_connect()* for doing this.

4.6.8 *tcp_connect()*

The first step is to do some more initializations of some of the fields of *tcp_opt* very specific to TCP protocol. These fields are related to mss, window size, mtu, and so on; for this we call *tcp_connect_init()*. The function also clears up retransmission-related fields in *tcp_opt* structure. Now we allocate the *sk_buff* structure (cs 4.30), which represents a packet on Linux (please refer to Chapter 5 for *sk_buff*).

Make room to store tcp header, i.e. Adjust the buffer data pointer to point to the location where the TCP header should go (see cs 4.31). Initialize the *cb* field of *sk_buff* (see cs 4.32). This field can contain any private data to be used by different

```
net/ipv4/tcp_output.c

1219          buff = alloc_skb(MAX_TCP_HEADER + 15, sk->allocation);
```

cs 4.30. *tcp_connect().*

```
net/ipv4/tcp_output.c

1223     /* Reserve space for headers. */
1224     skb_reserve(buff, MAX_TCP_HEADER);
```

cs 4.31. *tcp_connect().*

```
net/ipv4/tcp_output.c

1226     TCP_SKB_CB(buff)->flags = TCPCB_FLAG_SYN;
1227     TCP_ECN_send_syn(tp, buff);
1228     TCP_SKB_CB(buff)->sacked = 0;
1229     buff->csum = 0;
1230     TCP_SKB_CB(buff)->seq = tp->write_seq++;
1231     TCP_SKB_CB(buff)->end_seq = tp->write_seq;
1232     tp->snd_nxt = tp->write_seq;
1233     tp->pushed_seq = tp->write_seq;
1234
1235     /* Send it off. */
1236     TCP_SKB_CB(buff)->when = tcp_time_stamp;
1237     tp->retrans_stamp = TCP_SKB_CB(buff)->when;
```

cs 4.32. *tcp_connect().*

protocol layers. TCP keeps per packet control information here and is known as a control buffer for TCP. The control buffer is represented by *struct tcp_skb_cb*. The control buffer is provided with the following information:

- TCP flag is set to TCPCB_FLAG_SYN
- Sequence number
- Timestamp
- ACKing information

We are also intializing tcp_opt fields related to sequence number such as *snd_nxt, pushed_seq and retrans_stamp*. Our job is done, and we will queue the *sk_buff* at the head of the socket's write queue (see cs 4.33). Keep account of memory usage of the socket as a result of the *sk_buff* queuing (see cs 4.34). *sk→wmem_queued* keeps account of how much memory is allocated for the write queue, and *skb→ truesize* is the memory allocated for the *sk_buff* and the memory block allocated for *sk_buff* data. sk→forward_alloc keeps check on the total memory usage by

```
net/ipv4/tcp_output.c

1238          __skb_queue_tail(&sk->write_queue, buff)
```

cs 4.33. *tcp_connect().*

---

net/ipv4/tcp_output.c

1239   tcp_charge_skb()

cs 4.34. tcp_connect().

---

include/net/tcp.h

1681   sk->wmem_queued += skb->truesize;
1682   sk->forward_alloc -= skb->truesize;

cs 4.35. tcp_charge_skb().

socket. So, we update both here in tcp_charge_skb() (see cs 4.35). We need to transmit this *sk_buff* for further processing; call *tcp_transmit_skb()*. We don't pass the sk_buff just allocated to the function, but we pass just the clone of it. By clone it means that the new sk_buff structure is allocated and not the *sk_buff* data part. So, we have a new *sk_buff* structure that has a copy of the original sk_buff except for the data that is shared between the two. The new *sk_buff* is not owned by the socket.

4.6.9   *tcp_transmit_skb()*

This function is used to transmit the packets passed to it. *sk_buff* to be processed by the function don't have headers initialized, so it is the primary job of the functon to build the TCP header before transmitting it to the next layer for processing. First we want to know what TCP options are supported by protocol and gather that information from system control global variables *sys_ctl**. Accordingly, we increase the TCP header size to accommodate each option. Once we have the final TCP header size, we can adjust the sk_buff data pointer to point to the position where the TCP header should start. Finally, get the pointer to the data location (see cs 4.36). *skb→h.th* is the header field for the packet which points to transport layer (TCP in our case) header. Build header from information provided in *sock, tcp_ skb_cb* (control buffer) and *tcp_opt* structures. Associate sk_buff with the socket and modify the memory usage for the socket (see cs 4.37). We use functions specific to the inet family to build checksum and transmit the packet (*sk_buff*) for further

---

net/ipv4/tcp_output.c

226   th = (struct tcphdr *) skb_push(skb, tcp_header_size);
227   skb->h.th = th;

cs 4.36. tcp_transmit_skb().

---

net/ipv4/tcp_output.c

228   skb_set_owner_w(skb, sk);

cs 4.37. tcp_transmit_skb().

```
net/ipv4/tcp_output.c

1244        /* Timer for repeating the SYN until an answer. */
1245        tcp_reset_xmit_timer(sk, TCP_TIME_RETRANS, tp->rto);
```

cs 4.38. *tcp_connect().*

```
net/ipv4/af_inet.c

627              sock->state = SS_CONNECTING;
```

cs 4.39. *inet_stream_connect().*

processing by the next protocol layer (IP). These functions are registered by the socket. *tcp_opt's* field *af_specific* points to set of functions specific to ipv4/tcp and are pointing to i*pv4_specific*. So we call *tp→af_specific→send_check* pointed to by *tcp_v4_send_check()* is called to compute TCP checksum and finally *tp→af_ specific→queue_xmit* pointed to by *ip_queue_xmit()* is called to transmit the packet to IP layer for further process the packet. We wait here until we return from *ip_ queue_xmit()*. *tcp_transmit_skb()* returns with the error code set.

END OF *tcp_transmit_skb()*

We are back to *tcp_connect()* and now set SYN retransmit timer for retransmitting SYN if SYN/ACK is not received (see cs 4.38).

Return from *tcp_connect()*
END OF *tcp_connect()*

We are back to *tcp_v4_connect()* from where we just return with the error code set.

END OF *tcp_v4_connect()*

We are back to *inet_stream_connect()*, and here we set the socket state to connecting in case we get a success error code (see cs 4.39). Now we wait until we time out or we get the connection (three-way handshake is over) (see cs 4.40). *inet_wait_for_ connect()* makes the process sleep in socket's wait queue (sk→sleep) in INTER-RUPTABLE state (which means process can be aborted anytime while waiting for connect to get over). The process goes to sleep until

1. it is woken up by the soft IRQ on reception of SYN/ACK packet for the SYN,
2. timeout occurs, or
3. we receive ICMP error message.

If we don't encounter any error, *inet_wait_for_connect()* returns TRUE. If no signal is received by the current process, we receive some response from the peer. At this point in time, we are either connected or we received an error message about connection not established. We check this from the sock state (see cs 4.41).

```
net/ipv4/af_inet.c

637     timeo = sock_sndtimeo(sk, flags&O_NONBLOCK);
638
639     if ((1<<sk->state)&(TCPF_SYN_SENT|TCPF_SYN_RECV)) {
640         /* Error code is set above */
641         if (!timeo || !inet_wait_for_connect(sk, timeo))
642             goto out;
643
644         err = sock_intr_errno(timeo);
645         if (signal_pending(current))
646             goto out;
647     }
```

<u>cs 4.40</u>. *inet_stream_connect()*.

```
net/ipv4/af_inet.c

652         if (sk->state == TCP_CLOSE)
653     goto sock_error;
        ....
660         sock->state = SS_CONNECTED;
```

<u>cs 4.41</u>. *inet_stream_connect()*.

If we get connected, the socket state is set to *SS_CONNECTED*, and we return from here.

END OF *inet_stream_connect()*

We are back to *sys_connect()*. We return from here to the user application which invoked *connect()* systemcall with the error code set.

END OF *sys_connect()*

Figures 4.25a and 4.25b explain the complete flow for connect().

4.7   SUMMARY

Protocol-specific operation on the socket is accessed from *prot* field of the sock object. For the INET stream protocol, this is field is initialized to *tcp_prot*.

The *tcp_hashinfo* object has pointers to different hash tables for bind, established, and listening sockets.

tcp_bhash is an object of type *tcp_bind_hashbucket* pointing to bind hash table. This table is hashed based on the port number sockets are bound to them. The hash function takes post number as input to identity hash bucket for the socket in the table.

ehash is object of type *tcp_ehash_bucket* points to established hash table. Hashed on the destination and source port/IP.

tcp_listening_hash is a hash table of sock objects hashing all the listening sockets. Hashed on the listening port number.

tcp_bind_conflict() checks for any conflicts related to allocation of port.

tcp_port_rover stores the last allocated port number.

tcp_listen_opt is an object that keeps information about all connection requests for a listening socket.

syn_table field of *tcp_listen_opt* object of type *open_request*. This hashes in all the connection requests for the listening socket.

Once a three-way handshake is over, the connection request is moved from listeners SYN queue to accept queue, *tp→accept_queue*.

sock and *tcp_opt* objects are initialized for the new connection in the accept queue.

Once an application accepts a connection request in the accept queue, a BSD socket is created for the new connection and is associated with VFS.

___tcp_v4_lookup_established()* searches for established connections in the *ehash* table.

tcp_v4_lookup_listener() searches for listening sockets in the *tcp_listening_hash* hash table.

sk_buff AND PROTOCOL HEADERS

sk_buff is the network buffer that represents the network packet on Linux TCP/IP stack. *sk_buff* has three components: sk_buff, and linear-data buffer, and paged-data(struct *skb_shared_info*). When *sk_buff* is requested, we pass it the length of the linear data area. There are fields in the *sk_buff* which are pointers to transport layer, network layer, and link layer headers. Before passing on the *sk_buff* (network packet) to next protocol layer for processing, we make the data field of *sk_buff* to the start of next protocol layer header. The next protocol layer maps the data buffer pointed to by data field of *sk_buff* to the protocol header structure for that layer and accesses that protocol header. In the same way we construct the protocol headers for the outgoing packet. In this chapter we will see how protocol headers are built for the outgoing packets and extracted from the incoming packets.

We study various fields of *sk_buff* structure and functions manipulating head, tail, end, data, and len fields of *sk_buff*. We will study the data_len field of *sk_buff* and functions manipulating it. We need to study struct *skb_shared_info* and how it is used. Then we move down to descriptions of various functions specific to cloning and queuing *sk_buff*.

sk_buff contains linear and nonlinear data portions. Linear data are represented by the data field of *sk_buff*. Normally, we allocate one page of linear data only for IP segments that can be accommodated in a single page. In the case where the total IP segment length is more than one page, we have two options. First is to have a linear data area of length which can accommodate the entire segment, and second is to have a paged data area for the rest of packet (linear data = 1 page and (IP segment—1 page) length of IP segment in a paged data area of *sk_buff*). The

TCP/IP Architecture, Design, and Implementation in Linux. By S. Seth and M. A. Venkatesulu
Copyright © 2008 the IEEE Computer Society

latter is performed only if the output device's DMA channel doesn't support the scatter–gather technique. This chapter discusses the structure of the paged data area of sk_buff and discusses the routines to manipulate it.

There is also a provision to link all the fragments of the IP datagram in the case where the original datagram is fragmented by some intermediate router. Linux sk_buff has a pointer to such a fragmentation list which has all the IP fragments arranged in the same order. We study the sk_buff fragment list as part of *struct skb_shared_info* in this chapter.

We will study how the protocol headers are built as a packet (sk_buff) traverses down the protocol layers for transmission. At the same time we will also study how protocol headers are extracted by protocol layers as the packet (*sk_buff*) moves up the layers by manipulating *sk_buff* data field. This will make the *sk_buff* concept very clear as a Linux network buffer.

5.1   STRUCT *sk_buff*

sk_buff structure represents a packet on Linux. It consists of three segments:

- *sk_buff* structure, which is also referred to as a *sk_buffer* header
- Linear data block containing data
- Nonlinear data portion represented by *struct skb_shared_info*

The *sk_buff* structure contains fields that contain pointers to protocol-headers-specific data structures. Then there are fields that contain some control information for each protocol which may be used to build headers and also can also be used to decide the next action to be taken based on specific events. Some fields contain the IP checksum and also the next protocol information. We have some fields that manipulate actual packet data. *sk_buff* also contains information about the device from where the packet has arrived and about the device from where it has to leave the system. Whenever a new packet needs to be transmitted ot received over the interface, a new *sk_buff* structure is allocated along with the data block, and data are copied to the *sk_buff* and then only the packet is processed further. Each *sk_buff* for a connection may have some fields in common, but the others may differ. Depending on requirements, we can clone *sk_buff* (separate copy of *sk_buff* structure but sharing same data blocks) or make an exact copy of the *sk_buff* (duplicating the *sk_buff* with a separate copy of the data block). Let's look at the sk_buff structure in detail. Figures 5.1a and 5.1b have the definition of *sk_buff* struct. Let's look at each field in the sk_buff structure:

> *next and prev:* These fields link the related *sk_buffs* together. For example, when a packet is fragmented, each fragment of the original packet is linked through the *next* field. (We will further discover why these two fields are placed at the start in the same order, maybe to align it with *sk_buff_head*.)
>
> *list:* This is pointer to the queue (struct *sk_buff_head*) or list on which this *sk_buff* is currently placed.
>
> *sk:* Pointer to the socket to which this packet (*sk_buff*) belongs.
>
> *stamp:* This is the field keeping the timestamp of the point when the packet is transmitted or received.

include/linux/skbuff.h

```
129  struct sk_buff {
130      /* These two members must be first. */
131      struct sk_buff  * next;          /* Next buffer in list
             */
132      struct sk_buff  * prev;          /* Previous buffer in list          */
133
134      struct sk_buff_head * list;      /* List we are on
             */
135      struct sock    *sk;              /* Socket we are owned by           */
136      struct timeval  stamp;           /* Time we arrived
             */
137      struct net_device    *dev;       /* Device we arrived on/are leaving by    */
138
139      /* Transport layer header */
140      union
141      {
142          struct tcphdr   *th;
143          struct udphdr   *uh;
144          struct icmphdr  *icmph;
145          struct igmphdr  *igmph;
146          struct iphdr    *ipiph;
147          struct spxhdr   *spxh;
148          unsigned char   *raw;
149      } h;
150
151      /* Network layer header */
152      union
153      {
154          struct iphdr    *iph;
155          struct ipv6hdr  *ipv6h;
156          struct arphdr   *arph;
157          struct ipxhdr   *ipxh;
158          unsigned char   *raw;
159      } nh;
160
161      /* Link layer header */
162      union
163      {
164          struct ethhdr   *ethernet;
165          unsigned char   *raw;
166      } mac;
167
168      struct  dst_entry *dst;
             ....
176      char       cb[48];
177
178      unsigned int   len;              /* Length of actual data            */
179      unsigned int   data_len;
180      unsigned int   csum;             /* Checksum
             */
181      unsigned char  __unused,         /* Dead field, may be reused        */
182                     cloned,           /* head may be cloned (check refcnt to be sure). */
```

Figure 5.1a. Network buffer—Linux implementation of packet.

```
include/linux/skbuff.h

 183                              pkt_type,             /* Packet class */
 184                              ip_summed;              /* Driver fed us an IP checksum          */
 185        __u32      priority;          /* Packet queueing priority         */
 186        atomic_t     users;            /* User count - see datagram.c,tcp.c     */
 187        unsigned short  protocol;        /* Packet protocol from driver.         */
 188        unsigned short  security;        /* Security level of packet         */
 189        unsigned int   truesize;         /* Buffer size */

 190
 191        unsigned char  *head;            /* Head of buffer
               */
 192        unsigned char  *data;            /* Data head pointer
               */
 193        unsigned char  *tail;            /* Tail pointer
               */
 194        unsigned char  *end;             /* End pointer
               */
 195
 196        void          (*destructor)(struct sk_buff *);      /* Destruct function      */
 197 #ifdef CONFIG_NETFILTER
 198        /* Can be used for communication between hooks. */
 199        unsigned long   nfmark;
 200        /* Cache info */
 201        __u32       nfcache;
 202        /* Associated connection, if any */
 203        struct nf_ct_info *nfct;
 204 #ifdef CONFIG_NETFILTER_DEBUG
 205        unsigned int nf_debug;
 206 #endif
 207 #endif /*CONFIG_NETFILTER*/
 208
 209 #if defined(CONFIG_HIPPI)
 210        union{
 211             __u32  ifield;
 212        } private;
 213 #endif
 214
 215 #ifdef CONFIG_NET_SCHED
 216        __u32       tc_index;        /* traffic control index
 */
 217 #endif
 218 };
```

Figure 5.1b. Network buffer—Linux implementation of packet (*continued*).

dev: This is the pointer to the device, *struct net_device*, through which the packet is received or transmitted. The net_device keeps information about the network interface (data link layer) and operations specific to the device.

union h: This is a union of pointers to different transport layer headers. This field points to the offset in the packet data that is the start of transport layer header.

union nh: This is a union of pointers to different network layers headers supported by Linux. It points to the offset in the packet data that is the start of the network layer header.

union mac: This is a union of pointers to different mac layer headers supported by Linux. It points to the offset in the packet data that is the start of the mac layer header. We will see how these fields are made to point to the appropriate locations in the packet data so that they correctly access the start of the protocol headers.

dst: This points to dst_entry structure, which keeps the information about the route for a given destination and also some information specific to the network characterstics for a given connection such as pmtu, rtt, and so on; we study more about it in Section 14.8.

cb: This field keeps control information specific to the protocol. This may be used independently by each protocol layer. If we want to keep the same information across the layers, we can clone sk_buff. The socket layer can map these data to *struct inet_skb_parm*, and tcp can map this buffer to *struct tcp_skb_cb*. We will see the usage in later sections.

len: This field keeps the total length of the data associated with the sk_buff (packet length at any point of time).

data_len: This field is used only when we have nonlinear data (paged data) associated with the *sk_buff*. This field indicates the portion of the total packet length that is contained as paged data, which means that the linear data length will be $skb{\rightarrow}len - skb{\rightarrow}data\_len$. We will discuss more about it in Section 5.2.

csum: This is the checksum of the protocol at any point in time. Discuss more about it later.

cloned: This field keeps information that the *sk_buff* is the cloned one or the original one.

pkt_type: This field contains information about the type of the packet. The types generally are multicast, broadcast, loopback, host, other hosts, outgoing and so on; we will come to know more about it later.

ip_summed: This field indicates whether the driver calculated the IP checksum for us.

priority: This field keeps information about the queuing priority of the packet. This is based on the TOS field of the IP header.

users: This field keeps account of number of references to the *sk_buff*.

protocol: This field keeps the information of the next layer protocol and is set when a packet is processed by the current protocol layer.

security: This keeps the security level for the packet. We discuss it in more detail later.

truesize: This field keeps the information about the total memory allocated for this buffer. This includes the *sk_buff* structure size + the size of the data block allocated for this *sk_buff*.

head: This field points to the start of the linear data area (first byte of the linear-data area allocated for the *sk_buff*).

data: This field points to the start of the data residing in the linear-data area. The data residing in the linear-data area may not always start from the start of the linear-data area pointed to by head because of the reasons that we discuss in Section 5.4.2.

tail: This field points to the last byte of the data residing in the linear-data area.

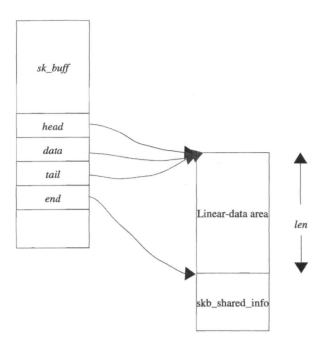

Figure 5.2. sk_buff when it is just as returned by skb_allocr().

end: This field points to the end of the linear-data area and is different from *tail*. The end of the data residing in the linear-data area may not always be at the end of the linear-data area, so we have *tail*. With this field we make sure that we don't use more than what is available.

Head, data, end, and tail fields manipulate the linear area, and we will see it in the latter part of the discussion. Whenever we allocate a new sk_buff, we provide the size of the linear-data area. At the same time, we initialize the four fields of sk_buff to point to linear-data area in appropriate positions. Figure 5.2 shows the position of four fields when a new sk_buff is allocated. We can see that when we request sk_buff for a given length *len* of linear-data area, we have fields of sk_buff set appropriately. We can also see the addition area reserved for *struct skb_shared_ info* at the end of the linear data area. This structure is shared across the sk_buff clones.

5.2 STRUCT *skb_shared_info* (Fig. 5.3)

This structure contains information about the nonlinear data area for the *sk_buff*. By nonlinear area, it means that the data contained by the *sk_buff* are just more than that can be accommodated in the linear data area. The data contained in the nonlinear data area is continuation of the data from the offset pointed to by *end* field of the *sk_buff*. The total length of the data is contained in linear and nonlinear data area. The total length of the *sk_buff* data is stored in *len* field, and the length of the nonlinear (paged) data area is stored in *data_len* field of *sk_buff*; please refer to Fig. 5.4. The paged-data area is possible only if DMA allows scatter–gather operations on the physically scattered pages.

```
include/linux/skbuff.h

122  struct skb_shared_info {
123      atomic_t       dataref;
124      unsigned int   nr_frags;
125      struct sk_buff *frag_list;
126      skb_frag_t     frags[MAX_SKB_FRAGS];
127  };
```

Figure 5.3a. Structure at the end of linear-data area containing *sk_buff* fragment info and nonlinear data info for *sk_buff*.

```
include/linux/skbuff.h

112  struct skb_frag_struct
113  {
114      struct page *page;
115      __u16 page_offset;
116      __u16 size;
117  };
```

Figure 5.3b. Structure, keeping information of nonlinear data for *sk_buff*.

dataref: This keeps the account of number of references for *skb_shared_info* object.

nr_frags: This field keeps the number of paged fragments for the *sk_buff*. It is an indication of the number of elements in the *frags[]* array containing paged data for *sk_buff*.

frag_list: This field keeps the pointer to the list of *sk_buffs* representing the fragments for the original packet (*sk_buff*, to which the *frag_list* belongs). We will see in the next section the live example explaining the field. If the original packet is fragmented, all the *sk_buffs* representing those fragments will be linked in this list and the total length of the original *sk_buff* is the sum of the lengths (*skb→len*) of each fragment in the frag_list list including the length of the original sk_buff. Please refer to Fig. 5.5.

frags: This field is the array of fragments containing the paged data for the sk_buff. The paged data are represented by struct *skb_frag_struct*. The length of data contained in the paged area (represented by *frags[]*) is the sum of the number of bytes contained in each page fragment (frags[i]→size) and is stored in *data_len* field of *sk_buff*.

5.3 *sk_buff* AND DMA—SKB_FRAG_STRUCT

This structure is a descriptor for each paged fragment containing paged data for the *sk_buff*.

page: This field is a pointer to the page structure containing paged data for the fragment. Each page fragment contains a maximum of one page of data.

The kernel virtual address to which this page is mapped can be obtained *page_address()*.

page_offset: This field is the offset for the page that points to the start of the data in this page.

size: This field is the total length of data contained in the page pointed by *page* field.

5.3.1   DMA and Fragmented *sk_buff* Containing Paged Data

Figure 5.4 shows linking of kernel data-structures to implement pagedata area for sk_buff.

5.3.2   *sk_buff* and IP Fragmentation

Figure 5.5 shows linking of sk_buff's to implement IP fragmentation.

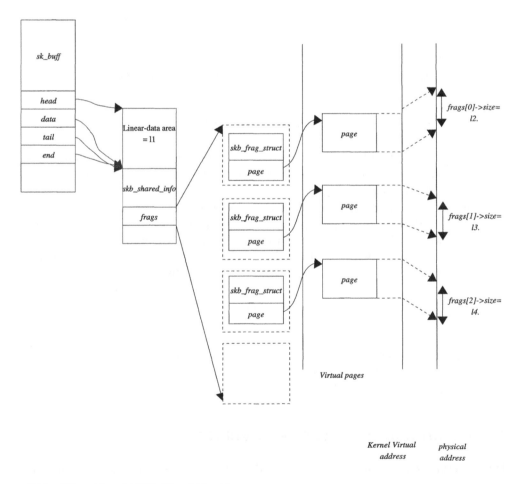

skb->len= l1(linear-data area) + (l2+l3+l4)(paged data area)

skb->data_len = (l2+l3+l4)(paged data area)

Figure 5.4. Paged data area organization for *sk_buff*.

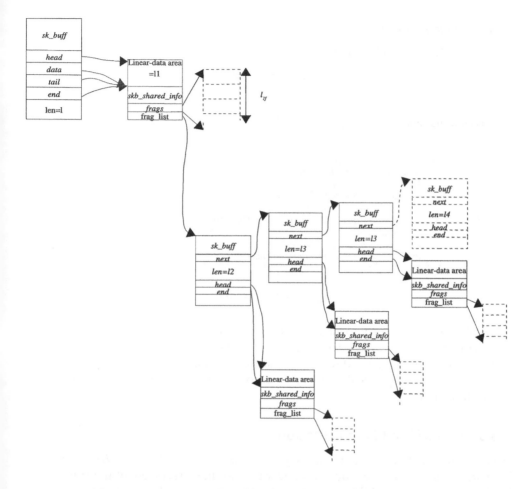

Total length of original sk_buff (l) = l_1 (length of linear-data area)+l_{1f}(length of paged area) +(l_2+l_3+l_4+.....+l_n)

Figure 5.5. Fragmentation and paged data area for *sk_buff*.

```
net/ipv4/tcp.c

1000    if (sk->route_caps&NETIF_F_SG) {
1001        int pgbreak = SKB_MAX_HEAD(MAX_TCP_HEADER);
```

cs 5.1. *select_size()*.

We can use a paged data area for *sk_buff* only if DMA supports the scatter–gather process on physically noncontagious pages. The fine example to understand the usage of the paged-data area is *tcp_sendmsg()*. If we look at this function, it is clear under what conditions we are making use of paged-data area. While allocating sk_buff, we need to actually decide on the length of the linear data area depending on whether DMA supports scatter–gather for physically noncontiguous pages. To decide on this, we call *select_size()* to get the size of the linear data area for the *sk_buff*. *select_size()* checks if DMA supports scatter–gather (see cs 5.1).

```
net/ipv4/ip_fragment.c

554        skb_shinfo(head)->frag_list = head->next;
```

cs 5.2. *ip_frag_reasm()*.

```
net/ipv4/ip_fragment.c

558        for (fp=head->next; fp; fp = fp->next)
559             head->data_len += fp->len;
560             head->len += fp->len;
561             if (head->ip_summed != fp->ip_summed)
562                  head->ip_summed = CHECKSUM_NONE;
563             else if (head->ip_summed == CHECKSUM_HW)
564                  head->csum = csum_add(head->csum, fp->csum);
565             head->truesize += fp->truesize;
566             atomic_sub(fp->truesize, &ip_frag_mem);
567        }
```

cs 5.3. *ip_frag_reasm()*.

If the above is true, we try to allocate one page of data for the linear-data area, and the rest of the data goes as a paged-data area where one page is allocated per *sk_buff* fragment for subsequent data. If the scatter–gather is not supported, we try to allocate contiguous physical memory to accommodate entire sk_buff data in the linear-data area.

5.3.3 *sk_buff* and Fragmentation

A good example to understand the usage of *frags_list (skb_shinfo(SKB)→frag_list)* is *ip_frag_reasm()*. The function is called when we have received all the fragments for the original packet. All the fragments for the original packet are linked together by *skb→next* in a chain of sk_buff pointed by *qp→fragments*. The packet fragments are arranged in the list in proper order. The list of fragments is pointed to by *head→next* where head is the first *sk_buff* in the list (the first packet in the list). The *head→next* is copied to list head's frag_list (cs 5.2).

Now head's len, data_len, csum, and truesize fields are updated to represent the complete packet including all the fragments that belong to the original packet (see cs 5.3).

5.4 ROUTINES OPERATING ON *sk_buff*

Let's look at the routines operating on *sk_buff*. Later on we will see how these routines are used in actual practice. First we will look at the routines that manipulate the linear-data area.

5.4.1 *alloc_skb()*

This function allocates a new *sk_buff*. We pass on the length of the data area and the mode of memory allocation. Data area is the block of memory allocated for the *sk_buff* where the packet is constructed. End of the linear data area is reserved for

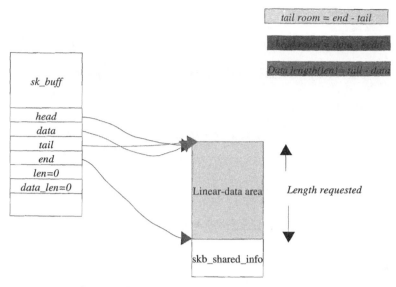

Figure 5.6. Status of *sk_buff* after it is allocated.

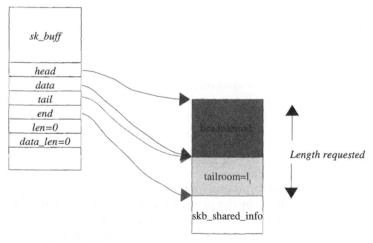

Figure 5.7. Status of *sk_buff* after call to *skb_reserve()*.

structure that keeps information of the paged-data area and fragments associated with the *sk_buff*. So, we allocate a *sk_buff* head and the data area of length 'len' bytes. The position of head, data, tail, and end pointers are shown in Fig. 5.6 when the *alloc_skb()* returns. We can see that the tail room is equal to the length of the data block requested for *sk_buff* just after allocation. Head room and data length are zero.

5.4.2 *skb_reserve()*

This function changes head and tail room for the sk_buff. It is called mostly to reserve space for the protocol headers. We pass length of the headroom we need to reserve for the protocol headers (Fig. 5.7). Whenever *sk_buff* is allocated to send a new TCP data, it allocates data space for the user data, protocol headers, and the

```
include/net/tcp.h

1710 static inline struct sk_buff *tcp_alloc_pskb(struct sock *sk, int size, int mem, int gfp)
1711 {
1712        struct sk_buff *skb = alloc_skb(size+MAX_TCP_HEADER, gfp);
1713
1714        if(skb) {
                   ....
1718                skb_reserve(skb, MAX_TCP_HEADER);
1719                return skb;
1722        } else {
1723            ...
1727 }
```

cs 5.4. *tcp_alloc_pskb()*.

```
include/linux/skbuff.h

786 static inline unsigned char *skb_put(struct sk_buff *skb, unsigned int len)
787 {
788     unsigned char *tmp=skb->tail;
789     SKB_LINEAR_ASSERT(skb);
790     skb->tail+=len;
791     skb->len+=len;
792     if(skb->tail>skb->end) {
793         skb_over_panic(skb, len, current_text_addr());
794     }
795     return tmp;
796 }
```

cs 5.5. *skb_put()*.

skb_shared_info. When we are constructing a packet, we reserve the maximum length that could be occupied by the protocol headers as headroom. Since there are some optional fields in the TCP/IP protocol headers, we allocate the tailroom as the sum of maximum header lengths (including all the optional header fields) of the protocols. For example, if we look at *tcp_alloc_pskb()*, it is clear that total data length allocated for *sk_buff* is requested length + MAX_TCP_HEADER. MAX_TCP_HEADER is the sum of maximum length of TCP header(64) + maximum length of IP header(64) + Maximum length of link layer(LL_MAX_HEADER) (see cs 5.4).

5.4.3 *skb_put()*

The routine is used to manipulate *sk_buff's* linear data area. The function reserves space for the segment data at the end of the linear data area, *skb→tail*. We record *sk_buff's* original *tail* field at line 788 (cs 5.5). At line 790, the *tail* field is incremented by requested length. Modified tail field expands *sk_buff's* total length, so we increment the *skb→len* by requested length at line 791. A sanity check is done at line 792 to make sure that the tail has not gone past the end of the linear data area

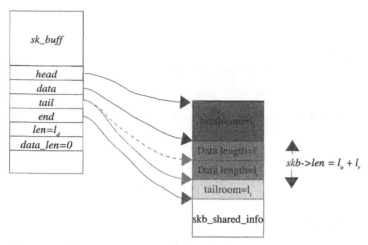

Figure 5.8. Status of *sk_buff* after call to *skb_put()*.

net/ipv4/tcp.c
1080	if (skb_tailroom(skb) > 0) {
1081	/* We have some space in skb head. Superb! */
1082	if (copy > skb_tailroom(skb))
1083	copy = skb_tailroom(skb);
1084	if ((err = skb_add_data(skb, from, copy)) != 0)
1085	goto do_fault;
1086	} else {
......

cs 5.6. *tcp_sendmsg()*.

(*skb→end*). If everything is OK, we return the original reference to *sk_buff's tail* field 795.

In most of the cases, user data go here or we can say that TCP/UDP payload is copied in here. It creates space for the segment payload (see Fig. 5.8). The dotted blue line in Fig. 5.8 shows the original position of the *skb→tail*, which is returned to the caller when *sk_buff's* length was l_o. After call to *skb_put()*, the solid gray line is the final position of *sk_buff's* tail field and the total *sk_buff's* length becomes $l_o + l_r$. Tail room is reduced by l_r. The caller directly uses the returned pointer to copy data.

The good example to explain this is *skb_add_data()* called from *tcp_sendmsg()*. Here we first check how much space is available at the tail end at line 1080 (cs 5.6) by calling *skb_tailroom()*. If some space is available, we find out if current request can be satisfied with the available tail room at line 1082. *skb_add_data()* is called at line 1084 to copy the data to the *sk_buff* linear data space. In *skb_add_data()* we call *csum_and_copy_from_use()* to copy data to *sk_buff*. The second argument is the location to where the data should be copied.

We call skb_put()(cs 5.7, line 985), which returns us the exact location in the *sk_buff* linear data area where the data should be copied (original location where skb→tail was pointing).

```
net/ipv4/tcp.c

978 static inline int
979 skb_add_data(struct sk_buff *skb, char *from, int copy)
980 {
          .....
985         csum = csum_and_copy_from_user(from, skb_put(skb, copy),
986                          copy, 0, &err);
          ......
994 }
```

cs 5.7. *skb_add_data()*.

5.4.4 *skb_push()*

This function manipulates the *data* field of *sk_buff* and acts only on linear data area. It pushes the *data* field closer to the head by the number of bytes provided as an argument to the function. The headroom is reduced by the number of bytes that data length has increased. Data field is deducted by length requested at line 817, cs 5.8. This shift of *data* field toward *head* causes overall *sk_buff* length to expand by the length requested so we increment *sk_buff* length at line 818. We do a sanity check at line 819 to make sure that the data field has not one past start of the buffer (line 819). If things are correct, reference to a data pointer is returned to the caller.

Figure 5.9 shows how a data field is manipulated by calling *skb_push()*. l_o was *sk_buff's* original length with a data field pointer represented by a dotted black line. l_r is the length requested by the caller of *skb_push()*. After *sk_buff* is processed by *skb_push()*, the total length of linear data area becomes $l_r + l_o$, and a data pointer is represented by a solid black line.

This is mainly called when we want to send a packet. The packet contains data and protocol headers. We need to add data, and each protocol layer will add its header as it passes through different layers. So, the topmost layer adds data and then its header. We have seen functions that will create headroom and the room for the user data. We create headroom by calling *skb_reserve()* and then room for user data by calling *skb_put()*. We copy user data in the data area pointed to by

```
include/linux/skbuff.h

815 static inline unsigned char *skb_push(struct sk_buff *skb, unsigned int len)
816 {
817    skb->data-=len;
818    skb->len+=len;
819    if(skb->data<skb->head) {
820       skb_under_panic(skb, len, current_text_addr());
821    }
822    return skb->data;
823 }
```

cs 5.8. *skb_push()*.

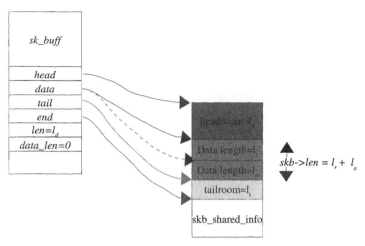

Figure 5.9. Status of *sk_buff* after call to *skb_push()*.

```
include/linux/skbuff.h
844 static inline unsigned char * skb_pull(struct sk_buff *skb, unsigned int len)
845 {
846    if (len > skb->len)
847        return NULL;
848    return __skb_pull(skb,len);
849 }
```

cs 5.9. *skb_pull()*.

skb→data. Now it is the chance to add the protocol header just before the start of user-data. For a more detailed example, refer to Section 5.5.1.

5.4.5 *skb_pull()*

The routine pulls down the data pointer by number of bytes specified as an argument to the function and returns the new data pointer. This manipulates *sk_buff's* linear data area by modifying its data field. It reduces *skb→len* by the number of bytes requested hence increasing headroom for *sk_buff's* linear data area. Let's look at the implementation. First we do some sanity check on the requested length. If it is more than the total *sk_buff's* length, we need to return NULL, indicating no action was taken (cs 5.9, line 846). If we can process the request, *__skb_pull()* is called at line 848.

__skb_pull() does the actual processing as requested by the caller. It reduces *sk_buff's* len field by the number of bytes requested because the request is to shrink the linear data area at line 827, cs 5.10. Next we make sure that the total length, just calculated at line 827, has not gone below the linear data area *length(skb→ data_len)*. If things are good, we increment the data pointer by the length of data requested at line 830 and return it to the caller.

```
include/linux/skbuff.h

825 static inline char *__skb_pull(struct sk_buff *skb, unsigned int len)
826 {
827     skb->len-=len;
828     if (skb->len < skb->data_len)
829         out_of_line_bug();
830     return  skb->data+=len;
831 }
```

<u>cs 5.10.</u> *__skb_pull()*.

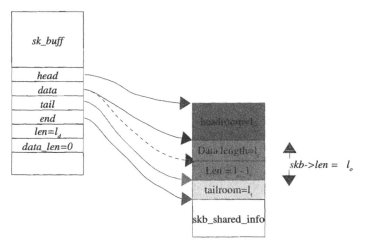

<u>Figure 5.10.</u> Status of *sk_buff* after call to *skb_push()*.

The routine is mostly used to access protocol headers when the packet arrives. Let's look pictorially as to what happens when sk_buff is processed by *skb_pull()* (see Fig. 5.10). Originally, *sk_buff's* total length (*skb→len*) was l_0 and *data* field is represented by a solid black line. Length requested to *skb_pull()* is l_r and final *data* field is represented by dotted black lines. The reference to data field represented as a dotted black line is returned by *skb_pull()* to its caller finally. For a more detailed example, see Section 5.6.

5.5 *sk_buff* BUILDS PROTOCOL HEADERS AS IT TRAVERSES DOWN THE PROTOCOL LAYERS

5.5.1 Tcp Header Is Added to *sk_buff*

We need to pre-pend the TCP header to sk_buff's data area just before the TCP payload. The situation is similar to Fig. 5.11 where we have copied l_d length (*skb→len*) of data starting at *skb→data*. Now we need to add a TCP header before a TCP payload—that is, before *skb→data*. TCP calls *tcp_transmit_skb()* to build a TCP header for the TCP segment. First it calculates the TCP header length, taking into consideration options that is used for current TCP connection. Once this is done,

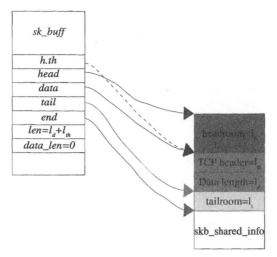

Figure 5.11. Status of *sk_buff* after TCP header is added to the outgoing packet.

```
net/ipv4/tcp_output.c

210             if(sysctl_tcp_window_scaling) {
211                  tcp_header_size += TCPOLEN_WSCALE_ALIGNED;
212                  sysctl_flags |= SYSCTL_FLAG_WSCALE;
213             }
      ......
226        th = (struct tcphdr *) skb_push(skb, tcp_header_size);
227        skb->h.th = th;
      .......
230        /* Build TCP header and checksum it. */
231        th->source       = sk->sport;
232        th->dest         = sk->dport;
233        th->seq          = htonl(tcb->seq);
```

cs 5.11. *tcp_transmit_skb().*

we call skb_push() to allocate room for the TCP header. This moves data toward the head by a number of bytes required for the TCP header as shown in Fig. 5.11. Now *skb→h.th* is made to point to *skb→data* (returned by *skb_push()*) in cs 5.11, line 226. We access the *skb→data* memory region as if it were *struct tcphdr* and initialize the fields of the *struct tcphdr*.

5.5.2   Ip Header Is Added to *sk_buff*

Now the packet containing a TCP header and a TCP payload is passed to the IP layer. IP creates its own header and adds it to the beginning of the packet (before *skb→data*). The example we take here is *ip_build_and_send_pkt()*. This function builds an IP header for the packet and sends it to the link layer. The IP options are already processed before we come here. So, we calculate the final IP header length and then call *skb_push()* to allocate space for IP header. This function returns the *skb→data* pointer.

We construct an IP header at the location pointed to by *skb→data* and finally make *skb→nh.iph* point to *skb→data* (line 147, cs 5.12) as shown in Fig. 5.12, which

```
net/ipv4/ip_output.c

122  int ip_build_and_send_pkt(struct sk_buff *skb, struct sock *sk,
123                   u32 saddr, u32 daddr, struct ip_options *opt)
124  {
125        struct rtable *rt = (struct rtable *)skb->dst;
126        struct iphdr *iph;
127
128        /* Build the IP header. */
129        if (opt)
130              iph=(struct iphdr *)skb_push(skb,sizeof(struct iphdr) +opt->optlen);
131        else
132              iph=(struct iphdr *)skb_push(skb,sizeof(struct iphdr));
133
134        iph->version  = 4;
135        iph->ihl      = 5;
136        iph->tos      = sk->protinfo.af_inet.tos;
        ........
147        skb->nh.iph   = iph;

        ......
158  }
```

cs 5.12. *ip_build_and_send_pkt()*.

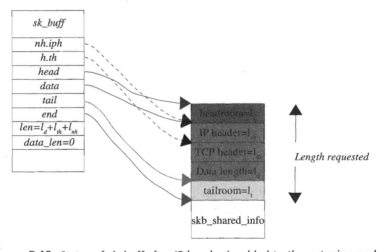

Figure 5.12. Status of *sk_buff* after IP header is added to the outgoing packet.

means that a reference of the location for the start of an IP header is stored in $skb \rightarrow nh.iph$ for later use and at the same time we have reference to the TCP header with sk_buff as $skb \rightarrow h.th$.

5.5.3 Link Layer Header Is Added to *sk_buff*

Until now we have added the transport layer header and the network layer header to the packet. It is the turn of the link layer to add its header. Considering that it is an ethernet frame, we will take the example of the *eth_header()* (see cs 5.13).

This routine pushes the data field by *ETH_HLEN* bytes toward the head as shown in Fig 5.13. We access the location pointed to by $skb \rightarrow data$ as the start of the ethernet header and build the header in this location. Finally the packet is ready

---

net/ethernet/eth.c

```
75  int eth_header(struct sk_buff *skb, struct net_device *dev, unsigned short type,
76          void *daddr, void *saddr, unsigned len)
77  {
78      struct ethhdr *eth = (struct ethhdr *)skb_push(skb,ETH_HLEN);
        .....
116 }
```

cs 5.13. *eth_header().*

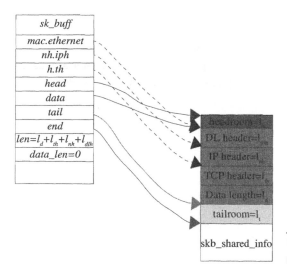

Figure 5.13. Status of *sk_buff* after link layer header is added to the outgoing packet.

to be transmitted. The total length of packet that will be transmitted is the area covered between *skb→tail* and *skb→data* in case we don't have any paged data area.

5.6.   *sk_buff* EXTRACTS PROTOCOL HEADERS AS IT TRAVERSES UP THE PROTOCOL LAYERS WHEN A PACKET ARRIVES

5.6.1   *sk_buff* Is Made to Point to a Datalink Layer Header Which Will Be Processed by Dalalink Driver

When a new packet arrives, a new *sk_buff* is allocated with the data buffer equal to the packet size. *sk_buff's* data field points to the start of the packet (ethernet header) as shown in Fig. 5.14. We will once again traverse from the link layer to the transport layer to look at how *skb_pull()* does the job of striping the protocol headers when the packet moves through different protocol layers. It is the job of the link layer driver to find out the next protocol layer from its header and then appropriately manipulate the pointers. Let's have a look at one of the Ethernet driver's receive routine *e100_rx()*. It gets the pointer to the received packet in the ring buffer and finds out the next layer protocol from the ethernet header field. It calls *eth_type_trans()*. *eth_type_trans()* pulls the data field of *sk_buff* to point to the IP header by pulling it down by the length of the ethernet header. This is done before the *sk_buff* is queued in the IP backlog queue. So just before queuing the *sk_buff* in the IP backlog queue, it looks as shown in cs 5.14.

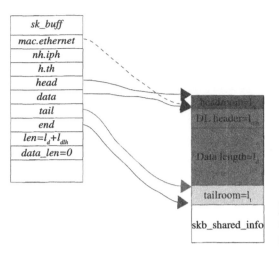

Figure 5.14. Status of *sk_buff* when new packet arrives on the interface, data points to start of data link header.

net/ethernet/eth.c

```
158  unsigned short eth_type_trans(struct sk_buff *skb, struct net_device *dev)
159  {
160      struct ethhdr *eth;
161      unsigned char *rawp;
162
163      skb->mac.raw=skb->data;
164      skb_pull(skb,dev->hard_header_len);
165      eth= skb->mac.ethernet;
         .....
207
```

<u>cs 5.14.</u> *eth_type_trans().*

5.6.2 *sk_buff* Is Made to Point to an ip Layer Header Which Will Be Processed by an IP Layer

Now the *sk_buff* is taken off the IP backlog queue and processed by the routine *netif_receive_skb()* that pulls *sk_buff* from the backlog queue. Here nh.raw is made to point to the data field of the *sk_buff*. So, we can directly access IP header as nh.iph (see cs 5.15, line 1435). So, the final *sk_buff* picture will look like Fig. 5.15.

5.6.3 *sk_buff* Is Made to Point to a tcp Layer Header Which Will Be Processed by a tcp Layer

Finally, an IP layer routine *ip_local_deliver_finish()* processes the packet for the next protocol and pulls the data field of *sk_buff* by the length of the IP header (including IP options) to point to the transport protocol header (see cs 5.16 line 227). So, finally the *sk_buff* is passed to the transport layer handler with h.th pointing to start of the transport layer header as shown in Fig. 5.16.

Finally, the transport layer needs to process the transport header packet. This is done in *tcp_v4_do_rcv()*. If the connection is found to be established and we have

```
net/core/dev.c

1415  int netif_receive_skb(struct sk_buff *skb)
1416  {
1417       struct packet_type *ptype, *pt_prev;
          .......
1435       skb->h.raw = skb->nh.raw = skb->data;
1494  }
```

<u>cs 5.15</u> *netif_receive_skb()*.

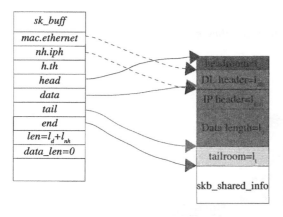

Figure 5.15. Linklayer has processed the packet and passes it to the network layer after making data point to start of network header.

```
net/ipv4/ip_input.c

219  static inline int ip_local_deliver_finish(struct sk_buff *skb)
220  {
221       int ihl = skb->nh.iph->ihl*4;
          .......
227       __skb_pull(skb, ihl);
          .......
237       skb->h.raw = skb->data;
          .......
285  }
```

<u>cs 5.16.</u> *ip_local_deliver_finish()*.

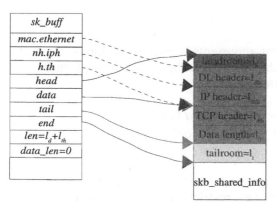

Figure 5.16. Network layer has processed the packet and has passed it to the transport layer after making data point to start of transport layer header.

```
net/ipv4/tcp_input.c

3210  int tcp_rcv_established(struct sock *sk, struct sk_buff *skb,
3211                   struct tcphdr *th, unsigned len)
3212  {
3213        struct tcp_opt *tp = &(sk->tp_pinfo.af_tcp);
       .......
3343                   __skb_pull(skb,tcp_header_len);
3344                   __skb_queue_tail(&sk->receive_queue, skb);
       ......

3449  }
```

cs 5.17. *tcp_rcv_established()*.

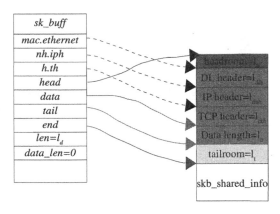

Figure 5.17. Transport layer has processed the packet and passed the data to the socket layer after making data point to the transport payload.

data in the TCP segment, we need to copy the data to the user application by calling *skb_copy_datagram_iovec()* from the offset l_{dth} starting from *skb→data*. If because of some reason, we are not able to copy data to the user application, we just pull the data field of the *sk_buff* by the length of the TCP header (including options) and queue it in the receive queue of the socket (see cs 5.17, line 3343). If the *sk_buff* is queued in the socket's receive buffer, the *sk_buff* looks as shown in Fig. 5.17.

We need to look at the other routines related to *sk_buff* like clone and paged *sk_buff*, which is an exercise until the next release of the book is available.

5.7 SUMMARY

sk_buff is a socket buffer header that represents a packet on Linux. Separate memory is allocated to store *sk_buff* data pointed to by *head* field of *sk_buff*.

Data area of *sk_buff* is divided into two parts:

- Linear data area manipulated by *head* and *end* fields of *sk_buff*.
- Paged data area managed by *skb_shared_info* object located at the end of the linear data area.

One page is allocated at a time to *skb_shared_info*. There is a limitation on number of pages allocated to paged data area. This restriction may cause a performance issue when we can't use the scatter–gather capability of the network controller in the case where complete segment can't be fit into paged data area. In such cases a big chunk of memory is allocated to linear data area, which is an expensive process.

skb_shared_info also manages IP fragments.

sk_buff has a back pointer to the socket to which it belongs. It can traverse anywhere in a stack with an identity.

skb_pull() removes data from the head of a buffer by moving the *data* pointer of *sk_buff* up in the memory, thereby creating head room. A routine is used to strip protocol headers as a packet moves up the stack.

skb_push() pushes a *data* pointer of *sk_buff* down in the memory, thereby reducing head space. This routine is used to build a protocol header when a packet is moving down the stack.

skb_reserve() reserves header room by moving *data* and *tail* pointers of *sk_buff* up in the memory by a given length.

6

MOVEMENT OF *sk_buff*
ACROSS PROTOCOL LAYERS

In this chapter we focus on the movement of sk_buff across protocol layers and discussion of only a TCP/IP over an ethernet link layer, which means the major kernel path through which *sk_buff* passes while in the transmission and reception process. We discuss the design of a TCP/IP stack here. In this chapter we see how firewall hooks are inserted and the way in which we find the route for the destination packet. We see how we attach an outgoing device with *sk_buff*, depending on the route. We cover ARP resolution for the outgoing packet in the chapter. At the same time we see how the incoming packet(*sk_buff*) traverses through the protocol layers. We need to see how *sk_buff* is processed in the network layer. In the IP layer we need to find a route for the packet, depending on the source and destination IP. If the packet needs to be forwarded, it will be routed through different path to the outgoing interface; otherwise it will be delivered locally. The IP layer has to process the packet to find out the next transport layer and send it to the transport layer for further processing. Finally, the transport layer has to demultiplex the packet and find out the socket to which the packet belongs. The idea is to discuss the how the packet is delivered to the next layer for processing when the packet is going up/ down the TCP/IP stack. We discuss the TCP/IP stack in brief and focus on the design of the stack implementation on Linux. The details of each is covered in individual chapters.

The entire discussion is divided into the following layers:

- Socket layer
- TCP layer

TCP/IP Architecture, Design, and Implementation in Linux. By S. Seth and M. A. Venkatesulu
Copyright © 2008 the IEEE Computer Society

- IP layer
- Link layer
- Packet scheduling layer, Qdisc
- softIRQ framework
- Transmission/reception

6.1   PACKET TRAVERSING DOWN THE TCP/IP STACK

This section addresses how the first packet for a given connection traverses down the TCP/IP stack when it has no information about the route and the outgoing device. Then we will see how the packet is generated and trickles down the protocol layers when we write data over the connected socket. In this section we will not discuss anything specific about TCP and IP processing but just the kernel framework that implements the network protocol.

When an application wants to connect to the server, it issues a connect on the server with the destination socket address as an argument to the connect systemcall. The socket address for inet protocol should contain a port number and an IP address. So, the connect only knows the port number of the service and the IP address of the host where the server needs to be contacted. Let's see step by step how we go about initializing the connection. The first thing that we need to do is to find the route for the given destination IP address. Here we check the kernel routing table for the destination IP address. If we don't get a valid route for the destination, we return error. There needs to be only one outgoing interface for a given route. If we have a valid route to a given destination, it should also contain information about the outgoing device. We cache the route along with the outgoing device with the connecting socket. Now we need to initialize ARP-specific information for the outgoing device if required. Since only Ethernet devices require such information and our discussion contains such a device, we need to initialize ARP information for the outgoing device and cache them. Outgoing interfaces such as PPP or PLIP don't require ARP to be initialized. Until now we have gotten the route for our destination in the connecting socket's cache. Data flow for packet down the TCP/IP stack is shown in Fig. 6.1(a) through 6.1(b).

TCP Layer. The next step is to build a TCP SYN packet for the destination as a first step to establish a connection. The TCP header is built for the SYN packet and and send it to the IP layer for building an IP header and further processing. The IP layer first checks if the cached route is still valid for the outgoing packet. If it is not valid, we once again try to get the valid route for the outgoing packet. This may happen because the route may have changed from the time we first found the route for the destination by the routing daemon because of failure in the link.

IP Layer. So, we once again repeat the steps for the new route; that is, we initialize the outgoing device for the route and also the ARP-specific information is initialized. If we are here, we have all the route specific information and we can go ahead with packet processing. We now build an IP header, and the IP layer does processing on the packet if required. Now we need to find out if there is a firewall policy that doesn't allow the packet to be sent out. If everything is OK, we do IP checksum for the packet just formed and place it on the IP header in the checksum slot. We do IP checksum here because the outgoing device may have changed and packet might need to be fragmented here. The next step is to masquerade the packet or do any modifications on the packet such as encryption and encapsulation packet (IPSec), if required. This is implemented by the way of a netfilter hook post route operation.

Link Layer. If everything is OK, we also build a link layer header because here we have a final valid output device for the packet. We can build a link layer header only if we have a hardware address for the destination IP. If this destination hardware is not yet known, we send out an ARP request now and get the hardware address for the destination IP in the ARP reply. We need to place it on the device queue for final transmission.

Packet Scheduler. We de-queue the packet from the device queue (this may not be the packet we just queued on the device queue because there may already be frames queued on the device). We try to transmit the packet by programming a device DMA for the current frame. Otherwise we requeue the packet on the device queue, queue the device on the CPU, and raise Tx IRQ on the CPU and return. When Tx softIRQ comes on the CPU, it just dequeues the packet from the device queue and starts transmitting it. Tx interrupt is raised after the packet is successfully transmitted. The packets (*sk_buff*) that are transmitted successfully are freed in the Tx interrupt.

In our last discussion we saw how the first-time connection setup is done which caches in important information such as route, device, and ARP. Now we will see how subsequent packets (*sk_buff*) are generated when we write data over the TCP socket.

Socket Layer. This is to discuss how a cached route is used by all the subsequent packets generated for the established connection. This will be explained by taking an example of TCP write over an established socket. We need to find a socket for the corresponding socket descriptor. Using file inode and private data, we can find the socket. Now we write data over connected sockets. When an application writes some data over the connected socket, the TCP either copies the data on last partial packet (*sk_buff* which is not yet full) or creates a new packet (*sk_buff*).

TCP Layer. Once the data are copied to the *sk_buff*, we need to consult the TCP state machine to check if we can send the packet now or wait for some event to occur before we can send it out. In case we are the only packet and are allowed to send the packet now, we will build the TCP header and send it to the IP layer. Otherwise, we queue the packet at the end of the the TCP send buffer queue. After queuing the packet on the TCP send buffer queue, we check if we need to send out the first packet on the send buffer. If so, we need to dequeue the first packet from the send buffer build the TCP header and give the packet to the IP layer for further processing. We initialize the TCP retransmit timer.

6.1.1 Path of Packet Traversal from Socket Layer to Device for Transmission

Figures 6.1(a) and 6.1(b) describes the date flow diagram for processing data down the stack. It describes how data is processed from socket layer to device layer unless transmitted, discussed in Section 6.1.

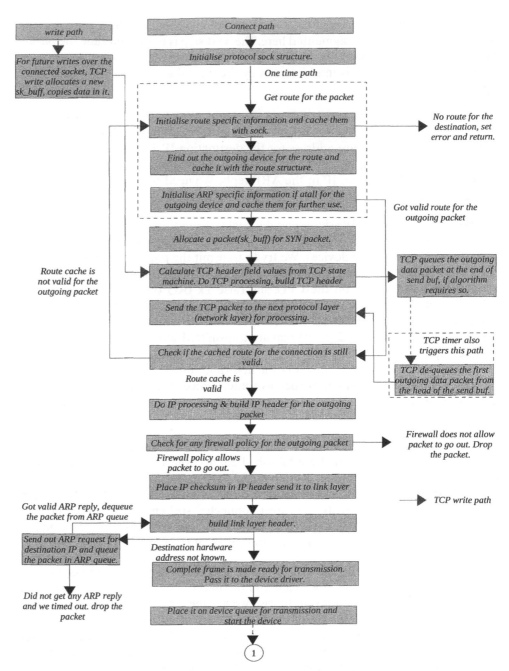

Figure 6.1a. Packet traversal down TCP/IP.

6.1.2 Kernel Path for TCP Packet Traversing Down the Stack

The outgoing packet (*sk_buff*) gets most of the information about route and next protocol layer from the *sock* structure. *sock* structure is initialized once and has all the information about the connection. Each outgoing packet gets all the required information from sock structure. With the help of an example, we will see how the

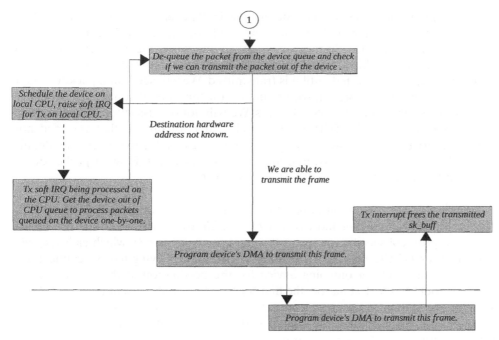

Figure 6.1b. Packet traversal down TCP/IP stack.

TCP packet is getting ready to be transmitted over IP network when it is built from scratch right from its allocation until it is transmitted out of the system. Each protocol has to add its header to the outgoing packet. The hardware layer adds information to the header which is more or less the same for all the outgoing packets for a given destination. The IP layer keeps information about the route to the destination. The IP header keeps information about the source and destination end points only, but the route will actually decide which interface it has to be transmitted. Once we know the route to the destination, we need not worry about the route for any future outgoing packets on this specific connection until that specific route is modified. Route-specific information is stored in *struct dst*, which has a pointer to the outgoing device as well. It is only the TCP layer whose header fields may change for each outgoing packet because it depends very much on the events and not on a one-time initialization. For TCP, most of the protocol-specific information is stored in a *tcp_opt* structure, which is linked with the sock structure as *sk→tp_pinfo.af_tcp*. Once the initial setup is over at the time of the connection setup, protocol layers use the same set of information for building protocol headers and maintaining the protocol state throughout the connection. Network interface is defined by *struct net_device*. This structure keeps device-specific information and also hardware-specific operations such as transmission and reception callback routines. In the case of the Ethernet framework, we have *struct neighbor* that is responsible for doing ARP and RARP. Neighbor framework manages the RARP/ARP table.

In this chapter we will take a simple example of initiating TCP/IP connection over the Ethernet interface. In this process we will go through the entire setup of the connection, which includes the setup for transport, the network, and the link layers. In Chapter 4 we discussed the flow of connect systemcall, but that was very much related to the socket connect describing TCP ports allocation and stuff. Here we will discuss connect from the point of view of kernel framework required to send the first packet out to the destination when we know nothing about the route and the outgoing device. Also, this discussion describes the entire path for the packet from the time it is generated until it is transmitted. We will see how a packet is built using the information stored in sock structure (at the time of connection setup) as it passes through different protocol layers. We will not discuss any protocol-specific details here but only the TCP/IP stack major functionality so that we need not wonder every time as to how are we getting any specific information. All the details about the protocols will be covered in the specific chapters. Flow of packet down the TCP/IP stack in kernel 2.4.20 is shown in Fig. 6.3.

Socket Layer. When an application wants to do a connect on a given TCP socket, it passes the socket address, *struct sockaddr*, to the kernel. Inside the kernel we make protocol-specific connect calls *inet_stream_connect()*, which calls *tcp_v4_connect()* for TCP. The socket over which we are we are trying to do a connect has no idea of the route or outgoing device for the destination at this point of time. Without route to the destination, the first SYN packet can't be sent anywhere. Let's see how we find out route specific information to route the very first packet. Once we have route information, we cache it with the socket for the connection so that we need not repeat the same step to find a route for each outgoing packet each time.

IP Layer Routing. In *tcp_v4_connect()* we start with *ip_route_connect()* that gets us route to the destination to which application wants to send connection request. Application passes sock address of the remote services. Based on the destination IP address, we find the route which contains information like outgoing device and the routines that will push the packet through the stack. This calls *ip_route_output()*, which will generate key for route entry search. Key is defined as *struct rt_key* that contains four fields:

- Destination IP (is must)
- Source IP (optional)
- Output interface (optional)
- Type of service (IP option and is optional)

The kernel routing table is cached in *rt_hash_table[]*. The hashing function has four inputs mentioned above. The route is defined as *struct rtable*, which has two parts:

- struct dst_entry
- Search key and fields for the route

dst_entry object contains route-specific information such as the following:

- It contains a pointer to an outgoing interface (*net_device* object).
- It contains a pointer to a neighbour object that manages ARP/RARP for the destination IP.

- It also caches in hardware-specific routines and address.
- It caches some of the path-specific protocol parameters like MSS, congestion window, reordering, and so on, so that it can be used by many TCP connections using the same route.

If we are able to find an entry in the kernel route cache, we return with the object *rtable* for the destination. If not, we need to look into the FIB table, which is a database for all the routes. All the routing information is a stored FIB database because the kernel routing cache is usage-based. Other than boot time entries, all other entries will be added and removed depending on the usage. We call *ip_route_output_slow()* to build routing information from FIB entries, if at all it exists. *fib_lookup()* is the routine that gets us the information about the route; based on the results, we create a new routing entry in the kernel routing cache. Object *rtable* is created for the new routing entry and is cached with *rt_hash_table[]* by calling *rt_intern_hash()*.

If it is Ethernet link and unicast packet, we resolve ARP for the destination. To associate the route with ARP, we need to initialize neighbor object for the route. We call *arp_bind_neighbor()* from *rt_intern_hash()* to resolve ARP for the destination. *arp_bind_neighbor()* looks up for cached neighbour entry in the global table *arp_tbl* by calling *__neigh_lookup_errno()*. If we get the entry from the cache, we return it and link it with the route for the connection (object *dst_entry*). Otherwise we create a new entry by calling *neigh_create()* from *__neigh_lookup_errno()* and hash it in the *arp_tbl* table. The hash function takes two inputs in this case:

1. Gateway address for the route
2. The outgoing device

Later in the discussion, we will see how to resolve ARP for the destination.

The route is returned to *tcp_v4_connect()* and is cached with the socket by calling *__sk_dst_set()*. This routine makes *sk→dst_cache* point to *dst_entry* object.

TCP Layer. The next step is to create SYN segment and transmit it. This is done in *tcp_connect()*. Here we initialize sequence numbers and queue the SYN segment in the socket's send queue. Finally, we call *tcp_xmit_skb()* to build a TCP header and push the packet to the IP layer for further processing. From here onwards, the path for the SYN packet and the TCP data packet will be the same. The TCP calls the internet address family-specific callback routine *tp→af_specific→queue_xmit* to pass the packet on to the next layer. This is initialized to *ip_queue_xmit()*. *af_specific* field of *tcp_opt* object is initialized at the time of socket initialization in *inet_create()* by a call to *sk→prot→init*, which is nothing but *tcp_v4_init_sock()*. For TCP it is initialized to an *ipv4_specific* containing a set of operations specific to TCP-IP.

IP Layer. *ip_queue_xmit()* checks if the route cached with the socket to the destination is valid by calling *__sk_dst_check()*. The route may have become obsolete because the packet was queued in TCP's transmit queue. If the route is no longer valid, we will try to find a new route for the destination by calling *ip_route_output()*. This routine goes through the same cycle of finding the route as discussed earlier. Once we have a valid route, we build an IP header and pass the IP datagram to be screened through the netfilter *NF_IP_LOCAL_OUT* using *NF_HOOK* macro.

Netfilter Hook. This framework implements firewall and extensions to the TCP/IP functionality. Here we will pass a packet to the netfilter hook to check if there is any firewall rule that is set for the packet generated locally. If so, a further decision is made based on the target set for the rule. Otherwise a callback routine passed to the hook will be executed, if we get clean chit. The callback routine in this case is *ip_queue_xmit2()*.

ip_queue_xmit2() is an intermediate routine before we pass on the packet from the IP layer to the packet scheduler. The routine is called both for locally generated packets and for a forwarded packet. It does some routine checks such as header room in the buffer. In the case where the header room is less than the size of the hardware address, we need to reallocate the buffer for the packet. This may happen because the routine for the destination has changed. We also compare the size of IP datagram against the current PMTU here. If the datagram size is found to exceed the PMTU, we need to fragment the packet. If the don't fragment bit is set for IP datagram, we need to send an ICMP message to the source TCP by calling *icmp_send()*. If we are allowed to fragment the packet, it is split into fragments by calling *ip_fragment()*. It is always preferable to ask TCP to resegment the packets instead of IP fragmenting it because one fragment loss means that the whole packet will be discarded. *ip_fragment()* splits the packet into smaller sizes and transmits them one by one by calling the callback routine registered with the socket *skb→dst→output*. This points to *ip_output()*.

In case we don't need to fragment the packet, we get an IP for the packet and add an IP checksum to the header by calling *ip_select_ident()* and *ip_send_check()*, respectively. We add an IP checksum here for the obvious reason that we may expect PMTU changed at this point. An output routine for the connection is called to push the packet further down the stack, *skb→dst→output* (= *ip_output()*).

Netfilter Hook. *ip_output()* effectively applies NAT on the packet, if NAT needs to be applied to the packet in case the kernel is compiled with the NAT option. If not, we directly call *ip_finish_output()*. Once again, *ip_finish_output()* does nothing additional but sends packet to netfilter check post to check if any post routing rule is applicable using macro NF_HOOK. Postrouting filtering may be required for IP Masquerading, NATing, Redirection, Ipsec, and so on. If so, the packet is modified and processed further by the target. If no rule applies, the callback routine *ip_finish_output2()* is called to push the packet down the stack.

ARP and Neighbor Framework. *ip_finish_output2()* needs to find out the hardware address for the destination IP in the case where a link layer being used in Ethernet. This is required to build a link layer header. If we already have the destination hardware address resolved, the packet is passed to the packet scheduler for transmission. We make a decision based on hardware caches for the route. If the route's hardware cache (*skb→dst→hh*) is initialized, the hardware address is resolved. Otherwise we may need to search in the ARP table for the destination IP entry. Neighbor framework manages and implements ARP/RARP on Linux.

In the case where the hardware cache (object hh_cache) is not initialized for the route, we call neighbour's output routine *dst→neighbor→output* (= *neigh_resolve_output()*) to resolve the hardware address. Neighbour operations are initialized at the time when the neighbour object is created in *neigh_create()*. Its output routines are initialized by calling a constructor routine specific to the neighbor table, *tbl→constructor* (= *arp_constructor()*). This initializes the neighbor's set of operations (*neigh→ops*) to *arp_generic_ops*.

neigh_resolve_output() is called to get a hardware address for the destination IP by issuing an ARP request. *__neigh_event_send()* is ultimately called down the line to initiate an ARP request in case we have not already resolved the ARP request or we are already in the process of probing (check flags in *neigh_event_send()*). *__neigh_event_send()* checks the flag and if it finds that the neigh entry is neither STALE nor is it in the process of sending ARP request, it calls *neigh→ops→solicit*(= *arp_solicit()*) to initiate arp request. *arp_solicit()* internally calls *arp_send()* that build ARP header and broadcasts the request. It also starts timer, *neigh_timer_handler()*, for the neighbor entry. This timer will manage IP datagrams that are queued up in the *neigh→arp_queue* queue waiting for ARP reply. Timer retransmits ARP request and set's timer once again to probe ARP request once again.

In the case where we have already sent out an ARP request, the IP datagram is queued in the *neigh→arp_queue* queue and return.

We receive ARP replies in the protocol handler *arp_rcv()*. The ARP packet is processed in *arp_process()*. If the reply is valid, *neigh_update()* is called that will ultimately send out all the IP datagrams that are queued in the ARP queue for the neighbour, *neigh→arp_queue*, using *skb→dst→neighbor→output*(= *neigh_resolve_output()*) callback routine.

Let's return to *neigh_resolve_output()*. Once we have the hardware address updated in the neighbor and our hardware cache (*dst→hh*) for the route is not updated, we do that by calling *neigh_hh_init()*. We build a link layer header for the IP datagram by calling the hardware-specific routine *dev→hard_header*. Finally, send the packet to the packet scheduler *neigh→ops→queue_xmit* (= *dev_queue_xmit()*) for transmission.

Once the hardware cache for the route in initialized, the next packet for the route can be sent out to the packet scheduler directly in *ip_finish_output2()* by directly calling dst→hh→output (= *dev_queue_xmit()*) for transmission.

Packet Scheduler and Hard Transmission. *dev_queue_xmit()* is a routine that checks if the packet has fragmented data and the device doesn't understand scatter–gather; in this case it tries to linearize the packet data by calling *skb_linearize()*. Also it checks if the IP checksum is not yet done; if the device is not capable of doing that, it does the IP checksum. Finally it queues the packet on the device queue (*dev→qdisc*) by calling *enqueue()* routine specific to the scheduler. Scheduler is defined by *Qdisc* object and its queue is pointed by *q* field. The generic enqueue routine for the device is *pfifo_enqueue()*.

Once we have a queued packet on the device queue, we need to wake up the device by calling *qdisc_run()*. In case device is already running, we need not worry and just return because somebody is already processing packet's from the device queue. Else, we need to process packets from the device queue by calling *qdisc_restart()*. This routine will start dequeuing packets on the device queue by calling the dequeue callback routine specific to the device discipline. The default dequeue routine for the device is *pfifo_dequeue()*.

pfifo_dequeue() dequeues one packet at a time from the device queue and calls the hard transmit routine for the device (*dev→hard_start_xmit*) if nobody has held the lock. In case somebody has held the lock and it is not us, we requeue the packet on the device queue by calling the *requeue()* callback routine from queue operations ($q{\to}ops$) and finally call *netif_schedule()* to schedule the device for transmission.

NET softIRQ. *netif_schedule()* schedules the device on the CPU output queue, *softnet_data[cpu].output_queue*, and raises the transmit soft IRQ(*NET_TX_SOFTIRQ*) by calling *cpu_raise_softirq()*. Later on when the Tx softIRQ is processed, the same dequeue routine for the device is called that will start processing packets queued on the device queue for final transmission.

Figure 6.2 shows link between the sock, *sk_buff*, *dst_entry*, *net_device*, neighbour, Qdisc and queue once it is ready for transmission.

6.2 ROUTED PACKET READY FOR TRANSMISSION

Figure 6.2 illustrates linking of kernel data-structures that links sk_buff, with route, outgoing device, CPU queue, arp table, queuing descipline queue etc.

6.3 KERNEL FLOW FOR A PACKET MOVING DOWN THE STACK

Figures 6.3(a) through 6.3(c) show flow of control to send TCP data down the stack. It shows major routines called to process data-through different layers unless transmitted. It also shows locations of queue moving down the stack where packets can be queued before transmission this queue is discussed in section 6.1.2.

6.4 PACKET TRAVERSING UP THE TCP/IP STACK
(see Figs. 6.4a–6.4b)

We start with the explanation of the reception process first. We have a flow diagram that indicates queuing of sk_buff at various stages when it is traversing up the stack from reception to the final socket's receive buffer. We divide the entire discussion into various stages explaining each step such as packet reception, soft IRQ processing, IP reception, firewall check, routing entry initialization, forwarding processing, local delivery, TCP entry point, backlog queue, prequeue, out-of-order-queue, socket receive queue, and so on. Data flow for the packet traversing up the stack is shown in Fig. 6.4(a) through 6.4(b).

Packet Reception and DMA. When a packet is completely DMAed in the ring buffer, receive interrupt is generated to remove the packet from the DMA ring buffer. The interrupt handler removes the packet from the DMA ring buffer and, after doing some sanity checks on the packet, queues it on per CPU receive *queue*. Once the packet is queued, it raises the Rx soft IRQ.

Rx SOFT IRQ. On return from the interrupt, we check if there is any soft IRQ to be processed. Since we just raised the Rx soft IRQ, it will be processed now. In Soft IRQ, Packet is completely processed through L3, L4 layer and packet is delivered to the Socket layer. The action is to remove the packet from CPU's input queue and find the next protocol layer (from the link layer header) to which the packet should be given for processing. Here the protocol switcher does the job of finding

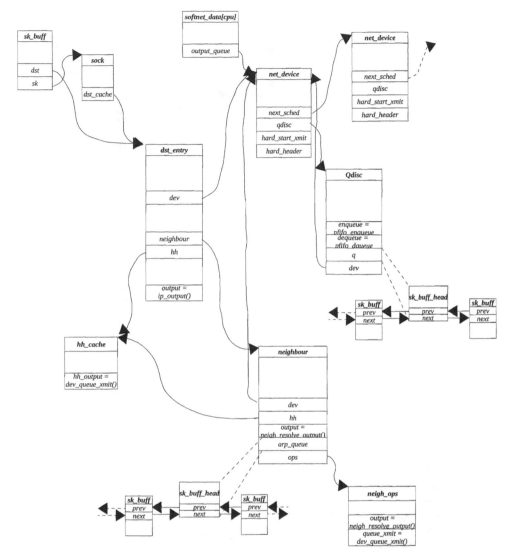

Figure 6.2. Linking of route-specific data structures when the packet is finally routed and ready for transmission.

the correct protocol layer. We will narrow down the discussion to TCP-IP protocols. The IP receive routine is called to process the packet.

Prerouting Netfilter Hook. Just at the entry, the IP enforces the netfilter hook before the route is finalized for the packet. The prerouting hook takes care of NAT/ IP Masquerading issues, Ipsec, and so on. Netfilter framework provides extended functionality to the TCP/IP stack. Once we pass through the filter, we need to find the route for the packet.

IP Layer. We try to determine the route for the packet. The packet may be destined for some other host in which it needs to be forwarded. In the case where the packet needs to be delivered, we need to find the next protocol layer to which the packet needs to be delivered. In the case of forwarding, we need to decrement the hop count for the packet; and if the hop count becomes zero, the packet

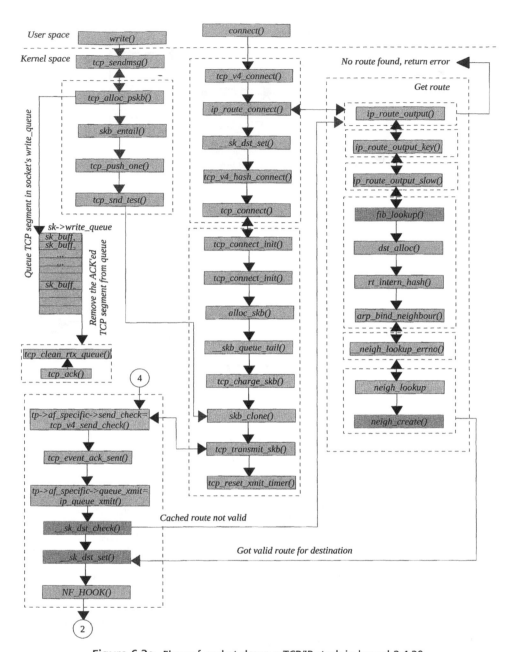

Figure 6.3a. Flow of packet down a TCP/IP stack in kernel 2.4.20.

needs to be dropped. In the case the link that the forwarded packet needs to take is the Ethernet and the destination is not directly connected to the link, the link layer address needs to be changed to that of the next hop.

Local Input Netfilter Hook. In the case where the packet needs to be delivered locally, we first need to pass the packet through the netfilter hook for the incoming packet. We need to check if the packet is acceptable or any firewall policy would reject the packet.

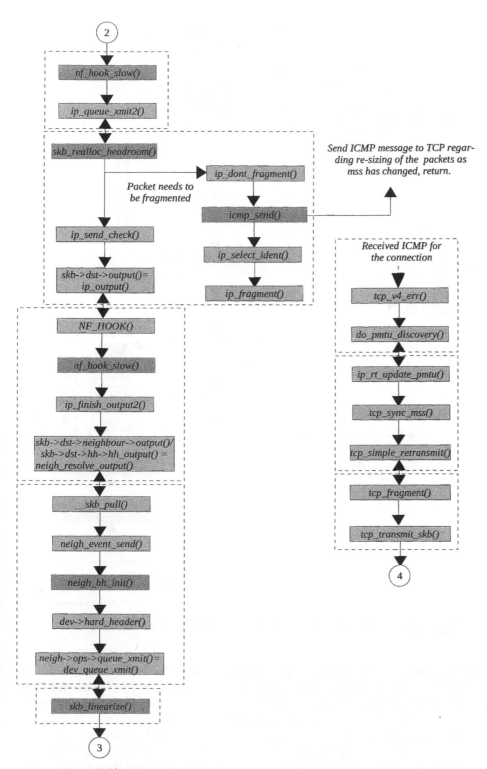

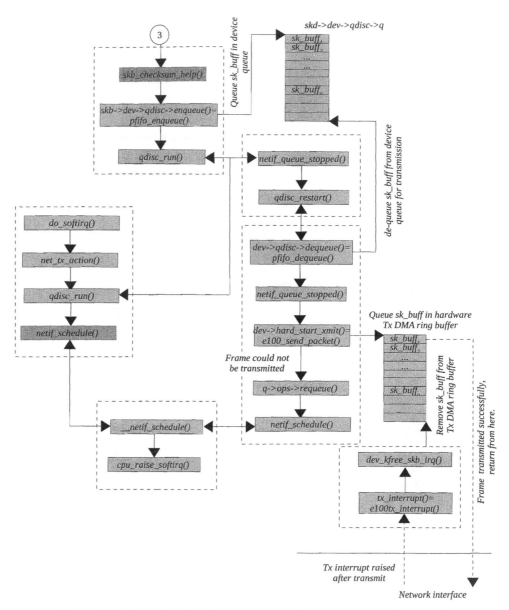

Figure 6.3c. Flow of packet down a TCP/IP stack in kernel 2.4.20 (*continued*).

TCP Layer. Once the packet is accepted, we need to check which protocol layer the packet belongs to. Protocol switcher once again does the job for us and finds out appropriate protocol specific handler. We call the protocol handler routine to process the packet. For the TCP, we check if this is a new connection request for any of the listening sockets or packet for already established connections. We have different hash tables for listening sockets and established connections. Once we have found the socket for the packet, we need to take appropriate action. In case this is a new connection request, we need to create a new request and send out SYN-ACK and wait for the final ACK. In the case of an established connection, we can either queue the packet on the backlog queue or just process it depending on whether the socket is being used by somebody or not. If we are queuing the packet in the backlog queue, the packets will be processed once the socket is released by the user.

In TCP processing, if we have TCP data in the new packet, either (a) we can directly copy it to the user buffer or (b) the data segment is queued in the socket's receive queue. TCP options are processed, and finally any pending outstanding data are sent along with the ACK for the new data or ACK may be delayed depending on conditions. If we receive out-of sequence data, ACK with SACK is sent out immediately.

Data that are queued in the receive buffer is eaten up by the application when it issues *recv* over the connected socket. Once the application has read data, it sends ACK in the case where ACK is pending or when the window is opened because space is generated in the receive buffer. Urgent byte is an exception and can be received as out-of-band data or can be read inline.

6.4.1 Path of Packet Traversal from Device (Reception) to Socket Layer

Figure 6.4(a) & 6.4(b) describes data flow diagram for processing data up the stack. It shows the processing of packet right from data reception stage at device layer through different protocol layers until it reaches the socket layer.

6.4.2 Kernel Path for TCP Packet Traversing Up the Stack

In this section we will see how the packet is handled inside the kernel while traversing up the stack. We will see entry points into a different kernel framework that implements the stack. Then we will have entry points into different protocol layers using a protocol switcher. There will be a short description for each entry point regarding its functionality. Flow of packet up the stack in kernel 2.4.20 is shown in Figs. 6.5(a–d).

Packet Reception. Receive interrupt for the NIC is generated once the packet is completely received through the DMA channel into the memory. Interrupt handling is a controller-specific process, but the common part in the reception of the packet is to pull out the packet from the DMA ring buffer. After doing some sanity check on the hardware header, place the packet on CPU's input queue, *softnet_ data[this_cpu]→input_pkt*_queue. This is per CPU queue designed to achieve better scalability on SMP architectures. We don't process the packet in the interrupt routine; otherwise the interrupt will be blocked for a long time. Instead we raise net Rx softIRQ, which will process the packet later. This is done by calling *netif_rx()*.

SoftIRQ. SoftIRQ is processed in various places:

1. Just after we returned from the interrupt in interrupt context.
2. SoftIRQ daemon running per CPU.
3. Whenever softIRQ on the CPU is enabled.

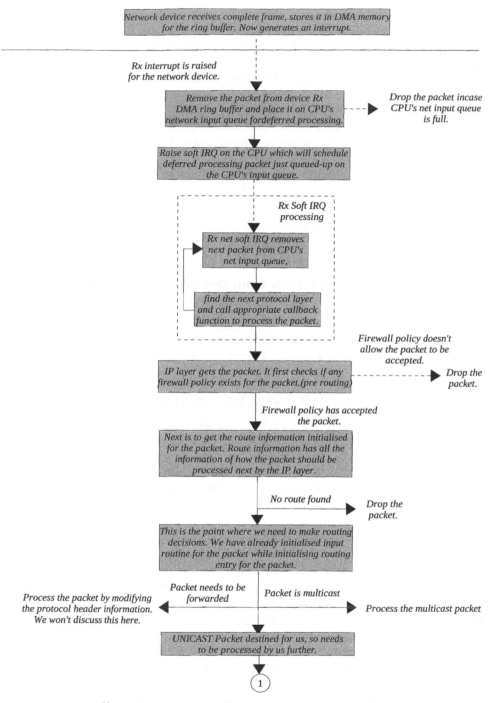

Figure 6.4a. Traversal of a packet up the TCP/IP stack.

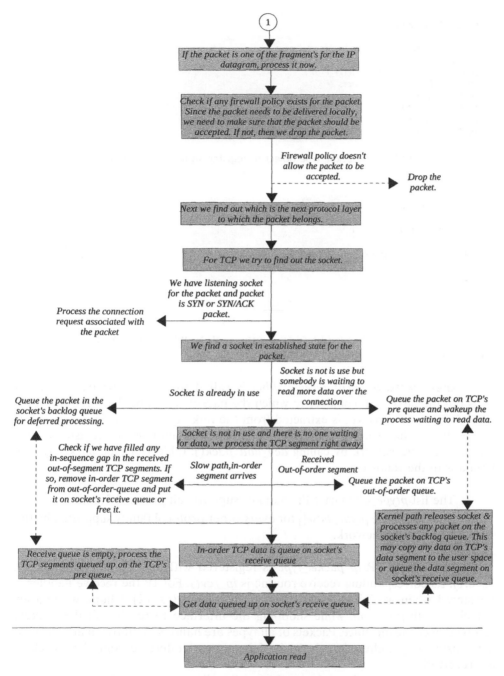

Figure 6.4b. Traversal of a packet up the TCP/IP stack (*continued*).

In the case where net Rx softIRQ is enabled, *net_rx_action()* is called just after we return from the interrupt. This will start processing the packet received in the CPU's input queue. The packet is processed completely in softIRQ. Even though we are in interrupt context, the interrupt for the controller is enabled so that NIC can continue to receive packets and queue them on CPU's input queue. Processing of

```
net/ipv4/ip_output.c

1001 static struct packet_type ip_packet_type =
1002 {
1003        __constant_htons(ETH_P_IP),
1004        NULL,  /* All devices */
1005        ip_rcv,
1006        (void*)1,
1007        NULL,
1008 };
```

cs 6.1. *ip_packet_type* object to register an IP packet handler.

```
net/ipv4/ip_output.c

1014 void __init ip_init(void)
1015 {
1016        dev_add_pack(&ip_packet_type);
          ....
1024 }
```

cs 6.2. *ip_init()*.

the packet starts with the protocol switching section where we find out which protocol will handle the packet.

Packet Switcher. *netif_receive_skb()* is called to process the packet, which finds out the next protocol layer to which the packet would be delivered. The protocol family of the packet is extracted from the link layer header. In our case, this will be IP. All the protocols supported by Ethernet technology are registered with the Ethernet framework by calling *dev_add_pack*(). Object of type *packet_type* is linked with the following:

1. The list *ptype_all* in case the handler supports all protocol families.
2. The hash table *ptype_base*[] for every other protocol family supported by the Ethernet framework.

In the case of IP, *ip_packet_type* is registered with the Ethernet framework (cs 6.1). Its corresponding receive routine is *ip_rcv()*. For IP, the receive handler is registered when we initialize the protocol in *ip_init()*(cs 6.2). I hope we register ourselves with *ptype_all*, while snooping the interface to receive all the packets received over the interface. Packets of all types are handled by those handlers listed in the list *ptype_all* filtered on the basis of the network interface from where packets are received.

Once we have sent the packet to the handlers listed in *ptype_all* in *netif_receive_ skb()*, we check the actual protocol that needs to be delivered to the packet by traversing through the hash table *ptype_base*. This is a table of length 15. The key to match the entry is the packet protocol as mentioned in the Ethernet header. The packet is fed to the IP handler callback routine *ip_rcv()* for further processing.

IP Layer. *ip_rcv()* is an entry point for IP packets processing. It first checks if the packet we have is destined for some other host (*PACKET_OTHERHOST*).

This may happen in the case where the interface is in the promisc mode. In such cases we just drop the packet.

We check the sanity of the IP header and checksum the packet by calling *ip_fast_csum()*. Before even finding the route for the packet, we pass it through netfilter hook *NF_IP_PRE_ROUTING*. Here the packet may be de-masqueraded or decrypted(IPSec) or NAT may be applied to the packet. The next step is to find the route for the packet. We call ip_route_input(), where *kb*→dst is initialized. This routine checks kernel routing table *rt_hash_table*. If there is no entry for the packet, FIB is consulted and the route is built. If the packet needs to be forwarded, the input routine is *ip_forward()*; otherwise it will be *ip_local_deliver()*.

ip_forward() decrements ttl in the IP header by 1 and checks if the packet needs to be discarded (in case ttl becomes zero). If the next hop is the gateway that is connected through the Ethernet link, the destination hardware address is changed. The packet is then scanned through the netfilter hook *NF_IP_FORWARD*. *ip_send()* is called to check if the packet needs to be fragmented. If so, it fragments the packet by calling *ip_fragment()*, which sends out each fragment through the packet output path *ip_finish_output()*. If no fragmentation is required, *ip_send()* sends the packet through the output path *ip_finish_output()*.

In the case where the packet needs to be delivered locally, *ip_local_deliver()* is called for further processing. This routine first checks if this is a fragment of IP datagram from the IP header. If so, it calls *ip_defrag()* to process the fragment.

IP Fragment Handling. This routine calls *ip_find()* to check if we have already received other fragments for the packet. The kernel maintains the hash table to manage fragmented IP datagrams *ipq_hash*. Fragments are hashed in the table based on destination, source IP address, packet ID, and protocol. *struct ipq* manages fragmented IP datagrams. All the received fragments of IP datagram are linked in the *fragments* field of this object. If we find an entry for the received fragment in the *ipq_hash* table and this is the last fragment for the IP datagram, *ip_frag_reasm()* is called to reassemble all the received fragments. Otherwise just queue the new fragment by calling *ip_frag_queue()*. The fragmentation handling unit installs a timer for each IP fragment that will expire after a certain time, if the complete packet is not assembled. *ip_expire()* is the timer callback routine initialized when the first fragment of the IP datagram is received and the new *ipq* object is created in *ip_frag_create()*. This routine sends out an ICMP message to the originator of the message that fragmentation–reassembly has timed out.

Coming back to *ip_local_deliver()*, if we obtained a full datagram or the fragment receive completed the IP datagram, we need to screen the packet through the netfilter hook NF_IP_LOCAL_IN. Here we check if there is any firewall rule to reject the received datagram. If the policy accepts the datagram, *ip_local_deliver_finish()* is called to find the next protocol to which the packet should be delivered.

INET Protocol Packet Switcher. We have come here from the IP layer. So, the next protocol switcher scans the datagram's protocol identifier through all L4 layer protocols that are supported by IP. The IP header for the received packet contains a protocol identifier field that corresponds to the next protocol layer to which the packet belongs (*skb*→*nh.iph*→*protocol*). There is a list of protocols that are supported by the IP and that are registered with the system. *inet_add_protocol()*

```
net/ipv4/af_inet.c

1102 static int __init inet_init(void)
1103 {
         ....
1127     for (p = inet_protocol_base; p != NULL;) {
1128         struct inet_protocol *tmp = (struct inet_protocol *) p->next;
1129         inet_add_protocol(p);
             ....
1131         p = tmp;
1132     }
         ....
1193     return 0;
1194 }
```

cs 6.3. inet_init().

```
net/ipv4/protocol.c

67 static struct inet_protocol tcp_protocol = {
68     handler:      tcp_v4_rcv,
69     err_handler:  tcp_v4_err,
70     next:         IPPROTO_PREVIOUS,
71     protocol:     IPPROTO_TCP,
72     name:         "TCP"
73 };
```

cs 6.4. Object *inet_protocol* to register the TCP packet handler.

is called to register INET protocol handlers with the IP. This routine adds the object of type *inet_protocol* to the global protocol table *inet_protos*. Protocol field in the *inet_protocol* field is matched against the protocol field in the IP header to find protocol handler for INET protocols.

For INET-TCP, UDP, and ICMP, protocol handlers are registered in *inet_init()*(cs 6.3). There are other INET protocols registered which we won't discuss here. For TCP, the protocol handler is *tcp_protocol*, which has a pointer to receive handler, *tcp_v4_rcv()* (see cs 6.4).

For TCP we find the receive handler routine as tcp_v4_rcv(), which is called from *ip_local_deliver_finish()*. Raw sockets are registered with the *raw_v4_htable* table. If we find any raw socket registered for the INET protocol to which the packet belongs, we pass a copy of the packet to raw socket by calling *raw_v4_input()*. Libpcap opens a raw socket to capture IP packets.

TCP Layer. *tcp_v4_rcv()* is the entry point for the TCP layer. First some of the fields from the TCP header are copied to the socket buffer (sk_buff), and the TCP checksum is done on the TCP header. We try to find out the socket to which the packet belongs by calling *__tcp_v4_lookup()*. This routine tries to find out if the packet belongs to an established connection where we try to match the source/destination IP and the source/destination port of the packet with the sockets in the established state. Established state sockets are maintained in the hash table *tcp_ehash*. *__tcp_v4_lookup_established()* searches for sockets in the established and time-wait state. If we don't find any socket in the established state here, we might have gotten a new connection request for any listening socket. For this we search for a listening socket with port numbers the same as the destination port in the listening socket's hash table *tcp_listening_hash*. The search for listening socket's is carried out in *tcp_v4_lookup_listener()*.

If we find the listening socket for the new request, we create a new open request, send SYN-ACK, and wait for final ACK by calling *tcp_v4_hnd_req()* from *tcp_v4_do_rcv()*. If the socket for the packet is in an established state, we either queue the packet in a backlog queue by calling *sk_add_backlog()* (if the socket is already in use by someone) or process the packet by calling *tcp_rcv_established()* from *tcp_v4_do_rcv()*.

tcp_rcv_established() processes the TCP segment. If we received in-sequence data in the packet, it is queued in the socket's receive buffer (*sk→receive_queue*); or if the application is waiting for data, it is directly copied to user buffer. If we receive out-of-order data, it is queued in *tp→out_of_order_queue*. If there are any data pending to be transmitted, we send them here along with the ACK for the new data.

Socket Layer. If we queued data in the receive queue, it is read by application when it issues *recv()*. Kernel routine to read data from TCP socket is *tcp_recvmsg()*. Data are read from the receive queue, and prequeue and socket buffers are freed. If we have an opened window, we send out an ACK immediately in this routine.

6.5 KERNEL FLOW FOR PACKET MOVING UP THE STACK

Figures 6.5(a) through 6.5(d) show flow control that implements packet processing while traversal up the stack from device layer to the socket layer. It shows major routines that are queues, called to process packets up the stack. It also shows implemented at various points while traversing up the stack where packets can be queued before reaching socket layer or before being forwarded. This is discussed in Section 6.4.2.

6.6 SUMMARY

The packet flows up the stack in three stages to reach from device to socket queue:

1. Network controller Rx DMA ring
2. CPU input queue, *softnet_data[cpu_id]→input_pkt_queue*
3. Socket queue, *sk→rcv_queue*

Packet flows down the stack in three stages to reach from socket layer to device:

1. Socket send queue, *sk→write_queue*
2. Device queue, *dev→q*
3. Network controller DMA Tx ring buffer.

Linux implements per CPU softIRQ for transmission and reception of packets. Packets are received and queued on the CPU's input queue. Rx softIRQ, NET_RX_

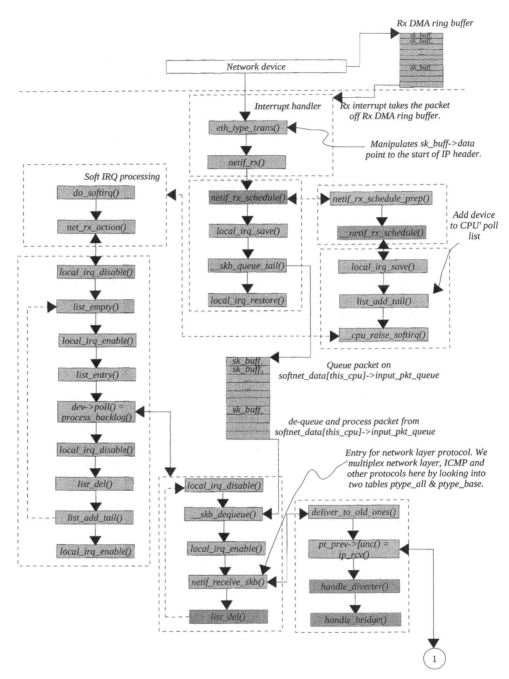

Figure 6.5a. Flow of a packet up a TCP/IP stack in kernel 2.4.20.

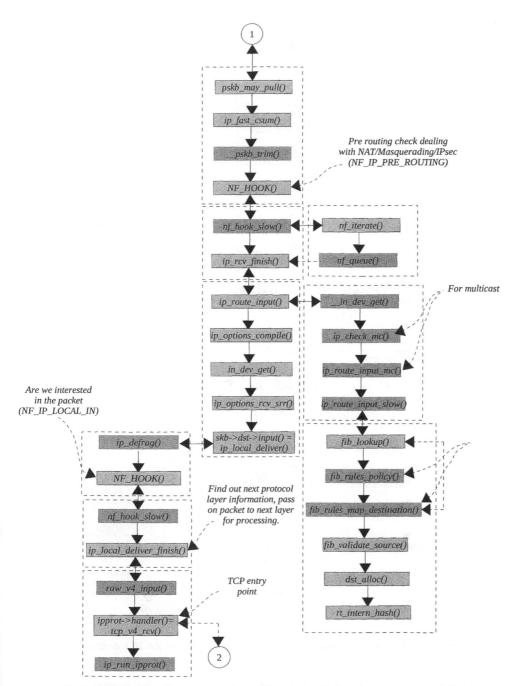

Figure 6.5b. Flow of a packet up a TCP/IP stack in kernel 2.4.20 (*continued*).

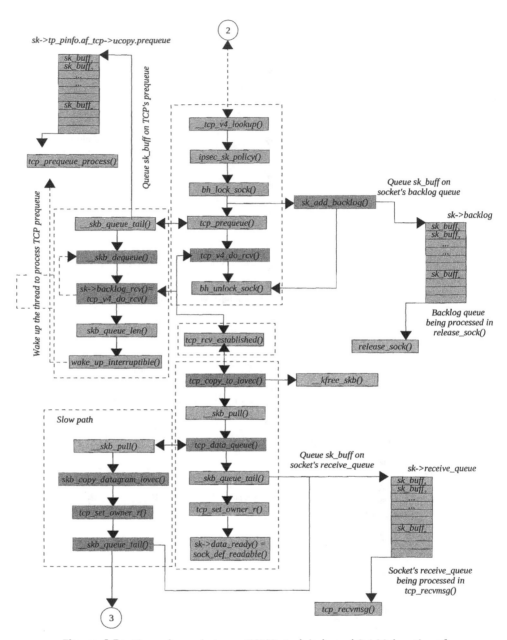

Figure 6.5c. Flow of a packet up a TCP/IP stack in kernel 2.4.20 (*continued*).

SOFTIRQ is raised on the CPU for further processing of the packet by a call to *netif_rx()*. On the SMP architecture, Rx softIRQs can be run parallelly on each CPU, thereby providing better scalability. On the transmission side, Tx soft IRQ, NET_TX_SOFTIRQ, is raised if we are not able to transmit the packet. Tx soft IRQ will be executed in the future and will start transmission of the packet queued on the device.

Received packets are processed completely in Rx softIRQ until it reaches the socket layer.

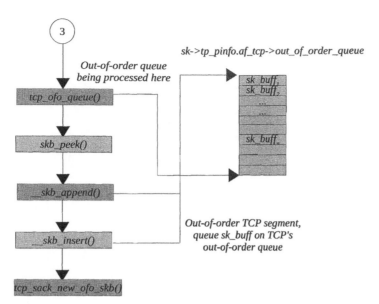

Figure 6.5d. Flow of a packet up a TCP/IP stack in kernel 2.4.20 (*continued*).

Callback routine to Rx softIRQ is *net_rx_action()*, whereas for Tx softIRQ it is *net_tx_action()*.

When the packet is going down the stack, it is the job of the routing engine to associate the outgoing device with the packet, which is done by calling *ip_route_output()*. Similarly, when the packet is received, routing is taken by calling *ip_route_input()*.

Ethernet protocol switching is done in *netif_receive_skb()*, where we get the handler for next protocol layer. INET protocol layer switching is done in *ip_local_deliver_finish()*.

The entry point for the TCP protocol is *tcp_v4_rcv()*. The socket for the TCP packet is identified in *__tcp_v4_lookup()*. *tcp_rcv_established()* is the entry point for established sockets.

TCP packets are processed with the socket lock (*sk→lock.slock*) held.

Extension to the IP stack is provided with the help of netfilter hooks. NF_IP_PRE_ROUTING and NF_IP_POST_ROUTING are two hooks that can be used by Ipsec, IP masquerading, and NAT modules.

neighbour framework implements ARP. The object of type *neighbour* is associated with the route and the *net_device* object. There is one *net_device* object per physical network interface.

dev_queue_xmit() routine is called to queue the packet on the device queue when the packet leaves the IP layer.

7

TCP SEND

TCP is a reliable protocol and applies flow control on the data being transmitted. It treats data as a stream of bytes and associates each byte with a sequence number. It requires each byte to be acknowledged. For flow control, TCP applies a sliding window protocol and congestion control algorithms. TCP has to consult the link layer and restricts the maximum size of the frame it can transmit from the interface. This restricts the maximum size of the segment that TCP can produce. TCP needs to discover the minimum transmission unit across the path that the packet takes to reach the destination. This is because If some link at an intermediate router offers a lower MTU than our interface MTU, the packet will be fragmented at the router, thereby hindering TCP and network performance.

Application needs not know anything about how data are sent to the peer. It just writes data in chunks over the TCP socket, and the rest is taken care of by the TCP segmentation unit. When data reach the TCP layer, they then break a big chunk into small units each of 1 mss size and queue them on the socket's send queue. Then we apply certain algorithms like Nagle's algorithm, sliding window protocol, and congestion window to check if the new segment can be transmitted.

We will first explain how TCP segmentation unit with and without scatter–gather DMA support. Then we learn about the policies to trigger transmission of segments. We will see how Nagle's algorithm is implemented to avoid transmission of small segments. There are different congestion control algorithms implemented in the core of TCP state machine that need to be taken into consideration here before we can transmit new buffer. Also, we will learn how a sliding window protocol is implemented. The process involved is explained in Figs. 7.5 (a) and 7.5 (b).

TCP/IP Architecture, Design, and Implementation in Linux. By S. Seth and M. A. Venkatesulu
Copyright © 2008 the IEEE Computer Society

7.1 TCP SEGMENTATION UNIT FOR SENDING DATA

In this section we will see how the big chunk of data to be sent over the socket requested by the user is broken into small segments by the segmentation unit. We will also see how the segmentation unit works when DMA supports the scatter–gather technique. See Figs. 7.6 (a) and 7.6 (b) for the flow control diagram.

7.1.1 Functioning of Segmentation Unit without Scatter–Gather Support (see cs-7.1 and cs-7.4)

When an application wants to write data over a TCP socket, finally *tcp_sendmsg()* is called inside the kernel. The segmentation unit works on the basic principle of breaking a big chunk of data into small chunks of 1 mss each. So, the first thing we do is get the cached in mss by calling *tcp_current_mss()* at line 1035. Next we get the number of the user buffers and the pointer to the user buffer at line 1038 and 1039, respectively. There are essentially two loops used to implement segmentation. The outer loop accesses the next user buffer in each iteration, and the inner loop generates segments from each user buffer. In the outer loop we access a pointer to the user buffer to be segmented and the length of the buffer at lines 1047 and 1048, respectively. We iterate in the inner loop until the entire buffer is used by the segmentation unit to generate segments.

Let's look at the implementation of the segmentation unit—that is, inner loop 1052–1184. Since we want to generate segments of 1 mss size, we first check if there is any partial segment in the transmit queue (*sk→write_queue*). By partial segment, I mean that the size of the segment is less than 1 mss. With this logic, a new segment is generated only after the existing segment is fully loaded. So, we always check the last segment in the queue to be partial at any point of time. The last segment for the socket can be accessed from the *prev* field of the queue head since it is a doubly linked link list, line 1055. We first check if there is any segment at the head of the transmit queue pointed to by *tp→send_head*. If this value is NULL, there is no point checking for partial segment because we know that the *prev* accessed at line 1055 is a back pointer to the transmit queue itself.

If the transmit queue is not empty, we check if the last segment in the queue is partial (length of the segment is less than the current mss) at line 1058. If we don't find a partial segment in the transmit queue, we need to create a new segment for the user data.

Before allocating memory for a new segment, we first check if the socket's quota for the send buffer has exceeded its limit by calling *tcp_memory_free()*. If we have enough memory, *tcp_alloc_pskb()* is called to allocate a new buffer for the TCP segment. If our hardware is aware of the scatter–gather technique, we allocate a buffer that fits into a single page. Otherwise, we get a buffer of length 1 mss (buffer that can hold 1 mss of TCP payload). In the case of a memory shortage, we need to wait for memory to be available, line 1069. Otherwise we queue the new segment at the tail of the transmit queue by calling *skb_entail()* (see Section 7.2.15 for more detail). Actually, Linux implements a transmit and retransmit queue as a single queue (*tp→write_queue*). *tp→send_head* marks the start of the transmit queue.

From line 1076, the code is common for both cases:

```
net/ipv4/tcp.c

1009 int tcp_sendmsg(struct sock *sk, struct msghdr *msg, int size)
1010 {
1011     struct iovec *iov;
1012     struct tcp_opt *tp;
        ....
1019     tp = &(sk->tp_pinfo.af_tcp);
1020
1021     lock_sock(sk);
        ....
1035     mss_now = tcp_current_mss(sk);
        ....
1038     iovlen = msg->msg_iovlen;
1039     iov = msg->msg_iov;

1046     while (--iovlen >= 0) {
1047         int seglen=iov->iov_len;
1048         unsigned char * from=iov->iov_base;
1049
1050         iov++;
1051
1052         while (seglen > 0) {
            ....
1055             skb = sk->write_queue.prev;
1056
1057             if (tp->send_head == NULL ||
1058                 (copy = mss_now - skb->len) <= 0) {
1059
1060 new_segment:
                    ....
1064                 if (!tcp_memory_free(sk))
1065                     goto wait_for_sndbuf;
1066
1067                 skb = tcp_alloc_pskb(sk, select_size(sk, tp), 0, sk->allocation);
1068                 if (skb == NULL)
1069                     goto wait_for_memory;
1070
1071                 skb_entail(sk, tp, skb);
1072                 copy = mss_now;
1073             }
            ....
1076             if (copy > seglen)
1077                 copy = seglen;
            ....
1080             if (skb_tailroom(skb) > 0) {
1081                 /* We have some space in skb head. Superb! */
1082                 if (copy > skb_tailroom(skb))
1083                     copy = skb_tailroom(skb);
1084                 if ((err = skb_add_data(skb, from, copy)) != 0)
1085                     goto do_fault;
1086             } else {
1087                 int merge = 0;
1088                 int i = skb_shinfo(skb)->nr_frags;
1089                 struct page *page = TCP_PAGE(sk);
1090                 int off = TCP_OFF(sk);
1091
1092                 if (can_coalesce(skb, i, page, off) && off != PAGE_SIZE) {
1093                     /* We can extend the last page fragment. */
1094                     merge = 1;
1095                 } else if (i == MAX_SKB_FRAGS ||
1096                     (i == 0 && !(sk->route_caps&NETIF_F_SG))) {
                    ....
1101                     tcp_mark_push(tp, skb);
1102                     goto new_segment;
1103                 } else if (page) {
                    ....
1108                     if (off == PAGE_SIZE) {
1109                         put_page(page);
1110                         TCP_PAGE(sk) = page = NULL;
1111                     }
1112                 }
1113
```

cs 7.1. *tcp_sendmsg()*.

- We created a new segment.
- We found partial segment in the transmit queue.

If the space found to exist in the selected segment is smaller than the data to be copied, we make an adjustment at line 1077. Next we check if any is space available in the linear area of the selected buffer. Now why do we make this additional check here when we know that for a new segment will have tail room? We do this test only for the case where we have identified a partial segment in the transmit queue. Even if it is a partial segment, we need this check because we might have paged data area for the partial segment. If our interface implements the scatter–gather technique, the segment extends to the paged data area when the linear data area is full (linear data area is limited to a single page for such cases). If there is room in the linear data area and the data to be copied are more than the space available, we make an adjustment at line 1083. Now we are ready to copy data to the identified segment by calling *skb_add_data()* at line 1084. We need to update TCP with the new data added to the send queue. We update write sequence (*tp→write_seq*) with the amount of data added to the write queue at line 1156. We also need to update the end sequence number of the segment to complete the sequence space covered by the segment at line 1157. Shift the user buffer pointer to point to the location where we need to start copying next at line 1159 and also update number of bytes copied at line 1160. If we have copied the entire data from the user buffer at line 1161, we try to send out the segment queued in the transmit queue by calling *tcp_push()* at line 1189. We release the socket user status and return the number of bytes.

In case we have not copied the entire user buffer to the socket buffer, we check if the segment we are working on is still partial or we are sending an OOB message at line 1164. If any one of the cases is TRUE, we would like to continue to iterate once again. In case the segment is still partial, we need to make it full. This will be the situation when we are filling paged data area because we are allocating 1 page per iteration. In the case of the OOB flag set, we will get out of the loop in the next iteration and get into *tcp_push()* where urgent data will be processed.

In case we have a full-sized segment at line 1164, we check if we need to force a push flag on the last segment in the transmit queue by calling *forced_push()* at line 1167. In case we need to tell the receiver to push data to the application at the earliest, mark the push sequence number as a write sequence number by calling *tcp_mark_push()* and call *__tcp_push_pending_frames()* at line 1169 to start transmitting pending segments in case we satisfy Nagle's algorithm, congestion window and send window. If we can't force the data to be pushed and there is only one segment in the transmit queue (line 1170), *tcp_push_one()* is called to push the segment from the transmit queue. We continue with segmentation for the rest of the user data by iterating in the inner loop.

7.1.2 Segmentation without Scatter–Gather Support

The application has written X bytes of data: $1\,mss = X + Y$ bytes. These segments are not yet transmitted because of any of the reasons which failed the send test. We generate two sk-buff's, one buffer is full and the other one is partially filled (see Fig. 7.1).

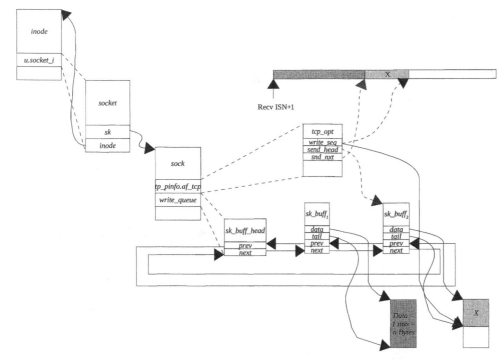

Figure 7.1. X bytes of data copied to socket buffer linear area.

7.1.3   1 mss of Data Written over the Socket

The application has written 1 mss of data. First the partial segment is filled to make it full-sized. Next we allocate one more segment to copy the rest of the X bytes. The send head is still pointing at segment 2, which is yet to be transmitted. (See Fig. 7.2.)

7.2   SEGMENTATION WITH SCATTER–GATHER TECHNIQUE
(E.g., Fig. 7.4, see cs 7.1 and cs 7.4 unless mentioned)

Until now we have seen how segmentation works for buffers with linear data area only where the interface is not scatter–gather capable. Now we extend our discussion to paged data area in segmentation. Our discussion starts from line 1086, where we come because there is no space left in the linear data area of the buffer and still the segment is seen as partial. This may happen because of two reasons:

- Our hardware is scatter–gather capable.
- Hardware doesn't implement the scatter–gather technique, which means that we can have data only in a linear-data area. In such cases, we allocate a big chunk of linear-data area of 1 mss. The only possibility to reach here is change of mss. Mss for the segment has gone up since a partial segment was created. Only in this case would we have allocated 1 mss of memory for a linear-data area where mss has now increased and the segmentation unit does not reallocate linear data area.

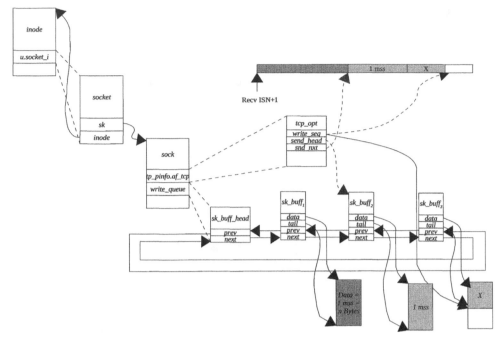

Figure 7.2. 1 mss of data copied to socket buffer linear area.

```
net/ipv4/tcp.c

954 #define TCP_PAGE(sk)   (sk->tp_pinfo.af_tcp.sndmsg_page)
955 #define TCP_OFF(sk)    (sk->tp_pinfo.af_tcp.sndmsg_off)
```

cs 7.2. Macros used for paged data area management.

So, we get ready for processing page data area. We get number of fragments already allocated for the buffer from *skb_shinfo(skb)→nr_frags* at line 1088. Current page that is partially filled can be accessed macro TCP_PAGE at line 1089 and offset within the page can be accessed from macro TCP_OFF at line 1090.

TCP_PAGE and TCP_OFF accesses *sndmsg_page and sndmsg_off* field of object *tcp_opt* for the connection (cs 7.2). Later in the discussion we will see when are these fields are initialized. Next, we check if data can be added to the existing partially filled page for the paged data area by calling *can_coalesce()*. If we can coalesce and we still have space left in the last modified page, we set a mark that new data should be merged to the last modified page. If we can't merge data with the existing page, we check if we can allocate another page. If the number of pages allocated has exceeded the limit for the buffer (= *MAX_SKB_FRAGS*) or we are allocating the first page and our hardware is not capable of scatter–gather, we need to allocate a new TCP segment CSK-buff. When our hardware is scatter–gather capable but current mss is so large that it can't be accommodated in a single segment, this is a cause for a network performance issue because we are not able to send full-sized segment because of buffer design limitation. This probably happens because mss has increased since the buffer was allocated. During buffer allocation,

```
net/ipv4/tcp.c

761 static inline void
762 fill_page_desc(struct sk_buff *skb, int i, struct page *page, int off, int size)
763 {
764     skb_frag_t *frag = &skb_shinfo(skb)->frags[i];
765     frag->page = page;
766     frag->page_offset = off;
767     frag->size = size;
768     skb_shinfo(skb)->nr_frags = i+1;
769 }
```

cs 7.3. *fill_page_desc()*.

we check if our hardware is scatter–gather capable; if it is capable, we also check if a full-sized segment can be accommodated in a single buffer (check select_size(), Section 9.1.1.). If so, we go for paged data area. Otherwise, we allocate a big chunk of memory that can accommodate full-sized segment. The other condition at line 1096 checks if we are allocating a page for the first fragment of the paged data area; if our interface is non scatter–gather, we need to allocate a new segment. This condition also arises from the fact that mss has changed since the buffer was allocated.

If we are not allowed to merge or we do not need to create a new segment, we check if the page TCP_PAGE() points to a valid page at line 1103. We may have a valid page that is FULL, because of which we are here. So, we check if the page is FULL at line 1108. If so, we release the page and initialize TCP_PAGE to NULL at line 1110 because the page is already full and we can't modify it anymore. If we didn't find the page that can be modified, try to allocate a page by calling *tcp_alloc_page()* at line 1116. This looks like another performance hit where we need to allocate 1 page of memory for each PAGE_SIZE of user data, which is an expensive operation. If we fail to allocate a page, we wait for memory to be available. Otherwise, we are ready to copy data to the newly allocated page.

We are here either because we found a partial page in which case we merge data to the existing page or we have allocated a new page. We adjust the bytes to be copied to the space available in the page at line 1122. We copy data to the page by calling *tcp_copy_to_page()*. We also update buffer fields specific to length and account for memory used to copy user buffer to the segment.

After copying data to the page, we need to update fragment information. In the case where we have merged data to the existing page, the last fragment's size needs to be updated at line 1139. In the case where we have allocated a new page to copy data, a new descriptor needs to be initialized. *fill_page_desc()* is called to initialize the descriptor at line 1141. We access a fragment from the index passed to the routine at line 764 (cs 7.3). *page, page_offset*, and *size* fields are initialized. *page_offset* is set to 0 here as an offset for partial page is maintained by *TCP_OFF* macro. *size* is the number of bytes copied to the page. Finally, *nr_frags* is incremented by 1 at line 768 (cs 7.3) because a new fragment is active now.

We need to hold an additional reference on the page by calling *tcp_get()* at line 1143 as it is being referred by *TCP_PAGE* macro. In the case where TCP_PAGE is not yet initialized and we have not filled the entire page, TCP_PAGE is initialized to point to the partial page at line 1146. Finally, TCP_OFF is initialized to point to a location where we need to copy the next byte in the page at line 1150.

```
net/ipv4/tcp.c
tcp_sendmsg() contd....

1114                    if (!page) {
1115                        /* Allocate new cache page. */
1116                        if (!(page=tcp_alloc_page(sk)))
1117                            goto wait_for_memory;
1118                        off = 0;
1119                    }
1120
1121                    if (copy > PAGE_SIZE-off)
1122                        copy = PAGE_SIZE-off;
                           ....
1125                    err = tcp_copy_to_page(sk, from, skb, page, off, copy);
                           ....
1138                    if (merge) {
1139                        skb_shinfo(skb)->frags[i-1].size += copy;
1140                    } else {
1141                        fill_page_desc(skb, i, page, off, copy);
1142                        if (TCP_PAGE(sk)) {
1143                            get_page(page);
1144                        } else if (off + copy < PAGE_SIZE) {
1145                            get_page(page);
1146                            TCP_PAGE(sk) = page;
1147                        }
1148                    }
1149
1150                    TCP_OFF(sk) = off+copy;
1151                }
1152
1153                if (!copied)
1154                    TCP_SKB_CB(skb)->flags &= ~TCPCB_FLAG_PSH;
1155
1156                tp->write_seq += copy;
1157                TCP_SKB_CB(skb)->end_seq += copy;
1158
1159                from += copy;
1160                copied += copy;
1161                if ((seglen -= copy) == 0 && iovlen == 0)
1162                    goto out;
1163
1164                if (skb->len != mss_now || (flags&MSG_OOB))
1165                    continue;
1166
1167                if (forced_push(tp)) {
1168                    tcp_mark_push(tp, skb);
1169                    __tcp_push_pending_frames(sk, tp, mss_now, 1);
1170                } else if (skb == tp->send_head)
1171                    tcp_push_one(sk, mss_now);
1172                continue;
1173
1174 wait_for_sndbuf:
1175                set_bit(SOCK_NOSPACE, &sk->socket->flags);
1176 wait_for_memory:
1177                if (copied)
1178                    tcp_push(sk, tp, flags&~MSG_MORE, mss_now, 1);
1179
1180                if ((err = wait_for_tcp_memory(sk, &timeo)) != 0)
1181                    goto do_error;
1182
1183                mss_now = tcp_current_mss(sk);
1184            }
1185        }
1186
1187 out:
1188     if (copied)
1189         tcp_push(sk, tp, flags, mss_now, tp->nonagle);
1190     TCP_CHECK_TIMER(sk);
1191     release_sock(sk);
1192     return copied;
1193
1194 do_fault:
1195     if (skb->len == 0) {
1196         if (tp->send_head == skb)
1197             tp->send_head = NULL;
1198         __skb_unlink(skb, skb->list);
1199         tcp_free_skb(sk, skb);
1200     }
         ....
1208     release_sock(sk);
1209     return err;
1210 }
```

cs 7.4. tcp_sendmsg().

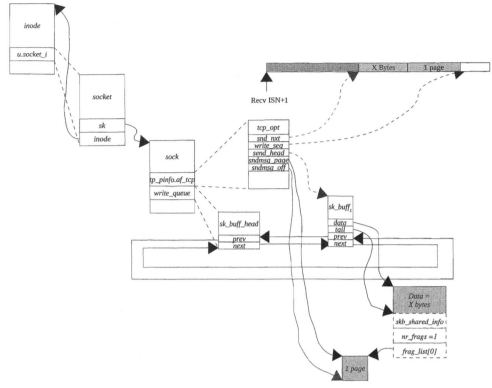

Figure 7.3. X bytes + (1 page) of data copied to a paged data area.

7.2.1   Segmentation with Scatter–Gather Support

Application has written X + 1 page bytes of data over the socket where mss = X + Y + (1 page) bytes (Fig. 7.3). Assume that the segment has not transmitted for some reason.

7.2.2   Application Writes Y Bytes over the Socket

Application has written Y bytes of data over the socket. Since the existing segment is partial, we allocate a new page for the next fragment in the paged data area to copy Y bytes (Fig. 7.4). Now we have a full-sized segment that is ready to be transmitted.

7.2.3   *can_coalesce()*

We have exceeded the number of fragments total allocated for a buffers' paged data area. We have a pointer to the buffer, a pointer to the page, and an offset passed as an argument to the routine. The caller wants to check if the page and offset as accessed from TCP_PAGE and TCP_OFF, respectively, are from the fragment last modified. We check the availability of space in the last modified fragment because we don't move to the next fragment until the current fragment is partially filled. The last modified fragment can be accessed from total the number of fragments allocated. At line 754 (cs 7.5), we access the last modified fragment. Next we compare the fragment page and offset with the page and offset passed as an argument.

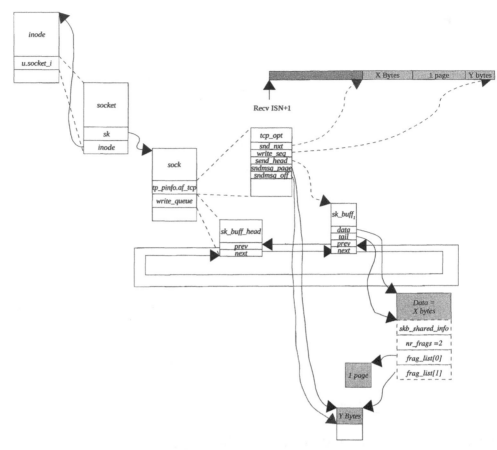

Figure 7.4. Data copied to a paged data area.

```
net/ipv4/tcp.c

750  static inline int
751  can_coalesce(struct sk_buff *skb, int i, struct page *page, int off)
752  {
753      if (i) {
754          skb_frag_t *frag = &skb_shinfo(skb)->frags[i-1];
755          return page == frag->page &&
756              off == frag->page_offset+frag->size;
757      }
758      return 0;
759  }
```

cs 7.5. can_coalesce().

7.2.4 tcp_copy_to_page()

The routine is called to copy data from a user buffer from a specified offset within the page and account for the memory usage by the socket buffer. We add the amount of coped bytes to total and paged area length of the buffer at line 969–970 (cs 7.6). So also we account for the overall memory usage by the buffer

```
net/ipv4/tcp.c

 957 static inline int
 958 tcp_copy_to_page(struct sock *sk, char *from, struct sk_buff *skb,
 959           struct page *page, int off, int copy)
 960 {
 961     int err = 0;
 962     unsigned int csum;
 963
 964     csum = csum_and_copy_from_user(from, page_address(page)+off,
 965                     copy, 0, &err);
 966     if (!err) {
 967         if (skb->ip_summed == CHECKSUM_NONE)
 968             skb->csum = csum_block_add(skb->csum, csum, skb->len);
 969         skb->len += copy;
 970         skb->data_len += copy;
 971         skb->truesize += copy;
 972         sk->wmem_queued += copy;
 973         sk->forward_alloc -= copy;
 974     }
 975     return err;
 976 }
```

<u>cs 7.6.</u> *tcp_copy_to_page().*

```
net/ipv4/tcp.c

 771 static inline void tcp_mark_push(struct tcp_opt *tp, struct sk_buff *skb)
 772 {
 773     TCP_SKB_CB(skb)->flags |= TCPCB_FLAG_PSH;
 774     tp->pushed_seq = tp->write_seq;
 775 }
```

<u>cs 7.7.</u> *tcp_mark_push().*

(*skb→truesize*). Account for the overall memory allocated for the socket's send buffer and account for the memory taken from the socket's memory pool at line 973.

7.2.5   *tcp_mark_push()*

This sets a PSH flag for the *sk_buff* and at the same time updates the push sequence with the latest write sequence (cs 7.7). We mark byte as PUSHED in the case where we have written more than half of the so far maximum window size from the last byte marked as pushed, or in the case where we have one full-sized TCP segment ready for transmission.

7.2.6   *forced_push()*

This checks if we have written out more than half of the maximum window size ever advertised by the peer. *tp→write_seq* indicates the sequence number of the unsent byte on the TCP stream. *tp→pushed_seq* is the sequence number associated with the byte in the TCP stream that was last marked pushed (cs 7.8). This forces the last segment to be sent out in the window to have a PSH flag set indicating the receiver to read all the data it has received so far if it has not yet done that.

```
net/ipv4/tcp.c

777 static inline int forced_push(struct tcp_opt *tp)
778 {
779      return after(tp->write_seq, tp->pushed_seq + (tp->max_window>>1));
780 }
```

cs 7.8. forced_push().

```
net/ipv4/tcp.c

806 static inline void
807 tcp_push(struct sock *sk, struct tcp_opt *tp, int flags, int mss_now, int nonagle)
808 {
809      if (tp->send_head) {
810          struct sk_buff *skb = sk->write_queue.prev;
811          if (!(flags&MSG_MORE) || forced_push(tp))
812              tcp_mark_push(tp, skb);
813          tcp_mark_urg(tp, flags, skb);
814          __tcp_push_pending_frames(sk, tp, mss_now, (flags&MSG_MORE) ? 2 : nonagle);
815      }
816 }
```

cs 7.9. tcp_push().

7.2.7 tcp_push()

The routine is called when we are either writing OOB data or we have consumed user buffer completely. We first check if there is anything to transmit (line 809). The first buffer of the send queue (sk→write_queue) is made to point tp→send_head, which means that the next TCP segment that is not yet transmitted is pointed to by tp→send_head. Now we check if we need to mark the PUSH flag for the TCP buffer. We mark the buffer as PUSH if the application has no more data to send or if we have written more than half the maximum receive window size observed so far since the last PUSHed byte (line 811, cs 7.9). Call forced-PUSHed to check this. The receive-window is advertised by the receiver of the TCP data; the sender TCP keeps track of this window. If so, we mark the last byte as PUSHed and also set the PUSH flag for the TCP segment (line 812). Now we call tcp_mark_urg(). This routine just checks if we are writing an OOB data. If so, we set the TCP in urgent mode (tp→urg_mode indicates that TCP connection is in urgent mode and it gets reset when we get ACK for the urgent byte). Now we initialize the urgent pointer for the urgent byte to tp→write_seq (tp→snd_up contains the sequence number of the send urgent pointer byte in the stream of TCP data). We initialize the send urgent pointer to the sequence number of the last byte written because we write only 1 byte as OOB data and we don't wait for any more data when we need to send urgent data. So, the urgent sequence number will be same as the sequence number of the last written byte. We finally set a URG flag for the TCP buffer (line 813). We are not discussing any urgent mode here, so we won't discuss more about it here. Now we call __tcp_push_pending_frames() at line 814 to try to send segments pending to be transmitted in the socket's write queue.

```
include/net/tcp.h
 1240  static __inline__ void __tcp_push_pending_frames(struct sock *sk,
 1241                              struct tcp_opt *tp,
 1242                              unsigned cur_mss,
 1243                              int nonagle)
 1244  {
 1245      struct sk_buff *skb = tp->send_head;
 1246
 1247      if (skb) {
 1248          if (!tcp_skb_is_last(sk, skb))
 1249              nonagle = 1;
 1250          if (!tcp_snd_test(tp, skb, cur_mss, nonagle) ||
 1251              tcp_write_xmit(sk, nonagle))
 1252              tcp_check_probe_timer(sk, tp);
 1253      }
 1254      tcp_cwnd_validate(sk, tp);
 1255  }
```

<u>cs 7.10.</u> __tcp_push_peding_frames().

7.2.8 __tcp_push_pending_frames()

This routine does all the work required to transmit TCP buffers queued up in the send queue so far. So, the first thing we check here is whether we have anything to transmit in the write queue (line 1247, cs 7.10). If the send queue is not empty, we call *tcp_skb_is_last()* (line 1248). This routine checks if we are the last and only buffer in the write queue. If this is not the last buffer in the write queue, we force Nagle's algorithm to be disabled (line 1249). This is because nothing can be added to the packet that needs to be transmitted first so we make sure that we can transmit the segment. In the case where there is only one segment, let Nagle's algorithm decide whether to transmit the packet now. Now we call *tcp_snd_test()* to make all the possible tests to check if we can transmit any unsent segment. If the test fails, we can't transmit any more data currently. In the case where the test passes, we call *tcp_write_xmit()* to try to send out segments to the allowable limits. In the case where both routines fail, we are not able to send out any new data. We check if the receiver has advertised zero-window and we need to reset the window probe timer by calling *tcp_check_probe_timer()* at line 1252.

7.2.9 tcp_snd_test()

This make all the possible tests to checks whether we can transmit segments in the transmit queue now. We make the following checks:

- Are we sending a segment without violating Nagle's algorithm?
- Do we need to send out an urgent byte?
- Are packets in flight greater than the current congestion window?
- Are we sending a FIN segment?
- Are we sending an out-of-window data?

If Nagle is enabled, we don't have to send out an urgent byte and Nagle's algorithm doesn't allow us to send out new data, and we defer transmission of segments. If we are not violating Nagle's rule or we are in an urgent mode, continue with other

```
include/net/tcp.h
1191  static __ inline __ int tcp_snd_test(struct tcp_opt *tp, struct sk_buff *skb,
1192                        unsigned cur_mss, int nonagle)
1193  {
          ....
1218      return ((nonagle==1 || tp->urg_mode
1219          || !tcp_nagle_check(tp, skb, cur_mss, nonagle)) &&
1220          ((tcp_packets_in_flight(tp) < tp->snd_cwnd) ||
1221          (TCP_SKB_CB(skb)->flags & TCPCB_FLAG_FIN)) &&
1222          !after(TCP_SKB_CB(skb)->end_seq, tp->snd_una + tp->snd_wnd));
1223  }
```

cs 7.11. tcp_snd_test().

```
include/net/tcp.h
1178  tcp_nagle_check(struct tcp_opt *tp, struct sk_buff *skb, unsigned mss_now, int nonagle)
1179  {
1180      return (skb->len < mss_now &&
1181          !(TCP_SKB_CB(skb)->flags & TCPCB_FLAG_FIN) &&
1182          (nonagle == 2 ||
1183          (!nonagle &&
1184          tp->packets_out &&
1185          tcp_minshall_check(tp))));
1186  }
```

cs 7.12. tcp_nagle_check().

checks to transmit a new segment. *tcp_nagle_check()* is called to check if Nagle is not violated. If any of the above-mentioned conditions is TRUE, we next check if the congestion window allows us to send out more segments. *packets_in_flight()* counts those segments that are transmitted but not yet ACKed and are neither SACKed nor considered lost. These segments are considered to be consuming the network resources. If the count exceeds the congestion window (line 1220, cs 7.11), we are fully utilizing the network resources for the connection. So, we can't send more, otherwise, we may end up congesting the network. FIN segment is an exception. Even if the connection is fully utilizing network resources, we can send out a FIN segment. The last check is to find out if we are not sending data out of the receivers window at line 1222. When we receive ACK for the new in-sequence data, window shifts toward right. *tp→snd_una* is updated to the acknowledged sequence number when we get ACK for new data and *tp→snd_wnd* is updated to window advertised by the receiver. So, the check reduces to the end sequence number of the segment being transmitted should not exceed end sequence number of the right edge of the send window.

7.2.10   *tcp_nagle_check()*

The very first check we make here is whether TCP segment is partial, *skb→len < mss* (line 1180, cs 7.12). If this condition fails it means that we have complete segment ready to be transmitted so we don't make more checks are return FALSE to *tcp_snd_test()*. Else we check if this is a FIN segment (line 1181). If it is a fin segment, we return FALSE to *tcp_send_test()*. Else we move on to the next check for TCP cork (line 1182). If we have set cork on the socket we return TRUE (When

```
include/net/tcp.h
 1157  static __inline__ int tcp_minshall_check(struct tcp_opt *tp)
 1158  {
 1159       return after(tp->snd_sml,tp->snd_una) &&
 1160            !after(tp->snd_sml, tp->snd_nxt);
 1161  }
```

cs 7.13. tcp_minshall_check().

we set cork on the socket stream, we can't send any TCP data until we release the cork). Otherwise we move on to the next check for Nagle's. If Nagle is not enabled, we return FALSE to *tcp_send_test()* (line 1183). Otherwise we move on to the next check to see if there are any packets which are sent out but not yet acknowledged (line 1184). If we have nothing unacknowledged, we just return FALSE. Otherwise we move on to the next check, which is to check if we have unacked small segments. For this we call *tcp_minshall_check()* (line 1185).

7.2.11   *tcp_minshall_check()*

This checks if tp→snd_sml (end sequence number of the last partial TCP segment, *skb*→*len* <*mss*) is less than or equal to the last unacknowledged byte (tp→snd_una). If not, we return FALSE (line 1159, cs 7.13), which means that we return FALSE if we have no unacknowledged small segments so far. Otherwise we still have an unacknowledged small segment. Now we check if we have not yet sent the small packet. If not yet sent (*tp→snd_sml > tp→snd_nxt*), we return FALSE. Otherwise we return TRUE (line 1160). There is SWS avoidance from the sender side to avoid sending too many small segments.

7.2.12   *tcp_write_xmit()*

Here we try to process all the TCP segments queued up at the socket's write queue one by one. For this we need to make a check for each segment to determine whether we can send it out or not. The next packet to send out can be accessed from *tp→send_head* (line 566, cs 7.14). At the same time we check if we can transmit this segment now by calling *tcp_snd_test()* (line 567). If we can send the segment now, the next thing we check is whether we have segment length more than the current mss. We may have changed the route to the destination. If segment length is more than the current segment, we fragment the segments further by calling tcp_fragment() (line 568–571) to avoid IP fragmentation, which is a heavy process. We discuss *tcp_fragment()* some time later. In case we need to fragment the segment, we come out of the loop (line 566–580). Otherwise we are all set to transmit the segment by calling *tcp_transmit_skb()*. We always pass a clone of the TCP segment to *tcp_transmit_skb()* and not the original *sk_buff* (line 574). The reason is that we want to maintain the original TCP buffer until it is ACKed. We will drop the reference for *sk_buff* once it is transmitted out of the hardware device. *tcp_transmit_skb()* actually builds TCP header, sends it to the IP layer for processing, and puts the final IP datagram on the device queue for hardware transmission. If this TCP segment could not be sent out successfully, we come out of the loop (line 566–580). Otherwise we need to update the send queue information and the

```
net/ipv4/tcp_output.c
546  int tcp_write_xmit(struct sock *sk, int nonagle)
547  {
548       struct tcp_opt *tp = &(sk->tp_pinfo.af_tcp);
549       unsigned int mss_now;
550
     ....
555       if(sk->state != TCP_CLOSE) {
556            struct sk_buff *skb;
557            int sent_pkts = 0;
558
         ....
564            mss_now = tcp_current_mss(sk);
565
566            while((skb = tp->send_head) &&
567                 tcp_snd_test(tp, skb, mss_now, tcp_skb_is_last(sk, skb) ? nonagle : 1)) {
568                 if (skb->len > mss_now) {
569                      if (tcp_fragment(sk, skb, mss_now))
570                           break;
571                 }
         ....
574                 if (tcp_transmit_skb(sk, skb_clone(skb, GFP_ATOMIC)))
575                      break;
576                 /* Advance the send_head.  This one is sent out. */
577                 update_send_head(sk, tp, skb);
578                 tcp_minshall_update(tp, mss_now, skb);
579                 sent_pkts = 1;
580            }
581
582            if (sent_pkts) {
583                 tcp_cwnd_validate(sk, tp);
584                 return 0;
585            }
586
587            return !tp->packets_out && tp->send_head;
588       }
589       return 0;
590  }
```

cs 7.14. tcp_write_xmit().

```
include/net/tcp.h
1163  static __inline__ void tcp_minshall_update(struct tcp_opt *tp, int mss, struct sk_buff *skb)
1164  {
1165       if (skb->len < mss)
1166            tp->snd_sml = TCP_SKB_CB(skb)->end_seq;
1167  }
```

cs 7.15. tcp_minshall_update().

TCP state machine variables and move on to process the next segment in the write queue.

If the segment is transmitted successfully, we update the send head to point to the next segment to be transmitted by calling *update_send_head()* at line 577. Now we need to update TCP variables that keep information of any small segments that are sent out recently by calling *tcp_minshall_update()* at line 578. If the most recent transmitted TCP segment had length less than the current mss, $tp \rightarrow snd\_sml$ is updated to the end sequence number of that small segment (cs 7.15). This is

```
net/ipv4/tcp_output.c
  48  void update_send_head(struct sock *sk, struct tcp_opt *tp, struct sk_buff *skb)
  49  {
  50      tp->send_head = skb->next;
  51      if (tp->send_head == (struct sk_buff *) &sk->write_queue)
  52          tp->send_head = NULL;
  53      tp->snd_nxt = TCP_SKB_CB(skb)->end_seq;
  54      if (tp->packets_out++ == 0)
  55          tcp_reset_xmit_timer(sk, TCP_TIME_RETRANS, tp->rto);
  56  }
```

cs 7.16. *update_send_head().*

used to check if we are transmitting a larger number of smaller segments while sending out the segments while Nagle is enabled (check *tcp_nagle_check()*). We have completely processed one TCP segment and sent it out. Now once again check if there is a TCP segment to be sent out (line 566). If we have consumed all the TCP segments in the write queue (*tp→send_head == NULL*), we come out of the loop.

7.2.13 *update_send_head()*

Here we update the *tp→send_head* to the next sk_buff in the write queue (line 50, cs 7.16). If we have just transmitted the last sk_buff in the write queue, we set tp→ send_head to NULL (line 51–52). Now we update the TCP variable that keeps account of what needs to be sent next, tp→snd_nxt. tp→snd_nxt is updated with the end sequence number of the segment just transmitted (line 53). TCP also keeps track of a number of packets that are sent out but are yet to be ACKed (*tp→ packets_out*). So, we increment *tp→packets_out* by one. If this is the first packet to be sent out or the first packet out and there is no outstanding ACKs (*tp→packets_ out* is decremented by one once an ACK for the segment is received), we set the retransmission timer for the packet just send out. If we are sending out the TCP segment when we already have unACKed segments in the queue, we don't update the TCP retransmission timer because the retransmission happens for any one segment for the TCP and this is the very first unACKed segment.

7.2.14 *tcp_push_one()*

This routine is called to send once we have a full-sized segment ready for transmission and we have only one segment in the transmit queue. It calls *tcp_snd_test()* to check if we can transmit the TCP segment right now (line 338, cs 7.17). We have already discussed the function in much detail before. We disable Nagle here because we don't have any unACKed segment here because this is the only segment in the write queue. If we are allowed to transmit the segment, we directly call *tcp_ transmit_skb()*, which builds the TCP/IP header and puts the IP datagram on the device queue for transmission. We initialize the send head (line 342) to NULL because this was the only segment in the write queue. Next we assign the end sequence number of the segment to the tp→snd_nxt (next byte to be sent, line 343).

```
net/ipv4/tcp_output.c
333  void tcp_push_one(struct sock *sk, unsigned cur_mss)
334  {
335      struct tcp_opt *tp = &(sk->tp_pinfo.af_tcp);
336      struct sk_buff *skb = tp->send_head;
337
338      if (tcp_snd_test(tp, skb, cur_mss, 1)) {
339          /* Send it out now. */
340          TCP_SKB_CB(skb)->when = tcp_time_stamp;
341          if (tcp_transmit_skb(sk, skb_clone(skb, sk->allocation)) == 0) {
342              tp->send_head = NULL;
343              tp->snd_nxt = TCP_SKB_CB(skb)->end_seq;
344              if (tp->packets_out++ == 0)
345                  tcp_reset_xmit_timer(sk, TCP_TIME_RETRANS, tp->rto);
346              return;
347          }
348      }
349  }
```

cs 7.17. tcp_push-one().

```
net/ipv4/tcp.c
782  static inline void
783  skb_entail(struct sock *sk, struct tcp_opt *tp, struct sk_buff *skb)
784  {
785      skb->csum = 0;
786      TCP_SKB_CB(skb)->seq = tp->write_seq;
787      TCP_SKB_CB(skb)->end_seq = tp->write_seq;
788      TCP_SKB_CB(skb)->flags = TCPCB_FLAG_ACK;
789      TCP_SKB_CB(skb)->sacked = 0;
790      __skb_queue_tail(&sk->write_queue, skb);
791      tcp_charge_skb(sk, skb);
792      if (tp->send_head == NULL)
793          tp->send_head = skb;
794  }
```

cs 7.18. skb_entail().

Finally, if this is the only unACKed segment sent out, we reset the retransmit timer for this segment.

7.2.15 skb_entail()

We initialize the start and end sequence for the segment to sequence number of the next unwritten byte, the reason being we don't know how much will be copied into the buffer. So, the end sequence number for the segment will be initialized only after we have copied data to the buffer. The buffer flag is initialized to *TCPCB_FLAG_ACK* because every TCP segment carries a minimum ACK flag. We queue the segment to the tail of the transmit queue at line 790. We then account for the socket memory allocated for the buffer by calling *tcp_charge_skb()* at line 791. If this is the first segment queued in the transmit queue, the send head (*tp→send_head*) is inititialized to point to this segment at line 793.

7.3 SENDING OOB DATA

Whenever we want to send out urgent byte, we do it by calling *send()* with *MSG_OOB* set in the user application. So, essentially we write only one byte as OOB data. In *tcp_sendmsg()* we write 1 byte either to existing segment or new segment and then continue in a loop at line 1165 (cs 7.4). we get out of inner loop here because seglen has become zero here because we had only 1 byte of data to copy. For the same reason, we get out of the outer loop because we had only 1 byte of data to copy. We call tcp_push() at line 1189 (cs 7.4) with flag set to *MSG_OOB*. From *tcp_push()* we call *tcp_mark_urg()* which in turn checks if *MSG_OOB* flag is ON. If that is the case, we set urgent mode (*tp→urg_mode*), set urgent pointer (*tp→snd_up*) to write sequence (*tp→write_seq*) and set URG flag for the TCP segment. Now urgent pointer will be set for all those segment's which are yet to be transmitted and for which following condition satisfy

sequence number >= urgent pointer >= sequence number + 0xffff

All those segments for which urgent pointer lies within start sequence number and 0xffff offset from the start sequence number for the segment, will have urgent pointer set (*tcp_transmit_skb()*, line 248).

We clear an urgent mode at the sender side in *tcp_clean_rtx_queue()* in case the segment for which urgent pointer is set is ACKed, and the ACKed segment contained marked urgent pointer, we clear the urgent mode at line 1781 (see Section 11.4.6). While building header for the TCP segment in *tcp_transmit_skb()*, we check if urgent mode is ON at line 247 (cs 7.19). We also check if the urgent pointer lies within the valid sequence range for the outgoing data segment at line 248 (*tcp_transmit_skb()*). If both of the above conditions satisfy, we set an urgent flag in the current segment's TCP header and also set the current urgent pointer.

```
net/ipv4/tcp_output.c

189 int tcp_transmit_skb(struct sock *sk, struct sk_buff *skb)
190 {
        ....
247     if (tp->urg_mode &&
248         between(tp->snd_up, tcb->seq+1, tcb->seq+0xFFFF)) {
249         th->urg_ptr  = htons(tp->snd_up-tcb->seq);
250         th->urg      = 1;
251     }
        ....
278     err = tp->af_specific->queue_xmit(skb);
279     if (err <= 0)
280         return err;
        ....
296 }
```

cs 7.19. tcp_transmit_skb().

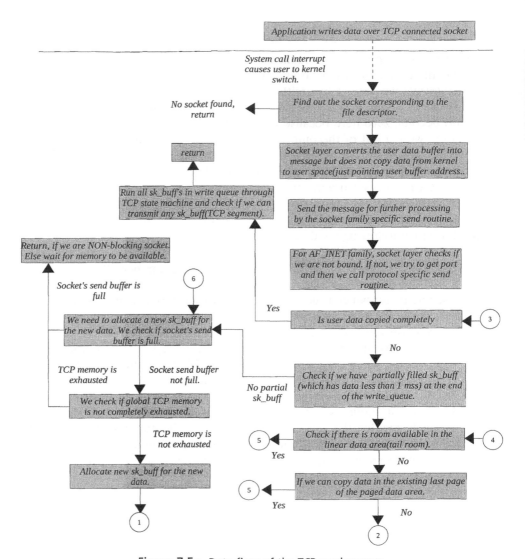

Figure 7.5a. Data flow of the TCP send process.

7.4 FLOW FOR TCP SEGMENTATION UNIT AND SEND PROCESS

Figures 7.5a and 7.5b are the data flow diagram for the processing of TCP data by segmentation unit. It describes how data is processed through segmentation unit, write queen and TCP state machine to send it down the stack. It also describes processing of urgent TCP data.

7.5 FUNCTIONAL LEVEL FLOW FOR SEGMENTATION AND SEND MECHANISM

Figures 7.6a and 7.6b show flow of control to implement processing of TCP data in the kernel. It shows major routines that are called to implement send side TCP data processing.

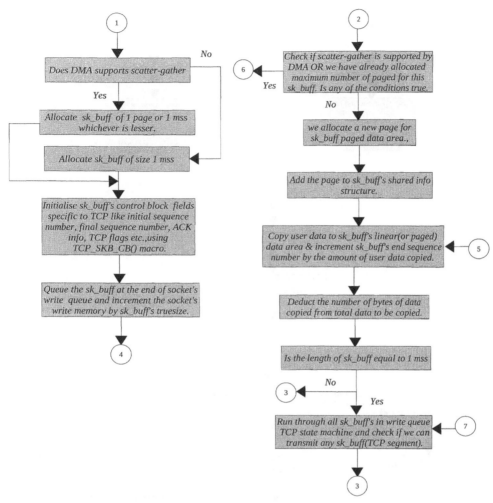

Figure 7.5b. DATA flow of TCP send process (*continued*).

7.6 SUMMARY

TCP sends out data in chunks of 1 mss. Maximum segment size is based on MTU, which is a link layer characteristic and can be retrieved from *tcp_current_mss()*.

tcp_alloc_pskb() allocates a new buffer for TCP data, and its minimum size is 1 mss or one page in case scatter–gather is supported.

skb_entail() queues up packet on the transmit buffer and also accounts for allocated buffer memory.

In the case where scatter–gather is supported by a network controller and mss is more than a single page, data are copied to *sk_buff's* paged data area. There is a limitation on the number of pages allocated to *sk_buff's* paged area. A segmentation unit looks slightly underperforming as far as memory allocation is concerned here. If the connection has very high mss with scatter–gather-capable NIC, we won't be able to take advantage of scatter–gather technique in the case where mss exceeds the limit imposed by number of pages that can be allocated to single *sk_buff*. Also, if the mss increases when we have partial segment in the transmit queue, we can't

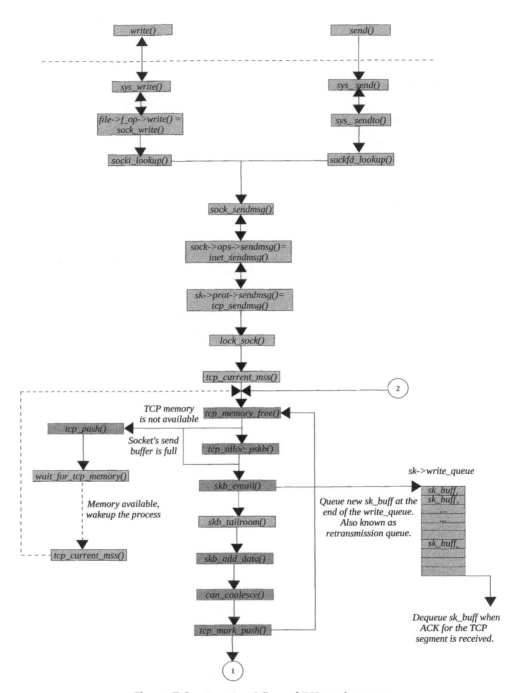

Figure 7.6a. Functional flow of TCP send process.

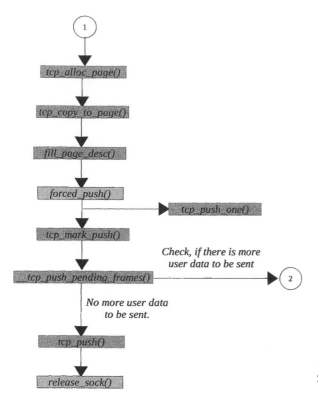

Figure 7.6b. Functional flow of TCP send process (*continued*).

reallocate memory for the partial segment to accommodate more data as per new mss. This would cause underperforming TCP.

tcp_push_one() tries to transmit one segment in the write queue. *__tcp_push_pending_frames()* tries to transmit more than one segment queued up in the write queue.

tp→send_head points to first segment in the write queue that needs to be transmitted next. This field marks the start of the transmit queue and separates it from the retransmit queue.

tcp_send_test() implements all the sender side algorithms like Nagle's algorithm, sliding window protocol, and congestion window test.

tcp_mark_urg() checks if we need to send out an urgent byte and sets TCP flag to indicate an urgent byte.

8

TCP RECEIVE

Application reads may request a kernel to receive normal or urgent data from a TCP socket. Kernel socket implementation has to differentiate between the two different types of requests. When an application wants to receive an urgent byte as OOB data, it has to take care of reading it at an appropriate time; otherwise, there is a chance of losing it.

TCP treats data as a stream of bytes. Only those bytes that are received in sequence are queued by a TCP receive buffer. Out-of-sequence data go into a separate queue, and data from this queue can't be considered to serve an application request.

Kernel processing of TCP data received can be divided into two parts. If an application is blocked to read data and in-sequence data are received, TCP directly copies data to a user buffer. The other way is to queue in-sequence data to a socket's receive queue, and the application request is served from the receive queue. The kernel implements the queuing mechanism for the received TCP segments, and there are more than one queue implemented.

In this chapter we will learn all about processing TCP data and about the design of receive queues. TCP data include normal and urgent data. We will learn about the queuing mechanism of TCP segments and about the processing sequence of the queues. We will also get to see how data are read from the socket buffers. There is a section that explains the receive mechanism from paged buffers as well. Then we have section on how an urgent byte is received both as inline and OOB data. There is a section that explains a blocking mechanism to receive data. Complete processing of receiving TCP data is explained in Figures 8.14(a) through 8.14(f).

TCP/IP Architecture, Design, and Implementation in Linux. By S. Seth and M. A. Venkatesulu
Copyright © 2008 the IEEE Computer Society

8.1 QUEUING MECHANISM

In this section we will see all the queues that exist for the incoming TCP packets. What is the design point of view to have all those queues, and in what sequence are they processed? There are three queues to receive incoming TCP segments:

- Backlog queue (*sk→backlog*)
- Prequeue queue (*tp→ucopy.prequeue*)
- Receive queue (*sk→receive_queue*)

sk→receive_queue contains processed TCP segments, which means that all the protocol headers are stripped and data are ready to be copied to the user application. *sk→receive_queue* contains all those data segments that are received in correct order. TCP segments in the other two queues are the ones that need to be processed.

Packets intended for TCP are first processed by *tcp_v4_rcv()* (cs 8.1). Here we need to make a decision on whether the packet needs to be processed or needs to be queued in either *backlog* or *prequeue* queues. We first hold a socket spin lock at line 1766. The bottom half is already disabled when this routine is entered because it is called from NET softIRQ. Next we check if any body is already using the socket at line 1768. sk→lock.users is one in case somebody is using the socket. The socket is in use when we are reading/writing/modifying the socket. If the socket is already in use, we first try to queue the TCP packet in the prequeue queue by calling *tcp_prequeue()* at line 1769. If for some reason we are not able to queue the TCP packet in a prequeue queue, we directly process the segment by calling *tcp_v4_do_rcv()* at line 1770. In our discussion, we are assuming that the socket is in an established state. So, the packet will be processed by calling *tcp_rcv_established()* from *tcp_v4_do_rcv()* (cs 8.1).

8.1.1 Processing in *tcp_rcv_established()*

Let's see how a TCP data packet is processed in *tcp_rcv_established()* (cs 8.2). We will not learn the entire processing of the data segment here, but only the data

```
net/ipv4/tcp_ipv4.c

1712 int tcp_v4_rcv(struct sk_buff *skb)
1713 {
          ....
1766      bh_lock_sock(sk);
1767      ret = 0;
1768      if (!sk->lock.users) {
1769          if (!tcp_prequeue(sk, skb))
1770              ret = tcp_v4_do_rcv(sk, skb);
1771      } else
1772          sk_add_backlog(sk, skb);
1773      bh_unlock_sock(sk);
          ...
1825 }
```

cs 8.1. *tcp_v4_rcv()*.

```
net/ipv4/tcp_input.c

3210 int tcp_rcv_established(struct sock *sk, struct sk_buff *skb,
3211                    struct tcphdr *th, unsigned len)
3212 {
3213      struct tcp_opt *tp = &(sk->tp_pinfo.af_tcp);
3214

         ....
3298          } else {
3299               int eaten = 0;
3300
3301               if (tp->ucopy.task == current &&
3302                    tp->copied_seq == tp->rcv_nxt &&
3303                    len - tcp_header_len <= tp->ucopy.len &&
3304                    sk->lock.users) {
3305                        __set_current_state(TASK_RUNNING);
3306
3307                        if (!tcp_copy_to_iovec(sk, skb, tcp_header_len)) {
                                ....
3318                             __skb_pull(skb, tcp_header_len);
3319                             tp->rcv_nxt = TCP_SKB_CB(skb)->end_seq;
3320                             NET_INC_STATS_BH(TCPHPHitsToUser);
3321                             eaten = 1;
3322                        }
3323               }
3324               if (!eaten) {
                        ....
3343                    __skb_pull(skb,tcp_header_len);
3344                    __skb_queue_tail(&sk->receive_queue, skb);
3345                    tcp_set_owner_r(skb, sk);
3346                    tp->rcv_nxt = TCP_SKB_CB(skb)->end_seq;
3347               }
         ....
3448      return 0;
3449 }
```

<u>cs 8.2.</u> *tcp_rcv_established().*

processing and queuing mechanism. First we look for the possibility of copying data directly to the user buffer. If that is not possible, we will strip the TCP header and queue the data segment in the receive queue.

There are certain conditions that need to be satisfied before we can copy TCP data directly to the user buffer. These are:

- The current process (*current*) should be the one that installed the receiver (*tp→ucopy.task*) at line 3301. It means that the chances of data being copied from softIRQ are very low because an interrupt can come anytime and it is not guaranteed that the same process may be running on the CPU that installed the receiver.
- (The copied sequence (*tp→copied_seq*) should be the same as the sequence number that is expected next (*tp→rcv_nxt*) at line 3302, which means that no outstanding data are there in the receive queue to be processed.
- TCP data contained in the segment should be maximum, equal to the length requested by the user (*tp→ucopy.len*) at line 3303. We do only one thing out of two: either copy data to the user buffer or queue the buffer to the receive queue. We don't queue a partially read segment on the receive queue; otherwise it will add further complexity and increase calculations.

· The final condition is that the routine should be called from socket user context. This will make sure that the data can't be directly copied to the user buffer from interrupt context (softIRQ), because *tcp_v4_rcv()* adds the TCP packet to the backlog queue in case somebody is already using the socket. So, we are sure that TCP data can be copied directly to the user buffer only from process context.

If all the above conditions are satisfied, we call *tcp_copy_to_iovec()* to copy TCP data from the packet being processed to the user buffer. This will also add copied length to *tp→ucopy.len* and *tp→copied_seq*. We also update *tp→rcv_nxt* to the end sequence of the processed packet at line 3319.

If we are not able to copy data to the user buffer because of any of the conditions above failing, we will queue a data segment at the end of the receive queue by calling *__skb_queue_tail()* at line 3344. We queue the buffer after stripping the TCP header so that we directly point to the data in the TCP segment. Update *tp→ rcv_nxt* as the end sequence of the segment.

8.1.2 *tcp_prequeue()*

The routine is called when we receive a TCP packet from *tcp_v4_rcv()*. This routine is called to queue a TCP packet in the prequeue queue, in the case where the receiver is installed by some user process (line 1328, cs 8.3). *tp→ucopy.task* points

```
include/net/tcp.h

1324 static __inline__ int tcp_prequeue(struct sock *sk, struct sk_buff *skb)
1325 {
1326     struct tcp_opt *tp = &sk->tp_pinfo.af_tcp;
1327
1328     if (tp->ucopy.task) {
1329         __skb_queue_tail(&tp->ucopy.prequeue, skb);
1330         tp->ucopy.memory += skb->truesize;
1331         if (tp->ucopy.memory > sk->rcvbuf) {
1332             struct sk_buff *skb1;
1333
1334             if (sk->lock.users)
1335                 out_of_line_bug();
1336
1337             while ((skb1 = __skb_dequeue(&tp->ucopy.prequeue)) != NULL) {
1338                 sk->backlog_rcv(sk, skb1);
1339                 NET_INC_STATS_BH(TCPPrequeueDropped);
1340             }
1341
1342             tp->ucopy.memory = 0;
1343         } else if (skb_queue_len(&tp->ucopy.prequeue) == 1) {
1344             wake_up_interruptible(sk->sleep);
1345             if (!tcp_ack_scheduled(tp))
1346                 tcp_reset_xmit_timer(sk, TCP_TIME_DACK, (3*TCP_RTO_MIN)/4);
1347         }
1348         return 1;
1349     }
1350     return 0;
1351 }
```

cs 8.3. *tcp_prequeue()*.

to the process that installed the receiver (for more details see Section 8.2, *tcp_recvmsg()*). We are called only if no one is using the socket currently, which essentially means that some user process wants to receive data and we are waiting for data over the socket. We can queue a TCP packet here only in one situation—that is, when we are waiting for a socket's wait queue in *tcp_data_wait()* called from *tcp_recvmsg()*.

First we queue a TCP packet on prequeue, *tp→ucopy.prequeue*, and account for the memory allocated by the user buffer (tp→ucopy.memory) at line 1329–1330. We actually don't process the TCP packets in the prequeue in the interrupt context (done usually in process context). But in the extreme case, where memory consumed by user buffer has stuck the upper limit (*sk→rcvbuf*) at line 1331, we need to process TCP segment's from the prequeue. We process all the segment in the prequeue one by one by calling callback routine *sk→backlog_rcv*, line 1337–1338. *backlog_rcv* points to *tcp_v4_do_rcv()*. The situation may arise in the case where packets are coming fast enough and the receiving process is not getting scheduled to process the prequeue. This is when we queue the first TCP segment on the preqeue (line 1343), the receiving process is woken up by calling *wake_up_interruptale()*. In the case where we are queuing the first TCP segment on the prequeue, the delayed ACK timer is reset in the case where ACK is not already scheduled to three-fourths of the minimum RTO value. We do this because we process the prequeue queue in the delay ACK timer if the application is not able to do it fast enough. We return values indicating whether we are able to queue the TCP segment on the prequeue.

8.1.3 Processing of Queues (see cs 8.4a and cs 8.4b unless mentioned)

TCP queues are processed mainly in two places:

- delay ACK timer, *tcp_delack_timer()*
- *tcp_recvmsg()*, when the application wants to receive data over the socket

Let's see how the queues are processed in *tcp_recvmsg()*. We process the queues as a user of the socket. We become a socket user by calling *lock_sock()* at line 1480 (cs 8.4a,b). Before entering tcp_recvmsg(), we can have data in the receive queue only. The reason for this is that the receiver is not installed for the socket, because of which the packets won't go into prequeue. Even if someone were holding the socket's user status because of which the packets were queued into a backlog queue, those packets would have been processed while the socket's user status is released. When the backlog queue is processed without the receiver being installed, the processed TCP data packets are queued into the receive queue. In the case where no one had socket's user status before entering this routine, all the segments received will be processed by *tcp_v4_rcv()* and the processed data packets will be queued in the receive queue.

So, the order will be to first process a receive queue. In the receive queue, only TCP data segments go which are received in order. We eat up data from the TCP receive queue in the loop 1524–1545. If we find the segment of our interest at line 1539, we consume data by jumping to a location and once again enter the same loop. Once we have completely processed a receive queue and we have copied the requested data, we return at line 1550.

```
net/ipv4/tcp.c

1467 int tcp_recvmsg(struct sock *sk, struct msghdr *msg,
1468          int len, int nonblock, int flags, int *addr_len)
1469 {
1470     struct tcp_opt *tp = &(sk->tp_pinfo.af_tcp);
          ....
1480     lock_sock(sk);
          ....
1502     do {
            ....
1523        skb = skb_peek(&sk->receive_queue);
1524        do {
1525            if (!skb)
1526                break;
                ...
1536            offset = *seq - TCP_SKB_CB(skb)->seq;
                ....
1539            if (offset < skb->len)
1540                goto found_ok_skb;
                ....
1544            skb = skb->next;
1545        } while (skb != (struct sk_buff *)&sk->receive_queue);
            ....
1549        if (copied >= target && sk->backlog.tail == NULL)
1550            break;
            ....
1590        if (tp->ucopy.task == user_recv) {
1591            /* Install new reader */
1592            if (user_recv == NULL && !(flags&(MSG_TRUNC|MSG_PEEK))) {
1593                user_recv = current;
1594                tp->ucopy.task = user_recv;
1595                tp->ucopy.iov = msg->msg_iov;
1596            }
1597
1598            tp->ucopy.len = len;
                ....
1628            if (skb_queue_len(&tp->ucopy.prequeue))
1629                goto do_prequeue;
                ....
1632        }
1633
1634        if (copied >= target) {
1635            /* Do not sleep, just process backlog. */
1636            release_sock(sk);
1637            lock_sock(sk);
1638        } else {
1639            timeo = tcp_data_wait(sk, timeo);
1640        }
1641
1642        if (user_recv) {
                .....
1647            if ((chunk = len - tp->ucopy.len) != 0) {
1648                net_statistics[smp_processor_id()*2+1].TCPDirectCopyFromBacklog += chunk;
1649                len -= chunk;
1650                copied += chunk;
1651            }
1652
1653            if (tp->rcv_nxt == tp->copied_seq &&
1654                skb_queue_len(&tp->ucopy.prequeue)) {
                ......
```

cs 8.4a. tcp_recvmsg().

```
net/ipv4/tcp.c   tcp_recvmsg() contd....

1655 do_prequeue:
1656                        tcp_prequeue_process(sk);
1657
1658                        if ((chunk = len - tp->ucopy.len) != 0) {
1659                                net_statistics[smp_processor_id()*2+1].TCPDirectCopyFromPrequeue += chunk;
1660                                len -= chunk;
1661                                copied += chunk;
1662                        }
1663                }
1664        }
        ....
1671        continue;
        ....
1730        } while (len > 0);
1731
1732        if (user_recv) {
1733            if (skb_queue_len(&tp->ucopy.prequeue)) {
1734                int chunk;
1735
1736                tp->ucopy.len = copied > 0 ? len : 0;
1737
1738                tcp_prequeue_process(sk);
1739
1740                if (copied > 0 && (chunk = len - tp->ucopy.len) != 0) {
1741                        net_statistics[smp_processor_id()*2+1].TCPDirectCopyFromPrequeue += chunk;
1742                        len -= chunk;
1743                        copied += chunk;
1744                }
1745            }
1746
1747            tp->ucopy.task = NULL;
1748            tp->ucopy.len = 0;
1749        }
        ....
1764        release_sock(sk);
1765        return err;
        ...
1770 }
```

cs 8.4b. tcp_recvmsg() (continued).

In case after completely processing a receive queue we could not satisfy an application request, we need to wait for some more data to arrive before we can return. So, we install a receiver at line 1590. Since this is the first time we have come here, we need to initialize *tp→ucopy* object. Structure ucopy is embedded in the *tcp_opt* structure and contains details of the user buffer. *prequeue* is a pointer to the queue where the TCP packets go when there is no socket user but receiver is installed. *task* is a pointer to the process that has installed the receiver. Using this field, we avoid copying data in a user buffer directly from interrupt context. *iov* is the pointer to the user buffer where data should be copied. *memory* keeps account of the amount of memory consumed by the buffers queued in the *prequeue* queue. *len* is the number of bytes we are interested in.

We initialize *task*, *iov*, and *len* fields of the *ucopy* object (cs 8.5). Next we check if there are any packets in the prequeue to be processed at line 1628. In the first iteration we should not see any packets in this queue because the receiver is just installed and we are still the user of the socket. *In tcp_v4_rcv()* we queue packets on this queue only if no one is using the socket and a receiver is installed.

```
include/net/sock.h

284        struct {
285               struct sk_buff_head      prequeue;
286               struct task_struct       *task;
287               struct iovec             *iov;
288               int                      memory;
289               int                      len;
290        } ucopy;
```

cs 8.5. Data structure to manage user buffer for copying tcp data.

Next we check if we have copied the requested data at line 1634. If so, we just release the socket's user status by calling *release_sock()* at line 1636 and then try to get the socket's user status by calling *lock_sock()* at line 1637. We do this because this will cause all the packets queued on the backlog queue to be processed in release_sock().All the packets arrived until the call to *release_sock()* will be queued on the backlog queue in *tcp_v4_rcv()* because socket is being used. We leave the routine after processing packets in the backlog queue this way even after all our requests are satisfied.

In the case where we have not copied all the data requested, we wait for data to be available by calling *tcp_data_wait()* at line 1639. We wait here until woken up due to the arrival of TCP packet for the socket or we experience timeout. On return from tcp_data_wait(), we might have packets in the prequeue (for more details see Section 8.1.4, *tcp_data_wait()*). The next step after waiting will be to test if the we have installed a receiver at line 1732. Since we are discussing the reception of data, this will always be non-NULL and will point to the process that wants to receive data. In the case where TRUNCATE flag is set, we don't have this set, but we don't care. So, the first check is made for the possibility of direct consumption of data during processing of packets. How is this possible? We may have copied data to the user buffer while releasing the socket's user status by calling *release_sock()* in *tcp_data_wait()*. Because a backlog queue will be processed here and since socket user status is retained by us, any TCP data packet processed will directly copy data in the user buffer in *tcp_rcv_established()*. If we have copied data to the user buffer, *tp→ucopy.len* will be decremented by copied length in *tcp_rcv_estbalished()* and we need to account for the copied data at line 1649–1650.

Next we check whether we can process a prequeue queue. Here we need to check for two conditions:

- Is there anything in the receive queue to be processed (line 1653)? If something is there in the receive queue to be processed, *tp→rcv_nxt* will be different from the *tp→copied_seq*; see Section 11.8, *tcp_rcv_established()*. If data are directly copied to the user buffer, the above two fields will have the same value.
- Is there anything in the prequeue to be processed (line 1654)?

To process the messages in the prequeue, there should be nothing in the receive queue to be eaten up; otherwise, things will mess up. We can have packets in the pre-queue to be processed at this point because of the small window between releasing and holding socket user status during which the receiver is already installed (see

Section 8.1.4, *tcp_data_wait()*). But, how do we have a situation where we have packets in the prequeue along with TCP data in the receive queue? In the small window when we have released socket's user status, we start queuing packets in the prequeue. On arrival of the first entry in the prequeue, we kick off a delay ACK timer in *tcp_prequeue()* called from *tcp_v4_rcv()*. If the delay ACK timer fires before we get the CPU, packets from the prequeue will be processed and all the data segments will be queued in the receive queue (as we are in the interrupt context). The delay ACK timer proceeds only if there is no user of the socket. After the prequeue is processed in the delay ACK timer, there can still be some time before we get the CPU and get the socket's user status. In this duration, packets arriving for the socket will be queued on the prequeue.

In the case where we are able to process packets on the prequeue because there was nothing in the receive queue to be processed, tcp_prequeue_process() is called to process the prequeue at line 1656. If there are any data segments on the pre-queue, data will be directly copied to the user process in tcp_recv_established() because we are the process who has installed a receiver as with the socket's user status on. Next we account for the copied data at line 1660–1661 and continue.

In case we are not able to process the packets on the prequeue because of pending data to be processed in the receive queue, we continue at line 1671. We repeat the processing from the start of the processing of the receive queue at line 1523. Consume all the data from the receive queue and we still fall short of data requested by the user; we will come to line 1628 from where we jump to line 1655 to process the prequeue. In the case where we have satisfied the request from the user by processing the receive queue and we still have packets in the prequeue, we process the prequeue before leaving the routine at line 1738 by calling *tcp_pre-queue_process()*. This will process all the data segments in the pre-queue and queue them in the receive queue. This makes sure that the next time we enter *tcp_recvmsg()*, the sequence of queue processing is maintained; that is, receive queue then prequeue and then backlog queue.

8.1.4   *tcp_data_wait()*

The routine is called when we want to wait for data to arrive over a socket. We add wait queue to the socket's wait queue $sk \rightarrow sleep$ and set the process state to *TASK_INTERRUPTIBLE* at line 1348 (cs 8.6). We set the SOCK_ASYNC_WAITDATA flag for the socket, which means that the socket is waiting for data to arrive asynchronously. Now we release the socket's user status by calling *release_sock()* at line 1351. As explained in Section 8.1.8, this will process all the TCP packets queued in the backlog queue. Now we check if the receive queue is empty at line 1353. Until releasing the socket's user status, whatever packets arrive will be queued in the backlog buffer in *tcp_v4_rcv()*. If the backlog queue was not empty and we received TCP data segments, they will be queued in the receive buffer. So, the receive buffer will not be empty in this case and we try to get the socket's user status for the process by calling lock_sock() at line 1356. Clear the SOCK_ASYNC_WAITDATA flag for the socket, remove the process from socket's wait queue at line 1359, set process state to TASK_RUNNING, and return.

In the case where there was nothing in the backlog queue or there were no TCP data segments by the time we released the socket's user status, we need to wait until data arrive by yielding our position at line 1354. We will be awakened either

```
net/ipv4/tcp.c

1342 static long tcp_data_wait(struct sock *sk, long timeo)
1343 {
1344      DECLARE_WAITQUEUE(wait, current);
1345
1346      add_wait_queue(sk->sleep, &wait);
1347
1348      __set_current_state(TASK_INTERRUPTIBLE);
1349
1350      set_bit(SOCK_ASYNC_WAITDATA, &sk->socket->flags);
1351      release_sock(sk);
1352
1353      if (skb_queue_empty(&sk->receive_queue))
1354          timeo = schedule_timeout(timeo);
1355
1356      lock_sock(sk);
1357      clear_bit(SOCK_ASYNC_WAITDATA, &sk->socket->flags);
1358
1359      remove_wait_queue(sk->sleep, &wait);
1360      __set_current_state(TASK_RUNNING);
1361      return timeo;
1362 }
```

cs 8.6. tcp_data_wait().

```
net/ipv4/tcp.c

1364 static void tcp_prequeue_process(struct sock *sk)
1365 {
1366      struct sk_buff *skb;
1367      struct tcp_opt *tp = &(sk->tp_pinfo.af_tcp);
              ....
1372      local_bh_disable();
1373      while ((skb = __skb_dequeue(&tp->ucopy.prequeue)) != NULL)
1374          sk->backlog_rcv(sk, skb);
1375      local_bh_enable();
              ....
1378      tp->ucopy.memory = 0;
1379 }
```

cs 8.7. tcp_prequeue_process().

whenever the TCP packet arrives or when we experience timeout. In either case, we just return from the routine.

There is a small window between releasing the socket's user status and reacquiring it at line 1356 where the current process is not the user of the socket. If no other process is using the socket in this duration, all the TCP packets intended for the socket will be queued in the prequeue queue because the receiver is installed.

8.1.5 *tcp_prequeue_process()*

The routine is called from process context, and is called from tcp_recvmsg() when we want to process packets queued in the prequeue (cs 8.7). We process packets in the prequeue with local bottom-half disabled. Disabling of the bottom-half is not required here because we already have acquired the socket's user status. Once the socket is in use, incoming TCP packets will be queued in the backlog queue. By disabling the local bottom half, we are actually deferring the processing of packets on the current CPU because they are processed in NET softIRQ.

```
include/net/sock.h

785 #define lock_sock(__sk) \
786 do {   spin_lock_bh(&((__sk)->lock.slock)); \
787        if ((__sk)->lock.users != 0) \
788            __lock_sock(__sk); \
789        (__sk)->lock.users = 1; \
790        spin_unlock_bh(&((__sk)->lock.slock)); \
791 } while(0)
```

<u>cs 8.8.</u> *lock_sock().*

```
net/core/sock.c

841 void __lock_sock(struct sock *sk)
842 {
843        DECLARE_WAITQUEUE(wait, current);
844
845        add_wait_queue_exclusive(&sk->lock.wq, &wait);
846        for(;;) {
847            current->state = TASK_UNINTERRUPTIBLE;
848            spin_unlock_bh(&sk->lock.slock);
849            schedule();
850            spin_lock_bh(&sk->lock.slock);
851            if(!sk->lock.users)
852                break;
853        }
854        current->state = TASK_RUNNING;
855        remove_wait_queue(&sk->lock.wq, &wait);
856 }
```

<u>cs 8.9.</u> *__lock_sock().*

8.1.6 *lock_sock()*

The routine is called when someone wants to read/modify/write to the socket. This macro grants socket user status to the caller. It holds socket spin lock *sk→lock.slock* and checks if somebody is already using the socket at line 787 (cs 8.8). If so, it has to wait for the user of the socket until it releases the user status by calling *__lock_sock()* at line 788. Once *__lock_sock()* returns, it means that someone has released the socket user status (*sk→lock.users == 0*). We are still holding the socket spin lock, so we become a user of the socket at line 789. At last we release the socket spin lock.

8.1.7 *__lock_sock()*

The routine essentially waits for the socket's lock wait queue (*sk→lock.wq*) until it is awakened by someone who releases the socket's user status (cs 8.9). By doing this, we loop forever by doing the following steps in each iteration:

1. Set the status of the current task to *TASK_UNINTERRUPTABLE* at line 847.
2. Release socket's spin lock at line 848.
3. Call *schedule()* to preempt the current process at line 849.
4. We return from schedule only after someone wakes us up (the one who releases hold on the socket user status, *release_sock()*).

```
include/net/sock.h

793 #define release_sock(__sk) \
794 do {    spin_lock_bh(&((__sk)->lock.slock)); \
795        if ((__sk)->backlog.tail != NULL) \
796            __release_sock(__sk); \
797        (__sk)->lock.users = 0; \
798        if (waitqueue_active(&((__sk)->lock.wq))) wake_up(&((__sk)->lock.wq)); \
799        spin_unlock_bh(&((__sk)->lock.slock)); \
800 } while(0)
```

cs 8.10. release_sock().

5. If the socket user status is still available, we break from the loop at line 852. Otherwise we iterate in a loop. Once someone holding the socket user status releases it, it wakes up everyone waiting for the status. Whoever gets CPU first will get the status, and the rest of them will once again wait until the next release.

Once we are out of the loop, we set the task status as TASK_RUNNING and remove the process from the socket's wait queue at line 855.

8.1.8   release_sock()

This macro is called when the user of the socket wants to release the user status on the socket. Hold the socket spin lock and first check if the backlog queue is empty at line 795. We need to check this because when the socket is in use, the incoming TCP packets in *tcp_v4_rcv()* are not processed immediately but are queued in the backlog queue. These packet's should be processed when the user of the socket is releasing the status. This way we maintain the order of packet processing. After holding the socket user status, no new TCP packet is processed until the socket user status is released by the process.

In the case where the backlog queue is not empty, we need to process all the TC packets queued in the backlog queue by calling *__release_sock()* at line 796 (cs 8.10). Once we have processed the backlog queue, the socket user status is released at line 797. If we have any processes queued in the socket's wait queue, *sk→lock. wq*, we wake up all the processes sleeping on this wait queue by calling *wake_up()* at line 798. Release socket's spin lock and return.

8.1.9   __release_sock()

We process the TCP packets on the backlog queue here. The idea is to process the backlog queue until it is empty. We can't process the TCP packet with the socket lock held, so while processing the packet's from the queue we release the socket lock. We have two loops to implement the idea. The outer loop is iterated until we have empty backlog queue. The inner loop processes one packet at a time from the backlog queue until all are processed by calling *sk→backlog_rcv, tcp_v4_do_rcv()*.

The first time we enter the routine, we detach the chain of packets from the queue at line 860 and then enter the inner loop after releasing the socket lock at

```
net/core/sock.c

858 void __release_sock(struct sock *sk)
859 {
860     struct sk_buff *skb = sk->backlog.head;
861
862     do {
863         sk->backlog.head = sk->backlog.tail = NULL;
864         bh_unlock_sock(sk);
865
866         do {
867             struct sk_buff *next = skb->next;
868
869             skb->next = NULL;
870             sk->backlog_rcv(sk, skb);
871             skb = next;
872         } while (skb != NULL);
873
874         bh_lock_sock(sk);
875     } while((skb = sk->backlog.head) != NULL);
876 }
```

cs 8.11. __release_sock().

line 864 (cs 8.11). Once all the packets in the chain are processed, we come out of the inner loop, hold the socket lock, and check if there is any packet in the backlog queue to be processed at line 875. If there is anything to be processed, we detach the chain at line 863 and proceed further to process the chain. We make this check at the end of the outer loop because there is a window between the socket spin lock being held and released. In this duration if the packets arrive, they will be queued in the backlog queue in *tcp_v4_rcv()* because the socket is still in use by the current process processing the backlog queue.

8.2 PROCESSING OF TCP DATA FROM THE RECEIVE QUEUE
(see cs 8.12a and 8.12b unless mentioned)

In the previous section we saw how queues are designed to work such that TCP data integrity is maintained and we leverage prequeue design to copy data efficiently to the user buffer. In this section we will learn how data are copied from the receive queue and the processing of receive buffers. This section covers only normal data receive, and Section 8.3 will cover urgent byte processing.

To copy data from socket buffer to the user land, we rely on the following fields:

1. *tp→copied_seq* is the sequence number of the byte that is copied to the user land. This is updated whenever we copy data to the user buffer in *tcp_recvmsg()* and also in *tcp_copy_to_iovec()* when data are directly copied to user buffer.
2. *skb→len* is the length of the socket buffer (TCP payload).
3. *TCP_SKB_CB(skb)→seq* is the sequence number corresponding to the first byte of the socket buffer.

We are interested in all those bytes that are received in-sequence. Each byte has a sequence number associated with it. Data segments queued in the receive queue have no hole is the sequence space. Moreover, each segment has its own sequence space—that is, start and end of the data sequence numbers. So, we can exactly know how much is copied and what needs to be copied. Even in the case of overlapping sequence spaces of the segments, we have no problem because each byte is marked with sequence number and we can avoid copying common data twice.

In this section we will see how data are copied from the socket buffer to the user buffer. In this discussion we assume that all the data we are interested in comes from the receive queue. We will have examples with paged and linear data sections each. When we enter tcp_recvmsg(), the copied sequence number is marked at line 1494 (cs 8.12a). Next we need to find out the segment that contains the byte that corresponds to sequence number next to the copied sequence in the receive buffer in a loop 1524–1545. For each buffer we calculate the offset within the buffer from the copied sequence and the start sequence number for the buffer at line 1536. If the offset is smaller than the length of the buffer, we have the buffer, line 1540. Otherwise we move on to the next buffer at line 1544. We copy data from the buffer by jumping to line 1673.

We found the buffer from where we need to copy data, and now we need to find how much data need to be copied from the buffer from the total length of the buffer and the offset within the buffer at line 1675. If the length requested by the user application is less than the number of unread bytes within the buffer, we adjust the number of bytes that can be copied at line 1677. Now we are ready to copy data with the offset and number of bytes from an identified buffer by calling *skb_copy_datagram_iovec()* at line 1697. We don't know if the data need to be copied from the linear data area or paged data area or from fragments. This part is taken care of by *skb_copy_datagram_iovec()*. We will learn more about it in Section 8.2.2. We have already read data from the buffer and now need to account for the same. So, we increment the copied sequence by the number of bytes read at line 1706, the total number of bytes copied to the user buffer, and the number of bytes remaining to be copied at lines 1707–1708. We check if complete buffer is consumed at line 1715 (cs 8.12b). If we still have data left in the buffer, it means that the number of bytes requested has been served and we need to return because the outer loop condition will fail at line 1730. In the case where the application has requested more data and the buffer just read couldn't satisfy the request, we move on to the next buffer by iterating through the outer loop. In this case, we have consumed the entire data from the current buffer and need to unlink it from the receive buffer by calling *tcp_eat_skb()* at line 1721. Once we come out of the loop after reading in all the requested by the application, we have actually created some space in the socket's receive buffer for more data to be received. In this case, we need to advertise the new window to the sender. We may be opening a window here, so we should notify the sender which must be waiting to send in data. For this we call *cleanup_rbuf()* at line 1756.

8.2.1 *cleanup_rbuf()*

This routine is called to check if we can send an ACK after application has read data from the socket buffer. First we check if the ACK was scheduled by calling

```
net/ipv4/tcp.c

1467 int tcp_recvmsg(struct sock *sk, struct msghdr *msg,
1468          int len, int nonblock, int flags, int *addr_len)
1469 {
1470      struct tcp_opt *tp = &(sk->tp_pinfo.af_tcp);
          ....
1480      lock_sock(sk);
          ....
1491      if (flags & MSG_OOB)
1492          goto recv_urg;
          ....
1494      seq = &tp->copied_seq;
          ....
1500      target = sock_rcvlowat(sk, flags & MSG_WAITALL, len);
          ....
1502      do {
          ....
1507          if (copied && tp->urg_data && tp->urg_seq == *seq)
1508              break;
          ....
1523          skb = skb_peek(&sk->receive_queue);
1524          do {
1525              if (!skb)
1526                  break;
              ...
1536              offset = *seq - TCP_SKB_CB(skb)->seq;
              ....
1539              if (offset < skb->len)
1540                  goto found_ok_skb;
              ....
1544              skb = skb->next;
1545          } while (skb != (struct sk_buff *)&sk->receive_queue);
          ....
1549          if (copied >= target && sk->backlog.tail == NULL)
1550              break;
          ....
1673 found_ok_skb:
1674          /* Ok so how much can we use? */
1675          used = skb->len - offset;
1676          if (len < used)
1677              used = len;
          ....
1680          if (tp->urg_data) {
1681              u32 urg_offset = tp->urg_seq - *seq;
1682              if (urg_offset < used) {
1683                  if (!urg_offset) {
1684                      if (!sk->urginline) {
1685                          ++*seq;
1686                          offset++;
1687                          used--;
1688                          if (!used)
1689                              goto skip_copy;
1690                      }
1691                  } else
1692                      used = urg_offset;
1693              }
1694          }
1695
1696          if (!(flags&MSG_TRUNC)) {
1697              err = skb_copy_datagram_iovec(skb, offset, msg->msg_iov, used);
1698              if (err) {
1699                  /* Exception. Bailout! */
1700                  if (!copied)
1701                      copied = -EFAULT;
1702                  break;
1703              }
1704          }
1705
1706          *seq += used;
1707          copied += used;
1708          len -= used;
          ....
```

cs 8.12a. tcp_recvmsg().

```
net/ipv4/tcp.c  tcp_recvmsg() contd....,

1715            if (used + offset < skb->len)
1716                continue;
        ....
1720            if (!(flags & MSG_PEEK))
1721                tcp_eat_skb(sk, skb);
1722            continue;
        ....
1730        } while (len > 0);
        ....
1756        cleanup_rbuf(sk, copied);
        ....
1764        release_sock(sk);
1765        return err;
        ....
1767 recv_urg:
1768        err = tcp_recv_urg(sk, timeo, msg, len, flags, addr_len);
1769        goto out;

            ...
1770 }
```

cs 8.12b. *tcp_recvmsg()* (continued).

tcp_ack_scheduled() at line 1291 (cs 8.13). If so, we can send ACK under following conditions:

1. Is the ACK blocked at line 1293? This may happen if the delayed ACK timer was intercepted by us as we are holding user status. Since we are called from *tcp_sendmsg()* holding user status, if the delayed ACK fires, ACK will be blocked. So, before releasing socket's user status, we are called. It is our job to send out blocked ACK in such cases.

2. We have not ACKed data of length greater than 1 mss at line 1295. $tp \rightarrow rcv\_wup$ is synced with $tp \rightarrow rcv\_nxt$ only when we send ACK.

3. When we have emptied the receive buffer, and there is data flow only in one direction ($tp \rightarrow ack.pingpong$ is not set).

In the case where none of the above conditions is TRUE, we still can send out an ACK if we have read some data because we might be opening the window. If the receive side of the socket is not shut down (we won't receive any data in this case) and the application has read some data before coming here (line 1316), we check if the window has opened. We get the last advertised window from *tcp_receive_window()* at line 1317. Next we check if twice of the window advertised is smaller than the window clamp (line 1320), and we calculate the new window by calling __tcp_select_window()* at line 1321. This routine will take into consideration space available in the receive buffer. If we have read enough data from the socket buffer, the window to be advertised will increase considerably. In the case where the new window calculated is more than twice of the window advertised last (line 1328), we need to send an ACK. This condition also satisfies the condition where the window is opened from zero.

We send an ACK by calling *tcp_send_ack()* at line 1333 if any of the conditions discussed above is satisfied.

```
net/ipv4/tcp.c

1280 static void cleanup_rbuf(struct sock *sk, int copied)
1281 {
1282      struct tcp_opt *tp = &(sk->tp_pinfo.af_tcp);
1283      int time_to_ack = 0;
           ....
1291      if (tcp_ack_scheduled(tp)) {
           ....
1293          if (tp->ack.blocked
           ....
1295              || tp->rcv_nxt - tp->rcv_wup > tp->ack.rcv_mss
           ....
1302              || (copied > 0 &&
1303              (tp->ack.pending&TCP_ACK_PUSHED) &&
1304              !tp->ack.pingpong &&
1305              atomic_read(&sk->rmem_alloc) == 0)) {
1306              time_to_ack = 1;
1307          }
1308      }
           ....
1316      if(copied > 0 && !time_to_ack && !(sk->shutdown&RCV_SHUTDOWN)) {
1317          __u32 rcv_window_now = tcp_receive_window(tp);
           
1320          if (2*rcv_window_now <= tp->window_clamp) {
1321              __u32 new_window = __tcp_select_window(sk);
               ....
1328              if(new_window && new_window >= 2*rcv_window_now)
1329                  time_to_ack = 1;
1330          }
1331      }
1332      if (time_to_ack)
1333          tcp_send_ack(sk);
1334 }
```

cs 8.13. _cleanup_rbuf()_.

8.2.2 _skb_copy_datagram_iovec()_

The routine is called to copy data from a socket buffer to a user buffer. We are passed a socket buffer (_sk_buff_) from where data need to be copied (offset within the buffer), a user buffer where data should be copied, and the length of data to be copied. The buffer is divided into two parts:

1. Linear data area
2. Paged data area or shared data area

First we read data from the linear data area and then get data from the paged data area. We first calculate linear data area length at line 208 (cs 8.14). _skb→len_ is the total length of the buffer, and _skb→data_len_ is the total length of the paged data area. If our offset is within the paged data area, we call _memcpy_toiovec()_ at line 214 to copy data from a given offset into the buffer to the user buffer. In the case where our request is satisfied from the linear data area, we return at line 216–217. If more data are requested, paged data are looked into for more data. We increment the offset by the amount of data copied at line 218.

Let's see how we get data from the paged data area. A number of fragments in the paged data area are stored in _skb_shinfo(skb)→nr_frags. skb_shinfo()_ is a

```
net/core/datagram.c

204  int skb_copy_datagram_iovec(const struct sk_buff *skb, int offset, struct iovec *to,
205                      int len)
206  {
207      int i, copy;
208      int start = skb->len - skb->data_len;
             ....
211      if ((copy = start-offset) > 0) {
212          if (copy > len)
213              copy = len;
214          if (memcpy_toiovec(to, skb->data + offset, copy))
215              goto fault;
216          if ((len -= copy) == 0)
217              return 0;
218          offset += copy;
219      }
             ....
222      for (i=0; i<skb_shinfo(skb)->nr_frags; i++) {
223          int end;
             ....
227          end = start + skb_shinfo(skb)->frags[i].size;
228          if ((copy = end-offset) > 0) {
229              int err;
230              u8 *vaddr;
231              skb_frag_t *frag = &skb_shinfo(skb)->frags[i];
232              struct page *page = frag->page;
233
234              if (copy > len)
235                  copy = len;
236              vaddr = kmap(page);
237              err = memcpy_toiovec(to, vaddr + frag->page_offset +
238                              offset-start, copy);
239              kunmap(page);
240              if (err)
241                  goto fault;
242              if (!(len -= copy))
243                  return 0;
244              offset += copy;
245          }
246          start = end;
247      }
248
249      if (skb_shinfo(skb)->frag_list) {
250          struct sk_buff *list;
251
252          for (list = skb_shinfo(skb)->frag_list; list; list=list->next) {
                 ....
257              end = start + list->len;
258              if ((copy = end-offset) > 0) {
259                  if (copy > len)
260                      copy = len;
261                  if (skb_copy_datagram_iovec(list, offset-start, to, copy))
262                      goto fault;
263                  if ((len -= copy) == 0)
264                      return 0;
265                  offset += copy;
266              }
267              start = end;
268          }
269      }
270      if (len == 0)
271          return 0;
272
273  fault:
274      return -EFAULT;
275  }
```

cs 8.14. *skb_copy_datagram_iovec()*.

macro that accesses the end of the linear data area where the *skb_shared_info* object for the buffer exists. For more details on *skb_shared_info* object, see Section 5.2. Each fragment is represented as an *skb_frag_t* object containing a pointer to the page (*frag→page*), offset within the page (*frag→page_offset*) and length of each fragment (*frag→size*). There is an array of *skb_frag_t* objects, *skb_shinfo(skb)→ frags* containing fragments. Data are stored sequentially in the successive elements of the array *skb_shinfo(skb)→frags*.

So, we traverse through all the fragments in a loop 222–247 to copy data until either the required data are copied or we have consumed all the data from the paged area. We use the same logic to find out whether the offset lies in the given fragment as we use for the linear data area. Offset and length of the fragment are calculated with respect to the base of the linear data area. For this reason, when we switch from linear to paged data area, the offset is recalculated as the amount of data copied from the linear data area at line 218. For each fragment we first calculate the total length of the buffer including the fragment at line 227. Next, we check if there is anything that can be copied from current fragment at line 228. In the case where we have already copied entire data from the current fragment, the new length is calculated as the cumulative length of the current fragment starting from the linear data area at line 246 and we access the next fragment from the array.

If we have data to be copied from a fragment and the number of bytes remaining in the page to be copied is more than the requested length, we adjust the amount that can be copied to the requested length at line 235. Next we access virtual address of the page for the fragment at line 236. We now copy number of required bytes from the page offset (*frag→page_offset*) starting from page virtual address to the user buffer by calling *memcpy_toiovec()* at line 237. If we have copied the entire data, return at line 243. Otherwise we calculate the new offset at line 244 by adding the copied length to it and start all over again.

In the case where we have fragmented buffer (IP datagram was received as fragments) and we have consumed all the data from paged data area, fragments (*skb_shinfo(skb)→frag_list*) of the buffer will contain rest of the data. Overall length of the main buffer is the sum of the lengths of all the fragments including itself. So, we find out if the next offset lies in any of the fragments while traversing the fragment list, line 252–268. once we find the fragment, we call *skb_copy_datagram_iovec()* recursively at line 261 and process the linear and paged data section of each fragment in the same way as we did for the main buffer.

8.2.3 Reading Data from Receive Buffer without Paged Data Area

Let's take an example of how we consume data from the receive buffer. We assume that the buffers in the receive buffer contain only linear data area and are not fragmented. Let's assume that we have received two full-sized segments as shown in Fig. 8.1. The application issues three reads of size X bytes, n bytes, and $(n - X)$ bytes, respectively. Let's see what happens to the buffers in the receive queue.

8.2.4 *X* Bytes Requested from the Application

After the first read of X bytes, the receive buffer will be as shown in Fig. 8.2. Since complete data from the first buffer is not completely consumed, it remains in the

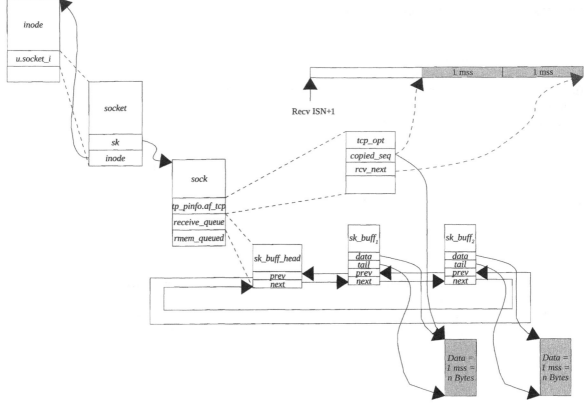

Figure 8.1. 2 mss of data to read from the receive buffer.

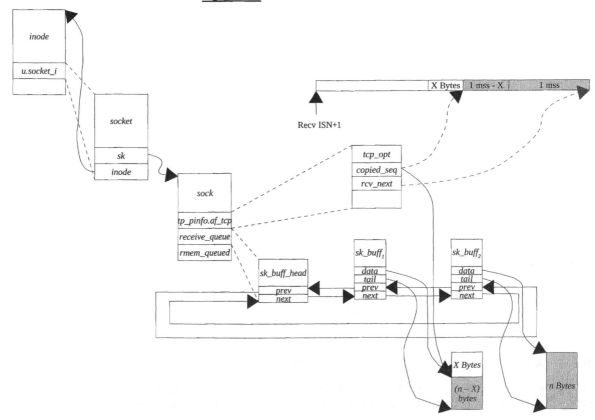

Figure 8.2. *X* bytes copied to the application buffer.

queue. From the sequence number and sequence space of the buffer, we can find out the exact byte from where we need to start reading next.

8.2.5 1 mss = *n* Bytes Requested from the Application

In the second read, application requests for n bytes (=1 mss) of data. At this time we have completely consumed first buffer in the receive queue, so it unlinked from the queue. Only $(n - X)$ bytes are remaining in the second buffer on the receive queue (Fig. 8.3), which will be consumed in the third read.

8.2.6 *n* − *X* Bytes Requested from the Application

The receive queue as seen after the third read of $(n - X)$ bytes is shown in Fig. 8.4. Here copied sequence is same as receive next because all the data in the receive queue are consumed.

8.2.7 Consumption of Data from a Paged Buffer

In this example we see how data are copied from the buffer with a paged data area. Suppose we have a total of $n + 2$ pages of data from the buffer. n bytes come from the linear data area and two pages come from the paged data area as shown in

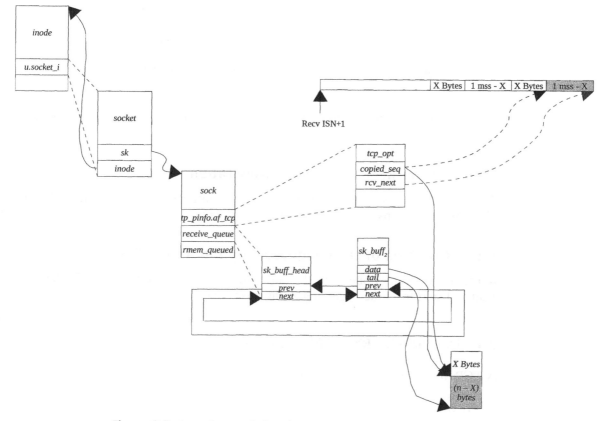

Figure 8.3. 1 mss data copied to the application buffer.

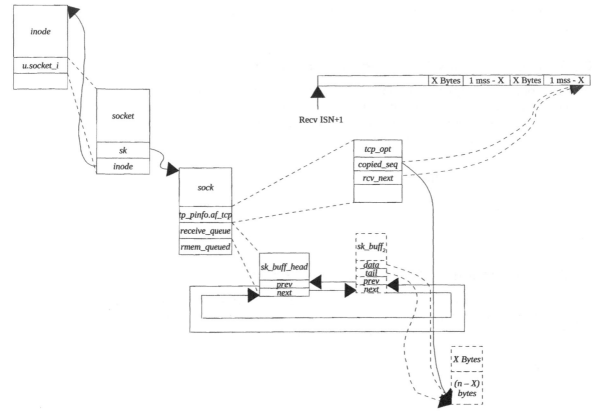

Figure 8.4. Complete data from a socket buffer are copied to a user buffer.

Fig. 8.5. The application issues 2 reads of *n* bytes and 1 page each. Let's see how data is copied in this case.

8.2.8 *n* Bytes Requested by the Application

After the first read of *n* bytes, the picture of the buffer will be as shown in Fig. 8.6. These bytes are consumed from the linear data area.

8.2.9 One Page of Data Requested by the Application

In the second read of one page, the buffer looks like as shown in Fig. 8.7. The next read will start from the beginning of the next page.

8.3 TCP URGENT BYTE PROCESSING

A TCP urgent byte can be read in two different modes:

1. Inline
2. Out-of-band

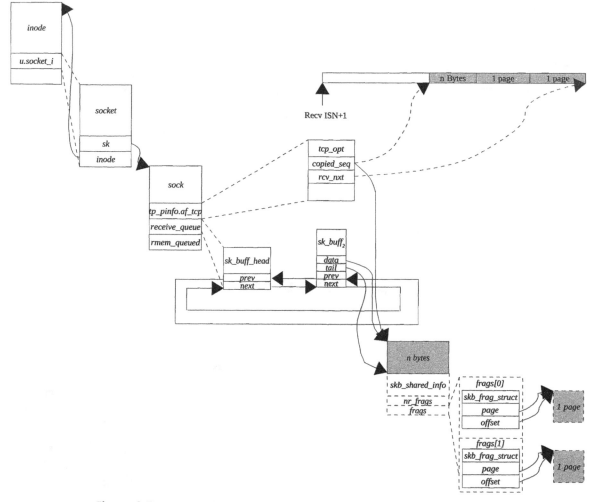

Figure 8.5. Data in a linear and paged data area of socket.

The default mode for a socket to receive an urgent byte is out-of-band. Out-of-band data are a socket level abstraction and have nothing to do with TCP byte-of-stream. In both the cases, the TCP transmits and receives an urgent byte as normal data. Once the urgent byte is received, it depends on the mode of reception of an urgent byte from where the urgent byte will be read. See cs 8.15 for all the codes referring to *tcp_recvmsg()*.

8.3.1 Urgent Byte Read as OOB Data

If an application wants to read an urgent byte as out-of-band data, it needs to issue *recv()* with an MSG_OOB set. There are ways to inform the application that the urgent data have arrived. It is up to the application to handle such events at the proper time and take the appropriate action to read the urgent byte. In the case where urgent byte is read inline, we don't need to issue *recv()* with an MSG_OOB flag set because it is read from the stream of bytes directly. *tcp_recvmsg()* is called

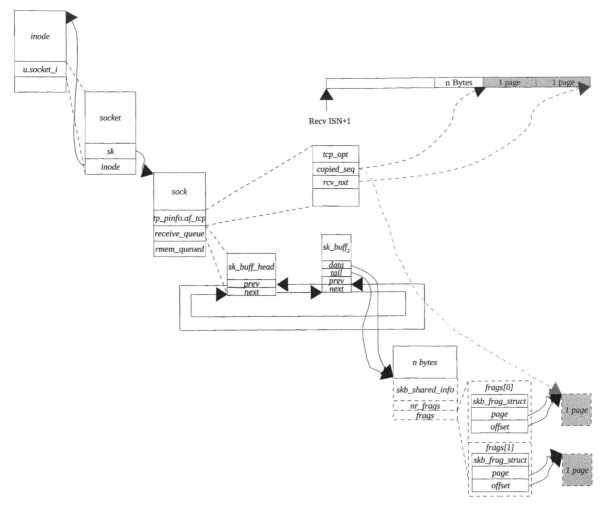

Figure 8.6. *n* bytes of data copied from a linear data area.

in the kernel to read an urgent byte. We start with reading an urgent byte as out-of-bound data by calling *tcp_recv_urg()* at line 1768 in *tcp_recvmsg()*.

8.3.2 *tcp_recv_urg()*

The very first thing we check here is whether we have any urgent byte to be read. For this we check three conditions at line 1224 (cs 8.15):

1. If the *sk→urginline* field is set, it means that we are supposed to read an urgent byte inline. This is the wrong request to read an urgent byte.
2. If the above fails, we need to check if *tp→urg_data* are still set, which means that we may have an urgent byte to be read. If not set, we just return with an error number set. We will see later that if an application reads past an urgent pointer mark without reading an urgent byte, that urgent byte is lost.

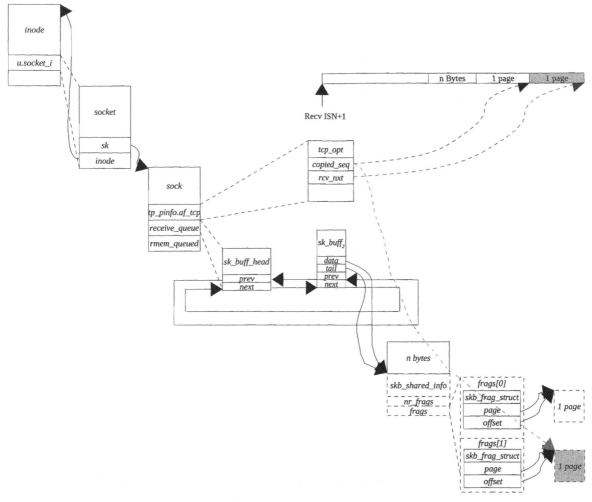

Figure 8.7. One page of data copied from a paged data area.

So, it is up to the application to read an urgent byte at the appropriate time.

3. If *tp→urg_data* is nonzero, we need to check if a TCP_URG_READ bit is set. If this flag is set, it means that an urgent byte is already read. So, we return with an appropriate error number set. A misbehaving application might issue more than one *recv()* for one urgent data notification.

Next we do some socket-related checks and check if the urgent data validity flag, TCP_URG_VALID, is set. This flag is set when we receive an urgent byte in *tcp_urg()* (see Section 11.7). If so, we read an urgent byte stored in the lower 8 bits of *tp→urg_data*. If we are just peeking urgent data, we won't set TCP_URG_READ flag set. Otherwise we clear everything and set the read flag indicating that the urgent byte is already read. If the number of bytes to be read is more than 1 and the message is not to be truncated, we read one byte of data in the user buffer at line 1242. Note that even with the MSG_PEEK flag set, we can read an urgent byte

```
net/ipv4/tcp.c

1217 static int tcp_recv_urg(struct sock * sk, long timeo,
1218              struct msghdr *msg, int len, int flags,
1219                int *addr_len)
        ....
1224    if (sk->urginline || !tp->urg_data || tp->urg_data == TCP_URG_READ)
1225        return -EINVAL; /* Yes this is right ! */
        ....
1230    if (tp->urg_data & TCP_URG_VALID) {
1231        int err = 0;
1232        char c = tp->urg_data;
1233
1234        if (!(flags & MSG_PEEK))
1235            tp->urg_data = TCP_URG_READ;
        ....
1238        msg->msg_flags|=MSG_OOB;
1239
1240        if(len>0) {
1241            if (!(flags & MSG_TRUNC))
1242                err = memcpy_toiovec(msg->msg_iov, &c, 1);
1243            len = 1;
1244        } else
        ....
1248    }
        ....
1259    return -EAGAIN;
1260 }
```

cs 8.15. tcp_recv_urg().

but do not set the TCP_URG_READ flag because the subsequent *recv()* will consume the urgent byte.

8.3.3 Urgent Mode Processing and Reading an Urgent Byte as Inline Data (see cs 8.12a and 8.12b unless mentioned)

We remain in urgent mode until we read the data past an urgent pointer mark. We do this in a normal data receive path in *tcp_recvmsg()*. Here we will see what happens when an urgent pointer is marked and we are reading normal data. In this section we will also see how a TCP urgent byte is read when we are receiving an urgent byte as inline data. From cs 8.12(a) and (b) (see *tcp_recvmsg()*) we are trying to read data from a socket's receive buffer. There are two loops here, and the outer loop (lines 1502–1730) makes sure that we get the amount of data requested wherein we may have to wait for the data or process the data from the prequeue, and it also does the job of copying data to a user buffer and performing processing related to urgent data. The inner loop (1524–1545) looks if there is any data to be read from a socket's receive buffer and if any data are to be read from the buffer, it provides us the buffer (*sk_buff*) from where data need to be copied (1539). It makes use of *tp→copied_seq* (line 1494) to find the buffer from where the requested data need to be copied to the user buffer. *tp→copied_seq* is the sequence number of the last byte in the stream of bytes which has been copied to the user buffer. We get the difference of the copied sequence and the start sequence number of the buffer as an offset in the buffer. If the offset is more than the buffer length, we have already copied the entire buffer so we move on to the next buffer. Once we have found the buffer, which means that the offset is less than the buffer length, we try to process the required data from the buffer in the outer loop by jumping to line 1673.

In the outer loop, we first check whether we have any valid urgent pointer at line 1507. In the case where we have valid urgent pointer, set ($tp{\rightarrow}urg\_data$). We discontinue reading any more data in the case where we have read some normal data and have already copied data ($tp{\rightarrow}copied\_seq$) pointed to by an urgent pointer mark ($tp{\rightarrow}urg\_seq$). Linux implementation supports both theories of urgent byte, where one says that an urgent byte is one byte ahead of the urgent pointer mark and the other one says that an urgent byte is exactly pointed to by an urgent pointer mark. We make these adjustments only at the time of reception of an urgent pointer (see Section 11.7.1). So, at this time we need not worry about any theory and consider that an urgent byte is pointed to by one byte ahead of an urgent pointer. If we have read a byte pointed to by an urgent pointer ($tp{\rightarrow}urg\_seq$), the next byte to be read is the urgent byte. So, if we are reading normal data, we will continue to read until we have read data up to an urgent pointer mark ($tp{\rightarrow}urg\_seq$) and return to the application even if more data are requested. The application can then check if an urgent pointer mark has reached. If so, an application can issue *recv()* of 1 byte to read in urgent byte. So, the condition at line 1507 makes sure that we should continue to read normal data until an urgent pointer mark and then stop. If we are entering the loop for the first time and next byte to be read is urgent byte, we go ahead and read it.

Let's discuss what happens when application issues read for normal data where urgent byte has already been received. Once we find a buffer that contains the next byte to be read, we jump to line 1673. First we check how much is already being read in the buffer at line 1675. Let's assume that the urgent byte also lies in the same buffer·(see Fig. 8.8).

Suppose an application issues a read of *n* bytes of normal data. The first byte is found to exist in the buffer as shown in Fig. 8.9. Our request can be satisfied by this buffer alone. We check if urgent data exist at line 1680. If the urgent data exist, we try to find out the offset of the urgent byte with respect to the sequence number corresponding to the last read byte. In the case where the urgent byte offset is more than the number of normal bytes that an application has requested, we just read the requested number of bytes and return it to the application as shown in Fig. 8.10.

In the case where an application has requested number of bytes beyond the urgent pointer mark and the current buffer can satisfy the request, we return the number of bytes until an urgent pointer mark (line 1692). Figure 8.11 and Figure 8.12 show a buffer state just after we return to the application. A good application design should try to sense an urgent data mark and then issue a read of 1 byte of data to read an urgent byte. Otherwise, we check if the next byte to be read is pointed to by an urgent pointer mark (a copied sequence is the same as an urgent pointer mark). If that is the case, the next byte to be read is an urgent byte. We take two different paths from here, depending on whether the socket is set to receive an urgent byte as out-of-band data ($sk{\rightarrow}urginline$ not set) or as inline data.

In the case where an urgent byte is received as out-of-band data, $sk{\rightarrow}urginline$ is not set. We know that the next byte is an urgent byte, and we skip reading the urgent byte. We will read the urgent byte from a different channel. In this case, we increment the copied sequence ($tp{\rightarrow}copied\_seq$) by 1 at line 1685. Next we check

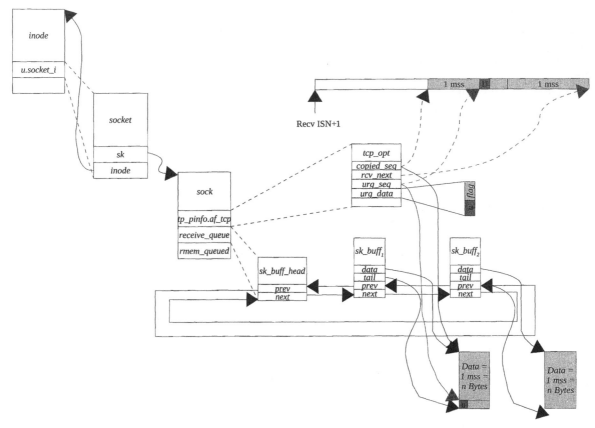

Figure 8.8. Urgent byte is received.

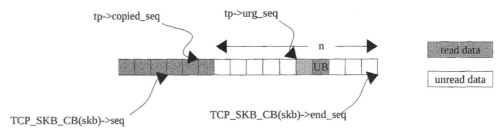

Figure 8.9. Urgent byte is covered by the sequence space of data requested by the application.

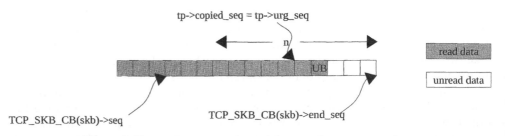

Figure 8.10. Application is returned data until an urgent pointer.

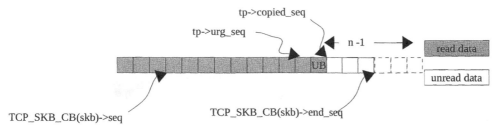

Figure 8.11. Application has read data past an urgent pointer.

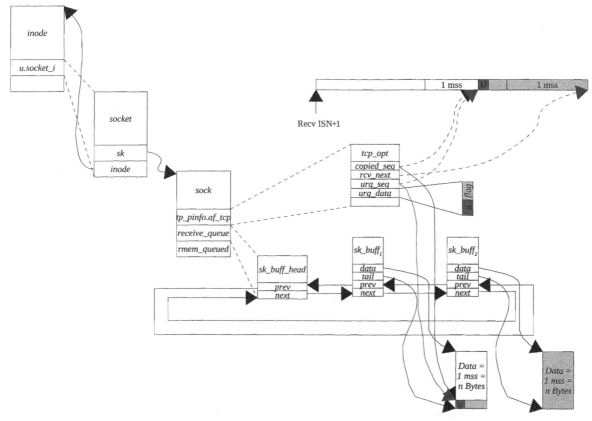

Figure 8.12. Application is returned data until an urgent pointer.

if the user has requested more than 1 byte, and we go ahead by reading the required number of bytes and skipping the urgent byte (line 1697) and then process the TCP urgent state at line 1710. In the case where the user has requested for only one byte, nothing needs to be copied to the user buffer and we jump to line 1710 for further processing of an urgent state.

An urgent byte is received inline. We don't skip an urgent byte and start reading the requested number of bytes starting from the next byte—that is, urgent byte. If *tp→urginline* is set, a good application design will request only 1 byte of urgent byte once it senses that the next byte to be read is an urgent byte.

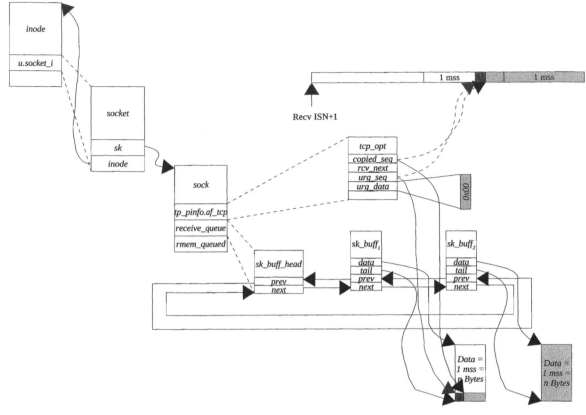

Figure 8.13. Application is returned data until an urgent pointer.

The next step is to process a TCP urgent state starting at line 1710. Since we have already read an urgent byte as shown in Fig. 8.11, we need to reset the flags related to an urgent state. We check the following:

1. If urgent data are valid (*tp→urg_data* is nonzero).
2. If an urgent byte has been read (*tp→copied_seq > tp→urg_seq*).

An urgent mode for the connection, once we have read data past an urgent byte, will be as shown in Fig. 8.13. If both of the above conditions are TRUE, *tp→urg_data* is reset and then we check if we can get back to the fast path of TCP processing. If we entered a slow path just because a new urgent pointer was received, a fast path will be enabled here.

8.4 DATA FLOW DIAGRAM FOR RECEIVING DATA OVER THE TCP SOCKET

Figures 8.14(a) through 8.14(f) show data flow diagram to implement reception of TCP data at the socket layer. They describe processing of different receive queues and also reception of TCP urgent data.

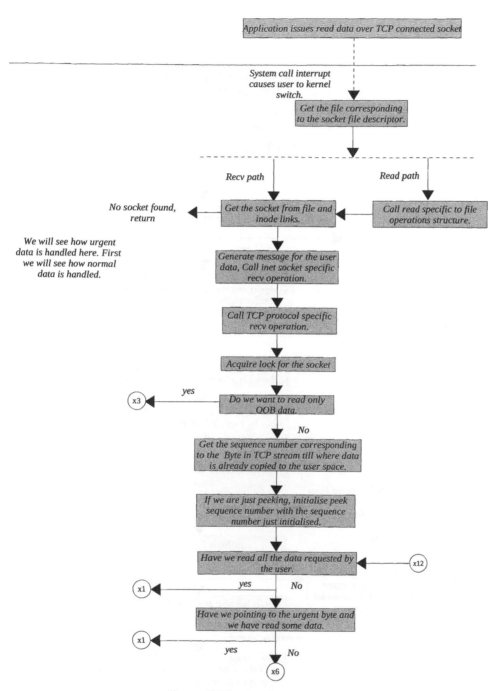

Figure 8.14a. Receive process.

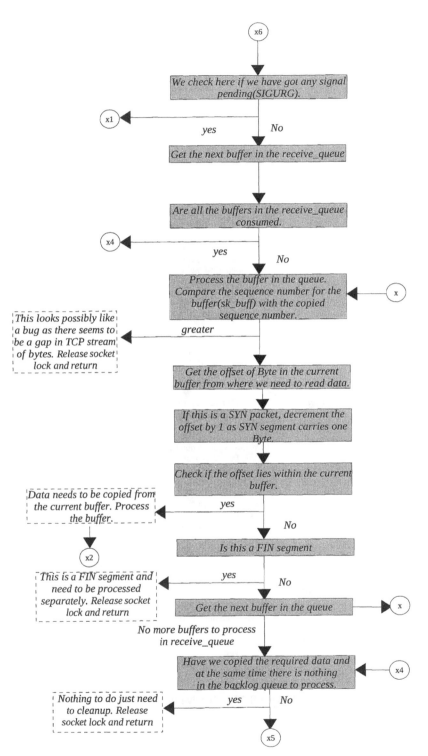

Figure 8.14b. Receive process (*continued*).

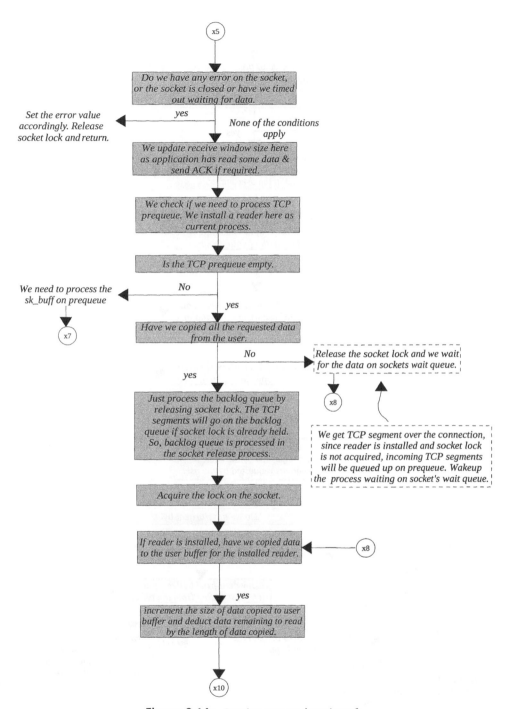

Figure 8.14c. Receive process (*continued*).

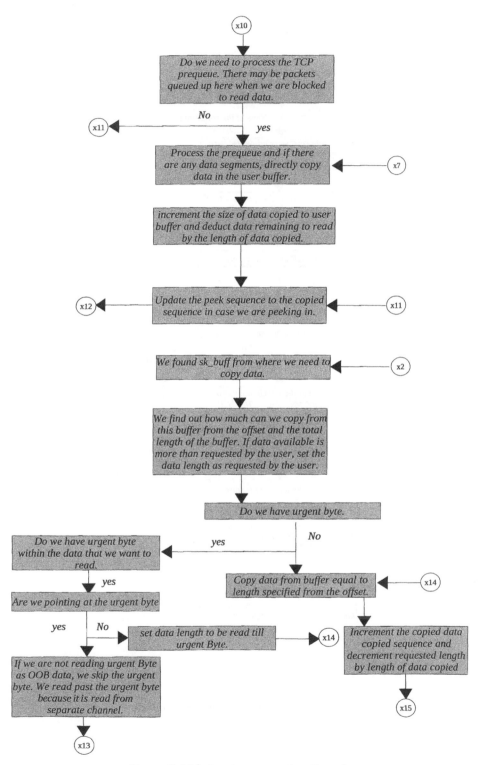

Figure 8.14d. Receive process (*continued*).

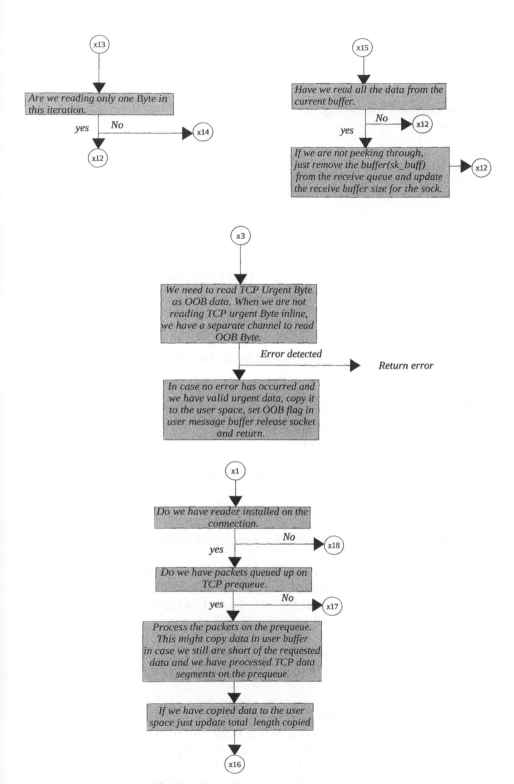

Figure 8.14e. Receive process (*continued*).

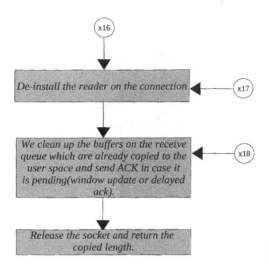

Figure 8.19. Receive process (*continued*).

8.5 SUMMARY

Incoming TCP data segments are processed from three different queues in the following order:

- Receive queue (*sk→receive_queue*)
- TCP prequeue (*tp→ucopy.prequeue*)
- Backlog queue (*sk→backlog*)

A backlog queue is processed when we release a socket's lock by calling *release_sock()*.

TCP segments are queued in the queue holding a socket spin lock by calling *bh_lock_sock()* in *tcp_v4_rcv()*.

TCP segments are processed from the queue after locking the socket by calling *lock_sock()* in *tcp_recvmsg()*.

tp→copied_seq is a sequence number associated with the byte in the TCP stream of bytes until data are copied to the application buffer.

tcp_data_wait() is called to wait for TCP data when the socket is blocking.

sk→urginline is a flag that indicates whether we are receiving a TCP urgent byte as out-of-band data or inline.

tp→urg_seq stores an urgent byte as well as flags associated with urgent data processing. In the case where we are receiving a TCP urgent byte as OOB data, it is read from here.

tcp_recv_urg() is called to receive an urgent byte in the case where we are receiving an urgent byte as OOB data.

tcp_eat_skb() is called to release a socket buffer from a receive queue once all the data from the buffer are already copied to a user application.

cleanup_rbuf() is called to check if ACK needs to be generated once data are read. This is required in the case where we have an opened window because an application has consumed data from the receive queue.

9

TCP MEMORY MANAGEMENT

Each TCP socket has send and receive buffers of fixed size. The reason for fixing buffer size is to allow each connection to fairly use system resources. If there was no limit on the size of the socket buffers, one connection on which data are communicated at a very fast rate would have left other connections starving for memory. Data from receive buffer are consumed when application issues receive a request on the TCP socket. Similarly, data from the send buffer is consumed only when data are ACKed.

TCP applies flow control on the connection when any of the buffers is full. Because of the difference rate of consumption of data and rate of arrival of data, we need a buffer. Linux does not allocate memory for socket buffers in one go. Memory is allocated in small chunks so that on every allocation we will can keep track of memory usage by socket and also overall system-wide memory usage by TCP. We will see how a socket's send and receive side buffer management is done in the current discussion.

9.1 TRANSMIT SIDE TCP MEMORY MANAGEMENT
(see cs 9.1 unless mentioned)

When we need to send out data over a TCP socket, new buffer needs to be allocated containing data. This buffer in Linux is represented by *struct sk_buff*. It contains complete TCP packet information as well as pointer to TCP payload. In this section we will see how memory is allocated for TCP buffer in *tcp_sendmsg()*. We will also

---

TCP/IP Architecture, Design, and Implementation in Linux. By S. Seth and M. A. Venkatesulu
Copyright © 2008 the IEEE Computer Society

check how a socket blocks in the case where memory is not available for the new buffer and how the sleeping socket is awakened when the memory is available. See Figure 9.1 for overview of send side TCP memory management memory.

When there is no partial packet at the head of the transmit queue, we need to allocate a new buffer (*sk_buff* object) to send out requested data over the socket, lines 1057–1058 (cs 9.1). In this case, the first thing that we do is check if the TCP memory quota is over for the socket by calling *tcp_memory_free()* at line 1064 (cs-9.1).

The routine (cs-9.2) checks if memory allocated for a socket's write buffer ($sk \rightarrow$ *wmem_queued*) is less than the maximum limit on the send buffer ($sk \rightarrow sndbuf$). If the condition is TRUE, we can allocate memory for the new send buffer; otherwise we need to wait for TCP memory to be available. The reason for nonavailability of

```
net/ipv4/tcp.c

1009 int tcp_sendmsg(struct sock *sk, struct msghdr *msg, int size)
1010 {
1011     struct iovec *iov;
         ....
1057             if (tp->send_head == NULL ||
1058             (copy = mss_now - skb->len) <= 0) {
1059
1060 new_segment:
         ....
1064             if (!tcp_memory_free(sk))
1065                 goto wait_for_sndbuf;
1066
1067             skb = tcp_alloc_pskb(sk, select_size(sk, tp), 0, sk->allocation);
1068             if (skb == NULL)
1069                 goto wait_for_memory;
1070
1071             skb_entail(sk, tp, skb);
1072             copy = mss_now;
1073         }


1114             if (!page) {
1115                 /* Allocate new cache page. */
1116                 if (!(page=tcp_alloc_page(sk)))
1117                     goto wait_for_memory;
1118                 off = 0;
1119             }
         ....
1176 wait_for_memory:
1177         if (copied)
1178             tcp_push(sk, tp, flags&~MSG_MORE, mss_now, 1);
1179
1180         if ((err = wait_for_tcp_memory(sk, &timeo)) != 0)
1181             goto do_error;
1182
1183         mss_now = tcp_current_mss(sk);
1184     }
1185 }
         ....
1208     release_sock(sk);
1209     return err;
1210 }
```

cs 9.1. *tcp_sendmsg()*.

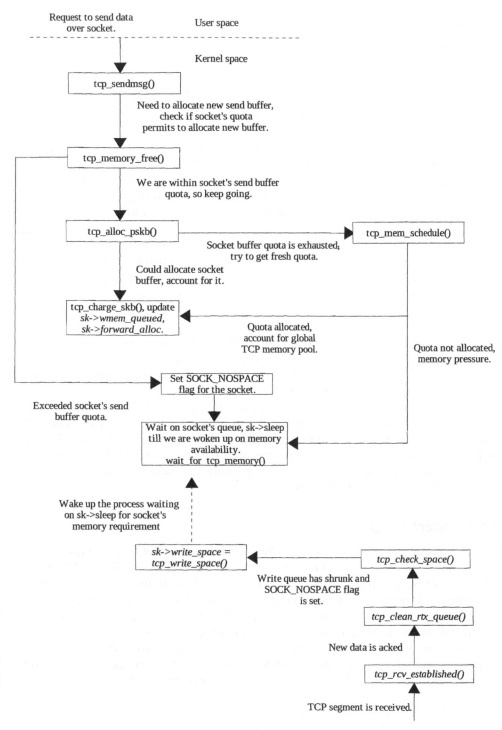

Figure 9.1. TCP memory management for send buffer.

```
net/ipv4/tcp.c

680 static inline int tcp_memory_free(struct sock *sk)
681 {
682        return sk->wmem_queued < sk->sndbuf;
683 }
```

cs 9.2. *tcp_memory_free().*

memory is that the socket buffers in the write queue are either not transmitted or not acknowledged. In this case we jump to line 1175, set *SOCK_NOSPACE* flag for the socket, and wait for memory to be available by calling *wait_for_tcp_memory()* at line 1180. We call *tcp_alloc_pskb()* to allocate memory for the socket send buffer. In the case where hardware is not capable of doing scatter–gather DMA(*NETIF_F_SG* bit is not set for *sk→route_caps*), this will allocate memory for a TCP payload of size 1 mss. Otherwise, if the hardware is scatter–gather-enabled and the paged area of single sk_buff can accommodate 1 mss of data, this routine should allocate 1 page of memory. Otherwise, it should allocate memory for the complete 1 mss as a linear data area. See Section 9.1.1 for more details on *select_size()*. In the case where *tcp_alloc_pskb()* fails to allocate a buffer of required length, we need to wait for memory to be available at line 1180 by calling *wait_for_tcp_memory()*. This memory requirement is different from the requirement at line 1065, which is because the socket's send buffer is already full. In case, buffer is allocated successfully, we need to account for allocated memory for the write side socket by calling *skb_charge()* from *skb_entail()* at line 1071.

In the case where the hardware interface is capable of doing scatter–gather DMA, we don't allocate a big chunk of memory for linear data area to copy the entire 1 mss of data. If data require more than 1 page of space, pages are allocated as per the requirement in the paged date area (see Section 5.1). For this we call *tcp_alloc_page()* at line 1116. If we fail to allocate the page here, we need to wait for memory by jumping at line 1180.

9.1.1 *select_size()*

The size passed to *tcp_alloc_pskb()* is the one returned by *select_size()* (cs 9.3). We first take mss value as stored in *tp→mss_cache*. In the case where the NETIF_F_SG bit is not set for sk→route_caps (hardware is capable of doing scatter–gather), we calculate the length of the buffer; that is, 1 page—(*MAX_TCP_HEADER* + size of object *skb_shared_info)* by using macro *SKB_MAX_HEAD* (cs 9.4). *MAX_TCP_HEADER* is the maximum number of bytes occupied by TCP + IP + link layer headers along with options (cs 9.5). The end of the linear area of *sk_buff* should contain object *skb_shared_info*. So, *SKB_MAX_HEAD* macro called at line 1001 should return the actual TCP payload bytes that can be accommodated within a page.

Continuing with *select_size()* at line 1003, we check if the space left in a page can make a full-length TCP segment. If yes, it means that a complete segment can be accommodated in a single page. Otherwise, mss is big enough to be accommodated in a single page and we need to allocate pages in paged data area of sk_buff to make a full segment. We can allocate maximum up to (*MAX_SKB_FRAGS* − 1) pages for a single *sk_buff*. If our mss can be accommodated in a a single sk_buff's

```
net/ipv4/tcp.c

 996 static inline int select_size(struct sock *sk, struct tcp_opt *tp)
 997 {
 998      int tmp = tp->mss_cache;
 999
1000      if (sk->route_caps&NETIF_F_SG) {
1001           int pgbreak = SKB_MAX_HEAD(MAX_TCP_HEADER);
1002
1003           if (tmp >= pgbreak && tmp <= pgbreak + (MAX_SKB_FRAGS-1)*PAGE_SIZE)
1004                tmp = pgbreak;
1005      }
1006      return tmp;
1007 }
```

cs 9.3. select_size().

```
include/linux/skbuff.h

38 #define SKB_MAX_ORDER(X,ORDER)  (((PAGE_SIZE<<(ORDER)) - (X) - sizeof(struct skb_shared_info))&~(SMP_CACHE_BYTES-1))
39 #define SKB_MAX_HEAD(X)      (SKB_MAX_ORDER((X),0))
```

cs 9.4. Calculation of memory size for sk_buff.

```
include/net/tcp.h

263 #define MAX_TCP_HEADER (128 + MAX_HEADER)
```

cs 9.5. Maximum header size for a TCP packet, taking into account TCP/IP options and link layer header length.

paged data area, we return bytes returned by *SKB_MAX_HEAD* as pages can be allocated for the rest of the data. Otherwise, complete mss is returned wherein we need to allocate a big chunk of memory for *sk_buff's* linear area. In a nut shell, *select_size()* returns 1 page of data in case our hardware is capable of doing scatter–gather, given that the complete segment can be accommodated in paged area of single *sk_buff*. In all other cases, 1 mss is returned for the linear data area of *sk_buff*.

9.1.2 *tcp_alloc_pskb()*

This routine returns buffer (*sk_buff*) with pointer to the linear data area of size as requested. First we call *alloc_skb()* with linear data area length that is split as size of TCP payload (*size*) + *MAX_TCP_HEADER* at line 1712 (cs 9.6). If we are able to allocate *sk_buff* with the required length of linear data area, we need to check if our quota allows us to do that. *skb→truesize* contains the total length of memory allocated for this buffer, which includes (size of *sk_buff* object + length of linear data area). We will learn this in the next section. Next we will check if memory to be forward allocated for the socket is more than total size of the buffer allocated

```
include/net/tcp.h

1710 static inline struct sk_buff *tcp_alloc_pskb(struct sock *sk, int size, int mem, int gfp)
1711 {
1712     struct sk_buff *skb = alloc_skb(size+MAX_TCP_HEADER, gfp);
1713
1714     if (skb) {
1715         skb->truesize += mem;
1716         if (sk->forward_alloc >= (int)skb->truesize ||
1717             tcp_mem_schedule(sk, skb->truesize, 0)) {
1718             skb_reserve(skb, MAX_TCP_HEADER);
1719             return skb;
1720         }
1721         __kfree_skb(skb);
1722     } else {
1723         tcp_enter_memory_pressure();
1724         tcp_moderate_sndbuf(sk);
1725     }
1726     return NULL;
1727 }
```

cs 9.6. tcp_alloc_pskb().

($skb \rightarrow truesize$) at line 1716. If not, we need not worry and return a buffer at line 1719. Otherwise, we check if we can allocate required amount of memory for the buffer by calling *tcp_mem_schedule()* at line 1717. In the case where we are able to allocate memory for the buffer, we return the pointer to the allocated buffer. Learn more about scheduling of memory in Section 9.1.6.

In the case where we are not able to allocate memory for the buffer, we need to enter a TCP memory pressure zone by calling *tcp_enter_memory_pressure()* and also call *tcp_moderate_sndbuf()* to moderate our send buffer at line 1724. We enter memory pressure to globally let all the users of TCP sockets in the system know that we have memory crunch and need to wait until we memory is available. We moderate out send buffer so that we wait for memory to be available before even trying so hard (*tcp_memory_free()* should fail, Section 9.1).

9.1.3 alloc_skb()

The routine can also be called from interrupt context. So, we need to check if it is called from interrupt context and *__GFP_WAIT* flag is set. If so, we should disable the flag because we can't sleep in interrupt context; otherwise it will freeze the system. First, we try to allocate a buffer head (*sk_buff* object) from the pool by calling *skb_head_from_pool()* at line 180 (cs 9.7). We keep some of the freed *sk_buff's* in this pool so that we don't need to knock at the cache for getting sk_buff object, which is expensive. If we fail here, we allocate *sk_buff* from cache at line 182. If we don't get an *sk_buff* object from cache, we return NULL. We now allocate a memory chunk requested for the linear data area of *sk_buff* object by calling *kmalloc()* at line 189. If we succeed in getting the memory chunk, we initialize a *truesize* field of *sk_buff* to the size of memory block requested + size of *sk_buff* object at line 194. Next we make the head of the buffer point to the start of the memory chunk at line 197. We do other initializations here, but it is of no relevance to the topic.

```
net/core/skbuff.c

164 struct sk_buff *alloc_skb(unsigned int size,int gfp_mask)
165 {
166     struct sk_buff *skb;
167     u8 *data;
        ....
179     /* Get the HEAD */
180     skb = skb_head_from_pool();
181     if (skb == NULL) {
182         skb = kmem_cache_alloc(skbuff_head_cache, gfp_mask & ~ __GFP_DMA);
183         if (skb == NULL)
184             goto nohead;
185     }
        ....
188     size = SKB_DATA_ALIGN(size);
189     data = kmalloc(size + sizeof(struct skb_shared_info), gfp_mask);
190     if (data == NULL)
191         goto nodata;
        ...
194     skb->truesize = size + sizeof(struct sk_buff);
        ....
197     skb->head = data;
        ....
211     return skb;
212
213 nodata:
214     skb_head_to_pool(skb);
215 nohead:
216     return NULL;
217 }
```

cs 9.7. *alloc_skb().*

```
include/net/tcp.h

1734 static inline struct page * tcp_alloc_page(struct sock *sk)
1735 {
1736     if (sk->forward_alloc >= (int)PAGE_SIZE ||
1737         tcp_mem_schedule(sk, PAGE_SIZE, 0)) {
1738         struct page *page = alloc_pages(sk->allocation, 0);
1739         if (page)
1740             return page;
1741     }
1742     tcp_enter_memory_pressure();
1743     tcp_moderate_sndbuf(sk);
1744     return NULL;
1745 }
```

cs 9.8. *tcp_alloc_page().*

9.1.4 *tcp_alloc_page()*

This routine is called when we want to allocate a page for a TCP buffer (paged area of *sk_buff* object). This is called from *tcp_sendmsg()* at line 1116. We first check if we have already consumed all the forward allocated memory (*sk→forward_alloc*) at line 1736 (cs 9.8). We allocate memory in multiples of page size. We learn more about sk→forward_alloc in Section 9.1.6. We try to look for the possibility of allocating the single page memory quota for our socket by calling *tcp_mem_schedule()*

```
include/net/tcp.h

1679 static inline void tcp_charge_skb(struct sock *sk, struct sk_buff *skb)
1680 {
1681      sk->wmem_queued += skb->truesize;
1682      sk->forward_alloc -= skb->truesize;
1683 }
```

cs 9.9. tcp_charge_skb().

at line 1737. If permission is granted, alloc_page() is called to allocate a single page of memory.

In the case where we are not allowed additional page quota or a new page could not be allocated, we know that there is memory pressure. So, we call *tcp_enter_ memory_pressure()* to declare socket users that there is memory crunch for TCP memory pool. We also try to moderate the send buffer size so that we may not have to come along so far next time.

9.1.5 *skb_charge()*

Whenever we allocate a buffer (*sk_buff*) to send data over the socket, this routine is called to account for memory used by a socket. $sk \rightarrow wmem\_queued$ is the amount of memory used by the socket send buffer queued in the transmit queue and are either not yet sent out or not yet acknowledged (cs 9.9). We add the size of the buffer to $sk \rightarrow wmem\_queued$. We also decrement socket's *forward_alloc* field by the size of the buffer. We allocate memory in multiple pages in *tcp_mem_schedule()*. Whenever we free a socket buffer, this field is incremented by size of the socket buffer. More details are given in Section 9.1.7.

9.1.6 *tcp_mem_schedule()*

We are called whenever the forward allocated memory is exhausted, which means that the requirement of memory for a new socket buffer is less than the total memory currently available in the socket's quota ($sk \rightarrow forward\_alloc$). We are called from memory allocation routines such as *tcp_alloc_page(), tcp_alloc_pskb()*, and so on. We get the size of buffer to be allocated. This routine does all the required checks before actually allocating memory for the socket's buffer. These checks will be system-wide TCP memory pressure, socket's memory quota, and so on; and if all the condition's are satisfied, we get the requested quota.

First we round off the memory requirements to multiple of *TCP_MEM_ QUANTUM* size (1 page) by using macro TCP_PAGES at line 289 (cs 9.10). This provides us the number of pages that we need to allocate. So, we add total memory calculated to sk→forward_alloc at line 291. Add total memory allocated to a global TCP memory pool, *tcp_memory_allocated*, at line 292. Now we check if the total memory allocated via the TCP memory pool has exceeded the lower limit on the TCP memory pool (*sysctl_tcp_mem[0]*) at line 295. If the memory pool is not exceeded and memory pressure is indicated, we put off memory pressure at line 297. If memory allocated to TCP is underutilized, we should remove TCP memory pressure and we reach the requested memory quota.

```
net/ipv4/tcp.c

285 #define TCP_PAGES(amt) (((amt)+TCP_MEM_QUANTUM-1)/TCP_MEM_QUANTUM)
286
287 int tcp_mem_schedule(struct sock *sk, int size, int kind)
288 {
289     int amt = TCP_PAGES(size);
290
291     sk->forward_alloc += amt*TCP_MEM_QUANTUM;
292     atomic_add(amt, &tcp_memory_allocated);
            ...
295     if (atomic_read(&tcp_memory_allocated) < sysctl_tcp_mem[0]) {
296         if (tcp_memory_pressure)
297             tcp_memory_pressure = 0;
298         return 1;
299     }
            ...
302     if (atomic_read(&tcp_memory_allocated) > sysctl_tcp_mem[2]) {
303         tcp_enter_memory_pressure();
304         goto suppress_allocation;
305     }
            ....
308     if (atomic_read(&tcp_memory_allocated) > sysctl_tcp_mem[1])
309         tcp_enter_memory_pressure();
310
311     if (kind) {
312         if (atomic_read(&sk->rmem_alloc) < sysctl_tcp_rmem[0])
313             return 1;
314     } else {
315         if (sk->wmem_queued < sysctl_tcp_wmem[0])
316             return 1;
317     }
318
319     if (!tcp_memory_pressure ||
320         sysctl_tcp_mem[2] > atomic_read(&tcp_sockets_allocated)
321         * TCP_PAGES(sk->wmem_queued+atomic_read(&sk->rmem_alloc)+
322             sk->forward_alloc))
323         return 1;
324
325 suppress_allocation:
326
327     if (kind == 0) {
328         tcp_moderate_sndbuf(sk);
            ....
333         if (sk->wmem_queued+size >= sk->sndbuf)
334             return 1;
335     }
            ....
338     sk->forward_alloc -= amt*TCP_MEM_QUANTUM;
339     atomic_sub(amt, &tcp_memory_allocated);
340     return 0;
341 }
```

cs 9.10. tcp_mem_schedule().

If total memory allocated for the TCP pool has exceeded the higher limit (*sysctl_tcp_mem[2]*), we enter memory pressure by calling *tcp_enter_memory_ pressure()* at line 303. This routine sets *tcp_memory_pressure* to 1, in case it is not already set. We need to suppress allocation at this condition because we cannot utilize all the available memory for TCP socket requirement. So, we jump to line 327. If we have come here for send buffer memory requirements, we still have a chance to allocate memory. For this we first try to moderate send buffer size by calling tcp_moderate_sndbuf(). If we are able to shrink the same, we make sure that next attempt to send tcp data will block for memory as tcp_memory_free() fails and we return success ... Finally we reclaim whatever memory we allocated at the entry. *sk→forward_alloc* and *tcp_memory_allocated* are subtracted by the amount allocated, because we could not succeed.

In case we have not reached a hard limit, we check if we are entering a pressure zone at line 308. If so, we just mark TCP memory pressure by calling *tcp_enter_memory_pressure()*. In this case, we can allocate memory if the socket's buffer limit has not reached. If we have come here for receive buffer requirement and receive buffer memory allocated so far, (*sk→rmem_alloc*) is below receive allocation limits for the socket (*sysctl_tcp_rmem[0]*), and we got the allocation approved (line 312). If we are here for send buffer requirements and send buffer allocated so far, (*sk→wmem_queued*) is below send buffer allocation limit (*sysctl_tcp_wmem[0]*), and we got our allocation approved (line 315). In both cases if we fail because we have reached the memory allocation limits, we still have a chance to get our allocation approved in the following circumstances:

1. There is no memory pressure or,
2. If we consider the average memory consumed by each allocated socket in the system (*tcp_sockets_allocated*) the same as memory consumed by this socket (*sk→wmem_queued* + *sk→rmem_alloc* + *sk→forward_alloc*), the total memory consumed should not exceed the hard limit for TCP memory allocation (*sysctl_tcp_mem[2]*).

If any of the above conditions is TRUE, we can still get approval for the memory requirements. Otherwise we will dishonor the request.

9.1.7 *tcp_free_skb()*

This routine is called whenever we are freeing *sk_buff* allocated for TCP sockets. For example, we call this when a TCP segment in the retransmit queue is acknowledged. Here we set *queue_shrunk* field of *tcp_opt* object to 1 so that if there is a memory requirement for send buffer, we can wake up the socket as soon as we call *tcp_data_snd_check()* next (see Section 11.3.11). The *queue_shrunk* field indicates if some memory is released because write queue has shrunk. Next we decrement the memory allocated for send buffer by size of buffer being freed at line 1674 and also increment forward allocated memory (*sk→forward_alloc*) by size of the buffer being released; this memory goes in the socket's pool (cs 9.11). Finally we call __kfree_skb() to release the socket by calling the destructor routine for the buffer. For send buffer, this destructor routine is *sock_wfree()*.

9.1.8 *sock_wfree()*

This is a destructor routine for send buffer and is a common routine for any type of socket. It is called when the buffer (*sk_buff*) is being freed. It decreases total write memory allocated (*sk→wmem_alloc*) by size of the buffer. If configured, we wake up the socket by calling sk→write_space (=*sock_def_write_space()*) at line 652 to wake up the socket, in case it is waiting for memory requirements for send buffer.

```
include/net/tcp.h

1671 static inline void tcp_free_skb(struct sock *sk, struct sk_buff *skb)
1672 {
1673     sk->tp_pinfo.af_tcp.queue_shrunk = 1;
1674     sk->wmem_queued -= skb->truesize;
1675     sk->forward_alloc += skb->truesize;
1676     __kfree_skb(skb);
1677 }
```

cs 9.11. tcp_free_skb().

```
fnet/core/sock.c

645 void sock_wfree(struct sk_buff *skb)
646 {
647     struct sock *sk = skb->sk;
648
649     /* In case it might be waiting for more memory. */
650     atomic_sub(skb->truesize, &sk->wmem_alloc);
651     if (!sk->use_write_queue)
652         sk->write_space(sk);
653     sock_put(sk);
654 }
```

cs 9.12. sock_wfree().

```
net/core/sock.c

464 void tcp_write_space(struct sock *sk)
465 {
466     struct socket *sock = sk->socket;
467
468     if (tcp_wspace(sk) >= tcp_min_write_space(sk) && sock) {
469         clear_bit(SOCK_NOSPACE, &sock->flags);
470
471         if (sk->sleep && waitqueue_active(sk->sleep))
472             wake_up_interruptible(sk->sleep);
473
474         if (sock->fasync_list && !(sk->shutdown&SEND_SHUTDOWN))
475             sock_wake_async(sock, 2, POLL_OUT);
476     }
477 }
```

cs 9.13. tcp_write_space().

9.1.9 tcp_write_space()

This is a callback routine for write side TCP socket called whenever write queue is shrunk (send buffers are freed). Since write queue has shrunk (TCP segments are being acknowledged), there may be chance that the socket may be waiting for memory availability to write data over the socket. So, we call this routine to check if the write queue has shrunk enough to wake up the socket waiting for memory. The condition here is that the total memory left to completely exhaust the write socket buffer (returned from *tcp_wspace()*) should be at least equal to half of the memory allocated for the write socket buffers (*sk→wmem_queued*), line 468 (cs 9.13).

```
include/net/tcp.h

1044 static inline int tcp_min_write_space(struct sock *sk)
1045 {
1046        return sk->wmem_queued/2;
1047 }
1048
1049 static inline int tcp_wspace(struct sock *sk)
1050 {
1051        return sk->sndbuf - sk->wmem_queued;
1052 }
```

cs 9.14. *tcp_min_write_space()*.

```
include/net/tcp.h

1688 static inline void tcp_mem_reclaim(struct sock *sk)
1689 {
1690        if (sk->forward_alloc >= TCP_MEM_QUANTUM)
1691            __tcp_mem_reclaim(sk);
1692 }
```

cs 9.15. *tcp_mem_reclaim()*.

If the condition is TRUE and some process is waiting for socket's wait queue (line 471), we wake up the process by calling *wake_up_interruptable()* at line 472 because memory is now available. *tcp_wspace()* returns the amount of space left in the write queue to complete exhaust the send quota. *tcp_min_write_space()* returns half of the space occupied by the write queue (cs 9.14).

9.1.10   *tcp_mem_reclaim()*

This routine is called to reclaim the memory allocated for the socket's memory pool to TCP memory pool if the forward allocated memory for the socket is more than a unit of TCP memory allocation (1 page). It may happen that a lot of memory is being allocated for the socket's send buffer and the socket's memory pool is not being reused because a huge number of segments are transmitted before any one is acknowledged (high send window). Once all of these segments are acknowledged, the socket's memory pool (*sk→forward_alloc*) becomes huge even if it not being utilized fully, also consuming a huge amount of memory from a system-wide common TCP memory pool causing memory pressure (cs 9.15). So, frequently we need to check if we can reclaim memory from a socket's memory pool. This routine is called from timer callback routines such as tcp_delack_timer(), tcp_write_timer(), and so on.

9.1.11   *__tcp_mem_reclaim()*

In the case where the socket's memory pool contains more than a unit of TCP memory allocation (*TCP_MEM_QUANTUM*), we return a number of pages contained in the socket's memory pool from global TCP memory pool (*tcp_memory_allocated*), line 346 (cs 9.16). This will make availability of TCP memory globally.

```
net/ipv4/tcp.c

343 void __tcp_mem_reclaim(struct sock *sk)
344 {
345      if (sk->forward_alloc >= TCP_MEM_QUANTUM) {
346          atomic_sub(sk->forward_alloc/TCP_MEM_QUANTUM, &tcp_memory_allocated);
347          sk->forward_alloc &= (TCP_MEM_QUANTUM-1);
348          if (tcp_memory_pressure &&
349              atomic_read(&tcp_memory_allocated) < sysctl_tcp_mem[0])
350                  tcp_memory_pressure = 0;
351      }
352 }
```

cs 9.16. __tcp_mem_reclaim().

Next we keep a number of bytes, if at all left, within a page in the socket's memory pool, line 347. If there is a memory pressure and the total memory allocated from global TCP memory pool is less than the lower limit on the memory allocation (*sysctl_tcp_mem[0]*), we release memory pressure at lines 348–350.

9.1.12   *wait_for_tcp_memory()*

This routine is called when we need to wait for memory to be available for a send socket buffer. We call this routine in two cases:

- Either socket send buffer quota is full (*sk→wmem_queued >= sk→sndbuf*).
- There is memory pressure and we have not exhausted our send buffer quota.

Let's see how it works. We check if the routine is called because we could not allocate a quota for the socket because of memory pressure. The fact that the socket's send buffer quota is not yet exhausted is an indication of this, line 695. If that is the case, we need to set a new timeout value at line 696, so that we can wait for some time for some more free memory to be available with the system. Next we loop until one of the events happens:

- The socket encounters an error or the send side of the socket has been shut down, line 704 (cs 9.17).
- The timeout value has expired, line 706. In the first iteration we can get out of the loop if we are nonblocking.
- We obtained a signal. We check this by calling *signal_pending()* at line 708. We may get a signal because of which we are awakened from sleep.
- We obtained the socket's send buffer quota and we are not waiting for system to free more TCP memory, line 711. If we are called because the socket's send buffer was exhausted and now *tcp_memory_free()* returns TRUE, it means that the send buffer quota is now available. In this case, we should not wait for VM timewait. In the case where we had come here because the system memory in general is not available but the socket's send buffer quota exists, we should at least wait until VM timeout occurs so that some system memory is freed by now. VM timeout is calculated at line 696.

```
net/ipv4/tcp.c

688 static int wait_for_tcp_memory(struct sock * sk, long *timeo)
689 {
690     int err = 0;
691     long vm_wait = 0;
692     long current_timeo = *timeo;
693     DECLARE_WAITQUEUE(wait, current);
694
695     if (tcp_memory_free(sk))
696         current_timeo = vm_wait = (net_random()%(HZ/5))+2;
697
698     add_wait_queue(sk->sleep, &wait);
699     for (;;) {
700         set_bit(SOCK_ASYNC_NOSPACE, &sk->socket->flags);
701
702         set_current_state(TASK_INTERRUPTIBLE);
703
704         if (sk->err || (sk->shutdown & SEND_SHUTDOWN))
705             goto do_error;
706         if (!*timeo)
707             goto do_nonblock;
708         if (signal_pending(current))
709             goto do_interrupted;
710         clear_bit(SOCK_ASYNC_NOSPACE, &sk->socket->flags);
711         if (tcp_memory_free(sk) && !vm_wait)
712             break;
713
714         set_bit(SOCK_NOSPACE, &sk->socket->flags);
715         sk->tp_pinfo.af_tcp.write_pending++;
716         release_sock(sk);
717         if (!tcp_memory_free(sk) || vm_wait)
718             current_timeo = schedule_timeout(current_timeo);
719         lock_sock(sk);
720         sk->tp_pinfo.af_tcp.write_pending--;
721
722         if (vm_wait) {
723             vm_wait -= current_timeo;
724             current_timeo = *timeo;
725             if (current_timeo != MAX_SCHEDULE_TIMEOUT &&
726                 (current_timeo -= vm_wait) < 0)
727                 current_timeo = 0;
728             vm_wait = 0;
729         }
730         *timeo = current_timeo;
731     }
732 out:
733     current->state = TASK_RUNNING;
734     remove_wait_queue(sk->sleep, &wait);
735     return err;
736
737 do_error:
738     err = -EPIPE;
739     goto out;
740 do_nonblock:
741     err = -EAGAIN;
742     goto out;
743 do_interrupted:
744     err = sock_intr_errno(*timeo);
745     goto out;
746 }
```

cs 9.17. wait_for_tcp_memory().

In each iteration, set the current task state to *TASK_INTERRUPTIBLE*, line 702. We set *SOCK_NOSPACE* flag for the socket, line 714. Next we need to wait for memory to be available at line 717 in any of two cases:

- The socket's send buffer quota is exhausted.
- We have come here because of system memory crunch and our VM timeout is not exhausted.

If any of the above cases is TRUE, we call *schedule_timeout()* to wait for specified time, line 718. We don't hold a socket lock while going to sleep, so we release the socket lock at line 716. Once we are awakened because of timeout or we got a signal or somebody woke us up because the socket's send buffer has shrunk, we hold the socket's lock at line 719 and proceed.

When we return from *schedule_timeout()* and VM timeout is set, we need to recalculate the timeout value. In case we are interrupted, *schedule_timeout()* returns the time left in expiry of scheduled timeout. We reset VM timeout at line 728. If we are not woken up because of signal, we might have timed out or we are woken up because some one released TCP memory and woke us up. In the second iteration, we will block only if TCP memory crunch still exists (tcp-memory-free() returns FALSE) because VM timeout will be reset in first iteration in any case. In all the cases, we break from the loop. We come out of the loop, so we should set ourselves to the *TASK_RUNNING* state and remove ourselves from socket's wait queue, *sk→sleep*, at lines 733–734. In case of the nonblocking systemcall or if we have timed out, we set the error number to EAGAIN at line 741. In case the send side of socket has shut down, we set the error number to *EPIPE* at line 738. In case we are interrupted because of signal, we set the error number to *ERESTARTSYS* or *EINTR* depending of whether we were blocked forever or not, line 744.

9.2   RECEIVE SIDE TCP MEMORY MANAGEMENT

In this section we will see how memory is managed for receive socket buffers. We take a snapshot of *tcp_rcv_established()* to learn about socket buffer memory management. When we get a data segment, it gets processed in *tcp_rcv_established()*. If we got a data segment containing new data and data could not be copied to the user buffer, we need to queue it in the receive queue (*sk→receive_queue*). For queuing the received segment, we will consume the socket's resources such as memory. The socket's receive buffer quota should be accountable for queuing the received segment. Refer Fig. 9.7 for overview on receive side TCP memory management.

First we check if the memory requirement for the current segment (including size of *sk_buff*) can be satisfied from the already allocated socket's pool of memory (*sk→forward_alloc*) at line 3337 (cs 9.18). If not, we need to allocate a fresh quota for socket's memory pool, which we discuss later. In case we are able to satisfy the buffer requirement from the already allocated socket's memory pool, we queue the received buffer by pulling off the *data* field to point to the start of TCP payload in *sk_buff*. The buffer is queued up in the socket's receive_queue at line 3344. Next we account for the queued segment by calling *tcp_set_owner_r()* at line 3345.

tcp_set_owner_r() is called to account for the new segment queued to the socket's receive buffer. We associate buffer with the socket at line 1760 (cs 9.19).

```
net/ipv4/tcp_input.c

3210 int tcp_rcv_established(struct sock *sk, struct sk_buff *skb,
3211              struct tcphdr *th, unsigned len)
3212 {
3213     struct tcp_opt *tp = &(sk->tp_pinfo.af_tcp);
             ....
3324         if (!eaten) {
                 ....
3337             if ((int)skb->truesize > sk->forward_alloc)
3338                 goto step5;
                 ....
3343             __skb_pull(skb,tcp_header_len);
3344             __skb_queue_tail(&sk->receive_queue, skb);
3345             tcp_set_owner_r(skb, sk);
3346             tp->rcv_nxt = TCP_SKB_CB(skb)->end_seq;
3347         }
             ....
3429 step5:
         ....
3437     tcp_data_queue(sk, skb);
         ....
3441     return 0;
         ....
3446 discard:
3447     __kfree_skb(skb);
3448     return 0;
3449 }
```

cs 9.18. *tcp_rcv_established().*

```
net/ipv4/tcp_input.c

1758 static inline void tcp_set_owner_r(struct sk_buff *skb, struct sock *sk)
1759 {
1760     skb->sk = sk;
1761     skb->destructor = tcp_rfree;
1762     atomic_add(skb->truesize, &sk->rmem_alloc);
1763     sk->forward_alloc -= skb->truesize;
1764 }
```

cs 9.19. *tcp_set_owner_r().*

Destructor callback routine for the buffer is initialized to *tcp_rfree()* at line 1761. Next we account for memory allocated for the new receive buffer at line 1762. $sk \rightarrow$ *rmem_alloc* contains total memory allocated for the socket's receive buffer so that we can keep check on total allocation for the socket's receive queue. We take this field into account while advertising the receive window. Since memory allocated for the buffer is taken from the socket's memory pool ($sk \rightarrow$ *forward_alloc*), we need to account for it at line 1763.

Continuing with our discussion, we may face a condition where the socket's pool of memory is below the memory requirements for queuing a new buffer while processing a received segment in tcp_rcv_established(). In this case the segment is processed in *tcp_data_queue()*. In case we have received in-sequence or out-of-order data segment, memory management is done in the same way if the segment needs to be queued. For in-sequence data received, processing is done at lines

```
net/ipv4/tcp_input.c
2522 static void tcp_data_queue(struct sock *sk, struct sk_buff *skb)
2523 {
2524        struct tcphdr *th = skb->h.th;
2525        struct tcp_opt *tp = &(sk->tp_pinfo.af_tcp);
2526        int eaten = -1;
            ....
2545        if (TCP_SKB_CB(skb)->seq == tp->rcv_nxt) {
            ....
2568            if (eaten <= 0) {
2569 queue_and_out:
2570                if (eaten < 0 &&
2571                    (atomic_read(&sk->rmem_alloc) > sk->rcvbuf ||
2572                    !tcp_rmem_schedule(sk, skb))) {
2573                        if (tcp_prune_queue(sk) < 0 || !tcp_rmem_schedule(sk, skb))
2574                            goto drop;
2575                }
2576                tcp_set_owner_r(skb, sk);
2577                __skb_queue_tail(&sk->receive_queue, skb);
2578            }
            ....
2644        if (atomic_read(&sk->rmem_alloc) > sk->rcvbuf ||
2645            !tcp_rmem_schedule(sk, skb)) {
2646                if (tcp_prune_queue(sk) < 0 || !tcp_rmem_schedule(sk, skb))
2647                    goto drop;
2648        }
            ....
2657        tcp_set_owner_r(skb, sk);
            ....
2725    }
2726 }
```

cs 9.20. *tcp_data_queue().*

2569–2578; for an out-of-order data segment, it is done at lines 2644–2657 (cs 9.20).

Let's see how we proceed when the socket's memory pool is exhausted and we need to allocate a fresh quota pool for the socket from global TCP memory pool. First we check if total memory allocated for receive side socket buffer (*sk→rmem_alloc*) has exceeded the limit (*sk→rcvbuf*). The situation arrives when:

- The application is not getting the chance to read data queued up at the socket's receive queue.
- We have received a huge amount of out-of-order segments.

In the above case, we have a different strategy to manage some memory from the socket's pool. Now, we will look at a simpler case where the socket's receive buffer is still not full but the socket's pool of forward allocated memory is exhausted such that a new segment can't be accommodated. In this case, the condition at line 2571 fails and we call *tcp_rmem_schedule()* at line 2572 (cs 9.20).

tcp_rmem_schedule() checks if memory required for the received buffer (*skb→ truesize*) is available from the socket's memory pool (*sk→forward_alloc*), line 2516 (cs 9.21). In our case, we have come here because the socket's memory pool has become exhausted. In this case, we try to allocate memory to the socket's memory pool from the global TCP memory pool by calling *tcp_mem_schedule()*. For more

```
net/ipv4/tcp.c

 2514 static inline int tcp_rmem_schedule(struct sock *sk, struct sk_buff *skb)
 2515 {
 2516     return (int)skb->truesize <= sk->forward_alloc ||
 2517         tcp_mem_schedule(sk, skb->truesize, 1);
 2518 }
```

<u>cs 9.21.</u> *tcp_mem_schedule().*

details on *tcp_mem_schedule()*, see Section 9.1.6. Let's return to our discussion at line 2572 (cs 9.20). We got the requested memory for the receive buffer to the socket's memory pool from the TCP global memory pool. So, we need to account for the receive buffer by calling *tcp_set_owner_r()* at line 2576.

tcp_set_owner_r() is called to account for read side socket buffer memory. We first associate the received buffer with the socket at line 1760 at cs 9.19. The destructor callback routine is initialized to *tcp_free()*, which will be called when the buffer is freed. We need to account for allocated memory toward the read side buffer allocation (*sk→rmem_alloc*) at line 1762. We allocate this memory from the socket's memory pool (*sk→forward_alloc*), so we need to account for the socket buffer allocated.

Continuing with our discussion on *tcp_data_queue()*, what do we do if our read side memory quota is full, which means that the condition at line 2571 is TRUE? We call *tcp_prune_queue()* to check if we can squeeze in a receive queue and an out-of-order queue to generate some space for the arrived buffer. In the worst case we may also discard segments received out-of-order in order to generate space for the new in-sequence received data.

9.2.1 *tcp_prune_queue()*

tcp_prune_queue() is called when socket has exhausted its quota of receive buffer. The idea is that we can still try to generate some space out by collapsing queues. If we have come here because our quota for the receive buffer has exhausted (line 2878, cs 9.22), we try to increase the quota for the receive buffer and also pull up the receive window by calling *tcp_clamp_window()*. The quota for the receive window can be increased in case we don't have memory pressure as far as the TCP memory pool is concerned. See Section 9.2.2 for details on *tcp_clamp_window()*. On the other hand, if we have come here because of TCP memory pressure, we reduce receive a slow-start threshold to a minimum of 4 mss. We do this in order to restrict the window advertised to the sender to low value so that it can't transmit a huge amount of data. See Section 11.3.7 for more details.

Next we try to collapse an out-of-order queue by calling *tcp_collapse_ofo_queue()* at line 2883. Here we try to collapse a contiguous block of received segments based on some conditions. For more details see Section 9.2.3. Next we try to generate some space out by squeezing the receive queue (*tp→receive_queue*) at line 2884 by calling *tcp_collapse()*. If We have come here because of memory pressure, it means that we may still have a quota in the socket's memory pool. In the case where the socket's memory pool has enough memory but not enough for the caller, we try to release some memory from the socket's memory pool to the global TCP pool. We do this because the caller tries to allocate memory to the socket's memory pool from the global memory pool on return.

RECEIVE SIDE TCP MEMORY MANAGEMENT

```
net/ipv4/tcp_input.c

2870 static int tcp_prune_queue(struct sock *sk)
2871 {
2872     struct tcp_opt *tp = &sk->tp_pinfo.af_tcp;
         ....
2878     if (atomic_read(&sk->rmem_alloc) >= sk->rcvbuf)
2879         tcp_clamp_window(sk, tp);
2880     else if (tcp_memory_pressure)
2881         tp->rcv_ssthresh = min(tp->rcv_ssthresh, 4U*tp->advmss);
2882
2883     tcp_collapse_ofo_queue(sk);
2884     tcp_collapse(sk, sk->receive_queue.next,
2885         (struct sk_buff*)&sk->receive_queue,
2886         tp->copied_seq, tp->rcv_nxt);
2887     tcp_mem_reclaim(sk);
2888
2889     if (atomic_read(&sk->rmem_alloc) <= sk->rcvbuf)
2890         return 0;
         ....
2896     if (skb_queue_len(&tp->out_of_order_queue)) {
2897         net_statistics[smp_processor_id()*2].OfoPruned += skb_queue_len(&tp->out_of_order_queue);
2898         __skb_queue_purge(&tp->out_of_order_queue);
         ....
2905         if(tp->sack_ok)
2906             tcp_sack_reset(tp);
2907         tcp_mem_reclaim(sk);
2908     }
2909
2910     if(atomic_read(&sk->rmem_alloc) <= sk->rcvbuf)
2911         return 0;
         ....
2920     tp->pred_flags = 0;
2921     return -1;
2922 }
```

cs 9.22. tcp_prune_queue().

The next step is to check if we have generated some space after all the efforts. If so, we return at line 2890. Otherwise we have one more way of finding some space for the new arrival. We try to release buffers from an out-of-order queue by calling *__skb_queue_purge()* at line 2898, in case there are any. If SACK is enabled, we try to reset the SACK state by calling *tcp_sack_reset()* at line 2906. In this case, the next ACK will not have any SACK information and the peer should sense this and clear all the segments marked SACKed in its retransmit queue. We check if we have some space after purging an out-of-order queue at line 2910. If we succeed, return. Otherwise we badly failed after all the efforts, so we disable a fast path by resetting prediction flags at line 2920. It means that when the next segment arrives, it necessarily has to take a slow path in *tcp_recv_established()*.

9.2.2 *tcp_clamp_window()*

The routine is called when the socket's receive side memory is exhausted completely, which means that the memory allocated for the receive side socket buffers (*tp→rmem_alloc*) has exceeded the maximum limit on the allocation (*tp→rcvbuf*). This may happen because of two reasons:

1. Out-of-order segments have arrived eating up the receive buffer quota.
2. Application is not reading data.

```
net/ipv4/tcp_input.c

314 static void tcp_clamp_window(struct sock *sk, struct tcp_opt *tp)
315 {
316     struct sk_buff *skb;
317     unsigned int app_win = tp->rcv_nxt - tp->copied_seq;
318     int ofo_win = 0;
319
320     tp->ack.quick = 0;
321
322     skb_queue_walk(&tp->out_of_order_queue, skb) {
323         ofo_win += skb->len;
324     }
        ....
329     if (ofo_win) {
330         if (sk->rcvbuf < sysctl_tcp_rmem[2] &&
331             !(sk->userlocks&SOCK_RCVBUF_LOCK) &&
332             !tcp_memory_pressure &&
333             atomic_read(&tcp_memory_allocated) < sysctl_tcp_mem[0])
334                 sk->rcvbuf = min(atomic_read(&sk->rmem_alloc), sysctl_tcp_rmem[2]);
335     }
336     if (atomic_read(&sk->rmem_alloc) > sk->rcvbuf) {
337         app_win += ofo_win;
338         if (atomic_read(&sk->rmem_alloc) >= 2*sk->rcvbuf)
339             app_win >>= 1;
340         if (app_win > tp->ack.rcv_mss)
341             app_win -= tp->ack.rcv_mss;
342         app_win = max(app_win, 2U*tp->advmss);
343
344         if (!ofo_win)
345             tp->window_clamp = min(tp->window_clamp, app_win);
346         tp->rcv_ssthresh = min(tp->window_clamp, 2U*tp->advmss);
347     }
348 }
```

cs 9.23. tcp_clamp_window().

Both of these can in some proportion cause the socket to hit a memory bound. We first try to see if an out-of-order segment has contributed to memory consumption. So, we walk down the out-of-order queue (*tp→out_of_order_queue*) at lines 322–324 (cs 9.23) and calculate the total memory occupied by TCP data. Next we check if the memory is consumed by an out-of-order queue, and we try to increase the quota for the receive buffer. The reason for this is that the segments may be reordered in the network, thereby causing segments to reach out-of-order. So, we try to stretch the quota for the receive buffer because the missing segments may appear any time that may cause an application to read the entire data. We can increase the quota on the receive buffer under the following conditions:

1. Receive buffer quota is below *sysctl_tcp_rmem[2]*, which means that we have not yet come here for the socket.
2. Receive buffer lock is not held (it is held when the socket buffer is being modified by the user).
3. TCP memory pressure does not exist.
4. Total memory allocated through the TCP memory pool (*tcp_memory_allocated*) is below lower limits (*sysctl_tcp_mem[0]*).

If all the above condition's apply, we raise the quota on the receive buffer to *sysctl_tcp_rmem[2]* at line 334.

If the memory bound has come because application is not consuming TCP data, we don't try increasing the quota on the receive buffer. The reason for this is either lack of resources or misbehaving application.

Next we check if the total memory allocated for the receive buffer is still exceeding the quota. The condition may be false in the case where we got chance to raise the quota on the receive buffer to *sysctl_tcp_rmem[2]*. If so, we return. Otherwise, we try to reduce the window clamp and receive a slow-start threshold value. The window clamp puts a cap on the window size advertised, and a slow-start threshold value puts a limit on the window to be advertised at any instance (see Sections 11.3.7 and 11.3.5).

We first calculate the total TCP data stuck in an out-of-order segment and the receive queue (application window) at line 337. If the memory allocated for received buffers has reached double the limit on the receive quota (*tp→rcvbuf*), we half the total TCP data received at line 339. We modify the window clamp to the minimum of current window clamp and application window calculated only if there was no contribution from an out-of-order queue, line 345. The receive slow-start threshold value is calculated as the minimum of window clamp and twice mss (advertised at the time of three-way handshake).

9.2.3 *tcp_collapse_ofo_queue()*

Routine is called to collapse an out-of-order queue whenever memory quota for the receive queue is full to make some space for the newly arrived data segment. The idea is to find out buffers containing contiguous data and pass the chain of buffers to *tcp_collapse()* to try to collapse buffers in the chain. Let's see how we find segments with contiguous sequence space.

We start with the first buffer of the out-of-order queue and record the start and end sequence for this buffer at line 2835–2836, which will be the collapsible sequence space. We mark this buffer as the head of the chain at line 2837. Now we enter the loop 2839–2860 to start processing an out-of-order queue to find out contiguous buffers.

In each iteration we do the following:

We get a pointer to the next buffer in the queue at line 2840. Next we check if we need to collapse the chain. We do so in the following situation (we do all the checks with respect to the buffer accessed at line 2840):

1. If this is the last buffer in the queue at line 2844.
2. If the buffer comes after a hole in the TCP sequence space, line 2845. This can be detected from the sequence space for the segment being processed.
3. If the start sequence of the segment is more than the end of sequence space recorded so far.
4. If the hole is detected at the end of the current buffer—that is, the end sequence of the buffer is more than the start sequence recorded so far.

In the case where none of the conditions satisfy, the current buffer is contiguous with the buffer's inspected so far. So, we need to inspect the next buffer. Before doing that, we need to check if we need to expand the sequence space for collapse. So, we modify the collapsible start sequence to the start sequence of the buffer just inspected, in the case where the start sequence of the buffer is less than the

```
net/ipv4/tcp_input.c

2825 static void tcp_collapse_ofo_queue(struct sock *sk)
2826 {
2827     struct tcp_opt *tp = &(sk->tp_pinfo.af_tcp);
2828     struct sk_buff *skb = skb_peek(&tp->out_of_order_queue);
2829     struct sk_buff *head;
2830     u32 start, end;
2831
2832     if (skb == NULL)
2833         return;
2834
2835     start = TCP_SKB_CB(skb)->seq;
2836     end = TCP_SKB_CB(skb)->end_seq;
2837     head = skb;
2838
2839     for (;;) {
2840         skb = skb->next;
         ....
2844         if (skb == (struct sk_buff *)&tp->out_of_order_queue ||
2845             after(TCP_SKB_CB(skb)->seq, end) ||
2846             before(TCP_SKB_CB(skb)->end_seq, start)) {
2847             tcp_collapse(sk, head, skb, start, end);
2848             head = skb;
2849             if (skb == (struct sk_buff *)&tp->out_of_order_queue)
2850                 break;
2851             /* Start new segment */
2852             start = TCP_SKB_CB(skb)->seq;
2853             end = TCP_SKB_CB(skb)->end_seq;
2854         } else {
2855             if (before(TCP_SKB_CB(skb)->seq, start))
2856                 start = TCP_SKB_CB(skb)->seq;
2857             if (after(TCP_SKB_CB(skb)->end_seq, end))
2858                 end = TCP_SKB_CB(skb)->end_seq;
2859         }
2860     }
2861 }
```

cs 9.24. *tcp_collapse_ofo_queue()*.

collapsible start sequence recorded so far at lines 2855–2856 (cs 9.24). If the end sequence of the buffer is beyond the end sequence recorded so far for collapse, we record the end sequence for the buffer as a new value for the collapsible end sequence, lines 2857–2858.

In the case where we find the gap in the sequence space—that is, one of the condition's TRUE at lines 2844–2846—we need to try to collapse the buffers between start and end sequence space recorded so far. The first buffer is the one marked as head, and the last buffer is the one just inspected. We call *tcp_collapse()* at line 2847. Once we return from *tcp_collapse()*, we need to mark new head as the one just inspected because it will be the start of the new chain of buffers after the gap. The new collapsible sequence space is taken from the head of the buffer, and we start over again in the loop trying to find the new gap.

9.2.4 *tcp_collapse()* (see cs 9.26, unless mentioned)

In this routine we try to merge those segments, which are as follows:

```
include/net/tcp.h

1542 static inline int tcp_win_from_space(int space)
1543 {
1544     return sysctl_tcp_adv_win_scale<=0 ?
1545         (space>>(-sysctl_tcp_adv_win_scale)) :
1546         space - (space>>sysctl_tcp_adv_win_scale);
1547 }
```

cs 9.25. tcp_win_from_space().

1. Bloated segments where TCP data are very less as compared to total buffer size.
2. Overlapping of segments.

New buffers are created with size (*skb→truesize*) of around one page. Data from overlapping/bloated segments are copied into buffers of size one page. This will save us a lot of memory and will make room for a new segment when the receive queues are full. Let's see how this is achieved.

We would like to merge all the segments between a specified sequence space. So, start sequence, end sequence, start buffer, and the end buffer are fed to the routine by the caller. The chain of buffers passed to the routine don't have any holes in it.

We start with finding a segment that can be the starting point for the collapse process. Start traversing the list starting from the start buffer toward the end in the loop 2741–2767. The first condition we check is the segment we are not interested in. In the case where the end sequence of the segment is before the start sequence we are interested in (line 2743), we remove the buffer from the queue and continue with the next buffer in the list.

Next we check for the buffer that can be the start of a collapse operation. For a segment to be collapsed, the following conditions should be satisfied:

1. The segment should not be tagged as SYN/FIN, line 2757.
2. The segment should be bloated, line 2758.
3. The segment should be overlapping with the previous segment, line 2759.
4. The segment is overlapping with the next segment, lines 2760–2761.

We don't collapse the SY/FIN segment because it will add complexity to the situation later. By bloated segment we mean that the overall size of the buffer is much higher in comparison to the TCP payload it carries. *skb→truesize* is the total memory allocated for the buffer which accounts for buffer header (*sk_buff* object) and the number of bytes allocated for buffer data (containing actual packet). If the size as returned by *tcp_win_from_space()* is greater than the length of the TCP payload (*skb→len*), we consider this as bloated. On my machine, *tcp_win_from_space()* returns three-fourths of the value passed to the routine as *sys_tcp_adv_win_scale* is set to 2 (cs 9.25).

I think we have sysctl_tcp_adv_win_scale to compensate for the *sk_buff* header which accounts for the total receive memory usage. When the buffer is queued in any of the receive queues (including out-of-order queue), skb→len sums to the length of the TCP payload as all the headers are stripped by this time. So, the final equation sums to the following: If three-fourths of the total memory allocated by the buffer is greater than the total TCP payload the buffer carries, a big proportion of memory allocation has come from infrastructure overhead, that is, buffer head (*sk_buff*). In this case we try to collapse this segment.

The next case is overlapping segments. It may happen that the segments queued do overlap. Overlapping segments have common data and also have the packet header overhead, which also contributes to memory consumption. Each TCP segment queued in the receive queue amounts for sk_buff overhead and memory occupied by protocol headers which is no more required.

Let's say in the first iteration of the loop we didn't get any of the segments satisfying the criteria to be considered as a collapsible segment. We move on to the next segment at line 2766; before doing so, we replace our start sequence with the end sequence of the buffer being examined at line 2765. This is to detect overlapping; moreover, we can't collapse the segment that contains the start sequence number from the previous segment.

Let's assume we find a segment that is considered collapsible, so we break from the loop at line 2762. First we check that the buffer we are currently pointing to should not be SYN/FIN or the last segment in the chain to be examined at line 2768. We break from the loop only under two conditions: Either we have reached the end of the chain or we have found the collapsible buffer. If the buffer is found to have a SYN/FIN flag outside the loop, it necessarily means that this is the last buffer in the chain to be examined.

If we have found the collapsible segment, next we start with the process to collapse the buffers in the loop 2771–2819. The first thing we do at the start of the loop is to allocate a new buffer with true size of one page irrespective of the size of the segment being collapsed. For doing this, we actually need to calculate the exact size that should be passed to *alloc_skb()*. To *alloc_skb()*, we should pass the total length required for storing protocol headers (TCP + IP + link layer) and TCP payload. The routine itself allocates space for *skb_shared_info* at the end of the linear data area as shown in Fig. 9.2. We also want to restrict the total memory allocated for the buffer to be within one page, that is, *skb→truesize* to be one page. For this we need to calculate the header length for the collapsible segment as the rest of the parameters are fixed. *skb_headroom()* will actually return us the size occupied by the protocol headers at line 2773. Now we can calculate the total length that should be requested to *skb_alloc()*. Since we want total allocation for the buffer to not to exceed one PAGE, we calculate the size of the linear data area to be one PAGE

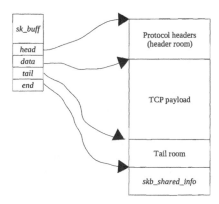

Figure 9.2. Memory layout of network buffer.

(size of *sk_buff* + protocol header length + size of *skb_shared_info*), lines 2774–2775. Since we have already calculated protocol header length, we pass the length of the linear data area as calculated above + protocol header length to *skb_alloc()*. So first we try to fill a new segment by copying data from collapsed segments and, once the segment is full, allocate new buffer in the same way as described above. In this loop we will cover all the segments until the end of sequence space has reached.

Once we have allocated a new buffer, the next step is to copy data from the collapsed buffers. First, reserve space to copy protocol headers at the head of the linear data area by calling *skb_reserve()* at line 2785. Now copy the header from an identified buffer to the new buffer at line 2786. We initialize certain sk_buff pointers that point directly into the linear data area to the start of protocol headers, lines 2787–2789. Copy the TCP control block at line 2790. Initialize the start and end sequence as a start sequence number for the new buffer at line 2791, and insert a new buffer prior to the buffer identified to be collapsed at line 2792. Next we account for the memory allocated for the new buffer from the socket's memory pool by calling *tcp_set_owner_r()*.

Next we need to copy the TCP payload from the collapsed buffers to the new buffer. We continue to copy data from the collapsed buffers to the new buffer until there is no space left in the new buffer. So, we may have *n* buffers collapsed to a single new buffer or *n* buffers collapsed to new *m* buffers where $n > m$. We can save on buffer head overhead (sk_buff) and also on overlapping segments. The loop where we copy data to the new buffer is lines 2796–2818. We first take the offset into the segment that needs to be collapsed from the start sequence number that needs to be collapsed at line 2797.

Next we calculate the total data that need to be copied from the segment from the start sequence number for data to be copied and the end sequence number for the segment at line 2798. If there are data from the collapsible segment to be copied, we take minimum of the data left in the collapsible segment for copying and space available in the new segment at line 2802. Next we copy data by calling *skb_copy_bits()* at line 2803. The third argument to *skb_copy_bits()* is a function call that will make room for new data to be copied in the new buffer and return the pointer to the location where data should go (*skb→data*). Increment the end sequence for the new buffer to indicate the sequence space it covers at line 2805. Account for the number of bytes copied at line 2806 and increment the start of the sequence number that needs to be copied next at line 2807. Next we check if all the data from the collapsible segment are copied at line 2809. If so, we need to unlink the copied collapsible segment from the chain and take the get next collapsible buffer for copying data. So, we call *__skb_unlink()* to remove the copied buffer from the chain at line 2811 and point to the next collapsible buffer at line 2814. If the new buffer has a SYN/FIN tag set or it is the last segment in the chain (line 2815), we stop there.

Just to explain how it works, we can assume that there are 'n' buffers passed to tcp_collapse() each of size TCP payload X bytes. New buffer generated to replace the collapsed ones can accommodate 2X bytes of TCP payload. Also assume that none of the buffer's have sequence spaces overlapping and there is no gap in the sequence spaces of the buffers. Figure 9.3 shows four buffers with contiguous TCP sequence spaces and rest of them are not shown. In Fig. 9.4, we have gone through first iteration and have copied the header from the first buffer in the new buffer and X bytes from the collapsed buffer to the new buffer. In Fig. 9.5, we have copied data from the second collapsible buffer into the new buffer. Now the new buffer is

```
net/ipv4/tcp_input.c

2733 static void
2734 tcp_collapse(struct sock *sk, struct sk_buff *head,
2735          struct sk_buff *tail, u32 start, u32 end)
2736 {
2737     struct sk_buff *skb;
         ....
2741     for (skb = head; skb != tail; ) {
2742         /* No new bits? It is possible on ofo queue. */
2743         if (!before(start, TCP_SKB_CB(skb)->end_seq)) {
2744             struct sk_buff *next = skb->next;
2745             __skb_unlink(skb, skb->list);
2746             __kfree_skb(skb);
2747             NET_INC_STATS_BH(TCPRcvCollapsed);
2748             skb = next;
2749             continue;
2750         }
         ....
2757         if (!skb->h.th->syn && !skb->h.th->fin &&
2758             (tcp_win_from_space(skb->truesize) > skb->len ||
2759             before(TCP_SKB_CB(skb)->seq, start) ||
2760             (skb->next != tail &&
2761             TCP_SKB_CB(skb)->end_seq != TCP_SKB_CB(skb->next)->seq)))
2762             break;
         ....
2765         start = TCP_SKB_CB(skb)->end_seq;
2766         skb = skb->next;
2767     }
2768     if (skb == tail || skb->h.th->syn || skb->h.th->fin)
2769         return;
2770
2771     while (before(start, end)) {
2772         struct sk_buff *nskb;
2773         int header = skb_headroom(skb);
2774         int copy = (PAGE_SIZE - sizeof(struct sk_buff) -
2775             sizeof(struct skb_shared_info) - header - 31)&~15;
2776
2777         /* Too big header? This can happen with IPv6. */
2778         if (copy < 0)
2779             return;
2780         if (end-start < copy)
2781             copy = end-start;
2782         nskb = alloc_skb(copy+header, GFP_ATOMIC);
2783         if (!nskb)
2784             return;
2785         skb_reserve(nskb, header);
2786         memcpy(nskb->head, skb->head, header);
2787         nskb->nh.raw = nskb->head + (skb->nh.raw-skb->head);
2788         nskb->h.raw = nskb->head + (skb->h.raw-skb->head);
2789         nskb->mac.raw = nskb->head + (skb->mac.raw-skb->head);
2790         memcpy(nskb->cb, skb->cb, sizeof(skb->cb));
2791         TCP_SKB_CB(nskb)->seq = TCP_SKB_CB(nskb)->end_seq = start;
2792         __skb_insert(nskb, skb->prev, skb, skb->list);
2793         tcp_set_owner_r(nskb, sk);
         ....
2796         while (copy > 0) {
2797             int offset = start - TCP_SKB_CB(skb)->seq;
2798             int size = TCP_SKB_CB(skb)->end_seq - start;
2799
2800             if (offset < 0) BUG();
2801             if (size > 0) {
2802                 size = min(copy, size);
2803                 if (skb_copy_bits(skb, offset, skb_put(nskb, size), size))
2804                     BUG();
2805                 TCP_SKB_CB(nskb)->end_seq += size;
2806                 copy -= size;
2807                 start += size;
2808             }
2809             if (!before(start, TCP_SKB_CB(skb)->end_seq)) {
2810                 struct sk_buff *next = skb->next;
2811                 __skb_unlink(skb, skb->list);
2812                 __kfree_skb(skb);
2813                 NET_INC_STATS_BH(TCPRcvCollapsed);
2814                 skb = next;
2815                 if (skb == tail || skb->h.th->syn || skb->h.th->fin)
2816                     return;
2817             }
2818         }
2819     }
2820 }
```

cs 9.26. *tcp_collapse()*.

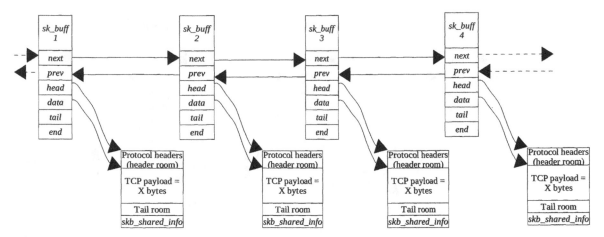

Figure 9.3. There are four buffers in the receive queue when we need to collapse the queue.

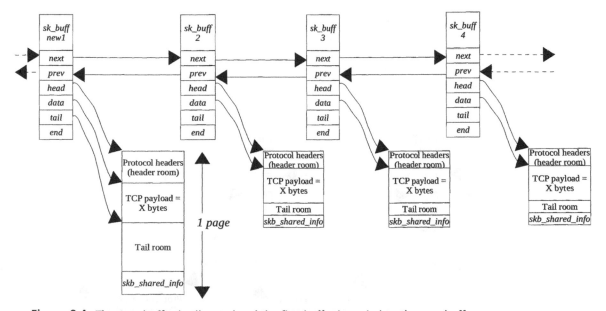

Figure 9.4. The new buffer is allocated and the first buffer is copied to the new buffer.

full and for the third buffer we have once again allocated a new buffer and copied the header from the third buffer into the new buffer. Once we have copied the TCP payload from the fourth buffer to the second new buffer, the final picture is as shown in Fig. 9.6. So, four segments are collapsed to two segments eliminating the overhead of two buffer heads.

9.2.5 __skb_queue_purge()

This routine is called to destroy the chain of buffers. It is mainly called to destroy an out-of-order queue when facing an acute shortage of resources. __skb_dequeue() returns the head of the chain and also removes the buffer from the chain (cs 9.27).

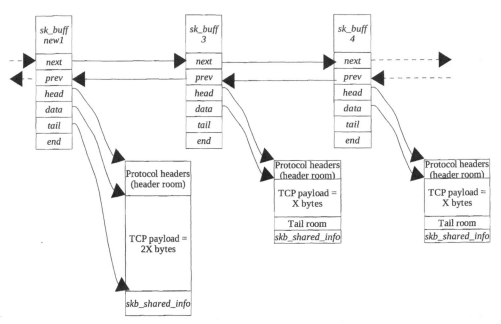

Figure 9.5. Data from two adjacent buffers are accommodated to a single page of the new buffer.

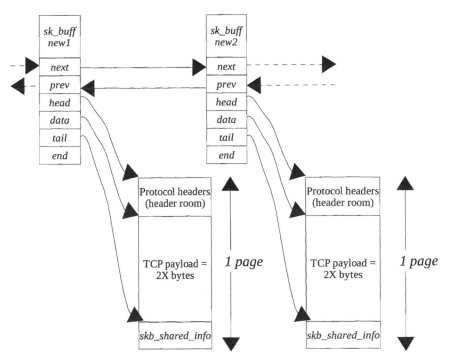

Figure 9.6. Finally we have two new buffers replacing four old buffers after collapsing the queue.

```
include/net/tcp.h

1009 static inline void __skb_queue_purge(struct sk_buff_head *list)
1010 {
1011     struct sk_buff *skb;
1012     while ((skb=__skb_dequeue(list))!=NULL)
1013         kfree_skb(skb);
1014 }
```

cs 9.27. __skb_queue_purge().

```
net/ipv4/tcp.c

354 void tcp_rfree(struct sk_buff *skb)
355 {
356     struct sock *sk = skb->sk;
357
358     atomic_sub(skb->truesize, &sk->rmem_alloc);
359     sk->forward_alloc += skb->truesize;
360 }
```

cs 9.28. tcp_rfree().

9.3 FREEING OF MEMORY ALLOCATED TO A RECEIVE BUFFER

Memory is returned to the socket's memory pool when data are read from the receive queue in *tcp_recvmsg()* by calling *tcp_eat_skb()*. This routine frees the buffer by calling *__kfree_skb()*, which calls the destructor callback routine of the receive buffer, *tcp_rfree()* (cs 9.28). In this routine, we deduct the size of the buffer (*skb→truesize*) from the total allocated memory for a read side socket buffer (*sk→rmem_alloc*). This will make room for one more data segment in the receive queue. Next we return memory associated with the buffer to the socket's memory pool (*sk→forward_alloc*) at line 359.

9.4 SYSTEM-WIDE CONTROL PARAMETERS ARE WORTH NOTICING WHEN IT COMES TO TCP MEMORY MANAGEMENT

tcp_memory_allocated: This is the total memory allocated to the TCP sockets system-wide.

sysctl_tcp_mem[0]: Memory allocated for TCP socket buffers is within limit, *tcp_memory_pressure* is reset.

sysctl_tcp_mem[1]: Under pressure. Pressure starts when overall TCP memory allocated just reaches this limit. We set global variable *tcp_memory_pressure* to indicate that TCP memory pressure has begun.

sysctl_tcp_mem[2]: We have reached hard limit with *tcp_memory_pressure* set. When overall TCP memory allocated has reached this limit, we start suppressing allocation of memory for TCP socket buffers.

tcp_memory_allocated: Each time we allocate memory quantum for TCP socket buffers, *tcp_memory_allocated* accounts for the memory allocated for socket buffer (TCP payload + *sk_buff*).

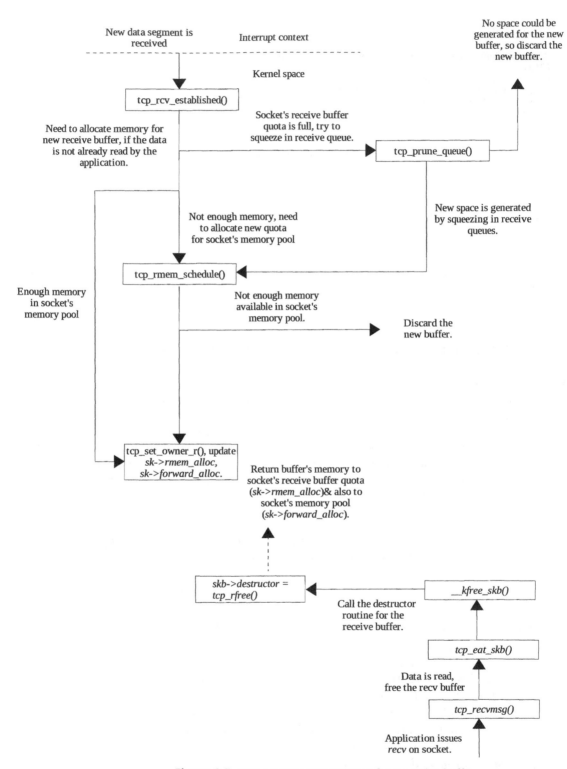

Figure 9.7. TCP memory management for a receive buffer.

sysctl_tcp_rmem[0]: Per socket lower limit on the total memory allocated for TCP read side. If *sk→rmem_alloc* goes beyond this limit, we can allocate additional memory for the read side only if the pressure is not there or if the total TCP memory allocated limit has not been reached (check *tcp_mem_schedule()*).

sysctl_tcp_rmem[1]: Per socket medium limit (default value of *sk→rcvbuf*) on the total memory allocated for the TCP read side, check *tcp_v4_init_sock()* when socket is initialized.

sysctl_tcp_rmem[2]: Per socket upper limit on the total memory allocated for a TCP socket read side buffer (upper cap on *sk→rcvbuf*). Check *tcp_fixup_rcvbuf()* and *tcp_clamp_window()*.

sysctl_tcp_wmem[0]: Per socket lower limit on the total memory allocated for the TCP write side. If *sk→wmem_queued* goes beyond this limit, we can allocate additional memory for write side only if the pressure is not there or if the total TCP memory allocated limit has not been reached (check *tcp_mem_schedule()*).

sysctl_tcp_wmem[1]: Per socket medium limit (default value for *sk→sndbuf*) on the memory allocated for the TCP write side, check *tcp_v4_init_sock()* when socket is initialized.

sysctl_tcp_wmem[2]: Per socket upper limit on the total memory allocated for TCP socket write side buffer (upper limit on *sk→sndbuf*).

9.5 SUMMARY

Memory for socket buffers is allocated in multiples of TCP_MEM_QUANTUM in *tcp_mem_schedule()*.

tcp_memory_allocated is a system-wide memory quota for TCP sockets.

Quota for send buffer and receive buffer can be increased, depending on total memory usage by TCP sockets system wide.

Segments in out-of-order queue also account for a socket's receive buffer quota.

Once the receive bugger is full, the TCP tries to generate some space by squeezing in receive queue and out-of-order queue in *tcp_collpse()*. If it is not able to generate space even after purging queues, the new data segment is dropped.

If the write is blocking and enough memory is not available to queue new data, *wait_for_tcp_memory()* blocks the process until memory is available to write new data.

Once data in the transmit queue are ACKed, *tcp_write_space()* tries to wake up the process sleeping in *wait_for_tcp_memory()* to start queuing new data.

10

TCP TIMERS

TCP is an event-driven state machine. Events happen asynchronously and we can't keep on looping to wait for an event to happen. Sometimes we need to wait for a small period of time to expire after which we can send ACK for better network utilization. On the other hand, we need to keep track of losses that are signaled when certain time lapses and we don't get an event. TCP has to take care of the data flow, depending on the resources advertised by the receiver. In the case where the sender finds that the receiver is falling short of resources, it needs to put a brake on the flow of data and keep tracking the event when it can send data again. There are a times when we need to check if the peer is still connected and our connection is still active where TCP connections are on for days (like telnet). New connection requests are queued up in a SYNQ until it is accepted. In the case where the accept queue is full and the application is not accepting new connections, we need to remove requests from the queue on timely basis. All these functionalities require a timely probe into the matter so that the proper action can be taken at right time. For this we need a timer to be introduced in TCP implementation. Let's take each TCP timer one by one to see their functioning and importance. TCP specifications recommend the following timers for functioning of the reliable transport protocol:

- Retransmit timer
- Delayed ACK timer
- Zero window probe timer (persistent timer)
- Keep-alive timer

TCP/IP Architecture, Design, and Implementation in Linux. By S. Seth and M. A. Venkatesulu
Copyright © 2008 the IEEE Computer Society

```
include/linux/timer.h

16 struct timer_list {
17      struct list_head list;
18      unsigned long expires;
19      unsigned long data;
20      void (*function)(unsigned long);
21 };
```

cs 10.1. *timer_list* object to register timer with kernel.

- TIME_WAIT timer
- SYN-ACK timer (timer for listening sockets)

Retransmit timer, delayed ACK timer, and zero-window probe timer are implemented as part of a core TCP state machine. Keepalive timer is implemented to manage established connections. TIME_WAIT timer is implemented to manage connections that are closed and waiting for 2*MSL time to expire. SYN-ACK timer is implemented to manage new connection requests. There are three routines provided by TCP to manage its timers:

- *tcp_reset_xmit_timer()*
- *tcp_reset_keepalive_timer()*
- *tcp_clear_xmit_timers()*

tcp_reset_xmit_timer() is a common routine to reset time for TCP state machine timers. As the name suggests, *tcp_reset_keepalive_timer()* is an interface to reset time for connection managing timers like keep-alive and syn-ack timers. *tcp_cleat_xmit_timers()* is called to clear/remove any of the installed TCP timers.

In this chapter we discuss various TCP timers and their implementation on Linux. We will try to explain the timers with the help of examples for better understanding. First there will be short description of how timers on Linux are implemented, and then we will take up one timer at a time.

10.1 TIMERS IN LINUX

Linux implements timers as *struct timer_list*. It has three members: *expires* stores the number of clock ticks after which the timer should fire, *data* contains any argument to be passed to the timer callback routine, and *function* is actually a callback routine to the timer that is actually executed when the timer expires (cs 10.1).

list is the pointer to the list head on which this timer should sit. *timerlist_lock* is a global timer lock to access the timer list. There are a set of routines to manipulate timers. We will discuss some of them here.

10.1.1 *mod_timer()*

Whenever we want to modify expire time for the timer, we call *mod_timer()* (cs 10.2). We hold a global timer spin lock *timerlist_lock* to modify the *expires* field for

```
kernel/timer.c

204 int mod_timer(struct timer_list *timer, unsigned long expires)
205 {
206      int ret;
207      unsigned long flags;
208
209      spin_lock_irqsave(&timerlist_lock, flags);
210      timer->expires = expires;
211      ret = detach_timer(timer);
212      internal_add_timer(timer);
213      spin_unlock_irqrestore(&timerlist_lock, flags);
214      return ret;
215 }
```

cs 10.2. mod_timer().

```
kernel/timer.c

196 static inline int detach_timer (struct timer_list *timer)
197 {
198      if (!timer_pending(timer))
199           return 0;
200      list_del(&timer->list);
201      return 1;
202 }
```

cs 10.3. detach_timer().

the timer. Call *detach_timer()* to detach the timer from the global list if already installed. Thereafter, *internal_add_timer()* is called to add a timer to the global list. *internal_add_timer()* has its own algorithm to find an appropriate global list to add the timer, depending on the expiry time for the timer. Once we get the pointer to the global list, we add the timer to the list by calling *list_add()*.

10.1.2 detach_timer()

This routine detaches the timer from the global list in case it is already installed. We call routine *timer_pending()* to check if the timer is already installed on the global list (cs 10.3). The next field of the timer's list head is NULL in the case where the timer is not installed. If it is installed, we call *list_del()*, which detaches the timer from the global list of timers.

10.1.3 del_timer()

Whenever we want to cancel timer, we first check if timer is already installed or not by calling *timer_pending()*. In the case where we find that the timer is already installed, we call *del_timer()* to remove the timer from the list. We once again hold global spin lock *timerlist_lock* to detach timer from the global list. We call *detach_timer()* to detach the timer from the global list and initialize *next* and *previous* field of the timer's list head to NULL, line 224 (cs 10.4).

```
kernel/timer.c

217 int del_timer(struct timer_list * timer)
218 {
219      int ret;
220      unsigned long flags;
221
222      spin_lock_irqsave(&timerlist_lock, flags);
223      ret = detach_timer(timer);
224      timer->list.next = timer->list.prev = NULL;
225      spin_unlock_irqrestore(&timerlist_lock, flags);
226      return ret;
227 }
```

cs 10.4. del_timer()

```
kernel/timer.c
164 void __tasklet_hi_schedule(struct tasklet_struct *t)
165 {
166      int cpu = smp_processor_id();
167      unsigned long flags;
168
169      local_irq_save(flags);
170      t->next = tasklet_hi_vec[cpu].list;
171      tasklet_hi_vec[cpu].list = t;
172      cpu_raise_softirq(cpu, HI_SOFTIRQ);
173      local_irq_restore(flags);
174 }
```

cs 10.5. __tasklet_hi_schedule().

10.1.4   When Are Timer Routines Executed?

Timer interrupt fires every 10ms—that is, one tick. This interrupt raises soft Inter-rupt to process timers by calling mark_bh() from do_timer(). To mark_bh() we pass offset in the bh_task_vec[]. mark_bh() calls tasklet_hi_schedule() to schedule the tasklet pointed to by bh_task_vec [TIMER_BH]. Here we first check if the tasklet is not already scheduled. In the case where it is not already scheduled, we schedule it by calling __tasklet_hi_schedule() (cs 10.5). This ensures that one tasklet is sched-uled on only one CPU and that also the same tasklet cannot be scheduled on the same CPU twice. This will schedule the timer tasklet on the CPU currently being executed on. The tasklet is added to per CPU list tasklet_hi_vec[cpu].list and sub-sequently HI_SOFTIRQ softirq is raised. On returning from timer interrupt, do_softirq() is executed, which will check for softirq's to be processed. Here, HI_SOFTIRQ is processed, which will also process *tasklet_hi_vec* list for that CPU. This list includes TIMER_BH tasklet, which gets executed as *timer_bh()*. *run_timer_list()* is called from *timer_bh()* to execute all the timers from the global list which have expired.

10.2   TCP RETRANSMIT TIMER

The timer is part of the TCP state machine to detect network congestion/loss of data. TCP maintains data integrity by sending out ACK for every byte of data that is received. The receiver doesn't remove transmitted data from the retransmit queue

```
net/ipv4/tcp_output.c

47 static __inline__
48 void update_send_head(struct sock *sk, struct tcp_opt *tp, struct sk_buff *skb)
49 {
        ....
54      if (tp->packets_out++ == 0)
55              tcp_reset_xmit_timer(sk, TCP_TIME_RETRANS, tp->rto);
56 }
```

cs 10.6. *update_send_head()*.

until it gets ACK for the transmitted data. So, the sender is not expected to wait forever to receive ACK for the transmitted data. The sender calculates RTO (retransmission timeout) based on RTT (round-trip time) calculated from timestamp options in the ACKing segment (check RFC 2988 and RFC 1323). When the first segment from the window is transmitted, we set a retransmit timer to expire after the RTO time interval. This is to make sure that we get an ACK within RTO time from the time when segment is transmitted. In case we don't get ACK, the retransmit timer would expire and signaling that all the data within the window is lost. So, our job will be to start transmitting lost segments starting from the head of the retransmit queue. This may happen because of network congestion causing some intermediate router to drop packets.

10.2.1 When Do We Set Retransmit Timer?

We set a retransmit timer when we are transmitting the first packet in the current window. *packets_out* is a field in the TCP state machine *struct tcp_opt* structure which keeps track of the packet's transmitted but not yet ACKed. We increment this field whenever we transmit a new segment. Just after transmitting a segment, we check if this field is zero. If so, we start the retransmit timer to expire after $tp \rightarrow rto$ ticks.

We can see that *update_send_head()* resets the retransmission timer for the first segment (lines 54–55, cs 10.6). This routine is called from *tcp_write_xmit()* after it has successfully transmitted a segment. We transmit a segment by calling different routines like *tcp_send_skb()*, *tcp_push_one()*, and *tcp_connect()*, and in each of these routines we make the same check and, if required, we reset the retransmit timer.

10.2.2 When Do We Reset or Cancel Retransmit Timers?

We need to reset a retransmit timer on each ACK we receive that advances a send window in *tcp_ack_packets_out()* called from *tcp_ack()→tcp_clean_rtx_queue()* (cs 10.7). RFC 2988 recommends that on reception of each ACK acking new data, we should reset the retransmit timeout to a new value of RTO. This gives some advantage to the remaining segments in the sense that their timeout is incremented by the time lapsed since the time they were transmitted. In the case where all the segments are ACKed, we remove retransmit timer by calling *tcp_clear_xmit_timer()* at line 1726. Otherwise we reset timer by calling *tcp_reset_xmit_timer()* at line 1728. This is the only place when we clear retransmit timer since we know that we are not waiting for any more ACKs.

```
net/ipv4/tcp_output.c

1723 static __inline__ void tcp_ack_packets_out(struct sock *sk, struct tcp_opt *tp)
1724 {
1725        if (tp->packets_out==0) {
1726             tcp_clear_xmit_timer(sk, TCP_TIME_RETRANS);
1727        } else {
1728             tcp_reset_xmit_timer(sk, TCP_TIME_RETRANS, tp->rto);
1729        }
1730 }
```

cs 10.7. tcp_ack_packets_out().

When we are retransmitting segments during loss-recovery process, we reset the retransmission timer in the case where we are retransmitting the first segment on the retransmit queue in *tcp_xmit_retransmit_queue()*. We set the retransmit timer for the very first unacknowledged segment; and since the first segment that is being retransmitted is lost we need to reset retransmit timer.

Let's see what happens when the retransmit timer expires. The timer expires because we have not gotten ACK for the very first segment transmitted in the current window. So, we consider all the segments in the current window which are not yet SACKed/lost as lost. We need to reduce the rate of transmission to avoid any more losses by performing slow-start. Finally we retransmit the head of the retransmit queue.

The retransmit timer not only takes care of retransmissions but also needs to adjust timeout values, reset routes, check if the number of retries has exceeded limit, and so on. Let's see what all it does. If no packets are transmitted, just return because we have nothing to retransmit at line 324 (cs 10.8). Next we check if the socket is still alive and not in the SYN_SENT/SYN_RECV state and if somehow the send window is closed, we need to timeout the connection in case we have not received any ACK from the peer for more than TCP_RTO_MAX. In case the socket is not timed out, we enter the loss state by entering slow-start (call *tcp_enter_loss()*), retransmit the head of the retransmit queue at line 347 (cs 10.8), and then invalidate the destination by calling *__sk_dst_reset()*. The reason for finding an alternate route for the connection may be that we are not able to communicate with the peer because of which we may not be able to get window updates. Then we reset the retransmit timer doubling timeout by jumping to line 406 (cs 10.8).

Next we check if we have actually exhausted all our retries by calling *tcp_write_timeout()* at line 352. tp→retransmits keeps account of the number of times we have tried retransmitting a lost segment. We have four system-wide control parameters here to timeout a connection:

- *sysctl_tcp_retries1*
- *sysctl_tcp_retries2*
- *sysctl_tcp_syn_retries*
- *sysctl_tcp_orphan_retries*

sysctl_tcp_retries1 is the maximum number of retries after which we need to check if the intermediate router has failed. If the number of retransmits exceeds this value, route-specific negative_advice routine is called (*dst→ops→negative_advice()*) from

```
net/ipv4/tcp_output.c

320 static void tcp_retransmit_timer(struct sock *sk)
321 {
322     struct tcp_opt *tp = &sk->tp_pinfo.af_tcp;
323
324     if (tp->packets_out == 0)
325         goto out;
        ....
329     if (tp->snd_wnd == 0 && !sk->dead &&
330         !((1<<sk->state)&(TCPF_SYN_SENT|TCPF_SYN_RECV))) {
            ....
342         if (tcp_time_stamp - tp->rcv_tstamp > TCP_RTO_MAX) {
343             tcp_write_err(sk);
344             goto out;
345         }
346         tcp_enter_loss(sk, 0);
347         tcp_retransmit_skb(sk, skb_peek(&sk->write_queue));
348         __sk_dst_reset(sk);
349         goto out_reset_timer;
350     }
351
352     if (tcp_write_timeout(sk))
353         goto out;
        ....
375     tcp_enter_loss(sk, 0);
376
377     if (tcp_retransmit_skb(sk, skb_peek(&sk->write_queue)) > 0) {
378         /* Retransmission failed because of local congestion,
379          * do not backoff.
380          */
381         if (!tp->retransmits)
382             tp->retransmits=1;
383         tcp_reset_xmit_timer(sk, TCP_TIME_RETRANS,
384                 min(tp->rto, TCP_RESOURCE_PROBE_INTERVAL));
385         goto out;
386     }
        ....
403     tp->backoff++;
404     tp->retransmits++;
405
406 out_reset_timer:
407     tp->rto = min(tp->rto << 1, TCP_RTO_MAX);
408     tcp_reset_xmit_timer(sk, TCP_TIME_RETRANS, tp->rto);
409     if (tp->retransmits > sysctl_tcp_retries1)
410         __sk_dst_reset(sk);
411
412 out:;
413 }
```

cs 10.8. tcp_retransmit_timer().

dst_negative_advice(). In the case of Ipv4, this is *ipv4_negative_advice()*, which sets *sk→dst* to NULL in case the route has become obsolete or the destination has expired. *rt_check_expire()* is run as a periodic timer for routing entries cached with the kernel to check old not-in-use entries.

sysctl_tcp_retries2 is the maximum number of retries the segment should be retransmitted after which we should give up on the connection.

sysctl_tcp_syn_retries is the number of retries allowed to retransmit a SYN segment after which we should give up.

For an orphaned socket (that is detached from the process context but exists to do some cleanup work), we have some more hard rules for number of retries. The maximum number of retries for an orphaned socket is *sysctl_tcp_orphan_retries*. Still we need to kill an orphaned socket in two cases even if it has not exhausted its retries (check *tcp_out_of_resources()*):

1. Total number of orphaned sockets has exceeded the system-wide maximum allowed number (*sysctl_tcp_max_orphans*).
2. There is acute memory pressure (*tcp_memory_allocated* > *sysctl_tcp_mem[2]*).

If we are here at line 375 of cs 10.8, we have not exhausted our retries. We need to call *tcp_enter_loss()* to enter into the slow-start phase (see Section 10.2.3). Thereafter, we try to retransmit the first segment from the retransmit queue at line 377 (cs 10.8). In case we fail to retransmit here, the reason for failure is local congestion. In this case, we don't back off the retransmit timeout value. We reset the retransmit timer with a minimum timeout value of *tp→rto* and *TCP_RESOURCE_PROBE_INTERVAL*. Since we need to probe availability of local resources more frequently than RTO, that is why we want the tcp retransmit timer to expire fast so that we can retransmit the lost segment.

If we are at line 403 of cs 10.8, we have retransmitted the lost segment (head of the retransmit queue) successfully. We increment *tp→back_off* and *tp→retransmits* by one. Even though we are not using the value of *tp→back_off* here, it is required by the zero-window probe timer. We take timeout value as minimum of *tp→rto* and *TCP_RTO_MAX* and store this value in *tp→rto* (RTO can't exceed beyond *TCP_RTO_MAX*). Finally we reset the retransmit timer to expire at the backoffed value of RTO, *tp→rto*, by calling tcp_reset_xmit_timer() at line 408 of cs 10.8. We now check if the maximum number of retries has exceeded the limit to reset route, at line 409. If so, we reset the route for the connection so that on next retransmit we are able to find a new route for the connection because the current route may be causing a problem.

While retransmitting a segment, we store the retransmission timestamp in *tp→retrans_stamp* for the very first segment retransmitted. We also increment *tp→retrans_out* and *tp→undo_retrans* by 1 every successful retransmission. *tp→retrans_out* is to keep track of the number of segments retransmitted, and tp→undo_retrans is to catch the number of D-SACKs which is required to check unnecessary retransmissions.

10.2.3   *tcp_enter_loss()*

We call *tcp_enter_loss()* to tag the lost segment from the current window and also reduce the rate of transmission of data by performing slow-start (cs 10.9). Let's see how is it done. We do reduce slow-start threshold only if it is not done in the current window, which means that within a window if multiple losses take place, we won't reduce the slow-start threshold every time. We reduce slow-start threshold to half of the congestion window for the reason that during slow-start we increment the congestion window by 1 every time we receive an ACK. So, the increment is exponential every RTT. If the current congestion window caused packet loss, we need

```
net/ipv4/tcp_input.c

 975 void tcp_enter_loss(struct sock *sk, int how)
 976 {
 977     struct tcp_opt *tp = &sk->tp_pinfo.af_tcp;
         ....
 982     if (tp->ca_state <= TCP_CA_Disorder ||
 983        tp->snd_una == tp->high_seq ||
 984        (tp->ca_state == TCP_CA_Loss && !tp->retransmits)) {
 985            tp->prior_ssthresh = tcp_current_ssthresh(tp);
 986            tp->snd_ssthresh = tcp_recalc_ssthresh(tp);
 987     }
 988     tp->snd_cwnd = 1;
 989     tp->snd_cwnd_cnt = 0;
 990     tp->snd_cwnd_stamp = tcp_time_stamp;
 991
 992     tcp_clear_retrans(tp);
         ...
 996     if (!how)
 997            tp->undo_marker = tp->snd_una;
 998
 999     for_retrans_queue(skb, sk, tp) {
1000            cnt++;
1001            if (TCP_SKB_CB(skb)->sacked&TCPCB_RETRANS)
1002                 tp->undo_marker = 0;
1003            TCP_SKB_CB(skb)->sacked &= (~TCPCB_TAGBITS)|TCPCB_SACKED_ACKED;
1004            if (!(TCP_SKB_CB(skb)->sacked&TCPCB_SACKED_ACKED) || how) {
1005                 TCP_SKB_CB(skb)->sacked &= ~TCPCB_SACKED_ACKED;
1006                 TCP_SKB_CB(skb)->sacked |= TCPCB_LOST;
1007                 tp->lost_out++;
1008            } else {
1009                 tp->sacked_out++;
1010                 tp->fackets_out = cnt;
1011            }
1012     }
1013     tcp_sync_left_out(tp);
1014
1015     tp->reordering = min_t(unsigned int, tp->reordering, sysctl_tcp_reordering);
1016     tp->ca_state = TCP_CA_Loss;
1017     tp->high_seq = tp->snd_nxt;
1018     TCP_ECN_queue_cwr(tp);
1019 }
```

cs 10.9. tcp_enter_loss().

to go back to the previous congestion window that provided an acceptable rate of data transmission. So, we divide the current congestion into two halves: The first half is for slow-start because it was in the previous congestion window, and the second half is for slow transmission of data (where congestion window is incremented every RTT). This will get us better congestion control in the second half session that got us into trouble. That is the reason we don't decrease slow-start threshold value twice for the same window. We just start with one congestion window every time we sense a loss through retransmission timer firing. Conditions to decrement slow-start threshold are as follows:

1. The TCP state should be less than disorder, which is nothing but open. If we are entering into the loss state from the open state, we have not yet reduced the slow-start threshold for the window of data.

2. If we have entered the loss state with all the data pointed to by tp→high_seq acknowledged. Once again it means that in whatever state we are (other than open state), all the data from the window that got us into the state, prior to retransmission timer expiry, has been acknowledged.

3. If the above two conditions fail, we still have one more condition that can demand reducing the slow-start threshold: If we are already in the loss state and have not yet retransmitted anything. The condition may arise in case we are not able to retransmit anything because of local congestion.

In case any of the above conditions is TRUE, we store the current slow-start threshold in *tp→prior_ssthersh* in case our current state is CWR or recovery. Otherwise we store three-fourths of the current cwnd or slow-start threshold, whichever is maximum at line 985. Slow-start threshold is set to half of the current congestion window by calling *tcp_recalc_ssthresh()* at line 986. Next we set send the congestion window to 1, and this finally completes the slow-start phase. We clear all the counters related to retransmissions by calling *tcp_clear_retrans()* at line 992, because we are going to do fresh calculations in the next step.

In case the second argument to *tcp_enter_loss()* is not set, we push *tp→undo_marker* so that we are eligible for undoing from the loss state. We set this argument only when we are called from *tcp_check_sack_reneging()* because the reason for entering into loss state is entirely different here. The reason is that whatever out-of-order segments have reached the receiver are discarded by the receiver and we need to retransmit all the data within the window once again. So, it is not the congestion state but the receiver's mismanagement that causes us to enter into the loss state. So, we cannot undo from the loss state.

Next we traverse the retransmit loop (lines 999–1012). First we check if any of the segments was retransmitted when we are entering into the loss state. In case something was already retransmitted, we unset tp→undo_marker, the reason being that we will never know if the Ack for packet appears from the retransmission or the original transmission. In the case where we get an ACK for retransmitted segment that is misinterpreted as an ACK for original segment and we undo from the loss state, this will be misleading (see Section 12.6.8). If the tp→undo_marker is unset, we are not eligible for undoing from the loss state. Next we check for the segment tags. In case the second argument for the routine *tcp_enter_loss()* is set, we just don't care for SACKed segments and mark all the segments as lost (line 1004), the reason being that we set the second argument only when we are called from *tcp_check_sack_reneging()* where we know that all the out-of-order segments are discarded by the receiver. Otherwise we increment the counter for each SACKed segment we encounter, line 1009. We also set *tp→facked_out* to the total segment traversed whenever we come across SACKed segment at line 1010.

We need to recalculate left out segments by calling tcp_sync_left_out() because all the counters were reset by call to *tcp_clear_retrans()*. Next we calculate reordering length to a minimum of current reordering length (*tp→reordering*) and *sysctl_tcp_reordering(3)*. Set TCP state to loss at line 1016. Mark the highest sequence number transmitted so far as *tp→high_seq* at line 1017. Set *TCP_ECN_QUEUE_CWR* for the TCP because we have just reduced C(ongestion) W(indow) by calling *TCP_ECN_queue_cwr()* at line 1018. The next new data segment that the sender sends will have a CWR bit set in the TCP header informing the receiver that it has reduced its congestion window.

10.2.4 *tcp_retransmit_skb()*

We need to explain that during retransmissions we adjust the segment length. In the case where the PMTU has changed and our segment length is more than the mss, we need to repacketize all the segment's by calling *tcp_fragment()* at line 834. This is a very common case, where we check if mss is changed before transmitting any segment (check *tcp_write_xmit()*). On the other hand, if the segment length of the retransmitted segment is less than 1 mss, we try to collapse the adjacent segment with the current segment in question to generate a full-length segment by calling *tcp_retrans_try_collapse()* at line 848 (cs 10.10). The following conditions should be satisfied to collapse the adjacent segments in the retransmit queue (lines 842–846):

1. The segment being retransmitted should not be SYN segment.
2. The length of the current segment is lesser than half of current mss.
3. The adjacent segment to be merged should not be a new segment; that is, it should be from the retransmit queue.
4. Both segments should not contain any paged data.
5. The system should allow us to collapse the segments; that is, *sysctl_tcp_retrans_collapse* should be set.

```
net/ipv4/tcp_output.c

812 int tcp_retransmit_skb(struct sock *sk, struct sk_buff *skb)
813 {
814     struct tcp_opt *tp = &(sk->tp_pinfo.af_tcp);
815     unsigned int cur_mss = tcp_current_mss(sk);
        ....
842     if(!(TCP_SKB_CB(skb)->flags & TCPCB_FLAG_SYN) &&
843         (skb->len < (cur_mss >> 1)) &&
844         (skb->next != tp->send_head) &&
845         (skb->next != (struct sk_buff *)&sk->write_queue) &&
846         (skb_shinfo(skb)->nr_frags == 0 && skb_shinfo(skb->next)->nr_frags == 0) &&
847         (sysctl_tcp_retrans_collapse != 0))
848             tcp_retrans_try_collapse(sk, skb, cur_mss);
        ...
872     err = tcp_transmit_skb(sk, (skb_cloned(skb) ?
873                     pskb_copy(skb, GFP_ATOMIC):
874                     skb_clone(skb, GFP_ATOMIC)));
875
876     if (err == 0) {
        ....
886             TCP_SKB_CB(skb)->sacked |= TCPCB_RETRANS;
887             tp->retrans_out++;
        ...
890             if (!tp->retrans_stamp)
891                 tp->retrans_stamp = TCP_SKB_CB(skb)->when;
892
893             tp->undo_retrans++;
        ...
898             TCP_SKB_CB(skb)->ack_seq = tp->snd_nxt;
899     }
```

cs 10.10. *tcp_retransmit_skb()*.

We store the timestamp of the retransmitted segment in the TCP control block, *TCP_SKB_CB(skb)→when* at line 870, which means that the timestamp is not retained from the original transmission. Once we have transmitted the segment correctly, we tag the segment as transmitted (*TCPCB_RETRANS*) at line 886 and also account for retransmission (*tp→retrans_out*) at line 887. We increment tp→ undo_retrans by 1 to account for D-SACKs at line 893.

10.2.5 *tcp_retrans_try_collapse()*

Here we try to merge the current retransmitted segment with the next segment in the retransmit queue by calling *tcp_retrans_try_collapse()* (cs 10.11).

The very first condition to continue with the merger is that both segments (retransmission and next segment) should not be in use at line 698, which means that the original transmission should not be there in the IP or device queue pending for transmission. If that is the case, TCP's data integrity will not be maintained. If the original segment (not yet transmitted) and the merged segment reach the receiver in the same sequence, data in the second segment will be discarded because of the same sequence number (considering retransmission). This can be checked from *tcp_cloned()*.

The next condition that disqualifies us from merging is that the next segment to be merged should not have been SACKed already at line 703. We can merge the two segments only if the receivers' window allows it to happen. If the merged data exceeds total available space in the receive *buffer* (*tp→snd_wnd*), we can't merge the two segments (line 707). Next we need to check if not enough tail room is available in the buffer being retransmitted to accommodate data from the next buffer (check being made at line 714) or if the sum of payload for both segments is exceeding the current mss. If any of the mentioned conditions is TRUE, we can't merge. We exit in case the former condition is TRUE because we are not going to add any data to the paged area nor are we going to reallocate memory in the linear area to accommodate new data (expensive operation). In case the latter condition is TRUE, we exit because we can't transmit more than mss.

If all the above-mentioned conditions are satisfied, we are eligible for merger. We first unlink the next segment from the retransmit list at line 719. If the next segment is hardware check-summed, we need to forcefully mark the original segment as hardware check-summed at line 722. In case the *CHECKSUM_HW* flag is not ON for the segment, we copy data from the next segment to the one being retransmitted at line 725 and also recalculate the checksum for the new data being copied at line 726. The CHECKSUM_HW flag is enabled for segments containing paged data, and here we are not dealing with any paged data. It appears that if we come here and the CHECKSUM_HW flag is ON, we are in trouble.

Next we update the sequence space of the merged segment (retransmit) by initializing the end sequence number from the next segment at line 730. We also merge control flags (*TCP_SKB_CB(skb)→flags*) of both the segment's at lines 733–734. Because the next segment being merged may contain PSH/FIN flags that should be set out for the new merged segment. If the segment being merged (next segment) was retransmitted, we need to account for it by decrementing the retransmission counter by 1 at line 741. This is because we are removing the segment and the merged segment is not yet retransmitted. We also account for the lost counter in the case where the segment being removed is marked lost at line 743, the reason

```
net/ipv4/tcp_output.c

 690 static void tcp_retrans_try_collapse(struct sock *sk, struct sk_buff *skb, int mss_now)
 691 {
 692     struct tcp_opt *tp = &sk->tp_pinfo.af_tcp;
 693     struct sk_buff *next_skb = skb->next;
         ...
 698     if(!skb_cloned(skb) && !skb_cloned(next_skb)) {
 699         int skb_size = skb->len, next_skb_size = next_skb->len;
 700         u16 flags = TCP_SKB_CB(skb)->flags;
             ...
 703         if(TCP_SKB_CB(next_skb)->sacked & TCPCB_SACKED_ACKED)
 704             return;
             ....
 707         if (after(TCP_SKB_CB(next_skb)->end_seq, tp->snd_una+tp->snd_wnd))
 708             return;
             ....
 714         if ((next_skb_size > skb_tailroom(skb)) ||
 715             ((skb_size + next_skb_size) > mss_now))
 716             return;
             ....
 719         __skb_unlink(next_skb, next_skb->list);
 720
 721         if (next_skb->ip_summed == CHECKSUM_HW)
 722             skb->ip_summed = CHECKSUM_HW;
 723
 724         if (skb->ip_summed != CHECKSUM_HW) {
 725             memcpy(skb_put(skb, next_skb_size), next_skb->data, next_skb_size);
 726             skb->csum = csum_block_add(skb->csum, next_skb->csum, skb_size);
 727         }
             ....
 730         TCP_SKB_CB(skb)->end_seq = TCP_SKB_CB(next_skb)->end_seq;
             ....
 733         flags |= TCP_SKB_CB(next_skb)->flags; /* This moves PSH/FIN etc. over */
 734         TCP_SKB_CB(skb)->flags = flags;
             ....
 739         TCP_SKB_CB(skb)->sacked |= TCP_SKB_CB(next_skb)->sacked&(TCPCB_EVER_RETRANS|TCPCB_AT_TAIL);
 740         if (TCP_SKB_CB(next_skb)->sacked&TCPCB_SACKED_RETRANS)
 741             tp->retrans_out--;
 742         if (TCP_SKB_CB(next_skb)->sacked&TCPCB_LOST) {
 743             tp->lost_out--;
 744             tp->left_out--;
 745         }
 746         /* Reno case is special. Sigh... */
 747         if (!tp->sack_ok && tp->sacked_out) {
 748             tp->sacked_out--;
 749             tp->left_out--;
 750         }
             ....
 755         if (tp->fackets_out)
 756             tp->fackets_out--;
 757         tcp_free_skb(sk, next_skb);
 758         tp->packets_out--;
 759     }
 760 }
```

cs 10.11. tcp_retrans_try_collapse().

being the same because the segment does not exist anymore and the new merged segment is not yet considered lost. In the case of Reno implementation, if our SACK count is nonzero, we decrement the SACK count by 1 (*tp→sacked_out*) at line 748. This is a special case of Reno where we SACKed counters but no segment is marked SACKed because SACK information is drawn from duplicate ACKs. If our FACK count is a positive nonzero value, we just decrement it by 1 because one segment is removed from the retransmit queue (line 756). The unlinked segment is freed at line 757, and the packet count is decremented by 1 at line 758 for the obvious reasons.

10.2.6 *skb_cloned()*

Whenever we transmit a segment, we clone it by calling *skb_clone()* and transmit the cloned segment. When we clone a segment, the *sk_buff* header is copied completely. The data part is shared here. The paged data are not copied; only the header part of paged data is copied. Since 'struct *skb_shared_info*' lies at the end of *sk_buff*, we need not copy it explicitly. We increment *skb_shinfo(skb)→dataref* by 1 when we are cloning *sk_buff*. When we check if the sk_buff is cloned, we check two flags in skb_cloned():

- *skb→cloned*
- *skb_shinfo(skb)→dataref*

Once a segment is transmitted, *skb→cloned* is set, which will always be set even if the *sk_buff* is transmitted. But additional *skb_shinfo(skb)→dataref* will be decremented by 1 once sk_buff is transmitted by calling *skb_release_data()*. So, *ck_buff* is considered cloned if the transmitted data are actually transmitted and are not queued up in the transmit queue or IP queue for transmission.

10.3 ZERO WINDOW PROBE TIMER

The receiver TCP advertises zero window whenever its receive buffer is full. This happens mainly because the application is not able to read the data fast enough to make room for the new TCP data in the socket's receive buffer. Whenever an application reads data from the receive buffer, it checks if enough space is generated in the receive buffer to advertise the new window to the sender. If so, it sends out an ACK segment advertising the new window. If this segment is lost, there will be deadlock between the sender and the receiver if the data are flowing only in one direction. To avoid this, the sender implements a zero window probe timer, also called a persistent timer to probe if the peer has opened window. It sends out 1 byte of data along with the zero-window probe. The macro defined for the persistent timer is

TCP_TIME_PROBE0

[**Note**: How probes are sent, *tcp_xmit_probe_skb()*: While sending out a probe segment, we don't queue up the probe segment and we send out sequence number that is one less than the last sent sequence number. In the case of urgent data, we send out two zero-length segments: one with sequence number same as Unacked sequence containing sequence number for the urgent byte (just urgent pointer) and the other one with sequence number UNA − 1. In both cases, the outgoing packets are not accounted for in packet count (tp→packets_out)].

```
include/net/tcp.h

1225 static __inline__ void tcp_check_probe_timer(struct sock *sk, struct tcp_opt *tp)
1226 {
1227      if (!tp->packets_out && !tp->pending)
1228          tcp_reset_xmit_timer(sk, TCP_TIME_PROBE0, tp->rto);
1229 }
```

cs 10.12. *tcp_check_probe_timer()*.

10.3.1 When Is the First Time Probe Timer Installed?

When we try to transmit a new segment, a check is made whether we can send out a new segment or not. There may be so many factors to decide on whether we can send out a new segment or not. One of the reasons can be that a window advertised by the receiver does not allow to receive any more data. We make these checks in many places when we want to send out new segments: *__tcp_push_pending_frames()* and *tcp_data_snd_check()*. *__tcp_push_pending_frames()* is called when we write data over the socket from an application in order to push out segments in the transmit queue. *tcp_data_snd_check()* is called when we receive a segment from the peer. The segment may be an ACK or DATA/ACK segment. While processing the received segment before sending out an ACK, we check if there are any data to be transmitted in the queue. If the data exist, we call *tcp_data_snd_check()* to piggyback data along with the ACK in *tcp_rcv_established()*.

These routines check if we can send out a new segment. If not, we call *tcp_check_probe_timer()* to check if the receive window is the cause that is not allowing us to send out new segments. *tcp_check_probe_timer()* checks if no outstanding unacknowledged data (*!tp→packets_out*) and no timer is installed (*!tp→pending*) at line 1227 (cs 10.12). From timers here we mean only retransmit and window probe timer's only. If there are no outstanding data that are unacknowledged, it means that only one condition can prevent more data to be pushed: a zero window advertised by the receiver. There is a common callback routine for retransmit timeout timer and zero-window probe timer. If a retransmit timer is already installed, it means that we are already probing a zero window because all the data are ACKed and there is nothing to be transmitted (possibility of retransmit timeout timer installed is ruled out). If the above two conditions are TRUE, we reset the zero-window timer with a timeout value of *tp→rto* at line 1228.

10.3.2 When Is the Probe Timer Canceled for the Connection?

We receive a window update from the receiver whenever the application reads data from a socket's receive queue and enough space is available in the receive buffer to accommodate at least 1 mss of data. Another way we can receive window update information is in response to the zero-window probe. While processing incoming ACK in *tcp_ack()* at line 1944 of cs 11.26, we just check if the valid ACK has come with no outstanding unacknowledged data. If that is the case, we know that this may be window update or ACK resulting from a zero-window probe. We just jump to line 1968 to process the window update. We first clear the probe count (*tp→probes_out*); furthermore, if any new segment is pending for transmission at line 1975 (*tp→send_head != NULL*), we call *tcp_ack_probe()* for further action (cs 11.26).

10.3.3 *tcp_ack_probe()*

This checks if the next segment to be transmitted is within the window opened by the peer at line 1825 (cs 10.13). If the end sequence of the head of the transmit queue (*tp→send_head*) is within the opened window sequence space, we can stop the zero-window probe by calling *tcp_clear_xmit_timer()* at line 1827, which means that the receiver has enough room to accommodate all the data in the head of the transmit queue in its receive buffer. On the other hand, if the end sequence is beyond the opened window as shown by dotted lines in Fig. 10.1, the receiver still doesn't have enough space to accommodate all the data from the head of the transmit queue. So, we continue with the zero-window probe timer by resetting the timer with timeout value governed by *tp→rto* and *tp→backoff*. Here, we don't have a backoffed timeout value for TCP state machine which means that we are not backing off retransmittion time out as *tp→rtof* & *tp→backoff* are not changed (line 1832). So, next zero-window-probe will not be backed off. Normally when a retransmission timer fires, the next retransmission timer is set to expire after twice the current timeout so that we don't retransmit too fast and worsen the congestion state. This is known as exponential backoff of RTO.

10.3.4 How Does the Window Probe Timer Work?

A single-timer callback routine, *tcp_write_timer()*, exists for both a retransmit timer and a window probe timer. *tcp_write_timer()* checks what routine to call, depending

```
net/ipv4/tcp_input.c

1819 static void tcp_ack_probe(struct sock *sk)
1820 {
1821      struct tcp_opt *tp = &(sk->tp_pinfo.af_tcp);
            ...
1825      if (!after(TCP_SKB_CB(tp->send_head)->end_seq, tp->snd_una + tp->snd_wnd)) {
1826           tp->backoff = 0;
1827           tcp_clear_xmit_timer(sk, TCP_TIME_PROBE0);
            ....
1831      } else {
1832           tcp_reset_xmit_timer(sk, TCP_TIME_PROBE0,
1833                     min(tp->rto << tp->backoff, TCP_RTO_MAX));
1834      }
1835 }
```

cs 10.13. *tcp_ack_probe()*.

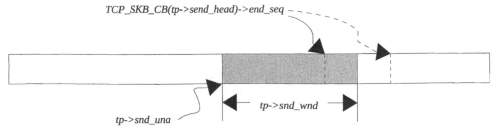

Figure 10.1. The window has opened enough to transmit new data.

on *tp→pending* flag. Very obviously, only one timer can be installed at any given point of time—that is, either retransmit or window-probe timer. When the window-probe timer expires, we call *tcp_probe_timer()* to transmit a zero-window probe segment.

10.3.5 *tcp_probe_timer()*

Here we do some cleanup checks and also resource management for the window probe timer. First we check if we have any unacknowledged data. If *tp→packets_out* is more than one, it means that we have transmitted some new segment after a zero-window probe timer was installed. This indicates that a window opened and a new segment got transmitted before the window probe timer could be canceled. The second condition we check here is whether we have any new segment to be transmitted. In this case again there is no point in having a window probe timer installed if there are no new data to be transmitted. In both the cases, we return without proceeding any further from line 279.

Next we check if the socket associated with the connection is already dead at line 299. If so, we need to check if the connection needs to be dropped because we can't allow the socket already detached from the application to hang on for a long time, thereby eating up resources. We call *tcp_out_of_resources()* to check if we can drop the connection immediately (for details on the routine, see Section 10.2.2). If the TCP socket is already in the dead state, we impose an additional penalty on the dead socket, that depends on the total number of orphaned sockets in the system. Which means that the dead connection should be closed in case there is no activity on the connection for a long time so that we are unnecessarily not utilizing resources. Otherwise, we check if the number of probes (*tp→probes_out*) already sent out has exceeded the system-wide control probe parameter (*sysctl_tcp_retries2*). If so, we just drop the connection by calling *tcp_write_err()* at line 309 (cs 10.14). If we still have another chance, *tcp_send_probe0()* is called to send out a zero-window probe at line 312.

10.3.6 *tcp_send_probe0()*

The routine tries to send out new data in case the window is opened by calling *tcp_write_wakeup()*. If a new segment is transmitted out, it is only because the window has opened enough. In this case, *tp→packets* will never be zero. Once again, if there is no segment in the transmit queue to be transmitted, there is no need to process the timer further. So, if a new segment is transmitted after a call to *tcp_write_wakeup()* or there are no new data to be transmitted (*tp→send_head equal to NULL*), we just return without processing any further.

If we are here, it means that we have not transmitted any new segment because the window has not opened. So, we are able to either transmit a window probe or not. If we are able to send out a window probe, just backoff RTO, increment the probe counter and reset the window probe timer to a new backoffed timeout value (lines 1433–1437, cs 10.15). Otherwise there was internal congestion at the driver level, so we reset the window probe timer to a minimum of *TCP_RESOURCE_PROBE_INTERVAL* and current backoffed RTO at line 1447.

10.3.7 *tcp_write_wakeup()*

This routine checks if the receiver has advertised enough window to transmit new data and transmits the new segment if permitted. First we check if the connection

```
net/ipv4/tcp_timer.c

272 static void tcp_probe_timer(struct sock *sk)
273 {
274     struct tcp_opt *tp = &sk->tp_pinfo.af_tcp;
275     int max_probes;
276
277     if (tp->packets_out || !tp->send_head) {
278         tp->probes_out = 0;
279         return;
280     }
            ...
297     max_probes = sysctl_tcp_retries2;
298
299     if (sk->dead) {
300         int alive = ((tp->rto<<tp->backoff) < TCP_RTO_MAX);
            ...
304         if (tcp_out_of_resources(sk, alive || tp->probes_out <= max_probes))
305             return;
306     }
307
308     if (tp->probes_out > max_probes) {
309         tcp_write_err(sk);
310     } else {
311         /* Only send another probe if we didn't close things up. */
312         tcp_send_probe0(sk);
313     }
314 }
```

cs 10.14. tcp_probe_timer().

```
net/ipv4/tcp_output.c

1419 void tcp_send_probe0(struct sock *sk)
1420 {
1421     struct tcp_opt *tp = &(sk->tp_pinfo.af_tcp);
1422     int err;
1423
1424     err = tcp_write_wakeup(sk);
1425
1426     if (tp->packets_out || !tp->send_head) {
             ....
1428         tp->probes_out = 0;
1429         tp->backoff = 0;
1430         return;
1431     }
1432
1433     if (err <= 0) {
1434         tp->backoff++;
1435         tp->probes_out++;
1436         tcp_reset_xmit_timer (sk, TCP_TIME_PROBE0,
1437                     min(tp->rto << tp->backoff, TCP_RTO_MAX));
1438     } else {
             ....
1445         if (!tp->probes_out)
1446             tp->probes_out=1;
1447         tcp_reset_xmit_timer (sk, TCP_TIME_PROBE0,
1448                     min(tp->rto << tp->backoff, TCP_RESOURCE_PROBE_INTERVAL));
1449     }
1450 }
```

cs 10.15. tcp_send_probe0().

```
net/ipv4/tcp_output.c

1373 int tcp_write_wakeup(struct sock *sk)
1374 {
1375        if (sk->state != TCP_CLOSE) {
1376            struct tcp_opt *tp = &(sk->tp_pinfo.af_tcp);
1377            struct sk_buff *skb;
1378
1379            if ((skb = tp->send_head) != NULL &&
1380                before(TCP_SKB_CB(skb)->seq, tp->snd_una+tp->snd_wnd)) {
1381                int err;
1382                int mss = tcp_current_mss(sk);
1383                int seg_size = tp->snd_una+tp->snd_wnd-TCP_SKB_CB(skb)->seq;
1384
1385                if (before(tp->pushed_seq, TCP_SKB_CB(skb)->end_seq))
1386                    tp->pushed_seq = TCP_SKB_CB(skb)->end_seq;
                          ....
1392                if (seg_size < TCP_SKB_CB(skb)->end_seq - TCP_SKB_CB(skb)->seq ||
1393                    skb->len > mss) {
1394                    seg_size = min(seg_size, mss);
1395                    TCP_SKB_CB(skb)->flags |= TCPCB_FLAG_PSH;
1396                    if (tcp_fragment(sk, skb, seg_size))
1397                        return -1;
1398                }
1399                TCP_SKB_CB(skb)->flags |= TCPCB_FLAG_PSH;
1400                TCP_SKB_CB(skb)->when = tcp_time_stamp;
1401                err = tcp_transmit_skb(sk, skb_clone(skb, GFP_ATOMIC));
1402                if (!err) {
1403                    update_send_head(sk, tp, skb);
1404                }
1405                return err;
1406            } else {
1407                if (tp->urg_mode &&
1408                    between(tp->snd_up, tp->snd_una+1, tp->snd_una+0xFFFF))
1409                    tcp_xmit_probe_skb(sk, TCPCB_URG);
1410                return tcp_xmit_probe_skb(sk, 0);
1411            }
1412        }
1413        return -1;
1414 }
```

cs 10.16. tcp_write_wakeup().

has already been closed at line 1375 (cs 10.16); if so, we return. We do the next check here:

1. if there is no new segment to be transmitted at line 1379 (*tp→send_head equal to NULL*).
2. If the above is FALSE, then we need to check if the window advertised by the receiver is big enough to transmit out new data at line 1380 (start sequence of segment < *SND.WND* + *SND_UNA*). Zero-window scenario at the render is shown in Figure 10.2.

If both of the above conditions satisfy, we calculate the size of the window that is opened at line 1383, shown as the shaded area in Fig. 10.3. Next we check if we need to fragment the segment to be transmitted. We need to fragment the segment in two cases:

TCP_SKB_CB(tp->send_head)->seq

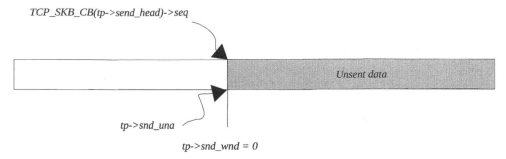

Figure 10.2. The window has not opened to transmit new data.

TCP_SKB_CB(tp->send_head)->seq

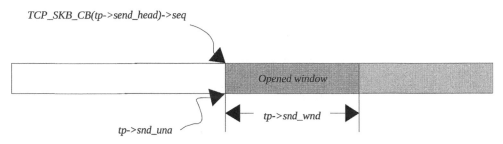

Figure 10.3. The window has opened enough to transmit new data.

1. The window opened is less than the segment length, line 1392.
2. The length of the segment is more than the current mss, line 1393.

In both cases, we fragment the segment into two parts. The segment is split: One part is equal to a minimum of window opened and current mss, and the other part contains the rest of the data. We call *tcp_fragment()* to fragment the segment. We set PUSH flag (*TCPCB_FLAG_PSH*) for the segment's control block. We then transmit the new segment at the head of the transmit queue at line 1401. In case we are able to transmit the segment properly, *update_send_head()* is called to update *tp→send_head* at line 1403.

In case the window has not yet opened as shown in Fig. 10.2, we just need to transmit a zero-window probe segment. We have two situations here. These are with and without urgent mode. Without urgent mode, we just transmit the window probe by calling *tcp_xmit_probe_skb()*. The sequence number sent out with this probe is one less than the unacknowledged sequence number in order to get fast ACK. With the urgent mode on, we transmit one more segment along with the probe segment. We send out one additional segment having an urgent flag set with a pointer to urgent data. This segment contains a sequence number that is equal to the unacknowledged sequence number (see line 1367 of *tcp_xmit_probe_skb()*).

10.4 DELAY ACK TIMER

TCP implements two modes of ACKing. These are:

1. Quick ACK
2. Delayed ACK

```
include/net/sock.h

271      struct {
272          __u8    pending;      /* ACK is pending */
273          __u8    quick;        /* Scheduled number of quick acks     */
274          __u8    pingpong;     /* The session is interactive         */
275          __u8    blocked;      /* Delayed ACK was blocked by socket lock*/
276          __u32   ato;          /* Predicted tick of soft clock       */
277          unsigned long timeout; /* Currently scheduled timeout       */
278          __u32   lrcvtime;     /* timestamp of last received data packet*/
279          __u16   last_seg_size; /* Size of last incoming segment      */
280          __u16   rcv_mss;      /* MSS used for delayed ACK decisions  */
281      } ack;
```

cs 10.17. to 'struct ack' implement ack management .

```
include/net/tcp.h

656 enum tcp_ack_state_t
657 {
658      TCP_ACK_SCHED  = 1,
659      TCP_ACK_TIMER  = 2,
660      TCP_ACK_PUSHED = 4
661 };
```

cs 10.18. ACK flags.

In some cases we need to ACK quickly so that the sender continues to pump in more data with the reception of ACK, because each ACK for new data increments the congestion window by one segment. Other cases where we need to ACK quickly is when we receive an out-of-order segment or when the gap in the received data is filled. In both cases we need to inform the sender about the event; otherwise in the former case, the sender may experience timeout unnecessarily entering into the loss state. In the latter case, the sender may continue to retransmit segments unnecessarily adding to network congestion. These are some of the reasons why we need quick ACKing. There are reasons for delayed ACKing also. In some cases we have an interactive session like telnet, rlogin, and so on, where each character typed needs to be echoed back. In such cases, if we generate ACK for each segment (containing one character), it will generate a huge number of segments in the network. In this case we delay ACK so that either the echoed character is piggybacked along with the ACK or some more characters are received before we can send out an ACK. In such cases, delayed ACK will save us a lot of ACK segments unnecessarily loading the network. Linux maintains all the ACK-related information with the help of *struct ack* (cs 10.17), which is embedded as part of *struct tcp_opt. Pending* field indicates the state of the ACK at any given point of time. There are three TCP ACK states as shown in (cs 10.18). *TCP_ACK_SCHED* indicates that the ACK is scheduled, *TCP_ACK_TIMER* indicates that the delayed ACK timer is already set, and the *TCP_ACK_PUSHED* flag indicates that the ACK is already pushed and needs to be sent out at the earliest.

```
include/net/tcp.h

663 static inline void tcp_schedule_ack(struct tcp_opt *tp)
664 {
665       tp->ack,pending |= TCP_ACK_SCHED;
666 }
```

cs 10.19. tcp_schedule_ack().

10.4.1 When Is the ACK Scheduled?

ACK is scheduled whenever we get data from the peer. We set the *TCP_ACK_SCHED* flag by calling *tcp_schedule_ack()*. (cs 10.19). We schedule ACK whenever we receive data in *tcp_event_data_recv()* called from *tcp_rcv_established()* and *tcp_data_queue()*. Then we directly schedule ACK whenever we receive *out-of-order segment, retransmitted segment, zero-window probe, out-of-window data, or partial segment* in all these events detected in *tcp_data_queue()*.

10.4.2 How and When Is the ACK Segment Sent?

There are a number of places where we need to make a decision whether to send segment immediately or to delay it. We can schedule an ACK by calling *tcp_schedule_ack()* but can't force an ACK based on the flag. There are certain conditions based on which we can send and ACK or delay it further. The simplest case we take here is from *tcp_rcv_established()* (cs 10.20). Whenever we receive in-sequence data in *tcp_rcv_established()*, we copy data directly to the user land process or queue it in a receive buffer. In case an application has read all the data that has arrived, we enter into block 3360–3364. In this case we check if we are in quick ack mode by calling *tcp_in_quickack_mode()*. See Section 10.4.3 for quick ACK mode.

If we are in quick ACK mode, ACK is generated immediately by call to *tcp_send_data()* at line 3361. In case we are not in quick ACK mode, we delay ACK for

```
net/ipv4/tcp_input.c

3210 int tcp_rcv_established(struct sock *sk, struct sk_buff *skb,
3211                  struct tcphdr *th, unsigned len)
3212 {
3213      struct tcp_opt *tp = &(sk->tp_pinfo.af_tcp);
         ....
3359           if (eaten) {
3360                if (tcp_in_quickack_mode(tp)) {
3361                     tcp_send_ack(sk);
3362                } else {
3363                     tcp_send_delayed_ack(sk);
3364                }
3365           } else {
3366                __tcp_ack_snd_check(sk, 0);
3367           }
         ...
3440      tcp_ack_snd_check(sk);
         ...
3449 }
```

cs 10.20. tcp_rcv_established().

```
net/ipv4/tcp_input.c

178 static __inline__ int tcp_in_quickack_mode(struct tcp_opt *tp)
179 {
180      return (tp->ack.quick && !tp->ack.pingpong);
181 }
```

cs 10.21. *tcp_in_quickack_mode().*

some more time by calling *tcp_send_delayed_ack()* (see Section 10.4.6). We delay ACK so that we can send out cumulative ACK for some more segment's that arrive quickly or it may wait for some data to be written so that data can be piggybacked along with the ACK.

In the case where data are not consumed by the application and it is queued up in the receive queue, we call __tcp_ack_snd_check() to do some more aggressive checking to send out an ACK. Please see Section 10.4.4. In the case where we have received out-of-window data, retransmission, out-of-order segment, or urgent pointer, we take slow path. In slow path, we check if ACK needs to be sent at line 3440 after processing the received segment. The ACK may be scheduled when we are here, but whether we need to delay it or send an ACK immediately will be checked by calling *tcp_ack_snd_check()*. For more details see Section 10.4.5.

10.4.3   Quick ACK Mode

In quick ACK mode, we check two fields from *struct ack. Pingpong* is set in case TCP connection is interactive like telnet, rlogin, and so on. In the case of interactive session, we don't ACK immediately because of the reason explained in Section 2.4. We enter quick ACK mode when we don't want to delay the ACKs such as out-of-order segments are received, segment fills hole in the received data, and so on. We call *tcp_enter_quickack_mode()* to enter quick ACK mode. We reset *pingpong* field and also initialize *quick* field of *struct ack. quick* field indicates the number of quick ACKs that we can send in a row and is decreased by one whenever an ACK is sent out by calling *tcp_dec_quickack_mode()* from *tcp_transmit_skb()*. So, we are in quick ACK mode if pingpong is reset and we still have quick ACK quota ($tp \rightarrow ack. quick > 0$) (cs 10.21).

10.4.4   __tcp_ack_snd_check()

In this routine we make some checks before we conclude whether to delay an ACK or to send it immediately. We can send an ACK immediately under the following conditions:

1. If the ACK is pending for more than full-segment-sized data. $tp \rightarrow rcv\_wup$ is updated to $tp \rightarrow rcv\_nxt$ when we send an ACK. If the difference of these two fields is more than received mss, ACK is pending for more than 1 mss of data. Along with this condition, we also need to have enough space in the receive buffer such that the window we are going to advertise is more than the last window (lines 3010–1014, cs 10.22). The latter condition ensures that fast

```
net/ipv4/tcp_input.c

3005 static __inline__ void __tcp_ack_snd_check(struct sock *sk, int ofo_possible)
3006 {
3007     struct tcp_opt *tp = &(sk->tp_pinfo.af_tcp);
         ...
3010     if (((tp->rcv_nxt - tp->rcv_wup) > tp->ack.rcv_mss
         ..
3014         && __tcp_select_window(sk) >= tp->rcv_wnd) ||
3015         /* We ACK each frame or... */
3016         tcp_in_quickack_mode(tp) ||
3017         /* We have out of order data. */
3018         (ofo_possible &&
3019         skb_peek(&tp->out_of_order_queue) != NULL)) {
3020             /* Then ack it now */
3021             tcp_send_ack(sk);
3022     } else {
3023             /* Else, send delayed ack. */
3024             tcp_send_delayed_ack(sk);
3025     }
3026 }
```

cs 10.22. __tcp_ack_snd_check().

ACKs should be sent out only if we have enough space in the receive buffer, because the rate at which new segments are transmitted depends on the rate at which ACKs are received. In the case where we have less space in the receive buffer because the application is reading slowly, we delay the ACK slightly so that the application gets enough time to read data in the receive queue before which new data should not arrive and fill the receive buffer. In this case, we are an eligible candidate for generating immediate ACK.

2. We have out-of-order data that can be detected from *tp→out_of_order_queue(!= NULL)* at line 3019. It means that we should generate an ACK immediately in order to tell the other end that we have received the segment out of order so that it should not experience timeout.

3. We are in quick ACK mode, if *tcp_in_quickack_mode()* returns TRUE at line 3016. See Section 10.4.3.

If any of the above conditions is TRUE, we call *tcp_send_ack()* to immediately generate an ACK; otherwise we call *tcp_send_delayed_ack()* in order to defer ACK for some more time.

10.4.5 *tcp_ack_snd_check()*

We call this routine in the slow path after processing the incoming segment just to check if ACK needs to be sent out from *tcp_rcv_established()*. Here, we first check if the ACK is scheduled. In case we got out-of-sequence data or retransmissions, ACK will be scheduled in *tcp_data_queue()* and we can send out an ACK segment here. Before this routine is called, we call *tcp_data_snd_check()* to check if there are any new data to be sent out. If new data are transmitted here, we have already ACKed the incoming segment. So, the ACK signal that was set in *tcp_data_queue()* will be reset and ACK need not be generated separately.

```
net/ipv4/tcp_input.c

3028 static __inline__ void tcp_ack_snd_check(struct sock *sk)
3029 {
3030       struct tcp_opt *tp = &(sk->tp_pinfo.af_tcp);
3031       if (!tcp_ack_scheduled(tp)) {
3032             /* We sent a data segment already. */
3033             return;
3034       }
3035       __tcp_ack_snd_check(sk, 1);
3036 }
```

<u>cs 10.23.</u> *tcp_ack_snd_check().*

If the ACK is not scheduled, we just return. Otherwise, we we need to make some more checks before we conclude whether an ACK should be sent out. So, we call __tcp_ack_snd_check() with a second argument as 1 (cs 10.23). This value signals that we should not ignore the possibility of an out-of-order segment being received, in which case we need to send out an ACK immediately (for details see Section 10.4.4).

10.4.6   *tcp_send_delayed_ack()*

In this routine we first try to adjust delay ACK timeout, depending on:

1. Current timeout, $tp \rightarrow ack.ato$
2. Smoothened rtt
3. Whether the ACK is in pingpong mode

In the case where the pingpong mode is on, we keep a lower limit on the maximum allowable timeout (HZ/5) as pinpong is enabled for interactive session. In the case where echo does not happen fast enough, we need not wait long enough to send the ACK back. Once we have smoothened the timeout value, we calculate timeout with respect to jiffies (number of ticks since the machine has booted) at line 1282. Next we check if the delayed ACK timer is already installed at line 1285. The reason for this may be:

1. The delayed ACK timer fired and got blocked because the socket was in use by some other thread (tp→ack.blocked is set) when the timer expired last. For details, see Section 10.4.8.
2. We got here much before the installed timer would expire.

In the latter case, if very little time is left for the installed timer to expire, we send out the ACK immediately. In the former case, we should process delayed ACK at the earliest because we already missed the delayed ACK timer for the reason that the socket was in use by someone else. If any of the above condition's is TRUE, we call *tcp_send_ack()* to send an ACK immediately at line 1290 and return (cs 10.24).

If both condition's are false, we need to reset delay ACK timer for which we are called. If the above calculated timeout is more than the current timeout ($tp \rightarrow$

```
net/ipv4/tcp_output.c

1253 void tcp_send_delayed_ack(struct sock *sk)
1254 {
1255      struct tcp_opt *tp = &sk->tp_pinfo.af_tcp;
1256      int ato = tp->ack.ato;
          ...
1281      /* Stay within the limit we were given */
1282      timeout = jiffies + ato;
1283
1284      /* Use new timeout only if there wasn't a older one earlier. */
1285      if (tp->ack.pending&TCP_ACK_TIMER) {
1286           /* If delack timer was blocked or is about to expire,
1287            * send ACK now.
1288            */
1289           if (tp->ack.blocked || time_before_eq(tp->ack.timeout, jiffies+(ato>>2))) {
1290                tcp_send_ack(sk);
1291                return;
1292           }
1293
1294           if (!time_before(timeout, tp->ack.timeout))
1295                timeout = tp->ack.timeout;
1296      }
1297      tp->ack.pending |= TCP_ACK_SCHED|TCP_ACK_TIMER;
1298      tp->ack.timeout = timeout;
1299      if (!mod_timer(&tp->delack_timer, timeout))
1300           sock_hold(sk);
1301 }
```

cs 10.24. tcp_send_delayed_ack().

ack.timeout), we take the the current delay ACK timeout at lines 1294–1295. The reason for this is that we are here with the timer already installed, so we should expire as per the schedule. Next we set *TCP_ACK_SCHED* and *TCP_ACK_TIMER* flags related to delayed ACK at line 1297. We set these flags here unconditionally because we don't know if the timer was already installed when we entered the routine. Next we modify a delayed ACK timer with the new timeout value by calling *mod_timer()* at line 1299. We hold a socket reference by calling *sock_hold()* at line 1300 in case *mod_timer()* returns 0. *mod_timer()* returns zero only if the timer was not already installed or had already expired. If it is already installed, the socket's reference is already held by the timer. The reference on the socket is released in the delay ACK timer routine which we are going to discuss next. We hold reference to socket so that the socket should not be destroyed before the timer expires.

10.4.7   *tcp_delack_timer()*

This is a callback routine for Delay ACK timer. We hold socket's spin lock and first check if the socket is already in use mainly because somebody is already accessing socket (*sk→lock.users != 0*) at line 216. If the socket is already being accessed somewhere else, we just set a blocked field at line 218 to indicate that the delay ACK timer was blocked because of a socket in use. We modify delay ACK timer with expiry time of *TCP_DELACK_MIN* at line 220. If the timer was not already installed, we need to hold additional reference on the socket by calling sock_hold() at line 221. We now release the socket lock and return.

In the case where the socket is not in use, the first thing we do is claim some memory for the socket by calling *tcp_mem_reclaim()* from TCP memory pool. For more detail, see Section 9.1. We do some clean checks such as if the socket is already closed or *TCP_ACK_TIMER* is not set at line 227. If any of these conditions is TRUE, we return. If we got fired before the expire time set for the timer at line 230, we modify the timer to the current timeout (*tp→ack.timeout*) value. If required, hold additional reference on the socket and return.

We are ready to handle delay ACK timer now. So, the first thing we do is to clear the *TCP_ACK_TIMER* bit, which indicates that the timer is installed. Next we check if the there is anything queued up in TCP's prequeue. This may happen because when an incoming segment is being processed in *tcp_v4_rcv()*, we first try to queue the segment in TCP prequeue by calling *tcp_prequeue()*. In case this is the first segment in the queue, we wake up the thread blocked to read data from the socket and also install delayed ACK in case ACK is not already scheduled. In case the timer fires before the sleeping thread gets the processor, we will process the prequeue first and then send the cumulative ACK. In case we have segments to be processed in the prequeue, they are processed in loop 242–243 by callback routine *sk→backlog_rcv()*, which is nothing but *tcp_rcv_established()*.

While processing segment's in the prequeue, we might have already sent out ACK. So, next we check if the ACK is already scheduled at line 248. If we are in interactive session (pingpong mode is turned off), we just inflate ACK timeout (*tp→ ack.timeout*) by backing off current timeout but not more than retransmission timeout at line 251. On the other hand, if it was interactive session and we have timed out, it means that we have not yet transmitted anything after we received data for a long time. For example, if this happens with telnet, rlogin server side TCP sessions and we have not echoed the characters typed from the client end TCP fast enough, we should leave pingpong mode of ACKing. Next thing we do is to send an ACK by calling *tcp_send_ack()* at line 259 (cs 10.25). We do some cleanup work, release lock on the socket by calling *bh_unlock_sock()*, release additional hold on the socket by calling *sock_put()*, and leave.

10.4.8   *tcp_reset_xmit_timer()*

This a common routine to reset timers for RTO, window probe, and delayed ACK timer. The second argument to the routine is the kind of timer, and the third argument is the expire time in ticks. The very first action we take here is that if the timeout passed to the routine is more than maximum RTO, we reduce it to TCP_RTO_MAX. Depending on the TCP timer, we take further action in the switch case. For RTO and window probe timers the callback routine is same, that is, *tcp_write_timer()*. Timer request for both these timers is processed in lines 876–879. We differentiate between these timers from *tp→pending* field. We set this field according to the timer type at line 876. Now we store the expiry time for the timer in *tp→ timeout* in *jiffies* (clock ticks) at line 877. Next we call *modify_timer()* to reset the timer with an expiry value as *tp→timeout*. If the timer is not already installed, we need to hold the reference for the socket at line 879 (cs 10.26).

Delay ACK timer is slightly different from these two timers in a way that we don't initialize *tp→pending* field here. Instead we just set *TCP_ACK_TIMER* bit in *pending* field of *struct ack*. Timeout for the delay ACK is set in *tp→ack.timeout* field. All the ACK status is maintained in *struct ack*, embedded in *struct tcp_opt*.

```
net/ipv4/tcp_output.c

210 static void tcp_delack_timer(unsigned long data)
211 {
212     struct sock *sk = (struct sock*)data;
213     struct tcp_opt *tp = &(sk->tp_pinfo.af_tcp);
214
215     bh_lock_sock(sk);
216     if (sk->lock.users) {
217         /* Try again later. */
218         tp->ack.blocked = 1;
219         NET_INC_STATS_BH(DelayedACKLocked);
220         if (!mod_timer(&tp->delack_timer, jiffies + TCP_DELACK_MIN))
221             sock_hold(sk);
222         goto out_unlock;
223     }
224
225     tcp_mem_reclaim(sk);
226
227     if (sk->state == TCP_CLOSE || !(tp->ack.pending&TCP_ACK_TIMER))
228         goto out;
229
230     if ((long)(tp->ack.timeout - jiffies) > 0) {
231         if (!mod_timer(&tp->delack_timer, tp->ack.timeout))
232             sock_hold(sk);
233         goto out;
234     }
235     tp->ack.pending &= ~TCP_ACK_TIMER;
236
237     if (skb_queue_len(&tp->ucopy.prequeue)) {
238         struct sk_buff *skb;
239
240         net_statistics[smp_processor_id()*2].TCPSchedulerFailed += skb_queue_len(&t241
242         while ((skb = __skb_dequeue(&tp->ucopy.prequeue)) != NULL)
243             sk->backlog_rcv(sk, skb);
244
245         tp->ucopy.memory = 0;
246     }
247
248     if (tcp_ack_scheduled(tp)) {
249         if (!tp->ack.pingpong) {
250             /* Delayed ACK missed: inflate ATO. */
251             tp->ack.ato = min(tp->ack.ato << 1, tp->rto);
252         } else {
253             /* Delayed ACK missed: leave pingpong mode and
254              * deflate ATO.
255              */
256             tp->ack.pingpong = 0;
257             tp->ack.ato = TCP_ATO_MIN;
258         }
259         tcp_send_ack(sk);
260         NET_INC_STATS_BH(DelayedACKs);
261     }
262     TCP_CHECK_TIMER(sk);
263
264 out:
265     if (tcp_memory_pressure)
266         tcp_mem_reclaim(sk);
267 out_unlock:
268     bh_unlock_sock(sk);
269     sock_put(sk);
270 }
```

cs 10.25. tcp_delack_timer().

```
include/net/tcp.h

862 static inline void tcp_reset_xmit_timer(struct sock *sk, int what, unsigned long when)
863 {
864     struct tcp_opt *tp = &sk->tp_pinfo.af_tcp;
865
866     if (when > TCP_RTO_MAX) {
        ....
870         when = TCP_RTO_MAX;
871     }
872
873     switch (what) {
874     case TCP_TIME_RETRANS:
875     case TCP_TIME_PROBE0:
876         tp->pending = what;
877         tp->timeout = jiffies+when;
878         if (!mod_timer(&tp->retransmit_timer, tp->timeout))
879             sock_hold(sk);
880         break;
881
882     case TCP_TIME_DACK:
883         tp->ack.pending |= TCP_ACK_TIMER;
884         tp->ack.timeout = jiffies+when;
885         if (!mod_timer(&tp->delack_timer, tp->ack.timeout))
886             sock_hold(sk);
887         break;
888
889     default:
890         printk(KERN_DEBUG "bug: unknown timer value\n");
891     };
892 }
```

cs 10.26. *tcp_reset_xmit_timer()*.

10.4.9 *tcp_write_timer()*

This is a callback routine for RTO and window probe timers. We process the timer with socket lock held by calling *bh_lock_sock()*. Next we check if the socket is being accessed by some other thread (*sk→lock.users != 0*). If so, we don't continue with processing of the timer; instead we defer the timer by *HZ/20* ticks by calling *mod_timer()* at line 424 (cs 10.27). We need to hold the additional reference on the socket in case the timer was not already installed at line 425 and return.

Next we check if the socket is closed or no timer is pending (*tp→pending == 0*) at line 429. If any of these conditions is TRUE, we return. If the timer has expired prematurely, line 432, we reset the timer with expiry time of *tp→timeout* ticks. Hold an additional reference on the socket in case timer is not already installed at line 434 and return.

If we are here, it is time to execute the TCP timer. Either RTO or window probe timer has timed out. tp→pending field stores the timer event—that is, which timer has expired. Depending on the pending timer, we call callback routine. On every exit from the timer callback routine, we release the socket lock and also release an additional reference on the socket by calling *bh_unlock_sock()* and *sock_put()*, respectively.

```
net/ipv4/tcp_timer.c

415 static void tcp_write_timer(unsigned long data)
416 {
417       struct sock *sk = (struct sock*)data;
418       struct tcp_opt *tp = &sk->tp_pinfo.af_tcp;
419       int event;
420
421       bh_lock_sock(sk);
422       if (sk->lock.users) {
423             /* Try again later */
424             if (!mod_timer(&tp->retransmit_timer, jiffies + (HZ/20)))
425                   sock_hold(sk);
426             goto out_unlock;
427       }
428
429       if (sk->state == TCP_CLOSE || !tp->pending)
430             goto out;
431
432       if ((long)(tp->timeout - jiffies) > 0) {
433             if (!mod_timer(&tp->retransmit_timer, tp->timeout))
434                   sock_hold(sk);
435             goto out;
436       }
437
438       event = tp->pending;
439       tp->pending = 0;
440
441       switch (event) {
442       case TCP_TIME_RETRANS:
443             tcp_retransmit_timer(sk);
444             break;
445       case TCP_TIME_PROBE0:
446             tcp_probe_timer(sk);
447             break;
448       }
449       TCP_CHECK_TIMER(sk);
450
451 out:
452       tcp_mem_reclaim(sk);
453 out_unlock:
454       bh_unlock_sock(sk);
455       sock_put(sk);
456 }
```

cs 10.27. *tcp_write_timer()*.

10.4.10 *tcp_clear_xmit_timer()*

This is a common routine to cancel TCP timers. The second argument to the routine
is the timer that needs to be canceled. For RTO and window probe timers we clear
$tp \rightarrow pending$ field at line 834 (cs 10.28). Additionally, we can remove a timer from
the list if it is installed (timer_pending() returns TRUE) and delete the installed
timer by calling *del_timer()*. If we delete a timer here, the additional reference
placed on the socket should be released here by calling __sock_put(). We delete the
timer from the global lost only if *TCP_CLEAR_TIMERS* is defined. In the case of
delayed ACK timer, we need to reset two fields tp→ack.pending and tp→ack.
blocked at lines 843–844. The rest of the deletion of the timer process is the same
as explained for the RTO timer above.

```
net/ipv4/tcp_timer.c

827 static inline void tcp_clear_xmit_timer(struct sock *sk, int what)
828 {
829        struct tcp_opt *tp = &sk->tp_pinfo.af_tcp;
830
831        switch (what) {
832        case TCP_TIME_RETRANS:
833        case TCP_TIME_PROBE0:
834              tp->pending = 0;
835
836 #ifdef TCP_CLEAR_TIMERS
837              if (timer_pending(&tp->retransmit_timer) &&
838                 del_timer(&tp->retransmit_timer))
839                    __sock_put(sk);
840 #endif
841              break;
842        case TCP_TIME_DACK:
843              tp->ack.blocked = 0;
844              tp->ack.pending = 0;
845
846 #ifdef TCP_CLEAR_TIMERS
847              if (timer_pending(&tp->delack_timer) &&
848                 del_timer(&tp->delack_timer))
849                    __sock_put(sk);
850 #endif
851              break;
852        default:
853              printk(timer_bug_msg);
854              return;
855        };
856
857 }
```

cs 10.28. tcp_clear_xmit_timer().

10.5 KEEPALIVE TIMER

The keepalive timer is used by TCP to probe the peer when there is no activity over the connection for a long time. This timer is used by interactive TCP connections where the connection may be in an idle state for a long time—for example, telnet, rlogin, and so on. Connections need to probe their peers by sending a TCP segment. The segment is sent with sequence number 1 less than the the highest acknowledged sequence number. When this segment reaches the other end, it should generate an ACK immediately thinking that it was retransmission. Once the ACK to the keepalive probe is received, we are sure that the peer is alive; otherwise we know that there is a problem. Let's see how this timer is implemented in Linux.

10.5.1 When Is Keepalive Timer Activated?

On Linux, the keepalive timer implements both a SYN ACK timer and a keepalive timer. This means that for any of these timers, we reset the same timer, that is, $tp \rightarrow$ *timer*. In this section we will only focus on the keepalive timer. The timer is started when a new connection is established in *tcp_create_openreq_child()*, only if the KEEP ALIVE option ($tp \rightarrow keepopen$) is enabled for the socket. This is done when an application issues the SO_KEEPALIVE socket option on the socket. This option is not enabled by default, which also means that the keepalive timer is not enabled for all the TCP connections by default.

10.5.2 How Is the Timer Reset?

The timer is reset by calling *tcp_reset_keepalive_timer()*, which kicks off the keepalive timer registered as *tp→timer* for the TCP connection. This timer is initialized as *tcp_keepalive_timer* in *tcp_init_xmit_timers()* at the time of opening a socket.

10.5.3 *tcp_keepalive_timer()*

Let's see how the keepalive timer functions. It first looks for the user of the socket. If so, we need to let the user of the socket complete its task and defer execution of the timer at some later time. We reset keepalive timer by calling *tcp_reset_ keepalive_timer()* to expire after *HZ/20* ticks at line 584, release socket hold and leave (cs 10.29a). The keepalive callback routine can act as a *SYN-ACK* timer by calling *tcp_synack_timer()* at line 589 to manage incoming connection request (discussed in Section 10.6.3), in case it is a listening socket. Next we check if the socket is in the *FIN_WAIT2* state, and the socket is already closed at line 593. If that is the case, we call *tcp_time_wait()* in case we have not expired *TCP_TIMEWAIT_ LEN* number of ticks. Otherwise if we have expired, we send out reset on the connection and remove the connection from our end. TIME_WAIT timer will be discussed in Section 10.7.2.

Next we check if the keepalive connection is not enabled (tp→keepalive) or the connection is in the closed state at line 606. If any of the conditions is TRUE, we release socket lock and return. We send the keepalive probe only if the segment has been idle for some time. So, next we check if any data segment was transmitted which is still unacknowledged (*tp→packets_out* is nonzero) or if there is anything in the send queue that needs to be sent next (*tp→send_head != NULL*) at line 612. If any of these conditions is TRUE, we reset the keepalive timer by calling tcp_ reset_keepalive_timer() at line 642, release the socket lock, and leave (cs 10.29b).

If we are here, we are eligible for sending out the keepalive probe if the time has actually expired. First we calculate the time elapsed since the last segment was received at line 615. Next we compare if the time since last segment was received has exceeded the probe time interval at line 617. *keepalive_time_when()* gets us probe time interval. The keepalive probe time interval is *tp→keepalive_time* in case it is set using socket options; otherwise it is *sysctl_tcp_keepalive_time*. If the timer has not expired, we calculate the next expiry as the time left for the keepalive timer to expire at line 635 and would reset the probe timer to expire in the near future. Otherwise, if the time has actually expired, the next check would be to see if the number of unacknowledged probes has exceeded the limit at lines 618–619. We increment *tp→probes_out* whenever the probe is sent out (is discussed ahead), and the counter is reset when we get an ACK when no outstanding unacknowledged data are there in the queue (see Section 10.4). If we have exceeded probe limits, the reset segment is sent out by calling *tcp_send_active_reset()* and the connection is closed, lines 620–621. In this case, we release the socket lock and leave.

If we have not exceeded the limit on the number of unacknowledged probes, we call *tcp_write_wakeup()* to send out a probe (see Section 10.3.7). If the probe segment is transmitted successfully, we increment the probe counter by 1 at line 625.

```
net/ipv4/tcp_timer.c

574 static void tcp_keepalive_timer (unsigned long data)
575 {
576     struct sock *sk = (struct sock *) data;
577     struct tcp_opt *tp = &sk->tp_pinfo.af_tcp;
578     __u32 elapsed;
579
580     /* Only process if socket is not in use. */
581     bh_lock_sock(sk);
582     if (sk->lock.users) {
583         /* Try again later. */
584         tcp_reset_keepalive_timer (sk, HZ/20);
585         goto out;
586     }
587
588     if (sk->state == TCP_LISTEN) {
589         tcp_synack_timer(sk);
590         goto out;
591     }
592
593     if (sk->state == TCP_FIN_WAIT2 && sk->dead) {
594         if (tp->linger2 >= 0) {
595             int tmo = tcp_fin_time(tp) - TCP_TIMEWAIT_LEN;
596
597             if (tmo > 0) {
598                 tcp_time_wait(sk, TCP_FIN_WAIT2, tmo);
599                 goto out;
600             }
601         }
602         tcp_send_active_reset(sk, GFP_ATOMIC);
603         goto death;
604     }
605
606     if (!sk->keepopen || sk->state == TCP_CLOSE)
607         goto out;
608
609     elapsed = keepalive_time_when(tp);
            ...
612     if (tp->packets_out || tp->send_head)
613         goto resched;
614
615     elapsed = tcp_time_stamp - tp->rcv_tstamp;
616
617     if (elapsed >= keepalive_time_when(tp)) {
618         if ((!tp->keepalive_probes && tp->probes_out >= sysctl_tcp_keepalive_probes) ||
619             (tp->keepalive_probes && tp->probes_out >= tp->keepalive_probes)) {
620             tcp_send_active_reset(sk, GFP_ATOMIC);
621             tcp_write_err(sk);
622             goto out;
623         }
624         if (tcp_write_wakeup(sk) <= 0) {
625             tp->probes_out++;
626             elapsed = keepalive_intvl_when(tp);
627         } else {
                ...
631             elapsed = TCP_RESOURCE_PROBE_INTERVAL;
632         }
633     } else {
634         /* It is tp->rcv_tstamp + keepalive_time_when(tp) */
635         elapsed = keepalive_time_when(tp) - elapsed;
636     }
```

cs 10.29a. *tcp_keepalive_timer()*.

```
include/net/tcp.h tcp_keepalive_timer contd .....

637
638        TCP_CHECK_TIMER(sk);
639        tcp_mem_reclaim(sk);
640
641 resched:
642        tcp_reset_keepalive_timer (sk, elapsed);
643        goto out;
644
645 death:
646        tcp_done(sk);
647
648 out:
649        bh_unlock_sock(sk);
650        sock_put(sk);
651 }
```

cs 10.29b. *tcp_keepalive_timer() (continued).*

Get the probe interval by calling *keepalive_intvl_when()*. In the case where the probe interval was not transmitted successfully, we need to send it at the earliest. So, the expiry time for the keepalive timer is reduced to *TCP_RESOURCE_PROBE_INTERVAL* at line 631, because we are not able to transmit because of lack of resources. Next we call tcp_mem_reclaim() to reclaim some memory. We do this here because if our connection has consumed its quanta of memory allocated, the next processing of the incoming segment will take it to the slow path. So, we do this check in advance here. Next we call tcp_reset_keepalive_timer() at line 642 to reset the keepalive probe timer to whatever expiry time we have calculated above. We release the socket lock and leave.

10.6   SYN-ACK TIMER

There is a timer maintained by Linux to manage connection requests that are not being accepted for a given period of time. The entire idea of having this timer is that if we are not able to accept more connections (accept queue is full) because the application is not able to get CPU or it is busy doing something else, we need to manage the connection request. There are two main cases where connection requests need to be managed:

1. Established connections are not being accepted because the accept queue is full and the application is not accepting new connections.
2. We don't get ACK for the SYN-ACK we sent; that is, the third step in the three-way handshake is not completed.

10.6.1   When Is the SYN-ACK Timer Activated?

The timer is activated when we get a connection request and there is no pending connection request in the listening socket's SYN queue to be processed. *lopt→qlen* is the counter that is incremented by 1 whenever a new connection requested arrives

```
include/net/tcp.h

1612 static inline void tcp_synq_added(struct sock *sk)
1613 {
1614     struct tcp_listen_opt *lopt = sk->tp_pinfo.af_tcp.listen_opt;
1615
1616     if (lopt->qlen++ == 0)
1617         tcp_reset_keepalive_timer(sk, TCP_TIMEOUT_INIT);
1618     lopt->qlen_young++;
1619 }
```

cs 10.30. *tcp_synq_added()*.

```
include/net/tcp.h

1601 static inline void
1602 tcp_synq_removed(struct sock *sk, struct open_request *req)
1603 {
1604     struct tcp_listen_opt *lopt = sk->tp_pinfo.af_tcp.listen_opt;
1605
1606     if (--lopt->qlen == 0)
1607         tcp_delete_keepalive_timer(sk);
1608     if (req->retrans == 0)
1609         lopt->qlen_young--;
1610 }
```

cs 10.31. *tcp_synq_removed()*.

by calling *tcp_synq_added()* (cs 10.30). Whenever the new connection moves from SYN queue to accept queue after three-way handshake, the counter is decremented by 1 by calling *tcp_synq_removed()*. In *tcp_synq_added()* we call *tcp_reset_keepalive_timer()* when we are processing the first connection request when no request is pending in the SYN queue to be processed.

10.6.2 When Is the SYN-ACK Timer Stopped?

The SYN-ACK timer stops when we find that the queue length (*lopt→qlen*) is zero, which means that there is no open request pending on the listening socket. So, all the open requests are now established and accepted since the SYN-ACK timer was reset. Whenever the connection requested is moved from SYN queue to accept queue after the three-way handshake is over, we decrement the counter by 1. If the counter becomes zero, we cancel the SYN-ACK timer in *tcp_synq_removed()* by calling *tcp_delete_keepalive_timer()* at lines 1606–1607 (cs 10.31).

In the case where SYN-ACK is not retransmitted even once, the connection request is considered young.

10.6.3 *tcp_synack_timer()*

In the case where the SYN queue is more than half-filled, we try to reserve half of the space for the young requests. Requests are young until they are retransmitted. The idea of SYN queue management is to keep most of the young entries and remove old ones from the queue which have been there for quite some time and have not yet been accepted or acknowledged. For this we have a timer per listening socket that expires after a given time interval *TCP_SYNQ_INTERVAL*. The value is *HZ/5*; that is, the timer expires five times per second. The individual entries in the SYN queue has its own expiry as *req→expires*. The timeout value for each request increases exponentially on each expiry. *req→retrans* counter is incremented by 1 every time SYN-ACK is retransmitted. Retransmission may happen because of two reasons:

1. The three-way handshake is over but there is no space in the accept queue for the new connection. In this case, *req→acked* is set.
2. The final ACK is not received for the request, which may be due to the SYN-ACK being lost, the final ACK being lost, or the peer not responding, and so on. In this case, *req→acked* is not set.

The very first retransmission converts a young request into a matured one, and *lopt→qlen_young* is decremented by 1.

Let's see how the idea is implemented. First we check if the SYN queue for the listening socket is more than half-filled at line 492 (cs 10.32). *lopt→max_qlen_log* is log base 2 of the maximum queue length. If the result of division of *lopt→qlen* by $2^{(lopt→max\_qlen\_log\ -1)}$ is a nonzero positive number, it means that our SYN queue is more than half full (equivalent to expression at line 492). For example, if *lopt→max_qlen_log* is 6, it means that the maximum queue length is 64. If the queue length is divided by 2^4 and the integral result is nonzero, it means that the queue length is minimum 32, which is half of 64.

So, once we are halfway through the queue length, we enter the block 492–501 to calculate the number of retries for the old entries which are not yet acknowledged. *thresh* is a local variable that is equal to the *max_retries* storing value that indicates a maximum number of retries for the retransmission, after which we should drop the connection request. We traverse in a loop 495–500, until *thresh* is greater than 2. In each iteration we decrement *thresh* by 1 and divide the number of young entries by 2. We also break from the loop when the length of the queue becomes less than the number of young entries in any iteration. This means that the higher the number of young entries, the lower the number of iterations we go around the loop and thus higher the *thresh*. The final value of *thresh* will decide as to how many times old unacknowledged connection requests in the SYN queue should be retransmitted before we drop those unacknowledged connection requests.

The maximum number of retries by default is the *sysctl_tcp_synack_retries* system-wide control parameter. The user can also set this value for the listening socket by using socket options *TCP_SYNCNT*. The final value of maximum number of retries for the SYN queue requests is decided by the socket option *TCP_DEFER_ACCEPT*. At line 504, maximum retries is set to *tp→defer_accept*, which is set by using the TCP_DEFER_ACCEPT socket option.

Next we need to calculate the total number of hash table entries be examined. There may be hundreds of requests in the SYN queue and we can't examine each open request every time that the SYN-ACK timer expires. So, we calculate a budget at line 506 which takes into account the HASH table size for the SYN queue, the time before which a new entry in the SYN queue should not be examined (*TCP_TIMEOUT_INIT*) and the time period for the SYN-ACK timer (*TCP_SYNQ_INTERVAL*).

```
net/ipv4/tcp_timer.c
462  static void tcp_synack_timer(struct sock *sk)
463  {
464      struct tcp_opt *tp = &(sk->tp_pinfo.af_tcp);
465      struct tcp_listen_opt *lopt = tp->listen_opt;
466      int max_retries = tp->syn_retries ? : sysctl_tcp_synack_retries;
467      int thresh = max_retries;
468      unsigned long now = jiffies;
469      struct open_request **reqp, *req;
470      int i, budget;
471
472      if (lopt == NULL || lopt->qlen == 0)
473          return;
             ....
492      if (lopt->qlen>>(lopt->max_qlen_log-1)) {
493          int young = (lopt->qlen_young<<1);
494
495          while (thresh > 2) {
496              if (lopt->qlen < young)
497                  break;
498              thresh--;
499              young <<= 1;
500          }
501      }
502
503      if (tp->defer_accept)
504          max_retries = tp->defer_accept;
505
506      budget = 2*(TCP_SYNQ_HSIZE/(TCP_TIMEOUT_INIT/TCP_SYNQ_INTERVAL));
507      i = lopt->clock_hand;
508
509      do {
510          reqp=&lopt->syn_table[i];
511          while ((req = *reqp) != NULL) {
512              if ((long)(now - req->expires) >= 0) {
513                  if ((req->retrans < thresh ||
514                      (req->acked && req->retrans < max_retries))
515                      && !req->class->rtx_syn_ack(sk, req, NULL)) {
516                          unsigned long timeo;
517
518                          if (req->retrans++ == 0)
519                              lopt->qlen_young--;
520                          timeo = min((TCP_TIMEOUT_INIT << req->retrans),
521                              TCP_RTO_MAX);
522                          req->expires = now + timeo;
523                          reqp = &req->dl_next;
524                          continue;
525                  }
526
527                  /* Drop this request */
528                  write_lock(&tp->syn_wait_lock);
529                  *reqp = req->dl_next;
530                  write_unlock(&tp->syn_wait_lock);
531                  lopt->qlen--;
532                  if (req->retrans == 0)
533                      lopt->qlen_young--;
534                  tcp_openreq_free(req);
535                  continue;
536              }
537              reqp = &req->dl_next;
538          }
539
540          i = (i+1)&(TCP_SYNQ_HSIZE-1);
541
542      } while (--budget > 0);
543
544      lopt->clock_hand = i;
545
546      if (lopt->qlen)
547          tcp_reset_keepalive_timer(sk, TCP_SYNQ_INTERVAL);
548  }
```

cs 10.32. tcp_synack_timer().

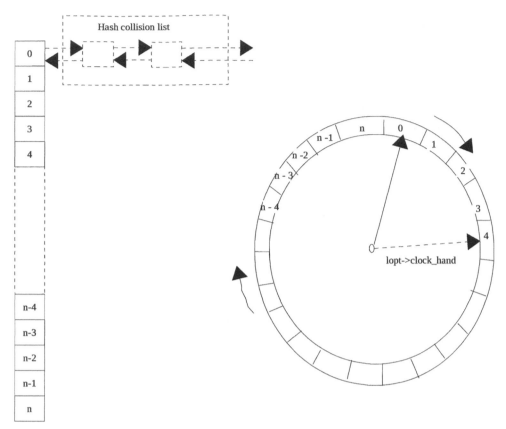

Figure 10.4. *SYN ACK* timer schedule.

We examine entries in the SYN queue table in a clock-arm manner. We have already calculated the number of hash table entries to be examined, so we start from the zeroth hash table entry and cover a number of hash table entries calculated above. We finally store the hash table index in lopt→clock_hand once we have exhausted our budget. Thus the next time the SYN-ACK timer expires, we start from the same hash table entry from where we left, line 507.

The clock works as shown in Fig. 10.4. If the length of the hash table is $n + 1$ and the fixed budget is 4, first processing will start from the zeroth entry. After processing, the clock arm will point to the fourth entry in the hash table. This value is stored in the clock arm *lopt→clock_hand*. The next time the SYN-ACK timer expires, we start from where *lopt→clock_hand* points. In each round all the requests in the collision list of the hash table entry is examined. If the hash function is not proper, we may have an uneven length of collision list in the each entry.

So, the number of requests examined on every timer expiry will be very much different. But the timer interval is so small (HZ/5) that each entry is examined at a very high rate.

We have two loops to examine entries in the SYN queue. The outer loop (509–542) advances us in the SYN queue hash table. The inner loop (511–538) takes us through each element in the hash collision list. In each iteration of the outer loop, we point to next entry in the hash table at line 510, where an increment is done at the end of the loop at line 540. Let's look at what is the inner loop is doing. We traverse through the collision list by accessing *dl_next* field of request structure. First we check if the request has timed out from *req→expires* at line 512.

- Next we check if the number of retransmissions for the request has not reached *thresh* calculated above at line 513.
- If it has exceeded (above condition fails), we once again check if the request being examined is already acknowledged (three-way handshake is over). We may have such requests in the SYN queue because the accept queue has overflown. We have a slightly different criterion for such requests. The maximum number of retries for already acknowledged requests is decided by either a user-defined value (*tp→defer_accept, tp→syn_retries*) or a system-wide control parameter *sysctl_tcp_synack_retries*.

If any of the above conditions is TRUE, we try to retransmit the SYN-ACK by calling the *rtx_syn_ack()* routine for the request, which is *tcp_v4_send_synack()* at line 515. In case we are able to retransmit SYN-ACK successfully, we increment the retransmit counter for the request at line 518. If this was the first retransmission for the request, we decrement the Young request counter by 1 at line 519 because this request has now matured. We calculate the next examination time for the request as exponentially incremented *TCP_TIMEOUT_INIT* or *TCP_RTO_MAX*, whichever is minimum at line 520. We set this timeout value for the request at line 522 and continue with the next element in the hash collision list.

If both conditions mentioned above fail, it means that the request has timed out in all the respects. We need to remove the connection from the hash collision list. We do this with *syn_wait_lock* held for the connection at line 528–530. Since a request has been dropped, we need to decrement the SYN queue length by 1 at line 531. If the request just dropped was young (*req→retrans* equal to 0), we decrement the young request counter by 1 at line 533. Next we free the open request by calling tcp_openreq_free() and continue with the next request in the collision list.

Once we have exhausted the budget, we come out of the outer loop and record the next hash table entry in lopt→clock_hand at line 544. If we still have requests in the SYN queue, we reset the SYN-ACK timer by calling *tcp_reset_keepalive_timer()* at line 547 and return. The callback routine for the SYN-ACK timer is the same as that for the keepalive timer.

10.7   TIME_WAIT TIMER

When the TCP connection enters the TIME_WAIT state, it needs to wait for 2 MSL seconds before the connection is completely dropped. The reason is to avoid any misunderstanding of the segments from this connection (delayed in the network) with the segments from the new reincarnation of the connection. So, we need to keep the old connection in TIME_WAIT state for the duration until we can expect that delayed segments from this connection can appear.

10.7.1   When Do We Trigger *TIME_WAIT* Timer?

We trigger the *TIME_WAIT* timer by calling *tcp_time_wait()* when we are closing the connection in *tcp_fin()* & *tcp_close()*. When we doing active close and receive

FIN/ACK from the peer, we enter into *TIME_WAIT* state and here we call *tcp_ time_wait()* to schedule expiry of the *TIME_WAIT* socket.

10.7.2 *tcp_time_wait()*

When we are entering into the *TIME_WAIT* state, we need to wait for 2 MSL seconds before we can destroy the connection completely. Linux implements this by having a list of time-wait socket entries in the form of *struct tcp_tw_bucket*. Each socket that goes into the *TIME_WAIT* state has a corresponding *tcp_tw_bucket* object. A list of time-wait buckets is maintained, and timers are triggered to fire at the appropriate time to examine time-wait buckets and destroy them. In this section we will see how all this is achieved.

Linux has two approaches to process *TIME_WAIT* sockets, depending on the time-wait period. We can have either a fixed period (considered as 2*MSL) or a variable waiting period calculated on the basis of the connection's RTO. This decision is made based on two factors:

1. Whether recycling of the *TIME_WAIT* socket is allowed (*sysctl_tcp_tw_ recycle* is enabled).
2. We can remember the timestamp from the most recent segment that is seen from the destination (peer for the connection going into the *TIME_WAIT* state).

In case both of the above conditions are TRUE, we just call *tcp_v4_remember_ stamp()* to check if the peer information exists in the global list. If it exists, we have timestamp information maintained that can be used to catch duplicate/retransmitted/delayed segments from the original connection in case a new reincarnation of the connection happens fast. We can enter the recycle mode for this time-wait socket, line 353.

Next we check if total number of time-wait buckets allocated (*tcp_tw_count*) has reached the limit, *sysctl_tcp_max_tw_buckets*, at line 355. If we have reached the limits, we don't register the socket in the *TIME_WAIT* state and close the connection. Otherwise, we allocate the *tcp_tw_bucket* object at line 356 and copy relevant information from the sock object to the *tcp_tw_bucket* object. We calculate RTO as 3.5 *tp→rto* at line 359. This will be used as expiry time in case the time-wait socket is eligible for recycling. Next we need to join the *TIME_WAIT* socket in the bind-hash list and remove the socket from established list by calling *__tcp_tw_hashdance()*.

Next we make sure that timeout for expiry of the time-wait socket is not less than the 3.5 RTO calculated, line 397–398. If we are eligible for the recycle mode, *tw→timeout* is set to 3.5 RTO, line 401. Otherwise, expiry time for the time-wait socket is set to *TCP_TIMEWAIT_LEN* at line 405. Now we need to schedule the time-wait socket by calling *tcp_tw_schedule()*. The fixed TIME_WAIT period, *TCP_TIMEWAIT_LEN*, considered by Linux is 60 sec (cs 10.33).

10.7.3 *tcp_tw_schedule()*

This routine is called to schedule the time-wait socket. The idea is to calculate the appropriate slot for the time-wait socket based on timeout ticks. Each slot is

include/net/tcp.h

317 #define TCP_TIMEWAIT_LEN (60*HZ)

cs 10.33. Time-wait timer frequency for any slot in the nonrecycle mode.

processed at equal time intervals. If we get the first slot, it means that we should be placed in the very next slot from the current scheduled slot that is going to expire first. First we calculate the slot for recycle mode; and if the value exceeds the recycle mode limit, we switch to non-recycle mode. The recycle mode timer expires every $2^{TCP\_TW\_RECYCLE\_TICK}$ ticks, which means that two consecutive slots will be processed at an interval of $2^{TCP\_TW\_RECYCLE\_TICK}$ clock ticks in recycle mode. So, we calculate the slot for the recycle mode at line 529 (cs 10.34), where we round up the timeout value to a multiple of $2^{TCP\_TW\_RECYCLE\_TICK}$ and divide the final value by $2^{TCP\_TW\_}$ $^{RECYCLE\_TICK}$. We hold global time-wait lock, *tw_death_lock*, at line 531 because we are going to manipulate the global time-wait chain. We first check if the time-wait bucket is already scheduled. If *pprev_death* field of the time-wait bucket is non-NULL, we are already linked in the global list. In this case, we remove the bucket from the list, lines 534–539. We decrement *tcp_tw_count* because we are going to reschedule it, which is going to increment the counter by 1. If the bucket was not already scheduled, we hold an additional reference on the bucket because we should not destroy the time-wait bucket before the timer expires. Next we check if the slot calculated based on recycle ticks is more than maximum slots held by the recycle time-wait table, *TCP_TW_RECYCLE_SLOTS*. Let's see how recycle and non-recycle time-wait timers are processed.

10.7.4 Nonrecycle Mode (see cs 10.34 unless mentioned)

This may happen when our timeout value is too high with the recycle mode or we are in the nonrecycle mode. In this case we take slow timer path. In the slow timer path, we expire for consecutive slots at fixed timer interval—that is, *TCP_TWKILL_PERIOD* as shown in Fig. 10.5. *TCP_TWKILL_PERIOD* is calculated by dividing time-wait length (60sec) by total number of slots, *TCP_TWKILL_SLOTS*. If our timeout value for expiry of this time-wait bucket is more than *TCP_TIMEWAIT_LEN*, the time-wait bucket should occupy the last slot with respect to the current scheduled slot, *tcp_tw_death_row_slot*, at line 546. Otherwise, we calculate the slot as dividing a rounded up timeout value to *TCP_TWKILL_PERIOD* by *TCP_TWKILL_PERIOD* at line 548. In any case, the slot should not go beyond *TCP_TWKILL_SLOTS*. Next we calculate the slot with respect to the current scheduled slot, *tcp_tw_death_row_slot*, at line 553. We keep the pointer to the entry in the *tcp_tw_death_row[]* table corresponding to the slot calculated above at line 554. *tcp_tw_timer* is the timer for nonrecycle mode operation. The timer is triggered when the first time-wait bucket entry arrives. Once the timer is triggered, it will continue to fire at equal intervals of *TCP_TWKILL_PERIOD* clock ticks (cs 10.35) for each slot irrespective of whether the slots have entries scheduled for it. The timer stops only when there is no entry in any of the slots and the tcp_tw_count has come down to zero. For more details see Section 10.7.6, which discusses *tcp_tw_timer* timer.

net/ipv4/tcp_timer.c

```
500 void tcp_tw_schedule(struct tcp_tw_bucket *tw, int timeo)
501 {
502     struct tcp_tw_bucket **tpp;
503     int slot;
        ...
529     slot = (timeo + (1<<TCP_TW_RECYCLE_TICK) - 1) >> TCP_TW_RECYCLE_TICK;
530
531     spin_lock(&tw_death_lock);
532
533     /* Unlink it, if it was scheduled */
534     if (tw->pprev_death) {
535         if(tw->next_death)
536             tw->next_death->pprev_death = tw->pprev_death;
537         *tw->pprev_death = tw->next_death;
538         tw->pprev_death = NULL;
539         tcp_tw_count--;
540     } else
541         atomic_inc(&tw->refcnt);
542
543     if (slot >= TCP_TW_RECYCLE_SLOTS) {
544         /* Schedule to slow timer */
545         if (timeo >= TCP_TIMEWAIT_LEN) {
546             slot = TCP_TWKILL_SLOTS-1;
547         } else {
548             slot = (timeo + TCP_TWKILL_PERIOD-1) / TCP_TWKILL_PERIOD;
549             if (slot >= TCP_TWKILL_SLOTS)
550                 slot = TCP_TWKILL_SLOTS-1;
551         }
552         tw->ttd = jiffies + timeo;
553         slot = (tcp_tw_death_row_slot + slot) & (TCP_TWKILL_SLOTS - 1);
554         tpp = &tcp_tw_death_row[slot];
555     } else {
556         tw->ttd = jiffies + (slot<<TCP_TW_RECYCLE_TICK);
557
558         if (tcp_twcal_hand < 0) {
559             tcp_twcal_hand = 0;
560             tcp_twcal_jiffie = jiffies;
561             tcp_twcal_timer.expires = tcp_twcal_jiffie + (slot<<TCP_TW_RECYCLE_TICK);
562             add_timer(&tcp_twcal_timer);
563         } else if ((long)(tcp_twcal_timer.expires - jiffies) > (slot<<TCP_TW_RECYCLE_TICK))
564             mod_timer(&tcp_twcal_timer, jiffies + (slot<<TCP_TW_RECYCLE_TICK));
565             slot = (tcp_twcal_hand + slot)&(TCP_TW_RECYCLE_SLOTS-1);
566         }
567         tpp = &tcp_twcal_row[slot];
568     }
569
570
571     if((tw->next_death = *tpp) != NULL)
572         (*tpp)->pprev_death = &tw->next_death;
573     *tpp = tw;
574     tw->pprev_death = tpp;
575
576     if (tcp_tw_count++ == 0)
577         mod_timer(&tcp_tw_timer, jiffies+TCP_TWKILL_PERIOD);
578     spin_unlock(&tw_death_lock);
579 }
```

cs 10.34. *tcp_tw_schedule()*.

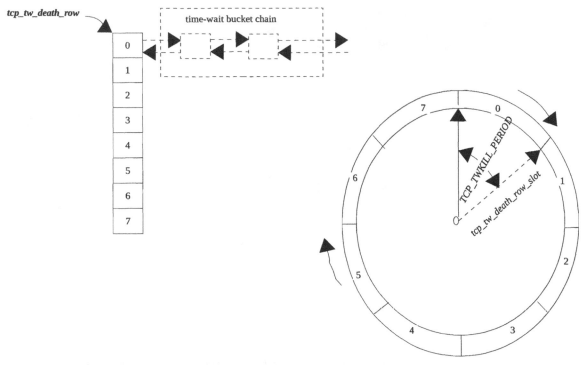

Figure 10.5. Time-wait timer schedule for the non-recycle mode.

include/net/tcp.h

```
352 #define TCP_TWKILL_SLOTS      8
353 #define TCP_TWKILL_PERIOD      (TCP_TIMEWAIT_LEN/TCP_TWKILL_SLOTS)
```

cs 10.35. Time-wait timer frequency.

Let's take an example for the slot calculation with slow timers. We take two timeout values –20 Hz ticks (20 sec) and *TCP_TIMEWAIT_LEN*. The slow timer fires after every *TCP_TWKILL_PERIOD* ticks, that is, 7 sec (7-Hz clock ticks). The first timeout value will be rounded off to multiple of 7 and then divide it by 7 to get the slot. We get slot 3 according to the above calculation for a timeout value of 20 sec. Since the current slot (*tcp_tw_death_row_slot*) is 2, our time-wait bucket should go in slot 6 as shown in Fig. 10.6. In the case where the timeout was greater than or equal to *TCP_TIMEWAIT_LEN*, we would have taken the last slot with respect to the current slot (i.e., slot 1) because the clock hand moves ahead by 1 slot on each expiry of the timer and the timer fires at an equal interval of *TCP_TWKILL_PERIOD* ticks.

10.7.5 Recycle Mode (see cs 10.34 unless mentioned)

In the recycle mode we have 32 slots, 0–31. The timer in this case can be scheduled to fire at any time that is a multiple of $2^{TCP\_TW\_RECYCLE\_TICK}$ as shown

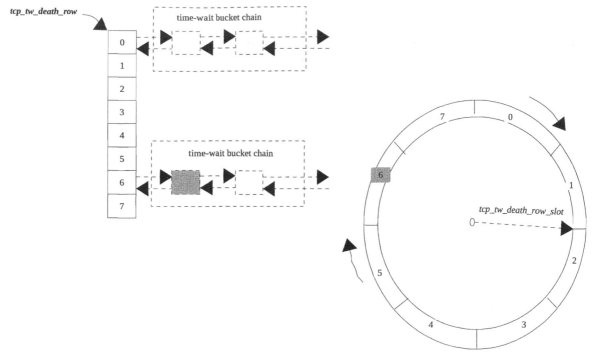

Figure 10.6. Time-wait timer in slot 6 is scheduled with respect to slot 1.

in Fig. 10.7. There are 32 slots, and each slot is processed at equal intervals of $2^{TCP\_TW\_RECYCLE\_TICK}$. TCP_TW_RECYCLE_TICK is calculated as defined in cs 10.36. It depends on Hz which is frequency of times Interrupt.

The timer used for processing of recycle mode time-wait sockets is *tcp_twcal_timer*. Hash bucket for this mode is *tcp_twcal_row[TCP_TW_RECYCLE_SLOTS]*. The scheme used here is slightly different from the one used for the non-recycle mode. Here we are allowed to modify expiry time for the timer whenever a new time-wait entry arrives. In the case where there is no entry in the time-wait hash bucket, *tcp_twcal_hand* is set to –1. Once the first entry arrives, we do the following:

- *tcp_twcal_hand* is set to 0, line 559.
- *tcp_twcal_jiffie* is another global variable that keeps the value of *jiffies* when the first entry arrives, line 560. This is used to compare with the expiry time of each slot. Will learn more in Section 10.7.7 that explains *tcp_twcal_tick()*.
- Timer expiry time is set as *jiffies* + slot*$2^{TCP\_TW\_RECYCLE\_TICK}$, line 561. *jiffies* contains number of clock ticks since the machine was booted. Even though this is the first entry that may go in any slot including 0, our arm (*tcp_twcal_hand*) is pointing at slot 0. We will see how this is taken care of in the timer routine.
- Next we trigger the timer by calling *add_timer()* at line 562.

In the case where we are going to add new a time-wait socket entry when the entries already exist—that is, the timer is already scheduled, we just check if the time

```
include/net/tcp.h

370 #define TCP_TW_RECYCLE_SLOTS_LOG      5
371 #define TCP_TW_RECYCLE_SLOTS        (1<<TCP_TW_RECYCLE_SLOTS_LOG)
        ....
377 #if HZ <= 16 || HZ > 4096
378 # error Unsupported: HZ <= 16 or HZ > 4096
379 #elif HZ <= 32
380 # define TCP_TW_RECYCLE_TICK (5+2-TCP_TW_RECYCLE_SLOTS_LOG)
381 #elif HZ <= 64
382 # define TCP_TW_RECYCLE_TICK (6+2-TCP_TW_RECYCLE_SLOTS_LOG)
383 #elif HZ <= 128
384 # define TCP_TW_RECYCLE_TICK (7+2-TCP_TW_RECYCLE_SLOTS_LOG)
385 #elif HZ <= 256
386 # define TCP_TW_RECYCLE_TICK (8+2-TCP_TW_RECYCLE_SLOTS_LOG)
387 #elif HZ <= 512
388 # define TCP_TW_RECYCLE_TICK (9+2-TCP_TW_RECYCLE_SLOTS_LOG)
389 #elif HZ <= 1024
390 # define TCP_TW_RECYCLE_TICK (10+2-TCP_TW_RECYCLE_SLOTS_LOG)
391 #elif HZ <= 2048
392 # define TCP_TW_RECYCLE_TICK (11+2-TCP_TW_RECYCLE_SLOTS_LOG)
393 #else
394 # define TCP_TW_RECYCLE_TICK (12+2-TCP_TW_RECYCLE_SLOTS_LOG)
395 #endif
```

cs 10.36. Logarithm of time-wait timer frequency depending on CPU frequency.

remaining for the timer to expire is more than the expiry time for our new time-wait entry at line 564. If that is the case, we reschedule the timer at line 564 by calling *mod_timer()* and set expiry time from new time-wait entry. If this is the case, a new entry would have gone into the slot that appears prior to current scheduled slot. So, the very next timer will process the slot corresponding to the new entry, and the current scheduled slot will be processed in the subsequent timers (explained with the help of Fig. 10.7). Next we calculate the new slot with respect to the current slot, *tcp_twcal_hand*, at line 566. For example, Fig. 10.8 shows that a new time-wait timer is added in slot 16 with respect current slot 0.

Next we add the new time-wait to the selected slot in the appropriate hash bucket using the *next_death* and *pprev_death* field of the *tcp_tw_bucket* object, lines 571–574. We increment *tcp_tw_count* by one. In the case where this is the first time-wait socket entry, we trigger *tcp_tw_timer* timer irrespective of timer mode. We release the global time-wait lock, *tw_death_lock* and leave.

10.7.6   *tcp_twkill()*

This is the timer callback routine for the *tcp_tw_timer* timer used for processing of time-wait sockets in the non-recycle mode. In the non-recycle mode, we have a timer that fires at equal time intervals of *TCP_TWKILL_PERIOD* to process each slot (cs 10.37). The timer fires for the slot irrespective of whether we have any time-wait sockets being there for that slot or not. We hold the *tw_death_lock* lock to access each bucket in the hash bucket collision list. With the *tw_death_lock* lock held (line 443), we check if there is no time-wait sockets to be processed in any of the slots at line 445. If so, we just return without rescheduling timer. This is one of the places where we stop the timer for the nonrecycle mode.

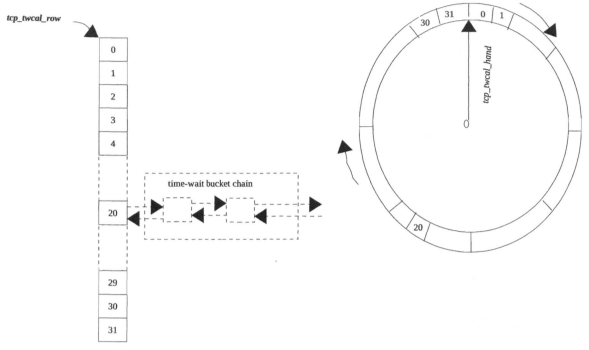

Figure 10.7. Time-wait timer slots for the recycle mode.

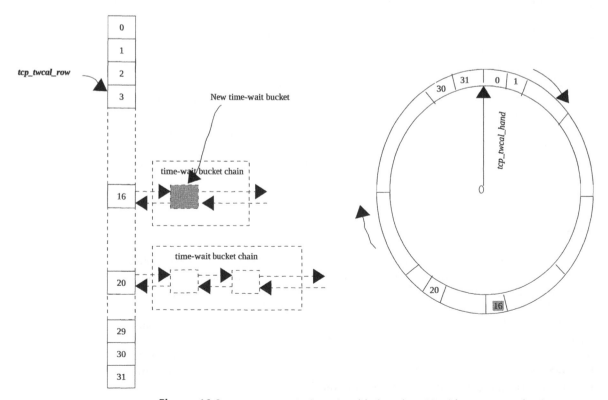

Figure 10.8. New time-wait timer is added to slots 16 with respect to slot 0.

```
net/ipv4/tcp_minisocks.c

432  static void SMP_TIMER_NAME(tcp_twkill)(unsigned long dummy)
433  {
434       struct tcp_tw_bucket *tw;
435       int killed = 0;
              ....
443       spin_lock(&tw_death_lock);
444
445       if (tcp_tw_count == 0)
446           goto out;
447
448       while((tw = tcp_tw_death_row[tcp_tw_death_row_slot]) != NULL) {
449           tcp_tw_death_row[tcp_tw_death_row_slot] = tw->next_death;
450           tw->pprev_death = NULL;
451           spin_unlock(&tw_death_lock);
452
453           tcp_timewait_kill(tw);
454           tcp_tw_put(tw);
455
456           killed++;
457
458           spin_lock(&tw_death_lock);
459       }
460       tcp_tw_death_row_slot =
461           ((tcp_tw_death_row_slot + 1) & (TCP_TWKILL_SLOTS - 1));
462
463       if ((tcp_tw_count -= killed) != 0)
464           mod_timer(&tcp_tw_timer, jiffies+TCP_TWKILL_PERIOD);
465       net_statistics[smp_processor_id()*2].TimeWaited += killed;
466  out:
467       spin_unlock(&tw_death_lock);
468  }
```

cs 10.37. tcp_twkill().

We are here because the time-wait bucket is not empty. But we don't know whether the current slot being processed has any entry to be processed. We start a loop here to process entries in the current slot, pointed to by tcp_tw_death_row[tcp_tw_death_row_slot]. Entries are accessed in the collision chain using the next_death field of the tcp_tw_bucket object. Once we have gotten the node to be processed (tcp_tw_bucket object) from the chain, we release the tw_death_lock lock at line 451. With this design of holding and releasing the lock for each node access, we can have tcp_tw_schedule() continue to do its job while the slot is being processed because there is a single lock for any time-wait table access. Next we unlink the time-wait socket from the time-wait hash table, tcp_ehash, and also from bind hash bucket, tcp_bhash, by calling tcp_timewait_kill(). We release an additional reference on the time-wait bucket while unlinking it from a different time-wait hash table in tcp_timewait_kill(). The additional reference was put on the time-wait socket when it was linked to these hashes by a call to __tcp_tw_hashdance() in tcp_time_wait(). Next we release one more reference on the time-wait bucket at line 454. This reference was put on the socket while adding in tcp_tw_schedule() when we are linking time-wait socket to the time-wait table slot. Counter is incremented every time to keep track of the number of sockets killed from the slot. This will help us in making a decision to stop the timer further down the line.

Once we have processed all the time-wait sockets in the slot, we calculate the next slot to be processed at lines 460–461. tcp_tw_death_row_slot moves like arm of

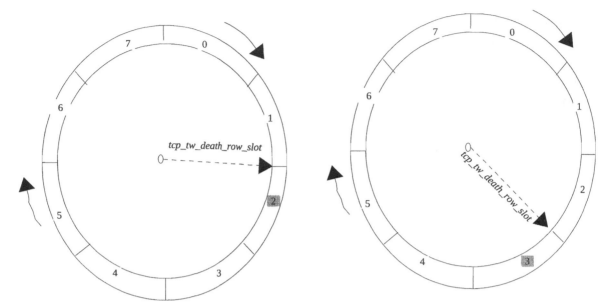

Figure 10.9. Movement of time-wait slot clock arm to point to the current slot being processed.

a clock in one direction as shown in Fig. 10.9. The slot wraps around itself once it has reached the maximum value of 7. Next we check if there are any more entries in the time-wait table to be processed over all at line 463. We do this by subtracting killed counter from *tcp_tw_count*. If entries exist, we reschedule *tcp_tw_timer* timer to expire after the *TCP_TWKILL_PERIOD* clock ticks. In the case where the next slot is empty, we don't care and we schedule the timer to process the next slot pointed to by *tcp_tw_death_row_slot*. This way we maintain simplicity of processing the slots at the correct time without too much manipulations at the cost of the timer firing unnecessarily for the slot that has nothing to be processed. But we never know if something can be added to the current slot before it is being processed in the next timer event after *TCP_TWKILL_PERIOD* clock ticks. Release the time-wait lock and return.

10.7.7   *tcp_twcal_tick()*

This is a timer callback routine for *tcp_twcal_timer* timer used in the recycle mode. This timer works slightly different from *tcp_tw_timer*. With this design, the timer is set to expire only for the slot at a minimum distance from the current scheduled slot. In *tcp_tw_schedule()* we can see that if the timer is already scheduled and that the new entry that needs to be scheduled earlier than the time left in expiry of the scheduled timer is more than the current entry, we reschedule the timer to expire early to process the latest entry. So, the chances of multiple nonvacant slots being processed on a single timer event are much lower. There is a boundary line case where the new entry arrives just at the boundary of $2^{TCP\_TW\_RECYCLE\_TICK}$ ticks where the condition mentioned above is not satisfied (time left for timer to expire is equal to $2^{TCP\_TW\_RECYCLE\_TICK}$ ticks). In this case we miss our opportunity to reschedule the

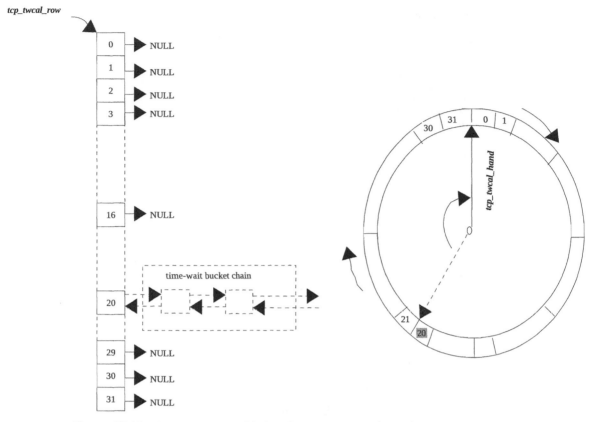

Figure 10.10. Time-wait timer added to slot 21 in nonrecycle mode.

timer but place the new entry in the slot. In this case, both slots will be processed when the next timer expires.

Let's see how the idea is implemented. We have two global variables here:

- *tcp_twcal_hand*
- *tcp_twcal_jiffie*

When the first entry is added to the hash table, *tcp_twcal_jiffie* is set to *jiffies* and *tcp_twcal_hand* is set to slot zero. Suppose the first entry is added to slot 20, depending on the timeout value as shown in Fig. 10.10(left). Since this is the first entry, all the slots will be vacant and will be pointing to NULL. The timer is set to expire at $20* 2^{TCP\_TW\_RECYCLE\_TICK}$ ticks. In this case, when the timer fires, let's see how loop 596–622 (cs 10.38) works. The loop does 32 iterations. In each iteration it checks if the current time is more than the time stored in *tcp_twcal_jiffie*. In the first iteration, we will surely have a value in *tcp_twcal_jiffie* less than current time since *tcp_twcal_jiffie* stores the value of *jiffies* when the first entry went into slot 20. At the end of each iteration we add $2^{TCP\_TW\_RECYCLE\_TICK}$ ticks to the value stored in *tcp_twcal_jiffie* because in each iteration we are moving to process the next slot, and the time period to process subsequent slots is $2^{TCP\_TW\_RECYCLE\_TICK}$ ticks. In the first iteration we pass the test, and so we are all set to process slot 0. This part is same

```
net/ipv4/tcp_minisocks.c

581 void SMP_TIMER_NAME(tcp_twcal_tick)(unsigned long dummy)
582 {
583     int n, slot;
584     unsigned long j;
585     unsigned long now = jiffies;
586     int killed = 0;
587     int adv = 0;
588
589     spin_lock(&tw_death_lock);
590     if (tcp_twcal_hand < 0)
591         goto out;
592
593     slot = tcp_twcal_hand;
594     j = tcp_twcal_jiffie;
595
596     for (n=0; n<TCP_TW_RECYCLE_SLOTS; n++) {
597         if ((long)(j - now) <= 0) {
598             struct tcp_tw_bucket *tw;
599
600             while((tw = tcp_twcal_row[slot]) != NULL) {
601                 tcp_twcal_row[slot] = tw->next_death;
602                 tw->pprev_death = NULL;
603
604                 tcp_timewait_kill(tw);
605                 tcp_tw_put(tw);
606                 killed++;
607             }
608         } else {
609             if (!adv) {
610                 adv = 1;
611                 tcp_twcal_jiffie = j;
612                 tcp_twcal_hand = slot;
613             }
614
615             if (tcp_twcal_row[slot] != NULL) {
616                 mod_timer(&tcp_twcal_timer, j);
617                 goto out;
618             }
619         }
620         j += (1<<TCP_TW_RECYCLE_TICK);
621         slot = (slot+1)&(TCP_TW_RECYCLE_SLOTS-1);
622     }
623     tcp_twcal_hand = -1;
624
625 out:
626     if ((tcp_tw_count -= killed) == 0)
627         del_timer(&tcp_tw_timer);
628     net_statistics[smp_processor_id()*2].TimeWaitKilled += killed;
629     spin_unlock(&tw_death_lock);
630 }
```

cs 10.38. tcp_twcal_tick().

as the one explained in section 10.6.3, where we traverse through the collision hash list (lines 600–607) by accessing the *next_death* field of object *tcp_tw_bucket*. In each iteration we call *tcp_timewait_kill()* to unlink the time-wait socket from the time-wait hash table and from the bind hash table. Thereafter, we call *tcp_tw_put()* to release an additional reference held on the time-wait bucket in *tcp_tw_schedule()*. Finally we increment the killed counter by 1 in order to keep track of the number of entries in the time-wait table subsequently.

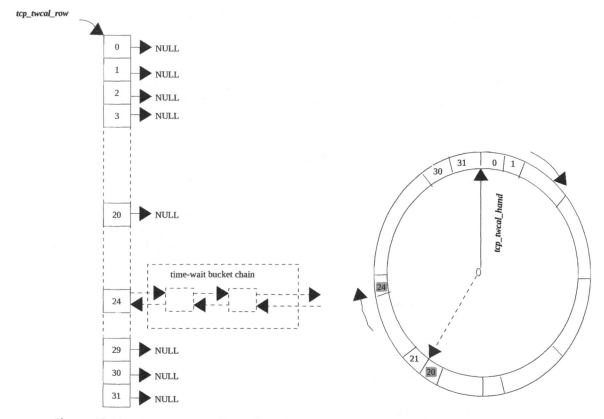

Figure 10.11. After processing timers from slot 20, we need to process slot 24.

In this case, slots 0–19 are empty (no entries for time-wait buckets). So, until the 20th iteration, we simply increment the slot number at line 621 and add time period ($2^{TCP\_TW\_RECYCLE\_TICK}$ ticks) to the value stored in *tcp_twcal_jiffie* at line 620 and do nothing. The condition at line 597 is TRUE until the 20th iteration because the timer has expired after $20 * 2^{TCP\_TW\_RECYCLE\_TICK}$ ticks since the entry was received. Once we are at the 20th iteration, we process all the time-wait entries in the 20th slot. In the next iteration, we find that the value of clock ticks has exceeded the current value of *jiffies*. So, we enter the else part (lines 608–619). Since this is the first time we have entered this block, we store the number of ticks calculated at the end of each iteration in *tcp_twcal_jiffie* and store the value of slot 21 (next to slot processed recently) in *tcp_twcal_hand*.

Next we check if the current slot has any entries, line 615. If there are entries in the slot, we schedule the timer to expire after $2^{TCP\_TW\_RECYCLE\_TICK}$ ticks (since value of ticks calculated until now at line 620 is *jiffies* $+ 21 * 2^{TCP\_TW\_RECYCLE\_TICK}$ ticks). And we leave. In the next timer, *tcp_twcal_hand* will be pointing to the 21st slot as shown by dotted lines in Fig. 10.10(right). In our case, all the slots from 21 to 31 are empty. So, in each iteration we enter the else part (lines 608–619) and find that there is nothing in the slot to be processed. We come out of the loop and set tcp_twcal_hand to −1 at line 623; −1 signifies that there is no entry in the time-wait table. In this case, *tcp_twcal_hand & tcp_twcal_jiffie* will be reinitialized in *tcp_tw_schedule()*.

In the above case, if the 20th and 24th slots had entries, the final scene would have been (as shown in Fig. 10.11).

- *tcp_twcal_hand* would be pointing to the 21st slot.
- The timer would be set to expire after 4* $^{2TCP\_TW\_RECYCLE\_TICK}$ ticks.
- *tcp_twcal_jiffie* would be set to current value of *jiffies*.

With this kind of setup, if we get time-wait socket entries for slot 22 or 23 before the clock passes the 21st slot, the timer can be rescheduled with a new expiry time to process the closest slots first.

10.7.8   __tcp_tw_hashdance()

This routine is called when a connection moves into the *TIME_WAIT* state. In this case, we need to link the *TIME_WAIT* socket to the bind-hash table, unlink it from the established state, and link it in the time-wait hash table. The socket is already hashed in the bind hash table *tcp_bhash[]* using socket's *num* field. We get the head of the hash table entry at line 310 (cs 10.39) in order to hold the bind hash spin lock

```
net/ipv4/tcp_minisocks.c

300 static void __tcp_tw_hashdance(struct sock *sk, struct tcp_tw_bucket *tw)
301 {
302     struct tcp_ehash_bucket *ehead = &tcp_ehash[sk->hashent];
303     struct tcp_bind_hashbucket *bhead;
304     struct sock **head, *sktw;
        ....
310     bhead = &tcp_bhash[tcp_bhashfn(sk->num)];
311     spin_lock(&bhead->lock);
312     tw->tb = (struct tcp_bind_bucket *)sk->prev;
313     BUG_TRAP(sk->prev!=NULL);
314     if ((tw->bind_next = tw->tb->owners) != NULL)
315         tw->tb->owners->bind_pprev = &tw->bind_next;
316     tw->tb->owners = (struct sock*)tw;
317     tw->bind_pprev = &tw->tb->owners;
318     spin_unlock(&bhead->lock);
319
320     write_lock(&ehead->lock);
        ....
323     if (sk->pprev) {
324         if(sk->next)
325             sk->next->pprev = sk->pprev;
326         *sk->pprev = sk->next;
327         sk->pprev = NULL;
328         sock_prot_dec_use(sk->prot);
329     }
        ....
332     head = &(ehead + tcp_ehash_size)->chain;
333     sktw = (struct sock *)tw;
334     if((sktw->next = *head) != NULL)
335         (*head)->pprev = &sktw->next;
336     *head = sktw;
337     sktw->pprev = head;
338     atomic_inc(&tw->refcnt);
339
340     write_unlock(&ehead->lock);
341 }
```

cs 10.39. __tcp_tw_hashdance().

at line 311. When we are binding the socket to a port, we make *sk→prev* point to the bind bucket, *tcp_bind_hashbucket* object, which corresponds to its entry in the bind hash collision list. We link object *tcp_tw_bucket* with the chain of sockets (*tb→owners*) associated with the *tcp_bind_bucket* object, lines 314–317. Next we need to remove the socket's entry from the established list. For this we need to hold the established hash table head lock. We get access to the established hash list lock by accessing *tcp_ehash_bucket* object corresponding to the socket. This index in the *tcp_ehash[]* table is stored in the socket's *hashent* field, line 302. We hold the established hash table head lock at line 320 and now unlink the socket from the hash table, *tcp_ehash[]*, lines 323–329. The socket is linked through the *next* and *pprev* field in the established collision hash chain. Next we need to link the socket in the time-wait hash bucket. There is no separate bucket for time-wait sockets; instead, the bucket is a part of the tcp_ehash[] table. The lower half of the *tcp_ehash[]* is used for time-wait sockets. So, to access the head of the hash bucket, we just need to add *tcp_ehash_size* to the head of the established hash bucket, line 332. The socket is linked through next and pprev field in the time-wait hash collision chain, lines 334–337.

10.8 SUMMARY

struct timer_list is the object that is initialized to register timer.

mod_timer() and del_timer() are the interfaces provided by the Linux kernel to manipulate timers.

mark_bh() is called to raise *HI_SOFTIRQ* softIRQ from the timer interrupt and schedules the timer tasklet for which the callback routine is *timer_bh()*.

tcp_reset_xmit_timer() is a common timer callback routine to register retransmit, zero-window probe, and delayed-ACK timer.

tcp_reset_keepalive_timer() is an interface to reset the keepalive timer.

tcp_clear_xmit_timers() is an interface to clear TCP timers.

tcp_ack_packets_out() resets retransmit to expire after RTO when new data are ACKed in *tcp_ack()*.

tcp_delack_timer() is a callback routine for the delayed-ACK timer.

tcp_retransmit_timer() is a callback routine for the retransmit timer.

tcp_check_probe_timer() is called to reset the zero-window probe timer in case we are not able to transmit new data and we have no unacknowledged data. The routine is called from *__tcp_push_pending_frames()* and *__tcp_data_snd_check()*.

tcp_probe_timer() is a callback routine to handle zero-window probe.

tcp_synq_added() is called to register the SYNQ timer for a new connection request. SYNQ timer is implemented as part of the keepalive timer. The keepalive timer callback routine calls *tcp_synack_timer()* in case the socket is in the listen state.

tcp_time_wait() is a callback routine for the time-wait timer.

The *TIME_WAIT* timer operates in two modes: recycle and nonrecycle mode. Those *TIME_WAIT* connections are processed in the recycle mode, for whom the last received timestamp information is available in a peer list.

In the non-recycle mode, the time-wait timer fires at a fixed interval of *TCP_TWKILL_PERIOD* ticks, whereas in the recycle mode the timer fires in multiples of $2^{TCP\_TW\_RECYCLE\_TICK}$ ticks.

11

TCP CORE PROCESSING

TCP is a full duplex stream protocol where data can flow in both directions. Each side has to apply flow control. When a TCP segment is received, it may contain data or may be plane ACK. If it contains data, it may be in-sequence data or out-of-order data. If it is in-sequence data, it is queued on the socket's receive queue or is immediately consumed by the application. In case we received new data, ACK may be generated immediately or delayed slightly so that combined ACK for more than one data segment can be generated together.

Before sending out an ACK, we need to check what information we have gotten from the peer. We need to process ACK generated by the peer. This includes the processing of (a) TCP options such as SACK and DSACK (b) advertised window, and (c) TCP flags such as ECE and CWR. The timestamp option is processed to calculate RTO and also to check against PAWS. The ACK sequence number will provide information about what data have reached the receiving TCP in-sequence. We update our retransmit queue based on this information and also update the congestion window. This information along with the advertised window will be used to make a decision on whether we can transmit new data.

SACK/DSACK and ACK sequence number will be used to sense congestion. If we sense congestion or early loss of data, the congestion control algorithm can be applied.

If the TCP urgent flag is set, we need to enter the urgent mode until we receive an urgent byte. In case we received out-of-order segments, an immediate ACK needs to be scheduled in order to let the sender TCP know about it at the earliest. If we

TCP/IP Architecture, Design, and Implementation in Linux. By S. Seth and M. A. Venkatesulu
Copyright © 2008 the IEEE Computer Society

have received an ACK segment without any data, it may be a window probe or because the peer has an opened window.

Once the incoming ACK is processed, TCP needs to check if any data are pending to be transmitted. It needs to check if new data can be transmitted. If the congestion window and the window advertised allow us to transmit new data, we transmit data from a transmit queue. This will require calculation of the window to be advertised. If data are transmitted here, an ACK for any new data that has arrived will also be sent out along with data.

In this chapter we will discuss how incoming TCP segments are processed. It is this place where we receive and queue TCP data. We process TCP options here and sense the state of the peer as well as state of the network. We do receive socket buffer management here when our socket's memory pool runs out of stock. We process ACK for the incoming segments. The decision on whether to update window advertised by the sender is made here. SACK processing and the cleaning of the retransmit queue are done here based on ACKed segments. On the basis of the received segment size, we grow the send window size here to be advertised to the peer. We will see how this is done. Congestion control algorithms are implemented here, and they are discussed separately in a different chapter. But we will see under what conditions decisions are made to divert our path to congestion state processing. We now try to send out any data that need to be sent out in the transmit queue along with the ACK for the received data. Once we have processed incoming segment, we check if the ACK needs to be sent out immediately or deferred.

11.1 TCP INCOMING SEGMENT PROCESSING

In this section we will see how the incoming segment is processed. A single point entry to process TCP segments is *tcp_rcv_established()*. Linux has two approaches to process incoming TCP segment: fast and slow path. In fast path we do minimal processing such as processing incoming data, sending ACK/data, and storing a time-stamp received from the peer, whereas in the slow path we take care of out-of-order segments, PAWS, socket's memory management, urgent data, and so on. Linux manages to differentiate between the two modes of processing by implementing a prediction flag. The prediction flag is the fourth word of the TCP header, which includes TCP header length, flags, and advertised window.

11.1.1 Prediction Flags

When we are processing a TCP segment in *tcp_rcv_established()* at line 3241 of cs 11.7, we check if the fast path is enabled. The fast path usually is an indication of the following:

1. Either the data transaction is taking place in only one direction (which means that we are the receiver and not transmitting any data) or in the case where we are sending out data also, the window advertised from the other end is constant. The latter means that we have not transmitted any data from our side for quite some time but are receiving data from the other end. The receive window advertised by the other end is constant.
2. Other than PSH|ACK flags in the TCP header, no other flag is set (ACK is set for each TCP segment). The PSH flag is just an indication from the sender

Figure 11.1. Fourth word of TCP header is directly taken as a prediction flag in network byte order.

```
include/linux/tcp.h

97 union tcp_word_hdr {
98      struct tcphdr hdr;
99      __u32        words[5];
100 };
101
102 #define tcp_flag_word(tp) ( ((union tcp_word_hdr *)(tp))->words [3])
```

cs 11.1. Prediction flags related macro and data structure.

```
include/net/tcp_ecn.h

6 #define TCP_HP_BITS (~(TCP_RESERVED_BITS|TCP_FLAG_PSH))
```

cs 11.2. Macro to build prediction flags.

to read data fast and has nothing to do with anything special. This means that if any other flag is set such as URG, FIN, SYN, ECN, RST, and CWR, we know that something important is there to be attended and we need to move into the SLOW path.

3. The header length has changed. If the TCP header length remains unchanged, we have not added/reduced any TCP option and we can safely assume that there is nothing important to be attended, if the above two conditions are TRUE.

This flag is 32 bits long and contains the fourth word of the segment's TCP header as shown in Fig. 11.1, where HL is the header length in number of words. From the TCP header, we can directly get this value. Directly access the fourth word of the TCP header by using macro *tcp_flag_word*. If we AND this value with *MASK TCP_HP_BITS*, we can get the prediction flag (cs 11.1–11.3). *TCP_RESERVED_BITS* in network byte order is 0x0000000F. We ignore the PSH flag in the header prediction because it does not require any attention. So, *MASK TCP_HP_BITS* in network byte order becomes ~0x0000080F, which is 0xFFFFF7F0 shown in Fig. 11.2.

11.1.2 Building Prediction Flags

When we enter into the fast path, the prediction flag is built into *tp→pred_flags*. We call *__tcp_fast_path_on()* to do this (cs 11.4). Let's assume we are on X86 platform, we first build prediction flag in host byte order and then convert it to network byte order and store it in *tp→pred_flags* (26 is because of –2 bits for dividing header length by 4 because the last 4 bits of the tcp header's fourth word contains header length in number of words), shown in Fig. 11.3a,b.

In network byte order, *tp→pred_flags* will be finally as shown in Fig. 11.3b.

```
include/linux/tcp.h
104 enum {
105        TCP_FLAG_CWR = __constant_htonl(0x00800000),
106        TCP_FLAG_ECE = __constant_htonl(0x00400000),
107        TCP_FLAG_URG = __constant_htonl(0x00200000),
108        TCP_FLAG_ACK = __constant_htonl(0x00100000),
109        TCP_FLAG_PSH = __constant_htonl(0x00080000),
110        TCP_FLAG_RST = __constant_htonl(0x00040000),
111        TCP_FLAG_SYN = __constant_htonl(0x00020000),
112        TCP_FLAG_FIN = __constant_htonl(0x00010000),
113        TCP_RESERVED_BITS = __constant_htonl(0x0F000000),
114        TCP_DATA_OFFSET = __constant_htonl(0xF0000000)
115 };
```

cs 11.3. TCP flags and macro to access header length from TCP header (all in network byte order).

```
include/net/tcp.h

933 static __inline__ void __tcp_fast_path_on(struct tcp_opt *tp, u32 snd_wnd)
934 {
935        tp->pred_flags = htonl((tp->tcp_header_len << 26) |
936                ntohl(TCP_FLAG_ACK) |
937                snd_wnd);
938 }
```

cs 11.4. __tcp_fast_path_on().

0   31

| 4 bits | HL = 4 bits | Flags = 7 bits | Window = 16 bits |

Figure 11.2. TCP_HP_BITS in network byte order, 0xFFFFF7F0.

```
include/net/tcp.h

945 static inline void tcp_fast_path_check(struct sock *sk, struct tcp_opt *tp)
946 {
947        if (skb_queue_len(&tp->out_of_order_queue) == 0 &&
948        tp->rcv_wnd &&
949        atomic_read(&sk->rmem_alloc) < sk->rcvbuf &&
950        !tp->urg_data)
951            tcp_fast_path_on(tp);
952 }
```

cs 11.5. tcp_fast_path_check().

11.1.3   Condition to Enable the Fast Path

When the fast path is on, *tp→pred_flags* will be nonzero; otherwise it will be set to zero. We check certain conditions before moving into the fast path. These conditions are checked in *tcp_fast_path_check()* under the following conditions (cs 11.5, cs 11.6):

- If there is anything in the out-of-order queue, line 947
- If our receive window is not zero, line 948

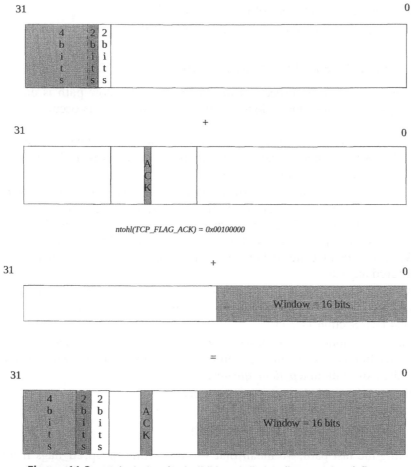

Figure 11.3a. Calculation for building prediction flags *tp→pred_flags*.

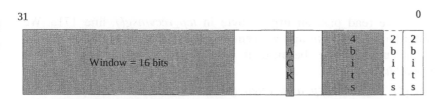

Figure 11.3b. Calculation for building prediction flags *tp→pred_flags (continued)*.

```
include/net/tcp.h

940 static __inline__ void tcp_fast_path_on(struct tcp_opt *tp)
941 {
942      __tcp_fast_path_on(tp, tp->snd_wnd>>tp->snd_wscale);
943 }
```

cs 11.6. *tcp_fast_path_on()*.

- If we are not running out of memory, line 949
- If we have not received any urgent pointer, 950

11.1.4 When to Enable the Slow Path

Whenever we want to be processed in a slow path, the slow path is enabled by resetting *tp→pred_*flags. This is done when the following events occur:

- We receive an out-of-order data segment in *tcp_data_queue()*, line 2651 (cs 11.44). We do it here because subsequent segments need to be processed in the slow path in *tcp_data_queue()*.
- We run short of memory and start dropping packets in our call to *tcp_prune_queue()*, line 2920 (cs 9.22). We do this because we have memory crunch and subsequent data packets will be dropped. If we don't enable the slow path here, the data packet will enter the fast path first in *tcp_rcv_established()*. When it finds that the socket's memory pool is empty, the slow path will be entered anyway.
- We get urgent pointer in *tcp_urg_check()*, line 3117. Urgent data are handled in the slow path in *tcp_rcv_established()* by calling *tcp_urg()* at line 3434 (see Section 11.7.1).
- Our send window drops down to zero in *tcp_select_window()*, line 172 (cs 11.18). In this case, we may get an out-of-window segment, which is handled in the slow path in *tcp_data_queue()*.
- The path is enabled for the new connection.

11.1.5 When to Enable the Fast Path

By enabling the fast path, we mean that we are setting tp→pred_flags from TCP header of the incoming segment under the conditions mentioned in Section 11.1.3 by calling *tcp_fast_path_check()*. The routine is called from three places:

- When we have read past an urgent byte in *tcp_recvmsg()*, line 1713. We have gotten an urgent byte and we remain in the slow path mode until we receive the urgent byte because it is handled in the slow path in *tcp_rcv_established()*.
- When the gap is filled in *tcp_data_queue()*. This may create some space in the receive buffer as the gap in received data is filled and we could have read data from the socket buffer. The slow path set due to receive memory crunch will be treated here.
- When the sender has updated its window in *tcp_ack_update_window()* (see Section 11.4.4). We do this because the window advertised in the incoming segment has changed because of which we have entered the slow path (assuming that nothing in the prediction flag has changed). If we don't set fresh prediction flags with the new advertised window, the next segment having the same send window will unnecessarily enter the slow path. By syncing prediction flags on first detection of the send window, we avoid subsequent packets being handled in the slow path given that nothing in the prediction changes after that.

11.1.6   Points to Remember about Prediction Flags

1. We start with the slow path first and once we receive the first segment, while processing the ACK received in *tcp_ack()*, we enter into the fast path by a call to *tcp_fast_path_check()* in case the advertised window has changed from the previous value (cs 11.26).

2. Once we enter the fast path, the advertised window and the TCP header length are recorded in *tp→pred_flags* as explained in Section 11.1.2. We ignore the PSH flag and also the ACK flag. The PSH flag does not indicate any noticeable change at the other end. All the TCP segments will have an ACK flag set except for the very first SYN segment sent out. In case any of the flags other than PSH and ACK is set, we will go process the segment through the slow path. May not enter slow path. If we get urgent flag set, we enable slow path (check *tcp_urg_check()*).

3. In the case where the receive window has changed, once again we take the slow path. This may or may not enable the slow path for the connection. Only the send window change alone does not qualify to enable the slow path. Since the send window has changed, we may have gotten a zero window or the other end might have opened the window; all these are special cases and are handled in the slow path.

4. In the case where the header length changes, it may mean that some option has changed (either withdrawn or introduced). It may also mean that we have gotten SACK blocks, in case SACK is supported.

5. Even if we have prediction flag intact, we can enter into the slow processing path in case out-of-order is received. In this case, we enable the slow path also in *tcp_data_queue()* (cs 11.44).

6. In case we receive the prediction flag intact and also no hole is seen in the data received, we can still enter into slow path processing in case we don't receive timestamp option or we sense PAWS.

7. We enable the slow path on other occasions where we fall short of memory for socket receive buffer and fail to make room for the new received TCP segment even after pruning the receive queues in *tcp_prune_queue()*. We allocate memory in advance for the receive socket in the slow path by calling *tcp_data_queue()*.

8. One more occasion where we enable slow path is when we are advertising 0 window in *tcp_select_window()* (cs 11.18). Out-of-window data are being processed in the slow path in *tcp_data_queue()*.

9. The slow path is enabled because of reception of an urgent pointer and also because of reception of out-of-order segments. We need to disable the slow path once we have read urgent byte and also when we have filled the gap in the received data. We try to undo the slow path once we have read past an urgent byte in *tcp_recvmsg()* at line 1713. We also try to disable the slow path once we receive a filled gap in the received data in *tcp_data_queue()*, line 2598 (cs 11.44).

10. The slow path is enabled when data are flowing in only one direction; that is, we are a receiver and not sending any data. In this case, since the window advertised will always be constant and the rest of the flag remains unchanged, we will be in the slow path.

11.2   FAST PATH PROCESSING (see cs 11.7 and cs 11.8 unless mentioned)

We discuss fast path processing of a received segment in *tcp_rcv_established()*. All the bits in the prediction flags should match TCP_HP_BITS bits in the TCP header of the received segment to enter fast path processing, line 3241 (cs 11.7). Once we have entered the slow path mode, prediction flags (tp→pred_flags) are set to zero. So in that case, none of the TCP_HP_BITS will match from the TCP header. Another necessary condition for entering the fast path is that the segment should be received in sequence, line 3242. If both of the above conditions are TRUE, we enter the fast path to process the segment. We check if the timestamp option is enabled in the TCP header at line 3251. If so, we access the end of the TCP header that should be the start of TCP timestamp option, 3252. If the code for the TCP timestamp option is incorrect, we will be processed in the slow path at line 3257. Otherwise we store the value of the received timestamp in *tp→rcv_tsval* and the echoed timestamp in *tp→rcv_tsecr* at lines 3261–3263. If the new timestamp received is less than the timestamp recorded earlier in tp→ts_recent, we need to process this situation in the slow path (line 3267) looking for the possibility of PAWS.

Next we check for a corrupted TCP header or TCP segment without any data. If the length of the TCP segment is just equal to the header length (line 3278), we can record received timestamp by calling *tcp_store_ts_recent()* only if no ACK is pending at line 3286. We will echo the timestamp from the very first segment received, in case more than one segment is cumulatively acknowledged as a result of delayed ACK. This done so that the peer should calculate RTO taking delayed ACK into account (RFC 1323). We process incoming ACK by calling *tcp_ack()* at line 3290 and try to send any pending data in the transmit queue by calling *tcp_data_snd_check()* at line 3292. Otherwise if the segment length is smaller than the minimum header length, there is an error.

In case we have received data, we first try to consume data if the receiver is installed by calling *tcp_copy_to_iovec()* at line 3307 (discussed in much detail in Section 8.2). In this case, we try to record timestamp received only if no ACK is pending at line 3316. Record the next sequence number to be received in *tp→rcv_nxt* from the end sequence of the received segment at line 3319. If we are not able to consume data, we try to queue it in the receive queue at line 3344 only if we have enough memory available in the socket's memory pool. Otherwise we try to get some memory into the socket's memory pool by entering the slow path at line 3338. Here also we record timestamp received, if no ACK is pending at line 3335.

We have consumed or queued up received data, and now we need to schedule ACK and also adjust the delayed ACK interval based on how fast we receive data. We also need to do a calculation for the receive window depending on the segment size received. All this is done by calling *tcp_event_data_recv()* at line 3349 (cs 11.8).

Next we check if new data are acknowledged at line 3351. If so, we process the incoming ACK by calling *tcp_ack()* at line 3353 with FLAG_DATA set. *tcp_ack()* will remove acknowledged segments from the retransmit queue generating space in the transmit queue. So, we call *tcp_data_snd_check()* to check if the socket is under memory pressure. If the socket is waiting for memory to be available, it wakes up the socket and finally it tries to send out any data in the transmit queue.

If we are able to transmit data in *tcp_data_snd_check()*, any pending ACK for the received data would have already been sent out. But nothing is guaranteed at

```
net/ipv4/tcp_input.c
3210 int tcp_rcv_established(struct sock *sk, struct sk_buff *skb,
3211              struct tcphdr *th, unsigned len)
3212 {
3213     struct tcp_opt *tp = &(sk->tp_pinfo.af_tcp);
         ....
3241     if ((tcp_flag_word(th) & TCP_HP_BITS) == tp->pred_flags &&
3242          TCP_SKB_CB(skb)->seq == tp->rcv_nxt) {
3243          int tcp_header_len = tp->tcp_header_len;
             ....
3251          if (tcp_header_len == sizeof(struct tcphdr) + TCPOLEN_TSTAMP_ALIGNED) {
3252              __u32 *ptr = (__u32 *)(th + 1);

3255              if (*ptr != ntohl((TCPOPT_NOP << 24) | (TCPOPT_NOP << 16)
3256                   | (TCPOPT_TIMESTAMP << 8) | TCPOLEN_TIMESTAMP))
3257                  goto slow_path;
3258
3259              tp->saw_tstamp = 1;
3260              ++ptr;
3261              tp->rcv_tsval = ntohl(*ptr);
3262              ++ptr;
3263              tp->rcv_tsecr = ntohl(*ptr);
                 ....
3266              if ((s32)(tp->rcv_tsval - tp->ts_recent) < 0)
3267                  goto slow_path;
                 ....
3276          if (len <= tcp_header_len) {
3277              /* Bulk data transfer: sender */
3278              if (len == tcp_header_len) {
                 ....
3283                  if (tcp_header_len ==
3284                      (sizeof(struct tcphdr) + TCPOLEN_TSTAMP_ALIGNED) &&
3285                      tp->rcv_nxt == tp->rcv_wup)
3286                      tcp_store_ts_recent(tp);
                     ....
3290                  tcp_ack(sk, skb, 0);
3291                  __kfree_skb(skb);
3292                  tcp_data_snd_check(sk);
3293                  return 0;
3294              } else { /* Header too small */
3295                  TCP_INC_STATS_BH(TcpInErrs);
3296                  goto discard;
3297              }
3298          } else {
                 ....
3301              if (tp->ucopy.task == current &&
3302                  tp->copied_seq == tp->rcv_nxt &&
3303                  len - tcp_header_len <= tp->ucopy.len &&
3304                  sk->lock.users) {
                     ....
3307                  if (!tcp_copy_to_iovec(sk, skb, tcp_header_len)) {
                         ....
3312                      if (tcp_header_len ==
3313                          (sizeof(struct tcphdr) +
3314                          TCPOLEN_TSTAMP_ALIGNED) &&
3315                          tp->rcv_nxt == tp->rcv_wup)
3316                          tcp_store_ts_recent(tp);

3319                          tp->rcv_nxt = TCP_SKB_CB(skb)->end_seq;
                         ....
3321                      eaten = 1;
3322                  }
3323              }
3324              if (!eaten) {
                     ....
3332                  if (tcp_header_len ==
3333                      (sizeof(struct tcphdr) + TCPOLEN_TSTAMP_ALIGNED) &&
3334                      tp->rcv_nxt == tp->rcv_wup)
3335                      tcp_store_ts_recent(tp);
3336
3337                  if ((int)skb->truesize > sk->forward_alloc)
3338                      goto step5;
                     ....
3344                  __skb_queue_tail(&sk->receive_queue, skb);
3345                  tcp_set_owner_r(skb, sk);
3346                  tp->rcv_nxt = TCP_SKB_CB(skb)->end_seq;
3347              }
                 ....
```

cs 11.7. tcp_rcv_established().

```
net/ipv4/tcp_input.c

tcp_rcv_established() contd....

3349                    tcp_event_data_recv(sk, tp, skb);
3350
3351                    if (TCP_SKB_CB(skb)->ack_seq != tp->snd_una) {
3352                        /* Well, only one small jumplet in fast path... */
3353                        tcp_ack(sk, skb, FLAG_DATA);
3354                        tcp_data_snd_check(sk);
3355                        if (!tcp_ack_scheduled(tp))
3356                            goto no_ack;
3357                    }
3358
3359                    if (eaten) {
3360                        if (tcp_in_quickack_mode(tp)) {
3361                            tcp_send_ack(sk);
3362                        } else {
3363                            tcp_send_delayed_ack(sk);
3364                        }
3365                    } else {
3366                        __tcp_ack_snd_check(sk, 0);
3367                    }
3368
3369 no_ack:
3370                    if (eaten)
3371                        __kfree_skb(skb);
3372                    else
3373                        sk->data_ready(sk, 0);
3374                    return 0;
3375                }
3376        }
```

cs 11.8. *tcp_rcv_established()*.

this point; that is, we are not sure that we are able to transmit new data. So, we check if ACK is still scheduled for the received data by calling tcp_ack_scheduled() at line 3355. If no ACK is scheduled, we are done. If we have copied received data to the user buffer, just free the buffer at line 3371. Otherwise, we have queued data in the receive queue and we need to wake up socket sleeping to receive more data by calling *sk→data_ready (= sock_def_readable())* at line 3373. If ACK is scheduled, then we need to make a decision on whether we need to send an ACK immediately or defer it, depending on many factors (lines 3359–3367). This is discussed in great detail in Section 10.4 (TCP timer chapter).

11.3 SLOW PATH PROCESSING (see cs 11.10 unless mentioned)

Slow path processing starts from line 3379. First we do some sanity check. If the length of the segment is less than the header length as specified in the TCP header field or if the checksum is incorrect as indicated by *tcp_checksum_complete_user()* at line 3379, we discard the segment. Next we do a PAWS check against wrapped timestamps. For this we first parse TCP options by calling *tcp_fast_parse_options()* at line 3385. If the timestamp option is present, we will proceed with the PAWS check; otherwise we proceed with slow path processing. When a timestamp option is present, we call *tcp_paws_discard()* at line 3386 to check if the packet can be dis-

```
net/ipv4/tcp_input.c

2186 static inline int tcp_sequence(struct tcp_opt *tp, u32 seq, u32 end_seq)
2187 {
2188     return !before(end_seq, tp->rcv_wup) &&
2189            !after(seq, tp->rcv_nxt + tcp_receive_window(tp));
2190 }
```

cs 11.9. *tcp_sequence().*

carded because PAWS has failed (see Section 11.3.13 for details). In the case where it is an RST segment, we will process the segment even if PAWS has failed but won't process the segment further otherwise. Next we check if the segment maintains sequence number integrity by calling *tcp_sequence()*.

11.3.1 *tcp_sequence()*

This checks if we have gotten a data segment that is completely acknowledged and we have all the bits from the segment already with us, line 2188. $tp{\rightarrow}rcv\_wup$ is synced with $tp{\rightarrow}rcv\_nxt$ when we are sending an ACK in *tcp_select_window()*. If the end sequence of the segment is below $tp{\rightarrow}rcv\_wup$, we should not accept this segment. We have already sent an ACK for all the data up to $tp{\rightarrow}rcv\_wup$. The second check we do here is that the start sequence of the segment should not be beyond the sequence number corresponding to the end of the receive window, 2189, which essentially means that the segment should not be out of window with respect to the acknowledged data. In this case we send a duplicate ACK (with DSACK) by calling *tcp_send_dupack()* at line 3411 (cs 11.10), if it is not RST segment and discard the packet. The sequence field for the RST segment should not be out-of-window, nor should it correspond to an already acknowledged sequence number (refer to RFC 793).

Now we are sure that the sequence field is valid for the segment and PAWS is also acceptable. If the segment has an RST bit on, we reset our side of connection without any formal TCP closing process by calling *tcp_reset()* at line 3416 (cs 11.10) and stop processing the segment any further. *tcp_reset()* wakes up any process waiting for socket's sleep queue and closes the TCP connection.

Now we check if the timestamp from the segment can be recorded as the most recent timestamp from the peer by calling *tcp_replace_ts_recent()* at line 3420 (cs 11.10).

11.3.2 *tcp_replace_ts_recent()*

This should make sure that we are not keeping a timestamp from out-of-order segments. Start of the sequence space for the segment should be maximum equal to the byte already acknowledged ($tp{\rightarrow}rcv\_wup$), line 2110 (cs 11.11). If the timestamp from the segment is more than the current recorded timestamp ($tp{\rightarrow}ts\_recent$), then we directly replace it with the new timestamp by calling *tcp_store_ts_recent()* at line 2120. Otherwise if the timestamp is less than the recorded timestamp, we need to check if the time elapsed since the timestamp was recorded is more than 24 days. If so, we replace the recorded timestamp with the one from the segment because the recorded timestamp is too old.

```
net/ipv4/tcp_input.c

tcp_rcv_established() contd....

3378 slow_path:
3379      if (len < (th->doff<<2) || tcp_checksum_complete_user(sk, skb))
3380          goto csum_error;
          ....
3385      if (tcp_fast_parse_options(skb, th, tp) && tp->saw_tstamp &&
3386          tcp_paws_discard(tp, skb)) {
3387          if (!th->rst) {
3388              NET_INC_STATS_BH(PAWSEstabRejected);
3389              tcp_send_dupack(sk, skb);
3390              goto discard;
3391          }
          ....
3397      }
          ....
3403      if (!tcp_sequence(tp, TCP_SKB_CB(skb)->seq, TCP_SKB_CB(skb)->end_seq)) {
          ....
3410          if (!th->rst)
3411              tcp_send_dupack(sk, skb);
3412          goto discard;
3413      }
3414
3415      if(th->rst) {
3416          tcp_reset(sk);
3417          goto discard;
3418      }
3419
3420      tcp_replace_ts_recent(tp, TCP_SKB_CB(skb)->seq);
3421
3422      if (th->syn && !before(TCP_SKB_CB(skb)->seq, tp->rcv_nxt)) {
3423          TCP_INC_STATS_BH(TcpInErrs);
3424          NET_INC_STATS_BH(TCPAbortOnSyn);
3425          tcp_reset(sk);
3426          return 1;
3427      }
3428
3429 step5:
3430      if(th->ack)
3431          tcp_ack(sk, skb, FLAG_SLOWPATH);
          ....
3434      tcp_urg(sk, skb, th);
          ....
3437      tcp_data_queue(sk, skb);
3438
3439      tcp_data_snd_check(sk);
3440      tcp_ack_snd_check(sk);
3441      return 0;
          ....
3446 discard:
3447      __kfree_skb(skb);
3448      return 0;
3449 }
```

cs 11.10. *tcp_rcv_established()*.

Continuing with *tcp_rcv_established()* at line 3422, if it is not an RST segment and has a SYN bit set, we need to handle it only if the sequence number is not less than the next expected sequence number, line 3422. This might happen because of retransmission of the SYN segment from the side that got a connection request, where both the original and retransmission reached the other end consecutively. If

```
net/ipv4/tcp_input.c

2107 extern __inline__ void
2108 tcp_replace_ts_recent(struct tcp_opt *tp, u32 seq)
2109 {
2110      if (tp->saw_tstamp && !after(seq, tp->rcv_wup)) {
             ....
2118          if((s32)(tp->rcv_tsval - tp->ts_recent) >= 0 ||
2119              xtime.tv_sec >= tp->ts_recent_stamp + TCP_PAWS_24DAYS)
2120                  tcp_store_ts_recent(tp);
2121      }
2122 }
```

cs 11.11. *tcp_replace_ts_recent()*.

the sequence number is less than the next expected sequence, we need to reset the connection because the peer may be buggy or we can sense some kind of attack. The SYN segment, even if retransmitted, will never have two different sequence numbers and no SYN bit will be set in more than one segment other than retransmission. The situation arises where the originator of the connection receives SYN/ACK (entered established state) and transmitted a final ACK which reached the other end slightly late. The other end retransmitted the segment because it didn't receive the final ACK.

Next we need to process incoming ACK by calling *tcp_ack()*, line 3431. The routine does some sanity checks on the ACK sequence, updates the send window, clears ACKed data from the retransmit queue, processes SACK information, manages the congestion window, and clears/resets the zero-window probe timer (see Section 11.4 for more details).

Once we have processed incoming ACK, we check if an urgent bit was set in the segment and need to process it if it exists; call *tcp_urg()* at line 3434. Here we check if we have gotten the urgent pointer. In the case where we have gotten the urgent pointer, we remain in urgent mode until we read data past the urgent pointer. For details see Section 11.7.

Now, process data in the segment by calling *tcp_data_queue()*. We may have entered the slow path because the socket's pool has exhausted its quota of memory, and we have gotten an out-of-order segment. Both cases are handled in *tcp_data_queue()*. If some data segment arrives that fills the hole, we take care of this situation here. Duplicate segments, out-of-window segments, and retransmissions are also handled here. We also set D-SACK in case the SACK option is enabled and we get duplicate segments. For more details see Section 11.8.

Check if any data are pending to be transmitted by calling *tcp_data_snd_check()* at line 3439. Since we might have ACKed some data increasing the congestion window, try to send data pending to be transmitted in the transmit queue. ACK of data in the retransmit queue may have generated some space in the socket's send buffer, and we try to wake up the process waiting for memory to be available in the write queue. See Section 11.3.11 for more details.

Finally, check if ACK is scheduled by calling *tcp_ack_snd_check()* at line 3440. If required, we need to send out any ACK for the received data; otherwise we start a delay ACK timer to defer sending ACK. We do this after sending out data at line 3439. If data are transmitted in *tcp_data_snd_check()*, we have already piggybacked pending ACK along with the data. In that case, there won't be any ACK scheduled.

11.3.3 *tcp_event_data_recv()*

The routine is called whenever we receive in-sequence data to take certain actions. These actions are as follows:

- Schedule ACK.
- Measure receive mss up until now. That is the size of the TCP payload of the received packet.
- Calculate a new delay ACK period based on the rate at which a data segment arrives.
- Grow a receive window based on the size of the received TCP segment.

tcp_schedule_ack() is called to schedule ACK for the received data sometime in the future or immediately at line 364. We call *tcp_measure_rcv_mss()* to cache in the maximum length of the TCP segment so far received. This will be used to calculate receive window size later. Next we calculate the delay-ACK timeout value

```
net/ipv4/tcp_input.c

360 static void tcp_event_data_recv(struct sock *sk, struct tcp_opt *tp, struct sk_buff *skb)
361 {
362     u32 now;
363
364     tcp_schedule_ack(tp);
365
366     tcp_measure_rcv_mss(tp, skb);
367
368     now = tcp_time_stamp;
369
370     if (!tp->ack.ato) {
        ....
374         tcp_incr_quickack(tp);
375         tp->ack.ato = TCP_ATO_MIN;
376     } else {
377         int m = now - tp->ack.lrcvtime;
378
379         if (m <= TCP_ATO_MIN/2) {
380             /* The fastest case is the first. */
381             tp->ack.ato = (tp->ack.ato>>1) + TCP_ATO_MIN/2;
382         } else if (m < tp->ack.ato) {
383             tp->ack.ato = (tp->ack.ato>>1) + m;
384             if (tp->ack.ato > tp->rto)
385                 tp->ack.ato = tp->rto;
386         } else if (m > tp->rto) {
            ....
390             tcp_incr_quickack(tp);
391             tcp_mem_reclaim(sk);
392         }
393     }
394     tp->ack.lrcvtime = now;
395
396     TCP_ECN_check_ce(tp, skb);
397
398     if (skb->len >= 128)
399         tcp_grow_window(sk, tp, skb);
400 }
```

cs 11.12. *tcp_event_data_recv()*.

(*tp→ack.ato*). In case we have not yet initialized it (very first segment has arrived), we initialize it to TCP_ATO_MIN and also initialize quick ack counter (*tp→ack. quick*) by calling *tcp_incr_quickack()*. This makes sure that we send out ACKs faster in the beginning because rate of transmission will depend on the rate of data being ACKed in the slow-start phase. If this is not the first data packet we have received, we need to calculate delay-ACK timeout based on the frequency at which data segments arrive. If data packets have arrived after more than RTO value, it may be because we have an opened window. In this case, we need to ACK quickly because the sender would like to push data quickly.

If our segment size is above 128 bytes, we need to check the possibility of incrementing the receive window by calling *tcp_grow_window()* at line 399. Linux adopts a strategy of forcing a slow start from the receiver's end. Since the sender can send a minimum of the congestion window and the advertised window, the receiver takes advantage by slowly incrementing the receive window. The idea is not only to reduce congestion in the network but also to take care of the receive buffer management. Consider a case where the sender is sending data in small chunks at high speed, and the application is not able to read data at such highspeed. In this case, data segments will be queued up on the receive queue causing receive queue to get full. If segments are so small that buffer overhead is eating up most of the space in the receive queue, a very small proportion of receive buffer space is used by data. In this case we need to prune the queue to generate some space in the receive queue, which is an expensive process. So in order to avoid pruning the queue too often, we manipulate the receive window to be advertised to the sender based on the size of the received data segment. We do this in *tcp_grow_window()*. If the sender is sending small segments, we don't increment the receive window so that the sender cannot transmit at a very high rate and the application can get a chance to read data from the queue.

11.3.4 *tcp_incr_quickack()*

Quickack counter is required to make a decision on whether we can send ACK immediately or defer it so that we can cumulatively send out ACK for more than one data segment received. This counter is decremented whenever a segment is transmitted (other than SYN segment) in *tcp_transmit_skb()*. We calculate a quick ACK counter based on the receive window and segment size received at line 159 (cs 11.13). We do this because on an average (receive window/segment size), a number of segments can be sent out by the sender at any given point of time. Quick

```
net/ipv4/tcp_input.c

157 static void tcp_incr_quickack(struct tcp_opt *tp)
158 {
159     unsigned quickacks = tp->rcv_wnd/(2*tp->ack.rcv_mss);
160
161     if (quickacks==0)
162         quickacks=2;
163     if (quickacks > tp->ack.quick)
164         tp->ack.quick = min(quickacks, TCP_MAX_QUICKACKS);
165 }
```

cs 11.13. *tcp_incr_quickack()*.

ACK count is just half of the number of such segments, meaning that one ACK can be sent out per two data segments received. The rest of the calculations show that quick ACK can assume a minimum 2 value and a maximum *TCP_MAX_QUICKACKS* value.

11.3.5 *tcp_grow_window()* (see cs 11.14 unless mentioned)

When we receive a data segment, we need to calculate a receive window that needs to be advertised to the sender, depending on the segment size received. The idea is to avoid filling the receive buffer with too many small segments when an application is reading very slowly and packets are transmitted at a very high rate, thus avoiding pruning of queues to make space in the receive queue. $tp \rightarrow window\_clamp$ is the maximum window that can be advertised and $tp \rightarrow rcv\_ssthresh$ is the slow-start threshold for the receiver side (cs 11.14). $tp \rightarrow rcv\_ssthresh$ functions very much similar to send congestion window. On reception of data segment from the sender, this value is recalculated based on the size of the segment, and later on this value is used as upper limit on the receive window to be advertised. The idea is not to use a complete receive buffer space to calculate the receive buffer. We reserve some space as an application buffer, and the rest is used to queue incoming data segments. An application buffer corresponds to the space that should compensate for the delay in time it takes for an application to read data from the socket buffer. If the application is reading more slowly than the rate at which data are arriving, data will be queued in the receive buffer. In order to avoid queue getting full, we advertise less receive window so that the sender can slow down the rate of data transmission and by that time the application gets a chance to read data from the receive buffer. We are advertising a receive window smaller than the space available in the receive buffer because of the application buffer space. *tcp_win_from_space()* returns us the value taking into account application space (cs 11.15). If *sysctl_tcp_adv_win_scale* is set to 2, one-fourth space will be reserved for user application for the reason explained above.

```
net/ipv4/tcp_input.c

240  static __inline__ void
241  tcp_grow_window(struct sock *sk, struct tcp_opt *tp, struct sk_buff *skb)
242  {
243        /* Check #1 */
244        if (tp->rcv_ssthresh < tp->window_clamp &&
245            (int)tp->rcv_ssthresh < tcp_space(sk) &&
246            !tcp_memory_pressure) {
             ....
252            if (tcp_win_from_space(skb->truesize) <= skb->len)
253                incr = 2*tp->advmss;
254            else
255                incr = __tcp_grow_window(sk, tp, skb);
256
257            if (incr) {
258                tp->rcv_ssthresh = min(tp->rcv_ssthresh + incr, tp->window_clamp);
259                tp->ack.quick |= 1;
260            }
261        }
262  }
```

cs 11.14. *tcp_grow_window().*

```
include/net/tcp.h

1542  static inline int tcp_win_from_space(int space)
1543  {
1544      return sysctl_tcp_adv_win_scale<=0 ?
1545          (space>>(-sysctl_tcp_adv_win_scale)) :
1546          space - (space>>sysctl_tcp_adv_win_scale);
1547  }
```

cs 11.15. *tcp_win_from_space()*.

```
include/net/tcp.h

1550  static inline int tcp_space(struct sock *sk)
1551  {
1552      return tcp_win_from_space(sk->rcvbuf - atomic_read(&sk->rmem_alloc));
1553  }
```

cs 11.16. *tcp_space()*.

We try to increment *tp→rcv_ssthresh* here whose effect will be seen while calculating a receive window in *tcp_select_window()*. The following conditions should be satisfied to qualify for increase in an *tp→rcv_ssthresh*:

1. *tp→rcv_ssthresh* should not have exceeded a maximum limit out on the receive window (*tp→window_clamp*), line 244.
2. *tp→rcv_ssthresh* has not yet exceeded the space available in the receive buffer as returned by the *tcp_space()*, line 245. tcp_space () returns total space available in socket's receive buffer (cs-11.16).
3. There should not be memory pressure, line 246. TCP enters into memory pressure when total memory allocated for TCP socket system exceeds a limit. In this case there is a chance that we may start pruning receive queues or start dropping packets, if the rate of data consumption by the application is lower than the rate of data being queued. So, we avoid increasing *tp→rcv_ssthresh* in case of memory pressure.

If all the above conditions are TRUE, we are an eligible candidate to increment *tp→rcv_ssthresh*. Next we check if the buffer is bloated at line 252. By bloated buffer we mean that the actual proportion of TCP data in the total size of the buffer is much lower, which effectively means that we have received a very small segment. If the buffer is bloated, most of the space will be taken away by the buffer head and we may need to prune the queues. If not bloated, we increment *tp→rcv_ssthresh* by twice the advertised mss. Otherwise we check for the possibility of incrementing tp→ rcv_ssthresh, depending on the degree of bloating of the segment with respect to the space available in the receive buffer by calling __tcp_grow_window() at line 255.

11.3.6 __tcp_grow_window() (see cs 11.17 unless mentioned)

We check the degree of bloat of segment with respect to the space available in the receive buffer. First we take half of the available space and true size of the buffer after taking an application buffer into account from both the buffers. We continue to loop until one of the conditions becomes true:

```
net/ipv4/tcp_input.c

223  static int
224  __tcp_grow_window(struct sock *sk, struct tcp_opt *tp, struct sk_buff *skb)
225  {
226      /* Optimize this! */
227      int truesize = tcp_win_from_space(skb->truesize)/2;
228      int window = tcp_full_space(sk)/2;
229
230      while (tp->rcv_ssthresh <= window) {
231          if (truesize <= skb->len)
232              return 2*tp->ack.rcv_mss;
233
234          truesize >>= 1;
235          window >>= 1;
236      }
237      return 0;
238  }
```

cs 11.17. __grow_tcp_window().

- tp→rcv_ssthresh is less than the total receive buffer space available, line 230.
- Total space occupied by buffer is at max equal to the segment length, line 231.

In each iteration we reduce total space available in the receive buffer and buffer size to half of the value. If we come out of the loop because the first condition becomes FALSE, we should not increment the receive window, the reason being that the buffer overhead is too huge to be accommodated in the available space. In a simpler way we can say that the degree of bloat is so much (very small segment) that even if we continue decrementing total space available and total buffer size by the same proportion, buffer overhead is too high even when total apace available in the receive buffer is less than the window to be advertised.

If the loop is exited because of later condition is TRUE, it means that buffer overhead is bearable because the segment length is good enough to be accommodated in the receive buffer. In this case, we may increment receive buffer by twice the maximum segment length seen so far.

11.3.7 How Do We Calculate Window to Be Advertised

We calculate receive window in *tcp_select_window()*. As discussed in Section 11.3.9, we know that there are two factors that decide on the receive window. They are *tp→window_clamp* and *tp→rcv_ssthresh*. The role of these two parameters is already discussed in Section 11.3.9, so it won't be repeated here. On reception of the data segment, we calculate *tp→rcv_ssthresh* and we use the parameter here to calculate the receive window.

First we get the current window from *tcp_receive_window()* at line 150 (cs 11.18). We calculate the new window based on the space available in the receive buffer, the upper limit on the receive window (*tp→window_clamp*), and *tp→rcv_ssthresh* by calling *__tcp_select_window()*. If the new window calculated is less than the current window, the new window is raised to the current window. We do this because the advertised window should not be allowed to shrink. The new window

```
net/ipv4/tcp_output.c

147 static __inline__ u16 tcp_select_window(struct sock *sk)
148 {
149     struct tcp_opt *tp = &(sk->tp_pinfo.af_tcp);
150     u32 cur_win = tcp_receive_window(tp);
151     u32 new_win = __tcp_select_window(sk);
152
        ....
154     if(new_win < cur_win) {
        ....
162         new_win = cur_win;
163     }
164     tp->rcv_wnd = new_win;
165     tp->rcv_wup = tp->rcv_nxt;
        ....
168     new_win >>= tp->rcv_wscale;
        ....
171     if (new_win == 0)
172         tp->pred_flags = 0;
173
174     return new_win;
175 }
```

cs 11.18. *tcp_select_window()*.

```
include/net/tcp.h

958 static __inline__ u32 tcp_receive_window(struct tcp_opt *tp)
959 {
960     s32 win = tp->rcv_wup + tp->rcv_wnd - tp->rcv_nxt;
961
962     if (win < 0)
963         win = 0;
964     return (u32) win;
965 }
```

cs 11.19. *tcp_receive_window()*.

as returned by *__tcp_select_window()* is 0, in case free space has fallen below 1 mss. But we can't advertise the zero window abruptly. In such cases, the current window as returned by *tcp_receive_window()* will get us the exact window to be advertised. Similarly, when a small window is opened (less than 1 mss), we don't advertise it unless a minimum 1 mss of window is opened. *__tcp_select_window()* takes care of this scenario (cs 11.18).

11.3.8 *tcp_receive_window()*

This is calculated as the last advertised window minus unacknowledged data length. $tp \to rcv\_wup$ is synced with next byte to be received ($tp \to rcv\_nxt$) only when we are sending ACK in *tcp_select_window()*. If there is no unacknowledged bytes, the routine returns the exact receive window advertised last (cs 11.19).

11.3.9 *__tcp_select_window()*

We are called to calculate the new window to be advertised. The new window is calculated on the basis of

```
net/ipv4/tcp_output.c
644 u32 __tcp_select_window(struct sock *sk)
645 {
646      struct tcp_opt *tp = &sk->tp_pinfo.af_tcp;
         ....
653      int mss = tp->ack.rcv_mss;
654      int free_space = tcp_space(sk);
655      int full_space = min_t(int, tp->window_clamp, tcp_full_space(sk));
656      int window;
657
658      if (mss > full_space)
659          mss = full_space;
660
661      if (free_space < full_space/2) {
662          tp->ack.quick = 0;
663
664          if (tcp_memory_pressure)
665              tp->rcv_ssthresh = min(tp->rcv_ssthresh, 4U*tp->advmss);
666
667          if (free_space < mss)
668              return 0;
669      }
670
671      if (free_space > tp->rcv_ssthresh)
672          free_space = tp->rcv_ssthresh;
         ....
682      window = tp->rcv_wnd;
683      if (window <= free_space - mss || window > free_space)
684          window = (free_space/mss)*mss;
685
686      return window;
687 }
```

cs 11.20. ___tcp_select_window().

1. The mss received so far (*tp→ack.rcv_mss*)
2. The total space in the socket's receive buffer obtained from *tcp_full_space()*
3. The space available in the receive buffer from *tcp_space()*
4. tp→rcv_ssthresh

tp→window_clamp is the upper limit on the total space in the receive buffer. We get the full space available in the socket's receive buffer at line 655 (cs 11.20). If the highest mss observed so far is higher than the maximum space in the socket's receive buffer, we need to slash mss to the maximum buffer size at line 659. We have to do this because our receive buffer should at least have space to receive a full-sized segment. Next we check if our receive buffer is half full, line 661. If so, we disable quick ACK mode at line 662. The reason is that we don't want to acknowledge data very fast to restrict the rate of data transmission by the sender so that the application gets enough time to eat up data in the receive buffer and leave enough space for the new data. If there is a memory pressure, we once again want to keep the advertised window tight. So, we restrict *tp→rcv_ssthresh* to be maximum four times advertised MSS at line 665. By doing this we are not shrinking the window but simply restricting the receive window to not to increase beyond its current value. If the new window calculated is less than the current window, *tcp_select_window()* takes the last advertised window as the current receive window. If the free space

```
include/net/tcp.h

1550 static inline int tcp_space(struct sock *sk)
1551 {
1552     return tcp_win_from_space(sk->rcvbuf - atomic_read(&sk->rmem_alloc));
1553 }
```

cs 11.21. tcp_space().

```
net/ipv4/tcp_input.c

2993 static __inline__ void tcp_data_snd_check(struct sock *sk)
2994 {
2995     struct sk_buff *skb = sk->tp_pinfo.af_tcp.send_head;
2996
2997     if (skb != NULL)
2998         __tcp_data_snd_check(sk, skb);
2999     tcp_check_space(sk);
3000 }
```

cs 11.22. tcp_data_snd_check().

available is less than the highest mss observed so far, we return 0. Next we check if the free space is more than $tp \rightarrow rcv\_ssthresh$ at line 671. If so, we adjust free space. This is the place where we are restricting the receive window to have a maximum value of $tp \rightarrow rcv\_ssthresh$. If the current window offered is within 1 mss of the free space (current window is greater than free space minus mss and also less than free space), we don't update the receive window at line 683. Otherwise the new window is taken as free space calculated above rounded to mss, line 684.

11.3.10 tcp_space()

Free space in the receive buffer is available from $tcp\_space()$ (cs 11.21). $sk \rightarrow rmem\_$ *alloc* is the amount of memory allocated for the socket's receive buffer, and $sk \rightarrow$ *rcvbuf* is the upper limit on the socket's receive buffer size. We take the application buffer into account as discussed in Section 11.3.5.

11.3.11 tcp_data_snd_check()

We are called to check if there are any data to be transmitted from the transmit queue while processing the incoming segment. We are called before sending an ACK so that we can piggyback ACK along with the data segment. We first check is there are any data to be transmitted by accessing the head of the transmit queue ($tp \rightarrow send\_head$) at line 2995. If there is nothing in the queue, we just check if some space is generated in the write queue by calling $tcp\_check\_space()$ at line 2999. We do this check here because we have just processed incoming ACK; and if new data are acknowledged, space is generated in the write queue. If space is generated in the write queue, we may need to wake up the socket sleeping on memory requirements in the write path. tcp_check_space() takes care of doing all this.

If there are any data to be transmitted, we try to transmit it by calling __tcp_ data_snd_check() at line 2998 (cs 11.22).

```
net/ipv4/tcp_input.c

2983 static void __tcp_data_snd_check(struct sock *sk, struct sk_buff *skb)
2984 {
2985        struct tcp_opt *tp = &(sk->tp_pinfo.af_tcp);
2986
2987        if (after(TCP_SKB_CB(skb)->end_seq, tp->snd_una + tp->snd_wnd) ||
2988            tcp_packets_in_flight(tp) >= tp->snd_cwnd ||
2989            tcp_write_xmit(sk, tp->nonagle))
2990                tcp_check_probe_timer(sk, tp);
2991 }
```

cs 11.23. __tcp_data_snd_check().

11.3.12 __tcp_data_snd_check()

We are called to check the possibility of transmitting any segment in the transmit queue. We make the following checks before the segment may be transmitted:

1. The segment should be within the window, line 2987 (cs 11.23).
2. Packets that are transmitted but have not yet left the network should be less than the congestion window, line 2988.
3. Nagle's algorithm is not violated.

If the above conditions are TRUE, tcp_write_xmit() is called to transmit any pending segment's in the write queue. tcp_write_xmit() once again makes all the necessary checks for all the segments in the transmit queue before transmitting them. If we fail to transmit segments because of any reason, we check if we need to start a zero-window probe timer by calling tcp_check_probe_timer().

11.3.13 tcp_paws_discard() (see cs 11.24 unless mentioned)

This routine is called to carry out the PAWS test against the timestamp value from the TCP segment. If the timestamp value from the TCP segment (tp→rcv_tsval) is less than the timestamp stored last (tp→ts_recent). We should carry out PAWS test. (Check Section 11.2 for details on timestamps.) This code follows the PAWS specification as mentioned in RFC 1323. The following conditions should be satisfied for the segment not to be discarded:

1. The difference between the timestamp value obtained in the current segment and last seen timestamp on the incoming TCP segment should be equal to TCP_PAWS_WINDOW (= 1), which means that if the segment that was transmitted 1 clock tick before the segment that reached here earlier TCP seq should be acceptable. It may be because of reordering of the segments that the latter reached earlier.
2. If the first condition passes and the timestamp difference is more than 1, we need to check if the 24 days have elapsed since last time timestamp was stored, line 2169. tp→ts_recent_stamp is updated whenever we update tp→ts_recent in tcp_store_ts_recent(). If last timestamp recorded is 24 days old, we discard further PAWS test and process the segment. For machine with

```
net/ipv4/tcp_input.c

2166 extern __inline__ int tcp_paws_discard(struct tcp_opt *tp, struct sk_buff *skb)
2167 {
2168     return ((s32)(tp->ts_recent - tp->rcv_tsval) > TCP_PAWS_WINDOW &&
2169         xtime.tv_sec < tp->ts_recent_stamp + TCP_PAWS_24DAYS &&
2170         !tcp_disordered_ack(tp, skb));
2171 }
```

cs 11.24. *tcp_paws_discard().*

```
net/ipv4/tcp_input.c

2147 static int tcp_disordered_ack(struct tcp_opt *tp, struct sk_buff *skb)
2148 {
2149     struct tcphdr *th = skb->h.th;
2150     u32 seq = TCP_SKB_CB(skb)->seq;
2151     u32 ack = TCP_SKB_CB(skb)->ack_seq;
2152
2153     return (/* 1. Pure ACK with correct sequence number. */
2154         (th->ack && seq == TCP_SKB_CB(skb)->end_seq && seq == tp->rcv_nxt) &&
             ....
2157         ack == tp->snd_una &&
             ....
2160         !tcp_may_update_window(tp, ack, seq, ntohs(th->window)<<tp->snd_wscale) &&
             ....
2163         (s32)(tp->ts_recent - tp->rcv_tsval) <= (tp->rto*1024)/HZ);
2164 }
```

cs 11.25. *tcp_disordered_ack().*

1-ms frequency, it will take approximately 24 days for timestamp value to wrap up.

3. If 24 days have not elasped, we need to still look for a more strict condition before which a segment can be considered to have failed PAWS. We check if this segment is not going to make any changes to the sequence or update window. For this we call *tcp_disordered_ack()*. For a segment to pass the PAWS check, this routine should return TRUE, line 2170.

The routine *tcp_disordered_ack()* checks if the ACK is harmless as far as PAWS is concerned (cs 11.25). The PAWS check passes in the following situations:

1. The segment doesn't carry any data and it is pure ACK in correct order, line 2154. The start sequence should be the same as the end sequence number and should also be the same as the next sequence number expected.
2. The ACK should not acknowledge any new data and at the same time should not acknowledge any old data. It should be a duplicate ACK, line 2157. Duplicate ACKs carry a valid timestamp.
3. ACK does not update the window, line 2160.
4. The timestamp received is within the replay window, line 2163.

In all we can say that this segment is a duplicate ACK that may carry D-SACK information.

11.4 PROCESSING OF INCOMING ACK (see cs 11.26 unless mentioned)

We process an incoming ACK in *tcp_ack()* while processing an incoming segment in *tcp_rcv_established()*. We will be updating retransmit queue by cleaning ACKed data. We update TAGS on the socket buffers based on the SACK information we get with the ACK. Based on the SACK information, we calculate lost/left-out segments. We update the send window conditionally in this routine. Congestion is sensed based on the SACK information or duplicate ACK, and accordingly we update the congestion window and also process the congestion state. In case we have already entered the congestion state, all the required processing is done in this routine. Let's see how all this is implemented.

We reject any ACK processing if we have gotten ACK for something that has not been transmitted yet ($tp \rightarrow snd\_nxt$) at line 1908 (cs 11.26). Similarly, if we have gotten an ACK for data that are already acknowledged ($tp \rightarrow snd\_una$) at line 1911, we won't process it but we may have gotten D-SACK/SACK information that we would like to be processed. So, we process SACK/D-SACK blocks in case they exist at line 1981 by calling *tcp_sacktag_write_queue()*.

Next we will try to update the send window advertised with the ACK segment. If we are processing the segment in the FAST mode and new data are acknowledged (line 1914), we immediately update the $tp \rightarrow snd\_wl1$ to the sequence number of the segment by calling *tcp_update_wl()* at line 1919. $tp \rightarrow snd\_wl$ is updated whenever we update the send window. We don't update the send window ($tp \rightarrow snd\_wnd$) here because it has not changed; otherwise we would have been processing the segment in the SLOW path (check prediction flags in Section 11.2). Even though we have not updated the send window, still $tp \rightarrow snd\_wl1$ could have changed because the left edge of the window might have advanced toward the right. It is just that send window has remained the same. $tp \rightarrow snd\_una$ is updated to the acknowledged sequence at line 1920.

If either we are processing in the FAST mode or we have not acknowledged any new data, some additional checks need to be done before updating the send window. In this case, we check if the ACK segment being processed carries data at line 1925. If so, we update flag *FLAG_DATA* that will be used later to detect a dubious ACK (duplicate ACK) because we don't know if the window is going to be updated or new data are ACKed in this path. Next we would like to check if the send window has changed and whether we need to update it by calling *tcp_ack_update_window()*.

Next, we check if there are any SACK blocks; if so, they need to be processed by calling *tcp_sacktag_write_queue()* at line 1933. The routine does all the necessary calculations to process SACK blocks. We also catch D-SACK in this routine. From the SACK block information we can have a fair estimation of packets that have left the network. Not only this, we can sense the state of the network congestion and guess reordering length using FACK.

Next we set the ECE flag at line 1936, in case the ECE bit is set in the TCP header. This is an indication from the peer that it has sense congestion at one of the intermediate routers. So we should reduce the transmission rate before we congest the network.

If we have nothing unacknowledged (line 1944), we have a pure ACK for the zero-window probe sent by us or which might be generated by the peer when it opened the window. In this case, we handle this situation by calling *tcp_ack_probe()*

net/ipv4/tcp_input.c

```
1896 static int tcp_ack(struct sock *sk, struct sk_buff *skb, int flag)
1897 {
1898     struct tcp_opt *tp = &(sk->tp_pinfo.af_tcp);
1899     u32 prior_snd_una = tp->snd_una;
1900     u32 ack_seq = TCP_SKB_CB(skb)->seq;
1901     u32 ack = TCP_SKB_CB(skb)->ack_seq;
         ....
1908     if (after(ack, tp->snd_nxt))
1909         goto uninteresting_ack;
1910
1911     if (before(ack, prior_snd_una))
1912         goto old_ack;
1913
1914     if (!(flag&FLAG_SLOWPATH) && after(ack, prior_snd_una)) {
         ....
1919         tcp_update_wl(tp, ack, ack_seq);
1920         tp->snd_una = ack;
1921         flag |= FLAG_WIN_UPDATE;
         ....
1924     } else {
1925         if (ack_seq != TCP_SKB_CB(skb)->end_seq)
1926             flag |= FLAG_DATA;
         ""
1930         flag |= tcp_ack_update_window(sk, tp, skb, ack, ack_seq);
1931
1932         if (TCP_SKB_CB(skb)->sacked)
1933             flag |= tcp_sacktag_write_queue(sk, skb, prior_snd_una);
1934
1935         if (TCP_ECN_rcv_ecn_echo(tp, skb->h.th))
1936             flag |= FLAG_ECE;
1937     }
         ....
1943     tp->rcv_tstamp = tcp_time_stamp;
1944     if ((prior_packets = tp->packets_out) == 0)
1945         goto no_queue;
1946
1947     prior_in_flight = tcp_packets_in_flight(tp);
         ....
1950     flag |= tcp_clean_rtx_queue(sk);
1951
1952     if (tcp_ack_is_dubious(tp, flag)) {
1953         /* Advanve CWND, if state allows this. */
1954         if ((flag&FLAG_DATA_ACKED) && prior_in_flight >= tp->snd_cwnd &&
1955             tcp_may_raise_cwnd(tp, flag))
1956             tcp_cong_avoid(tp);
1957         tcp_fastretrans_alert(sk, prior_snd_una, prior_packets, flag);
1958     } else {
1959         if ((flag&FLAG_DATA_ACKED) && prior_in_flight >= tp->snd_cwnd)
1960             tcp_cong_avoid(tp);
1961     }
1962
1963     if ((flag & FLAG_FORWARD_PROGRESS) || !(flag&FLAG_NOT_DUP))
1964         dst_confirm(sk->dst_cache);
1965
1966     return 1;
1967
1968 no_queue:
1969     tp->probes_out = 0;
         ....
1975     if (tp->send_head)
1976         tcp_ack_probe(sk);
1977     return 1;
1978
1979 old_ack:
1980     if (TCP_SKB_CB(skb)->sacked)
1981         tcp_sacktag_write_queue(sk, skb, prior_snd_una);
1982
1983 uninteresting_ack:
1984     SOCK_DEBUG(sk, "Ack %u out of %u:%u\n", ack, tp->snd_una, tp->snd_nxt);
1985     return 0;
1986 }
```

cs 11.26. *tcp_ack().*

at line 1975. The routine checks if the enough window is opened to transmit a segment; if so, we clear off the zero-window probe timer. Otherwise we reset the zero-window probe timer with timeout exponentially backed off. When we return to *tcp_rcv_established()*, a subsequent call to *tcp_data_snd_check()* will start transmitting the segments in case enough window is opened and will also wake up the socket if it is blocking.

Until this point, we have processed SACK, recorded the send window, and updated the last acknowledged byte. We now need to clean up the retransmit queue by removing acknowledged segments from the queue. We do this by calling *tcp_clean_rtx_queue()* at line 1950. This routine processes tags on the segments being acknowledged and so adjusts counters that keep account of retransmitted segments, sacked-out segments, lost segments, and finally unacknowledged segments. Since the routine modifies an unacknowledged segment counter, we need to record a number of segments on the flight prior to arrival of this segment by calling *tcp_packets_in_flight()* at line 1947. This is required to decide if we have acknowledged new data to detect partial ACK in case we are operating in the congestion state. Prior packets in flight is also required to calculate the next congestion window.

Next we check for any congestion indications at line 1952. We check if the ACK is dubious by calling *tcp_ack_is_dubious()*. This routine checks if we are about to enter the congestion state or are already in the congestion state. The next course of action will depend on the congestion state of the connection. In case ACK is not dubious, things are very straightforward and we need not take any special care and should look at the possibility of incrementing the send congestion window if we have ACKed new data. So, we have two checks at line 1959:

1. Is new data acknowledged?
2. Have we been utilizing the network at its full capacity?

If the number of segments transmitted is equal to the congestion window, the network is being utilized at its full capacity. We check this by comparing packets in flight prior (calculated at line 1947) to the segment being processed against the current send congestion window (*tp→snd_cwnd*). In case we get a cumulative ACK for more than one data segment transmitted, the rate of increment of the send congestion window will not be as fast as the increment in case each data segment is ACKed separately. Cumulative ACK for multiple segments indicates that more data segments have left the network. For the same congestion window we can send out more data, and the case looks similar to the network bandwidth being underutilized because ACKs are not generated at the same rate at which data are being transmitted.

If both the conditions are TRUE, we call *tcp_cong_avoid()* to check if we can increment the congestion window further, depending on whether we are doing *slow-start* or *congestion avoidance*.

In case we are dubious (see Section 11.4.2), we need to make one additional check along with the two tests performed for the nondubious case before we can try increasing the congestion window. We call *tcp_may_raise_cwnd()* to check the following conditions: (cs 11.27):

1. We may not have the ECE flag set in the TCP header of the ACKing segment. If it is already set, our congestion window should be below the slow-start threshold (*tp→snd_ssthresh*) at line 1845.

```
include/net/tcp.h

1843 static __inline__ int tcp_may_raise_cwnd(struct tcp_opt *tp, int flag)
1844 {
1845      return (!(flag & FLAG_ECE) || tp->snd_cwnd < tp->snd_ssthresh) &&
1846          !((1<<tp->ca_state)&(TCPF_CA_Recovery|TCPF_CA_CWR));
1847 }
```

cs 11.27. *tcp_may_raise_cwnd().*

```
include/net/tcp.h

1069 static __inline__ unsigned int tcp_packets_in_flight(struct tcp_opt *tp)
1070 {
1071      return tp->packets_out - tp->left_out + tp->retrans_out;
1072 }
```

cs 11.28. *tcp_packets_in_flight().*

2. We should not be in either the recovery (*TCP_CA_Recovery*) or the congestion window reduction state (*TCP_CA_CWR*).

In case the ECE flag is set, we are advised to slow down transmission rate. If we are in CWR state, we are once again advised not to increase the rate of data transmission because there may local congestion at the device driver level or we might have gotten the ECE flag set in the TCP header. If we are doing fast recovery (TCP_CA_Recovery), priority should be given to lost segments first and then we should try to transmit new segments. The current congestion window is assumed to have saturated the network in the fast recovery state, so we try to be conservative about congestion window.

If the ACK is dubious, we also need to do congestion state congestion processing by calling *tcp_fastretrans_alert()*. As already discussed, we may have sensed congestion or may be in the congestion state, and both these situations are handled in *tcp_fastretrans_alert()*. We handle fast-transmissions fast-recovery, partial ACK, reneging of SACK, and so on, in this routine. For more details, see Section 12.1.

11.4.1 *tcp_packets_in_flight()*

This routine gives us a fair estimation of the packets that are still in flight at any point of time (cs 11.28). By packets in flight, we mean that the segments have not left the network. How do we know this? We know the number of segments that are transmitted and are not yet acknowledged as *tp→packets_out*. Then we know the number of segments that have reached the other end but not in order with the help of SACK blocks as *tp→sacked_out*. If a loss is sensed, we have a rough estimate of lost segments as *tp→lost_out*. If there are no sudden spikes in RTT or network reordering doesn't increase abruptly, our loss estimation is correct. The number of segments that have left the network are the ones that are either SACKed or considered LOST. Then we have retransmitted segments as *tp→retrans_out*. When a segment is considered lost, we don't decrement *tp→packets_out* for the lost segment but instead compensate for lost segment by incrementing the lost count *tp→lost_out*. So, we balance the number of segments in flight. Once we retransmit this segment,

```
net/ipv4/tcp_input.c

1837 static __inline__ int tcp_ack_is_dubious(struct tcp_opt *tp, int flag)
1838 {
1839     return (!(flag & FLAG_NOT_DUP) || (flag & FLAG_CA_ALERT) ||
1840         tp->ca_state != TCP_CA_Open);
1841 }
```

cs 11.29. tcp_ack_is_dubious().

```
net/ipv4/tcp_input.c

100 #define FLAG_ACKED      (FLAG_DATA_ACKED|FLAG_SYN_ACKED)
101 #define FLAG_NOT_DUP    (FLAG_DATA|FLAG_WIN_UPDATE|FLAG_ACKED)
102 #define FLAG_CA_ALERT   (FLAG_DATA_SACKED|FLAG_ECE)
```

cs 11.30. Incoming ACK flags.

one extra segment is pumped in the network which is consuming network resources. That is why we consider *tp→retrans_out* while calculating packets in flight.

11.4.2 *tcp_ack_is_dubious()*

Here we have three checks to confirm that either we are already in the congestion state or have sensed congestion: (cs 11.29):

1. *FLAG_NOT_DUP* flag set by the current ACK. This indicates if we have a duplicate ACK.
2. *FLAG_CA_ALERT* flag set by the current ACK. This indicates if we need to be at alert because we have sensed congestion.
3. TCP state at present should not be set to open (TCP_CA_Open). We are already in one of the congestion states.

FLAG_NOT_DUP is defined as the combination of three flags: (cs 11.30):

1. FLAG_DATA
2. FLAG_WIN_UPDATE
3. FLAG_ACKED = *FLAG_DATA_ACKED|FLAG_SYN_ACKED*

If any of the above flags is set, we need to check for other conditions that we will discuss later. If none of the above is set, we have gotten a duplicate ACK. The reasons for this are as follows:

1. *FLAG_DATA* is set if we have gotten DATA. Even though we did not acknowledge any new data, this should not be considered as duplicate ACK with *FLAG_DATA* set. A simple example is to consider data flowing only in one direction where we are the receiver. In this case we will always get the same ACK sequence number because we are not sending anything. We can't consider all the ACKs as duplicate.

2. *FLAG_WIN_UPDATE* is set if either peer's receive window has either changed or it has acknowledged new data. The duplicate ACK we are discussing is the one that is generated once an out-of-sequence segment has been receive by the peer. Since this out-of-sequence segment doesn't shift the left edge of the window toward the right, it won't change its receive window. If the segment doesn't acknowledge new data and doesn't carry any new data but it changes the send window, it can be considered as window update from the peer and not as duplicate ACK.

3. *FLAG_ACKED* is set if new data are ACKed or we got SYN segment. In both the cases, this can't be considered as duplicate ACK.

FLAG_CA_ALERT has two parts, *FLAG_DATA_SACKED* and *FLAG_ECE*. If any of these flags are set, we need to take action because we have sensed congestion.

FLAG_DATA_SACKED is set when we get SACK blocks. This is an indication that segments have reached the receiver out-of-order. This may be because of reordering of segments or because some segment is lost. We need to be watchful here.

FLAG_ECE is set when we get the ECE flag set in the TCP header. The other end received an indication from one of the intermediate routers about the congestion state at that router. The router may be loaded heavily and about to drop packets. In this situation it sets the EC flag in the IP header of the packet that is directed for the receiver. The receiver turns the ECE flag in the TCP header to indicate the sender of the congestion state. We need to take action to reduce the transmission rate in such condition.

If none of the above-mentioned conditions satisfy, we consider ACK as dubious only if we are already in a congestion state; that is, TCP state is anything other than *TCP_CA_Open*.

11.4.3 *tcp_cong_avoid()*

This routine implements a congestion control algorithm during slow start and fast retransmission. In Section 10.2.3 (explaining slow start) and Section 12.5.5 (explaining fast retransmission), we can see that whenever we sense congestion, we adjust $tp \rightarrow snd\_ssthresh$ and $tp \rightarrow snd\_cwnd$ as explained by Jacobson (SIGCOM 88). $tp \rightarrow snd\_ssthresh$ is slow-start threshold. Once the send congestion window ($tp \rightarrow snd\_cwnd$) exceeds this value, we enter into the recovery state where the rate of increment of the congestion window is a function of RTT and not number of ACKs returned, whereas before the congestion window exceeds the slow-start threshold, we are into slow-start algorithm where congestion window increases exponentially with RTT (increments by 1 with reception of each ACK). In ideal conditions, calculation shows that when we are operating at full network capacity, we can send out segments equal to the congestion window without waiting for ACK for any of these segments. In such case, the rate at which segments are ACKed per RTT is equal to the congestion window. Once we have recovered from the congestion state, we call $tcp\_undo\_cwr()$ where we set ssthresh to the value prior to entering the congestion state.

The very first condition that we check here is if we are in the slow-start phase (line 1701). If so, we increment the congestion window by 1 only if the send congestion window clamp ($tp \rightarrow snd\_cwnd\_clamp$) is not exceeded. Initially, ssthresh is set

```
net/ipv4/tcp_input.c

1699 static __inline__ void tcp_cong_avoid(struct tcp_opt *tp)
1700 {
1701      if (tp->snd_cwnd <= tp->snd_ssthresh) {
1702          /* In "safe" area, increase. */
1703          if (tp->snd_cwnd < tp->snd_cwnd_clamp)
1704              tp->snd_cwnd++;
1705      } else {
             ....
1709          if (tp->snd_cwnd_cnt >= tp->snd_cwnd) {
1710              if (tp->snd_cwnd < tp->snd_cwnd_clamp)
1711                  tp->snd_cwnd++;
1712              tp->snd_cwnd_cnt=0;
1713          } else
1714              tp->snd_cwnd_cnt++;
1715      }
1716      tp->snd_cwnd_stamp = tcp_time_stamp;
1717 }
```

cs 11.31. *tcp_cong_avoid().*

to a very high value, so the congestion window keeps increasing until we experience congestion (loss of segments or duplicate ACKs). At this point we recalculate ssthresh to half of the congestion window or 2, whichever is higher (see Section 10.2.3). If both conditions are TRUE, we increment the congestion window by 1 (line 1704, cs 11.31).

In case we have entered the recovery state, which means that the send congestion window has exceeded the slow-start threshold (lines 1706–1715), Linux takes the path of the incrementing congestion window per '*current congestion window*'— that is, $tp \rightarrow snd\_cwnd$, the number of ACKs received. This is because the congestion window is assumed to be saturating the network at any given point of time by making full utilization of the available network bandwidth under a given network congestion state. Each time we receive an ACK, we do the following:

1. We check if the counter ($tp \rightarrow snd\_cwnd\_cnt$) is equal to the current congestion window.
2. If 1 is FALSE, we increment the the congestion window counter ($tp \rightarrow snd\_cwnd\_cnt$) (line 1714).
3. Otherwise we are ready to increment the congestion window only if we are not exceeding the cwnd clamp (line 1710). If we pass this post, increment the congestion window and reset the congestion window counter (line 1712).

11.4.4   *tcp_ack_update_window()*

We first check if the window can be updated by calling *tcp_may_update_window()*. If the window is allowed to be updated, we set the flag *FLAG_WIN_UPDATE* at line 1872 (cs 11.32). Since the window is being updated, we record the sequence number of the segment in $tp \rightarrow snd\_wl1$ by calling *tcp_update_wl()*. If the new window advertised is more than the recorded send window, we sync up the send window at line 1876. In this case, we also check if we need to switch to FAST path by calling *tcp_fast_path_check()* (see Section 11.1.3 for details on PATH). We do it here because the window has changed and if are already in FAST path, prediction flag

```
net/ipv4/tcp_input.c

1865 static int tcp_ack_update_window(struct sock *sk, struct tcp_opt *tp,
1866                        struct sk_buff *skb, u32 ack, u32 ack_seq)
1867 {
1868     int flag = 0;
1869     u32 nwin = ntohs(skb->h.th->window) << tp->snd_wscale;
1870
1871     if (tcp_may_update_window(tp, ack, ack_seq, nwin)) {
1872         flag |= FLAG_WIN_UPDATE;
1873         tcp_update_wl(tp, ack, ack_seq);
1874
1875         if (tp->snd_wnd != nwin) {
1876             tp->snd_wnd = nwin;
                 ....
1881             tcp_fast_path_check(sk, tp);
1882
1883             if (nwin > tp->max_window) {
1884                 tp->max_window = nwin;
1885                 tcp_sync_mss(sk, tp->pmtu_cookie);
1886             }
1887         }
1888     }
1889
1890     tp->snd_una = ack;
1891
1892     return flag;
1893 }
```

cs 11.32. tcp_ack_update_window().

```
net/ipv4/tcp_input.c

1852 static __inline__ int
1853 tcp_may_update_window(struct tcp_opt *tp, u32 ack, u32 ack_seq, u32 nwin)
1854 {
1855     return (after(ack, tp->snd_una) ||
1856         after(ack_seq, tp->snd_wl1) ||
1857         (ack_seq == tp->snd_wl1 && nwin > tp->snd_wnd));
1858 }
```

cs 11.33. tcp_may_update_window().

needs to be initialized as it takes the window into account. If the new window advertised is more than the largest window seen so far, we sync up *tp→max_window*. Finally, the acknowledged sequence number is synced up at line 1890.

11.4.5 *tcp_may_update_window()*

We can update the window under the following conditions (RFC 793, p. 72):

1. If new data are acknowledged, line 1855 (cs 11.33).
2. If the first condition fails, the sequence number of the segment should be higher than the sequence number last recorded (*tp→snd_wl1*) when the window was updated, line 1856. The reason for this check is that it gives an indication of the latest scenario at the other end as it carries new data with respect to the segment that updated the window last.

3. If both condition fail, we check if the sequence number of the segment is same as *tp→snd_wl1*, but the window advertised is more than the last recorded send window (*tp→snd_wnd*), line 1857. This condition may arise because the peer has opened the window.

We don't update the window in the case where the sequence is less than the *tp→snd_wl1* because the segment may have arrived out-of-order and have an incorrect window. This segment was transmitted prior to the one that has updated the window last, so we discard the window update in this case.

11.4.6 *tcp_clean_rtx_queue()*

The routine is called while we are processing incoming ACK (cs 11.34). The routine removes the acknowledged segment from the retransmit queue. If the segment is tagged as SACKED, retransmitted, or lost, the routine updates counters specific to SACKed-out segments, lost segments, and retransmitted segments associated with the segment.

In this routine we traverse through each segment in the write queue until we find a segment beyond *tp→snd_una* (line 1749). *tp→snd_una* is already updated to the next unacknowledged byte before we are called. Next we need to check if data were ACKed or if it was a SYN segment that was ACKed. Since we have ACKed some data, we are here. If it is a SYN segment that is ACKed, it is ok since SYN carries one byte. Otherwise we have ACKed data. In both the cases we set FLAG. The next step is to process the tag on the segment.

If the segment is tagged, first we check if the segment was ever retransmitted. If so, we set the FLAG_RETRANS_DATA_ACKED flag; and at the same time if the segment is tagged as retransmitted, *tp→retrans_out* is decremented by 1 (lines 1767–1770). Otherwise if the segment was never retransmitted and RTT is not yet recorded (line 1772), we calculate RTT based on the current timestamp and the time recorded when the segment was transmitted. We don't calculate RTT for retransmitted segment (line 1773). If the segment was SACKed out, we need to decrement the SACK counter (line 1775). If the segment is marked lost, the lost counter is decremented by 1. If this segment is marked to contain an urgent pointer, we check if the urgent mode is set (see Section 11.7.1). If set, we check if the segment covers the urgent pointer (lines 1779–1780). If both are true, an urgent byte is ACKed and we unset the urgent mode.

Otherwise the segment that is ACKed was not tagged (neither retransmitted nor SACKed, and neither was marked lost) and we have not yet calculated RTT, and we can record RTT (line 1784). Next we check if the segments are FACKed out, and we decrement the FACKed segments by 1 (line 1786). Decrement a number of transmitted packets by 1. Remove the ACKed segment from the retransmit queue by calling (line 1788).

The next step is to estimate RTO based on either TCP timestamp option or the new rtt calculated above. This is done by calling *tcp_ack_update_rtt()*. We have three fields, which are used to calculate RTO:

1. *tp→srtt* smoothened RTT. On reception of RTT value each time, we calculate the error based on the srtt and the new value. It is calculated as 7/8(srtt) + 1/8 (new value).

2. *tp→mdev*. This is the mean deviation in calculation of RTT, and once again it is calculated as 3/4 (mdev) + 1/4 of new deviation.

3. *tp→rttvar* is called a variant in the rtt calculation.

Finally, RTO is calculated as

$$1/8 \text{ (smoothened RTT)} + \text{variance RTT}$$

```
net/ipv4/tcp_input.c

1733 static int tcp_clean_rtx_queue(struct sock *sk)
1734 {
          ....
1740
1741     while((skb=skb_peek(&sk->write_queue)) && (skb != tp->send_head)) {
1742         struct tcp_skb_cb *scb = TCP_SKB_CB(skb);
1743         __u8 sacked = scb->sacked;
             ....
1749         if (after(scb->end_seq, tp->snd_una))
1750             break;
             ....
1759         if(!(scb->flags & TCPCB_FLAG_SYN)) {
1760             acked |= FLAG_DATA_ACKED;
1761         } else {
1762             acked |= FLAG_SYN_ACKED;
1763             tp->retrans_stamp = 0;
1764         }
1765
1766         if (sacked) {
1767             if(sacked & TCPCB_RETRANS) {
1768                 if(sacked & TCPCB_SACKED_RETRANS)
1769                     tp->retrans_out--;
1770                 acked |= FLAG_RETRANS_DATA_ACKED;
1771                 seq_rtt = -1;
1772             } else if (seq_rtt < 0)
1773                 seq_rtt = now - scb->when;
1774             if(sacked & TCPCB_SACKED_ACKED)
1775                 tp->sacked_out--;
1776             if(sacked & TCPCB_LOST)
1777                 tp->lost_out--;
1778             if(sacked & TCPCB_URG) {
1779                 if (tp->urg_mode &&
1780                     !before(scb->end_seq, tp->snd_up))
1781                     tp->urg_mode = 0;
1782             }
1783         } else if (seq_rtt < 0)
1784             seq_rtt = now - scb->when;
1785         if(tp->fackets_out)
1786             tp->fackets_out--;
1787         tp->packets_out--;
1788         __skb_unlink(skb, skb->list);
1789         tcp_free_skb(sk, skb);
1790     }
1791
1792     if (acked&FLAG_ACKED) {
1793         tcp_ack_update_rtt(tp, acked, seq_rtt);
1794         tcp_ack_packets_out(sk, tp);
1795     }
             ...
1816     return acked;
1817 }
```

cs 11.34. *tcp_clean_rtx_queue()*.

```
net/ipv4/tcp_input.c

1723 static __inline__ void tcp_ack_packets_out(struct sock *sk, struct tcp_opt *tp)
1724 {
1725      if (tp->packets_out==0) {
1726           tcp_clear_xmit_timer(sk, TCP_TIME_RETRANS);
1727      } else {
1728           tcp_reset_xmit_timer(sk, TCP_TIME_RETRANS, tp->rto);
1729      }
1730 }
```

cs 11.35. *tcp_ack_packets_out()*.

Finally, we need to adjust the retransmit timer depending on whether we still have unacknowledged packets (*tp→packets_out* >0) by calling *tcp_ack_packets_out()*. If we have acked all the data, the retransmit timer should be stopped (line 1726, cs 11.35). Otherwise we should set the retransmit timer to the current value of RTO for the next segment to be ACKed (line 1728).

We return the flags set in the routine that will be used later to determine the course of action.

11.5 PROCESSING OF SACK BLOCKS

When we receive an ACK, we need to process SACK blocks if the TCP sack option is enabled and we have received SACK blocks. *TCP_SKB_CB(skb)→sacked* is initialized to offset corresponding to the start of the SACK option in the TCP header for the segment received. This is done while processing optional fields in the TCP header in *tcp_rcv_established()* by a call to *tcp_fast_parse_options()*. Let's see how SACK blocks received are processed by calling *tcp_sacktag_write_queue()* from *tcp_ack()*.

11.5.1 *tcp_sacktag_write_queue()* (see cs 11.36 to cs 11.41 unless mentioned)

We get access to SACK information as shown in Fig. 11.4. Before we are called from *tcp_ack()*, we have already updated the unacknowledged byte field in the TCP state machine (*tp→snd_una*). But we have stored the unacknowledged byte field to be used further to find out duplicate ACKs and ACKs for very old segments.

0 = SACK option.
1 = total length of the SACK optional field.

Our consideration here is that the segments which are still in the flight may be reordered. So, we store *tp→packets_out* for further use. If none of the segments were SACKed out prior to arrival of this segment, we initialize FORWARD ACKed (*tp→fackets_out*) segment count to 0 at line 773. The reason is that forward ACKed segments are calculated based on the latest SACK information (Mathis, 1996). This will give the latest picture of the network congestion at any given point of time.

In the Fig. 11.5, we have four SACKed segments, but the number of FACKed segments is 12. We process all the SACK blocks associated with the arrived ACK.

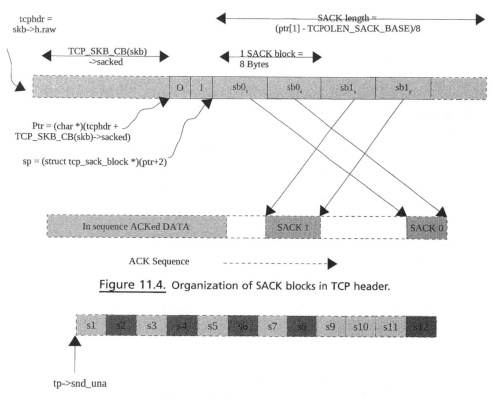

Figure 11.4. Organization of SACK blocks in TCP header.

Figure 11.5. SACKed segments.

There may be D-SACK blocks or SACK blocks which may have SACKed new data. We need to update the state of each individual segment in the retransmit queue. We may have a new SACK block that has selectively ACKed a never retransmitted segment or a retransmitted segment or lost segment. The SACK block may have filled the GAP that causes the right edge of the window to move toward the right. We may end up modifying FACK information in the TCP state machine. We may sense reordering of segments in case we get a SACK block that fills up a never retransmitted old hole. And we update reordering information here. D-SACK is also an indication of segment reordering. D-SACK is generated when the receiver receives a segment that is partly or completely received as out-of-order segment and resides in out-of-order queue. Hole is created in sending TCP sequence space when we get SACK block as a result of packet re-ordering or loss of segments.

The very first thing that we do here is to check if we got D-SACK (duplicate SACK). The information about D-SACK is stored in the first block SACK block. RFC 2883 says that D-SACK is generated in the case where the receiver receives the following:

1. A segment that advances the right edge of the window toward the right such that it covers the hole and spans across the segment in the out-of-order queue as shown in Fig. 11.6. $sb0_s < tp \rightarrow snd\_una$ (or sequence number of the ACKing segment), line 787 (cs 11.36).
2. A segment that may not advance the right edge of the window, but the new segment is completely covered by the existing segment in the out-of-order segment and the new segment may also span across multiple segments in the

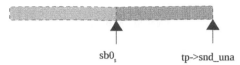

sb0$_s$ tp->snd_una

Figure 11.6. SACKed segments covered by ACK.

---

net/ipv4/tcp_input.c

```
759 static int
760 tcp_sacktag_write_queue(struct sock *sk, struct sk_buff *ack_skb, u32 prior_snd_una)
761 {
762     struct tcp_opt *tp = &(sk->tp_pinfo.af_tcp);
763     unsigned char *ptr = ack_skb->h.raw + TCP_SKB_CB(ack_skb)->sacked;
764     struct tcp_sack_block *sp = (struct tcp_sack_block *)(ptr+2);
765     int num_sacks = (ptr[1] - TCPOLEN_SACK_BASE)>>3;
766     int reord = tp->packets_out;
767     int prior_fackets;
768     u32 lost_retrans = 0;
769     int flag = 0;
770     int i;
771
772     if (!tp->sacked_out)
773         tp->fackets_out = 0;
774     prior_fackets = tp->fackets_out;
775
776     for (i=0; i<num_sacks; i++, sp++) {
777         struct sk_buff *skb;
778         __u32 start_seq = ntohl(sp->start_seq);
779         __u32 end_seq = ntohl(sp->end_seq);
780         int fack_count = 0;
781         int dup_sack = 0;
            ....
784         if (i == 0) {
785             u32 ack = TCP_SKB_CB(ack_skb)->ack_seq;
786
787             if (before(start_seq, ack)) {
788                 dup_sack = 1;
789                 tp->sack_ok |= 4;
790                 NET_INC_STATS_BH(TCPDSACKRecv);
791             } else if (num_sacks > 1 &&
792                 !after(end_seq, ntohl(sp[1].end_seq)) &&
793                 !before(start_seq, ntohl(sp[1].start_seq))) {
794                 dup_sack = 1;
795                 tp->sack_ok |= 4;
796                 NET_INC_STATS_BH(TCPDSACKOfoRecv);
797             }
            ....
801             if (dup_sack &&
802                 !after(end_seq, prior_snd_una) &&
803                 after(end_seq, tp->undo_marker))
804                 tp->undo_retrans--;
            ....
810             if (before(ack, prior_snd_una-tp->max_window))
811                 return 0;
812         }
```

cs 11.36. *tcp_sacktag_write_queue().*

Figure 11.7. New SACK block covered by already SACKed segments.

out-of-order queue as shown in Fig. 11.7 (see Section 11.8). $sb0_s >= sb1_s$ && $sb0_e <= sb1_e$ (lines 791–793).

In both of the above cases, we enable D-SACK option for the TCP connection ($tp \rightarrow sack\_ok$) and we set a duplicate SACK flag.

Next we check if the D-SACK is generated for the data that are already ACKed because the retransmitted segment reached before the original segment was ACKed or vice versa. In this case the end sequence of the SACK block should be within the ACKed sequence prior to arrival of this segment, and the end sequence should also be after the $tp \rightarrow undo\_marker$ (which is set to $tp \rightarrow snd\_una$ when we enter the recovery phase and *retransmit* data, lines 801–803). We will decrement $tp \rightarrow undo\_retrans$ by 1 in such a case because D-SACK is generated because of retransmission of the segment after we entered the recovery/loss state. In all, it means that D-SACK is generated because of retransmission of a segment that was considered lost when we entered the recovery phase. But the segment reached the receiver later because of reordering. $tp \rightarrow undo\_retrans$ keeps account of number of retransmitted segments (see Section 10.2.4). We never know when the duplicate segment reaches the receiver.

Finally we check if we got ACK for too old data (line 810); that is, ACK acknowledges one window of old data. This ACK segment might have got stuck in the network for sometime before it reached before we got ACK for the latest data that are received in sequence. In this case we discard the SACK because the SACK information may be too old to consider and return.

$tp \rightarrow undo\_retrans$ is also related to $tp \rightarrow undo\_marker$ in the way that whenever D-SACK is generated, we check if the end of the SACK is after $tp \rightarrow undo\_marker$. If so, D-SACK is because of the retransmitted segment that was assumed lost wherein the original segment arrived late at the receiving end. When DSACK is received, we need to decrement the $tp \rightarrow undo\_retrans$ if the end sequence of the SACK block is not higher than the ACK sequence prior to the arrival of the segment being processed and at the same time higher than $tp \rightarrow undo\_marker$, which means that D-SACK is generated because of the retransmission due to current congestion state as $tp \rightarrow undo\_marker$ is set once we enter congestion state. $tp \rightarrow undo\_retrans$ helps in detecting false retransmits in recovery/loss state. Isis also helpful in detecting spurious RTO.

$tp \rightarrow retrans\_out$, on the other hand, takes care of the retransmitted segments marked as lost. This will be helpful in detecting partial ACKing in the congestion state. With the help of these two fields, we can always know what amount of reordering is happening in the network.

We check if we have received SACK for the data that were transmitted ahead of $tp \rightarrow high\_seq$. $tp \rightarrow high\_seq$ is set to the highest sequence number that has been transmitted at that point of time when we enter loss or recovery state. It may happen that the congestion window allows us to transmit more data before we enter the OPEN state. In such a case, we may transmit data with sequence higher than $tp \rightarrow high\_seq$ in recovery state.

```
net/ipv4/tcp_input.c(tcp_sacktag_write_queue() continue....)
814        /* Event "B" in the comment above. */
815        if (after(end_seq, tp->high_seq))
816            flag |= FLAG_DATA_LOST;
817
818        for_retrans_queue(skb, sk, tp) {
819            u8 sacked = TCP_SKB_CB(skb)->sacked;
820            int in_sack;
           ....
825            if(!before(TCP_SKB_CB(skb)->seq, end_seq))
826                break;
827
828            fack_count++;
829
830            in_sack = !after(start_seq, TCP_SKB_CB(skb)->seq) &&
831                !before(end_seq, TCP_SKB_CB(skb)->end_seq);
           ....
834            if ((dup_sack && in_sack) &&
835                (sacked & TCPCB_RETRANS) &&
836                after(TCP_SKB_CB(skb)->end_seq, tp->undo_marker))
837                tp->undo_retrans--;
           ....
840            if (!after(TCP_SKB_CB(skb)->end_seq, tp->snd_una)) {
841                if (sacked&TCPCB_RETRANS) {
842                    if ((dup_sack && in_sack) &&
843                        (sacked&TCPCB_SACKED_ACKED))
844                        reord = min(fack_count, reord);
845                } else {
846                    /* If it was in a hole, we detected reordering. */
847                    if (fack_count < prior_fackets &&
848                        !(sacked&TCPCB_SACKED_ACKED))
849                        reord = min(fack_count, reord);
850                }
```

cs 11.37. tcp_sacktag_write_queue().

If we get a SACK that covers *tp→high_seq*, we consider that some data are lost here (line 815, cs 11.37). Otherwise we would have gotten ACK for the entire data transmitted so far, if SACK blocks are generated because segments got reordered in the network instead of getting lost. We set a data loss flag in this case and will check later if we actually lost any data or not. Let's see how the SACK blocks arrived with the TCP segment processed. Here we traverse the entire retransmit queue for each SACK block (loops 818–910). The segments in the retransmit queue may already be tagged. These segments are marked either retransmitted, SACKed, lost, or none of these.

1. If the segment was retransmitted, it is marked as *TCPCB_RETRANS*.
2. If the segment is SACKED, it is marked as *TCPCB_SACKED_ACKED*.
3. If the segment is LOST, it is marked as *TCPCB_LOST*.

The next step will be to find out the segment which is covered by the current SACK block. It may also have happened that the SACK block is generated for the segment that is already ACKed as part of in-sequence data. We will sense reordering for the case where a new SACK block is generated for never retransmitted data or a D-SACK block is generated. Finally we tag the segments in the retransmit queue according to the new events. Components of a TCP state machine related to reordering of segments, FACKed out segments, and SACKed out segments are also modified accordingly.

We will examine each segment in the out-of-order queue for every SACK block in the following way:

The segments in the retransmit queue are arranged in order of increasing start sequence number. So, if we find that the end sequence of the SACK block is below the start sequence of the segment, we just skip through this SACK block and move on to the next SACK block (line 825). If not so, the SACK block is covered by at least one of the segments in the retransmit queue. This condition will make us traverse all those segments in the retransmit queue which are within the end sequence of the SACK block.

Each time we iterate through the inner loop for a given SACK block, we increment the FACK count by 1 (line 828). This way we can keep account of the FACKed segments while processing each SACK block. We will retain the FACK count from the SACK block that forwards ACK's highest sequence number.

We check if the SACK block completely covers the segment. If so, we mark the segment as within SACK. One SACK segment may cover more than one segment in the case where more than one contiguous (but not in-sequence) segment reaches the receiver. We will process each segment that is covered by the SACK block one-by-one.

If the current segment is within the SACK block and the SACK block is marked as a duplicate SACK, we check if the segment under consideration is marked as retransmitted (line 835). If all the conditions are true and the end sequence number of the segment is after the undo mark, $tp{\to}undo\_marker$ (line 836). We need to account for the retransmitted segment that caused D-SACK by decrementing $tp{\to}undo\_retrans$. An end sequence of the segment occurring after an undo marker means that the segment was retransmitted after TCP entered loss/recovery state.

Next we check if the current segment is ACKed by the received segment (line 840). If so, we will check if this was result of reordering or not. If the segment is ACKed, we check if the segment was retransmitted (line 841). If so, we check if it is a duplicate SACK; this segment is covered by the SACK (line 842), and the segment is also marked as being SACKed previously. In this case we encountered reordering. We record reordering as a minimum of reorder segments and forward ACKed segments (line 844). Reordering segments is initialized to packets sent out but not yet ACKed ($tp{\to}packets\_out$). Otherwise if the segment was not retransmitted and the segment under consideration was not SACKed, it means that the hole was filled because the segment arrived late out-of-order. If FACK count at this point is less than the FACK recorded earlier, we update the FACK count. In this case, we continue with the next segment in the retransmit queue. Since a segment is ACKed completely, we will remove this from the retransmit queue in $tcp\_clean\_rtx\_queue()$.

We are here because the current segment under examination is not ACKed. The next step is to check if the current segment was retransmitted and probably the retransmission is also lost. At the time of retransmission, in $tcp\_retransmit\_skb()$, we store the sequence number to be transmitted next in $TCP\_SKB\_CB(skb){\to}ack\_seq$. This will help us detect if the retransmissions are lost in case the TCP has entered the RECOVERY state. In case we enter the LOSS state, all those segments

```
net/ipv4/tcp_input.c(tcp_sacktag_write_queue() continue....)

        ....
854     }
855
856     if ((sacked&TCPCB_SACKED_RETRANS) &&
857         after(end_seq, TCP_SKB_CB(skb)->ack_seq) &&
858         (!lost_retrans || after(end_seq, lost_retrans)))
859         lost_retrans = end_seq;
860
861     if (!in_sack)
862         continue;
863
864     if (!(sacked&TCPCB_SACKED_ACKED)) {
865         if (sacked & TCPCB_SACKED_RETRANS) {
            ....
870             if (sacked & TCPCB_LOST) {
871                 TCP_SKB_CB(skb)->sacked &= ~(TCPCB_LOST|TCPCB_SACKED_RETRANS);
872                 tp->lost_out--;
873                 tp->retrans_out--;
874             }
875         } else {
            ....
879             if (!(sacked & TCPCB_RETRANS) &&
880                 fack_count < prior_fackets)
881                 reord = min(fack_count, reord);
882
883             if (sacked & TCPCB_LOST) {
884                 TCP_SKB_CB(skb)->sacked &= ~TCPCB_LOST;
885                 tp->lost_out--;
886             }
887         }
```

cs 11.38. tcp_sacktag_write_queue().

which are not yet SACKed are marked as lost in *tcp_enter_loss()* but we are not sure of LOST segments in the case of the RECOVERY state.

If the SACK block ends after the highest sequence number to be transmitted next was marked at the time when the segment was retransmitted, it means that some data were pushed ahead of $tp{\rightarrow}snd\_nxt$ and are also SACKed. If this is the case, we are alarmed of this retransmission being lost. We just mark the end sequence of the SACK block here, and later we may need to check which segments need to be marked as lost based on the marked sequence number (line 859, cs 11.38). At this point we need to check if the segment being examined is covered by the SACK block (line 830). If segment is not covered by the SACK block, we continue with the next segment (line 861). Otherwise we will process the SACK further.

Now there are two possibilities: Either the segment under examination is already SACKed or not. If the segment is already SACKed, we check if the current block is a duplicate SACK; and if the segment that is covered by the duplicate SACK is marked retransmitted, we update reordering based on segments FACKed so far for this SACK block (lines 896–897, cs 11.39). Otherwise the segment being examined is SACKed. If this segment was retransmitted, we update loss and retransmit counts only if the segment is already marked as lost. We also update the segment TAG by clearing retransmit and loss flags in this case. The reason for doing this is that if the segment is not marked lost, we may have retransmission in the flight for which we may get D-SACK later when we decrement $tp{\rightarrow}retrans\_out$ by 1 at line 908.

```
net/ipv4/tcp_input.c(tcp_sacktag_write_queue() continue....)

888
889            TCP_SKB_CB(skb)->sacked |= TCPCB_SACKED_ACKED;
890            flag |= FLAG_DATA_SACKED;
891            tp->sacked_out++;
892
893            if (fack_count > tp->fackets_out)
894               tp->fackets_out = fack_count;
895        } else {
896           if (dup_sack && (sacked&TCPCB_RETRANS))
897              reord = min(fack_count, reord);
898        }
           ....
905        if (dup_sack &&
906           (TCP_SKB_CB(skb)->sacked&TCPCB_SACKED_RETRANS)) {
907           TCP_SKB_CB(skb)->sacked &= ~TCPCB_SACKED_RETRANS;
908           tp->retrans_out--;
909        }
910    }
911  }
```

cs 11.39. tcp_sacktag_write_queue().

Otherwise we check if the segment was never retransmitted (line 897). If so, it is time to update reordering only if the FACK count for this segment is less than the number of segments forward ACKed prior to arrival of the ACK segment. The condition at line 880 is probably because we try to check here that the current segment is lower in order (fack_count) than the previously highest-order SACKed segment ($tp \rightarrow facked\_out$). If the new SACKed segment is marked lost, we clear the lost flag for the segment and also adjust the counter for lost segments (lines 883–885). We need to TAG the new SACKed segment as SACKed (line 889) and increment the counter that is specific to SACKed out segments by 1 (line 891). If the new segment FACKs a higher number of segments than recorded previously, we update the FACKed segments (line 893–894).

Next we check if the SACK block under consideration is D-SACK; if the segment covered by this block was retransmitted ($TCPCB\_SACKED\_RETRANS$ flag is set), we clear the retransmit tag and decrement the retransmit counter by 1.

Reordering length is the number of segments between the segments SACKed/ACKed with the highest sequence number ($tp \rightarrow facked\_out$) and the lowest sequence number (reord). That is why we are marking the minimum of the fack_count and previously recorded reorder. Finally, when we update reordering by calling $tcp\_update\_reordering()$, we just pass FACKed-out segments ($tp \rightarrow facked\_out$) – reord + 1, where 'reord' is calculated as segment lowest in the sequential order SACKed/ACKed so far which is recorded whenever we receive D-SACK or receive SACK for the hole which was never retransmitted.

11.6 REORDERING LENGTH

The first SACK arrives and SACK's seventh segment is in the retransmit queue; FACK should be set to the segment SACKed. $tp \rightarrow fackets\_out$ will be set to 7 as

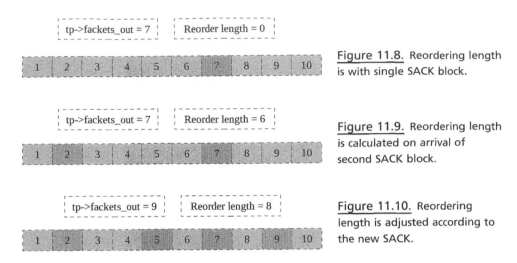

Figure 11.8. Reordering length is with single SACK block.

Figure 11.9. Reordering length is calculated on arrival of second SACK block.

Figure 11.10. Reordering length is adjusted according to the new SACK.

shown in Fig. 11.8. We can't detect reordering at this stage until we receive another SACK block or any D-SACK block.

The second SACK block arrives and SACK's second segment that is already in the retransmit queue. $tp \rightarrow fackets\_out$ is still set to 7. But now we have knowledge of reordering taking place in the network. Segments 2 and 7 are reordered and all other segments in between are also reordered in the network. So, reorder length in this case becomes 6 as shown in Fig. 11.9.

The third SACK block arrives SACKing segment 9 in the retransmit queue. Since the new segment SACKed is beyond the last FACKed segment, it means that this segment has arrived in order with respect to segments 6 and 7. This SACK indicates that the segment high in order so far has reached the receiver, which means that the FACKed segment should be updated to the new SACKed segment. $tp \rightarrow fackets\_out$ is set to 9, whereas reorder length updated as the new segment arrives as 8.

The next step is to spot those retransmitted segments in the retransmit queue which should be assumed lost. In the case where we are in the recovery state and we have a SACK block that covers the sequence number to be transmitted next ($tp \rightarrow snd\_nxt$) when the segment was retransmitted, the segment should be considered lost if not SACKed and not already marked lost. We mark such an event while processing the SACK block at line 859. The reason for this is that we may transmit the segment beyond the marked high sequence ($tp \rightarrow high\_seq$) when we enter the recovery stage if the congestion window allows. We may have entered the recovery state because of excessive reordering. If the SACK block is received covering a high sequence, it is assumed that the holes are lost. This is illustrated in Fig. 11.11a–d.

In this phase, we traverse through all the segments in the retransmit queue until (line 924, cs 11.40) we get a segment whose start sequence is beyond the lost retransmit mark (marked at line 859). We won't consider those segments (line 926) which have been just ACKed (will be removed from the queue in the next step). We will consider only those segments that are marked as retransmitted (line 927) because we want to check here if the retransmissions are lost. The very first thing we check here is that is the lost-retransmit mark is beyond the highest sequence mark recorded at the time of segment retransmission. If not so, we are not an eligible candidate to be assumed as lost. Otherwise we proceed further only in two cases.

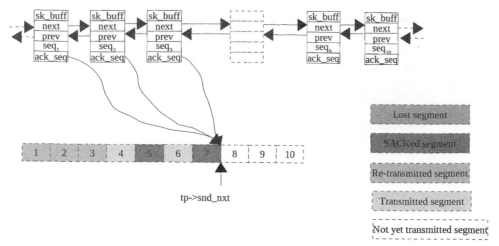

Figure 11.11a. Tracking lost retransmits.

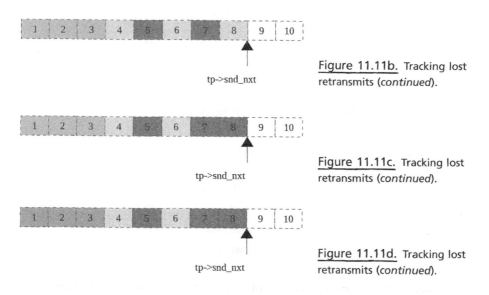

Figure 11.11b. Tracking lost retransmits (*continued*).

Figure 11.11c. Tracking lost retransmits (*continued*).

Figure 11.11d. Tracking lost retransmits (*continued*).

1. The FACK is enabled for the connection (line 929).
2. The lost retransmit mark is beyond the reordering limits for this segment, which essentially means that the SACKed block covers the segment that is beyond tolerant estimated reordering (*tp→reordering*) with respect to the highest sequence mark for the segment. We can't consider so much reordering, and the segment should be considered lost in case it not already SACKed (line 930). Segments 1, 2, and 3 are retransmitted, and they record the highest sequence to be transmitted at the time of transmission.

Segment's 1, 2, and 3 are retransmitted and segment 8 is transmitted (forward transmission). We get the SACK block for segment 8. In the case of FACK enabled, all those segments which are not marked LOST or are not SACKed and are retransmitted are marked LOST (i.e., segments 1, 2, and 3). For both cases, we clear the retransmit flag for this segment (line 931) and decrement the retransmit counter

```
net/ipv4/tcp_input.c(tcp_sacktag_write_queue() continue....)

     ....
919   if (lost_retrans && tp->ca_state == TCP_CA_Recovery) {
920      struct sk_buff *skb;
921
922      for_retrans_queue(skb, sk, tp) {
923         if (after(TCP_SKB_CB(skb)->seq, lost_retrans))
924            break;
925         if (!after(TCP_SKB_CB(skb)->end_seq, tp->snd_una))
926            continue;
927         if ((TCP_SKB_CB(skb)->sacked&TCPCB_SACKED_RETRANS) &&
928            after(lost_retrans, TCP_SKB_CB(skb)->ack_seq) &&
929            (IsFack(tp) ||
930             !before(lost_retrans, TCP_SKB_CB(skb)->ack_seq+tp->reordering*tp->mss_cache))) {
931            TCP_SKB_CB(skb)->sacked &= ~TCPCB_SACKED_RETRANS;
932            tp->retrans_out--;
933
934            if (!(TCP_SKB_CB(skb)->sacked&(TCPCB_LOST|TCPCB_SACKED_ACKED))) {
935               tp->lost_out++;
936               TCP_SKB_CB(skb)->sacked |= TCPCB_LOST;
937               flag |= FLAG_DATA_SACKED;
938               NET_INC_STATS_BH(TCPLostRetransmit);
939            }
940         }
941      }
942   }
943
944   tp->left_out = tp->sacked_out + tp->lost_out;
```

cs 11.40. tcp_sacktag_write_queue().

```
net/ipv4/tcp_input.c(tcp_sacktag_write_queue() continue....)

946   if (reord < tp->fackets_out && tp->ca_state != TCP_CA_Loss)
947      tcp_update_reordering(tp, (tp->fackets_out+1)-reord, 0);
      ...
955   return flag;
956 }
```

cs 11.41. tcp_sacktag_write_queue().

(line 932). And finally if the segment is not already marked lost or SACKed (line 934), we mark the segment as lost (line 936) and increment the lost counter (line 935). In the case where FACK is not enabled and reordering length is default 3 segments, we will not have marked any of the segments as lost.

We need to update the left-out segments based on new SACKed segments and lost-out segments. At last we update the reordering level. We update *tp→reordering* only if the lowest observed reordered segment is not the same as total FACKed-out segment (highest reorder segment), which means that we know that there is nothing to update. Update re-ordering, in case we sense reordering and are not in LOSS state (cs-11.41, line 946). In the state of loss, we are not sensitive to reordering because we have already reduced the congestion window to control congestion. Reorder length is calculated as the number of FACKed segments – the reorder segment that SACKed the hole closest to the ACKed sequence number or any such D-SACK block + 1.

This updates the *tp→reordering* field in case the new value of reordering is more than the existing value. Reordering is being used in the recovery state to assume retransmit lost or to enter recovery state from other states. We need this field to guess lost segment in *tcp_update_scoreboard()*.

tp→fackets_out and *tp→reordering* together can be used to guess lost-out segments. Reordering takes into account the lowest SACKed-out segment and the highest SACKed-out segment (*tp→facked_out*), and the rest of the segments from the start of the retransmit queue are processed to be marked as lost in *tcp_update_scoreboard()*. Since reordering length (*tp→reordering*) takes into account the highest and lowest SACKed segments, we assume that the segments that are missing in between these two may appear some time in the future out-of-order. In *tcp_update_scoreboard()* we try to mark the lost segments based on FACKed-out segments and reordering in case SACK is enabled. Thus, during the loss and recovery stage, we can retransmit only those segments which are marked lost by calling *tcp_xmit_retransmit_queue()* and at the same time we can transmit unsent segments in the retransmit queue (beyond *tp→high_seq*) if the congestion window allows.

11.7 PROCESSING TCP URGENT POINTER (see cs 11.42 unless mentioned)

We check if there are any urgent data to be processed in the slow path. We call tcp_urg() to process urgent data. As far as urgent data processing is concerned, specification says that we may or may not get an urgent byte with the segment containing an urgent pointer and an urgent flag set. The urgent pointer is a 16-bit number that is offset in the TCP segment (containing urgent pointer) starting from first byte of the TCP payload. It means that the urgent pointer points to the byte in the TCP data stream treated as an urgent byte. We may get an urgent pointer and urgent flag in the segment providing information about the urgent byte coming ahead. An urgent byte may be present in the same segment or in the segments to follow. We remain in the urgent mode until we receive an urgent byte. Once we have received a TCP urgent byte, the urgent mode is turned off. We process an urgent byte in the slow path, so the slow path is set once we receive the urgent pointer. *tcp_urg()* is called in *tcp_rcv_established()* (line 3434, cs 11.10) to process urgent data.

If we have a new urgent pointer, an URG flag will be set in the TCP header. Let's hope we got the new urgent pointer, so we call *tcp_check_urg()* at line 3127 (cs 11.42) to process the urgent pointer. We may have have URG flags set in the TCP header because of two reasons:

- It is a duplicate urgent pointer because urgent data are yet to be received.
- A new urgent pointer is received.

tcp_check_urg() makes all the necessary checks and either copies the urgent byte to the user space or wants us to do that. It also sends *SIGURG* to the process that is receiving urgent data. For details see Section 11.7.1. Now we need to check if the urgent byte has arrived along with the segment containing an urgent pointer (lines 3131–3134). If we have received an urgent byte, the *TCP_URG_VALID* bit is set for *tp→urg_data* and the urgent byte is stored in the *tp→urg_data* at line 3138. The *TCP_URG_VALID* flag means that the urgent byte is valid and is ready to be read. *tp→urg_data* is a 16-bit field where the higher 8 bits are used as control flags for urgent data and the lower 8 bits are used to store the urgent byte as shown in Fig. 11.12.

```
net/ipv4/tcp_input.c

3121 static inline void tcp_urg(struct sock *sk, struct sk_buff *skb, struct tcphdr *th)
3122 {
3123     struct tcp_opt *tp = &(sk->tp_pinfo.af_tcp);
         ....
3126     if (th->urg)
3127         tcp_check_urg(sk,th);
         ....
3130     if (tp->urg_data == TCP_URG_NOTYET) {
3131         u32 ptr = tp->urg_seq - ntohl(th->seq) + (th->doff*4) - th->syn;
             ....
3134         if (ptr < skb->len) {
3135             u8 tmp;
3136             if (skb_copy_bits(skb, ptr, &tmp, 1))
3137                 BUG();
3138             tp->urg_data = TCP_URG_VALID | tmp;
3139             if (!sk->dead)
3140                 sk->data_ready(sk,0);
3141         }
3142     }
3143 }
```

cs 11.42. tcp_urg().

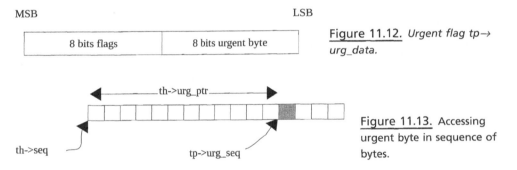

Figure 11.12. Urgent flag tp→ urg_data.

Figure 11.13. Accessing urgent byte in sequence of bytes.

Finally we wake up the process waiting on the socket's wait queue and the process polling exception event on the socket.

11.7.1 tcp_check_urg()

We are called when a new urgent pointer is signalled on incoming TCP segment. We need to clear any unread out-of-band urgent byte to make room for new OOB urgent byte. Linux implements both versions of the tcp urgent pointer. Some implementations assume that the TCP urgent byte is pointed by an urgent pointer, and the others consider the urgent byte to be one byte ahead of the urgent pointer. If *sysctl_tcp_stdurg* is set, an urgent byte is just one byte ahead of an urgent pointer. In the other case, an urgent byte is just the byte pointed to by an urgent pointer. This the reason why we decrement the urgent pointer by 1 here in the latter case (line 3054). Next we calculate the urgent pointer because what we get in the TCP header as an urgent pointer is the offset with respect to the sequence number of the segment containing an urgent pointer (see Fig. 11.13).

If we received an urgent pointer that is already being read, just ignore it (line 3058). The second thing we need to check here is if we received an urgent pointer

```
net/ipv4/tcp_input.c

3048 static void tcp_check_urg(struct sock * sk, struct tcphdr * th)
3049 {
3050     struct tcp_opt *tp = &(sk->tp_pinfo.af_tcp);
3051     u32 ptr = ntohs(th->urg_ptr);
3052
3053     if (ptr && !sysctl_tcp_stdurg)
3054         ptr--;
3055     ptr += ntohl(th->seq);
          ....
3058     if (after(tp->copied_seq, ptr))
3059         return;
          ...
3071     if (before(ptr, tp->rcv_nxt))
3072         return;
          ....
3075     if (tp->urg_data && !after(ptr, tp->urg_seq))
3076         return;
          ....
3079     if (sk->proc != 0) {
3080         if (sk->proc > 0)
3081             kill_proc(sk->proc, SIGURG, 1);
3082         else
3083             kill_pg(-sk->proc, SIGURG, 1);
3084         sk_wake_async(sk, 3, POLL_PRI);
3085     }
          ...
3102     if (tp->urg_seq == tp->copied_seq && tp->urg_data &&
3103         !sk->urginline &&
3104         tp->copied_seq != tp->rcv_nxt) {
3105         struct sk_buff *skb = skb_peek(&sk->receive_queue);
3106         tp->copied_seq++;
3107         if (skb && !before(tp->copied_seq, TCP_SKB_CB(skb)->end_seq))
3108             __skb_unlink(skb, skb->list);
3109             __kfree_skb(skb);
3110         }
3111     }
3112
3113     tp->urg_data = TCP_URG_NOTYET;
3114     tp->urg_seq = ptr;
          ....
3117     tp->pred_flags = 0;
3118 }
```

cs 11.43. tcp_check_urg().

for the data that have already been received in sequence before (line 3071, cs 11.43). This may happen in the case where we receive a segment having an urgent pointer pointing to a segment present in an out-of-order queue. This may be buggy implementation in the sending TCP.

Next we check if we received a duplicate urgent pointer. This may happen in the case where there are many segments yet to be transmitted in the write queue when an urgent byte is written. This urgent byte is not sent immediately but is sent out in correct order, but the urgent pointer is sent out in the segments that are sent out prior to the segment containing an urgent byte.

We are here because we received a new urgent pointer. So, we need to inform to the application that urgent data are received, and it must read the urgent byte at the earliest. So, we send out SIGURG to the application and also wake up any process polling for the urgent data (lines 3079–3085).

Next we check if an urgent byte is not yet read but it has been received and valid when the urgent byte is not received as inline data:

1. Urgent byte is not yet read ($tp \rightarrow urg\_seq == tp \rightarrow copied\_seq$).
2. Urgent data are still valid ($tp \rightarrow urg\_data \mathrel{!=} 0$).
3. We are not reading urgent data as inline ($sk \rightarrow urginline$ is not set).
4. We have already received an urgent byte ($tp \rightarrow copied\_seq \mathrel{!=} tp \rightarrow rcv\_nxt$). Since case 1 is TRUE, we have received data beyond urgent pointer.

If all the above conditions are TRUE, we need to increment the tp→copied sequence by 1. If the urgent byte to be read is the last byte of the first segment in the receive queue or is in the next segment, we remove the first segment from the queue. We do this for the reason that we want to void reading an urgent byte from the receive queue accidently in normal read when we are receiving an urgent byte as out-of-band data in *tcp_recvmsg()* (explained in Section 8.2). If OOB urgent byte is the last byte in the first TCP segment and we have read entire data in this segment until last byte, we should remove this segment.

Normally, an urgent byte is either the last byte of the segment or the only byte in the segment because as soon as we write an urgent byte, we can either append data to the existing segment and try to transmit it at the earliest or create a new segment and try to transmit it at the earliest. But this does not guarantee that an urgent byte should be at the end of the segment or is the only segment in the segment. This is because if we are not able to send urgent byte in the segment containing an urgent pointer, urgent byte is sent in one of the subsequent TCP segments. There may be data pending to be transmitted when urgent byte is queued in by the sender. In such case sender will signal urgent pointer in all the TCP Segment, unless urgent byte is transmitted.

Now we update the urgent data flag to *TCP_URG_NOTYET*, meaning that the urgent byte is yet to be read. Next we set the urgent pointer to *tp→urg_seq*. We need to disable the FAST mode (line 3117) because the urgent pointer is processed in the slow path (*tp→pred_flags* is reset).

From here we return to *tcp_urg()* with the new urgent pointer set and *tp→ urg_data* set to *TCP_URG_NOTYET* in case a new urgent pointer has arrived. Otherwise, no new urgent pointer has arrived (it may be a duplicate urgent pointer).

11.8 PROCESSING DATA SEGMENTS IN SLOW PATH (see cs 11.33 to 11.46 unless mentioned)

tcp_data_queue() is the routine called to process any data segment in the slow path. This routine is called from tcp_rcv_established() at line 3437 (cs 11.10). This routine does the following:

- It processes the data segment received in sequence.
- It gets the memory to the socket's memory pool from the TCP global pool or by pruning receive queues.
- It processes data segments from the out-of-order queue in case a new data segment fills the gap.

- It queues data in out-of-order segments in the ofo queue.
- It processes SACK/DSACK to be sent to the receiver in case SACK is enabled and we receive out-of-order segments.

Let's see how is this implemented. We discuss *tcp_data_queue()* in this section (cs 11.44). First we check how in-sequence data are processed. Then we look at processing of out-of-order segments and processing of SACK information. We first check if there are no data to be processed in the segment at line 2528. If so, we don't process the segment. We do processing of in-sequence data segments in the same way as we did in *tcp_rcv_established()*. We don't process the incoming timestamp here because it is already done by the caller. We copy data to the user buffer by calling *skb_copy_datagram_iovec()* at line 2560 in case the reader is installed and we are the one who installed it.

If we are not able to copy in-sequence data to the user buffer for any reason, we need to queue it in the socket's receive buffer at line 2577. What additional we do in this path before queuing is to check if the socket's memory pool is exhausted and we need to allocate more. If so, we try to allocate more memory to the socket's buffer pool by calling *tcp_rmem_schedule()* at line 2571. In case we are still not able to allocate memory, *tcp_prune_queue()* is called to squeeze out some memory by pruning the receive queue/out-of-order queue.

The rest of the operations are the same as we did in *tcp_rcv_established()*.

One additional check that we do in this path while processing in-sequence data segment is to check if the new segment has filled the gap in the received data sequence space. Segments received out-of-order are queued in the out-of-order queue (*tp→out_of_order_queue*). If the new segment fills the hole such that some of the segments can be removed from the out-of-order queue, we check this possibility by calling *tcp_ofo_queue()* at line 2586. We generate DSACK in the case where new segments cover partially or fully any segment in the out-of-order queue. In the case where all the gaps in the out-of-order queue are filled, we need to send immediate ACK by disabling the pingpong mode. We do this so that the sender should stop retransmitting; as with Reno implementation, we have no idea of how many segments are lost. We need to adjust the SACK list because some of the SACK blocks are eaten up by the *tcp_ofo_queue()*. So, we call *tcp_sack_remove()* at line 2596.

We also check if the FAST path can be enabled by calling *tcp_fast_path_check()* at line 2598. We do it here because all the segments from the out-of-order queue might have got processed as the hole is filled due to arrival of new segment.

In this part we covered how incoming data segments are processed in SLOW path when the segment has arrived in-sequence. Now let's see if we have received out-of-order. We will start from line 2607 (cs 11.45) where we check for retransmission. If the end sequence of the segment is not beyond the last in-sequence byte received so far (*tp→rcv_nxt*), it is a retransmission. In this case, we need to generate DSACK as per the specification by calling *tcp_dsack_set()* at line 2610. The sender keeps track of the false recovery mode or spurious retransmissions through DSACK received. We need to send an ACK at the earliest to let the sender know that it can repair its state, if it mistakenly sensed congestion. We call *tcp_enter_quickack_mode()* to disable delayed ACK and schedule ACK. Once we return to *tcp_rcv_established()* from here, ACK will be sent out by call to *tcp_ack_snd_check()*. We don't proceed further in this case.

Next we check if the segment is out of window at line 2621. *tcp_receive_window()* returns the current advertised window. In this case we need to ACK quickly and

```
net/ipv4/tcp_input.c

2522 static void tcp_data_queue(struct sock *sk, struct sk_buff *skb)
2523 {
2524     struct tcphdr *th = skb->h.th;
2525     struct tcp_opt *tp = &(sk->tp_pinfo.af_tcp);
         ....
2528     if (TCP_SKB_CB(skb)->seq == TCP_SKB_CB(skb)->end_seq)
2529         goto drop;
         ....
2545     if (TCP_SKB_CB(skb)->seq == tp->rcv_nxt) {
2546         if (tcp_receive_window(tp) == 0)
2547             goto out_of_window;
2548
2549         /* Ok. In sequence. In window. */
2550         if (tp->ucopy.task == current &&
2551             tp->copied_seq == tp->rcv_nxt &&
2552             tp->ucopy.len &&
2553             sk->lock.users &&
2554             !tp->urg_data) {
2555             int chunk = min_t(unsigned int, skb->len, tp->ucopy.len);
2556
2557             __set_current_state(TASK_RUNNING);
2558
2559             local_bh_enable();
2560             if (!skb_copy_datagram_iovec(skb, 0, tp->ucopy.iov, chunk)) {
2561                 tp->ucopy.len -= chunk;
2562                 tp->copied_seq += chunk;
2563                 eaten = (chunk == skb->len && !th->fin);
2564             }
2565             local_bh_disable();
2566         }
2567
2568         if (eaten <= 0) {
2569 queue_and_out:
2570             if (eaten < 0 &&
2571                 (atomic_read(&sk->rmem_alloc) > sk->rcvbuf ||
2572                 !tcp_rmem_schedule(sk, skb))) {
2573                 if (tcp_prune_queue(sk) < 0 || !tcp_rmem_schedule(sk, skb))
2574                     goto drop;
2575             }
2576             tcp_set_owner_r(skb, sk);
2577             __skb_queue_tail(&sk->receive_queue, skb);
2578         }
2579         tp->rcv_nxt = TCP_SKB_CB(skb)->end_seq;
2580         if(skb->len)
2581             tcp_event_data_recv(sk, tp, skb);
2582         if(th->fin)
2583             tcp_fin(skb, sk, th);
2584
2585         if (skb_queue_len(&tp->out_of_order_queue)) {
2586             tcp_ofo_queue(sk);
                 ....
2591             if (skb_queue_len(&tp->out_of_order_queue) == 0)
2592                 tp->ack.pingpong = 0;
2593         }
2594
2595         if(tp->num_sacks)
2596             tcp_sack_remove(tp);
2597
2598         tcp_fast_path_check(sk, tp);
2599
2600         if (eaten > 0) {
2601             __kfree_skb(skb);
2602         } else if (!sk->dead)
2603             sk->data_ready(sk, 0);
2604         return;
2605     }
         ....
```

cs 11.44. *tcp_data_queue()*.

```
net/ipv4/tcp_input.c  tcp_data_queue(contd....)
         ....
2607     if (!after(TCP_SKB_CB(skb)->end_seq, tp->rcv_nxt)) {
              ....
2610          tcp_dsack_set(tp, TCP_SKB_CB(skb)->seq, TCP_SKB_CB(skb)->end_seq);
2611
2612 out_of_window:
2613          tcp_enter_quickack_mode(tp);
2614          tcp_schedule_ack(tp);
2615 drop:
2616          __kfree_skb(skb);
2617          return;
2618     }
         ....
2621     if (!before(TCP_SKB_CB(skb)->seq, tp->rcv_nxt+tcp_receive_window(tp)))
2622          goto out_of_window;
2623
2624     tcp_enter_quickack_mode(tp);
2625
2626     if (before(TCP_SKB_CB(skb)->seq, tp->rcv_nxt)) {
              ....
2632          tcp_dsack_set(tp, TCP_SKB_CB(skb)->seq, tp->rcv_nxt);
              ....
2637          if (!tcp_receive_window(tp))
2638               goto out_of_window;
2639          goto queue_and_out;
2640     }
2641
2642     TCP_ECN_check_ce(tp, skb);
2643
2644     if (atomic_read(&sk->rmem_alloc) > sk->rcvbuf ||
2645         !tcp_rmem_schedule(sk, skb)) {
2646          if (tcp_prune_queue(sk) < 0 || !tcp_rmem_schedule(sk, skb))
2647               goto drop;
2648     }
         ....
2651     tp->pred_flags = 0;
2652     tcp_schedule_ack(tp);
         ....
2657     tcp_set_owner_r(skb, sk);
2658
2659     if (skb_peek(&tp->out_of_order_queue) == NULL) {
2660          /* Initial out of order segment, build 1 SACK. */
2661          if(tp->sack_ok) {
2662               tp->num_sacks = 1;
2663               tp->dsack = 0;
2664               tp->eff_sacks = 1;
2665               tp->selective_acks[0].start_seq = TCP_SKB_CB(skb)->seq;
2666               tp->selective_acks[0].end_seq = TCP_SKB_CB(skb)->end_seq;
2667          }
2668          __skb_queue_head(&tp->out_of_order_queue,skb);
2669     } else {
2670          struct sk_buff *skb1=tp->out_of_order_queue.prev;
2671          u32 seq = TCP_SKB_CB(skb)->seq;
2672          u32 end_seq = TCP_SKB_CB(skb)->end_seq;
2673
2674          if (seq == TCP_SKB_CB(skb1)->end_seq) {
2675               __skb_append(skb1, skb);
2676
2677               if (tp->num_sacks == 0 ||
2678                    tp->selective_acks[0].end_seq != seq)
2679                    goto add_sack;
              ....
2682               tp->selective_acks[0].end_seq = end_seq;
2683               return;
2684          }
              ....
```

cs 11.45. *tcp_data_queue().*

discard the segment. The sender may be misbehaving or we might have gotten urgent data or this may be a zero-window probe. Next we check if we received a partial segment at line 2626. We check only if the start sequence of the segment is below the sequence of the last byte received in-sequence, but we don't check for the end sequence. The reason is that we have already done that check at line 2607. Since some portion of the sequence space for the segment is already received, we need to generate DSACK for the overlapping segment at line 2632. We also need to check if our receive window is zero. If so, we schedule ACK in quick ACK mode and discard the segment. Otherwise, we need to receive this data segment as a normal in-sequence segment and queue it on the receive queue being processed at line 2570. If we are still processing a data segment, it is because we received an out-of-order segment. This segment needs to go into out-of-order queue (*tp→out_of_order_queue*). We first check if enough memory is available to queue the new segment, lines 2644–2646. If we fail here, the segment is dropped.

Otherwise we process the out-of-order segment further. We force the SLOW processing path by disabling the prediction flag at line 2651. The reason is understandable because we have received an out-of-order segment, and all the subsequent data segments should be processed in the SLOW path. Only in the SLOW path do we process the filling of holes in the received sequence space. We are already in the quick ACK mode and we also schedule ACK at line 2652 so that ACK should be sent at the earliest. We should be able to send immediate ACK in case an out-of-order segment is received at the earliest so that the sender is notified of loss and congestion. Charge socket receive buffers for the memory consumed by the new out-of-order segment by calling *tcp_set_owner_r()* at line 2657.

Now we start the process of finding the right place for the segment in the out-of-order queue. If this is the very first segment to go into the queue (line 2659), we initialize the first SACK block *tp→selective_acks[0]* and also the SACK-related fields for the connection (lines 2661–2667). Finally, queue the data segment in the out-of-order queue at line 2668. If we are not the first one to go on the queue, we need to find the proper position to insert the segment, depending on the sequence space of the segment. If we already have sk_buff in the out-of-order queue, we have many possibilities. We will check these one by one:

1. If the sequence space of the new segment starts beyond end sequence of the last segment in the out_of_order queue, queue it after the last segment in the out-of-order queue at line 2657. Either the new segment can expand the existing SACK block or we need to create a new SACK block. We will first try to look at the possibility of expanding the existing SACK block. We check if the new segment arrived is in-sequence with the last segment in the out-of-order queue, line 2674. If so, we need to check if we need to create new SACK block for the new segment.

2. If there is no SACK block (*tp→num_sacks = = 0*), line 2677, there can be a situation where we have sk_buffs in the out-of-order queue still *tp→num_sacks* be 0. The reason for this is that there can only be four SACK blocks at any given point of time (RFC-2018 requirements). Only the latest SACK blocks are listed in *tp→selective_acks*, and rest are discarded. This does not mean that the segments corresponding to the older SACK blocks are also discarded. It may happen that some of the GAPS get filled because of which *tp→num_sacks* has come down to 0. This does not mean that all the gaps are

filled, so we may have *tp→num_sacks* to drop down to 0 with segments still there in the out-of-order queue (see Sections 11.8.4 and 11.8.5).

3. The last segment in the out-of-order queue is not the latest one to arrive, line 2678. Since the SACK block corresponding to the latest out-of-order segment sits at the start of the SACK block array (RFC-2018 requirements), *tp→ selective_acks[0]*, we check if that is expandable.

If any of the above conditions is TRUE, we need to create a new SACK block for the new segment, for which we call *tcp_sack_new_ofo_skb()* at line 2724. For details, check Section 11.8.1. Otherwise we expand the latest SACK block at line 2682.

If we are at line 2687 (cs 11.46), we need to find the right place for the new segment in the out-of-order queue because the new segment was not in-sequence with the last segment in the out-of-order queue. Segments in the out-of-order queue

```
net/ipv4/tcp_input.c  tcp_data_queue(contd....)

        ....
2687        do {
2688            if (!after(TCP_SKB_CB(skb1)->seq, seq))
2689                break;
2690        } while ((skb1=skb1->prev) != (struct sk_buff*)&tp->out_of_order_queue);

        ....
2693        if (skb1 != (struct sk_buff*)&tp->out_of_order_queue &&
2694            before(seq, TCP_SKB_CB(skb1)->end_seq)) {
2695            if (!after(end_seq, TCP_SKB_CB(skb1)->end_seq)) {
2696                /* All the bits are present. Drop. */
2697                __kfree_skb(skb);
2698                tcp_dsack_set(tp, seq, end_seq);
2699                goto add_sack;
2700            }
2701            if (after(seq, TCP_SKB_CB(skb1)->seq)) {
2702                /* Partial overlap. */
2703                tcp_dsack_set(tp, seq, TCP_SKB_CB(skb1)->end_seq);
2704            } else {
2705                skb1 = skb1->prev;
2706            }
2707        }
2708        __skb_insert(skb, skb1, skb1->next, &tp->out_of_order_queue);

        ....
2711        while ((skb1 = skb->next) != (struct sk_buff*)&tp->out_of_order_queue &&
2712            after(end_seq, TCP_SKB_CB(skb1)->seq)) {
2713            if (before(end_seq, TCP_SKB_CB(skb1)->end_seq)) {
2714                tcp_dsack_extend(tp, TCP_SKB_CB(skb1)->seq, end_seq);
2715                break;
2716            }
2717            __skb_unlink(skb1, skb1->list);
2718            tcp_dsack_extend(tp, TCP_SKB_CB(skb1)->seq, TCP_SKB_CB(skb1)->end_seq);
2719            __kfree_skb(skb1);
2720        }
2721
2722 add_sack:
2723        if (tp->sack_ok)
2724            tcp_sack_new_ofo_skb(sk, seq, end_seq);
2725    }
2726 }
```

cs 11.46. *tcp_data_queue().*

Figure 11.14. DSACK block.

are arranged in the order of their sequence spaces. We start traversing the list in the reverse order, which means starting from the segment with a higher sequence number toward the lower ones in the order (traversing prev link in the list), loops 2687–2690. We break if (a) we find a segment with start sequence number at the maximum same as sequence number of the new segment or (b) we have traversed the entire list.

We would like to check if the new segments partially or fully overlap with any of the existing segment. This may happen as a result of retransmissions when both the original transmissions and retransmissions reach the receiver. Excessive reordering of segments in the network may result in this kind of scenario. In overlapping segment case, we are not at the end of the queue and the start sequence number of the new segment lies between the start and end sequence of the segment already in the queue. In case we have traversed the entire queue, the sequence space for the new segment is highest of all the queued segments. So, this new segment will be queued at the tail of the out-of-order queue, line 2708.

We can have a combination of any of the following scenarios:

1. *Queue(seq) < new_seg(seq) < Queue(end_seq)*
2. *Queue(seq) = new_seg(seq) < Queue(end_seq)*
3. *new_seg (end_seq) <= Queue(end_seq)*
4. *new_seg(end_seq) > Queue(end_seq)*

A. If conditions 1, 2, and 3 are TRUE, the new segment is completely covered by one of the segments in the out-of-order queue (Fig. 11.14). In this case, we set the DSACK by calling *tcp_dsack_set()* and we free the new segment, line 2698. If the SACK block corresponding to the selected segment exists in the queue, we need to shift the SACK block at the head of the SACK array, *tp→selective_acks[0]*, as per RFC 2883 (see Fig. 11.15 b). Otherwise we need to create a SACK block with the sequence space of the new segment. We call *tcp_sack_new_ofo_skb()* to manipulate the SACK array.

This is a duplicate segment, and the list need not be manipulated because all the bits in the new segment are already present. We only need to update DSACK information and create a new SACK block with the same start and end sequence as of the new segment.

B. If conditions 1 and 4 is true, the new segment partially overlaps the segment in the queue (Fig. 11.16). In this case we set a duplicate SACK by calling *tcp_dsack_set()* with sequence space of the new segment at line 2698. We insert the new segment just after the identified segment.

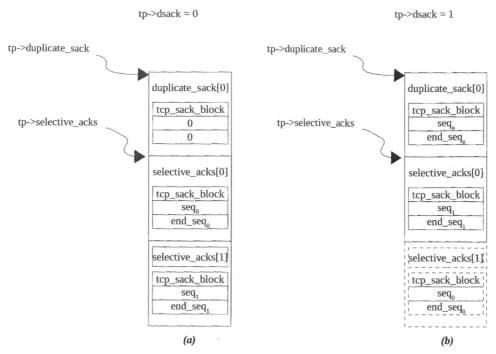

Figure 11.15. Generating DSACK blocks.

Figure 11.16. DSACK blocks generated in case new out-of-order segment spans across several segments in an out-of-order queue.

In the above case, we never know how many segments are being covered by the new segment. So, we traverse the segments ahead of the overlapping segment to check this in the loop, lines 2711–2720. We remove the segments that are covered by the new segment and also modify DSACK block.

C. If conditions 2 and 4 are true, new segment completely covers the identified segment in the queue (Fig. 11.17). In this case we are sure that the identified segment needs to be removed from the queue because all the bits are covered by the new segment. We insert the new segment ahead of the identified segment, line 2795. We try to remove all the segments in the queue which are covered by the new segment ahead in loop 2711–2720. Finally, add the new SACK block to $tp \rightarrow selective\_ack[]$. We will see if the duplicate SACK is generated for this case.

We don't find any overlapping segments for the new segment, and the new segment should be added just after the identified segment at line 2708. We are here after queuing the new segment in its proper place on the out-of-order queue. We

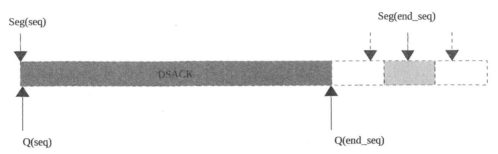

Figure 11.17. DSACK blocks generated in case new out-of-order segment completely covers segment in out-of-order queue.

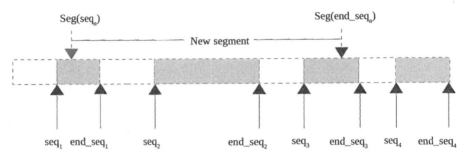

Figure 11.18. New segment covers segment 1 and segment 3 partially and segment 3 fully.

have queued the new segment in the list in the correct place—that is, just after the segment whose initial sequence number is below the initial sequence number of the new segment. But we don't know about the end sequence number of the new segment whether it spans across a few segments ahead of it. Now we need to check for all that segments those are covered partially/fully by the new segment as they need to be removed.

We traverse the list from the position where we have inserted the new segment in forward direction (accessing *skb→next*) in loop 2711–2720. The list is traversed until either (a) we have traversed the entire list (line 2711) or (b) the new segment extends into the next segment, line 2712. If these two conditions are not TRUE, the new segment does not cover the next segment in the list completely (line 2713).

In each iteration, we remove the segment that is being covered by the new segment at line 2717 and also extend DSACK information at line 2718. Here DSACK is extended until the end of the segment being covered. Once we get a segment that is partially covered by the new segment, DSACK is extended until the end of the new segment and we break.

Let's take an example where we received a new out-of-order segment [seq_n, end_seq_n] when we already have segments in the out-of-order queue as shown in Fig. 11.18. The segment finds its place after segment [seq_1, end_seq_1] in the out-of-order queue as $seq_1 < seq_n$ as shown in Fig. 11.19. Segment [seq_2, end_seq_2] is completely covered by the new segment, so it is removed from the out-of-order queue as shown in Fig. 11.20. DSACK generated for the new segment is shown in Fig. 11.21.

The last step to process D-SACK is to call *tcp_sack_new_ofo_skb()* from tcp_data_queue() at line 2729. We need to reorganize SACK information. If we already

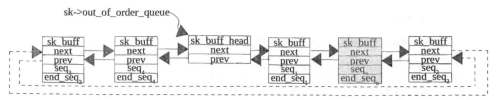

Figure 11.19. Position os new segment in out-of-order queue.

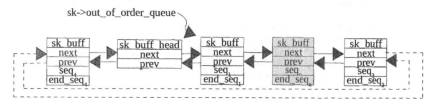

Figure 11.20. Segment 2 is eaten by new segment.

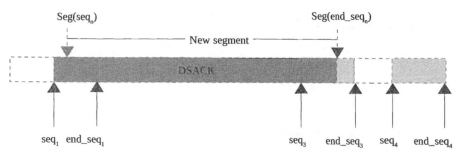

Figure 11.21. DSACK generated for the new segment.

have SACK block adjacent to the sequence space of the DSACK block generated for the new overlapping segment, we need to bring it to the beginning of the SACK array. Otherwise we need to create one. This is done in *tcp_sack_new_ofo_skb()*.

11.8.1 *tcp_sack_new_ofo_skb()*

We are called from tcp_data_queue() after the new segment has found its place in the out-of-order queue. We need to generate a SACK block for the new segment that can be an extension of any of the existing SACK block. If the new segment has overlapping sequence space with any of the existing segments in the out-of-order queue, we have already generated DSACK for this segment before being called. In this case we check if there exists any of the SACK blocks adjacent to the sequence space of the DSACK generated. Since SACK blocks are arranged in *tp→selective_acks[]* in the order they have arrived, so we need to search for all the SACK blocks in the array in loop 2405–2414 (cs 11.47). If we find a SACK block with sequence space overlapping with the sequence space of DSACK at line 2406, the sequence field of the SACK block is extended to take care of DSACK sequence space in *tcp_sack_extend()* itself. We need to get the identified SACK block to the top of the SACK list (*tp→selective_acks[0]*) in loop 2408–2409. We look at the possibility of eating up SACK blocks covered by the new SACK block by calling *tcp_sack_maybe_coalesce()* at line 2411 and then returning.

```
net/ipv4/tcp_input.c

2395 static void tcp_sack_new_ofo_skb(struct sock *sk, u32 seq, u32 end_seq)
2396 {
2397     struct tcp_opt *tp = &(sk->tp_pinfo.af_tcp);
2398     struct tcp_sack_block *sp = &tp->selective_acks[0];
2399     int cur_sacks = tp->num_sacks;
2400     int this_sack;
2401
2402     if (!cur_sacks)
2403         goto new_sack;
2404
2405     for (this_sack=0; this_sack<cur_sacks; this_sack++, sp++) {
2406         if (tcp_sack_extend(sp, seq, end_seq)) {
2407             /* Rotate this_sack to the first one. */
2408             for (; this_sack>0; this_sack--, sp--)
2409                 tcp_sack_swap(sp, sp-1);
2410             if (cur_sacks > 1)
2411                 tcp_sack_maybe_coalesce(tp);
2412             return;
2413         }
2414     }
             ....
2422     if (this_sack >= 4) {
2423         this_sack--;
2424         tp->num_sacks--;
2425         sp--;
2426     }
2427     for(; this_sack > 0; this_sack--, sp--)
2428         *sp = *(sp-1);
2429
2430 new_sack:
2431     /* Build the new head SACK, and we're done. */
2432     sp->start_seq = seq;
2433     sp->end_seq = end_seq;
2434     tp->num_sacks++;
2435     tp->eff_sacks = min(tp->num_sacks+tp->dsack, 4-tp->tstamp_ok);
2436 }
```

cs 11.47. *tcp_sack_new_ofo_skb().*

In case we are not able to find any SACK block of interest, a new SACK block is generated matching the DSACK sequence space, lines 2432–2433, and is placed at the top of the SACK array. We can't send more than four SACK blocks. So we need to remove the furthest SACK block from the array in case we are going to add a fifth SACK block. Since the new SACK block needs to be added at the top of the array, we generate space for it in a loop 2427–2428 by shifting the SACK blocks toward the end of the array by one position traversing the array in the reverse direction.

For the example considered in Section 11.8, SACK blocks are arranged as shown in Fig. 11.22a. After call to *tcp_sack_maybe_coalesce()* SACK blocks are arranged as shown in Fig. 11.22b. Segment [seq$_1$, end_seq$_1$] and segment [seq$_3$, end_seq$_3$] are partially covered but [seq$_1$, end_seq$_1$] is fully covered. So, it reduces to one extended SACK block [seq$_1$, end_seq$_3$].

11.8.2 *tcp_sack_maybe_coalesce()*

tcp_sack_maybe_coalesce() is used to see if the new extended SACK block extends into any of the existing SACK block region (cs 11.48). If that is the case, all those

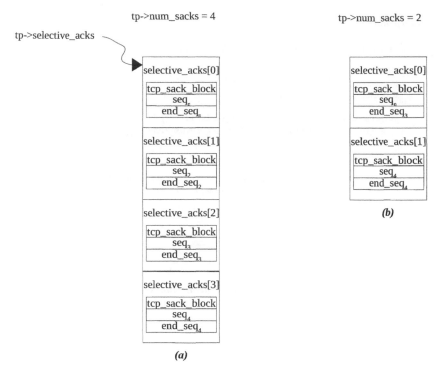

Figure 11.22. Organization of SACK blocks after new out-of-order segmentarrived.

SACK blocks are removed from the selective ACK array and is coalesced with the new extended SACK block. We check if the first SACK block overlaps with any of the existing SACK block (in the outer loop 2365–2377) at line 2366. We traverse through the SACK blocks starting from the second SACK block. If we find any of the SACK blocks being overlapped with the new SACK block (zeroth SACK block), we need to remove the SACK block from the array by shifting the SACK block by one position toward the beginning (loop 2374–2375). The removed SACK block is already merged with the new SACK block (zeroth SACK block) by calling *tcp_sack_extend()* at line 2366, if the sequence spaces overlap.

11.8.3 *tcp_sack_extend()*

tcp_sack_extend() tries to find the possibility of extending the SACK block if the sequence space provided to the routine overlaps with the SACK block. We are extending the SACK block with respect to the sequence space, provided that the following conditions are satisfied at line 2299:

- The start of the sequence space is at maximum equal to the end sequence of the SACK blocks.
- The start sequence of the SACK block is at maximum equal to the end of the sequence space.

If either of the conditions is FALSE, we will have a hole in the sequence space.

```
net/ipv4/tcp_input.c

 2356 static void tcp_sack_maybe_coalesce(struct tcp_opt *tp)
2357 {
2358      int this_sack;
2359      struct tcp_sack_block *sp = &tp->selective_acks[0];
2360      struct tcp_sack_block *swalk = sp+1;
          ....
2365      for (this_sack = 1; this_sack < tp->num_sacks; ) {
2366          if (tcp_sack_extend(sp, swalk->start_seq, swalk->end_seq)) {
2367              int i;
              ....
2372              tp->num_sacks--;
2373              tp->eff_sacks = min(tp->num_sacks+tp->dsack, 4-tp->tstamp_ok);
2374              for(i=this_sack; i < tp->num_sacks; i++)
2375                  sp[i] = sp[i+1];
2376              continue;
2377          }
2378          this_sack++, swalk++;
2379      }
2380 }
```

cs 11.48. tcp_sack_maybe_coalesce().

```
net/ipv4/tcp_input.c

2296 static __inline__ int
2297 tcp_sack_extend(struct tcp_sack_block *sp, u32 seq, u32 end_seq)
2298 {
2299      if (!after(seq, sp->end_seq) && !after(sp->start_seq, end_seq)) {
2300          if (before(seq, sp->start_seq))
2301              sp->start_seq = seq;
2302          if (after(end_seq, sp->end_seq))
2303              sp->end_seq = end_seq;
2304          return 1;
2305      }
2306      return 0;
2307 }
```

cs 11.49. tcp_sack_extend().

Next we check if the left edge or the right edge of the SACK block can be extended, depending on the new sequence space lines 2300–2303.

1. sequence space [seq, end_seq] that can't be extended using tcp_sack_extend() with the SACK block(sp) as there is a hole in the sequence spaces and the SACK block, refer Fig. 11.23.
2. sequence space [seq, end_seq] that can be extended using tcp_sack_extend() with the SACK block(sp) as the sequence spaces and the SACK block are overlapping (see Fig. 11.24).

11.8.4 tcp_ofo_queue()

This routine checks if the new in-sequence data segment received fills the hole in the received out-of-sequence data so far (cs 11.50). It checks sequence spaces of the

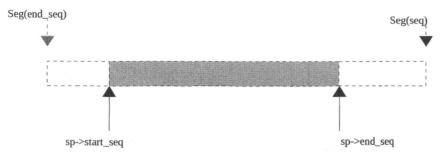

Seg(end_seq)   Seg(seq)

sp->start_seq   sp->end_seq

Figure 11.23. Sequence spaces are not overlapping, not eligible for SACK extension.

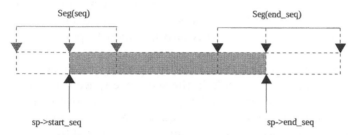

Seg(seq)   Seg(end_seq)

sp->start_seq   sp->end_seq

Figure 11.24. Overlapping sequence spaces, eligible for SACK extension.

```
net/ipv4/tcp_input.c

2479 static void tcp_ofo_queue(struct sock *sk)
2480 {
2481     struct tcp_opt *tp = &(sk->tp_pinfo.af_tcp);
2482     __u32 dsack_high = tp->rcv_nxt;
2483     struct sk_buff *skb;
2484
2485     while ((skb = skb_peek(&tp->out_of_order_queue)) != NULL) {
2486         if (after(TCP_SKB_CB(skb)->seq, tp->rcv_nxt))
2487             break;
2488
2489         if (before(TCP_SKB_CB(skb)->seq, dsack_high)) {
2490             __u32 dsack = dsack_high;
2491             if (before(TCP_SKB_CB(skb)->end_seq, dsack_high))
2492                 dsack_high = TCP_SKB_CB(skb)->end_seq;
2493             tcp_dsack_extend(tp, TCP_SKB_CB(skb)->seq, dsack);
2494         }
2495
2496         if (!after(TCP_SKB_CB(skb)->end_seq, tp->rcv_nxt)) {
2497             SOCK_DEBUG(sk, "ofo packet was already received \n");
2498             __skb_unlink(skb, skb->list);
2499             __kfree_skb(skb);
2500             continue;
2501         }
             ....
2506         __skb_unlink(skb, skb->list);
2507         __skb_queue_tail(&sk->receive_queue, skb);
2508         tp->rcv_nxt = TCP_SKB_CB(skb)->end_seq;
2509         if(skb->h.th->fin)
2510             tcp_fin(skb, sk, skb->h.th);
2511     }
2512 }
```

cs 11.50. tcp_ofo_queue().

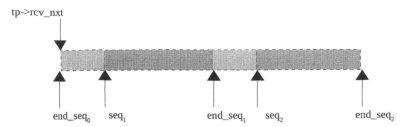

tp->rcv_nxt

end_seq$_0$ seq$_1$ end_seq$_1$ seq$_2$ end_seq$_2$

Figure 11.25. Sequence space for received out-of-order segments.

segments in the out-of-order queue. If we have filled a hole, all the in-sequence data are transferred from the out-of-order queue to the receive queue. One thing that we need to remember is that the new in-sequence data segment that fills the hole is already processed and $tp \rightarrow rcv\_nxt$ is also modified to point to the end of this segment before we are called.

We loop in 2485–2511 until we have traversed all the segments in the out-of-order queue or we find another hole in the sequence space (line 2486). We unlink all those segments from the out-of-order queue which are covered partially or fully by tp→rcv_nxt and place them the receive queue. In each iteration, we update tp→ rcv_nxt to the end sequence of the segment which is moved from the out-of-order queue to the receive queue at line 2508 because this is the sequence number received in-sequence so far. If the new segment doesn't cover any of the segment in the out-of-order queue but just fills the gap at the boundary, we need not process DSACK. If the new segment partially or fully covers any of the out-of-order segment's sequence space, the condition at line no 2489 will be true. Once again, we check if the out-of-order segment is covered fully; if so, the condition at line 2491 will be true and we set the end of the DSACK block to the end of the segment. DSACK mark is set to the end of the segment just to make sure that in the next iteration we make correct judgment about the DSACK. We call *tcp_dsack_extend()* to either initialize DSACK block if it does not exist else extend the same. In case we have overlapping out-of-order segments, in the next iteration we will once again have to extend DSACK. In this case, DSACK will be generated for which the end sequence will be within the ACK sequence, which is a valid case.

Finally we remove all those segments partially or fully covered by the new segment from the out-of-order queue (line 2506) and queue them in the receive queue (line 2507). In both examples explained below, we have the following SACK and DSACK blocks before we reorganize SACK blocks in *tcp_sack_remove()*. *tcp_sack_remove()* is called immediately after this routine to remove any SACK blocks that are covered by $tp \rightarrow rcv\_next$.

Let's see how it works with the help of an example. If we have two segments received out-of-order as shown in Fig. 11.26. Sequence space for the received data is shown in Fig. 11.25. There is only one segment in the receive queue as shown in Fig. 11.27. We take two different examples where different scenarios are presented in a way that a hole is filled by a new segment and how DSACK is generated.

We get segment that partially covers segment [seq$_1$, end_seq$_1$] as shown in Fig. 11.28. such that seq$_1$ <= $tp \rightarrow rcv\_nxt$ < end_seq$_1$. Once we have gone through processing in *tcp_ofo_queue()*, the receive queue looks as shown in Fig. 11.29. This queue will have overlapping segments since we don't do any truncation in this routine. The receive routine takes care of this while reading data. The out-of-order queue will

sk->out_of_order_queue

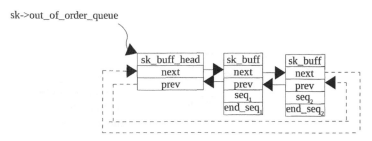

Figure 11.26. Out-of-order segments.

sk->receive_queue

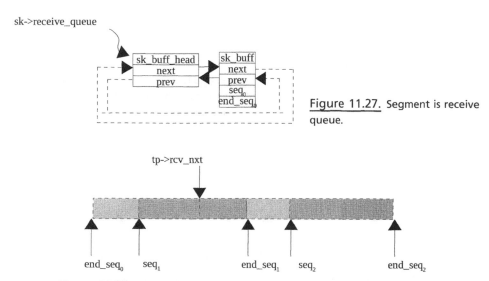

Figure 11.27. Segment is receive queue.

tp->rcv_nxt

Figure 11.28. New ACK partially covers a segment in an out-of-order queue.

sk->receive_queue

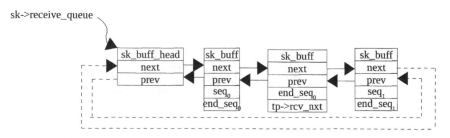

Figure 11.29. Out-of-order queue after queuing a new segment.

be left with only one segment [seq_2, end_seq_2] because it is not being covered by $tp{\rightarrow}rcv\_nxt$ as shown in Fig. 11.30. The final sequence space is shown in Fig. 11.31.

Next we take an example of the case where the new in-sequence data segment fully covers the segment as shown in Fig. 11.32. The sequence spaces before we enter the routine are

$$tp{\rightarrow}rcv\_nxt > end\_seq_1$$
$$n = tp{\rightarrow}rcv\_nxt - end\_seq_1$$

sk->out_of_order_queue

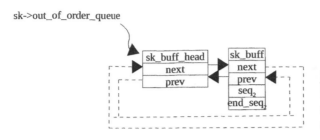

Figure 11.30. Only one segment is left in an out-of-order queue as an in-sequence segment is moved to receive queue.

tp->rcv_nxt

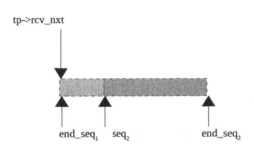

Figure 11.31. Sequence space after shuffling of a segment from an out-of-order queue to a receive queue.

tp->rcv_nxt

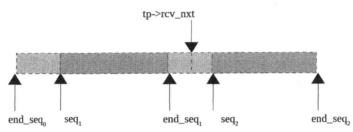

Figure 11.32. New ACK covers the sequence space of one segment completely in the out-of-order queue.

sk->receive_queue

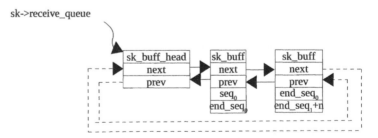

Figure 11.33. New segment is queued on the receive queue.

Here, segment [seq_1, end_seq_1] is covered completely by the new segment so it is removed from both the queues as all the bits are already there in the receive queue as shown in Fig. 11.33. The out-of-order queue will have only one segment in the queue [seq_2, end_seq_2] as shown in Fig. 11.30. The final sequence space will show only one hole as shown in Fig. 11.34.

In both cases, the DSACK block will be same because the specifications say so. The DSACK block should be completely covered by a big SACK block, and minimum their boundaries should match exactly. See Fig. 11.35.

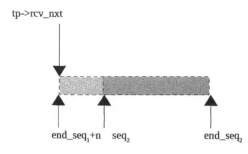

tp->rcv_nxt

end_seq$_1$+n seq$_2$ end_seq$_2$

Figure 11.34. Sequence space after the new segment is moved to receive queue.

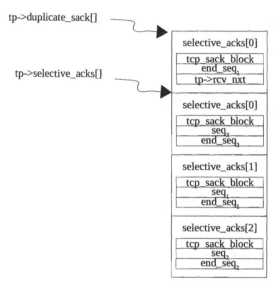

tp->duplicate_sack[]

tp->selective_acks[]

selective_acks[0]

| tcp_sack_block |
| end_seq$_1$ |
| tp->rcv_nxt |

selective_acks[0]

| tcp_sack_block |
| seq$_3$ |
| end_seq$_3$ |

selective_acks[1]

| tcp_sack_block |
| seq$_1$ |
| end_seq$_1$ |

selective_acks[2]

| tcp_sack_block |
| seq$_2$ |
| end_seq$_2$ |

Figure 11.35. SACK blocks adjusted to accommodate DSACK block because of segment received overlapping with segment in out-of-order queue.

11.8.5 tcp_sack_remove()

We are called from *tcp_data_queue()* after a hole in the sequence space of the received data is filled by a new data segment. In this process we have removed some of the segments from an out-of-order queue to the receive queue. We need to modify SACK blocks in this case. Here we look out for the SACK blocks which are covered by *tp→rcv_nxt*. This is the only place where we check if SACK information needs to be reset because we might have removed all the segments from the out-of-order queue as the hole is being filled (lines 2447–2451, cs 11.51). We return if the out-of-order queue is empty after resetting the SACK state. We traverse all the SACK blocks currently active for the session (loop 2453–2469). Those SACK blocks that are fully covered by the latest event of packet arrival need to be removed. If the start sequence of the SACK block is covered by tp→rcv_nxt, the end sequence necessarily has to be covered also. We take care of this aspect in *tcp_ofo_queue()*. If we find one such SACK block, we remove it by left-shifting all the SACK blocks one position starting from the SACK block next to the one that has been identified until the end of the SACK block array (loop 2462–2463). Finally, we sync up the SACK count in case any SACK block has been removed, and we also update effective number of SACK blocks (considering DSACK) at lines 2471–2472. An effective number of SACK blocks (*tp→eff_sacks*) is used to build a SACK block in the TCP header.

If we consider the example in Section 11.8, the final SACK blocks will have a SACK block with sequence space [seq$_1$, end_seq$_1$] removed. The reason for this is

```
net/ipv4/tcp_input.c

2440 static void tcp_sack_remove(struct tcp_opt *tp)
2441 {
2442      struct tcp_sack_block *sp = &tp->selective_acks[0];
2443      int num_sacks = tp->num_sacks;
          ....
2447      if (skb_queue_len(&tp->out_of_order_queue) == 0) {
2448           tp->num_sacks = 0;
2449           tp->eff_sacks = tp->dsack;
2450           return;
2451      }
2452
2453      for(this_sack = 0; this_sack < num_sacks; ) {
2454           /* Check if the start of the sack is covered by RCV.NXT. */
2455           if (!before(tp->rcv_nxt, sp->start_seq)) {
2456                int i;
                ....
2462                for (i=this_sack+1; i < num_sacks; i++)
2463                     tp->selective_acks[i-1] = tp->selective_acks[i];
2464                num_sacks--;
2465                continue;
2466           }
2467           this_sack++;
2468           sp++;
2469      }
2470      if (num_sacks != tp->num_sacks) {
2471           tp->num_sacks = num_sacks;
2472           tp->eff_sacks = min(tp->num_sacks+tp->dsack, 4-tp->tstamp_ok);
2473      }
2474 }
```

cs 11.51. tcp_sack_remove().

that the SACK block is covered entirely by *tp→rcv_nxt* because the new data segment filled the hole. Figure 11.36 is the scene of SACK blocks before we are called, and Fig. 11.36b is after the SACK block [seq$_1$, end_seq$_1$] is removed.

11.9 OVERVIEW OF CORE TCP PROCESSING

An overview of core TCP processing is presented in Fig. 11.37.

11.10 SUMMARY

tp→pred_flags is the way to implement SLOW and FAST paths for TCP packet processing. It takes into account TCP header length, flags (other than ACK/PSH), and window advertised. This makes life simpler in a fast path when we have data flow only in one direction and we do minimum processing to process data and send back ACK and escape so many conditional checks.

    tp→ucopy manages a user buffer and keeps information about the details such as

- Pointer to the thread that wants to read data from TCP socket
- Pointer to user buffer
- Length of data to be read in the user buffer

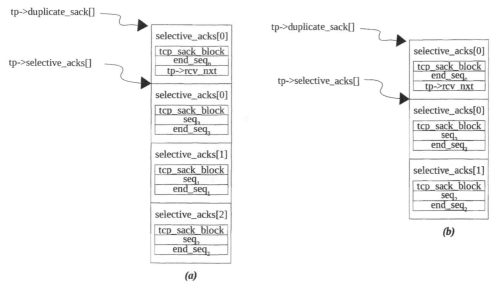

Figure 11.36. SACK blocks adjusted to follow the DSACK format.

TCP data are directly copied to the user buffer if they are received in-sequence and if a receiver is installed for the socket and we are processing the packet in a user context.

The TCP timestamp option is used to check PAWS in *tcp_paws_discard()*.

The new timestamp from the arrived segment is replaced by the older one after all the conditions applied in *tcp_replace_ts_recent()*.

Incoming ACK is processed in *tcp_ack()*. It processes the following:

- Acknowledgment sequence number to clean up retransmit queue
- SACK/DSACK blocks
- ECE flags
- Duplicate ACKs
- Congestion control

Incoming SACK/DSACK are processed in *tcp_sacktag_write_queue()*.

tcp_packets_in_flight() gives a number of packets that are considered consuming network resources. This is a simple calculation based on the total number of packets transmitted minus the number of packets that have left the network (lost + SACKed).

tcp_clean_rtx_queue() removes segments from the retransmit queue which have been ACKed.

tcp_cong_avoid() calculates congestion window depending on whether we are in a slow-start phase or in congestion recovery.

tcp_ack_probe() checks if we need to stop probing timer.

tcp_urg() processes TCP urgent data if there is any in the segment being processed.

tcp_data_queue() takes care of out-of-order segments and is also called to manage a socket's memory pool.

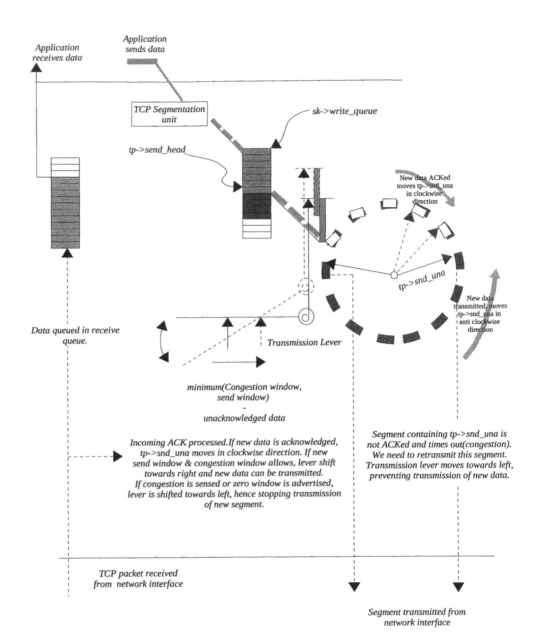

Figure 11.37. Core TCP processing.

tcp_data_snd_check() transmits any data that are pending in the transmit queue and that the congestion state allows. This is called once an incoming segment is processed completely.

tcp_ack_snd_check() sends out ACK if any ACK is pending. This is called after the call to *tcp_data_snd_check()*; otehwise we may end up sending two segments—ACK and data segments—separately.

12

TCP STATE PROCESSING

Sender TCP sends a data segment and it expects ACK for the sent data. The rate of transmission of data increases with the ACK received because the congestion window increases exponentially in the slow-start phase. We keep increasing the data transmission rate until we saturate the network by utilizing full network capacity. On further increasing the transmission rate, we may see one of the intermediate routers dropping packets because it is not able to handle it. In an ideal condition, this causes all the packets transmitted within the window to be dropped as they are all transmitted in a row. TCP comes to know about the loss when it doesn't get ACK for the first segment transmitted in the current window and it times out. We need to start retransmission of the lost segments in such a case and slow down the rate of data transmission.

Above is one of the examples of congestion. There are different situations where we can sense congestion. One of the algorithms where we can detect early congestion is fast recovery and fast retransmission. With this algorithm, we can detect loss much before we experience timeout by counting duplicate ACKs.

Using an ECN (explicit congestion notification) bit in the IP header, one of the intermediate routers can tell the receiver TCP about the congestion it is encountering. This is a proactive approach from the router to notify TCP much in advance about the congestion state. The receiver TCP then sends a congestion notification to the sender by setting an ECE flag in the TCP header. This way the sender TCP reduces the rate of data transmission which can save us from loss due to a packet being dropped at the router facing congestion.

There are certain smart algorithms designed that will detect false retransmissions in the case of both (a) fast retransmission and fast recovery and (b) RTO. With

TCP/IP Architecture, Design, and Implementation in Linux. By S. Seth and M. A. Venkatesulu
Copyright © 2008 the IEEE Computer Society

the help of these algorithms, we can get better network performance when we enter into the loss state because packets are being delayed in the network or ACKs get lost.

In this chapter we are going to see handling of the TCP congestion state. We will see under what conditions we enter and exit the TCP congestion state. Then we will also learn how we control data transmission and retransmission in the congestion state. We will cover the calculation of reordering length and logic of the retransmission of lost segments. Complete congestion control logic is implementation in *tcp_fastretrans_alert()*. We divide the routine into different sections:

- Processing in the TCP congestion state
- Processing exit from the congestion state

12.1 OVERVIEW OF STATE PROCESSING
(see cs 12.1 unless mentioned)

Let's start with *tcp_fastretrans_alert()*. We call this routine *from tcp_ack()* on reception of an ACK segment after processing the ACKed segment and the SACKed segment only when the ACK is found dubious (see Section 11.4.2). It simply means that we enter here when we sense congestion for the first time or to process TCP already in the congestion state (other than OPEN state). We implement the following algorithms in this routine:

1. False retransmissions
2. Recovery from a different congestion state
3. Sensing a false congestion state due to delay in transmission of packets
4. Recovering to an open state from all the congestion states here

We mark the segment as duplicate (line 1494, cs 12.1) only if its ACK sequence number is the same as the previously ACKed sequence number and any of the bits in *FLAG_NOT_DUP* is not set for this segment (see Section 11.4.2).

We need to complete the preliminary work before processing TCP states. We check if all the packets sent out are ACKed by the segment being processed at line 1498. In such cases, the SACK count is also reset because Reno implementation simulates SACKed segments based on duplicate ACKs. In the case where SACK is supported, we account for the SACK count once a SACKed-out segment is ACKed in-sequence (see Section 11.4.6). But in the case of Reno, segments are never marked SACKed out so we take care of the Reno Sack count here. In the case where the SACK count is zero, the FACK count should also necessarily be to zero (line 1502) because the FACK count is derived only if at least one segment is SACKed out.

Irrespective of whichever state we are currently in, if an ECE flag is found in the TCP header, we reset a prior slow-start threshold at line 1507. The reason for this is congestion that is sensed by one of the intermediate routers. If we don't do this and we are about to undo from a non-open state, we may end up increasing the congestion window to a very high value in *tcp_undo_cwr()*, thereby aggravating the congestion conditions.

In the case where the SACK count is nonzero, we check for reneging SACKs. We check this by calling *tcp_check_sack_reneging()*. Reneging SACK means that we need to destroy all the SACK information so far sent by the receiver because

```
net/ipv4/tcp_input.c

1489 static void
1490 tcp_fastretrans_alert(struct sock *sk, u32 prior_snd_una,
1491                int prior_packets, int flag)
1492 {
1493     struct tcp_opt *tp = &(sk->tp_pinfo.af_tcp);
1494     int is_dupack = (tp->snd_una == prior_snd_una && !(flag&FLAG_NOT_DUP));
         ...
1498     if (!tp->packets_out)
1499         tp->sacked_out = 0;
1500     /* 2. SACK counts snd_fack in packets inaccurately. */
1501     if (tp->sacked_out == 0)
1502         tp->fackets_out = 0;
         ....
1506     if (flag&FLAG_ECE)
1507         tp->prior_ssthresh = 0;
1508
1509     /* B. In all the states check for reneging SACKs. */
1510     if (tp->sacked_out && tcp_check_sack_reneging(sk, tp))
1511         return;
1512
1513     /* C. Process data loss notification, provided it is valid. */
1514     if ((flag&FLAG_DATA_LOST) &&
1515         before(tp->snd_una, tp->high_seq) &&
1516         tp->ca_state != TCP_CA_Open &&
1517         tp->fackets_out > tp->reordering) {
1518             tcp_mark_head_lost(sk, tp, tp->fackets_out-tp->reordering, tp->high_seq);
1519             NET_INC_STATS_BH(TCPLoss);
1520     }
1521
1522     /* D. Synchronize left_out to current state. */
1523     tcp_sync_left_out(tp);
         ....
```

cs 12.1. tcp_fastretrans_alert().

either the receiver is buggy or the receiver is not able to handle out-of-order segments correctly because of any reason.

Next we check if DATA is actually lost in the case where the *FLAG_DATA_ LOST* flag is set. This flag is set in *tcp_sacktag_write_queue()* when we get SACK that covers *tp→high_seq*. We enter *tcp_sacktag_write_queue()* only if SACK is enabled and we received a SACK block. If we are in the congestion state and we receive a SACK block that covers *tp→high_seq*, it means that the new segment transmitted after the lost segment was retransmitted got SACKed. This gives us indication that the new segment reached before the retransmitted segment reached the receiver. In this case, we can assume that the data in the window are lost. We check for some more conditions here before declaring that the data are lost.

- The very first condition we check here is if in-sequence data acknowledged so far is below *tp→high_seq*, which means that the segment covering *tp→ high_seq* has reached the receiver as an out-of-order segment that has been SACKed (line 1515).
- We are in any congestion state other than an OPEN state at line 1516. It may happen that TCP has entered into the congestion state incorrectly because of either reordering or fast RTO. In such cases, we are able to undo from the congestion state with *tp→high_seq* already set. In this case, we may have condition at line 1515 true with condition at line 1516 false.

• Finally we check if the number of FACKed segments is greater than the reordered segments at line 1517. This surely means that some of the segments at the start of the retransmit queue can be considered lost. The segments that need to be marked lost are all those segments from the beginning of the queue which are not yet SACKed.

If all the above conditions are TRUE, we are in a non-open state and have SACKed $tp \rightarrow high\_seq$, and facked-out segments are more than the reordering count. In such cases, we try to mark all those retransmitted segments from the start of the retransmitted queue as lost until we find the first SACKed segment. This is because the reordering length is the difference between the facked-out segments and the position of the first SACKed-out segment lower down the order in the retransmit queue (see Section 11.6). Call *tcp_mark_head_lost()* at line 1518. This is a special case where we may need to mark the head lost because it may happen that we are not already in the fast retransmit mode. With the indication of a SACK block covering $tp \rightarrow high\_seq$, we can start fast retransmit and we don't cover this case anywhere.

At line 1530 (see *fast_netrans_alert()*), check if we can undo from any of the congestion states in case we have ACKed data beyond $tp \rightarrow high\_seq$. While entering into any state other than *TCP_CA_Open*, we mark highest sequence number so far transmitted as $tp \rightarrow high\_seq$.

If we have come to the next stage, it means that either we are unable to undo from congestion states or we are going to enter any of the non-open states other than loss state. Whether we received a duplicate ACK or received an ACK for the new data, for any state, processing is done here. We get TCP states processed beyond line 1569 (cs 12.5).

If we are at line 1631 (cs 12.8), it means that we have entered the recovery state (*TCP_CA_Recovery*) or we were already in this state. The final step is to estimate the number of segments lost based on the reordering or number of duplicate segments received (in the case of Reno) by calling *tcp_update_scoreboard()* and then finally we need to retransmit the lost segment (i.e., fast retransmission). In the case where the congestion window allows transmission of new data and we have new segments to be transmitted in the write queue, we can do so. The SACK option provides much better control on the choice of segments that need to be retransmitted because we know the exact holes in the data segments received by the receiver. We also moderate the congestion window each time we come here.

12.2 TCP STATES

The following TCP states are processed here:

• *TCP_CA_CWR*
• *TCP_CA_Disorder*
• *TCP_CA_Recovery*
• *TCP_CA_Loss*

We will cover the processing of each state one at a time.

12.2.1 *TCP_CA_CWR*

This is set by calling *tcp_enter_cwr()* under the following conditions:

Driver Senses Local Congestion. This TCP state indicates that the congestion window has been reduced. Mainly the reason is that the device is congested. The device is not able to transmit a segment because of huge traffic for this packet priority at the device level.

We Received an ECE Flag Set in a TCP Header. The other reason this TCP state is entered is when we get a TCP segment that has an ECE (explicit congestion echo, RFC-3168) flag set. A receiver TCP sets this flag in the TCP header when it receives a CE segment (indication of congestion in the IP header, set by any of the routers on the way). On reception of a TCP segment with an ECE flag set, ACK is considered dubious because *FLAG_CA_ALERT* includes an ECE flag. Suppose we are in an open state when we got a TCP segment with an ECE flag set, and we enter *tcp_fastretrans_alert()* from *tcp_ack()*. Here we need to process OPEN state; and if we have not sensed any congestion, we call *tcp_try_to_open()*. Here we call *tcp_enter_cwr()* to enter into the *TCP_CA_CWR* state.

ICMP Resource Quench Is Received over the Connection. The error message is generated by the router to the source of the packet in case it is about to drop the packet. This ICMP message is outdated, but some of the router implementations still support it. *RFC 1122* suggests that on reception of such an error message, TCP is supposed to back off the congestion window in order to slow down the transmission rate. Instead of resorting to a slow start, Linux enters into the recovery state by simply setting a slow-start threshold to half of the congestion window. We handle the ICMP resource quench error in tcp_v4_error() by calling tcp_enter_cwr(). Section 12.2.2 explains what happens when we enter the TCP_CA_CWR state in terms of a congestion window, a slow-start threshold, and a highest sequence mark.

12.2.2 Undoing from *TCP_CA_CWR*

We process the *TCP_CA_CWR* state in *tcp_fastretrans_alert()* and exit the congestion state only if we get ACK for the last byte transmitted at the time of entering the CWR state line 1541 (cs 12.2).

We adjust the send congestion window to a minimum of current congestion window and slow-start threshold value by calling *tcp_complete_cwr()*. We don't increment the congestion window on reception of ACK in case we are in the CWR state because of a restriction imposed by *tcp_may_raise_cwnd()*. We will see in a later section that the congestion window can be reduced on reception of ACK in this state (until we ACK *tp→high_seq*). We return to the open state at line 1543 (cs 12.2) and go ahead for next step of processing open state.

12.3 PROCESSING OF DUPLICATE/PARTIAL ACKS IN RECOVERY STATE

We receive a duplicate ACK; and if it is Reno implementation, we call *tcp_add_reno_sack()* to increment SACK count emulated for Reno at line 1573 (cs 12.5). We

```
net/ipv4/tcp_input.c  tcp_fastretrans_alert() contd....

              ....
1538            case TCP_CA_CWR:
              ....
1541                if (tp->snd_una != tp->high_seq) {
1542                    tcp_complete_cwr(tp);
1543                    tp->ca_state = TCP_CA_Open;
1544                }
1545                break;
              ....
```

cs 12.2. tcp_fastretrans_alert().

also check if the reordering length needs to be modified because of the duplicate ACK received. tcp_check_reno_reordering() is called from tcp_add_reno_sack(). The idea to check reordering is simple. If the sum of lost and sacked segments is more than the packets transmitted, it means that some of the segments that were considered lost and retransmitted were actually not lost but instead reached late. This happened because of reordering of segments. In this case the original transmissions and the retransmissions both got received, and duplicate ACK was generated for both.

In the case where sacked-out segments have exceeded our expectations at line 1195 (cs 12.21), we adjust the sacked-out segments as the difference between packets transmitted and lost segments at line 1196. Then we call *tcp_update_reordering()* to update the reordering length to a number of packets transmitted in the current window at line 1197 (cs 12.21). In Reno, we have no idea which segment caused the generation of duplicate ACK and we are equating packets sacked and packets lost to exceed the total length of the transmission; we need to assume that the entire transmission is reordered.

If we are at line 1574 (cs 12.5), it is because we received ACK paritially for new data. We will try to remove Reno SACKs in case of Reno implementation by calling *tcp_remove_reno_sacks()* at line 1577 (cs 12.5). The number of segments ACKed is calculated based on number of packets transmitted (*tp→packets_out*) before and after arrival of the ACK at line 1575 (cs 12.5). When new data are ACKed, *tp→packets_out* is decremented by the number of segments covered by the new ACK sequence number in *tcp_clean_rtx_queue()*.

We check if we can undo from received partial ACK by calling *tcp_try_undo_partial()* at line 1578 (cs 12.5). We check if the partially ACKed data exist because of original transmission and not retransmission. We don't switch to an open state here but only revert to a congestion state prior to entering congestion in case we received ACK for original transmissions. The return value of *tcp_try_undo_partial()* will decide if we want to mark more segments as lost and carry on with retransmits later at line 1634 (cs 12.8). TRUE return value is considered similar to duplicate ACK because duplicate ACK will force *tcp_update_scoreboard()* to be called later at line 1632 (cs 12.8).

12.3.1 *tcp_remove_reno_sacks()*

tcp_remove_reno_sacks() recalculates SACKed-out segments based on the ACK we received. Since Reno implementation can't see what all the segments have reached, it assumes that each duplicate ACK means that a segment has reached the receiver after the hole. If SACK count is n, it means that $n - 1$ segments after one hole has

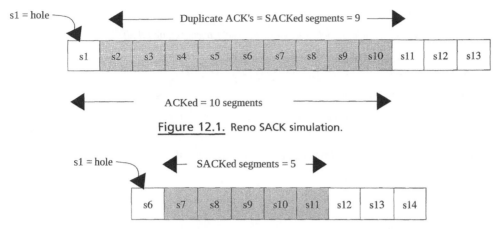

Figure 12.1. Reno SACK simulation.

Figure 12.2. Partial ACKing causes recalculation of SACK.

```
net/ipv4/tcp_input.c

1212 static void tcp_remove_reno_sacks(struct sock *sk, struct tcp_opt *tp, int acked)
1213 {
1214     if (acked > 0) {
1215         /* One ACK acked hole. The rest eat duplicate ACKs. */
1216         if (acked-1 >= tp->sacked_out)
1217             tp->sacked_out = 0;
1218         else
1219             tp->sacked_out -= acked-1;
1220     }
1221     tcp_check_reno_reordering(tp, acked);
1222     tcp_sync_left_out(tp);
1223 }
```

cs 12.3. *tcp_remove_reno_sack().*

reached the receiver (Fig. 12.1) when the reality may be very different. If we have ACKed $n + 1$ segments, where n is the number of sacked-out segments (duplicate ACKs), Reno SACK counter is reset because all the sacked out segments are covered by the ACK (line 1217, cs 12.3).

Otherwise if segments covered by ACK is less than SACKed-out segments, we decrement the SACKed-out segments by ACKed segments –1 (1 for hole) at line 1219. In the above example if five segments are ACKed, then the scenario would be as shown in Fig. 12.2.

Finally, we update Reno reordering length by calling *tcp_check_reno_reordering()* at line 1221 in *tcp_remove_reno_sacks()* as explained in Section 12.6.7.

12.3.2 *tcp_try_undo_partial()*

Here, we don't want to leave recovery and enter an open TCP state because of the partial ACK. In the case of Reno implementation or with SACK, if the FACKed-out segment is greater than reordering length, we want to mark new segments as lost for retransmission by calling *tcp_update_scoreboard()* because partial ACK has filled up some of the holes. That is the reason why we set the flag if any of the above two cases is true. If we received partial ACK because the packet got delayed and reached the receiver before the retransmitted segment could reach, we will try to

```
net/ipv4/tcp_input.c

1395 static int tcp_try_undo_partial(struct sock *sk, struct tcp_opt *tp, int acked)
1396 {
1397      /* Partial ACK arrived. Force Hoe's retransmit. */
1398      int failed = IsReno(tp) || tp->fackets_out>tp->reordering;
1399
1400      if (tcp_may_undo(tp)) {
            ....
1404          if (tp->retrans_out == 0)
1405              tp->retrans_stamp = 0;
1406
1407          tcp_update_reordering(tp, tcp_fackets_out(tp)+acked, 1);
            ....
1410          tcp_undo_cwr(tp, 0);
            ....
1417          failed = 0;
1418      }
1419      return failed;
1420 }
```

cs 12.4. tcp_try_undo_partial().

slightly improve the condition by opening a congestion window to increase the flow
of data transmission. If the ACK covers all the retransmitted segments, it shouldn't
necessarily mean that retransmitted segments filled the hole. It may also happen
that the original packets that reached the receiver prior to retransmissions got
delayed. Is such cases we are able to undo in case we received partial ACK. It may
also happen that only a few of the retransmitted segments got covered by the ACK.
If all the retransmitted segments got ACKed, $tp \rightarrow retrans\_out$ should be zero and
we reset a retransmit timestamp at line 1405 (cs 12.4). We update the reordering
length because some of the SACKed-out segments are eaten up by the ACK by
calling $tcp\_update\_reordering()$ at line 1407. Then we call $tcp\_undo\_cwr()$ with a
second argument as 0. It means that we can set a congestion window to the value
prior to entering the congestion state but can't set ssthresh to the value prior to
entering congestion. This means that we can inject more segments into the network,
but the rate of increment of the congestion window will be 1 per RTT. Since we are
able to undo from partial ACK, we can expect more segments to be delayed in the
network. That is the reason we don't want to retransmit more segments but can
either transmit new segments or do forward retransmissions (reset flag) at line 1417.
We return the flag at line 1419. We return TRUE in case we are not able to undo
from partial ACK, and Reno Implementation or Facked out segments are more than
current reorder length (line 1398). Otherwise we return FALSE. Reno implementation does not take care of SACK, with SACK implementations, we can predict
reordering of Segments in the network and congestion state. This is the reason we
return TRUE for every partial ACK for Reno implementations. Reno is highly
sensitive to Partial ACKs because SACK implementation Provides much closer
estimate of re-ordering.

12.4 PROCESSING OF DUPLICATE/PARTIAL ACKs IN LOSS STATE

When we enter a loss state, we assume that all the segments from the last window
which are not already marked either lost or SACKed are lost. In most of the cases

when a retransmit timer times out, either we have lost all the segments from the last window or we are experiencing *spurious retransmission* assuming that all the packets are following the same path. But rate of transmission can be inflated with loss state with Reno implementation. We enter loss state when:

a. The retransmit timer times out by calling *tcp_enter_loss()* from *tcp_retransmit_timer()*.

b. We get SACK reneging SACK by calling *tcp_enter_loss()* from *tcp_check_sack_reneging()*. Here we are not sure of the SACK state of the receiver, so we discard all the data transmitted within the last window and enter into a loss state.

c. PMTU has changed and needs to do a path MTU discovery and needs to retransmit everything that is not marked SACK/lost by calling *tcp_simple_retransmit()* from *do_pmtu_discovery()*. In this case we enter into a loss state but without reducing the congestion window to 1 but reduce the slow-start threshold to half of the congestion window, which means doing congestion avoidance. We don't want to undo from the loss state here until we get ACK for $tp{\rightarrow}high\_seq$ because the idea here is to just reduce the rate at which the congestion window should be increased on arrival of ACK.

We enter a loss state mostly when the retransmit timer expires—that is, when we don't get ACK for the very first segment transmitted in the current window within RTO time (see Section 10.2.2). Here we consider that all the segments that were transmitted within the window are lost and we transmit only the head of the retransmit queue. When we get an ACK, we will know exactly as to what action should be taken depending on whether we received a duplicate ACK or ACK for the data that we retransmitted. In case we receive ACK for the retransmitted segment, it means that the loss is proven and we continue retransmitting lost segments. Or we receive partial ACK from the original segment, and we know that the packet got delayed in the network. In these cases, we undo from the loss state and in case of SACK implementation we enter into the open state, which may finally fall into the recovery phase. With Reno implementation, we continue with the loss state until $tp{\rightarrow}high\_seq$ is ACKed (cs 12.5). We call *tcp_try_undo_loss()* to check partial ACKing in the loss state at line 1584. If we are able to undo, we return only if TCP state has not opened (cs 12.5, line 1589). If the TCP state has opened, because of partial ACK we may look for the possibility of entering into the recovery state and we proceed with default processing of the TCP state at line 1592 (cs 12.5).

12.4.1 *tcp_try_undo_loss()*

Let's see what happens when we receive duplicate ACK/partial ACK as a result of original segment reaching the receiver slightly late. Let's take each case one-by-one:

1. In the case where none of the segments was lost when the retransmit timer fired, this happened because the packet got delayed in the network or there was a sudden spike in RTO. Here we retransmit the lost segment (head of the list) and wait for the first ACK. We received an ACK that ACKs the head of the list from the window at the time when we enter the loss state. But the

```
net/ipv4/tcp_input.c  tcp_fastretrans_alert() contd....

1570    case TCP_CA_Recovery:
1571        if (prior_snd_una == tp->snd_una) {
1572            if (IsReno(tp) && is_dupack)
1573                tcp_add_reno_sack(tp);
1574        } else {
1575            int acked = prior_packets - tp->packets_out;
1576            if (IsReno(tp))
1577                tcp_remove_reno_sacks(sk, tp, acked);
1578            is_dupack = tcp_try_undo_partial(sk, tp, acked);
1579        }
1580        break;
1581    case TCP_CA_Loss:
1582        if (flag&FLAG_DATA_ACKED)
1583            tp->retransmits = 0;
1584        if (!tcp_try_undo_loss(sk, tp)) {
1585            tcp_moderate_cwnd(tp);
1586            tcp_xmit_retransmit_queue(sk);
1587            return;
1588        }
1589        if (tp->ca_state != TCP_CA_Open)
1590            return;
1591        /* Loss is undone; fall through to processing in Open state. */
1592    default:
```

cs 12.5. tcp_fastretrans_alert().

ACK was generated for the original transmission and not for the retransmitted segment which we can detect from the echoed timestamp. In this case we are able to undo from the loss state because the original transmission succeeded. In the case of Reno implementation, we don't exit the state until we ACK something more than $tp \rightarrow high\_seq$.

2. In the case where packets are being routed through different internet paths, some of the packets are dropped and others are delayed, thus leading to retransmission timeout. In this case, out-of-order segments may reach the receiver generating duplicate ACKs (with SACK, in case SACK is enabled). In such cases, we know that all the segments from the last window is not lost and we should undo from the loss state. In such cases, we can exit from the loss state only in the case where SACK is enabled; otherwise we exit the state only when $tp \rightarrow high\_seq$ is ACKed. RFC 1323 specifies that the timestamp echoed with the duplicate ACK generated for out-of-order segment is from the segment that was last received in-sequence.

Under the above-mentioned situations, $tcp\_may\_undo()$ returns TRUE. Let's see what happens when we undo from loss state. We clear the $TCPCB\_LOST$ bit from each segment in the retransmit queue (loop 1427–1429, cs 12.6). This means that none of the segment is considered lost, and the loss counter is reset at line 1431. We also recalculate the segments that have left the network because they comprise two components: lost segments and SACKed segments. Since the lost-out segments equal zero, we initialize left-out segments to sacked-out segments. The number of retransmissions is zeroed out here at line 1435. If our TCP is Reno implementation, we will wait until $tp \rightarrow high\_seq$ is acknowledged. Otherwise we enter the open state

```
net/ipv4/tcp_input.c

1423 static int tcp_try_undo_loss(struct sock *sk, struct tcp_opt *tp)
1424 {
1425     if (tcp_may_undo(tp)) {
1426         struct sk_buff *skb;
1427         for_retrans_queue(skb, sk, tp) {
1428             TCP_SKB_CB(skb)->sacked &= ~TCPCB_LOST;
1429         }
1430         DBGUNDO(sk, tp, "partial loss");
1431         tp->lost_out = 0;
1432         tp->left_out = tp->sacked_out;
1433         tcp_undo_cwr(tp, 1);
1434         NET_INC_STATS_BH(TCPLossUndo);
1435         tp->retransmits = 0;
1436         tp->undo_marker = 0;
1437         if (!IsReno(tp))
1438             tp->ca_state = TCP_CA_Open;
1439         return 1;
1440     }
1441     return 0;
1442 }
```

cs 12.6. *tcp_try_undo_loss()*.

```
net/ipv4/tcp_input.c

1021 static int tcp_check_sack_reneging(struct sock *sk, struct tcp_opt *tp)
1022 {
1023     struct sk_buff *skb;
1024
        ....
1031     if ((skb = skb_peek(&sk->write_queue)) != NULL &&
1032         (TCP_SKB_CB(skb)->sacked & TCPCB_SACKED_ACKED)) {
1033         NET_INC_STATS_BH(TCPSACKReneging);
1034
1035         tcp_enter_loss(sk, 1);
1036         tp->retransmits++;
1037         tcp_retransmit_skb(sk, skb_peek(&sk->write_queue));
1038         tcp_reset_xmit_timer(sk, TCP_TIME_RETRANS, tp->rto);
1039         return 1;
1040     }
1041     return 0;
1042 }
```

cs 12.7. *tcp_check_sack_reneging()*.

because SACK implementations have good control over the congestion state. We may enter the recovery state depending on the number of segments SACKed out immediately.

12.4.2 *tcp_check_sack_reneging()*

This routine checks if we need to destroy all the SACK block received from the peer because it may be buggy. If so, we need to enter into the loss state because all the SACKed segments are marked lost. The indication is that the first segment in the write queue is marked as SACKed at line 1032 (cs 12.7). This should never be the case because if the first unACKed segment in the write queue has reached the receiver, then it should be ACKed as in-sequence data. If this segment is SACKed, it means that this in-order segment is still lying in the out-of-order queue even though there is no hole in the data received prior to this segment. In this case, we mark all the segments in the retransmit queue as lost by calling *tcp_enter_loss()* at line 1035. We refer to this routine with the second argument as 1, which means that we want to mark all the segments in the retransmit queue as lost and at the same time we don't initialize *tp→undo_marker*. *tp→undo_marker* remains uninitialized, which means that we don't want to undo from the loss state because we know that something is messed up at the receiver and so far it is not able to handle unacknowledged segments properly and we need to retransmit all of them once again. We start the slow-start algorithm here. Transmit the first segment in the retransmit queue at line 1037 and reset the retransmit timer at line 1038.

12.5 DEFAULT PROCESSING OF TCP STATES
(see cs 12.8 unless mentioned)

For default processing of TCP states we have a common code. We come here in case TCP has entered any of the congestion state and we received got an ACK for data that are below *tp→high_seq* (recorded at the time when we entered congestion state) under different conditions for each TCP state. We also enter here in case we are in the OPEN state and we received a first duplicate ACK. We will discuss processing of each state separately. Here we will discuss only the default processing of TCP state. We refer to cs 12.8, line 1593–1634.

In case it is Reno implementation, we need to update the Reno SACK in case we have received a duplicate ACK. In case we have ACKed new data, we need to reset Reno SACK counters. Since Reno implementation has no idea which segment has reached the receiver out-of-order, it just increments the SACK counter on reception of every consecutive duplicate ACK by calling *tcp_add_reno_sack()* at line 1597. Similarly, it resets the SACK counter when new data are ACKed by calling *tcp_reset_reno_sack()* at line 1595. This way Linux TCP implementation simulates SACK for SACKless Reno implementation.

In case we have reached the default processing of TCP state and we have ACKed the new data line 1594, we reset Reno SACK information by calling *tcp_reset_reno_sack()* (cs 12.9).

The next step is to check if we can undo from disorder state (*TCP_CA_Disorder*), which means that we have just sensed reordering but have not entered the recovery state. In this case we try to undo DSACK by calling *tcp_try_undo_dsack()* at line 1601. It may happen that we received acknowledged *tp→high_seq* and recovered from congestion to the OPEN state without undoing from the congestion state. So *tp→undo_marker* and *tp→undo_retrans* will still be nonzero. This means that we may still have retransmissions in the network which may reach the destination later generating DSACK. If we received a duplicate ACK containing DSACK from the window that got us into the congestion state causing *tp→undo_retrans* to become zero, we try to undo congestion window reduction. It means that the original transmissions for all the retransmitted data during the congestion state have reached the receiver generating DSACK. So, our retransmission was false. We won't leave the current state (i.e., *TCP_CA_Disorder*) but will reset the congestion state variables

```
net/ipv4/tcp_input.c  tcp_fastretrans_alert() contd....

        ....
1592    default:
1593        if (IsReno(tp)) {
1594            if (tp->snd_una != prior_snd_una)
1595                tcp_reset_reno_sack(tp);
1596            if (is_dupack)
1597                tcp_add_reno_sack(tp);
1598        }
1599
1600        if (tp->ca_state == TCP_CA_Disorder)
1601            tcp_try_undo_dsack(sk, tp);
1602
1603        if (!tcp_time_to_recover(sk, tp)) {
1604            tcp_try_to_open(sk, tp, flag);
1605            return;
1606        }
1608        /* Otherwise enter Recovery state */
        ....
1615        tp->high_seq = tp->snd_nxt;
1616        tp->prior_ssthresh = 0;
1617        tp->undo_marker = tp->snd_una;
1618        tp->undo_retrans = tp->retrans_out;
1619
1620        if (tp->ca_state < TCP_CA_CWR) {
1621            if (!(flag&FLAG_ECE))
1622                tp->prior_ssthresh = tcp_current_ssthresh(tp);
1623            tp->snd_ssthresh = tcp_recalc_ssthresh(tp);
1624            TCP_ECN_queue_cwr(tp);
1625        }
1626
1627        tp->snd_cwnd_cnt = 0;
1628        tp->ca_state = TCP_CA_Recovery;
1629    }
1630
1631    if (is_dupack || tcp_head_timedout(sk, tp))
1632        tcp_update_scoreboard(sk, tp);
1633    tcp_cwnd_down(tp);
1634    tcp_xmit_retransmit_queue(sk);
1635 }
```

cs 12.8. *tcp_fastretrans_alert().*

```
net/ipv4/tcp_input.c

1225 static inline void tcp_reset_reno_sack(struct tcp_opt *tp)
1226 {
1227     tp->sacked_out = 0;
1228     tp->left_out = tp->lost_out;
1229 }
```

cs 12.9. *tcp_reset_reno_sack().*

values that were set prior to entering the congestion state. We leave the *TCP_CA_Disorder* state only when something above *tp→high_seq* is acked.

The next step is to see if we need to enter the fast-retransmission fast-recovery state (*TCP_CA_Recovery*). We check all the conditions to enter into the recovery state by calling tcp_time_to_recovery() at line 1603. We are here only if we have entered *tcp_fastretrans_alert()* in any of the four states:

1. *TCP_CA_Open*
2. *TCP_CA_Disorder*
3. *TCP_CA_CWR*
4. *TCP_CA_Loss*

We discuss these once we discuss the processing of these states. If *tcp_time_to_ recover()* returns TRUE, it is an indication that we are entering into a fast-retransmit fast-recovery state (*TCP_CA_Recovery*). In the case where the routine returns FALSE, we can't enter into the recovery state. So, we check the possibility of entering the disorder or CWR state by calling *tcp_try_to_open()*. The TCP disorder state indicates that packets are getting reordered in the network or we may have just recovered from the congestion state but are not yet completely undone (see Section 12.6.3). Before entering into the recovery state, we always first enter into the disorder state. The disorder state is an initial indication of congestion as explained in Section 12.6.3, where we discuss how we enter into the disorder state.

In the case where *tcp_time_to_recover()* returns TRUE, it is time to enter the fast-recovery state (*TCP_CA_Recovery*). Starting from line 1615, we mark $tp \rightarrow high\_seq$ to the next sequence number to be transmitted ($tp \rightarrow snd\_nxt$). $tp \rightarrow prior\_ ssthresh$ is reset here because we set it once again only if we have not received congestion notification. We set $tp \rightarrow undo\_marker$ to the first unacknowledged sequence number. $tp \rightarrow undo\_retrans$ is set to $tp \rightarrow retrans\_out$. $tp \rightarrow retrans\_out$ may be set while entering the recovery state in case we have undone from the loss state because of duplicate ACKs generated as a result of an out-of-order segment from the window that got us into the congestion state. Or we may have exited the loss state on reception of a partial ACK from the original transmission, and we can catch DSACKs from this window now.

The next step is to set $tp \rightarrow prior\_ssthresh$ to the current value as returned by *tcp_current_ssthresh()* at line 1622. *tp_current_ssthresh()* returns maximum of $tp \rightarrow snd\_ssthresh$ or three-fourths of the current congestion window. This is recorded so that we can revert to these values in case we are able to undo from this state (false entry into congestion state by calling *tcp_undo_cwr()*). Next is to bring down the value of the slow-start threshold, which is standard practice. We set the slow-start threshold to half of the congestion window or 2, whichever is maximum.

Call *TCP_ECN_queue_cwr()* to set the *TCP_ECN_QUEUE_CWR* flag, ensuring that we send out the CWR bit with the new data segment to inform the other end that we have a reduced congestion window.

We are here if we have just entered the recovery state or we received a partial or duplicate ACK in the recovery state. In the next step we will see how we mark lost segments, and then we will learn how we select segments to be retransmitted starting from line 1631. We call *tcp_update_scoreboard()* to update lost segments within the window in two cases:

1. If the segment we are processing is a duplicate ACK.
2. In the case where the head of the segment has timed out and *tcp_head_ timedout()* returns TRUE (see Section 12.5.2).

In the case where we received a duplicate ACK, we may have updated reordering and also Facked out segments. We may need to update lost-out segments here for retransmission. Also, in the case where the head of the segment is timing out and we have entered into the recovery state because of this reason (see Section 12.5.2), we need to mark the head lost. Let's see how we mark segments lost in *tcp_update_ scoreboard()* in Section 12.5.4.

Next is to reduce the congestion window in case we have just entered the recovery state or are processing ACK in the recovery state by calling *tcp_cwnd_down()*. For each duplicate ACK that we receive in the recovery state, we make room for at least one segment to be transmitted or retransmitted. Even for Reno, we count each duplicate ACK as a sacked-out segment. The left-out segment will be incremented by 1. *tcp_cwnd_down()* initializes cwnd to a minimum of congestion window and packets in flight + 1, making room for transmitting or retransmitting one segment. If SACK is implemented, we know exactly which segment to mark lost and retransmit, but in the case of Reno implementation we just retransmit segments from the head of the list one at a time.

Next we call *tcp_xmit_retransmit_queue()* at line 1634 to initiate retransmission of the segments marked as lost. We may also do forward retransmissions here. Let's see how *tcp_xmit_retransmit_queue()* works in Section 12.5.5.

12.5.1 *tcp_time_to_recover()* (see cs 12.10 unless mentioned)

This routine checks we need to enter the recovery state. *tp→lost_out* is incremented in *tcp_mark_head_lost()* even if we are in a disorder state or an open state. This happens in *tcp_fastretrans_alert()* when a *FLAG_DATA_LOST* flag is set. Otherwise there is no other way we call *tcp_time_to_recover()* with *tp→lost_out* more than zero (cs 12.10). We might have entered *tcp_fastretrans_alert()* in any of the congestion states as stated above, but we may leave the congestion state and enter the open state (because of *tp→high_seq* being ACKed).

```
net/ipv4/tcp_input.c

1152 static int
1153 tcp_time_to_recover(struct sock *sk, struct tcp_opt *tp)
1154 {
1155        /* Trick#1: The loss is proven. */
1156        if (tp->lost_out)
1157            return 1;
1158
1159        /* Not-A-Trick#2 : Classic rule... */
1160        if (tcp_fackets_out(tp) > tp->reordering)
1161            return 1;
              ....
1166        if (tcp_head_timedout(sk, tp))
1167            return 1;
              ....
1172        if (tp->packets_out <= tp->reordering &&
1173            tp->sacked_out >= max_t(__u32, tp->packets_out/2, sysctl_tcp_reordering) &&
1174            !tcp_may_send_now(sk, tp)) {
              ....
1178            return 1;
1179        }
1180
1181        return 0;
1182 }
```

cs 12.10. *tcp_time_to_recover()*.

```
net/ipv4/tcp_input.c

1044 static inline int tcp_fackets_out(struct tcp_opt *tp)
1045 {
1046      return IsReno(tp) ? tp->sacked_out+1 : tp->fackets_out;
1047 }
```

cs 12.11. *tcp_fackets_out()*.

If no segment is marked lost, the next condition we check here is the number of Facked-out segments that have exceeded reordering length. See Section 11.6 to know more about reordering length. If the condition is true, it means that some of the segments at the beginning of the retransmit queue are considered lost because the rest of them covered by reorder length are considered as being reordered in the network and will appear sooner or later. In the case of SACK implementation, we exactly know FACKed-out segments, but in Reno implementation we hardly have an idea of it. So, we consider only SACKed-out segments (number of duplicate ACKs + 1) as FACKed-out segments in Reno implementation (line 1046, cs 12.11). We add one because we consider one segment lost at the head of the retransmit queue in the case of Reno Implementation. This a classic rule to enter into the fast-retransmit fast-recovery state where if we get three duplicate ACKs, we consider the head of the list as lost and retransmit the head of the list. With FACK/SACK, we know exactly what is lost and how much to transmit that we see later.

Next we check if the head of the retransmit queue has timed out by calling *tcp_head_timedout()* at line 1166. The retransmission timer is reset on reception of each ACK. The packet should be ACKed within an estimated RTO. If the time for the packet exceeds RTO, it is another way to signal early retransmission.

If we are at line 1172, we have not entered fast-recovery state because of the following:

1. No packet is lost.
2. Head if the transmit queue has not timed out.
3. Facked segments has not exceeded reordering length.

We still can enter into the fast-recovery state. We have reordering length calculated from the SACK information calculated from the last window. In the current window, in this case, we may be misled and can detect congestion here. In the case where the number of packets sent out (*tp→packets_out*) is less than the reordering length and the SACKed out segments are more than the maximum of half the number of the packets transmitted so far and *sysctl_tcp_reordering* (line 1173), we can enter into the recovery state if there is nothing to be sent out (*tcp_may_send_now()* returns FALSE, line 1174).

12.5.2 *tcp_head_timedout()*

We try to find out if the head of the retransmit queue is not ACKed even after it has elapsed more than RTO since it was transmitted. Timestamp is stored in each segment (skb→when) when it is transmitted in *tcp_transmit_skb()*. When we receive ACK for a segment, we set a retransmission timeout timer for the next segment in

```
net/ipv4/tcp_input.c

1049 static inline int tcp_skb_timedout(struct tcp_opt *tp, struct sk_buff *skb)
1050 {
1051      return (tcp_time_stamp - TCP_SKB_CB(skb)->when > tp->rto);
1052 }

1054 static inline int tcp_head_timedout(struct sock *sk, struct tcp_opt *tp)
1055 {
1056      return tp->packets_out && tcp_skb_timedout(tp, skb_peek(&sk->write_queue));
1057 }
```

cs 12.12. tcp_skb_timedout().

tcp_ack()→tcp_ack_packets_out(). The timeout value for the retransmission timer is set to *tp→rto*, even though the next segment was transmitted much earlier. So, timeout for the next segment is slightly overestimated by time lapsed since it was transmitted and the ACK for the previous segment arrived. We can detect early timeout for the retransmit queue head by calling *tcp_head_timedout()*. The routine checks if the time lapsed since the head of the retransmit queue was transmitted has exceeded the RTO. The retransmit timer won't fire for the next segment (head of the retransmit queue) even if the segment has elapsed more than RTO (*tp→rto*) because the retransmit timer is started only after the ACK for the previous segment was received (cs- 12.12). But, early indication of timing out from *tcp_head_timedout()* can save us from entering into the loss state in the case where the segment is slightly delayed in the network, which is very expensive. In this routine we check if there are any segments which are transmitted (tp→packets_out > 0). If so, we check if the head of the list has timed out by using the buffer's timestamp stored at the time when it is transmitted (*TCP_SKB_CB(skb→when)*) (cs- 12.12, line 1051). If the head of the retransmit queue has timed out, we enter into the fast-recovery state.

12.5.3 *tcp_try_to_open()* (see cs 12.13 unless mentioned)

The routine checks if we need to enter into the CWR state or the disorder state. We adjust the congestion window for these states by trying to bring it down as we need to keep congestion under control to avoid serious loss. We are called only in open, C(ongestion)W(indow)R(eduction), and disorder TCP states. So, we initialize *tp→left_out* to *tp→sacked_out* at line 1452 because nothing is marked lost in these states. If *tp→retrans_out* is set to zero, *tp→retrans_stamp* is set to zero. It may happen that we have left the congestion state without undoing from the state. If we come here just after entering the open state from the congestion state, we will try to reset *tp→retrans_stamp* in case *tp→retrans_out* is set to zero at line 1455. We enter into the open state from the congestion state only after all the retransmitted segments are ACKed. So, *tp→retrans_out* should become zero. In such cases, we should try to reset *tp→retrans_stamp* because it records the timestamp of the first retransmitted segment. If we don't do this here, and the very next instance we need to retransmit the segment, we will still have the older value in *tp→retrans_stamp* and will not set the new value (check *tcp_retransmit_skb()* at line 890). This may provide us wrong results in case we are detecting false retransmissions in *tcp_may_ undo()*. *tp→retrans_stamp* is useful to check false retransmission (see Section 12.6.8).

Next is if ECE flag is set, we enter into the CWR state here by calling *tcp_enter_cwr()*. This is the place where we can enter into the CWR state in case we received an ECE flag set in the packet being processed currently. Here, we reduce the slow-start threshold to half of the congestion window or minimum 2 and the send congestion window is reduced to a value so that we should be able to send a maximum of one segment. *tp→undo_marker* is not set because we are sure that we are not retransmitting anything in this state (*tp→undo_marker* should be set to undo from the congestion state; refer to *tcp_may_undo()*). If we are not retransmitting anything, we should not expect any test for false retransmissions and delayed packets. Check Section 12.2.1 for details on entering the CWR state.

The next action will be based on the TCP state. As stated earlier, we are here only in three TCP states: *TCP_CA_Open, TCP_CA_CWR*, and *TCP_CA_Disorder*. We may have entered the CWR state in this routine itself because of the ECE flag set. If the CWR state is set, we just call *tcp_cwnd_down()* to simply try to reduce the congestion window on the reception of every second ACK. In *tcp_cwnd_down()* we also try to keep the congestion window such that at the most one new segment can be transmitted which is calculated as *packets_in_flight()* + 1. Otherwise if the congestion window is less than the number of packets in flight + 1, we wait for more segments to be ACKed before we can transmit any new segment.

If the TCP state is other than *TCP_CA_CWR*, then, we are processing either the *TCP_CA_Open* state or the TCP_CA_Disorder state here. If we have entered *tcp_fastretrans_alert()* in the open state, it may be because we received the first duplicate ACK. In such cases, *tp→left_out* will be a nonzero positive number because it is set to the number of SACKed-out segments. In Reno implementation, SACKed-out segments are emulated as duplicate ACKs.

We may have entered *tcp_fastretrans_alert()* with the TCP state as a loss and have just left these states (because *tp→high_seq* is ACKed with this segment). In this case, if we are not able to undo from the congestion states, *tp→undo_retrans* and *tp→undo_marker* will still be set to the congestion state value.

In both of the above cases, we just set the TCP state to disorder at line 1466 (cs 12.13). Next we check if the state is something other than *TCP_CA_Open* (can only be a disorder state), We set the state to the disorder state and set *tp→high_seq* to the highest sequence number transmitted so far at line 1470. Finally, we call *tcp_moderate_cwnd()* to slow down the rate of transmission. By calling *tcp_moderate_cwnd()*, we actually restrict ourselves to sending out a maximum of three new segments from here. This way we enter into the disorder state.

In the case where we are already in the disorder state and received an ACK, we just call *tcp_moderate_window()* to bring down the transmission rate and do nothing.

12.5.4   *tcp_update_scoreboard()* (see cs 12.14 unless mentioned)

In the case where FACK is implemented, we take difference of FACKed-out segment and disorder length to estimate the lost segments. Otherwise we assume that only the head of the retransmit queue is lost. In the example shown in Fig. 12.3, 12 segments are transmitted in a window and out of 12 segments, only 3 segments are SACKed, that is, s4, s8, and s12. In this case, the FACK count is 12 and the reorder length is 9—that is, number of segments covered between highest and lowest SACKed segments (see Section 11.6). So, the number of segments that will be

```
net/ipv4/tcp_input.c

1450 static void tcp_try_to_open(struct sock *sk, struct tcp_opt *tp, int flag)
1451 {
1452      tp->left_out = tp->sacked_out;
1453
1454      if (tp->retrans_out == 0)
1455           tp->retrans_stamp = 0;
1456
1457      if (flag&FLAG_ECE)
1458           tcp_enter_cwr(tp);
1459
1460      if (tp->ca_state != TCP_CA_CWR) {
1461           int state = TCP_CA_Open;
1462
1463           if (tp->left_out ||
1464               tp->retrans_out ||
1465               tp->undo_marker)
1466               state = TCP_CA_Disorder;
1467
1468           if (tp->ca_state != state) {
1469               tp->ca_state = state;
1470               tp->high_seq = tp->snd_nxt;
1471           }
1472           tcp_moderate_cwnd(tp);
1473      } else {
1474           tcp_cwnd_down(tp);
1475      }
1476 }
```

cs 12.13. tcp_try_to_open().

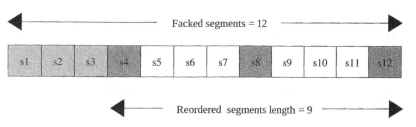

Figure 12.3. Partial ACKing causes recalculation of SACK.

marked as lost in this window when we call *tcp_update_scoreboard()* will be 3, that is, s1, s2, and s3.

In the case where SACK is not supported or it is Reno implementation, we have little or no idea of reordering and the segments that have reached the receiver. So, in this case we mark only one segment at the head of the retransmit queue as lost.

We call *tcp_mark_head_lost()* to mark the segments lost. The second argument to the routine is the number of segments to be marked lost, and the third argument is the highest sequence that marks the right edge of the window. Beyond this sequence number, we should not consider any segment as lost. For details on *tcp_mark_head_lost()* see Section 12.6.11.

In the case where head of the retransmit queue has timed out, we check for each segment in the retransmit queue which has timed out in loop 1272–1278 (cs 12.14). If the segment is found to have timed out and it has not yet been retransmitted or SACKed out or marked lost (*TCPCB_TAGBITS* for the segment is not set),

```
net/ipv4/tcp_input.c

1253 static void tcp_update_scoreboard(struct sock *sk, struct tcp_opt *tp)
1254 {
1255      if (IsFack(tp)) {
1256           int lost = tp->fackets_out - tp->reordering;
1257           if (lost <= 0)
1258                lost = 1;
1259           tcp_mark_head_lost(sk, tp, lost, tp->high_seq);
1260      } else {
1261           tcp_mark_head_lost(sk, tp, 1, tp->high_seq);
1262      }
           ....
1269      if (tcp_head_timedout(sk, tp)) {
1270           struct sk_buff *skb;
1271
1272           for_retrans_queue(skb, sk, tp) {
1273                if (tcp_skb_timedout(tp, skb) &&
1274                     !(TCP_SKB_CB(skb)->sacked&TCPCB_TAGBITS)) {
1275                     TCP_SKB_CB(skb)->sacked |= TCPCB_LOST;
1276                     tp->lost_out++;
1277                }
1278           }
1279           tcp_sync_left_out(tp);
1280      }
1281 }
```

cs 12.14. *tcp_update_scoreboard()*.

we mark the segment as lost and increment the lost counter. This is just a proactive approach or a protective way to sense any congestion and retransmit at least one segment so that the retransmit timer does not experience timeout and we can avoid the loss state. Finally, we calculate the segments that have left the network by calling tcp_sync_left_out() at line 1279 since we have sensed lost segments.

12.5.5 *tcp_xmit_retransmit_queue()* (see cs 12.15 unless mentioned)

As discussed above, on reception of each duplicate ACK or if the head of the retransmit queue has timed out, we update lost segment information. First we consider normal retransmissions based on the number of segment's marked lost (*tp→lost_out*). Thereafter we need to make a decision between forward retransmission and transmitting new segments in case we still have enough congestion window to pump out more segments.

If *tp→lost_out* is some positive number, we traverse through the retransmit queue (lines 919–941, cs 12.15) and for each segment in the retransmit queue we do the following things:

1. Check if the congestion window is greater than packets in flight at line 922. If so, we can pump out more segments in the network; otherwise we return.
2. Check if the segment is marked lost at line 925. If it is marked lost, we try to retransmit this segment only if the segment is not yet SACKed or retransmitted at line 926. If the error code returned from *tcp_retransmit_skb()* is nonzero, there was some problem and the segment could not be

net/ipv4/tcp_input.c

```
911  void tcp_xmit_retransmit_queue(struct sock *sk)
912  {
913      struct tcp_opt *tp = &(sk->tp_pinfo.af_tcp);
914      struct sk_buff *skb;
915      int packet_cnt = tp->lost_out;
916
917      /* First pass: retransmit lost packets. */
918      if (packet_cnt) {
919          for_retrans_queue(skb, sk, tp) {
920              __u8 sacked = TCP_SKB_CB(skb)->sacked;
921
922              if (tcp_packets_in_flight(tp) >= tp->snd_cwnd)
923                  return;
924
925              if (sacked&TCPCB_LOST) {
926                  if (!(sacked&(TCPCB_SACKED_ACKED|TCPCB_SACKED_RETRANS))) {
927                      if (tcp_retransmit_skb(sk, skb))
928                          return;
929                      if (tp->ca_state != TCP_CA_Loss)
930                          NET_INC_STATS_BH(TCPFastRetrans);
931                      else
932                          NET_INC_STATS_BH(TCPSlowStartRetrans);
933
934                      if (skb == skb_peek(&sk->write_queue))
935                          tcp_reset_xmit_timer(sk, TCP_TIME_RETRANS, tp->rto);
936                  }
937
938                  if (--packet_cnt <= 0)
939                      break;
940              }
941          }
942      }
         ....
947      if (tp->ca_state != TCP_CA_Recovery)
948          return;
949
950      /* No forward retransmissions in Reno are possible. */
951      if (!tp->sack_ok)
952          return;
         ....
961      if (tcp_may_send_now(sk, tp))
962          return;
963
964      packet_cnt = 0;
965
966      for_retrans_queue(skb, sk, tp) {
967          if(++packet_cnt > tp->fackets_out)
968              break;
969
970          if (tcp_packets_in_flight(tp) >= tp->snd_cwnd)
971              break;
972
973          if(TCP_SKB_CB(skb)->sacked & TCPCB_TAGBITS)
974              continue;
975
976          /* Ok, retransmit it. */
977          if(tcp_retransmit_skb(sk, skb))
978              break;
979
980          if (skb == skb_peek(&sk->write_queue))
981              tcp_reset_xmit_timer(sk, TCP_TIME_RETRANS, tp->rto);
982
983          NET_INC_STATS_BH(TCPForwardRetrans);
984      }
985  }
```

cs 12.15. *tcp_xmit_retransmit_queue()*.

retransmitted. In that case, we just return and don't try for the second time. In case we are able to retransmit the segment and this was the first segment in the write queue, we reset the retransmit timer at lines 934–935, the same as we do for plane transmission of a segment where we set the retransmit timer for the first segment and we reset the retransmit timer once some data gets ACKed. Next is to decrement the lost segment count. If the count is zero, we come out of the loop at lines 938–939; otherwise we traverse in the loop for the next segment.

The above was retransmission on demand, and now we check for the possibility of forward retransmission—that is, those segments that are not yet SACK/retransmitted/lost. Here we also have the choice of transmitting new data segments that are not yet transmitted. We are allowed to do forward retransmissions only if we are in the recovery state and not in the loss state, line 947. The reason for this is that the loss state indicates acute congestion as packets are getting dropped by some intermediate router and we assume that all the segments in the window being lost. So we want to transmit very limited segments in a controlled way in a loss state. Another reason is that we may expect original retransmissions reaching the receiver, causing partial ACKing or duplicate ACKs that may get us out of the loss state. One more reason we keep retransmitting slowly is that we may have entered the loss state because of false retransmissions.

We are an eligible candidate for forward retransmission only if SACK is implemented, else return (line 951). The reason for this is that we have a fair idea of which segments to transmit and have controlled retransmissions with SACK in place.

While in forward retransmission, Linux has a choice of retransmitting un-ACKed segments from the current window or transmitting new segment. Linux prefers transmitting new data segments once it has retransmitted marked lost segments in case congestion window allows. First we check if there are any new segments to be transmitted by calling *tcp_may_send_now()* at line 961. This should ensure that there *tp→send_head* is non-NULL and that all other conditions are also satisfied related to Nagles, algorithm, the congestion window, and the receiver's window. If for any reason we are not able to transmit a new segment, we try to retransmit segments from the retransmit queue which are not marked as Lost/Sack/retransmitted. We traverse through the queue in the loop 966–984. We make the same checks as in the loop 934–935. The only difference is that there we knew the exact number of segments and we don't try for anything above the specified number of segments. Here, we look for the possibility of transmitting segments that are covered by FACKed-out segments, the condition at line 967.

12.5.6 *tcp_packet_delayed()* (see cs 12.23)

From this logic we can conclude that we can undo from loss state as soon as we get a duplicate ACK from the window that got us into congestion because the timestamp echoed will always be less than the timestamp for the first retransmitted segment. We get back to the congestion state prior to entering the congestion state, but we exit the loss state only if SACK is supported over the connection; otherwise we remain in the loss state even with a high rate of data transmission. We undo from the recovery state only if we received an ACK that ACKed full (tp→high_seq) or partial (current tp→snd_una is higher than the value before the ACK being processed arrived) data but not from retransmission but from original transmissions (tp→retrans_stamp > tp→rcv_tsecr). For the same reason, *tcp_try_undo_recovery()* is called only when we get partial/full data ACKed, whereas *tcp_try_undo_loss()* is called irrespective of the fact that we obtained a duplicate ACK or data ACKed in *tcp_fastretrans_alert()*.

12.6 PROCESSING OF TCP NON-OPEN STATES WHEN ACKED BEYOND *tp→high_seq* (see cs 12.19)

The first thing we check here is if we have entered this routine in the open state. If so, we should not have any retransmissions pending (*tp→retrans_out* should be zero). We enter into the congestion state once we have retransmitted a segment because of any reason. In the open state since there are no retransmissions, we need not have the *tp→retrans_stamp* set. So, we reset it here at line 1529. This is important because we may be sensing congestion and may need to retransmit segments. If *tp→retrans_stamp* is set, we won't be able to record retransmission timestamp for our first retransmission (check tcp_retransmit_skb()) and this will mislead us in detecting false retransmissions.

   If we have not entered the routine in the open state, we check if we can exit from any of the congestion states. We exit the congestion state if *tp→high_seq* (highest sequence number transmitted when we enter the congestion state, i.e., *tp→snd_nxt*) recorded at the time of entering the congestion state has been ACKed at line 1530. In the case where *tp→high_seq* is ACKed with the segment being processed, we have different processing for each TCP congestion state. Let's look at them one-by-one.

12.6.1   *TCP_CA_Loss*

When we enter the loss state, all the transmitted segments within the window which are not SACKed out are marked lost (see Section 10.2.2 for retransmission timer). In the case of Reno implementation, all the segments within the window are marked lost because we have no idea which segment is SACKed. We mark the highest sequence number that is transmitted in *tp→high_seq* at the time we enter the loss state. We leave the loss state when *tp→high_seq* is ACKed. This is because we would like to be in the congestion state until all the data within the window at the time of entering the congestion state has reached the receiver in correct order. Thereafter we can start pushing out data gradually in the network. So, no new data are pumped in the network until *tp→high_seq* is ACKed. We need to reset *tp→retransmits* (number of attempts to retransmit the same segment without getting ACK) here. We check if we can undo from the recovery state by calling *tcp_try_undo_recovery()*. In *tcp_try_undo_recovery()* we first check if we did false retransmission because of underestimated RTO or packets getting late in the flight by calling *tcp_may_undo()*. If it returns TRUE, we undo from the state by calling *tcp_undo_cwr()*. The routine reverts the congestion variables back to the value that was set prior to entering congestion state (see Section 12.6.10) and reset *tp→undo_marker*. Whether we can leave the congestion state will depend on the TCP implementation and sequence number ACKed. With Reno implementation, we don't want to leave the loss state until something above *tp→high_seq* is ACKed to avoid false fastretransmissions.

This is very well documented in RFC 2582. The idea is that we may have retransmitted three segments after entering the loss state. When those segments reach the receiver, it will generate a duplicate ACK when those segments are already there in the out-of-order queue. In the case of Reno implementation, we have no idea of SACK/DSACK, so these duplicate ACKs should not be confused with the fast-recovery state we wait for until something above the high sequence is ACKed. New data (above *tp→high_seq*) are transmitted only after we have retransmitted all the lost segments and the congestion window allows us to do so. So, new data ACKed means that we have already ACKed new data that are beyond the window that moved us into the congestion state. In this case, we just moderate the congestion window and continue to send out new segments in the loss state until something beyond *tp→high_seq* is ACKed. The reason that we are doing this in the loss state is that there may be reordering taking place in the loss state also that may lead to retransmission of segments causing false fast recovery when the retransmitted segments cause duplicate ACKs when *tp→high_seq* is ACKed.

In the case of SACK implementation, we exit the congestion state (loss) as soon as we ACK *tp→high_seq* because the duplicate ACK for the above-explained case will carry DSACK and will differentiate these duplicate ACKs from fast recovery. In the case where we are not able to exit the loss state, we return with TCP_CA_Loss state; otherwise we need to process the open state further.

12.6.2 *TCP_CA_CWR*

The following two flags are used to exchange ECN information:

- *TCP_ECN_QUEUE_CWR*
- *TCP_ECN_DEMAND_CWR*

ECN-related information is maintained in the *tp→ecn_flags* field. How does ECN work? Whenever an ECN field is set in an IP header (set by the intermediate router), the receiver TCP sets an ECE flag in the TCP header. The ECN field is checked by calling *TCP_ECN_check_ce()*. The routine is called from *tcp_event_data_recv()* and *tcp_data_queue()*. An ECN flag is checked by calling *INET_ECN_is_ce*(TCP_SKB_CB(skb)→flags). It checks if the flag's zeroth and first bits are set. If so, a TCP_ECN_DEMAND_CWR bit is set for *tp→ecn_flags*. Now it means that the receiver is demanding a CWR bit in the TCP header. If the *TCP_ECN_DEMAND_CWR* bit is set in *tp→ecn_flags*, we set an ECE flag in the next TCP segment that is transmitted by calling *TCP_ECN_send()* in *TCP_ECN_send()*.

Once the sender receives the TCP segment with an ECE flag set (check is made in *TCP_ECN_rcv_ecn_echo()* called from *tcp_ack()*), we enter into the *TCP_CA_CWR* state by calling *tcp_enter_cwr()* called from *tcp_try_to_open()* in case we are in an open state or a disorder state but not in any other TCP state. From *tcp_enter_cwr()* we call *TCP_ECN_queue_cwr()* to set a *TCP_ECN_QUEUE_CWR* bit in *tp→ecn_flags* field. In the very next new data segment that we transmit, we check if we need to set a CWR flag in the TCP header by calling *TCP_ECN_send()* from *tcp_transmit_skb()*. In *TCP_ECN_send()*, we check if the new data segment is being transmitted at lines 52 and 53 and if the *TCP_ECN_QUEUE_CWR* bit is set (cs 12.16). If so, we set the CWR flag in the TCP header and also clear the *TCP_ECN_QUEUE_CWR* bit in *tp→ecn_flags* so that every time we don't send out the TCP

```
include/net/tcp_ecn.h

47 static __inline__ void
48 TCP_ECN_send(struct sock *sk, struct tcp_opt *tp, struct sk_buff *skb, int tcp_header_len)
49 {
50      if (tp->ecn_flags & TCP_ECN_OK) {
51           /* Not-retransmitted data segment: set ECT and inject CWR. */
52           if (skb->len != tcp_header_len &&
53               !before(TCP_SKB_CB(skb)->seq, tp->snd_nxt)) {
54                INET_ECN_xmit(sk);
55                if (tp->ecn_flags&TCP_ECN_QUEUE_CWR) {
56                     tp->ecn_flags &= ~TCP_ECN_QUEUE_CWR;
57                     skb->h.th->cwr = 1;
58                }
59           } else {
60                /* ACK or retransmitted segment: clear ECT|CE */
61                INET_ECN_dontxmit(sk);
62           }
63           if (tp->ecn_flags & TCP_ECN_DEMAND_CWR)
64                skb->h.th->ece = 1;
65      }
66 }
```

cs 12.16. *TCP_ECN_send().*

```
include/net/tcp_ecn.h

70 static __inline__ void
71 TCP_ECN_accept_cwr(struct tcp_opt *tp, struct sk_buff *skb)
72 {
73      if (skb->h.th->cwr)
74           tp->ecn_flags &= ~TCP_ECN_DEMAND_CWR;
75 }
```

cs 12.17. *TCP_ECN_accept_cwr().*

segment with a CWR flag set. The receiver checks for a CWR flag in the TCP header by calling *TCP_ECN_accept_cwr()* from *tcp_data_queue()*; because an additional flag is set in the TCP header, it will take a slow path and *tcp_data_queue()* will be called. Here we make a check if CWR flags is set. Once we have received CWR for the ECE flag, we clear off the *TCP_ECN_DEMAND_CWR* bit (cs-12.17). It means that our ECE request is being heard by the sender, and it has reduced its congestion window to slow down the rate of data transmission and no more TCP segments will be sent out with ECE flags set.

   Important: When we enter the CWR state by calling *tcp_enter_cwr()*, we adjust the congestion window to a minimum of current congestion window and (packets in flight + 1), which means that at the most we can send only one new segment until segments in flight are ACKed. We don't leave this state until something higher than *tp→high_seq* (recorded at the time of entering TCP CWR state) is ACKed. The CWR state is maintained only for a single window of TCP data. Once data above *tp→high_seq* are ACKed, we leave the CWR state to enter the open state and also adjust the congestion window to a minimum of slow-start threshold and congestion window. We need to wait for anything above *tp→high_seq* to be ACKed in order to make sure that the CWR bit has reached the receiver. The CWR bit is sent in the very next new segment after we have received an ECE bit from the receiver. When we receive an ECE bit, we enter into the CWR state setting $tp{\rightarrow}high\_seq$ to $tp{\rightarrow}$ snd_nxt. So, the next new segment carrying data beyond $tp{\rightarrow}high\_seq$ will contain a CWR bit. If we leave the state without the receiving end receiving data segment with CWR bit, it may cause a problem because the sender has exited from the CWR state but has not received a CWR bit. This will cause every ACK to carry an ECE bit set from the receiver once again, causing the sender to enter into CWR state. In case nothing above $tp{\rightarrow}high\_seq$ is ACKed, we don't leave the CWR state and continue our processing in default processing of a TCP state by calling $tcp\_try\_to\_open()$ (only if we don't enter into the recovery state).

For *TCP_CA_CWR* state processing in $tcp\_try\_to\_open()$, we always try to adjust CWR such that at the most we can send out only one segment on reception of ACK. The congestion window is adjusted to the minimum of congestion window and (packets in flight + 1) by calling $tcp\_cwnd\_down()$.

12.6.3 *TCP_CA_Disorder* (see cs 12.19 unless mentioned)

We acknowledged all the data that were transmitted until we enter the disorder state, so we need to take action. As explained in Section 12.5.3, we enter the disorder state in two cases in routine $tcp\_try\_to\_open()$:

1. From the open state when we receive first the duplicate ACK.
2. When we exit the congestion state (loss) and enter the open state on ACKing $tp{\rightarrow}high\_seq$ but without undoing from congestion. This means that $tp{\rightarrow}$ $undo\_retrans$ and $tp{\rightarrow}undo\_marker$ are set with a TCP open state, which means that we are not reverting back to the congestion state prior to entering the congestion. With SACK implementation, we can still get DSACK for the retransmissions which will indicate if the congestion state was entered incorrectly.

In the latter case, we know that retransmissions are still there in the flight and can expect them in the form of DSACK. So, in case we get ACK for $tp{\rightarrow}high\_seq$ in the disorder state, we call $tcp\_try\_undo\_dsack()$ at line 1548 to check if we received DSACK that clears off $tp{\rightarrow}undo\_retrans$ field.

The next step is to check if we can undo from the disorder TCP state. There are three conditions to exit the disorder state:

1. Is $tp{\rightarrow}undo\_marker$ reset?
2. Is it Reno implementation (SACK is disabled)?
3. If condition 2 is false, have we received ACK for data above $tp{\rightarrow}high\_seq$.

If we have entered the disorder state from the open state without $tp{\rightarrow}undo\_marker$ set (reception of the first duplicate ACK) or call to $tcp\_try\_undo\_dsack()$ might have cleared $tp{\rightarrow}undo\_marker$. In the case where $tp{\rightarrow}undo\_marker$ is set, we can still enter the open state in case this is Reno implementation because we have nothing like DSACK to catch. Still we can undo from the disorder state in the case where SACK is implemented and we have ACKed something above $tp{\rightarrow}high\_seq$ because this makes sure that all the data from the window at the time of entering the congestion state have reached the receiver properly. In the case where we are entering open state, we reset $tp{\rightarrow}undo\_marker$.

```
net/ipv4/tcp_input.c

1383 static void tcp_try_undo_dsack(struct sock *sk, struct tcp_opt *tp)
1384 {
1385     if (tp->undo_marker && !tp->undo_retrans) {
1386         DBGUNDO(sk, tp, "D-SACK");
1387         tcp_undo_cwr(tp, 1);
1388         tp->undo_marker = 0;
1389         NET_INC_STATS_BH(TCPDSACKUndo);
1390     }
1391 }
```

cs 12.18. *tcp_try_undo_dsack().*

Once we have exited the disorder state, we process open state in default processing of TCP states as mentioned in Section 12.5. In case we are in the *TCP_CA_Disorder* state and could not ACK *tp→high_seq* the processing of ACK received takes place in default processing of the TCP state as described in Section 12.5. Processing takes place in *tcp_try_to_open()* in case we are not entering into the fast-recovery state. We just call *tcp_moderate_cwnd()* to reduce the congestion window to slow down the rate of data transmission to send a maximum of three new segments and return.

12.6.4 *tcp_try_undo_dsack()* (see cs 12.18)

This routine is called to check if the DSACK is received that may open the TCP state. If so, we are able to undo from the congestion state prior to entering the recovery state. On reception of each DSACK within the window, *tp→undo_retrans* is decremented by 1 (see Section 11.5.1).

We call *tcp_undo_cwr()* to get us back to the congestion state prior to entering congestion by adjusting *tp→snd_ssthresh* and *tp→snd_cwnd*. This is to increment the rate of data transmission. We reset *tp→undo_marker*, which is a clear indication that we can no longer undo from the congestion state for a current window.

12.6.5 *TCP_CA_Recovery* (see cs 12.19 unless mentioned)

We have acknowledged all the data that were transmitted until the time we entered the recovery state. So, we process the recovery state between lines 1558 and 1564. In case we have ACKed *tp→high_seq* in the recovery state, we reset *tp→sacked_out* in the case of Reno implementation. This is done because we have ACKed all the data within the window transmitted at the time when we entered the recovery state. Reno emulates duplicate ACKs as SACKed-out segments. Duplicate ACKs were a result of data loss or reordering of segments within the window marked by *tp→high_seq*. Once we ACK tp→high_seq, should reset the SACK counter because SACK implementation will automatically have the SACK count set to 0 as all the holes in the window are filled when we ACK *tp→high_seq*. In Reno implementation, we need to reset the SACK counter here because there is no way we can detect the filling of holes. Next we check if we can try undo recovery by calling *tcp_try_undo_recovery()*. Here we check if our retransmission was false by calling *tcp_may_undo()*. If so, we revert back to the congestion variables that were set prior to entering congestion state by calling *tcp_undo_cwr()* and we reset *tp→undo_marker*. Irrespec-

```
net/ipv4/tcp_input.c tcp_fastretrans_alert()..... cont

1527   if (tp->ca_state == TCP_CA_Open) {
1528       BUG_TRAP(tp->retrans_out == 0);
1529       tp->retrans_stamp = 0;
1530   } else if (!before(tp->snd_una, tp->high_seq)) {
1531       switch (tp->ca_state) {
1532       case TCP_CA_Loss:
1533           tp->retransmits = 0;
1534           if (tcp_try_undo_recovery(sk, tp))
1535               return;
1536           break;
1537
1538       case TCP_CA_CWR:
1539           /* CWR is to be held something *above* high_seq
1540            * is ACKed for CWR bit to reach receiver. */
1541           if (tp->snd_una != tp->high_seq) {
1542               tcp_complete_cwr(tp);
1543               tp->ca_state = TCP_CA_Open;
1544           }
1545           break;
1546
1547       case TCP_CA_Disorder:
1548           tcp_try_undo_dsack(sk, tp);
1549           if (!tp->undo_marker ||
                   ...
1552               IsReno(tp) || tp->snd_una != tp->high_seq) {
1553               tp->undo_marker = 0;
1554               tp->ca_state = TCP_CA_Open;
1555           }
1556           break;
1557
1558       case TCP_CA_Recovery:
1559           if (IsReno(tp))
1560               tcp_reset_reno_sack(tp);
1561           if (tcp_try_undo_recovery(sk, tp))
1562               return;
1563           tcp_complete_cwr(tp);
1564           break;
1565       }
```

cs 12.19. *tcp_fastretrans_alert()*.

tive of whether we are able to undo from the recovery state, the next step is for exiting the recovery state. In the case of Reno implementation, we should ACK something beyond *tp→high_seq* to exit the recovery state. This is done in order to avoid entering a false fast-recovery state in case the retransmissions for segments below *tp→high_seq* generate duplicate ACKs. In the case of SACK/DSACK implementation, DSACKs are generated for each such duplicate ACKs, so we need not worry and exit the recovery state as soon as *tp→high_seq* is ACKed. In the latter case we are not able to exit the recovery state, so we moderate the congestion window by calling *tcp_moderate_cwnd()* to slow down the data transmission rate until we get ACK beyond *tp→high_seq*. In the case where we exit the recovery state, the next step is to continue processing for the open state; otherwise we return with the recovery state from the routine.

12.6.6 *tcp_add_reno_sack()*

Reno implementation does not have any idea of any out-of-order segments that are received by the peer. We try to simulate SACK-out segments from the duplicate acknowledgments we receive. This makes our work simpler by having a common

```
net/ipv4/tcp_input.c

1203 static void tcp_add_reno_sack(struct tcp_opt *tp)
1204 {
1205      ++tp->sacked_out;
1206      tcp_check_reno_reordering(tp, 0);
1207      tcp_sync_left_out(tp);
1208 }
```

cs 12.20. *tcp_add_reno_sack().*

```
net/ipv4/tcp_input.c

1188 static void tcp_check_reno_reordering(struct tcp_opt *tp, int addend)
1189 {
1190      u32 holes;
1191
1192      holes = max(tp->lost_out, 1U);
1193      holes = min(holes, tp->packets_out);
1194
1195      if (tp->sacked_out + holes > tp->packets_out) {
1196           tp->sacked_out = tp->packets_out - holes;
1197           tcp_update_reordering(tp, tp->packets_out+addend, 0);
1198      }
1199 }
```

cs 12.21. *tcp_check_reno_reordering().*

routine for SACK as well as Reno implementations. In *tcp_add_reno_sack()* we increment the SACK counter (*tp→sacked_out*) by 1, and we call *tcp_check_reno_reordering()* in order to check if we need to update the Reno reordering length. Finally we call *tcp_sync_left_out()* at line 1207 (cs 12.20) to update the segments that have left the network that is the sum of SACKed-out and lost-out segments. We do it here because we have a new Reno SACK.

12.6.7   *tcp_check_reno_reordering()*

The routine tries to calculate the reordering length for Reno implementations where we have no idea of out-of-order segments received by the peer. Normally, with SACK implementation, we can calculate the reordering length from SACK block highest and lowest sequence spaces. With Reno, we have no such case. Reordering can be observed only if we receive more than expected duplicate ACKs. This may happen in case the lost segment reaches the receiver out-of-order after we have already retransmitted it. In such cases, we get a duplicate ACK for the retransmitted segment which will be one more than expected. We can safely assume this as reordering. In such cases where the sum of SACKed-out segments and lost segments is more than the segments so far transmitted within the window (line 1195, cs 12.21), we need to update reordering length as the number of packets transmitted but not yet ACKed within the window (*tp→packets_out*) by calling *tcp_update_reordering()* at line 1197.

12.6.8   *tcp_may_undo()* (see cs 12.22 unless mentioned)

The routine checks if we can revert back to the open state because we may have entered the congestion state incorrectly. When the TCP enters into any state other

```
net/ipv4/tcp_input.c

1350 static inline int tcp_may_undo(struct tcp_opt *tp)
1351 {
1352      return tp->undo_marker &&
1353           (!tp->undo_retrans || tcp_packet_delayed(tp));
1354 }
```

cs 12.22. tcp_may_undo().

```
net/ipv4/tcp_input.c

1312 static __inline__ int tcp_packet_delayed(struct tcp_opt *tp)
1313 {
1314      return !tp->retrans_stamp ||
1315           (tp->saw_tstamp && tp->rcv_tsecr &&
1316            (__s32)(tp->rcv_tsecr - tp->retrans_stamp) < 0);
1317 }
```

cs 12.23. tcp_packet_delayed().

than open because of congestion, we record the highest sequence number transmitted so far (tp→high_seq), the slow-start threshold and congestion window are adjusted to slow down the rate of transmission of segments, and we record the slow-start threshold prior to entering the congestion state. We record tp→high_seq so that once this sequence is acknowledged, we can try to undo from the congestion state.

Undoing from state means that if we were misled into the congestion state because of a packet delayed in the network, reordering of segments, and underestimated RTOs, we can resume the same state as it was before. After entering into congestion state, we may retransmit segments marked lost. We can sense undoing from the state in case we find that the original transmissions are succeeding. We do this by calling tcp_may_undo().

We check that if tp→undo_marker is set, this is set to unACKed sequence number (tp→snd_una) when we enter the congestion state. If this field is set, we know that we are eligible for undoing from the congestion state. We proceed further to check if we can undo from the congestion state. Next we check is whether tp→undo_retrans is 0. If this field is zero, it means that either we have not retransmitted anything or whichever segment was retransmitted has been DSACKed, indicating that the original segments were not lost and they also reached the destination along with the retransmitted segments. It may also happen that the ACKs to the segment transmitted earlier were lost and when we retransmitted them, we got DSACKs for those retransmitted segments. If tp→undo_retrans is nonzero, it means that we have retransmitted something. We check if packets got delayed in the network but reached the destination by calling tcp_packet_delayed().

12.6.9 tcp_packet_delayed() (see cs 12.23 unless mentioned)

We undo from the congestion state only if we got DSACKs for all retransmitted segments (tp→undo_retrans equal to 0) or our original transmissions successfully reached the receiver (tcp_packet_delayed() returned TRUE because tp→rcv_tsecr < tp→retrans_stamp).

      tp→retrans_stamp → is the timestamp when the first segment was retransmitted.

      tp→rcv_tsecr → is the echoed timestamp from the receiver.

If *tp→rcv_tsecr* < *tp→retrans_stamp*, it means that the echoed timestamp was from the original transmission because the retransmission timestamp is higher than the echoed timestamp. If the echoed timestamp was greater than the timestamp of the first retransmission, it means that the retransmission has filled the hole. To understand which timestamp is echoed in the case of reordering, just check RFC 1323. According to this document, we echo the timestamp from the last segment that advanced the left window in case we receive an out-of-order segment. When a segment arrives that fills a gap, we echo back the timestamp from this segment. The reason for this is that the segment that fills the gap represents the true congestion state of the network. See Section 11.8.

12.6.10 *tcp_undo_cwr()*

In case we are about to undo from any of the non-open (congestion) states, we may revert back to the congestion state prior to entering the congestion state. There are two congestion state variables: slow-start threshold and congestion window. We record the slow-start threshold value before entering the congestion state in *tp→prior_ssthresh*, and the slow-start threshold is initialized to half of the congestion window at that time. While undoing from the congestion state, we call *tcp_undo_cwr()* to revert back to the original congestion state, in case the prior threshold recorded in *tp→prior_ssthresh* is greater than the current slow-start threshold value. Since half of the congestion window was recorded in the slow-start threshold (*tp→snd_ssthresh*), we initialize the congestion window to the maximum of current congestion window and double the slow-start threshold value (line 1337) since during the congestion state the congestion window may have increased to a high value if the number of packets in flight is too high at the time of congestion. This will increase the data transmission to a very high value. If the prior slow-start threshold is zero, we don't revert back to the slow-start threshold value recorded prior to going into the congestion state, and the congestion window is initialized as a maximum of current congestion window and a slow-start threshold value (line 1344, cs 12.24).

    Finally, we try to moderate congestion window in case we have reverted back to the congestion window prior to congestion. This may inflate the congestion to a very high value, suddenly causing a burst of packets in the network difficult to handle. We call *tcp_moderate_cwnd()*. It may happen that all the ACKs from the last window were lost and on reretransmission after we got ACK for all the data, thereby causing congestion window to grow up to very high value. This may cause a burst of segment to be transmitted. The congestion window is initialized to a minimum of current congestion window and packets in flight + maximum burst (cs-12.25). Linux assumes maximum burst to be 3, which means that even with delayed ACK, it can send out a maximum of 3 segments.

12.6.11 *tcp_mark_head_lost()*

This routine is called to mark a specified number of segments lost starting from the head of the retransmit queue. The number of segments is the minimum of the

```
net/ipv4/tcp_input.c

1334 static void tcp_undo_cwr(struct tcp_opt *tp, int undo)
1335 {
1336     if (tp->prior_ssthresh) {
1337         tp->snd_cwnd = max(tp->snd_cwnd, tp->snd_ssthresh<<1);
1338
1339         if (undo && tp->prior_ssthresh > tp->snd_ssthresh) {
1340             tp->snd_ssthresh = tp->prior_ssthresh;
1341             TCP_ECN_withdraw_cwr(tp);
1342         }
1343     } else {
1344         tp->snd_cwnd = max(tp->snd_cwnd, tp->snd_ssthresh);
1345     }
1346     tcp_moderate_cwnd(tp);
1347     tp->snd_cwnd_stamp = tcp_time_stamp;
1348 }
```

cs 12.24. tcp_undo_cwr().

```
net/ipv4/tcp_input.c

1286 static __inline__ void tcp_moderate_cwnd(struct tcp_opt *tp)
1287 {
1288     tp->snd_cwnd = min(tp->snd_cwnd,
1289                 tcp_packets_in_flight(tp)+tcp_max_burst(tp));
1290     tp->snd_cwnd_stamp = tcp_time_stamp;
1291 }
```

cs 12.25. tcp_moderate_cwnd().

```
net/ipv4/tcp_input.c

1232 static void
1233 tcp_mark_head_lost(struct sock *sk, struct tcp_opt *tp, int packets, u32 high_seq)
1234 {
1235     struct sk_buff *skb;
1236     int cnt = packets;
         ....
1240     for_retrans_queue(skb, sk, tp) {
1241         if (--cnt < 0 || after(TCP_SKB_CB(skb)->end_seq, high_seq))
1242             break;
1243         if (!(TCP_SKB_CB(skb)->sacked&TCPCB_TAGBITS)) {
1244             TCP_SKB_CB(skb)->sacked |= TCPCB_LOST;
1245             tp->lost_out++;
1246         }
1247     }
1248     tcp_sync_left_out(tp);
1249 }
```

cs 12.26. tcp_mark_head_lost().

number of segments as specified by the caller and *tp→high_seq* recorded so far
(line 1241, cs 12.26). The segments are marked lost only if they are neither
SACKed/retransmitted or not already marked lost (lines 1243–1246). Finally, we
need to synchronize the segments that have left the network by calling
tcp_sync_left_out()

```
include/net/tcp.h

1098 static inline void tcp_sync_left_out(struct tcp_opt *tp)
1099 {
1100      if (tp->sack_ok && tp->sacked_out >= tp->packets_out - tp->lost_out)
1101           tp->sacked_out = tp->packets_out - tp->lost_out;
1102      tp->left_out = tp->sacked_out + tp->lost_out;
1103 }
```

cs 12.27. *tcp_sync_left_out().*

12.6.12 *tcp_sync_left_out()*

This routine is called when we need to update segments that have left the network (cs 12.27). This is required when we have updated SACKed-out segments or lost-out segments. In the case where SACKed-out segments have exceeded the number of segments already transmitted minus the number of segments considered lost, we need to equate the SACKed-out segments to the difference of these two (line 1101). This may happen in the case of Reno SACK implementation, where every duplicate ACK is considered to be a SACKed-out segment. The duplicate ACK may also be generated from retransmits failing the packet conservation law. Finally, the number of segments that have left out the network is calculated as the sum of the number of segments lost out and the number of segments SACKed.

12.7 SUMMARY

In this chapter we have seen how *tcp_fastretrans_alert()* implements the logic of TCP congestion state enter and exit logic. There are four TCP congestion states that are processed:

- *TCP_CA_CWR*, congestion window reduction. This is set because of local congestion or we received a TCP segment with an ECE flag set.
- *TCP_CA_Disorder*. TCP enters this state when it senses congestion for the first time because of SACK blocks or duplicate ACK. TCP enters this state before entering recovery.
- *TCP_CA_Recovery*. TCP enters the recovery state when we get an early indication of congestion because of duplicate ACKs and the retransmission head timing out.
- *TCP_CA_Loss*. TCP enters the loss state when we experience timeout or we reject all the SACK blocks in *tcp_check_sack_reneging()* as the receiver has destroyed its out-of-order queue.

The two congestion state variables are implemented as follows:

- *tp→snd_cwnd*, which is send side congestion window that is manipulated by different congestion control algorithms and rate at which ACK is received.
- *tp→snd_ssthresh*, which is sender's slow-start threshold to mark the start of the recovery algorithm.

- *tp→high_seq* is used as an exit condition when TCP has entered any of the congestion state.
- *tcp_may_undo()* is used to detect false entry into the congestion state and spurious RTO.
- *tcp_xmit_retransmit_queue()* implements the fast retransmission algorithm.
- Linux simulates Reno SACK by incrementing the SACK count on reception of duplicate ACK.
- *tcp_update_scoreboard()* implements logic of updating lost segment based on FACK count for SACK implementation.

13

NETLINK SOCKETS

This chapter starts with the introduction of netlink sockets and the different types of protocol families supported. Then gives a detailed explanation of how netlink sockets are registered at boot time. In addition, we will explain how the kernel and user netlink sockets are created. Then we see the details of netlink data structures and the format of netlink packet. Finally we will go through the details of how a netlink user and a kernel socket interact.

13.1 INTRODUCTION TO NETLINK SOCKETS

Netlink is a bidirectional communication method for transferring the data between kernel modules and user space processes. This functionality is provided using the standard socket APIs for user space processes and an internal kernel API for kernel modules.

The supported netlink families are as follows:

- *NETLINK_ROUTE:* It is used for queueing disciplines, to update the IPV4 routing table.
- *NETLINK_SKIP:* Reserved for ENskip.
- *NETLINK_USERSOCK:* Reserved for user mode socket protocols.
- *NETLINK_FIREWALL:* Receives packets sent by the IPv4 firewall code.
- *NETLINK_TCPDIAG:* TCP socket monitoring.

TCP/IP Architecture, Design, and Implementation in Linux. By S. Seth and M. A. Venkatesulu
Copyright © 2008 the IEEE Computer Society

- *NETLINK_NFLOG:* Netfilter/iptables ULOG.
- *NETLINK_ARPD:* To update the arp table.
- *NETLINK_ROUTE6:* To update the IPV6 routing table.

Why Netlink Sockets?

- Netlink sockets support multicast, and one process can multicast messages to a netlink group of addresses.
- They provide BSD socket-style APIs.
- Netlink sockets are asynchronous, and they provide queuing of messages for socket.
- For any new feature support, only the protocol type has to be implemented.

13.2 NETLINK SOCKET REGISTRATION AND INITIALIZATION AT BOOT TIME

At boot time when the netlink module (net/netlink/af_netlink.c) gets loaded, the *module_init* function calls the *netlink_proto_init()* initialization routine (cs 13.1).

In the *netlink_proto_init()* routine, the *sock_register()* function gets called at line 1013 with '*netlink_family_ops*' as parameter.

'*netlink_family_ops*' is of type *net_proto_family* struct, and in case of netlink protocol it is defined as shown in cs 13.2, where *PF_NETLINK* is the family of protocol type. *netlink_create* is the create function for the socket of *PF_NETLINK*.

The main purpose of the *sock_register()* function is to advertise the protocol handler's address family and have it linked into the socket module (cs 13.3).

```
net/netlink/af_netlink.c
1005 static int __init netlink_proto_init(void)
1006 {
          . . .
1013     sock_register(&netlink_family_ops);
          . . .
1017     return 0;
1018 }
```

cs 13.1. *Netlink_proto_init ( ).*

```
net/netlink/af_netlink.c

1000 struct net_proto_family netlink_family_ops = {
1001     PF_NETLINK,
1002     netlink_create
1003 };
```

cs 13.2. *Netlink_proto_family.*

```
net/socket.c
  1620 int sock_register(struct net_proto_family *ops)
  1621 {
         . . .
  1630      if (net_families[ops->family] == NULL) {
  1631           net_families[ops->family]=ops;
  1632           err = 0;
  1633      }
         . . .
  1636 }
```

cs 13.3. sock_register ( ).

```
net/socket.c
  133 static struct net_proto_family *net_families[NPROTO];
```

cs 13.4. net_families.

```
init/main.c
  475 static void __init do_basic_setup(void)
  476 {
       . . .
  541      sock_init();
       . . .
  553 }
```

cs 13.5. do_basic_setup ( ).

At line 1630 (cs 13.3) the *sock_register()* checks for the socket system call protocol family entry in the *net_families* table and at line 1631 it inserts the protocol family entry in the *net_families* table (in this case it is a netlink protocol).

The *net_families* table is an array of *struct net_proto_family* pointers where all the protocol families are registered, *net_families* is defined as shown in cs 13.4 where NPROTO is the minimum number of protocol that can be registered. It's value is set to 32 in kernel.

13.3 HOW IS THE KERNEL NETLINK SOCKET CREATED?

At Linux booting when the CPU subsystem is up and running and memory and process management works, the function *do_basic_setup()* does network initialization by calling the function *sock_init()* at line 541 as shown in cs 13.5.

The *sock_init()* function initializes all the address (protocol) families at lines 1677 and 1678 (cs 13.6). Here we are interested in the initialization of the protocols module, particularly about the netlink protocol. For initializing the netlink protocol there is a function called *rtnetlink_init()* which gets called at line 1717 to initalize and create the kernel netlink socket.

The *rtnetlink_init()* creates a netlink socket in the kernel for handling the user requests (cs 13.7). It calls the routine '*netlink_kernel_create*' with parameters such as *NETLINK_ROUTE* and *rtnetlink_rcv* function pointer at line 523.

```
net/socket.c
1666 void __init sock_init(void)
1667 {
         . . .
1677      for (i = 0; i < NPROTO; i++)
1678           net_families[i] = NULL;

1717      rtnetlink_init();
          . . .
1729 }
```

cs 13.6. sock_init ( ).

```
net/core/rtnetlink.c
518 void __init rtnetlink_init(void)
519 {
        . . .
523      rtnl = netlink_kernel_create(NETLINK_ROUTE, rtnetlink_rcv);
         . . .
530 }
```

cs 13.7. rtnetlink_init ( ).

The *netlink_kernel_create()* function first allocates a socket by calling the routine *sock_alloc()* at line 715. Then it initializes the socket type to *SOCK_RAW* at line 718 (cs 13.8).

At line 720 the kernel netlink socket is created by calling the function *netlink_create()* and then initializes the sock struct pointer sk to point to the socket object of socket struct at line 724 which is dynamically allocated in the *netlink_create()* function. Also it initializes the *data_ready* function pointer of sock struct to point to the *netlink_data_ready()* function, and then it checks if there is a second input parameter is passed; if yes, then it initializes the *af_netlink→data_ready* function pointer to the second input parameter at line 727, which is *rtnetlink_rcv* for netlink protocol. Finally, it adds the entry of this socket in *nl_table* (see Section 13.5) by calling the routine *netlink_insert* at line 729.

13.4 HOW IS THE USER NETLINK SOCKET CREATED?

The user space netlink socket is created by the socket() system call, for example,

fd = socket(AF_NETLINK, SOCK_RAW, protocol);

where *AF_NETLINK* is the address family and the *SOCK_RAW* is socket type.
The following protocol families are supported by the netlink socket:

NETLINK_ROUTE
NETLINK_FIREWALL
NETLINK_ARPD

```
net/netlink/af_netlink.c

707 netlink_kernel_create(int unit, void (*input)(struct sock *sk, int len))
708 {
709     struct socket *sock;
710     struct sock *sk;
711
    . . .
715     if (!(sock = sock_alloc()))
716         return NULL;
717
718     sock->type = SOCK_RAW;
719
720     if (netlink_create(sock, unit) < 0) {
721         sock_release(sock);
722         return NULL;
723     }
724     sk = sock->sk;
725     sk->data_ready = netlink_data_ready;
726     if (input)
727         sk->protinfo.af_netlink->data_ready = input;
728
729     netlink_insert(sk, 0);
730     return sk;
731 }
```

cs 13.8. *netlink_kernel_create ( ).*

NETLINK_IP6_FW
NETLINK_NFLOG
NETLINK_ROUTE6
NETLINK_TAPBASE
NETLINK_TCPDIAG
NETLINK_XFRM

Here We Will Discuss the NETLINK_ROUTE Protocol. The *NETLINK_ ROUTE* protocol is used for updating the routing table, to link parameters for setting up network interfaces, to address for setting up ip address for network interface, for queuing disciplines, for traffic classes, for setting up of filters for traffic classes, for neighbor setups, and for setting up of rules for the routing. It controls the Linux networking routing system.

For example, the user command used for updating the routing table is 'ip,' and that for the queuing discipline and traffic classes is 'tc' using NETLINK sockets for the *NETLINK_ROUTE* protocol.

LINK Parameter Messages. The LINK messages allows a *NETLINK_ROUTE* protocol user to set and retrieve information about the network interfaces on the system. It consists of the following message types:

RTM_NEWLINK
RTM_DELLINK
RTM_GETLINK

The ADDR Messages. The ADDR messages allows a *NETLINK_ROUTE* protocol user to set/unset the IP address on the network interface on the system. It consists of the following message types:

RTM_NEWADDR
RTM_DELADDR
RTM_GETADDR

The ROUTE Messages. The ROUTE messages allow a *NETLINK_ROUTE* protocol user to update the routing table. It consists of the following message types:

RTM_NEWROUTE
RTM_DELROUTE
RTM_GETROUTE

The QDISC Messages. The QDISC messages allows a *NETLINK_ROUTE* protocol user to add/delete the qdisc to the queuing discipline of the system. It consists of the following message types:

RTM_NEWQDISC
RTM_DELQDISC
RTM_GETQDISC

The CLASS Messages. The CLASS messages allow a *NETLINK_ROUTE* protocol user to add/delete a class to the qdisc of the queuing discipline of the system. It consists of the following message types:

RTM_NEWCLASS
RTM_DELCLASS
RTM_GETCLASS

The FILTER Messages. The FILTER messages allows a *NETLINK_ROUTE* protocol user to add/delete a filter to the class of qdisc of the queuing discipline of the system. It consists of following message types:

RTM_NEWFILTER
RTM_DELFILTER
RTM_GETFILTER

The socket() is a system call which is then resolved in the kernel. It calls the *sys_socketcall()*, which in turn calls *sys_socket()*; *sys_socket()* calls the *sock_create()*, and based on the family in this case it is netlink; and *sock_create()* calls the netlink_create. This function creates the socket and initializes the operations of protocol performed with socket. It initializes the *sock→ops* to be *&netlink_ops*, where *netlink_ops* is a list of function pointers for various operation to be performed on netlink sockets (cs 13.9).

```
net/netlink/af_netlink.c
 979 struct proto_ops netlink_ops = {
 980      family:       PF_NETLINK,
 981
 982      release:        netlink_release,
 983      bind:          netlink_bind,
 984      connect:        netlink_connect,
 985      socketpair:      sock_no_socketpair,
 986      accept:         sock_no_accept,
 987      getname:        netlink_getname,
 988      poll:          datagram_poll,
 989      ioctl:         sock_no_ioctl,
 990      listen:         sock_no_listen,
 991      shutdown:        sock_no_shutdown,
 992      setsockopt:      sock_no_setsockopt,
 993      getsockopt:      sock_no_getsockopt,
 994      sendmsg:        netlink_sendmsg,
 995      recvmsg:        netlink_recvmsg,
 996      mmap:          sock_no_mmap,
 997      sendpage:       sock_no_sendpage,
 998 };
```

cs 13.9. netlink_ops.

13.5 NETLINK DATA STRUCTURES

Kernel Data Structures

- *nl_table*
- *rtnetlink_link*

13.5.1 *nl_table*

nl_table is an array of pointers to sock structures (socket linked list). Its size is set to *MAX_LINKS* (32). It is defined in kernel as shown in cs 13.10. Each element of *nl_table* array represents a NETLINK protocol family—for example, *NETLINK_ ROUTE*, NETLINK_FIREWALL, and so on, as shown in Fig. 13.1 and each NETLINK protocol family contains a pointer to the socket (struct sock) linked list. The *nl_table* is looked up based on the protocol when there is a communication between user and kernel space for the netlink socket; and based on the protocol, the socket (struct sock) linked list is searched for sock that has the same pid with the current process. Once the sock struct is found in the sock list for the protocol in the *nl_table*, then it enqueues the skbuff (contains netlink packet) into the sock's receive queue.

```
net/netlink/af_netlink.c
 66 static struct sock *nl_table[MAX_LINKS];
```

cs 13.10. nl_table.

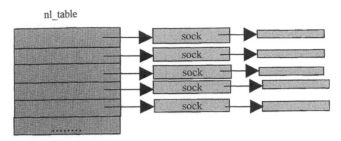

Figure 13.1. *nl_table data structure.*

13.5.2 *rtnetlink_link*

rtnetlink_links is defined as an array of pointers to *rtnetlink_link* data structure (cs 13.11). Each *rtnetlink_link* data structure corresponds to a rtnetlink command—for example, *RTM_NEWQDISC*, which is a command for adding a new qdisc. Here the *rtnetlink_link* is shown in cs 13.12.

> doit: pointer to a function which will be called based on the command in the control message.
>
> dumpit: pointer to a function to clear data after completion of command or on error.

Each entry in the *rtnetlink_links* table corresponds to a particular family such as *AF_NETLINK*.

The *rtnetlink_link* data structure contains the doit and dumpit function pointers (Fig. 13.2). The *rtnetlink_links* table gets initialized while registering the *net_device* if *CONFIG_NET_SCHED* is defined in the case of queueing discipline.

The *rtnetlink_links* gets initialized in *pktsched_init()* from *net/sched/sch_api.c* in the case of queuing discipline (cs 13.13).

In *pktsched_init ( )*, at line 1167 we declare a data structure *rtnetlink_link* and then directly assign the global *rtnetlink_links* table address based on the address

```
net/core/rtnetlink.c
    81 struct rtnetlink_link * rtnetlink_links[NPROTO];
```

cs 13.11. *rtnetlink_links.*

```
include/linux/rtnetlink.h
    553 struct rtnetlink_link
    554 {
    555      int (*doit)(struct sk_buff *, struct nlmsghdr *, void *attr);
    556      int (*dumpit)(struct sk_buff *, struct netlink_callback *cb);
    557 };
```

cs 13.12. *rtnetlink_link.*

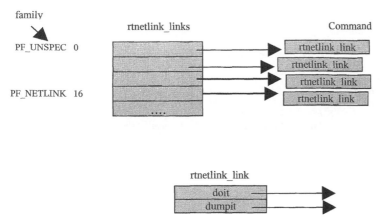

Figure 13.2. *rtnetlink_links* and *rtnetlink_link* data structure.

```
net/sched/sch_api.c
    1165 int    init pktsched_init(void)
    1166 {
    1167      struct rtnetlink_link *link_p;
              . . .
    1180      link_p = rtnetlink_links[PF_UNSPEC];
              . .
    1186      if (link_p) {
    1187          link_p[RTM_NEWQDISC-RTM_BASE].doit = tc_modify_qdisc;
    1188          link_p[RTM_DELQDISC-RTM_BASE].doit = tc_get_qdisc;
    1189          link_p[RTM_GETQDISC-RTM_BASE].doit = tc_get_qdisc;
    1190          link_p[RTM_GETQDISC-RTM_BASE].dumpit = tc_dump_qdisc;
    1191          link_p[RTM_NEWTCLASS-RTM_BASE].doit = tc_ctl_tclass;
    1192          link_p[RTM_DELTCLASS-RTM_BASE].doit = tc_ctl_tclass;
    1193          link_p[RTM_GETTCLASS-RTM_BASE].doit = tc_ctl_tclass;
    1194          link_p[RTM_GETTCLASS-RTM_BASE].dumpit = tc_dump_tclass;
    1195      }

              . . .
```

cs 13.13. *pktsched_init ( ).*

family (used as an index for the array) at line 1180. Here the address family is *PF_UNSPEC*. The *rtnetlink_links* global table is viewed as a two-dimensional array, its row corresponds to family, and each column on a row corresponds to command (*struct rtnetlink_link*) in that family. Then based on the type—for example, *RTM_NEWQDISC* (which acts as command for adding the new qdisc)—the doit function pointer of struct *rtnetlink_link* for *RTM_NEWQDISC* type points to function *tc_modify_qdisc( )* at line 1187. Similarly from lines 1188 to 1194, based on other type the doit and dumpit function pointer gets initialized for struct *rtnetlink_link* (command).

Similarly the queuing discipline filter function pointers for adding filter to the class are initialized in function *tc_filter_init()* (cs 13.14).

We can see that for adding/deleting/getting the filter doit function pointers are initialized to *tc_ctl_tfilter ()* function at lines 441–443.

```
net/sched/cls_api.c
  432 int __init tc_filter_init(void)
  433 {
  434      struct rtnetlink_link *link_p = rtnetlink_links[PF_UNSPEC];

  440      if (link_p) {
  441          link_p[RTM_NEWTFILTER-RTM_BASE].doit = tc_ctl_tfilter;
  442          link_p[RTM_DELTFILTER-RTM_BASE].doit = tc_ctl_tfilter;
  443          link_p[RTM_GETTFILTER-RTM_BASE].doit = tc_ctl_tfilter;
  444          link_p[RTM_GETTFILTER-RTM_BASE].dumpit = tc_dump_tfilter;
  445      }
```

cs 13.14. tc_filter_init ( ).

```
net/ipv4/devinet.c
  952 static struct rtnetlink_link inet_rtnetlink_table[RTM_MAX-RTM_BASE+1] =
  953 {
            . . .
  959      { inet_rtm_newaddr,   NULL,            },
  960      { inet_rtm_deladdr,   NULL,            },
  961      { NULL,               inet_dump_ifaddr, },
  962      { NULL,               NULL,            },
  963
  964      { inet_rtm_newroute,  NULL,            },
  965      { inet_rtm_delroute,  NULL,            },
  966      { inet_rtm_getroute,  inet_dump_fib,   },
  967      { NULL,               NULL,            },
            . . .
  974 #ifdef CONFIG_IP_MULTIPLE_TABLES
  975      { inet_rtm_newrule,   NULL,            },
  976      { inet_rtm_delrule,   NULL,            },
  977      { NULL,               inet_dump_rules, },
  978      { NULL,               NULL,            },
            . . .
  984 #endif
  985 };
```

cs 13.15. inet_rtnetlink_table.

In case of the routing, this table is defined as *inet_rtnetlink_table* and it gets initialized as part of *inet_init()*. For routing, *inet_rtnetlink_table* is declared as in net/ipv4/devinet.c as shown in cs 13.15.

13.6 OTHER IMPORTANT DATA STRUTURES

13.6.1 *struct nlmsghdr*

The nlmsghdr is a standard message header for each message sent or received for the netlink protocol (cs 13.16).

nlmsg_len is the length of total amount of data in the message including the header itself.

```
include/linux/netlink.h
  26 struct nlmsghdr
  27 {
  28      __u32      nlmsg_len;     /* Length of message including header */
  29      __u16      nlmsg_type;    /* Message content */
  30      __u16      nlmsg_flags;   /* Additional flags */
  31      __u32      nlmsg_seq;     /* Sequence number */
  32      __u32      nlmsg_pid;     /* Sending process PID */
  33 };
```

cs 13.16. *nlmsghdr.*

nlmsg_type defines the format of the data which follow the netlink header.

nlmsg_flags defines various control flags.

nlmsg_seq is used by a process that creates the netlink request messages to correlate those requests with their responses.

nlmsg_pid is the sending process PID.

13.6.2 *struct msghdr*

The msghdr data structure contains the netlink message that will be passed to the kernel (cs 13.17). *msg_iov* is a pointer of type iovec, where iovec is as shown in cs 13.18.

```
include/linux/socket.h
  33 struct msghdr {
  34      void   *    msg_name;       /* Socket name           */
  35      int        msg_namelen;    /* Length of name        */
  36      struct iovec * msg_iov;    /* Data blocks           */
  37      __kernel_size_t msg_iovlen;   /* Number of blocks       */
  38      void   *    msg_control;   /* Per protocol magic (eg BSD file descrip    tor passing) */
  39      __kernel_size_t msg_controllen; /* Length of cmsg list */
  40      unsigned    msg_flags;
  41 };
```

cs 13.17. msghdr.

```
include/linux/uio.h
  19 struct iovec
  20 {
  21      void *iov_base;        /* BSD uses caddr_t (1003.1g requires void *) */
  22      __kernel_size_t iov_len; /* Must be size_t (1003.1g) */
  23 };
```

cs 13.18. iovec.

The iovec structure consists of two elements: the pointer to data and the length of the data.

iov_base points to the netlink packet (netlink message header plus data).
iov_len contains the length of this packet to be passed to the kernel.

13.7 NETLINK PACKET FORMAT

Figure 13.3 shows the format of the netlink socket in the case of queuing disciplines. The parameters have to be filled in the above format before passing the netlink socket in the kernel. Based on the parameters, the appropriate action is performed by the spefic kernel module.

In the case of the routing table, only the struct tcmsg is replaced by the rtmsg. So the netlink packet for the queuing discipline consists of

struct nlmsghdr: netlink message header.

struct tcmsg: for setting up classes, qdisc type, and filters.

struct rtattr and attributes (parameters to be passed to buffer)

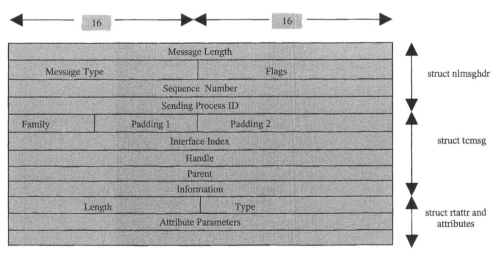

Figure 13.3. Netlink packet format.

13.8 NETLINK SOCKET EXAMPLE—tc COMMAND FOR Adding a qdisc

In this section we see how the netlink socket is used in 'tc' command implementation, e.g., tc qdisc add dev etho root handle 1:0 cbq bandwidth 10 mbit.

13.8.1 tc Command Flow in User Space for Adding a qdisc

Figure 13.4 shows tc command user space flow diagram. Here we are not covering details about the tc command user space flow. From Fig 13.4, it's clear that how

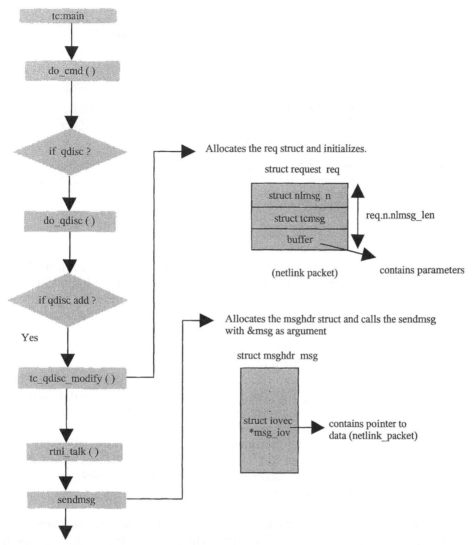

Figure 13.4. tc command user space flow diagram.

request and msghdr structures are allocated. After allocating these structures *sendmsg() sys_call* get invoked and enters the kernel mode with request and msghdr details.

13.8.2 tc Command in Kernel Space

In this section the details about TC command implementation in kernel space are outlined.

13.8.2.1 sys_sendmsg ( ). This function gets invoked in kernel space for a *sendmsg()* systen call. The main parameter to *sys_sendmsg()* is struct msghdr msg. The msg struct includes a pointer to the netlink packet (struct req). The

```
net/socket.c
1343 asmlinkage long sys_sendmsg(int fd, struct msghdr *msg, unsigned flags)
1344 {
1345     struct socket *sock;

1350     struct msghdr msg_sys;

1354     if (copy_from_user(&msg_sys,msg,sizeof(struct msghdr)))
1355         goto out;

1376     err = verify_iovec(&msg_sys, iov, address, VERIFY_READ);

1403     err = sock_sendmsg(sock, &msg_sys, total_len);

```

cs 13.19. *sys_sendmsg ( ).*

sys_sendmsg () creates a new data structure of the same type as struct msghdr msg from user space. The new data structure is declared as *msg_sys* at line 1350.

Then at line 1354 using *copy_from_user*, copy each element from the user space msg struct to the kernel space new data structure *msg_sys*. The iovec element of *msg_sys* contains a pointer to the netlink packet which will be verified and copied by calling the *verify_iovec ( )* function at line 1376. Finally, the *sock_sendmsg* is invoked at line 1403 with argument *msg_sys* passed to it (cs 13.19).

13.8.2.2   sock_sendmsg ( ). The *sock_sendmsg( )* declares a data structure *scm_cookie* at line 503 (cs 13.20). Its main purpose is to hold information about the socket control messages (uid, gid, pid, etc., of the process). This *scm_cookie* data structure is initialized by calling the function *scm_send( )* at line 505. And finally the function pointer *sendmsg* at line 507 is invoked; here the operation pointer points to the *netlink_ops* data structure, and the sendmsg in *netlink_ops* points to *netlink_sendmsg*. So *netlink_sendmsg* is invoked.

13.8.2.3   netlink_sendmsg ( ). In *netlink_sendmsg* a new *sk_buff skb* is allocated at line 600 for copying the netlink data. Then at line 618 (cs 13.21) *memcpy_fromiovec ( )* copies the *msg→msg_iov* (message buffer), which contains the pointer

```
net/socket.c
500 int sock_sendmsg(struct socket *sock, struct msghdr *msg, int size)
501 {
502     int err;
503     struct scm_cookie scm;
504
505     err = scm_send(sock, msg, &scm);
506     if (err >= 0) {
507         err = sock->ops->sendmsg(sock, msg, size, &scm);
508         scm_destroy(&scm);
509     }
510     return err;
511 }
```

cs 13.20. *sock_sendmsg ( ).*

```
net/netlink/af_netlink.c
565 static int netlink_sendmsg(struct socket *sock, struct msghdr *msg, int len,
566                 struct scm_cookie *scm)
567 {

600     skb = alloc_skb(len, GFP_KERNEL);

618     if (memcpy_fromiovec(skb_put(skb,len), msg->msg_iov, len)) {
619         kfree_skb(skb);
620         goto out;
621     }

623     if (dst_groups) {
624         atomic_inc(&skb->users);
625         netlink_broadcast(sk, skb, dst_pid, dst_groups, GFP_KERNEL);
626     }
627     err = netlink_unicast(sk, skb, dst_pid, msg->msg_flags&MSG_DONTWAIT);

631 }
```

cs 13.21. *netlink_sendmsg ( ).*

to netlink packet to the *sk_buff* skb's data area. After copying the netlink packet to *sk_buff*, at line 625 or 627 *netlink_broadcast( )* or the *netlink_unicast( )* with skb as main parameter is called based on the value of dstgroups (which checks for multiple process broadcast or for the single process).

13.8.2.4   netlink_unicast ( ).   The *netlink_unicast ( )* gets the socket's protocol from the sock structure (passed as a parameter *ssk→protocol*) at line 412 (cs 13.22). Then it calls the function *netlink_lookup()* to find the corresponding linked list from the global netlink table (i.e., nl_table). After getting the corresponding linked list, it then searches the linked list for the sock struct with the same pid. Then based on the mode defined when the socket was created, it calls the *add_wait_queue( )* to put the current process into the socket's wait queue and set the process's state to *TASK_INTERRUPTIBLE*. Again, it continuously checks for the state for running

```
net/netlink/af_netlink.c
408 int netlink_unicast(struct sock *ssk, struct sk_buff *skb, u32 pid, int nonblock)
409 {

412     int protocol = ssk->protocol;

419     sk = netlink_lookup(protocol, pid);

442         __set_current_state(TASK_INTERRUPTIBLE);
443         add_wait_queue(&sk->protinfo.af_netlink->wait, &wait);

450             __set_current_state(TASK_RUNNING);
451             remove_wait_queue(&sk->protinfo.af_netlink->wait, &wait)


463     skb_queue_tail(&sk->receive_queue, skb);
464     sk->data_ready(sk, len);
```

cs 13.22. *netlink_unicast ( ).*

the current process; and if there is no overload, it then changes the current process state to *TASK_RUNNING* at line 450. Finally, at line 463 enqueues the *sk_buff* to the socket's receive queue and calls the function *sk→data_ready(sk_len)* at line 464. This function pointer is initialized to *netlink_data_ready( )* function (see Section 13.3).

13.8.2.5 netlink_data_ready ( ). The *netlink_data_ready( )* again invokes the *data_ready* function pointer of rtnetlink socket, which is *rtnetlink_rcv( )* function at line 690 (cs 13.23).

13.8.2.6 rtnetlink_rcv ( ). The *rtnetlink_rcv ( )* dequeues each skbuff from the socket's receive in a while loop at line 443 (cs 13.24) and calls the function *rtnetlink_rcv_skb ( )* at line 444 for each *sk_buff* for processing the data.

13.8.2.7 rtnetlink_rcv_skb ( ). The *rtnetlink_rcv_skb( )* typecasts the *skb→data* pointer at line 405 (cs 13.25) to struct nlmsghdr, which is the netlink header structure. This *skb→data* is the starting address of the netlink packet (see Section 13.7 for more information). Then *rtnetlink_rcv_skb ()* calls the function *rtnetlink_rcv_msg()* with netlink header struct as one of the parameters at line 411.

```
net/netlink/af_netlink.c
687 void netlink_data_ready(struct sock *sk, int len)
688 {
689      if (sk->protinfo.af_netlink->data_ready)
690          sk->protinfo.af_netlink->data_ready(sk, len);
         . . . .
```

cs 13.23. *netlink_data_ready ( ).*

```
net/core/rtnetlink.c
435 static void rtnetlink_rcv(struct sock *sk, int len)
436 {
437      do {
             . . . .
442
443          while ((skb = skb_dequeue(&sk->receive_queue)) != NULL) {
444              if (rtnetlink_rcv_skb(skb)) {
445                  if (skb->len)
446                      skb_queue_head(&sk->receive_queue, skb);
447                  else
448                      kfree_skb(skb);
449                  break;
450              }
451              kfree_skb(skb);
452          }
453
454          up(&rtnl_sem);
455      } while (rtnl && rtnl->receive_queue.qlen);
456 }
```

cs 13.24. *rtnetlink_rcv ( ).*

```
net/core/rtnetlink.c
397 extern __inline__ int rtnetlink_rcv_skb(struct sk_buff *skb)
398 {

405         nlh = (struct nlmsghdr *)skb->data;

411         if (rtnetlink_rcv_msg(skb, nlh, &err)) {

419         }

425 }
```

cs 13.25. *rtnetlink_rcv_skb ( )*.

13.8.2.8 rtnetlink_rcv_msg ( ). The *rtnetlink_rcv_msg ( )* first extracts the type and family of the netlink socket at lines 289 and 299 (cs 13.26) from the netlink packet(nlh) passed as an input parameter to this function. The doit and dumpit function pointers are stored in the *rtnetlink_link* in the *rtnetlink_links* table. Family and type were setup in the tc (user space code of tc). Finally, based on the family row and type column, the doit function is called at line 378. In this case for adding a qdisc, the *tc_modify_qdisc( )* function is called. Similarly, for adding a filter in that case, doit will point to *tc_ctl_filter*; and for deleting/or getting the qdisc, doit will point to the *tcl_get_qdisc( )* function.

```
net/core/rtnetlink.c
272 rtnetlink_rcv_msg(struct sk_buff *skb, struct nlmsghdr *nlh, int *errp)
273 {

289     type = nlh->nlmsg_type;

299     type -= RTM_BASE;

305     family = ((struct rtgenmsg*)NLMSG_DATA(nlh))->rtgen_family;

311     link_tab = rtnetlink_links[family];
312     if (link_tab == NULL)
313         link_tab = rtnetlink_links[PF_UNSPEC];
314     link = &link_tab[type];

374     if (link->doit == NULL)
375         link = &(rtnetlink_links[PF_UNSPEC][type]);

378     err = link->doit(skb, nlh, (void *)&rta);

390 }
```

cs 13.26. *rtnetlink_rcv_msg ( )*.

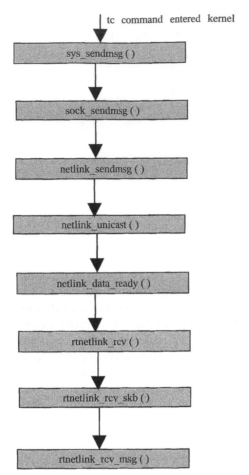

Figure 13.5. TC command flow in kernel space.

13.9   FLOW DIAGRAM FOR tc COMMAND IN KERNEL SPACE

Figure 13.5 shows the TC command flow in kernel space. For more details refer to Section 13.8.2.2.

13.10   SUMMARY

What happens in user space?

1. It creates a netlink socket and binds it to the address structure.
2. It allocates the request message.
3. It allocates a message structure msg.
4. It calls system call sendmsg.

What happens in kernel space?

1. The received msg structure and the necessary data structure gets copied to kernel space by *copy_from_user* and verify iovec.
2. It creates *sk_buff* and uses *memcpy_from_iovec* to copy the msg's iovec to the data area of *sk_buff*.
3. It searches the *nl_table* with the sock that has the same pid as the current process.
4. It enqueues the *sk_buff* in the socket's receive queue and then dequeues each *sk_buff* in the receive queue.
5. It extracts the family and type from the *sk_buff*, and based on the family and type values, it checks the *rtnetlink_link* table for calling the appropriate doit function, which takes the appropriate actions.

14

IP ROUTING

The Internet is designed to communicate between any two networks that don't have any idea about each other's location. The unit of information carrier in the Internet is a packet that contains an Internet protocol header that carries enough information for the packet to take it to its destination. So far, we learned about the transport layer protocol that carries information enough to identify the consumer of the Internet data at the two ends of the connection. But it says nothing about what path the packet is taking in the Internet to reach the destination or what path should be taken by the packet to reach the destination.

The Internet is a huge and complex web of networks interconnected with each other. There is a basic Internet backbone that connects the networks useful for providing services at the periphery of the Internet backbone. These periphery networks are either Internet consumers or services provided over the Internet. Each host providing service over the Internet has a unique I(nternet)P(rotocol) address that should be known to all the consumers of the service to avail it. It is difficult to remember the IP address of each host on the Internet providing service, so these IP addresses are mapped to the names. These names are called domain names and are resolved by D(omain)N(ame)S(ervice). So, to cut it short we can say that to reach a specific host on the Internet, we need to know the Fully Qualified Domain Name of the host. DNS will resolve the domain name and get a corresponding IP address. This is all about how hosts on the Internet are identified. But the question still remains as to how these hosts are reached from anywhere in the Internet. We will not go into the details of DNS functionality but will be focused on understanding the Internet.

TCP/IP Architecture, Design, and Implementation in Linux. By S. Seth and M. A. Venkatesulu
Copyright © 2008 the IEEE Computer Society

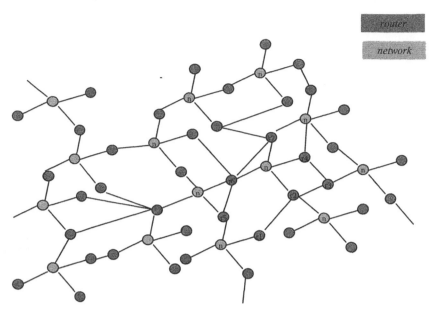

Figure 14.1. Internet with complex web of routers and networks.

Figure 14.1 shows how the Internet is designed. It has mainly two components namely, router and network. Two different networks are connected via a router, and two or more than two routers are also connected to each other directly. Note that all the entities in the Internet are public and can be seen by every other entity in the Internet. The packet that traverses between the two networks may take different routes at the same time, depending on the intermediate router configuration. The packet is routed out of the network through the router, also called gateway. The gateway will have information about its next hop (router) which is stored in the database maintained by the routing subsystem also called as routing table. Once it knows the route for the packet (next hop), it also knows from which interface it can reach the next hop. The packet is transmitted out of the interface to reach the next hop. Once the packet reaches the next hop, the routing table is consulted on that router to find the next hop if that is not the final destination for the packet. So, this way each router knows the next hop for the packet and if the route to the destination is not found in the routing table, the packet is dropped. Let's consider an example of a packet starting from network n1 and destined for network n5. The packet can take two different paths, namely, [r5, r6, r7] and [r1, r2, r3, r4]. The path taken may depend on different factors router configuration and link status at different routers. We will discuss this later.

The routing table can be built mainly in two different ways. One is statically, which is done at the system boot-up time and by the administrator by issuing commands such as *ifconfig, route*, and so on. Another way to add an entry to the routing table is dynamically, which is done by routing daemons. Routing daemons are mainly very much dominant in the Internet backbone, where different routers need to tell each other's neighboring router about its routing table. Or routers can also demand a certain part of the routing table from neighboring routers, and all this is done by routing daemons that understand routing protocols. There are various routing protocols such as RIP (routing information protocol), OSPF (open shortest path first), BGP (broader gateway protocol), and so on.

RIP. With RIP, each router broadcasts information about the neighboring network to all the other networks linked with the router. Among other information, the most important is the network ID, netmask, and the distance of the network from the router (hop count). This way, each neighboring router will have its routing table updated for all remotely connected networks. RFC 1388 covers the specification for the protocol.

OSPF. RIP has some shortcomings as regards to the information it provides and also the features. This protocol provides information about the link status of each connected network to every other network it is directly connected to. This way it is very effective as far as recovery of routes is concerned. For example, if a link to a specific network goes down, there may be some other link which may get us to that network. Not only this, it also provides information about different routes based on TOS. Most importantly, OSPF is multicast, as compared to broadcast, which brings down network load. The specification is covered by RFC 1247.

Today's Internet is very different from the Internet at the time it was just introduced. Many more features are added to make on-demand services available on the Internet. The Internet is fair to each of its users as long as resource allocation is concerned. But nowadays, Internet service providers are providing on-demand services. With the introduction of multimedia and application requiring a huge bandwidth, the Internet resources need to be shared fairly among the consumers of high and nominal bandwidth based on demand.

With these features, ISPs can pump out data at a higher rate for the high-bandwidth consumers based on demand. Among many features, some of them added to the routing subsystem are

- Policy routing
- TOS

In the current chapter, we will discuss all these features along with the routing concepts and its implementation in detail.

14.1 ROUTING

When a packet is generated locally or is received from any of the interfaces, it has to consult a routing subsystem for the routing decisions based on the destination IP address. The route basically decides on the outgoing interface to which the packet should be transmitted so that the packet is closer to its destination. This is the very basic functionality of the routing subsystem. If the route is defined for the packet, it is routed via a defined interface for the route; otherwise the packet is dropped and an ICMP message is sent to the originator of the packet.

Routing works on very simple rules, which are defined as follows:

1. First try to find out matching entry for complete destination IP address of the packet.

2. If there is no match found, then all the network entries are matched against the destination IP address.
3. If there is no matching network found for the destination, we take the default route in case any exist.

The above is a very basic type of routing. An example of a routing table is covered in Section 14.2, which explains how to interpret *netstat* output. '*netstat -nr*' reads kernel routing table entries and displays them. *ifocnfig* output shows configuration of the network interface. It shows all the physical and virtual interfaces configured for the interface. The physical interface is configured with the netmask and IP address. There can be multiple IP addresses assigned to the physical interface. In doing so, we are creating virtual interfaces associated with each IP address. The virtual interfaces can be configured for eth0 as eth0:1, eth0:2, and so on. The purpose of having multiple IP address configured for the same NIC is that we can remain connected to different subnets on the same physical network.

Routing entries have following basic entities:

Network	Gateway	Interface
192.168.1.0/24	0.0.0.0	eth0
192.168.1.1	0.0.0.0/0	eth0

Network means the network we are trying to match, gateway is the next hop gateway to reach the network, and interface is the network interface through which we can reach the network. There are flags and metrics associated with each entriy, and they are used to identify the route. These are discussed in Section 2.13. In the above example, 192.168.1.0/24 means network 192.168.1 with netmask of 24 bits (255.255.255.0). This network is directly reachable via interface eth0 because gateway entry for this is 0.0.0.0. So, all the packets destined for the 192.168.1 network will be routed via eth0. How do we know that a packet is destined for a specific network? We use the network field of the entry (i.e., 192.168.1.0/24) to find this out. If the 24 most significant bits of a packet's destination IP match the network ID for the route (i.e., 192.168.1), the packet is destined for network 192.168.1.

Another entry is 0.0.0.0/0, which means that this is a default route. If none of the entries in the table match against the destination IP address for the packet, this entry will be used to route the packet. For this entry, the destination network is 0.0.0.0 and the netmask is 0 bit (0.0.0.0), which means that the destination is not at all matched for the packets using this route. But there is a gateway field set for the default entry which is reachable through interface eth0. This essentially means that destination is not reachable directly and will use default gateway 192.168.1.1 to further route the packet. In other words, gateway for the default entry is also called next hop for the route. So, the packets using this route will have destination IP address as it is, but the destination link layer address will be that of the default gateway (192.168.1.1).

As shown in Fig. 14.2, there are hosts H1, H2, H3, H4, and so on, on the network 192.168.1.0/24, and each one of them will have the two routing entries: one for the local network and the other one for default gateway. The GW is the default gateway with IP 192.168.1.1. The default gateway will have minimum of two interfaces: one connected to the network 192.168.1.0/24 and the other one connected to the Internet (via ISP). GW will route all the packets destined for the Internet through the second interface PPP0 (dial out connection to the ISP).

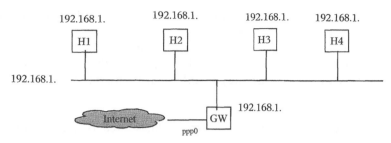

Figure 14.2. Network segment pointing to default gateway to access internet.

To further explain routing decisions, let's take a simple example where a packet is generated for host 192.168.1.3 from host 192.168.1.2. The routing table at 192.168.1.2 is consulted, which first looks if there is any entry for destination host. This means that it checks if any entry exists with matching host 192.168.1.3. Since no such entry exists, it will check if there is any entry with matching network ID. An entry for network 192.168.1.0/24 matches network ID for the destination 192.168.1.3. So, this route is picked up and the packet is transmitted out through interface eth0.

In another example, there is a packet that is destined for 192.168.2.3 and is generated from 192.168.1.2. First the matching entry for destination IP 192.168.2.3 is searched in the routing table. Since it does not exist, we check if there is any matching entry for the destination network ID. There is only one entry for the network in the routing table, that is, 192.168.1.0/24. The destination network for the packet does not match this entry. So, finally the default route is selected to route this packet through interface eth0. In this case, the packet is sent to the default gateway 192.168.1.1 to finally route the packet in its final destination. In this case, the destination link layer address in the Ethernet frame is that of the default gateway (192.168.1.1) rather than the destination IP (192.168.1.2).

The above example explains very simple configurations. There may be complex scenario where we may end up having thousands of entries in the routing table. The routing table may not be statically configured but may be updated dynamically by the routing daemons. But whatever be the case, the routing decisions are based on the very simple three rules as stated above. There are many features added to the routing subsystem some for enhancing performance and others for on-demand services.

14.2 POLICY-BASED ROUTING

As discussed until now, the packets reach their destination in the Internet based on the routing information (next hop) at each router. This is the simplest way to see the packet traversing through the Internet. With the advancement and on-demand usage of the Internet services, there is something more required other than just routing the packet correctly to its final destination. For example, in demand-based Internet services, one user may require a high bandwidth for streaming multimedia whereas another user just needs enough bandwidth to browse through the Internet. If we take another example, it may be for security reasons that we would like to separate out routes for a different cadre of employee for the same/different services.

All these requirements need adding a new feature to the routing subsystem which will route packets based on certain policies.

Current implementation on Linux takes into account the following criteria to build a policy to route a packet that has originated from the system locally or that has originated elsewhere (forwarding). List the entities used to build policy to route a packet:

Destination Net ID. This is derived from the source IP and by applying an appropriate netmask to it.

Source net ID. This is derived from the destination IP and by applying an appropriate netmask to it.

TOS. The IP header has a type-of-service field that is used by the routers to queue the packet in different queues to achieve differential services.

Forward Mark. In the case where multiple routing tables are configured on the system, the packets are marked by the routing subsystem to use a specific route. We take this also into consideration while setting policy for the route (*CONFIG_IP_ROUTE_FWMARK*).

Incoming Interface. This is the interface from which the packet is arrived (in case of packets to be forwarded). This allows us to provide differential services for packets arriving from different networks.

Class ID. CONFIG_NET_CLS_ROUTE.

Figure 14.3 illustrates a typical example of routing policy configured on router R1 to divert intranet traffic through different routers R2 & R3. It may be configured because of resource utilization or security reasons.

For configuring policy-based routing we use the "ip rule" command. The rule option consists of a selection criteria based on which we use the routing table from the multiple routing tables.

Here we are adding the ip rule for the following:

1. The packets with source address 'ipaddr1' should use the routing table 1 (dev is eth0).
2. The packets with source address 'ipaddr2' should use the routing table 2 (dev is eth1).

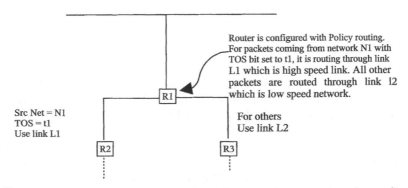

Figure 14.3. Traffic an R1 is routed through routers R2 and R3 based on policy.

Policy routing acts as a load balancing for the outgoing packets.
First we start with adding the default route to the routing tables 1 and 2:

1. # ip route add default via 'ipaddr1' dev eth0 tab 1.
2. # ip route add default via 'ipaddr2' dev eth1 tab 2.

Then add the policy rule to the routing table based on the source address:

1. # ip rule add from 'ipaddr1' tab 1 priority 500.
2. # ip rule add from 'ipaddr2' tab 2 priority 600.

Here the ip rule command configures the routing table selection based on the source
ipaddress. Check Sections 14.11 and 14.12.8 for more details.

14.3 MULTIPATHING

There may be situations where we can have multiple gateways to the public network
from the local network. For example, we can have multiple connections to the ISP
from a single host that is acting as a gateway for the private network, which means
that we have many alternatives to reach the public network. One of the reasons for
having this kind of setup is to make arrangements for higher availability of the
Internet for the private network. If one of the ISPs goes down, the public network
may still be available via another ISP. When all the ISPs are up, we need to make
arrangements to distribute the load fairly across different ISP connections. It is up
to the administrator to setup distribution of load across all the connected ISPs. The
algorithm to distribute load across multiple gateways is implemented as part of
multipathing in a routing subsystem.

We have discussed a simple example where we have multiple connections to
ISP for the outgoing Internet traffic where we can use multipathing to our advantage. There may be other examples where we can use the same concept to balance
load. One example is if we have certain service running on different hosts connected
to a single host acting as load balancer. Any traffic bound to this service will go
through the load balancer, which in turn will have multipathing configured to
distribute incoming traffic to different servers, hence balancing loads (Fig. 14.5).
Similarly, we can have multipathing configured on the router to better distribute
traffic across different links for the same route (Fig. 14.4).

CONFIG_IP_ROUTE_MULTIPATH is a kernel option to configure
multipathing.

fib_select_multipath() (See cs 14.2 unless mentioned) is called from *ip_route_
output_slow()/ip_route_input_slow()* to select a default gateway from multiple gateways when the kernel is compiled with the *CONFIG_IP_ROUTE_
MULTIPATH* option. As shown in Figure 14.6 multipathing parameters are
embedded in fib_nh (nexthop) object entries for each gateway.

fi→fib_power → *cumulative power allocated to all the nexthop entries.*

nh→nh_power→ *individual power allocated to each next hop entry
(consumable).*

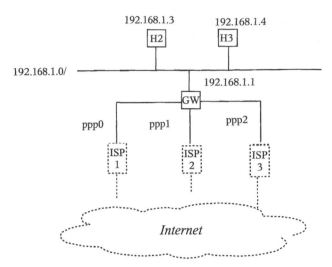

Figure 14.4. GW does multipathing.

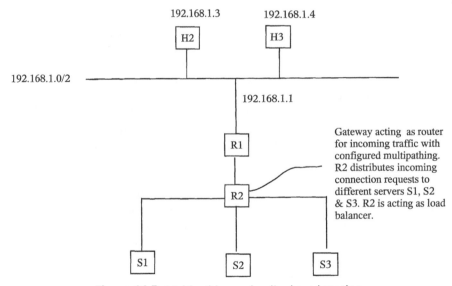

Figure 14.5. Multipathing and policy-based routing.

> ***nh→nh_weight→*** *static weight assigned to each hop entry. Power to each entry is assigned this value when they are exhausted.*

The algorithm works like this: If the complete power of the route is not exhausted (*fi→fib_power* > 0), we need to select one of the gateways from the list of entries for the route. Here we are not very sure which gateway entry we are going to select because it will not depend on the power left with the entry. Selection of entry is based on the initial power calculated, which is given as (line 980)

$$jiffies \ \% \ fi{\to}fib\_power$$

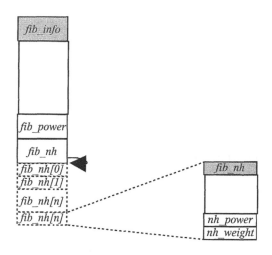

Figure 14.6. *fib_info and fib_nh objects designed for multipathing.*

jiffies is a system variable that is incremented on each clock tick and rolls over when it attains 2^{32} on a 32-bit machine. So, the value of the calculated weight is always between $0 - fi \rightarrow fib\_power$. So, we never know what value the weight will have.

We try to match the entry with weight, more than or the same as the weight calculated (loop 982–992). If we received the match, we use the gateway associated with the entry to route packets for the requested route. If the power of this entry is not exhausted and the route is alive, we have selected this entry (line 983). In this case, we decrement the power for the entry (line 985), decrement the cumulative power for the route (line 986), and assign the index corresponding to the selected next hop entry to the result (line 987) and return.

In case, the weight calculated is more than the weight of the entry, the weight is subtracted from the current entries' weight, and the next entry is checked against the new reduced weight. Like this the search goes on until we find the suitable entry with weight more than (or equal to) the calculated weight. With this algorithm, we get either fair selection or in worst cases the reverse case also. In the worst case, the entry with the lowest weight may first get exhausted and then the entries with higher values may get selected. The other extreme would be that higher weights may get exhausted before the lower-powered entries because we are calculating weight randomly (see Fig. 14.7). We manipulate the next hop entries with *fib_multipath_lock* lock held.

We need to check how the entries are arranged in the list (are they according to the weights?).

Once the entire power for the route gets exhausted ($fi \rightarrow fib\_power == 0$), the fresh allocation takes place (lines 960–973). Here we go through the list of entries and add the individual power of each entry ($nh \rightarrow nh\_power$) in case the entry is not dead (line 962). We also replenish the power of each entry at line 963. Once we have come out of the loop, the cumulative power calculated is assigned to the route's power (line 966).

change_nexthops(). This macro traverses through the nexthop entries for the route. The *fib_nh* field of the *fib_info* object points to the list of nexthop entries of

```
net/ipv4/fib_semantics.c

64 #define change_nexthops(fi) { int nhsel; struct fib_nh * nh; \
65 for (nhsel=0, nh = (struct fib_nh*)((fi)->fib_nh); nhsel < (fi)->fib_nhs; nh++, nhsel++)
    ......
79 #define endfor_nexthops(fi) }
```

cs 14.1. *Declaration of nexthops.*

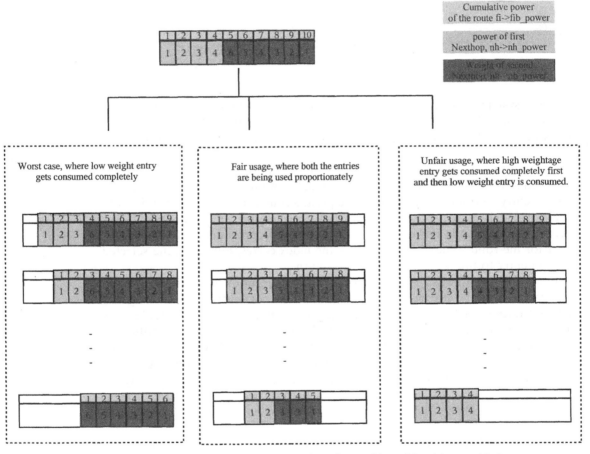

Figure 14.7. Selection of nexthops with multipathing enabled.

type *fib_nh*. The *fib_nhs* field of the object *fib_info* indicates the maximum number of nexthop entries (cs 14.1).

endfor_nexthops(). This macro just ends the loop by closing braces.

FIB_RES_NH. Once nexthop is selected for the route, it is accessed using macro *FIB_RES_NH* later to build the routing cache entry (cs 14.3, Fig. 14.7).

```
net/ipv4/fib_semantics.c

952 void fib_select_multipath(const struct rt_key *key, struct fib_result *res)
953 {
954     struct fib_info *fi = res->fi;
955     int w;
956
957     spin_lock_bh(&fib_multipath_lock);
958     if (fi->fib_power <= 0) {
959         int power = 0;
960         change_nexthops(fi) {
961             if (!(nh->nh_flags&RTNH_F_DEAD)) {
962                 power += nh->nh_weight;
963                 nh->nh_power = nh->nh_weight;
964             }
965         } endfor_nexthops(fi);
966         fi->fib_power = power;
967         if (power <= 0) {
968             spin_unlock_bh(&fib_multipath_lock);
969             /* Race condition: route has just become dead. */
970             res->nh_sel = 0;
971             return;
972         }
973     }
        .....
980     w = jiffies % fi->fib_power;
981
982     change_nexthops(fi) {
983         if (!(nh->nh_flags&RTNH_F_DEAD) && nh->nh_power) {
984             if ((w -= nh->nh_power) <= 0) {
985                 nh->nh_power--;
986                 fi->fib_power--;
987                 res->nh_sel = nhsel;
988                 spin_unlock_bh(&fib_multipath_lock);
989                 return;
990             }
991         }
992     } endfor_nexthops(fi);
        ....
995     res->nh_sel = 0;
996     spin_unlock_bh(&fib_multipath_lock);
997 }
```

cs 14.2. fib_select_multipath ().

```
include/net/ip_fib.h

101 #define FIB_RES_NH(res)    ((res).fi->fib_nh[(res).nh_sel])
```

cs 14.3. FIB_RES_NH.

14.4 RECORD ROUTE OPTIONS (RFC 791) AND PROCESSING BY LINUX STACK

As discussed in Section 14.1, the routing subsystem bothers only about the next hop for the given destination. It selects the best possible route for the given destination, in case there are many choices. So, it is always left to the routing subsystem to decide

Figure 14.8. Format for record-route option.

on the next hop router for the given destination. But, there is a feature extended to the IP wherein the user can supply its own build chain of next hops to reach a specified destination. On the other hand, the IP option is provided which can record the next hop value at each router that a packet reaches. The usage of these options is not well-defined, but to me it looks like these options are mainly used for network diagnostics purposes. For example, traceroute uses a strict-route-record option to determine routes taken by a packet to reach a specific destination. The proper ICMP error code is returned in case the strict-record-route option is set and the next hop is unknown at any point of time.

14.4.1 Record Routing

The IP option requires that each router should record its address when reached by the packet. This way we get a complete list of routers when the packet reaches its final destination. This list of routers is copied back to the IP datagram in reply to the IP datagram that has recorded the route so that the originator of the packets gets the route to the destination.

The format for the record-route option is shown in Fig. 14.8.

Zeroth byte contains opcode for record route, that is, $0x7$.

First byte is the total length of the record-route option data.

Second byte contains the offset from the start of the record-route option where the next entry should be copied. The router will need this field to copy the IP address when the option is set.

There can be a maximum of nine entries that can be recorded using this option.

14.5 SOURCE ROUTING

This option entitles the originator of the IP datagram to specify its own route for a given destination, which essentially means that the user will provide an IP layer with complete set of next hops (in the correct sequence) which the IP datagram should follow to reach the destination. It is similar to the record-route option except that the list of next hops is specified by the originator of the datagram and is not recorded by the intermediate routers. If it is found that any of the routes as mentioned in the list of next hops is not reachable at any point of time, an ICMP error message is returned to the originator of the IP datagram. There are two options here.

14.5.1 Strict Record Routing

When this option is set in the IP datagram, the router has to strictly follow the same path as specified by the list of next hops. This means that if the next hop router is not found at any intermediate router, the datagram will be dropped and the ICMP error message will be returned to the originator. The message format is the same for the option as described in Fig. 14.8. The opcode for the option is 0x89 and it can have maximum of nine next hop values. The ptr field is modified by each router to point to the next value in the list so that the next router uses this field to identify the next hop for the packet.

14.5.2   Loose Record Routing

The option is similar to a strict-route option except that the IP datagram is allowed to take different paths while traversing between the two consecutive next hops as mentioned in the option list. This essentially means that any of the next hops speci-fied in the list may not be directly reachable but is surely reachable. The opcode for the option is 0x83 and can have a maximum of eight entries. Ptr is used in the same way as it is done for strict-route option.

14.5.3   SRR Processing Implementation

In *ip_rcv_finish()*, we first process IP options from the IP header *ip_options_ compile()*. If SRR/LSRR is set in the IP header, *opt→srr* will be set to point to the start of the SRR option in the IP header. We first check if the SRR option is sup-ported by the interface on which the packet is received by using macro *IN_DEV_ SOURCE_ROUTE* at line 353 (cs 14.4, cs 14.5). If the option is not supported for either IP or the incoming interface, we drop the packet; otherwise we call *ip_ options_rcv_srr()* to further process the SRR option.

```
net/ipv4/ip_input.c

306 static inline int ip_rcv_finish(struct sk_buff *skb)
307 {
308    struct net_device *dev = skb->dev;
309    struct iphdr *iph = skb->nh.iph;
       ....
346       if (ip_options_compile(NULL, skb))
347          goto inhdr_error;
       ....
349       opt = &(IPCB(skb)->opt);
350       if (opt->srr) {
351          struct in_device *in_dev = in_dev_get(dev);
352          if (in_dev) {
353             if (!IN_DEV_SOURCE_ROUTE(in_dev)) {
                   ....
357                in_dev_put(in_dev);
358                goto drop;
359             }
360             in_dev_put(in_dev);
361          }
362          if (ip_options_rcv_srr(skb))
363             goto drop;
364       }
       ....
374 }
```

cs 14.4. *ip_rcv_finish ()*.

```
include/linux/inetdevice.h

43 #define IN_DEV_SOURCE_ROUTE(in_dev) (ipv4_devconf.accept_source_route && (in_dev)->cnf.accept_source_route)
```

<u>cs</u> 14.5. *IN_DEV_SOURCE_ROUTE.*

14.5.3.1   *ip_options_compile().* This is a routine that is called from *ip_rcv_finish()*, where IP options are processed from the received packet. The *IPOPT_SSRR, IPOPT_LSRR* and *IPOPT_RR* record-route options are identified from the IP header here, and a sanity check is made against the format for these options.

If the record-route options are identified, the *rr* field of the *ip_options* object is made to point to the start of the option string in the IP header. If we have not reached the end of the list or the packet has not reached the final destination, the *is_changed* and *rr_needaddr* fields of the *ip_options* object are set. These fields will be used later by the forwarding subsystem will see later. We will copy the IP address of the next hop in the IP header location as specified by the *ptr* field of the option and increment the *ptr* field to point to the next copy location.

If any of the source-route option is identified, *srr* field of the *ip_options* object is made to point to the start of the option string in the IP header. If the strict-route option is set, the *is_strictroute* field of the *ip_options* object is also set here which will be used later by the forwarding subsystem.

Note: *PACKET_HOST* means that the packet belongs to the host (i.e., US) and it is a unicast packet. In a promiscuous mode, the Ethernet driver collects all the packets which don't even belong to us and sends it to the IP layer for further processing. In the case where the packets don't belong to us, those are marked by the Ethernet driver as *PACKET_OTHERHOST* in *eth_type_trans()*. These packets are dropped by the IP layer in *ip_rcv()*. All those packets which belong to us are not marked as PACKET_HOST and *skb→pkt_type* remains zero, which means that any packet for which *pkt_type* is zero belongs to us (*PACKET_HOST*).

[*IPCB* macro provides a pointer to IP control block pointed to by cb field of skb. This field can be used by any protocol layer for option processing. In the case of IP, this control block is mapped to *struct inet_skb_parm*. To access IP options from IPCB, we need to access *opt* field of struct *inet_skb_parm*. The Opt field is embedded type *ip_options* in *struct inet_skb_parm*.]

14.5.3.2   *ip_options_rcv_srr().* In lines 582–587 the route is calculated for the source and destination IP addresses for the packet before the routine is called (cs 14.6). So, the route checked here is for the packet destination. If the route type is *RTN_UNICAST*, it means that the destination IP does not belong to any of the IP configured for the host. In the case of the strict route, this is not acceptable. The packet at each step should reach the exact destination as specified by the destination IP in the packet. In the case of the loose record route option, we may reach the destination (specified by destination IP in the IP header) through one or more hops. That is the reason why even if the route for the destination is not the local host (line 582), we consider this packet if the packet has a loose record route option set (line 583); otherwise we discard the packet sending an ICMP message to the originator of the packet.

net/ipv4/ip_options.c

```
566 int ip_options_rcv_srr(struct sk_buff *skb)
567 {
568     struct ip_options *opt = &(IPCB(skb)->opt);
569     int srrspace, srrptr;
570     u32 nexthop;
571     struct iphdr *iph = skb->nh.iph;
572     unsigned char * optptr = skb->nh.raw + opt->srr;
573     struct rtable *rt = (struct rtable*)skb->dst;
        ....
577     if (!opt->srr)
578         return 0;
579
580     if (skb->pkt_type != PACKET_HOST)
581         return -EINVAL;
582     if (rt->rt_type == RTN_UNICAST) {
583         if (!opt->is_strictroute)
584             return 0;
585         icmp_send(skb, ICMP_PARAMETERPROB, 0, htonl(16<<24));
586         return -EINVAL;
587     }
588     if (rt->rt_type != RTN_LOCAL)
589         return -EINVAL;
590
591     for (srrptr=optptr[2], srrspace = optptr[1]; srrptr <= srrspace; srrptr += 4) {
592         if (srrptr + 3 > srrspace) {
593             icmp_send(skb, ICMP_PARAMETERPROB, 0, htonl((opt->srr+2)<<24));
594             return -EINVAL;
595         }
596         memcpy(&nexthop, &optptr[srrptr-1], 4);
597
598         rt = (struct rtable*)skb->dst;
599         skb->dst = NULL;
600         err = ip_route_input(skb, nexthop, iph->saddr, iph->tos, skb->dev);
601         rt2 = (struct rtable*)skb->dst;
602         if (err || (rt2->rt_type != RTN_UNICAST && rt2->rt_type != RTN_LOCAL)) {
603             ip_rt_put(rt2);
604             skb->dst = &rt->u.dst;
605             return -EINVAL;
606         }
607         ip_rt_put(rt);
608         if (rt2->rt_type != RTN_LOCAL)
609             break;
610         /* Superfast 8) loopback forward */
611         memcpy(&iph->daddr, &optptr[srrptr-1], 4);
612         opt->is_changed = 1;
613     }
614     if (srrptr <= srrspace) {
615         opt->srr_is_hit = 1;
616         opt->is_changed = 1;
617     }
618     return 0;
619 }
```

cs 14.6. *ip_options_rcv_srr ()*.

In loop 591–613, we are traversing through list of next hops listed in the strict route IP options pointed to by *skb→nh.raw+opt→srr*. We do some sanity checking on the srr string, if the format is not proper, the ICMP message is generated for an improper parameter (line 593). nexthop is copied from srrptr, which is offset into the srr option string pointing to the nexthop router (line 596). We check routing entry for the next hop by calling *ip_route_input()* at line 600. On return, route is either defined or not. If not, an error is returned; otherwise we get a valid entry that is updated in the dst field of skb. We need to make checks here on the type of route that is associated with the nexthop selected at line 602. If the route is not unicast (directly connected or gateway) and at the same time is also not a route for the local machine (*RTN_LOCAL*), it means that the route is invalid. It means that the we have not reached the destination, nor can we reach the next hop router directly from any of the interfaces configured on the host. We return with an error here. In the case where one of the conditions is false—that is, either the route is a directly connected one or we are the ones that the next hop points to—we will proceed further. Further, we make a check if the route for the next hop selected points to us at line 608. If so, we continue with the nexthop search jumping to the next entry in the srr option string and copy the current next hop as pointed to by SRR pointer to the destination address in the IP header. If not, we got the nexthop to route the packet to its next destination. We return with *srr_is_hit* and *srr_is_changed* set if we have not reached past the end of the list (line 617). If one of the nexthop from the SRR list is successfully found, the dst field of skb will be pointing to the route that will be used later to route the packet by the forwarding module.

14.5.3.3   *ip_forward_options()*. This routine is called from *ip_forward_finish()*, which is the final call by a forwarding subsystem while forwarding a packet. *ip_forward_options()* needs to update some of the fields in the IP header options based on the IP options processed in *ip_options_compile()* when the datagram is received. We will check how SRR and RR-related options are processed here. In *ip_options_rcv_srr()* we found out the route for the packet in case the SRR option is set. Also for the RR option, we did most of the processing in *tcp_options_compile()*. For the RR I option, we try to modify the IP address recorded so far for the current hop (in *ip_options_compile()*) depending on the IP addresses of the forwarding interface as permitted by scope of the IPs configured on the interface. We do this to take care of the administrative scopes of the IP address as set for the interface and also to record actual nodes from where the packet is forwarded with an SRR/RR option for the IP set. Similarly, for the SRR IP option, we do the same and also modify the pointer to the next hop as to be seen by the next hop router.

At line 523, we access IP options then we access routing table information at line 525 and finally we access the IP header for the packet at line 526 (cs 14.7). The *rr_needaddr* field of the *ip_options* object is set only if RR option is set in *ip_options_compile()*. We call *ip_rt_get_source()* at line 530 to copy the appropriate source address in the location specified by the pointer for RR option. The pointer for the RR option is already modified to point to the new location to copy the next hop router in *ip_options_compile()*. At line 533 we check if *srr_is_hit* field of *ip_options* object is set. This is set in *ip_options_compile* in the case where SRR option in the IP header is set. If this field is set, we try to loop through the next hop list starting from the location as specified by the pointer to SRR option (lines 538–546). In each iteration we try to match the next hop route entry in the SRR list with the

```
net/ipv4/ip_options.c

521 void ip_forward_options(struct sk_buff *skb)
522 {
523    struct ip_options * opt  = &(IPCB(skb)->opt);
524    unsigned char * optptr;
525    struct rtable *rt = (struct rtable*)skb->dst;
526    unsigned char *raw = skb->nh.raw;
       ....
528    if (opt->rr_needaddr) {
529       optptr = (unsigned char *)raw + opt->rr;
530       ip_rt_get_source(&optptr[optptr[2]-5], rt);
531       opt->is_changed = 1;
532    }
533    if (opt->srr_is_hit) {
534       int srrptr, srrspace;
535
536       optptr = raw + opt->srr;
537
538       for ( srrptr=optptr[2], srrspace = optptr[1];
539          srrptr <= srrspace;
540          srrptr += 4
541          ) {
542          if (srrptr + 3 > srrspace)
543             break;
544          if (memcmp(&rt->rt_dst, &optptr[srrptr-1], 4) == 0)
545             break;
546       }
547       if (srrptr + 3 <= srrspace) {
548          opt->is_changed = 1;
549          ip_rt_get_source(&optptr[srrptr-1], rt);
550          skb->nh.iph->daddr = rt->rt_dst;
551          optptr[2] = srrptr+4;
552       } else if (net_ratelimit())
       ....
563    }
564 }
```

cs 14.7. ip_forward_options.

destination IP address for the route set for the packet in *ip_options_rcv_srr()*. If a match is found and is not the last entry (line 547), we try to replace the entry in the SRR list for the current router with the IP address of the forwarding interface as permitted by the scope value by calling *ip_rt_get_source()* at line 549. At line 550, we modify the destination field of the IP header from the destination IP address in the routing entry. At line 551, the SRR pointer is modified to point to the next location as seen by the net hop router where the packet is being forwarded.

The processing of the SRR option is shown in Fig. 14.9. The packet originating from host H1 has an SR set with a list of next hops R1, R2, R3, ... , Rn and a pointer set to 3 (first next hop in the list). When the packet emerges from the first router R1 from the interface with IP IP1, this IP is recorded, replacing R1 in SRR option field. The pointer is incremented to point to the next hop, that is, R2. This repeats as the packet emerges from each router, and finally we have a list of IP addresses of the forwarding router interfaces replacing the IP addresses of the routers specified by the end user. This list is copied in the reply so that the originator of the packet knows exactly how the packet has traversed.

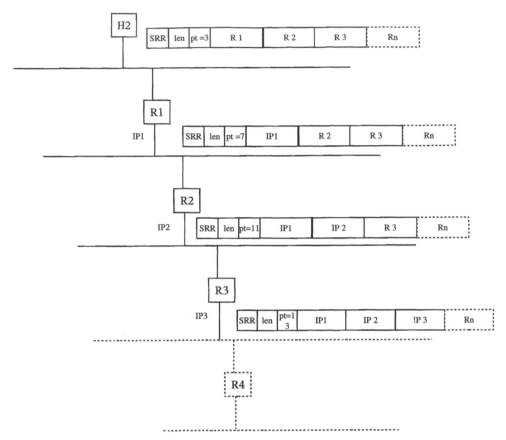

Figure 14.9. Packet with SRR IP option being modified as it emerges from each router interface.

```
include/net/ip_fib.h

111 #define FIB_RES_PREFSRC(res)        ((res).fi->fib_prefsrc ? :
  __fib_res_prefsrc(&res))
```

cs **14.8.** *FIB_RES_PREFSRC.*

14.5.3.4 ip_rt_get_source(). In this routine we try to get the source IP address for the interface used by the selected route and return it to the caller. If an incoming interface is not provided (line 1168), the source IP for the interface is just the source IP as specified by the route itself. Otherwise we try to look up the routing table using a key for the route to find out the preferable source IP address for the route, and we call *fib_lookup()* at line 1170. In case the result indicates that the route is of type NAT, we need to find the NATed source address for the packet by calling *inet_select_addr()* for a given gateway with universal scope at line 1173. Otherwise, we try to get the most preferable source IP address for the interface used by the route using macro *FIB_RES_PERFSRC* (cs 14.8, cs 14.9). If the preferred source is set for the route (*fib_prefsrc*), *else __fib_res_prefsrc()* is called to the return source with universal scope (using outgoing interface and the gateway information).

```
net/ipv4/route.c

1163 void ip_rt_get_source(u8 *addr, struct rtable *rt)
1164 {
1165    u32 src;
1166    struct fib_result res;
1167
1168    if (rt->key.iif == 0)
1169       src = rt->rt_src;
1170    else if (fib_lookup(&rt->key, &res) == 0) {
1171 #ifdef CONFIG_IP_ROUTE_NAT
1172       if (res.type == RTN_NAT)
1173          src = inet_select_addr(rt->u.dst.dev, rt->rt_gateway,
1174                RT_SCOPE_UNIVERSE);
1175       else
1176 #endif
1177          src = FIB_RES_PREFSRC(res);
1178       fib_res_put(&res);
1179    } else
1180       src = inet_select_addr(rt->u.dst.dev, rt->rt_gateway,
1181             RT_SCOPE_UNIVERSE);
1182    memcpy(addr, &src, 4);
1183 }
```

cs 14.9. *tp_rt_get_source.*

If no results are returned by the route lookup, *inet_select_addr()* is directly called at line 1180 to find the source IP with universal scope (also using gateway information for the route) for the route. We do this because there may be a different source IP configured for the interface for administrative reasons. Finally we copy the identified source address to return to the caller at line 1182.

14.6 LINUX KERNEL IMPLEMENTATION OF ROUTING TABLE AND CACHES

Let's start with the flow of how the routing table and routing caches are maintained by the kernel.

We will draw a diagram of how routing tables are updated, how they are accessed, and different paths in the linux kernel. Also, we will explain the relation between routing table and the routing cache (Fig. 14.10).

14.7 ROUTING CACHE IMPLEMENTATION OVERVIEW

The routing cache is the fastest caching method for finding the route (Fig. 14.11). The FIB also offers a method to find the route, but the lookup time is greater and for each single packet to run a FIB query impacts the performance, whereas the routing cache reduces the lookup time for finding the route information.

A single routing cache is shared in the case where multiple routing tables are configured for policy routing. The routing cache keeps every route that is in use or used recently in a hash table. It also maintains timers and counters to remove the route that is no longer in use.

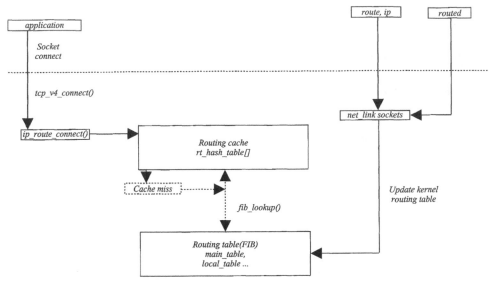

Figure 14.10. Route cache and FIB.

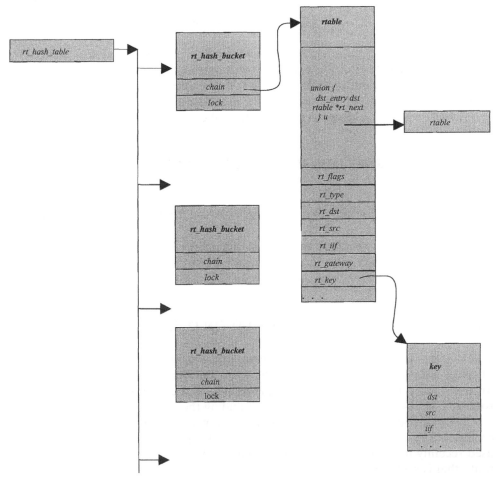

Figure 14.11. Routing cache implementation overview.

```
net/ipv4/route.c
194 static struct rt_hash_bucket  *rt_hash_table;
```

cs 14.10. *rt_hash_bucket declaration.*

The routing cache is a single hash table which includes the cache entries. cs 14.10 shows that the routing cache hash table is an array of *rt_hash_bucket* structures.

Each *rt_hash_bucket* structure contains the chain element and the read/write spin lock. The chain element includes the list of ratable structures that represent the cache entries.

When an IP layer wants to find a route, based on the hash value it goes to the proper *hash_bucket* and searches the chain of cached routes for the match. If a match is not found, then the FIB is accessed to find the match.

The routing cache is initialized in *ip_rt_init()* function called by *ip_init ()* fucntion. The size of the routing cache hash table depends upon the physical memory in the system. At boot time a message is displayed which displays the size of the hash table.

The *rt_hash_bucket* is selected based on the hash value, which is a combination of source, destination, and TOS values.

The routing cache in IP is defined in kernel as a pointer called *rt_hash_table*, which points to a single array of *rt_hash_bucket* structures.

14.7.1 Routing Cache Data Structures

struct rt_hash_bucket. This structure contains a list of rtable and a read–write lock for accessing the rtable from the list (cs 14.11).

Chain: This includes the list of rtable structures that represent the routing table entries.

Lock: Read/write spin lock for accessing the routing cache entries.

struct rtable. An rtable data structure is used to store a routing table entrry in the routing cache. It represents each destination route entry in the routing cache (cs 14.12).

*union {dst_entry dst; rtable *rt_next;}u.* Both *dst* and **rt_next* are used concurrently. The *dst* next pointer and **rt_next* points to the same memory location. Here

```
net/ipv4/route.c
189 struct rt_hash_bucket {
190      struct rtable   *chain;
191      rwlock_t        lock;
192} __attribute__(( __aligned__ (8)));
193
```

cs 14.11. *rt_hash_bucket.*

```
include/net/route.h

62 struct rtable
63 {
64     union
65     {
66          struct dst_entry      dst;
67          struct rtable         *rt_next;
68     } u;
69
70     unsigned          rt_flags;
71     unsigned          rt_type;
72
73     __u32             rt_dst; /* Path destination    */
74     __u32             rt_src; /* Path source         */
75     int               rt_iif;
76
77     /* Info on neighbour */
78     __u32             rt_gateway;
79
80     /* Cache lookup keys */
81     struct rt_key     key;
82
83     /* Miscellaneous cached information */
84     __u32             rt_spec_dst; /* RFC1122 specific destination */
85     struct inet_peer  *peer; /* long-living peer info */
86
87 #ifdef CONFIG_IP_ROUTE_NAT
88     __u32             rt_src_map;
89     __u32             rt_dst_map;
90 #endif
91 };
```

cs 14.12. *rtable.*

the pointer to the next rtable can be accessed as either a pointer to a destination cache entry through *dst* or a routing table entry pointer through *rt_next*. The union is used to embed the *dst_entry* structure into the rtable structure. The socket buffer *sk_buff* for an outgoing packet contains a pointer to the destination cache entry; this *dst* would also be used as a pointer to the routing cache entry for the packet. This cache entry is sometimes used to decide to send the packet to the destination by avoiding lookup into global routing tables.

rt_flags. This contains routing cache flags (can also be used in a routing table). This flag value is used to determine the accessibility or reachability of the destination route. It can be any of these flags shown in cs 14.13. Important flags from above list are:

RTCF_DEAD: Indicates that the route is dead.
RTCF_ONLINK: Indicates that the destination route is locally reachable network.
RTCF_BROADCAST: Indicates that the destination route is a broadcast route.
RTCF_MULTICAST: Indicates that the destination route is a multicast route.
RTCF_LOCAL: Indicates that the destination is a local route.

```
/* IPv4 routing cache flags */

#define RTCF_DEAD      RTNH_F_DEAD
#define RTCF_ONLINK    RTNH_F_ONLINK
#define RTCF_NOTIFY    0x00010000
#define RTCF_DIRECTDST 0x00020000
#define RTCF_REDIRECTED 0x00040000
#define RTCF_TPROXY    0x00080000

#define RTCF_FAST      0x00200000
#define RTCF_MASQ      0x00400000
#define RTCF_SNAT      0x00800000
#define RTCF_DOREDIRECT 0x01000000
#define RTCF_DIRECTSRC 0x04000000
#define RTCF_DNAT      0x08000000
#define RTCF_BROADCAST 0x10000000
#define RTCF_MULTICAST 0x20000000
#define RTCF_REJECT    0x40000000
#define RTCF_LOCAL     0x80000000

#define RTCF_NAT       (RTCF_DNAT\RTCF_SNAT)
```

cs 14.13. *IPV4 routing cache flags.*

RTN_UNSPEC	0	
RTN_UNICAST	1	Gateway or direct route
RTN_LOCAL	2	Accept locally
RTN_BROADCAST	3	Accept locally as broadcast, send as broadcast
RTN_ANYCAST	4	Accept locally as broadcast, but send as unicast *
RTN_MULTICAST	5	Multicast route
RTN_BLACKHOLE	6	Drop the packets
RTN_UNREACHABLE	7	Destination is unreachable
RTN_PROHIBIT	8	Administratively prohibited
RTN_THROW	9	Not in this table
RTN_NAT	10	Translate this address
RTN_XRESOLVE	11	Use external resolver

cs 14.14. *Route types.*

rt_type. This is a type of route that indicates whether the route is UNICAST, MULTICAST, and so on, and specifies whether the route is for a single destination or for all destinations or to a group of machines in a network. It can be any of the routes listed in cs 14.14.

rt_src and rt_dst. The source and the destination address.

rt_gateway. Address of next hop gateway.

rt_key. Key used for searching the cache entry for destination route.

_u32 rt_spec_dst. Specific destination for the use of UDP socket users to set the source address.

_ *u32 rt_src_map* and _ *u32 rt_dst_map*. Used for the NAT if configured in kernel.

peer. This is a pointer to *inet_peer* structure, which is used to store the information related to the recent communication to the remote host. This is 'Long-Living IP Peer Information.'

struct dst_entry. This structure contains protocol-independent destination cache definitions and pointers to the destination-specific input and output functions and data.

next. Pointer to the next *dst_entry* instance from the list for same route cache hash table's bucket.

```
include/net/dst.h
    27 struct dst_entry
    28 {
    29      struct dst_entry      *next;
    30      atomic_t              __refcnt;      /* client references   */
    31      int                   __use;
    32      struct net_device     *dev;
    33      int                   obsolete;
    34      int                   flags;
    35 #define DST_HOST           1
    36      unsigned long         lastuse;
    37      unsigned long         expires;
    38
    39      unsigned              mxlock;
    40      unsigned              pmtu;
    41      unsigned              window;
    42      unsigned              rtt;
    43      unsigned              rttvar;
    44      unsigned              ssthresh;
    45      unsigned              cwnd;
    46      unsigned              advmss;
    47      unsigned              reordering;
    48
    49      unsigned long         rate_last;    /* rate limiting for ICMP */
    50      unsigned long         rate_tokens;
    51
    52      int                   error;
    53
    54      struct neighbour      *neighbour;
    55      struct hh_cache       *hh;
    56
    57      int                   (*input)(struct sk_buff*);
    58      int                   (*output)(struct sk_buff*);
    59
    60 #ifdef CONFIG_NET_CLS_ROUTE
    61      __u32                 tclassid;
    62 #endif
    63
    64      struct dst_ops        *ops;
    65
    66      char                  info[0];
    67 };
```

cs 14.15. *dst_entry*.

refcnt. Reference count to keep track for entries in use or deleted.

use. Number of times this entry has been used.

dev. Pointer to the egress device to be used for packet transmission to reach the next destination.

lastuse. Timestamp to indicate when this entry was used last time. This field is useful for the garbage collector ro clear the dst structs that are not in use.

expires. Timestamp to indicate when this entry would expire.

pmtu. Max packet size for this route.

neighbor. Pointer to the ARP cache neighbor structure for this route.

hh. Pointer to a hardware header cache.

(*input). Pointer to the post routing input function for this route.

(*output). Pointer to the output function for this route (*dev_queue_xmit()*).

ops. Pointer to an operational structure of *dst* that is *dst_ops* struct that contains family, protocol, and operational functions for the route cache.

tclassid. Used in class-based queueing discipline for queueing of the packets; represents a classid.

14.8 MANAGING ROUTING CACHE

As discussed in Section 14.6, whenever a new route is created, there is a route cache miss. When a Linux machine is acting as a router, it gets a huge number of packets with different origins and destinations. This may cause a huge number of entries in the routing table. These entries take up a huge amount of system memory. This requirement raises the need to clean up the kernel routing cache on a regular basis. The entries in the routing cache are added for each new route but are not destroyed as soon as the connection associated with the packet is closed or the incoming packet for which an entry is made is already processed. We need to cache entries in the kernel routing cache for some time so that we can reuse it for connections/ packets using the same route. The sole aim of having a routing cache table is to save a huge amount of time creating routing entry by re-using entries already created for the route. But what about stale entries in the cache or entries that are no longer in use? To manage such unused entries, a routing subsystem introduces timers that will be fired periodically to check if there are any entries that are no longer in use or have become stale and will remove those entries from the routing cache.

For every packet that enters the system whether originated locally or from a different host, the route needs to be defined. The route is created based on various criteria from the information available in the kernel FIB (see Section 14.12.3). This

```
net/ipv4/route.c

1999 int ip_route_output_key(struct rtable **rp, const struct rt_key *key)
2000 {
2001    unsigned hash;
2002    struct rtable *rth;
2003
2004    hash = rt_hash_code(key->dst, key->src ^ (key->oif << 5), key->tos);
2005
2006    read_lock_bh(&rt_hash_table[hash].lock);
2007    for (rth = rt_hash_table[hash].chain; rth; rth = rth->u.rt_next) {
2008        if (rth->key.dst == key->dst &&
2009            rth->key.src == key->src &&
2010            rth->key.iif == 0 &&
2011            rth->key.oif == key->oif &&
2012 #ifdef CONFIG_IP_ROUTE_FWMARK
2013            rth->key.fwmark == key->fwmark &&
2014 #endif
2015            !((rth->key.tos ^ key->tos) &
2016               (IPTOS_RT_MASK | RTO_ONLINK))) {
2017            rth->u.dst.lastuse = jiffies;
2018            dst_hold(&rth->u.dst);
2019            rth->u.dst.__use++;
2020            rt_cache_stat[smp_processor_id()].out_hit++;
2021            read_unlock_bh(&rt_hash_table[hash].lock);
2022            *rp = rth;
2023            return 0;
2024        }
2025    }
2026    read_unlock_bh(&rt_hash_table[hash].lock);
2027
2028    return ip_route_output_slow(rp, key);
2029 }
```

cs 14.16. ip_route_output_key ().

routing entry is cached for all the packets/connections that need to be routed using the same route. When a connection is established for the first time, the route cache is consulted first to check if the entry is cached in for the route by calling *ip_route_output_key()* (cs 14.16). This routine traverses the chain of routing entries to find out if they have hit the cache (loop 2007–2025). In each iteration we check the entry for matching route key (lines 2008–2016). If we miss the cache, FIB is consulted to build a routing entry for the requested route by calling *ip_route_output_slow*() (line 2028) which will finally add an entry to the cache. If we hit the cache, the following action is taken:

1. *lastuse* field of the routing entry (object *dst_entry*) is updated with current value of *jiffies* (line 2017). *lastuse* field of the route indicates when was the routing cache entry last hit. This value indicates how old the entry is as in when it was last used.

2. *dst_hold()* is called for the route at line 2018 to increment reference count for the routing cache entry. This value indicates the number of references to the cached routing entry. The cached entry can be destroyed only if the there is no one referencing the cached entry; that is, nobody is using the cached entry.

3. *_use* field of the object *dst_entry* is incremented by one. This field is not used while destroying the cached routing entry and should not be confused with reference count(*_refcnt*). This is incremented whenever there is a cache hit for the entry and is used for statistical purpose. Similarly, on line 2020 we update statistical data for the cache hit on the CPU.

14.8.1 Routing Cache for Local Connections

Let's have a look at how the routing cache is consulted when a TCP connection is initiated. The *tcp_v4_connect()* routine is called within the kernel when a new TCP connection request is made from the user application (cs 14.17). It calls *ip_route_connect()* at line 773 to get route for the destination. If route for the destination is found, it is returned as first argument to the routine; otherwise error is returned. The simple step to get routing information is to first check the kernel routing cache and if an entry does not exist, build new routing entry from the information provided in FIB and cache it in kernel routing cache. *ip_route_connect()* does some sanity checks and calls *ip_route_output_key()* to search kernel routing cache for the routing entry requested for the connection. If the routing entry is found in the cache, we hold reference for the routing entry as explained in Section 14.12.2. We cache the routing information for the socket by calling *_sk_dst_set()* at line 783. This routine makes a *dst_cache* field for the socket (sock object), to point to the new route (*dst_entry* object). The route information will be used for all the packets sent out on this socket connection.

Whenever a packet is sent out over the socket connection, cached in route information is checked for its validity in *ip_queue_xmit()* (cs 14.18). Before the packet is processed by the IP layer, *_sk_dst_check()* is called at line 354. This routine returns NULL in the case where the cached routing entry is marked obsolete; otherwise it returns a value cached in by the socket (pointed to by *sk→dst_cache*) at the time of connection setup in *tcp_v4_connect()*. In case the route is obsoleted, we call *ip_route_output()* to build routing entry for the destination at line 367. We cache in the new routing entry with the socket by calling *_sk_dst_set()* at line 371. The routing entry is also pointed to by each outgoing packet, and this is done by calling *dst_clone()* at line 374. *dst_clone()* increments the reference count of the routing entry (*dst_entry* object) so that it should not be destroyed before the packet is finally sent out.

```
net/ipv4/tcp_ipv4.c

751 int tcp_v4_connect(struct sock *sk, struct sockaddr *uaddr, int addr_len)
752 {
753    struct tcp_opt *tp = &(sk->tp_pinfo.af_tcp);
       ....
773    tmp = ip_route_connect(&rt, nexthop, sk->saddr,
774             RT_CONN_FLAGS(sk), sk->bound_dev_if);
       ....
783    __sk_dst_set(sk, &rt->u.dst);
       ....
853 }
```

cs 14.17. tcp_v4_connect ().

```
net/ipv4/ip_output.c

339 int ip_queue_xmit(struct sk_buff *skb)
340 {
341    struct sock *sk = skb->sk;
          ....
349    rt = (struct rtable *) skb->dst;
350    if (rt != NULL)
351       goto packet_routed;
352
353    /* Make sure we can route this packet. */
354    rt = (struct rtable *)__sk_dst_check(sk, 0);
355    if (rt == NULL) {
          ....
367       if (ip_route_output(&rt, daddr, sk->saddr,
368                 RT_CONN_FLAGS(sk),
369                 sk->bound_dev_if))
370          goto no_route;
371       __sk_dst_set(sk, &rt->u.dst);
          ...
373    }
374    skb->dst = dst_clone(&rt->u.dst);
          ....
407 }
```

cs 14.18. *ip_queue_xmit ().*

14.8.2 __sk_dst_check()

__sk_dst_check() checks if the route exists (dst != NULL) and is obsolete (dst→ obsolete > 0) at line 1100 (cs 14.19). If both are TRUE, it calls a check routine specific to IP version. In case of Ipv4, this routine points to *ipv4_dst_check()*. This routine just calls *dst_release()* to decrement the reference count of the *dst_enrty* object and returns NULL. Essentially we call *ipv4_dst_check()* only if the route has become obsolete, and in that case the reference count for the route is decremented by 1 because we are not referring to this routing entry anymore (*sk→dst_cache* is set to NULL at line 1101. In Section 14.8.3, we will see under what conditions the routing entry is marked obsolete.

```
include/net/sock.h

1095 static inline struct dst_entry *
1096 __sk_dst_check(struct sock *sk, u32 cookie)
1097 {
1098    struct dst_entry *dst = sk->dst_cache;
1099
1100    if (dst && dst->obsolete && dst->ops->check(dst, cookie) == NULL) {
1101       sk->dst_cache = NULL;
1102       return NULL;
1103    }
1104
1105    return dst;
1106 }
```

cs 14.19. *__sk_dst_check ().*

14.8.3 Link Failure and Reporting to Routing Subsystem

In this section we will see how the routing cache entry is invalidated when link failure associated with the route is indicated. The final step in packet transmission is to build a link layer header. For this, the hardware address corresponding to the destination IP should be made available. The neighboring subsystem is consulted to resolve the hardware address. It sends out an ARP request and queues the packet in its queue. A timer is installed for this ARP request so that we can check the ARP results asynchronously. *neigh_timer_handler()* is the routine that is run when the neighbor timer expires (cs 14.20). In this routine we check if we have exhausted the maximum number of retries to send out ARP requests without getting ARP reply at line 650. If so, we will do error handling for each queued packet on the neighbor queue waiting for ARP resolution in a loop 663–667. We call neighbor-specific error handling routine, *neigh→ops→error_report*, at line 665. This points to *arp_error_report()*.

   arp_error_report() calls a routine to free *sk_buff* and also makes sure that the routing entry associated with the packet is removed from the system at the earliest by calling *dst_link_failure()*.

```
net/core/neighbour.c

619 static void neigh_timer_handler(unsigned long arg)
620 {
621    unsigned long now = jiffies;
622    struct neighbour *neigh = (struct neighbour*)arg;
       ....
650    if (atomic_read(&neigh->probes) >= neigh_max_probes(neigh)) {
651       struct sk_buff *skb;
       ....
663       while(neigh->nud_state==NUD_FAILED && (skb=_skb_dequeue(&neigh->arp_queue)) != NULL) {
664          write_unlock(&neigh->lock);
665          neigh->ops->error_report(neigh, skb);
666          write_lock(&neigh->lock);
667       }
       ....
667    }
       ....
686    neigh_release(neigh);
687 }
```

cs 14.20. *neigh_timer_handler ()*.

14.8.4 *dst_link_failure()*

This gets reference to the *dst_entry* object from the *dst* field of the packet (line 142) (cs 14.21). Next we check if this field is not NULL and link failure operation specific to the route (*dst→ops→link_failure !=NULL*) is defined at line 143. If so, we make a call to link a failure routine for the route at line 144. For Ipv4, this operation is defined as *ipv4_link_failure()*.

14.8.5 *ipv4_link_failure()*

This routine sends out an ICMP error message to the originator of the packet reporting error 'destination not reachable.' The routing entry for the packet is

```
include/net/dst.h

140 static inline void dst_link_failure(struct sk_buff *skb)
141 {
142    struct dst_entry * dst = skb->dst;
143    if (dst && dst->ops && dst->ops->link_failure)
144       dst->ops->link_failure(skb);
145 }
```

cs 14.21. *dst_link_failure.*

```
net/ipv4/route.c

1134 static void ipv4_link_failure(struct sk_buff *skb)
1135 {
         ....
1138    icmp_send(skb, ICMP_DEST_UNREACH, ICMP_HOST_UNREACH, 0);
1139
1140    rt = (struct rtable *) skb->dst;
1141    if (rt)
1142       dst_set_expires(&rt->u.dst, 0);
1143 }
```

cs 14.22. *ipv4_link_failure ().*

referred to at line 1140 (cs 14.22). If it exists, the route is all set to be expired at the earliest by calling *dst_set_expires()* at line 1142. The timeout value we are providing is 0, which means that we want this route to expire whenever the next routing cache timer is run (see Section 14.8.10 for more details).

14.8.6   *dst_set_expires()*

We first calculate the expiry value relative to the current value of *jiffies* at line 149 (cs 14.23). The sanity check at line 151 to keep a minimum value of expiry to 1

```
include/net/dst.h

147 static inline void dst_set_expires(struct dst_entry *dst, int timeout)
148 {
149    unsigned long expires = jiffies + timeout;
150
151    if (expires == 0)
152       expires = 1;
153
154    if (dst->expires == 0 || (long)(dst->expires - expires) > 0)
155       dst->expires = expires;
156 }
```

cs 14.23. *dst_set_expirese ().*

because of the requirements in the routing cache timer (Section 14.8.10). Next we check if the expiry of route is set to 0 or the route is set to expire at a much later time than the value calculated above (line 154). In any case, we set the value of the routes expiry to the value calculated at line 149. I suppose that a zero value of the routes expiry means that the route should never be destroyed.

14.8.7 Routing Cache for the Incoming Packets

The routing subsystem is consulted for every incoming packet in the same way it is done for outgoing packet. We need to know if the incoming packet needs to be delivered locally, needs to be forwarded, is a multicast or a broadcast packet, and so on. All this information is available from the routing entry corresponding to the packet, and a further course of action is decided based on this information.

ip_route_input() is called from *ip_rcv_finish()* to get routing information for the packet (cs 14.24). First the hash bucket is identified for the packet, and then the collision list for the bucket is traversed (loop 1648–1665) to match the routing entry. Once we have the matching routing entry for the packet, the *lastuse* field of the *dst_entry* object is updated to value of *jiffies* at line 1657. This value indicates when the entry was last used, and we can see the details in Section 14.8.11. Next we increment the reference count for the routing entry by calling *dst_hold()* at line 1658. We do this to avoid destruction of the routing entry before the packet is either sent out of the system or delivered locally. Usage count of the routing entry is incremented for kernel statistics at line 1659, and a hit count for the routing entry on the CPU is incremented at line 1660 for kernel stats. The *dst* field of the packet is made to

```
net/ipv4/route.c

1637 int ip_route_input(struct sk_buff *skb, u32 daddr, u32 saddr,
1638         u8 tos, struct net_device *dev)
1639 {
        ....
1647    read_lock(&rt_hash_table[hash].lock);
1648    for (rth = rt_hash_table[hash].chain; rth; rth = rth->u.rt_next) {
1649        if (rth->key.dst == daddr &&
1650            rth->key.src == saddr &&
1651            rth->key.iif == iif &&
1652            rth->key.oif == 0 &&
1653 #ifdef CONFIG_IP_ROUTE_FWMARK
1654            rth->key.fwmark == skb->nfmark &&
1655 #endif
1656            rth->key.tos == tos) {
1657            rth->u.dst.lastuse = jiffies;
1658            dst_hold(&rth->u.dst);
1659            rth->u.dst.__use++;
1660            rt_cache_stat[smp_processor_id()].in_hit++;
1661            read_unlock(&rt_hash_table[hash].lock);
1662            skb->dst = (struct dst_entry*)rth;
1663            return 0;
1664        }
1665    }
1666    read_unlock(&rt_hash_table[hash].lock);
        ....
1698    return ip_route_input_slow(skb, daddr, saddr, tos, dev);
1699 }
```

cs 14.24. *ip_route_input ().*

point to the routing entry (*dst_entry* object) at line 1662 for further processing by the IP layer. In the case where the routing entry is not found in the kernel routing cache, we call *ip_route_input_slow()*.

14.8.8 Routing Cache Timer

As mentioned earlier, we need to keep a constant eye on the routing cache entries as they grow in size on a busy system making a huge number of network connections per seconds or a busy router. A single routing table entry in FIB may lead to hundreds of kernel routing cache entries. Each connection to different hosts on the remote network (single routing table entry in FIB) will have one routing cache entry. The routing entries in the kernel routing cache may be lying unused for a long time, taking up system memory. To manage these situations, a timer is installed to monitor routing cache entries at some preset time intervals.

There are two system-wide timers related to routing cache management:

- *rt_periodic_timer*
- *rt_flush_timer*

rt_flush_timer and *rt_periodic_timer* timers are initialized at the system bootup time in routine *ip_rt_init()*, but only an *rt_periodic_timer* timer is installed at line 2525 (cs 14.25). The timer routine for *rt_periodic_timer* and *rt_flush_timer* are *rt_check_expire* and *rt_run_flush*, respectively. We discuss these timers in detail in the sections that follow.

14.8.9 *rt_periodic_timer*

As the name suggests, this is a periodic timer that is kicked off at the boot-up time when a routing subsystem is initialized. Once started, this timer will never stop but may not necessarily happen at fixed frequency. In this section we will see the role of this timer and how it calculates the next expiry time.

The routine registered to execute when this timer fires is *rt_check_expire()*. The routine checks for all those routing entries in the cache which have expired by this

```
net/ipv4/route.c

2459 void __init ip_rt_init(void)
2460 {
2461    int i, order, goal;
          ...
2517    rt_flush_timer.function = rt_run_flush;
2518    rt_periodic_timer.function = rt_check_expire;
          ....
2523    rt_periodic_timer.expires = jiffies + net_random() % ip_rt_gc_interval +
2524            ip_rt_gc_interval;
2525    add_timer(&rt_periodic_timer);
          ...
2532 }
```

cs 14.25. *ip_rt_init e ( ).*

time. Expired entries are removed from the kernel routing cache so that it should not be used any more. Later in this section we will see what to do with the expired entry. First we will learn how to identify the expired routing entries in the cache.

1. *lastuse* field of the *dst_entry* object (embedded in rtable object) is used to identify if the routing entry has expired. As discussed in Section 14.12.2, this field is updated with the value of *jiffies* whenever there is cache-hit for route lookup in *ip_route_output_key()/ip_route_input()*. In the timer, we check the value of *expires* field of *dst_entry* object to identify the expired entry.

2. *expires* field of the *dst_entry* object is set to the value (with respect to *jiffies*) that indicates the number of clock ticks, after which this entry should be removed from the routing cache. *expires* field is set by call to *dst_set_expires()* whenever we want to remove the entry forcefully even if the entry is in use and has not yet aged.

rt_hash_log is the base 2 logarithm of *rt_hash_mask*, where *rt_hash_mask* is the number of buckets in the routing cache, *rt_hash_table*. Calculation of 't' doesn't make any sense because it is not used anywhere. It is used just to calculate the number of times the outer loop should be traversed, which is never less than the number of hash buckets in the *rt_hash_table*. The outer loop 376–407 starts at a fixed value of 't' that is $ip\_rt\_gc\_interval*2^{rt\_hash\_log}$ (cs 14.26). In each iteration, 't' is decremented by *ip_rt_gc_interval* until 't' becomes zero. This essentially means that the loop will iterate for number of turns that equals number of hash buckets in the routing hash table *rt_hash_table*. Instead, *rt_hash_mask* could have been used to do this. If there are huge number of entries, the outer loop is terminated when the next timer interrupt has fired, in which case *jiffies* > now will be true at line 405.

We start from the next routing cache hash bucket entry from where we left last (line 380). When we are entering the routing for the first time, it will be the zeroth hash bucket. The reason for this is that *rover* is a local variable that is declared 'static' (line 371). We grab the lock for the hash bucket at line 383 and start traversing the routing entries in the hash bucket in the inner loop 384–401. Once we have traversed all the entries in the hash bucket, the lock is released at line 402. If another timer interrupt has happened while we are here processing routing caches, the value of *jiffies* would have incremented by 1. So, the condition at line 405, if TRUE, indicates that we have spent the entire time between two clock ticks in this routine. We stop processing in this case; otherwise for a system with huge number of entries in the routing hash table, CPU will always be busy processing routing caches. When we are leaving the routine (outer loop), *rover* is set to the current hash bucket at line 408 and a timer is reset to fire after *ip_rt_gc_interval* ticks from now at line 409.

Processing within the inner loop (381–401) will do all the expiry check for each routing entry in the hash bucket. First check is whether the expiry field of the *dst_entry* object is set. This is set in case we want to forcefully remove the routing cache entry from the system (by call to *dst_set_expires()*)—for example, when link failure is detected. When the entry has expired (condition at line 387 is FALSE), we delink the current routing entry at line 399 and free the current entry at line 400 by a call to *rt_free()*. Otherwise the entry has not expired (condition at line 387 is TRUE), the timeout value is halved at line 388, and we move to the next entry (line 389). The reason why we half the timeout value here for the next entry here is because

```
net/ipv4/route.c

369 static void SMP_TIMER_NAME(rt_check_expire)(unsigned long dummy)
370 {
371    static int rover;
372    int i = rover, t;
373    struct rtable *rth, **rthp;
374    unsigned long now = jiffies;
375
376    for (t = ip_rt_gc_interval << rt_hash_log; t >= 0;
377         t -= ip_rt_gc_timeout) {
378        unsigned tmo = ip_rt_gc_timeout;
379
380        i = (i + 1) & rt_hash_mask;
381        rthp = &rt_hash_table[i].chain;
382
383        write_lock(&rt_hash_table[i].lock);
384        while ((rth = *rthp) != NULL) {
385            if (rth->u.dst.expires) {
     ....
387                if ((long)(now - rth->u.dst.expires) <= 0) {
388                    tmo >>= 1;
389                    rthp = &rth->u.rt_next;
390                    continue;
391                }
392            } else if (!rt_may_expire(rth, tmo, ip_rt_gc_timeout)) {
393                tmo >>= 1;
394                rthp = &rth->u.rt_next;
395                continue;
396            }
     ....
399            *rthp = rth->u.rt_next;
400            rt_free(rth);
401        }
402        write_unlock(&rt_hash_table[i].lock);
     ....
405        if ((jiffies - now) > 0)
406            break;
407    }
408    rover = i;
409    mod_timer(&rt_periodic_timer, now + ip_rt_gc_interval);
410 }
```

cs 14.26. *SMP_TIMER_NAME ( )*.

the routing entries are organized in the hash bucket chain in the order they arrive. The old entries can be found at the head and latest entries at the tail. The reason for this kind of arrangement is that when a new entry is entered, it is checked against all the entries in case the matching entry already exists. In this process we reach the end of the chain where the new entry is inserted (check *rt_intern_hash()*).

In the case where the expire fields of the *dst_entry* object are not set, we are not forcing the entry to expire but still the entry can be removed from the system depending on its age and value. We call *rt_may_expire()* at line 392 to check expiry of the routing entry with respect to its age. We pass two timeout values to this routine: The second argument (first timeout value) is the reduced timeout value for the much latest entries, and the third argument (second timeout value) is the fixed timeout value *ip_rt_gc_timeout*. In section 14.8.11, we will see how these two values are used. If the route is not in use, *rt_may_expire()* returns an indication to remove the entry from the cache in case the entry is at least *ip_rt_gc*-timeout ticks old. If the entry has not expired, we half the timeout value for the very latest entries and move on to the next routing entry (line 393–394). If both the tested conditions fail, we need to remove the entry from the routing cache as the route has expired.

14.8.10 *rt_may_expire()*

This routine makes various checks on the routing cache entry regarding its expiry. First we check if anybody is referencing the routing entry (reference count for the entry) at line 352 (cs 14.27). If the route is being used, we don't check anything else and just return failure. Next is to check if expiry for the route is set (forceful removal of the route) at line 356. If so, the expiry check is made with current *jiffies* value to see if we have expired. In case we have expired, we return success (indicating expiry of the entry). In case it is not forced expiry for the entry or the entries forced expiry has not timed out, we need to do some more expiry checks. Now we calculate the age of the route using lastuse field of *dst_entry* object (line 359), which is updated whenever there is a cache hit. If the age of the entry has not expired as per the first timeout considered (line 361), the route can still be removed. In this case we check if the entry can be cleaned fast by calling *rt_fast_clean()*. *rt_fast_clean()* checks if this is multicast/broadcast route (cs 14.28, line 337) and if we are not the latest entry in the chain (*rth→u.rt_next != NULL*).

If any of these conditions is FALSE, *rt_may_expire()* returns false, if the entry has not aged. If either entry has expired against the first timeout value (age > tmo1) or *rt_fast_clean()* returns TRUE, the route can still be valid. Here we need to check for another set of conditions at line 362. If the route has not expired against the second timeout value (age ⇐ tmo2), we call *rt_valuable()* to check if the route is valuable. *rt_valuable()* checks if expiry time is set for the route and some other conditions which are of less relevance. If the route is valuable and the route has not timed out, we keep it. Else we return TRUE if any of the conditions at line 362 is

```
net/ipv4/route.c

347 static __inline__ int rt_may_expire(struct rtable *rth, int tmo1, int tmo2)
348 {
    ....
352    if (atomic_read(&rth->u.dst.__refcnt))
353        goto out;
354
355    ret = 1;
356    if (rth->u.dst.expires && (long)(rth->u.dst.expires - jiffies) <= 0)
357        goto out;
358
359    age = jiffies - rth->u.dst.lastuse;
360    ret = 0;
361    if ((age <= tmo1 && !rt_fast_clean(rth)) ||
362        (age <= tmo2 && rt_valuable(rth)))
363        goto out;
364    ret = 1;
365 out:    return ret;
366 }
```

cs 14.27. *rt_may_expire ( ).*

```
net/ipv4/route.c

333 static __inline__ int rt_fast_clean(struct rtable *rth)
334 {
        ....
337    return (rth->rt_flags & (RTCF_BROADCAST | RTCF_MULTICAST)) &&
338        rth->key.iif && rth->u.rt_next;
339 }
340
341 static __inline__ int rt_valuable(struct rtable *rth)
342 {
343    return (rth->rt_flags & (RTCF_REDIRECTED | RTCF_NOTIFY)) ||
344        rth->u.dst.expires;
345 }
```

cs 14.28. rt_fast_clean ( ).

FALSE. In any case, if route has timed out against second timeout value provided to the routine, we return TRUE.

[**Note**: In the case where we are called from rt_check_expire(), the second argument is *ip_rt_gc_timeout*. If the route times out against *ip_rt_gc_timeout* and the route is not in use, the route is removed from the cache.]

14.8.11   dst_free()

The routine is called to free the *dst_entry* object and also to free any resources associated with it. First we check if the entry is obsolete and is already there on the garbage list (*dst_garbage_list*) at line 118 (cs 14.29). If so, we just return at line 119. If we are not on the garbage list, next check is for the references to this routing entry. If someone is already using the routing cache entry (*dst→__refcnt > 0*), we will defer freeing of the cache entry by calling *__dst_free()* at line 124. In case no one is referring to the routing cache entry, we will free the *dst_entry* object by calling *dst_destroy()* at line 121 and return.

```
include/net/dst.h

115 static inline
116 void dst_free(struct dst_entry * dst)
117 {
118    if (dst->obsolete > 1)
119        return;
120    if (!atomic_read(&dst->__refcnt)) {
121        dst_destroy(dst);
122        return;
123    }
124    __dst_free(dst);
125 }
```

cs 14.29. dst_free ( ).

14.8.12 __dst_free()

The routine puts routing cache entry (*dst_entry* object) on the garbage list to be freed asynchronously by the *dst_gc_timer* timer. We hold *dst_lock* to manipulate *dst_garbage_list*. In case there is no interface device (*dst→dev*) associated with the route or the associated interface is down (line 126, cs 14.30), we set input and output routine associated with the route to *dst_discard* and *dst_blackhole*, respectively. We do this to ignore any packets that are sent or received using the route. We set an obsolete field to 2 at line 130, indicating that the entry is already on the garbage list. Next we add the route at the start of the garbage list using the next field of the *dst_entry* obect (line 131–132). It means that the latest entries reside at the head of the list.

Whenever a new entry is made to the garbage list *dst_garbage_list* (check __dst_free()), *dst_gc_timer_inc* is reinitialized to *DST_GC_INC* (5 Hz) and *dst_gc_timer_expires* is initialized to *DST_GC_MIN* (1 Hz) and *dst_gc_timer* timer is set to expire after one second by calling *add_timer()*, in case there was no fresh entry in the garbage list which has even expired once. If there is even one entry on the garbage list which has expired even once, *dst_gc_timer_inc* would always be more than *DST_INC_MIN* (check Section 14.8.15).

```
include/net/dst.h

119 void __dst_free(struct dst_entry * dst)
120 {
121    spin_lock_bh(&dst_lock);
       ....
126    if (dst->dev == NULL || !(dst->dev->flags&IFF_UP)) {
127       dst->input = dst_discard;
128       dst->output = dst_blackhole;
129    }
130    dst->obsolete = 2;
131    dst->next = dst_garbage_list;
132    dst_garbage_list = dst;
133    if (dst_gc_timer_inc > DST_GC_INC) {
134       del_timer(&dst_gc_timer);
135       dst_gc_timer_inc = DST_GC_INC;
136       dst_gc_timer_expires = DST_GC_MIN;
137       dst_gc_timer.expires = jiffies + dst_gc_timer_expires;
138       add_timer(&dst_gc_timer);
139    }
140
141    spin_unlock_bh(&dst_lock);
142 }
```

cs 14.30. __dst_free ( ).

14.8.13 dst_destroy()

This is the routine that is finally called to free the route and associated resources when the route has expired and there is no one referring this route. The *hh_cache* object contains cached-in hardware (NIC)-related information for the route. If nobody is referring to the cached object (line 150, cs 14.31), free it at line 151. If there is ARP associated with the route (*dst→neighbour*), just free it by calling

```
net/core/dst.c

144 void dst_destroy(struct dst_entry * dst)
145 {
146     struct neighbour *neigh = dst->neighbour;
147     struct hh_cache *hh = dst->hh;
148
149     dst->hh = NULL;
150     if (hh && atomic_dec_and_test(&hh->hh_refcnt))
151         kfree(hh);
152
153     if (neigh) {
154         dst->neighbour = NULL;
155         neigh_release(neigh);
156     }
157
158     atomic_dec(&dst->ops->entries);
159
160     if (dst->ops->destroy)
161         dst->ops->destroy(dst);
162     if (dst->dev)
163         dev_put(dst->dev);
    ....
167     kmem_cache_free(dst->ops->kmem_cachep, dst);
168 }
```

cs 14.31. dst_destroy ( ).

neigh_release() at line 155. This frees the *neighbour* object and also the resources associated with it, in case we were the ones last referring it. The destroy method of *dst* operations is called to destroy the *dst_ops* object at line 161. If there is an interface associated with the route (*dst→dev*), we decrement the reference count on the device by calling *dev_put()* at line 162. If we are the last one to refer the device, it is unregistered from the system and freed. *dst_entry* object is returned to the cache from where it was allocated at line 167.

14.8.14 dst_run_gc()

This routine is run whenever *dst_gc_timer* expires. It checks if any routing entry on the *dst_garbage_list* needs to be destroyed. If any such entry is found, *dst_destroy()* is called to free the routing entry (*dst_entry* object) and also any resources associated with it.

First we try to acquire *dst_lock* by a call to *spin_trylock()* at line 49 (cs 14.32). If we could not get the lock, we reset the timer (*dst_gc_timer*) to expire after one-tenth of a second at line 50 and return. Otherwise, we delete the timer and move ahead to manipulate the garbage list. The list (*dst_garbage_list*) is traversed in the loop 57–65. For each entry we check if the reference count has become zero at line 58. If somebody is already referring to the routing entry, we move to the next entry and continue (line 59). Otherwise, we remove the entry from the list at line 63 (remember *dstp* is double pointer) and call *dst_destroy()* at line 64 to free the *dst_entry* object. Once we have traversed the entire list, we check if there is any entry left on the list at line 66. If there is nothing left in the *dst_garbage_list*, *dst_gc_timer_*

```
tnet/core/dst.c

44 static void dst_run_gc(unsigned long dummy)
45 {
46     int   delayed = 0;
47     struct dst_entry * dst, **dstp;
48
49     if (!spin_trylock(&dst_lock)) {
50         mod_timer(&dst_gc_timer, jiffies + HZ/10);
51         return;
52     }
53
54
55     del_timer(&dst_gc_timer);
56     dstp = &dst_garbage_list;
57     while ((dst = *dstp) != NULL) {
58         if (atomic_read(&dst->__refcnt)) {
59             dstp = &dst->next;
60             delayed++;
61             continue;
62         }
63         *dstp = dst->next;
64         dst_destroy(dst);
65     }
66     if (!dst_garbage_list) {
67         dst_gc_timer_inc = DST_GC_MAX;
68         goto out;
69     }
70     if ((dst_gc_timer_expires += dst_gc_timer_inc) > DST_GC_MAX)
71         dst_gc_timer_expires = DST_GC_MAX;
72     dst_gc_timer_inc += DST_GC_INC;
73     dst_gc_timer.expires = jiffies + dst_gc_timer_expires;
       ....
78     add_timer(&dst_gc_timer);
79
80 out:
81     spin_unlock(&dst_lock);
82 }
```

cs 14.32. dst_run_gc ( ).

inc is initialized to DST_GC_MAX (120 Hz = 150 sec) at line 67 and the timer is not restarted.

dst_gc_timer_expires keeps the value of next expiry of the *dst_gc_timer* timer and can assume a maximum of DST_GC_MAX (120 Hz = 120 sec). If there is any entry still on the list which is being referred, expiry time of the timer is incremented by DST_GC_MAX (5 Hz = 5 sec) at line 70. *dst_gc_timer_inc* is incremented in multiples of DST_GC_INC (5 Hz) every time *dst_gc_timer* timer expires, in this case. *dst_gc_timer* is installed with the new calculated value of *dst_gc_timer_expires* at line 78. Now we release *dst_lock* at line 81 and return.

14.8.15 Interface down and *rt_flush_timer*

rt_flush_timer is used for the forced flush of a routing cache because of any reason such as interface down, routing table is flushed, and so on; *rt_run_flush* is a routine

```
net/ipv4/route.c

417 static void SMP_TIMER_NAME(rt_run_flush)(unsigned long dummy)
418 {
419     int i;
420     struct rtable *rth, *next;
421
422     rt_deadline = 0;
423
424     for (i = rt_hash_mask; i >= 0; i--) {
425         write_lock_bh(&rt_hash_table[i].lock);
426         rth = rt_hash_table[i].chain;
427         if (rth)
428             rt_hash_table[i].chain = NULL;
429         write_unlock_bh(&rt_hash_table[i].lock);
430
431         for (; rth; rth = next) {
432             next = rth->u.rt_next;
433             rt_free(rth);
434         }
435     }
436 }
```

cs 14.33. *SMP_TIMER_NAME ( )*.

installed for *rt_flush_timer* timer. Let's look at the functionality of *rt_flush_timer*. We initialize *rt_deadline* to 0 and we will see later (Section 14.8.17) how the value of *rt_deadline* does matter. We traverse through all the bucket in the routing cache bucket in the outer loop (lines 424–435, cs 14.33). *rt_hash_mask* is the number of buckets in the kernel routing hash table *rt_hash_table*. This value is calculated in *ip_rt_init()* at kernel boot-up time where resources are allocated for routing caches. If there are any routing entries in the hash bucket (line 427, cs 14.33), the chain is detached at line 428. We release the hash bucket lock at line 429 and traverse the routing entries chain in the inner loop (lines 431–434). We call *rt_free()* for each routing entry (*dst_entry* object) in the chain to free these entries one at a time. This way complete routing cache is flushed.

14.8.16 *rt_cache_flush()*

When a network interface card is brought down or it comes down, *fib_inetaddr_event()* is called as notifier callback routine registered for the device. We call *rt_cache_flush()* with a negative argument when the *NETDEV_DOWN* tag is set. In this section we will see how *rt_cache_flush()* works and under what conditions it will start the *rt_flush_timer* timer.

We record current *jiffies* at line 444 (cs 14.34) and also mark if we are being called from soft IRQ at line 445. *in_softirq()* returns the softIRQ counter on the current CPU. If it is nonzero positive value, it means that the current CPU is processing softIRQ from where we are being called. If delay from the caller is a negative value, we set it to a minimum delay value of *ip_rt_min_delay* (= 2 sec). We try to acquire the *rt_flush_lock* lock after making sure that the softIRQ is disabled locally at line 450.

```
net/ipv4/route.c

442 void rt_cache_flush(int delay)
443 {
444     unsigned long now = jiffies;
445     int user_mode = !in_softirq();
446
447     if (delay < 0)
448         delay = ip_rt_min_delay;
449
450     spin_lock_bh(&rt_flush_lock);
451
452     if (del_timer(&rt_flush_timer) && delay > 0 && rt_deadline) {
453         long tmo = (long)(rt_deadline - now);
        ....
462         if (user_mode && tmo < ip_rt_max_delay-ip_rt_min_delay)
463             tmo = 0;
464
465         if (delay > tmo)
466             delay = tmo;
467     }
468
469     if (delay <= 0) {
470         spin_unlock_bh(&rt_flush_lock);
471         SMP_TIMER_NAME(rt_run_flush)(0);
472         return;
473     }
474
475     if (rt_deadline == 0)
476         rt_deadline = now + ip_rt_max_delay;
477
478     mod_timer(&rt_flush_timer, now+delay);
479     spin_unlock_bh(&rt_flush_lock);
480 }
```

cs 14.34. rt_cache_flush ( ).

If the timer is already installed, we delete it by a call to *del_timer()* at line 452. In case there was no timer installed, we move to line 469. Here we check if the delay provided by the caller is zero or a negative value. The logic says that if no timer was installed, we need to urgently flush the routing cache only if the delay provided is zero. In this case, we directly call *rt_run_flush()*. Remember that *rt_run_flush()* is the callback routine for the *rt_flush_timer* timer. In this case, we directly flush the routing cache and return. Otherwise, if timer is not installed and the delay provided was negative or more than 0, we need to freshly install the timer at line 478.

If the *rt_flush_timer* timer was installed and the delay provided by the caller is a positive value and *rt_deadline* is also a positive value, we try to recalculate the delay (expiry time for the *rt_flush_timer*). All these conditions being TRUE means that the timer was installed and the route cache has not been flushed. *rt_run_flush()* can be called from an outside *rt_flush_timer* from *rt_cache_flush()*. *rt_deadline* is zero only when *rt_flush_timer* is being run or has just run before we came here because it is reset in *rt_run_flush()*. We calculate timeout value from the value of *rt_deadline*, which was set when the timer was last installed from this routine.

If we are not called from soft IRQ (timer) and timeout is not very huge (line 462), we set timeout to 0. If the delay provided is more than the timeout value calculated so far, we set delay to the value of timeout at line 466. If *rt_deadline* is zero, it means that either *rt_flush_timer* has already expired or it was never installed and the route was never flushed. In this case, *rt_deadline* is set to *ip_rt_max_delay* ticks with respect to current *jiffies*. If someone tries to flush caches with negative or positive delays and nobody has flushed the routing caches since we have installed the timer, the new delay will be calculated for that timer based on *rt_deadline* value set here.

14.9   IMPLEMENTATION OVERVIEW OF FORWARDING INFORMATION BASE (FIB)

The Forwarding Information Base (FIB) represents the internal routing structure in the kernel. It contains the routing information (Fig. 14.12). When the IP layer sends the request for identifying the route for the destination address and if the entry is not found in the routing cache, then the IP layers does the FIB lookup with most specific zones and searches the table until it finds a match. When it finds the match, the FIB updates the routing cache with the match so that the next time the IP layer can find the route in the routing cache.

Structure *fib_table* represents the routing table in the kernel. This is defined as an array variable; as illustrated in cs 14.35. This *fib_table* structure contains a pointer to the *fn_hash* structure which contains a table of *fn_zone* structures. One zone for each bit in the netmask (i.e., 32 Zones) and each zone can have entries for networks or hosts which can be identified by the number of bits. For example, a netmask of 255.255.0.0 has 16 bits, and this will correspond to zone 16; also a netmask of 255.255.255.0 has 24 bits and corresponds to zone 24.

Each *fn_zone* structure also contains a pointer to the hash table of nodes represented by the *fib_node* structure. The *fib_node* structure contains the pointer to the *fib_info* structure which contains the actual data of an routing table entry. If several routing table entries have the same hash value, then the corresponding *fib_node* structures are linked in the linear list.

14.9.1   *struct fib_table*

The *fib_table* structure represents a routing table (cs 14.36). It contains a table identifier and pointers to routing table functions (lookup, insert, delete, hash, etc.). It also contains a hash table structure which has a pointer to zone structures.

tb_id. This is a table identifier. There are up to 255 different routing tables that can be created. Each routing table in the system is identified by table identifier. By

```
net/ipv4/fib_frontend.c
    60
    61 struct fib_table *fib_tables[RT_TABLE_MAX+1];
    62
```

cs 14.35. *Declaration of fib_table.*

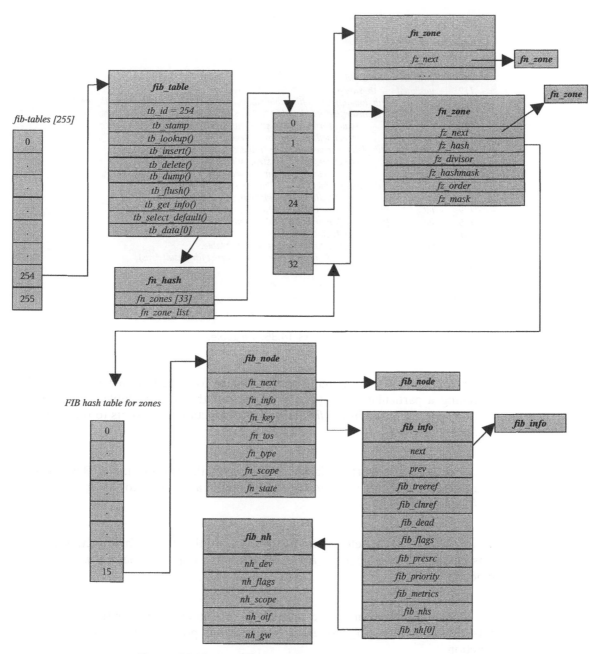

Figure 14.12. FIB implementation overview.

default there are two tables: local and main. Identifiers for local and main tables are 255 and 254.

tb_stamp. This is an unused element.

fib_table. This structure contains function pointers to create/delete/lookup, and so on, for entries in the routing table.

```
include/net/ip_fib.h
  116 struct fib_table
  117 {
  118       unsigned char   tb_id;
  119       unsigned        tb_stamp;
  120       int             (*tb_lookup)(struct fib_table *tb, const struct rt_key *key, struct fib_result *res);
  121       int             (*tb_insert)(struct fib_table *table, struct rtmsg *r,
  122                               struct kern_rta *rta, struct nlmsghdr *n,
  123                               struct netlink_skb_parms *req);
  124       int             (*tb_delete)(struct fib_table *table, struct rtmsg *r,
  125                               struct kern_rta *rta, struct nlmsghdr *n,
  126                               struct netlink_skb_parms *req);
  127       int             (*tb_dump)(struct fib_table *table, struct sk_buff *skb,
  128                               struct netlink_callback *cb);
  129       int             (*tb_flush)(struct fib_table *table);
  130       int             (*tb_get_info)(struct fib_table *table, char *buf,
  131                               int first, int count);
  132       void            (*tb_select_default)(struct fib_table *table,
  133                                   const struct rt_key *key, struct fib_result *res);
  134
  135       unsigned char   tb_data[0];
  136 };
```

cs 14.36. *fib_table*.

tb_lookup(). This is a routing table lookup for matching a key—that is, for searching a particular route (destination) from the routing table. This function pointer gets initialized in the *fib_hash_init ( )* function and points to the *fn_hash_lookup( )* function.

tb_insert. This inserts/updates the entries in the routing table. This function pointer gets initialized in *fib_hash_init ( )* function and points to the *fn_hash_insert ( )* function.

tb_delete (). This deletes entries from the routing table. This function pointer gets initialized in the *fib_hash_init ( )* function and points to the *fn_hash_delete ( )* function.

tb_dump(). This dumps the contents of a routing table. This function pointer gets initialized in the *fib_hash_init ( )* function and points to the *fn_hash_dump ( )* function.

tb_flush (). This frees the entries in the table (i.e., the *fib_info* structures) if the *RTNH_F_DEAD* flag is set. This function pointer gets initialized in the *fib_hash_init ( )* function and points to the *fn_hash_flush ( )* function.

tb_select_default (). This selects one route from several existing default routes. This function pointer gets initialized in the *fib_hash_init ( )* function and points to the *fn_hash_select_default ( )* function.

tb_get_info (). Output entries in the /proc/net/route format. This function pointer gets initialized in the *fib_hash_init ( )* function and points to the *fn_hash_get_info ( )* function.

tb_data[0]. This is a variable-sized area for which memory is allocated along with *fib_table struct. tb_data[0]* contains a pointer to the FIB hash table (*fn_hash*). This *fn_hash* structure has an *fn_zone* structure table that contains pointers to the zones based on the netmasks and the zone list.

14.9.2   *struct fn_hash*

The *fn_hash* structure consists of an array of pointers to *fn_zone* structures, where each *fn_zone* structure represents a zone (collection of routes) for the same netmask length and a pointer to the zones list (cs 14.37).

fn_zone[33]. This is an array of pointers of type *fn_zone* struct; it contains a pointers to the table of zones where each *fn_zone* structure represents a zone (collection of routes) for same netmask length.

fn_zone_list. This is a pointer to the first non-empty zone with more specific netmask (i.e., longest netmask length) in the zones list; that is, it points to the head of the list fron the active zones list.

```
net/ipv4/fib_hash.c

104 struct fn_hash
105 {
106        struct fn_zone  *fn_zones[33];
107        struct fn_zone  *fn_zone_list;
108 };
```

cs 14.37. fn_hash.

14.9.3   *struct fn_zone*

This represents an active zone for the same netmask length, and it contains hashing information and a pointer to the hash table node (cs 14.38). It manages all the entries for the same netmask.

fz_next. This is a pointer to the next non-empty zone in the zones list. The head of the list is kept in the *fn_zone_list* field of the *fn_hash* structure.

fz_hash. This is a pointer to the hash table of nodes for this zone, where the hash table of nodes is an array of *fib_node* structures which represent a single route entry for the routing table. This hash table is organized based on the key value (dst address, netmask, tos, etc.).

fz_nent. This is the number of routes (nodes, i.e., *fib_node* structs in hash table) in this zone.

```
net/ipv4/fib_hash.c

85 struct fn_zone
86 {
87      struct fn_zone *fz_next;      /* Next not empty zone */
88      struct fib_node **fz_hash;    /* Hash table pointer */
89      int        fz_nent;      /* Number of entries */
90
91      int      fz_divisor;  /* Hash divisor */
92      u32        fz_hashmask;  /* (1<<fz_divisor) - 1 */
93 #define FZ_HASHMASK(fz) ((fz)->fz_hashmask)
94
95      int      fz_order;    /* Zone order */
96      u32        fz_mask;
97 #define FZ_MASK(fz)    ((fz)->fz_mask)
98 };
```

cs 14.38. fn_zone.

fz_divisor. This is a hash divisor (number of buckets in the hash table). Normally, this value will be 0xf except for prefix (netmask) length 0. If netmask length is 0, the *fz_divisor* value is 1.

fz_hashmask. This is a bit mask used to mask the hash value for indexing in the hash table bucket to select the *fib_node's* list for traversing. Normally, this value is 0xf.

fz_order. This is the fixed prefix length for this zone (bit length of the netmask).

fz_mask. This is a zone netmask. There are total 32 zones for a *fib_table*, and each zone has a specific netmask. This field contains the zone netmask.

14.9.4 *struct fib_node*

This represents a single (destination) route entry from the routing table; it describes each host network route (cs 14.39).

fn_next. fib_node structures are organized in a hash table. This is a pointer to next *fib_node* from the *fib_node's* list in a single bucket of a hash table.

fn_info. This structure contains protocol- and hardware-specific information for the *fib_node* structure; it also maintains common features of the routes.

fn_key. This structure contains a destination network prefix (hash table key—least significant 8 bits of the destination address).

fn_type. This field represents a type of address. The significance of this field is that it indicates whether a destination is a single machine, all machines, or a group of machines in a network. It can be any of the values of UNICAST, BROADCAST, MULTICAST, LOCAL, and so on, listed in cs 14.40.

```
net/ipv4/fib_hash.c

68 struct fib_node
69 {
70      struct fib_node      *fn_next;
71      struct fib_info      *fn_info;
72 #define FIB_INFO(f)      ((f)->fn_info)
73      fn_key_t             fn_key;
74      u8                   fn_tos;
75      u8                   fn_type;
76      u8                   fn_scope;
77      u8                   fn_state;
78 };
```

cs 14.39. *fib_node.*

RTN_UNSPEC	0	
RTN_UNICAST	1	Gateway or direct route
RTN_LOCAL	2	Accept locally
RTN_BROADCAST	3	Accept locally as broadcast, send as broadcast
RTN_ANYCAST	4	Accept locally as broadcast, but send as unicast *
RTN_MULTICAST	5	Multicast route
RTN_BLACKHOLE	6	Drop the packets
RTN_UNREACHABLE	7	Destination is unreachable
RTN_PROHIBIT	8	Administratively prohibited
RTN_THROW	9	Not in this table
RTN_NAT	10	Translate this address
RTN_XRESOLVE	11	Use external resolver

cs 14.40. *Route types.*

RT_SCOPE_UNIVERSE	0	indicates that the destination address is more than one hop away
RT_SCOPE_SITE	200	indicates interior route within the site
RT_SCOPE_LINK	253	indicates that the destination address is for the local network
RT_SCOPE_HOST	254	indicates that the destination address is for the local host
RT_SCOPE_NOWHERE	255	indicates that there is no route to the destination address

cs 14.41. *Route scopes.*

fn_scope. This field represents a scope of this route. The significance of this field is that it indicates the distance to a destination host or network. It can be any of the values listed in cs 14.41.

fn_state. This field stores flags for *fib_node*; they can be either of two flags, namely, *FN_S_ZOMBIE* or *FN_S_ACCESSED*, where *ZOMBIE* nodes are considered nonusable, and it is likely that deleted routes or dead *interface.ACCESSED* nodes are usable nodes and are currently active.

14.9.5 *struct fib_info*

This contains protocol- and hardware-specific information which basically define a destination route (cs 14.42).

fib_next and fib_prev. This points to the *next* and *prev fib_nodes* from the *fib_node*'s list in a single bucket of the hash table.

fib_treeref. Reference count to track the number of *fib_node* structures holding a reference on this *fib_node* instance.

fib_clntref. Reference count to track number of successful routing lookups.

fib_dead. Indicates route entry is removed from the table.

fib_flags. Represents any of *RTNH_F_DEAD*, *RTNH_F_PERVASIVE*, and *RTNH_F_ONLINK* flags. Of these *RTNH_F_DEAD* is currently in use and indicates that nexthop is dead (used by multipath only).

fib_protocol. This identifies the source of the route—that is, the protocol that installed the route. The possible values for this field are listed in cs 14.43.

fib_prefsrc. This contains the preferred source address. This is selected either by the user while configuring the route or by calling the function *inet_select_addr ( )*.

```
include/net/ip_fib.h

57 struct fib_info
58 {
59       struct fib_info      *fib_next;
60       struct fib_info      *fib_prev;
61       int                  fib_treeref;
62       atomic_t             fib_clntref;
63       int                  fib_dead;
64       unsigned             fib_flags;
65       int                  fib_protocol;
66       u32                  fib_prefsrc;
67       u32                  fib_priority;
68       unsigned             fib_metrics[RTAX_MAX];

73       int                  fib_nhs;
74 #ifdef CONFIG_IP_ROUTE_MULTIPATH
75       int                  fib_power;
76 #endif
77       struct fib_nh        fib_nh[0];
78 #define fib_dev              fib_nh[0].nh_dev
79 };
```

cs 14.42. *fib_info.*

RTPROT_UNSPEC Invalid field.

RTPROT_REDIRECT Route installed by the ICMP redirects, not used by current IPV4.

RTPROT_KERNEL Route installed by kernel.

RTPROT_BOOTRoute installed by the ip route and route commands.

RTPROT_STATICRoute installed by the administrater.

cs 14.43. *Fib protocols.*

fib_priority. This indicates the priority of the route: The smaller the value, the higher the priority. Default value is 0 when not set.

fib_power. This field is used only when multipath routing is enabled in kernel.

fib_nh[0]. This element is an *fib_nh* structure array that contains information about the output interface used and the next hop along the route. Several equivalent routes get the same destination in FIB query; this array represents these routes.

fib_nhs. This represents the number of entries in *fib_nh[0]*. The value of this field is greater than one only when multipath routing is enabled in the kernel.

14.9.6 *struct fib_nh*

This contains the pointer to the net device and the next hop gateway for this route. Apart from this, it contains more information required for multipath routing and the class used for queueing if class-based queuing is activated (cs 14.44).

```
include/net/ip_fib.h

37 struct fib_nh
38 {
39      struct net_device         *nh_dev;
40      unsigned            nh_flags;
41      unsigned char        nh_scope;
42 #ifdef CONFIG_IP_ROUTE_MULTIPATH
43      int              nh_weight;
44      int              nh_power;
45 #endif
46 #ifdef CONFIG_NET_CLS_ROUTE
47      __u32            nh_tclassid;
48 #endif
49      int             nh_oif;
50      u32            nh_gw;
51 };
```

cs 14.44. *fib_nh.*

nh_dev. This is a pointer to the *net_device* structure.

nh_scope. This is the scope of the route used to get to the next hop (for more inforamtion on scopes refer routing scopes section).

nh_flags. This represents any of the *RTNH_F_DEAD, RTNH_F_PERVASIVE,* and *RTNH_F_ONLINK* flags. Of these, *RTNH_F_DEAD* is currently in use and indicates that nexthop is dead (used by multipath only).

nh_weight and nh_power. This is used only when multipath routing is configured in kernel.

nh_oif. This is the output interface id to be used—that is, the index of the interface.

nh_gw. IP address of the next router.

nh_tclassid. This is used in a class-based queueing discipline for queueing of the packets, and represents a classid.

14.9.7 *struct fib_rule*

This data structure represents the rule or policy defined by the user for selection of the routing table from the multiple routing tables in the system (cs 14.45). This is used only if policy routing is configured in the kernel.

```
net/ipv4/fib_rules.c

52 struct fib_rule
53 {
54      struct fib_rule *r_next;
55      atomic_t    r_clntref;
56      u32        r_preference;
57      unsigned char  r_table;
58      unsigned char  r_action;
59      unsigned char  r_dst_len;
60      unsigned char  r_src_len;
61      u32        r_src;
62      u32        r_srcmask;
63      u32        r_dst;
64      u32        r_dstmask;
65      u32        r_srcmap;
66      u8         r_flags;
67      u8         r_tos;
68 #ifdef CONFIG_IP_ROUTE_FWMARK
69      u32        r_fwmark;
70 #endif
71      int        r_ifindex;
72 #ifdef CONFIG_NET_CLS_ROUTE
73      __u32       r_tclassid;
74 #endif
75      char        r_ifname[IFNAMSIZ];
76      int         r_dead;
77 };
```

cs 14.45. *fib_rule.*

r_next. This is the pointer to the next *fib_rule* in the global list of rules maintained by the kernel. By default, this global list has a local, main, and default rule.

r_clntref. This is the reference count of the rule instance being used.

r_preference. This is the priority of the rule. The three default rules in the system—that is, local, main, and default rules have 0, 0x7ffe, and 0x7fff—are assigned. *local_rule* value 0 has the highest priority. The user can assign the priority to the rule using ip rule command or if it is not asssinged by the user, then kernel will assign the priority that is one less than priority of the last added rule.

r_table. This is the routing table to be used for finding the destination route if this rule is applied to the packet.

r_action. This field contains the policy action type, and there are five types of policy actions. They are *RTN_UNICAST, RTN_NAT, RTN_UNREACHABLE, RTN_BLACKHOLE,* and *RTN_PHOHIBIT.* If the type is *RTN_UNICAST, RTN_NAT*, then we have a matching rule; otherwise, for any other policy action we return error.

r_dst_len and r_src_len. This stands for length of destination and source IP address, in terms of bits.

r_src and r_srcmask. This stands for source IP address and netmask.

r_dst and r_dstmask. This stands for destination IP address and netmask.

r_flags. This is currently not in use.

r_tos. This is the IP header's TOS field value.

r_ifindex. This represents the output interface id.

r_ifname[IFNAMSIZ]. This represents the name of the device.

r_tclassid. This is used in class-based queueing discipline for queueing of the packets, represents a classid.

r_dead. This field value is 0 when the rule is available.

14.10 ADDING NEW ENTRY IN ROUTING TABLE USING ip COMMAND (RT NETLINK INTERFACE)

Routing tables can be updated from the user space using the RT Netlink interface. For more details on how RT Netlink works, refer to the netlink chapter (Chapter 13).

Here we will see details about the only two options of the 'ip commnad' and the kernel functions invoked when these options are used—that is, for updating the routing table and adding a new rule (policy) for a new routing table.

1. ip route option
2. ip rule option

For more details refer to the Linun manual page for 'ip command.'
The following functions are registered in net/ipv4/devinet.c : inet_rtnetlink_table[]:

1. *inet_rtm_newroute()*
2. *inet_rtm_delroute()*
3. *inet_dump_fib()*

Any of these functions are invoked when the ip command is run from the user space with route option for adding, deleting, and displaying routing table.

1. *inet_rtm_newrule*
2. *inet_rtm_delrule*
3. *inet_dump_rules*

Any of these functions are invoked when the ip command is run from the user space with a rule option for adding new rule either new or existing routing table.

14.10.1   What Happens When the ip Command Is Run with a Route Option for Adding an Entry in the Routing Table?

The RT Netlink interface uses the netlink packet for communication with the kernel. When the ip command is run with the 'route add' option to update the routing table, a netlink packet is created in the user space; and when this packet reaches the kernel, the doit function in the *inet_rtnetlink_table* indexed by *RTM_NEWROUTE* is called (see Chapter 13 for more details) and the function *inet_rtm_newroute()* gets invoked.

14.10.2   *inet_rtm_newroute ()*

This function adds a new route to the FIB.
The main input parameters passed to this function are *sk_buff* struct, netlink header nlmsghdr struct, and the pointer to the optional data (user arguments) of type void which can be typecasted to FIB internal interface struct *kern_rta* through struct rtattr (for more details on struct rttr, see Chapter 13).
So at line 369 (cs 14.46) we are assigning the optional arguments pointer to struct rttr, and at line 370 the *NLMSG_DATA* (for more details on *NLMSG_DATA* see Chapter 13) macro takes you to the start of the rtmessage (struct rtmsg) in the netlink packet.
At line 372 the *inet_check_attr()* function loops through the optional parameter list and creates an array of parameters consisting of only the data; this is later typecasted to struct *kern_rta*, which is an FIB internal interface. Then at line 375 we call the function *fib_new_table ()*, which allocates memory for *fib_table* and initializes the function pointers by calling the function *fn_hash_init ()*. And finally at line 377 if *fib_table* is returned by *fib_new_table()*, then *fn_hash_insert()* gets called since *tb→tb_insert* is initialized to *fn_hash_insert()* in the *fn_hash_init ()* function.

```
net/ipv4/fib_frontend.c
 366 int inet_rtm_newroute(struct sk_buff *skb, struct nlmsghdr* nlh, void *arg)
 367 {
 368       struct fib_table * tb;
 369       struct rtattr **rta = arg;
 370       struct rtmsg *r = NLMSG_DATA(nlh);
 371
 372       if (inet_check_attr(r, rta))
 373           return -EINVAL;
 374
 375       tb = fib_new_table(r->rtm_table);
 376       if (tb)
 377           return tb->tb_insert(tb, r, (struct kern_rta*)rta, nlh, &NETLINK_CB(skb));
 378       return -ENOBUFS;
 379 }
```

cs 14.46. *inet_rtm_newroute ( ).*

The *fn_hash_insert()* function adds a new entry into the routing table.

Here the important data structures for interaction between user space and kernel for adding the routing table entry or adding a new rule to the routing table:

1. struct rtmsg
2. struct *kern_rta*

14.10.3   *struct rtmsg*

This structure is used for representing the user arguments set through the command line for adding a new routing entry in the routing table (cs 14.47).

rtm_family. This contains information about the supported address family, for example, *AF_INET* (IP protocol).

```
include/linux/rtnetlink.h
 83 struct rtmsg
 84 {
 85       unsigned char       rtm_family;
 86       unsigned char       rtm_dst_len;
 87       unsigned char       rtm_src_len;
 88       unsigned char       rtm_tos;
 89
 90       unsigned char       rtm_table;      /* Routing table id */
 91       unsigned char       rtm_protocol;   /* Routing protocol; see below */
 92       unsigned char       rtm_scope;      /* See below */
 93       unsigned char       rtm_type;       /* See below */
 94
 95       unsigned            rtm_flags;
 96 };
```

cs 14.47. *rtmsg.*

rtm_dst_len and rtm_src_len. This represents the number of bits used to create a 32-bit or smaller netmask for *AF_INET* addresses for both source and destination addresses.

rtm_tos. This is a ToS field in the IP header.

rtm_table. This contains routing table ID.

rtm_protocol. This refers to the routing message protocol—for example, *RTPROT_UNSPEC, RTPROT_KERNEL*, and so on.

rtm_scope. This refers to the route message scope—for example, *RT_SCOPE UNIVERSE*, and so on.

rtm_type. This refers to the type of the route—for example, *UNICAST*, and so on.

rtm_flags. Any of these three values—*RTM_F_NOTIFY*—notify the user route change.

RTM_F_CLONED. This route is cloned.

RTM_F_EQUALIZE. This route is not implemented yet.

14.10.4 *struct kern_rta*

This data structure represents the FIB internal values. It is used for assigning the values to the FIB data structures whenever there is an update to the routing table (cs 14.48).

rta_dst. This is the destination address.

rta_src. This is the source address.

```
include/net/ip_fib.h
21 struct kern_rta
22 {
23      void      *rta_dst;
24      void      *rta_src;
25      int       *rta_iif;
26      int       *rta_oif;
27      void      *rta_gw;
28      u32       *rta_priority;
29      void      *rta_prefsrc;
30      struct rtattr  *rta_mx;
31      struct rtattr  *rta_mp;
32      unsigned char  *rta_protoinfo;
33      unsigned char  *rta_flow;
34      struct rta_cacheinfo *rta_ci;
35 };
```

cs 14.48. *kern_rta.*

rta_iif. This is the input internal network interface.

rta_oif. This is the output network interface.

rta_gw. This contains gateway IP address.

rta-prefsrc. This is the preferred source address (used by RFC 1122 as part of UDP multihoming).

14.10.5   *fn_hash_insert ()*

This function is called for adding/inserting route information in the fib table. The *fib_table* pointer and the netlink message parameters (main structures are struct rtmsg and struct rta) are passed to this function. It starts with extracting the individual parameters from the netlink message struct and then checks if the zone is already existing; if not, then it allocates and initializes the new zone by calling the function *fib_new_zone()* at line 455 (cs 14.51).

After assigning the new zone, new hash key value is generated by using the destination and the netmask value by calling the function *fz_key()* at line 464.

The function *fz_key()* builds the hash key by AND-ing the destination address with the zone's netmask (cs 14.49). Now before getting the hash index from the hash table, *fib_info* struct is allocated and initialized in *fib_create_info()* at line 467.

The zone-specific *fz_hash* table is a table of *fib_node* structures as shown in Fig 14.13. We have seen that the memory is already allocated for *fz_hash* table in *fib_new_zone()*. By using the hash key, we can get the hash table index from the *fz_hash* table at line 477 by calling the function *fz_chain_p()* (cs 14.50) and then check for the *fib_node* list using the hash index.

The function *fz_chain_p()* calculates the hash index from *fz_hash* table by calling the function *fn_hash ()* based on the key value and returns a pointer to pointer to the *fib_node* for that hash index.

```
net/ipv4/fib_hash.c
123 static __inline__ fn_key_t fz_key(u32 dst, struct fn_zone *fz)
124 {
125      fn_key_t k;
126      k.datum = dst & FZ_MASK(fz);
127      return k;
128 }
```

<u>cs 14.49.</u> *fz_key ( ).*

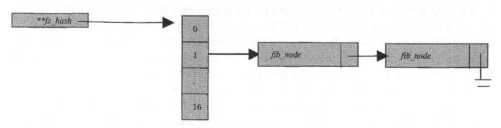

Figure 14.13. *fz_hash pointer.*

```
net/ipv4/fib_hash.c
    130 static __inline__ struct fib_node ** fz_chain_p(fn_key_t key, struct fn_zone *fz)
    131 {
    132        return &fz->fz_hash[fn_hash(key, fz).datum];
    133 }
```

cs 14.50. fz_chain_p ( ).

Using the new *fib_node* list address from the hash index returned by *fz_chain_p()*, scan the list to check that the destination address (hash key) is already existing.

There are four cases to check for scanning the list:

1. Scan the list to find the first route with the same destination at line 483 (cs 14.51).
2. If 'CONFIG_IP_ROUTE_TOS' is defined, then scan the list to find route with the same destination and tos at line 492.
3. If any of the above scan checks returns *fib_node* for the hash key, then check for the state of the *fib_node* for ZOMBIE at line 500. If the state is ZOMBIE, then delete the old *fib_node* and insert the new *fib_node* in *fib_node_list*.
4. If *fib_node* state is not ZOMBIE, then scan the list with an additional check for the *fib→priority* of *fib_node* at line 511; and again if such a key exists, then replace the *fib_node* with the new one.

(ZOMBIE nodes are considered nonusable and are likely to be deleted routes or a dead interface.) If this is a new entry, then all the scan checks will fail and finally the memory for the new entry (*fib_node*) is allocated at line 564 from the *fib_node* cache. Then this new entry (*fib_node*) will initialize to type, tos, scope values and the *fib_info* pointer from line 570 to line 576.

And finally this new entry (*fib_node*) is inserted into the *fib_node_list* at line 584.

14.10.6 *fn_new_zone()*

fn_new_zone() basically gets the struct *fn_hash* pointer and the destination address bit length as parameters. It starts with allocating and initializing the new zone struct (*fn_zone*) at line 229 and then checks for the destination address bit length at line 234. If bit length is zero, then the hash table will have a single entry and the divisor in this case will be 1. For any bit length apart from zero, the hash table will have 16 entries and the divisor in this case will be always 16. After calculating the hash table size for the zone, it then allocates and initializes *fz→fz_hash* table space for this zone at line 241. Next assign the bit length (netmask length) value to the *fz→order* and *fz→mask* with the netmask for this zone at lines 247 and 248.

Before inserting this new zone into the zones list, we need to identify the first non-empty zone with more specific netmask (i.e., longest netmask length). The significance for doing this is that the lookup algorithm used to find the route from the routing table is the longest prefix match (LPM), which starts the lookup with the zone having the longest prefix (netmask) length.

```
net/ipv4/fib_hash.c
432 static int
433 fn_hash_insert(struct fib_table *tb, struct rtmsg *r, struct kern_rta *rta,
434          struct nlmsghdr *n, struct netlink_skb_parms *req)
435 {

454      fz = table->fn_zones[z];
455      if (!fz && !(fz = fn_new_zone(table, z)))
456          return -ENOBUFS;
457
           .............
464          key = fz_key(dst, fz);
465      }
466
467      if ((fi = fib_create_info(r, rta, n, &err)) == NULL)
468          return err;
469
           ...........
473      (z==32 || (1<<z) > fz->fz_divisor))
474          fn_rehash_zone(fz);
475 #endif
476
477      fp = fz_chain_p(key, fz);
     . .
483      FIB_SCAN(f, fp) {

. . .
492      FIB_SCAN_KEY(f, fp, key) {
. . .

500 if (f && (f->fn_state&FN_S_ZOMBIE) &&
. . .

511FIB_SCAN_TOS(f, fp, key, tos) {

. . .

564      new_f = kmem_cache_alloc(fn_hash_kmem, SLAB_KERNEL);
. . .

570      new_f->fn_key = key;
571 #ifdef CONFIG_IP_ROUTE_TOS
572      new_f->fn_tos = tos;
573 #endif
574      new_f->fn_type = type;
575      new_f->fn_scope = r->rtm_scope;
576      FIB_INFO(new_f) = fi;

584      *fp = new_f;
```

cs 14.51. fn_hash_insert ( ).

14.10.6.1 Why LPM Algorithm for Routing Table Lookup? IP performs
the steps in following order to find the destination route in its routing table:

1. It searches for a matching host address (IP address).
2. It searches for a matching network address.
3. It searches for a default entry (The default entry is a network address with
   0).

A matching host address (host's IP address) is always used before matching a network address. If both host address and network address are not matched, then we use the default entry (default route) which is a network address with ID 0 for which a default gateway address is defined in the routing table.

The *fn_zone[33]* array field of the *fn_hash* struct of *fib_table* maintains a list of zones based on the netmask length, and each zone represents each bit in the netmask (32-bit).

fn_zone[0] represents the default entry (default route).

fn_zone[32] represents the more specific route.

At lines 251 and 252 (cs 14.52) we identify the first non-empty zone with the longest netmask length based on the *fz→fz_order* value. Then we check if the new zone's netmask length is greater than the found longest netmask length zone. It is then that we insert the new zone as the longest netmask length after this found longest netmask length zone and initialize the *fn_zone_list* to this new zone at lines

```
net/ipv4/fib_hash.c

225 static struct fn_zone *
226 fn_new_zone(struct fn_hash *table, int z)
227 {
228     int i;
229     struct fn_zone *fz = kmalloc(sizeof(struct fn_zone), GFP_KERNEL)      ;

233     memset(fz, 0, sizeof(struct fn_zone));
234     if (z) {
235         fz->fz_divisor = 16;
236         fz->fz_hashmask = 0xF;
237     } else {
238         fz->fz_divisor = 1;
239         fz->fz_hashmask = 0;
240     }
241     fz->fz_hash = kmalloc(fz->fz_divisor*sizeof(struct fib_node*), G     FP_KERNEL);

246     memset(fz->fz_hash, 0, fz->fz_divisor*sizeof(struct fib_node*));
247     fz->fz_order = z;
248     fz->fz_mask = inet_make_mask(z);

251     for (i=z+1; i<=32; i++)
252         if (table->fn_zones[i])
253             break;

255     if (i>32) {

257         fz->fz_next = table->fn_zone_list;
258         table->fn_zone_list = fz;
259     } else {
260         fz->fz_next = table->fn_zones[i]->fz_next;
261         table->fn_zones[i]->fz_next = fz;
262     }
263     table->fn_zones[z] = fz;
```

cs 14.52. *fn_new_zone ( )*.

257 and 258. The *fn_zone_list* contains the earlier longest netmask length zone. Otherwise, if the new zone's netmask is less than the found longest netmask length zone, then we insert the new zone before the found longest netmask length zone at lines 260 and 261. Finally at line 263 we add this new zone to the table's zone list.

14.10.7 *fib_create_info()*

The main parameters passed to this function are the *rtmsg* struct and the *kern_rta* struct (netlink message). It starts with allocating the memory for the *fib_info* struct at line 446 (cs 14.53). Here the total memory allocated to *fib_info* is size of *fib_info* and the size of *fib_nh* with number of elements (*fib_nh*) required for this *fib_info*. The *fib_nh* struct is one of the elements (declared as array) of *fib_info* struct, and it should be allocated at the end of *fib_info* struct so that the memory will be contiguous. After allocating the memory, the *fib_info* struct elements are initialized based on the values in *rtmsg* and the *kern_rta* struct.

```
net/ipv4/fib_semantics.c
 421 struct fib_info *
 422 fib_create_info(const struct rtmsg *r, struct kern_rta *rta,
 423          const struct nlmsghdr *nlh, int *errp)
 424 {
        ......
 446     fi = kmalloc(sizeof(*fi)+nhs*sizeof(struct fib_nh), GFP_KERNEL);   447      err = -ENOBUFS;
 448     if (fi == NULL)
 449         goto failure;
 450     fib_info_cnt++;
 451     memset(fi, 0, sizeof(*fi)+nhs*sizeof(struct fib_nh));
 452
 453     fi->fib_protocol = r->rtm_protocol;
 454     fi->fib_nhs = nhs;
 455     fi->fib_flags = r->rtm_flags;
 456     if (rta->rta_priority)
 457         fi->fib_priority = *rta->rta_priority;
        ......
 483 #ifdef CONFIG_NET_CLS_ROUTE
 484         if (rta->rta_flow && memcmp(&fi->fib_nh->nh_tclassid, rt a->rta_flow, 4))
 485             goto err_inval;
 486 #endif
 487 #else
 488         goto err_inval;
 489 #endif
 490     } else {
 491         struct fib_nh *nh = fi->fib_nh;
 492         if (rta->rta_oif)
 493             nh->nh_oif = *rta->rta_oif;
 494         if (rta->rta_gw)
 495             memcpy(&nh->nh_gw, rta->rta_gw, 4);
 496 #ifdef CONFIG_NET_CLS_ROUTE
 497         if (rta->rta_flow)
 498             memcpy(&nh->nh_tclassid, rta->rta_flow, 4);
 499 #endif
 500         nh->nh_flags = r->rtm_flags;
        . . . . . .
```

cs 14.53. *fib_create_info.*

14.10.8 *fn_hash_insert ()*

Fig 14.14 shows the *fn_hash_insert()* flow diagram for more details refer to Section 14.10.5.

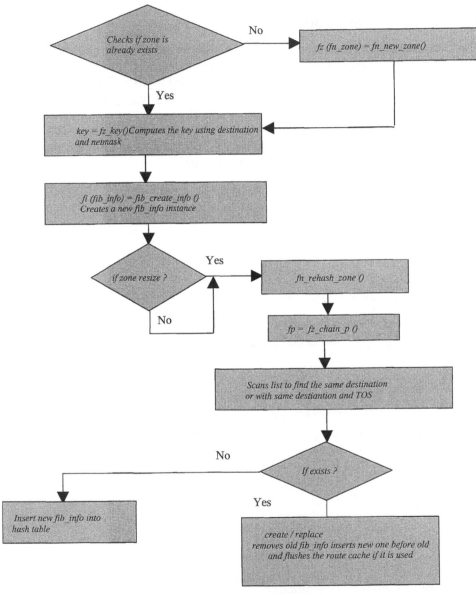

Figure 14.14. *fn_hash_insert ( )* flow.

14.11   WHAT HAPPENS WHEN THE ip COMMAND IS RUN WITH A RULE OPTION FOR ADDING AN ENTRY IN THE ROUTING TABLE?

The RT Netlink interface uses the netlink packet for communication with the kernel. When the ip command is run with a 'rule add' option to update the new routing table (created by using ip route command prior to adding new rule) or existing routing table, the netlink packet is created in the user space; and when this packet reaches the kernel, the doit function in the *inet_rtnetlink_table* indexed by *RTM_NEWRULE* is called (see Chapter 13 for more details) and the function *inet_rtm_newrule()* gets invoked.

14.11.1 *inet_rtm_newrule()*

This function adds a new rule or policy to the new or existing routing table.

The main input parameters passed to this function are *sk_buff* struct, netlink header *nlmsghdr* struct, and the pointer to the optional data (user arguments) of type void which can be typecasted to the FIB internal interface struct *kern_rta* through struct *rtattr* (for more details on struct rttr refer Netlink chapter), at line 164 (cs 14.54) we are assigning the optional arguments pointer to struct *rttr* and at line 165 *NLMSG_DATA* (for more details on *NLMSG_DATA* see Chapter 13) macro takes you to the start of the rtmessage (struct *rtmsg*) in the netlink packet.

Any ip rule can be added to the routing table. For example, a rule can be that packets coming from 'this' source address should use 'this' routing table for lookup. At line 176 we get the routing table id which signifies that a new ip rule is going to be added to this routing table. If routing table id is unspecified, then we allocate a unique new table id at line 180 by calling the function *fib_empty_table ( )*. Then allocate a new *fib_rule* struct at line 186 for defining the new rule for the routing table and initialize it at line 189.

Now we copy the user data to the newly allocated the *fib_rule* structure. The user data are source address, destination address, gateway address, type of address, flags.table id, and so on.

```
net/ipv4/fib_rules.c

162 int inet_rtm_newrule(struct sk_buff *skb, struct nlmsghdr* nlh, void *arg)
163 {
164      struct rtattr **rta = arg;
165      struct rtmsg *rtm = NLMSG_DATA(nlh);
166      struct fib_rule *r, *new_r, **rp;
167      unsigned char table_id;
168

176      table_id = rtm->rtm_table;
177      if (table_id == RT_TABLE_UNSPEC) {
178          struct fib_table *table;
179          if (rtm->rtm_type == RTN_UNICAST || rtm->rtm_type == RTN_NAT) {
180              if ((table = fib_empty_table()) == NULL)
181                  return -ENOBUFS;
182              table_id = table->tb_id;
183          }
184      }
185
186      new_r = kmalloc(sizeof(*new_r), GFP_KERNEL);
    . . .
189      memset(new_r, 0, sizeof(*new_r));
                                                    cont . . .
```

cs 14.54. *inet_rtm_newrule ( )*.

```
net/ipv4/fib_rules.c
inet_rtm_newrule () cont...

191          memcpy(&new_r->r_src, RTA_DATA(rta[RTA_SRC-1]), 4);
193          memcpy(&new_r->r_dst, RTA_DATA(rta[RTA_DST-1]),

195          memcpy(&new_r->r_srcmap, RTA_DATA(rta[RTA_GATEWAY-1]), 4);
196     new_r->r_src_len = rtm->rtm_src_len;
197     new_r->r_dst_len = rtm->rtm_dst_len;
198     new_r->r_srcmask = inet_make_mask(rtm->rtm_src_len); 4);

199     new_r->r_dstmask = inet_make_mask(rtm->rtm_dst_len);
200     new_r->r_tos = rtm->rtm_tos;

205     new_r->r_action = rtm->rtm_type;
206     new_r->r_flags = rtm->rtm_flags;

208          memcpy(&new_r->r_preference, RTA_DATA(rta[RTA_PRIORITY-1]), 4);
209     new_r->r_table = table_id;
210     if (rta[RTA_IIF-1]) {
211         struct net_device *dev;
212         memcpy(new_r->r_ifname, RTA_DATA(rta[RTA_IIF-1]), IFNAMSIZ);
213         new_r->r_ifname[IFNAMSIZ-1] = 0;
214         new_r->r_ifindex = -1;
215         dev = __dev_get_by_name(new_r->r_ifname);
216         if (dev)
217             new_r->r_ifindex = dev->ifindex;
218     }
221          memcpy(&new_r->r_tclassid, RTA_DATA(rta[RTA_FLOW-1]), 4);

                                                                cont...
```

cs 14.55. *inet_rtm_newrule ( ) (continued).*

The most important data is the priority that would be assigned to the *fib_rule r_preference* field at line 208. Its significance is that it plays an important role in deciding the position for this new *fib_rule* in the global list of *fib_rules* defined in the kernl. If a network interface is provided, we get the *net_device* pointer before copying the device pointer in the *fib_rule*. Finally, copy the flow id (realm) used in the queueing discipline for identifying the class is copied at line 221 (cs 14.55).

After copying the user data into the new *fib_rule* struct now, this new rule has to be added into the *fib_rules* global list maintained by the kernel. By default, there are three rules in the system local, main, and default rules. The priority of these rules are 0, 32766, and 32767. This list is sorted in increasing order based on the priority (0 is the highest priority rule). Any new rule added would be inserted between the *loca_rule* and the *main_rule*. We do this by getting the address of the global *fib_rules* list at line 224 (cs 14.56). Before traversing through this list for inserting a new rule, if priority (*r_preference*) is provided by the user, then we check at line 235 if there is any rule which has a priority value greater than this new rule, if it is then we insert this new rule before tht rule in the rules. If the priority value is not provided by the user at line 225, then before checking the condition at line 235 we decide the priority value for this new rule at line 230 and then continue to traverse the list and insert this new rule.

```
net/ipv4/fib_rules.c
inet_rtm_newrule () cont ...
  224      rp = &fib_rules;
  225      if (!new_r->r_preference) {
  226          r = fib_rules;
  227          if (r && (r = r->r_next) != NULL) {
  228              rp = &fib_rules->r_next;
  229              if (r->r_preference)
  230                  new_r->r_preference = r->r_preference - 1;
  231          }
  232      }
  233
  234      while ( (r = *rp) != NULL ) {
  235          if (r->r_preference > new_r->r_preference)
  236              break;
  237          rp = &r->r_next;
  238      }
  239
  240      new_r->r_next = r;
  
  242      write_lock_bh(&fib_rules_lock);
  243      *rp = new_r;
  244      write_unlock_bh(&fib_rules_lock);
                                                    cont ...
```

cs 14.56. *inet_rtm_newrule ( ) (continued).*

14.11.2 FIB Initialization

Linux supports 255 routing tables, and each routing table is identified by the table id. By default, local (id = 255) and main (id = 254) tables are used. If policy routing is defined, multiple tables can be configured and used for the route lookup. If policy routing is not configured, then only the local and main routing tables are used and the lookup to find the route is done only in these tables. The local table has the highest precedence. Figure 14.15 shows the details about FIB initialization.

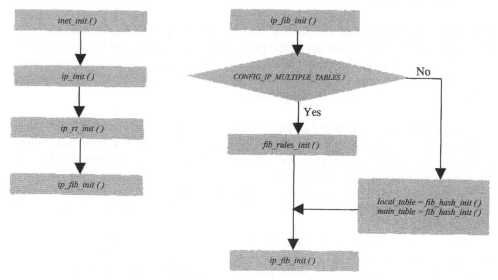

Figure 14.15. FIB initialization flow diagram.

The local table consists of routes to local and broadcast addresses. This table is maintained by the kernel automatically. Any routing lookup request has to go through the local table first, and the significance of this table is to determine whether a packet has to be delivered locally or has to be forwarded. The local table is searched first for any routing lookup request, and this saves lookup time if the packet has to be delivered locally and there is no need to search other tables. The contents of the local table can be viewed by running the command:

 # ip route show table local

The main table consists of all the normal routes, and these routes are inserted by the 'ip route' command when no other table is mentioned. This can be manually configured, and the kernel uses this table to calculate the routes to destination. The contents of the local table can be viewed by running the command:

 # ip route show table
#route -n
#netstat -nr

The *inet_init ( )* function called by socket.c on kernel starup is responsible to set the IP module up by invoking the function *ip_init ( )*.

The *ip_init ( )* function initializes the IP subsytem and registers the packet type and the subprotocol initializers. To initialize the routing subsystem, it invokes the function *ip_rt_init ( )*.

The *ip_rt_init ( )* function does the two important initializations to the routing code:

1. It sets up the routing cache (defines the size of the cache and the memory allocation, starts the cache-related timers, etc.)
2. It calls the function *ip_fib_init ( )*, which initializes the default routing tables (FIB for IPV4).

The *ip_fib_init ( )* function checks if *CONFIG_IP_MULTIPLE_TABLES* (Policy Routing) is defined in the kernel. If the policy routing is defined in the kernel, then the *fib_rules_init ( )* function is invoked to set up the policy-based routing; otherwise, it calls the *fib_hash_init ( )* function to set up the default routing tables (local and main table only) which are defined globally.

14.11.2.1   fib_hash_init ( ). This function initializes and allocates a *fib_table* in the kernel. A FIB slab cache is allocated at line 899 (cs 14.57), from which *fib_node* structures will be allocated for various FIB entries. Then a new *fib_table* is allocated at line 904. At least two *fib_table* instances are present in the kernel; if policy routing is enabled, then there are more instances of *fib_table* in the kernel for different routing tables. After allocating the *fib_table*, we initialize the various field of *fib_table*.

First the *tb_id* field is set to the table number at line 908, which is passed as an input parameter. Then we set the various function pointers in the *fib_table* struct to point to the *fn_hash_lookup, fn_hash_insert*, and so on, functions from lines 909 to 914. Finally the *tb_data* field of *fib_table* is initialized using the memset at line 918. This field is an anonymous pointer and is further used to point to an *fn_hash* struct

```
net/ipv4/fib_hash.c
 890 #ifdef CONFIG_IP_MULTIPLE_TABLES
 891 struct fib_table * fib_hash_init(int id)
 892 #else
 893 struct fib_table * __init fib_hash_init(int id)
 894 #endif
 895 {
 896     struct fib_table *tb;
 897
 898     if (fn_hash_kmem == NULL)
 899         fn_hash_kmem = kmem_cache_create("ip_fib_hash",
 900                             sizeof(struct fib_node)    ,
 901                             0, SLAB_HWCACHE_ALIGN,
 902                             NULL, NULL);
 903
 904     tb = kmalloc(sizeof(struct fib_table) + sizeof(struct fn_hash),
    GFP_KERNEL);
 908     tb->tb_id = id;
 909     tb->tb_lookup = fn_hash_lookup;
 910     tb->tb_insert = fn_hash_insert;
 911     tb->tb_delete = fn_hash_delete;
 912     tb->tb_flush = fn_hash_flush;
 913     tb->tb_select_default = fn_hash_select_default;
 914     tb->tb_dump = fn_hash_dump;
 . . .
 918     memset(tb->tb_data, 0, sizeof(struct fn_hash));
 919     return tb;
 920 }
```

cs 14.57. fib_hash_init ().

which contains array of *fz_zone* struct, and this in turn contains an array of *fib_node* hash structures.

14.11.2.2   *fib_rules_init ( ).* This function registers the callback function *fib_rules_event ( )* (cs 14.58). The rules list is already statically linked, and it doesn't do any intializations.

The *fib_rules_event ( )* function is invoked whenever a new network device is registerd or unregistered. The *fib_rules_attach ( )* and *fib_rules_detach ( )* functions are called for all rules to correct all the ifindex entries to any event of register or unregister network device.

14.12   FIB TRAVERSAL FLOW DIAGRAM

Figure 14.16 shows details about destination route lookup for the outgoing packet. The destination route lookup is done first in route cache if it's not found then search the FIB detabase.

14.12.1   *ip_route_output()*

The main arguments to *ip_route_output* (cs 14.59) function is the source and desti- nation address, tos, and the output interface. It initializes the *rt_key* structure with

```
net/ipv4/fib_rules.c

382 static int fib_rules_event(struct notifier_block *this, unsigned long event, void *ptr)
383 {
384     struct net_device *dev = ptr;
385
386     if (event == NETDEV_UNREGISTER)
387         fib_rules_detach(dev);
388     else if (event == NETDEV_REGISTER)
389         fib_rules_attach(dev);
390     return NOTIFY_DONE;
391 }
392
393
394 struct notifier_block fib_rules_notifier = {
395     notifier_call: fib_rules_event,
396 };
    . . .

464 void __init fib_rules_init(void)
465 {
466     register_netdevice_notifier(&fib_rules_notifier);
467 }
```

cs 14.58. fib_rules_event().

```
include/net/route.h
140 static inline int ip_route_output(struct rtable **rp,
141                              u32 daddr, u32 saddr, u32 tos, int oif)
142 {
143     struct rt_key key = { dst:daddr, src:saddr, oif:oif, tos:tos };
144
145     return ip_route_output_key(rp, &key);
146 }
```

cs 14.59. ip_route_output ().

the saddr, daddr, tos, and oif values at line 143 and calls the function *ip_route_output_key()* for getting the routing cache entry.

14.12.2 ip_route_output_key ()

The *rt_key* struct is passed as an argument to this function from *ip_route_output()*. This *rt_key* struct is used to find the hash index for *rt_hash_table* so that the appropriate chain from *rt_hash_bucket* of routing entries are searched. At line 2004 (cs 14.60) it calls the *rt_hash_code()* function to calculate the hash value. Once the hash value is returned from *rt_hash_code()*, then at line 2006 it acquires the *rt_hash_table* lock for reading the entries from *rt_hash_table* for comparison with the hash key.

The hash value returned from *rt_hash_code* is used to search the appropriate hash queue from *rt_hash_table* to find an entry that matches the key with respect to destination & source address and tos & oif values (if *CONFIG_IP_ROUTE_*

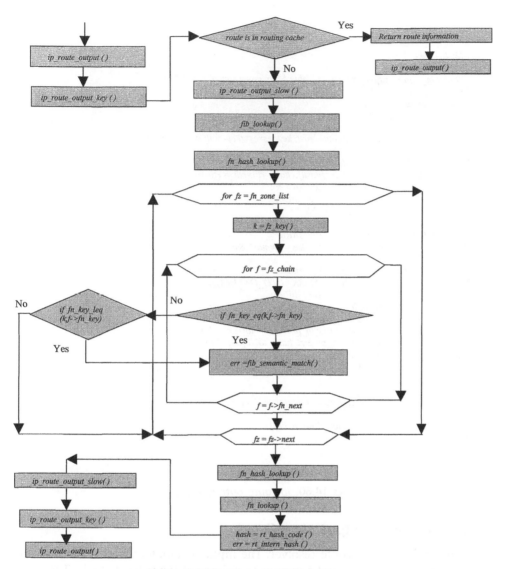

Figure 14.16. *FIB traversal flow diagram.*

FWMARK is enabled in the kernel, then the mark value is also used for matching the key, i.e., at line 2007 to 2011).

If an entry is found for the input key from hash queue of *rt_hash_table*, then since we are going to use this routing cache entry, so at line 2017 the routing cache entries' last time of use should be updated so that the garbage collection routine for cleaning the entries from the chain should be aware of this. And *dst_hold()* is called at line 2018, and this function simply increments the reference count so that this can't be deleted if its in use. Finally at line 2022, *rp is set to this found entry from the chain and then returns.

If the matching key is not found from the *rt_hash_table*—that is, the condition fails at line 2008—then we exit from the loop and finally call the function *ip_route_ output_slow* at line 2028, which uses the FIB to construct the new routing entry.

```
net/ipv4/route.c

1999 int ip_route_output_key(struct rtable **rp, const struct rt_key *key)
2000 {
2001     unsigned hash;
2002     struct rtable *rth;
2003
2004     hash = rt_hash_code(key->dst, key->src ^ (key->oif << 5), key->tos);
2005
2006     read_lock_bh(&rt_hash_table[hash].lock);
2007     for (rth = rt_hash_table[hash].chain; rth; rth = rth->u.rt_next) {
2008         if (rth->key.dst == key->dst &&
2009             rth->key.src == key->src &&
2010             rth->key.iif == 0 &&
2011             rth->key.oif == key->oif &&
2012 #ifdef CONFIG_IP_ROUTE_FWMARK
2013             rth->key.fwmark == key->fwmark &&
2014 #endif
2015             !((rth->key.tos ^ key->tos) &
2016                 (IPTOS_RT_MASK | RTO_ONLINK))) {
2017             rth->u.dst.lastuse = jiffies;
2018             dst_hold(&rth->u.dst);
2019             rth->u.dst.__use++;
2020             rt_cache_stat[smp_processor_id()].out_hit++;
2021             read_unlock_bh(&rt_hash_table[hash].lock);
2022             *rp = rth;
2023             return 0;
2024         }
2025     }
2026     read_unlock_bh(&rt_hash_table[hash].lock);
2027
2028     return ip_route_output_slow(rp, key);
2029 }
```

cs 14.60. *ip_route_output_key ().*

14.12.3 *ip_route_output_slow ()*

This function is a major route resolver. The input parameters to this function are routing key (*rt_key* struct) and a pointer to pointer of type struct rtable. The main functionality of this function is to search the FIB database based on the input routing key; and if the match entry is found, then create a new route cache entry. The new route cache entry is returned as a pointer and stored in **rp, which is an input parameter of type struct rtable.

It mainly delivers an IP packet locally or to a remote destination. Any IP packet created by the host system must have an source address; so whenever a packet is transmitted, the destination should know the source of the received packet to send a reply back to the source.

The main significance of this routine is that it checks for the IP source address and selects the egress device for the packet transmission. It checks for both the IP source address and egress device. If the source address is given, then it selects the egress device by doing local routing table lookup; or else if the egress device is already known, then it selects the source address based on the egress device. Finally, if the route lookup is successful for the IP packet, then it creates and initializes a

```
net/ipv4/route.c

1705 int ip_route_output_slow(struct rtable **rp, const struct rt_key *oldkey)
1706 {
1707     struct rt_key key;
1708     struct fib_result res;
         . . . . .
1717     tos         = oldkey->tos & (IPTOS_RT_MASK | RTO_ONLINK);
1718     key.dst     = oldkey->dst;
1719     key.src     = oldkey->src;
1720     key.tos     = tos & IPTOS_RT_MASK;
1721     key.iif     = loopback_dev.ifindex;
1722     key.oif     = oldkey->oif;
1723 #ifdef CONFIG_IP_ROUTE_FWMARK
1724     key.fwmark      = oldkey->fwmark;
1725 #endif
1726     key.scope       = (tos & RTO_ONLINK) ? RT_SCOPE_LINK :
1727                             RT_SCOPE_UNIVERSE;
1728     res.fi      = NULL;
1729 #ifdef CONFIG_IP_MULTIPLE_TABLES
1730     res.r       = NULL;
1731 #endif


                                                         cont...
```

cs 14.61. ip_route_output_slow ().

new route cache table entry and inserts it into the route cache. It also identifies whether the packet is of multicast, broadcast, or unicast type. It also provides support for multipath routing if configured in kernel for the next hop selection, or it selects the default gateway for the next hop. Multicast routing is also supported if defined in kernel.

The key (struct *rt_key*) and res (struct *fib_result*) are two important local variables at lines 1707 and 1708 (cs 14.61), where the struct *rt_key* contains information about the destination, source, input, and output interface, the tos, and the forwarding mark. The 'key' variable is of type struct *rt_key*, gets initialized to values pointed by oldkey, which is also of type struct *rt_key*, and is passed as an input parameter. The 'res' variable is of type struct *fib_result*, which is later passed as an input parameter to *fib_lookup* () function and gets the route information required. It is also used to build the new routing cache entry, where the *fib_result* struct contains information about the route—that is, prefixlen, next hop details, scope of route, and type of address. The input parameter 'oldkey' contains the information about the route, and the *ip_route_output_slow* ( ) starts with copying the values from oldkey to local variables for building the new search key.

At line 1717, before assigning the *oldkey→tos* value, we are checking whether the flag *RTO_ONLINK* is set or not, where '*RTO_ONLINK*' is used to indicate that the destination is no more than one hop away and reachable via a link layer protocol. This flag is important for scope value of the new key element of struct *rt_key*. From lines 1718 to 1722, new key values of key variables are getting assigned from the input parameter oldkey; that is, first the destination and source address are copied into the new search key, followed by the tos value and the output

```
net/ipv4/route.c
ip_route_output_slow cont ...
  1733        if (oldkey->src) {
  1734            err = -EINVAL;
  1735            if (MULTICAST(oldkey->src) ||
  1736                BADCLASS(oldkey->src) ||
  1737                ZERONET(oldkey->src))
  1738                goto out;
  1739

  1741            dev_out = ip_dev_find(oldkey->src);
  1742            if (dev_out == NULL)
  1743                goto out;

                                                              cont . . .
```

cs 14.62. *ip_route_output_slow () (continued).*

interface identifier. Initially the input interface identifier is pointed to the loopback device at line 1721 and at line 1724; if *CONFIG_IP_ROUTE_FWMARK* is defined, then the new mark (netfilter) value is assigned to key.fwmark. The value of key. scope at line 1726 depends on the flag '*RTO_ONLINK*.' If *RTO_ONLINK* flag is set, then the scope of the route must be *RT_SCOPE_LINK*; otherwise it is *RT_SCOPE_UNIVERSE*. The key.scope indicates the distance to the destination IP address (local network, host, universe, etc.). For more information on scopes, see Section 14.12.7. Then the *fib_info* pointer is initialized to NULL at line 1728. If policy routing is defined in the kernel '*CONFIG_MULTIPLE_TABLES*,' then the fibrule struct (i.e., res.r) at line 1730 is initially set to NULL.

Here we check for the source address from the search key at line 1733 (cs 14.62). As mentioned earlier, any IP packet must have the source address so that the destination can send back the reply. If we have the source address at line 1733, then we need to test whether this is of type MULTICAST, BADCLASS, or ZERONET at line 1735, and any source address cannot be of these types. If there is any chance of either of these types occurring, then we return the error to the caller by jumping to the label out at line 1738.

Then we need to check if this source address is one of our local addresses that is assigned to one of the network interfaces of the system. So we call the function *ip_dev_find ( )* at line 1741 to identify the interface with this source address. This function returns the pointer to the *net_device* struct associated with the source address; that is, we get the network interface from which the packet has to be transmitted. For more information on *ip_dev_find*, refer to Section 14.12.4.

At lines 1753 and 1754, the egress device is not provided by the search key and the destination is multicast or a limited broadcast address (cs 14.63). If the destination is a multicast address, then a group of hosts or systems on the same subnet or different subnet (or WAN) can receive the packet, whereas in the case of broadcast packets they can be received by all the hosts on the subnet. So here the source address plays an important role in communication since the destination can be a group of hosts or all the hosts in the link. This is the case of the special hack as per the comments in the code at lines 1755–1769, which gives more details about this hack. So the check is made at lines 1753 and 174 for this case. If the condition at lines 1753 and 1754 is true, then the output interface identifier of the new search

```
net/ipv4/route.c
ip_route_output_slow cont ...
    1753            if (oldkey->oif == 0
    1754                && (MULTICAST(oldkey->dst) || oldkey->dst == 0xFFFFFFFF)) {
                    . . .
    1770                key.oif = dev_out->ifindex;
    1771                goto make_route;
    1772            }
    1773        if (dev_out)
    1774            dev_put(dev_out);
    1775        dev_out = NULL;
    1776    }

cont . . .
```

cs 14.63. *ip_route_output_slow ()* (continued).

key is the output interface associated with the device returned by the *ipdev_find* ( ) function as explained earlier. So it uses the returned *net_device* from the *ip_dev_find* ( ). Then it jumps to the label *make_route*. Here the packet can be routed without doing the *fib_lookup* since we have all the routing information.

Finally, release the device by calling the *dev_put* ( ) function and set the *dev_out* to NULL at line 1775. This is the case where an output interface is provided, so we check for the source address; if it is not provided, we get the source address. If the output interface identifier is specified in the search key, then we get the *net_device* by calling the function *dev_get_by_index* ( ) at line 1778 (cs 14.64). If the returned value is NULL, then jump to label out and return error at line 1781. The function *__in_dev_get( )* returns the void **ip_ptr* element of the *net_device* structure at line 1782; if not, the device is released and an error is returned. The *ip_ptr* element points to the instance of *in_device* struct. This *in_device* struct contains the important element *ifa_listof type in_ifaddr* struct, which is an IP ifaddr chain (list of struct *ifa_list*). This is important that each physical *net_device* on the system may be assigned alias IP addresses and labels (eth0:0, eth0:1, etc.)

If the destination is a local multicast address, then a group of hosts or systems on the same subnet can receive the packet, whereas in the case of broadcast packets they can be received by all the hosts on the subnet. The source address is required here before transmitting these types of packets since it is the important key for the communication because the destination can be a group of hosts or all the hosts in the link.

So if the destination is the local multicast or the broadcast address at line 1787 and if the source address is not provided in the key but output interface identifier is specified, then we retrieve the source address of the output device by calling the function *inet_select_addr* ( ) (for more information on *inet_select_addr*, see Section 14.12.6). The scope here is *RT_SCOPE_LINK* (for more information on scopes, see Section 14.12.7). The reason for link scope is that the local multicast, broadcast, and limited broadcast destinations are on the same subnet. Here the destination address is with scope *RT_SCOPE_LINK*, so we have the route information and hence it jumps to label *make_route* without doing the route lookup at line 1791.

```
net/ipv4/route.c
ip_route_output_slow cont ...

1777        if (oldkey->oif) {
1778            dev_out = dev_get_by_index(oldkey->oif);
1779            err = -ENODEV;
1780            if (dev_out == NULL)
1781                goto out;
1782            if (__in_dev_get(dev_out) == NULL) {
1783                dev_put(dev_out);
1784                goto out;      /* Wrong error code */
1785            }
1786
1787            if (LOCAL_MCAST(oldkey->dst) || oldkey->dst == 0xFFFFFFFF) {
1788                if (!key.src)
1789                    key.src = inet_select_addr(dev_out, 0,
1790                                    RT_SCOPE_LINK);
1791                goto make_route;
1792            }
1793            if (!key.src) {
1794                if (MULTICAST(oldkey->dst))
1795                    key.src = inet_select_addr(dev_out, 0,
1796                                    key.scope);
1797                else if (!oldkey->dst)
1798                    key.src = inet_select_addr(dev_out, 0,
1799                                    RT_SCOPE_HOST);
1800            }
1801        }

                                                                        cont . . .
```

cs 14.64. *ip_route_output_slow () (continued).*

If the source address is not specified in the search key at line 1793 and then if it is for the general multicast (can be same subnet or on WAN), then we retrieve the IP source address by calling the function *inet_select_address ( )* (for more information on *inet_select_addr*, see Section 14.12.6) using the key scope as an input parameter. Otherwise, if the destination address is not specified, then the scope *RT_SCOPE_HOST* is passed as an input parameter to *inet_select_address ( )* to get the source IP address for the output device.

This is a case wherein the destination address is not specified in the search key. If it is not specified, then we assign the source address from the search key as the destination address at line 1804 (cs 14.65). If the source address from the search key is also NULL, then both the destination and source address is set to the loopback address at line 1806. Then release the device line 1808 and use the loopback device at line 1809 for sending packets to this machine. The type of the address is *RTN_LOCAL*, and it finally jumps to the label *make_route* without doing the route lookup because it is not required since it is for a local machine.

The function *fib_lookup()* is invoked at line 1817 (cs 14.66) to resolve the destinations address by finding a specific route. A more detailed description about *fib_lookup* is explained in Section 14.12.8.

In the case where *fib_lookup()* fails here, it falls into the block at line 1818. If an output interface is specified by the search key at line 1819, then it is still possible

```
net/ipv4/route.c
ip_route_output_slow cont ...
    1803        if (!key.dst) {
    1804            key.dst = key.src;
    1805            if (!key.dst)
    1806                key.dst = key.src = htonl(INADDR_LOOPBACK);
    1807            if (dev_out)
    1808                dev_put(dev_out);
    1809            dev_out = &loopback_dev;
    1810            dev_hold(dev_out);
    1811            key.oif = loopback_dev.ifindex;
    1812            res.type = RTN_LOCAL;
    1813            flags |= RTCF_LOCAL;
    1814            goto make_route;
    1815        }

                                                        cont ...
```

cs 14.65. *ip_route_output_slow () (continued).*

```
net/ipv4/route.c
ip_route_output_slow cont ...
    1817        if (fib_lookup(&key, &res)) {
    1818            res.fi = NULL;
    1819            if (oldkey->oif) {

    1838                if (key.src == 0)
    1839                    key.src = inet_select_addr(dev_out, 0,
    1840                                RT_SCOPE_LINK);
    1841                res.type = RTN_UNICAST;
    1842                goto make_route;
    1843            }
    1844            if (dev_out)
    1845                dev_put(dev_out);
    1846            err = -ENETUNREACH;
    1847            goto out;
    1848        }

                                                        cont ...
```

cs 14.66. *ip_route_output_slow () (continued).*

to send the packet. First it checks for the source address from the key; and if it is not provided, then it gets the source address of the device by invoking the function *inet_select_addr ( )* at line 1839. Here the assumption is made that the destination address is on the link, hence the scope *RT_SCOPE_LINK*. The type of the address is set to *RTN_UNICAST* at line 1841. Then it jumps to the label *make_route* at line 1842. If the egress device is not provided by the key (i.e., condition at line 1844 becomes false), then release the device by calling the *dev_put ( )* function and set the *dev_out* to NULL at line 1845 and set the error to destination unreachable and then jump to label out at line 1847.

The variable res has type *fib_result* struct, and it is updated and returned by the fib_lookup ( ) function. Here we are checking the address type for *RTN_LOCAL*

```
net/ipv4/route.c
ip_route_output_slow cont ...
    1854        if (res.type == RTN_LOCAL) {
    1855            if (!key.src)
    1856                key.src = key.dst;
    1857            if (dev_out)
    1858                dev_put(dev_out);
    1859            dev_out = &loopback_dev;
    1860            dev_hold(dev_out);
    1861            key.oif = dev_out->ifindex;
    1862            if (res.fi)
    1863                fib_info_put(res.fi);
    1864            res.fi = NULL;
    1865            flags |= RTCF_LOCAL;
    1866            goto make_route;
    1867        }

                        cont . . .
```

cs 14.67. *ip_route_output_slow ()* (continued).

at line 1854 (cs 14.67). *RTN_LOCAL* flag indicates that the packet is routed locally.

If the source address is not specified in the search key, then we assign the source address from the search key as the destination address at line 1856 (source address and destination address are same). Then release the device at line 1860 and use the loopback device at line 1859 for sending packets to this machine. Release the reference to the *fib_table* by calling the *fib_info_put ( )* function. *RTCF_LOCAL* is an indication that the route is specific to the local IP address. For the routes that are destined to or originate from one of local interfaces, the routes have an *RTCF_LOCAL* bit set. Finally, jump to the label *make_route*.

The multipath route selection happens only when the multipath support (*CONFIG_IP_ROUTE_MULTIPATH*) is enabled in the kernel. If the multipath support is enabled in the kernel, then we check to see if the *fib_lookup ( )* function returns to the route with more than one next hop (routers), that is, $res.fi \rightarrow fib \rightarrow nhs$ >1. And also check for the if egress device is not provided with the search key. If both these conditions are true, then only the *fib_select_multipath ( )* functions gets called to select the route from the multiple routes. For more information on multipath routing see Section 14.3.

The default route selection happens only if the prefix length (netmask) of the route is 0; that is, the route returned by *fib_lookup ( )* and the type of the address is *RTN_UNICAST* and also the egress device in not provided by the search key. If these three conditions are true at line 1874, then only the *fib_select_default ( )* function is invoked at line 1875 (cs 14.68) to select the right default gateway. The input parameters to the *fib_select_default ( )* function are search key, and the *fib_result* struct was returned by the *fib_lookup ( )* function.

A check is made if the source IP address is still NULL at line 1877. If it is NULL, then the *FIB_RES_PRESRC* macro is used to get the IP address at line 1878. The *FIB_RES_PRESRC* macro retrieves the source IP address from the $fi \rightarrow fib\_prefsrc$ field of the *fib_info* struct field. If this fib_info field is also NULL, then the *inet_select_address ( )* function is invoked to get the source IP address from the *net_device*.

```
net/ipv4/route.c
ip_route_output_slow cont ...

1869 #ifdef CONFIG_IP_ROUTE_MULTIPATH
1870     if (res.fi->fib_nhs > 1 && key.oif == 0)
1871         fib_select_multipath(&key, &res);
1872     else
1873 #endif
1874     if (!res.prefixlen && res.type == RTN_UNICAST && !key.oif)
1875         fib_select_default(&key, &res);
1876
1877     if (!key.src)
1878         key.src = FIB_RES_PREFSRC(res);
1879
1880     if (dev_out)
1881         dev_put(dev_out);
1882     dev_out = FIB_RES_DEV(res);
1883     dev_hold(dev_out);
1884     key.oif = dev_out->ifindex;
                                    cont ...
```

cs 14.68. *ip_route_output_slow () (continued).*

```
net/ipv4/route.c
ip_route_output_slow cont ...

1886 make_route:
1887     if (LOOPBACK(key.src) && !(dev_out->flags&IFF_LOOPBACK))
1888         goto e_inval;
1889
1890     if (key.dst == 0xFFFFFFFF)
1891         res.type = RTN_BROADCAST;
1892     else if (MULTICAST(key.dst))
1893         res.type = RTN_MULTICAST;
1894     else if (BADCLASS(key.dst) || ZERONET(key.dst))
1895         goto e_inval;

1900     if (res.type == RTN_BROADCAST) {
1901         flags |= RTCF_BROADCAST | RTCF_LOCAL;
1902         if (res.fi) {
1903             fib_info_put(res.fi);
1904             res.fi = NULL;
1905         }
                                    cont ...
```

cs 14.69. *ip_route_output_slow () (continued).*

Finally, release the *net_device* if *dev_out* is holding it at line 1881 and then set the *dev_out* using macro *FIB_RES_DEV* (from *fib_info* struct of *fib_result* struct) at line 1882. Also set the value of *key.oif* using the *dev_out*'s ifindex at line 1884.

Here first we are checking if the source address is LOOPBACK, and the selected the output device has an *IFF_LOOPBACK* flag set at line 1887 (cs 14.69). If not jump to label e_inval at line 1888 and return error.

```
net/ipv4/route.c
ip_route_output_slow cont ...
   1906        } else if (res.type == RTN_MULTICAST) {
   1907             flags |= RTCF_MULTICAST|RTCF_LOCAL;
   1908             read_lock(&inetdev_lock);
   1909             if (!__in_dev_get(dev_out) ||
   1910                 !ip_check_mc(__in_dev_get(dev_out), oldkey->dst))

       . . .

   1923        rth = dst_alloc(&ipv4_dst_ops);
   1924        if (!rth)
   1925             goto e_nobufs;

                                                              cont . . .
```

cs 14.70. *ip_route_output_slow () (continued).*

Then check for the following:

1. *key.dst* == 0XFFFFFFFF at line 1890; if it is, then set the type of address to *RTN_BROADCAST*.
2. The destination address is multicast at line 1892; if it is, then set the type of address to *RTN_MULTICAST*.
3. If the destination address is BADCLASS or ZERONET at line 1894, then jump to label *e_inval* and return error.

If the *res.type* (type of address) is *RTN_BROADCAST* at line 1900, then the *fib_info* struct associated will be released at line 1903 by calling the function *fib_info_put ( )*.

If the *res.type* is *RTN_MULTICAST*, then check the multicast list of the *net_device* by acquiring *inetdev_lock*.

The *function __in_dev_get( )* returns the void **ip_ptr* element of the *net_device* structure. The *ip_ptr* element points to the instance of *in_device* struct. This *in_device* struct contains the important element *mc_list* of type *ip_mc_list struct*. To check the destination, the IP address is multicast and the function *ip_check_mc ( )* is invoked.

Allocate the memory for the rtable struct *rth* (route cache entry) at line 1923 (cs 14.70).

Then copy most of the elements of the oldkey structure from line 1928 to 1933 (cs 14.71), which is used to create route the key-for-key struct embedded in rtable struct *rth*. The *rth→key* struct will be used in subsequent route cache olookups and must match the input key.

Then copy the elements used to route the packet to *rt_fields* of the route cache element from line 1943 to 1947. These are the elements that are actually used in building and routing the packet. Setup the function that will be used to transmit the packet at line 1949.

The output function used to transmit the packets is set to *ip_output ( )* at line 1949 (cs 14.72).

Then check for the flags at line 1953 for local delivery and line 1957 for multicast that this route is terminating on the local machine or different and based on that

```
net/ipv4/route.c
ip_route_output_slow cont ...

1927        atomic_set(&rth->u.dst.__refcnt, 1);
1928        rth->u.dst.flags= DST_HOST;
1929        rth->key.dst   = oldkey->dst;
1930        rth->key.tos   = tos;
1931        rth->key.src   = oldkey->src;
1932        rth->key.iif   = 0;
1933        rth->key.oif   = oldkey->oif;
             . . .
1937        rth->rt_dst    = key.dst;
1938        rth->rt_src    = key.src;
             . . .
1943        rth->rt_iif    = oldkey->oif ? : dev_out->ifindex;
1944        rth->u.dst.dev = dev_out;
1945        dev_hold(dev_out);
1946        rth->rt_gateway = key.dst;
1947        rth->rt_spec_dst= key.src;
1948
                                cont . . .
```

cs 14.71. *ip_route_output_slow () (continued).*

```
net/ipv4/route.c
ip_route_output_slow cont ...

1949        rth->u.dst.output=ip_output;
             . . .
1953        if (flags & RTCF_LOCAL) {
1954            rth->u.dst.input = ip_local_deliver;

1956        }
1957        if (flags & (RTCF_BROADCAST | RTCF_MULTICAST)) {

1960                rth->u.dst.output = ip_mc_output;

1962        }
1963 #ifdef CONFIG_IP_MROUTE
1964        if (res.type == RTN_MULTICAST) {
1965            struct in_device *in_dev = in_dev_get(dev_out);
1966            if (in_dev) {
1967                if (IN_DEV_MFORWARD(in_dev) &&
1968                    !LOCAL_MCAST(oldkey->dst)) {
1969                    rth->u.dst.input = ip_mr_input;
1970                    rth->u.dst.output = ip_mc_output;
1971                }
1972                in_dev_put(in_dev);
1973            }
1974        }
1975 #endif
1976        }
                                cont . . .
```

cs 14.72. *ip_route_output_slow () (continued).*

```
net/ipv4/route.c
ip_route_output_slow cont ...
    1978        rt_set_nexthop(rth, &res, 0);
    1979
    1980        rth->rt_flags = flags;
    1981
    1982        hash = rt_hash_code(oldkey->dst, oldkey->src ^ (oldkey->oif << 5), tos);
    1983        err = rt_intern_hash(hash, rth, rp);
    1984 done:
    1985        if (free_res)
    1986            fib_res_put(&res);
    1987        if (dev_out)
    1988            dev_put(dev_out);
    1989 out:   return err;
    1991 e_inval:
    1992        err = -EINVAL;
    1993        goto done;
    1994 e_nobufs:
    1995        err = -ENOBUFS;
    1996        goto done;
    1997 }
```

cs 14.73. *ip_route_output_slow* () (continued).

set the *ip_function* for delivery of packets. In case of local delivery of packets the output function is set to *ip_local_deliver* ( ) and for the multicasting the output function is set to *ip_mc_output* ( ) function.

The *CONFIG_IP_MROUTE* option at line 1963 is enabled in kernel if the machine acts as a router for multicast destination addresses.

The *rt_set_nexthop()* at line 1978 sets the next-neighbor parameters including pmtu.

And finally find the hash code value by calling the function *rt_hash_code()* at line 1982. This hash code value is used by the function *rt_intern_hash()* at line 1983 to search in the respective hash queue of *rt_hash_table*. The rp parameter passed to *ip_route_output_slow* as the location at which a pointer to a new route cache entry should be returned.

14.12.4 *ip_dev_find* ( )

The *ip_dev_find* ( ) function returns the network device configured within this machine for the source IP address provided as input parameter to this function. It starts with initializing the *rt_key* struct at line 151 (cs 14.74). The only field used here for the *rt_key* struct is the *dst* element. The input source IP address is copied to the *dst* field of the *rt_key* struct before doing the lookup in the local table at line 152. If the policy routing (*CONFIG_IP_MULTIPLE_TABLES*) is defined in the kernel, then initially we set the *fib_rule* struct to NULL at line 154.

Then we proceed with the local table lookup to find the source address with the network device. The local table here consists of local and broadcast address information within this machine. The lookup routine called through the function pointer *tb_lookup* at line 157 is *fn_hash_lookup* ( ) (for more information on lookup, see Section 14.12.8.1) function. After successful local table lookup, the most important check is made at line 160 for the routing type of the source address found. If

```
net/ipv4/fib_frontend.c
  145 struct net_device * ip_dev_find(u32 addr)
  146 {
  147      struct rt_key key;
  148      struct fib_result res;
  149      struct net_device *dev = NULL;
  150
  151      memset(&key, 0, sizeof(key));
  152      key.dst = addr;
  153 #ifdef CONFIG_IP_MULTIPLE_TABLES
  154      res.r = NULL;
  155 #endif
  156
  157      if (!local_table || local_table->tb_lookup(local_table, &key, &r      es)) {
  158          return NULL;
  159      }
  160      if (res.type != RTN_LOCAL)
  161          goto out;
  162      dev = FIB_RES_DEV(res);
  163      if (dev)
  164          atomic_inc(&dev->refcnt);
  165
  166 out:
  167      fib_res_put(&res);
  168      return dev;
  169 }
```

cs 14.74. ip_dev_find ().

it is not *RTN_LOCAL* type, otherwise this is a invalid entry in the table. The *RTN_LOCAL* signifies that the address found is configured on the local interface of the system.

If the routing type of the source address from local table lookup is *RTN_LOCAL*, then get the reference to the *net_device* by calling the macro *FIB_RES_DEV* at line 162. Finally, increment the use count in the *net_device* struct at line 164 and return the *net_device* pointer at line 168 before releasing the reference in the *fib_table* by calling the function *fib_res_put ( )* function.

14.12.5 __in_dev_get ( )

The function *__in_dev_get( )* returns the void **ip_ptr* element of the *net_device* structure (cs 14.75).

```
include/linux/inetdevice.h
  134 static __inline__ struct in_device *
  135 __in_dev_get(const struct net_device *dev)
  136 {
  137      return (struct in_device*)dev->ip_ptr;
  138 }
```

cs 14.75. in_device.

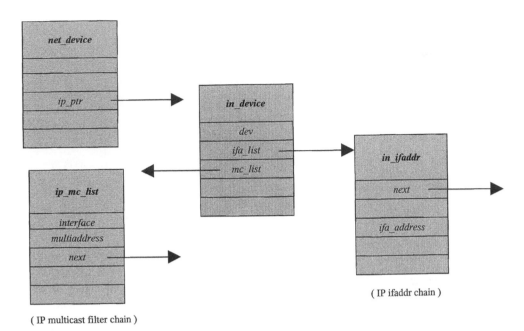

Figure 14.17. *ifa_list and mc_list.*

The *ip_ptr* element points to the instance of *in_device* struct. This *in_device* struct contains the important element *ifa_list* of type *in_ifaddr* struct which is an IP ifaddr chain (list of struct *ifa_list*) (Fig. 14.17). This is important that each physical *net_device* on the system may be assigned alias IP addresses and labels (e.g., eth0:0, eth0:1, and so on).

14.12.6 *inet_select_addr ( )*

This function (cs 14.76) selects the IP address (i.e., source IP) configured on the network device. If there are multiple IP addresses configured on the device, it selects the appropriate IP address based on the inputs provided. Why source address selection?

For any IP packet created on the host system, it has to select the some source address before sending that packet to the destination address. This source information is important for the destination system to know from where the packet has arrived, so that it can deliver a reply to the source. If source information is not provided to the destination system, then half of the communication will never arrive and the reply is lost.

Linux selects the source address using the following rules:

- The application may be already using the socket, so the source address is already selected or may request the source address using *bind ( )* call.
- It performs route lookup to find the destination route. If the destination route is found, then it checks the src parameter from the route; if it is not found, then the kernel selects this source address for communication.
- If application or route lookup doesn't provide the source address, then the kernel searches the list of IP addresses configured for the network interface.

```
net/ipv4/devinet.c
718 u32 inet_select_addr(const struct net_device *dev, u32 dst, int scope)
719 {
        . . .
724     in_dev = __in_dev_get(dev);
        . . .
731     for_primary_ifa(in_dev) {
732         if (ifa->ifa_scope > scope)
733             continue;
734         if (!dst || inet_ifa_match(dst, ifa)) {
735             addr = ifa->ifa_local;
736             break;
737         }
738         if (!addr)
739             addr = ifa->ifa_local;
740     } endfor_ifa(in_dev);
        . . .
744     if (addr)
745         return addr;

753     for (dev=dev_base; dev; dev=dev->next) {
754         if ((in_dev=__in_dev_get(dev)) == NULL)
755             continue;
        . . .
758         for_primary_ifa(in_dev) {
759             if (ifa->ifa_scope != RT_SCOPE_LINK &&
760                 ifa->ifa_scope <= scope) {
761                 read_unlock(&in_dev->lock);
762                 read_unlock(&inetdev_lock);
763                 read_unlock(&dev_base_lock);
764                 return ifa->ifa_local;
765             }
766         } endfor_ifa(in_dev);
```

cs 14.76. *inet_select_addr ().*

Here the *inet_select_addr ( )* function comes into the picture, it performs the lookup into the list of address configured on the interface and selects the appropriate IP address.

The Network Interface Card (NIC) can be configured for a single IP address or multiple IP addresses. If multiple addresses are set for a NIC, then some of the addresses are called primary while others are called secondary. Each IP address configured on the NIC must have a netmask; either this is provided by the user while configuring the IP address or the system would assign the default netmask based on the IP address class.

A single subnet or multiple subnets can be configured on the NIC, and each subnet would have multiple addresses. The distinction between the primary and secondary addresses can be automatically done by the system. The first address configured on the subnet is the primary address, and thereafter any IP address configured is called a secondary address. For example, if there are three subnets configured for the NIC, there are three primary addresses, and each subnet would have one primary address and the rest of the addresses of the specific subnets are called a secondary address. The interface can have many primary and secondary addresses.

A system can be configured with a single interface or multiple interfaces, and any of the interfaces in turn can be configured with a single IP address or multiple

IP addresses with different subnets. The selection of the IP address is straightforward in the case of a single IP configured on the interface.

The input parameters to the *inet_select_addr ( )* function are the *net_device* pointer, IP address (not local to the system), and the scope. If the input IP address is zero, then any primary address configured on the ingress device would be selected. The selection of the source IP address from multiple IP addresses configured on the ingress device is based on the input scope provided and the location of the destination address. Selection based on the scope is important here since the destination has to in turn reply to the source with the same scope.

The scope can be *RT_SCOPE_LINK/HOS/SITE/UNIVERSE*.

The *in_device* instance has the list of IP addresses configured on the *net_device*. We get the pointer to the *in_device* instance at line 724 (cs 14.76). Then using the kernel provided macro *for_primary_ifa*, we browse through the list of IP addresses configured for the *net_device*. The *for_primary_ifa* macro is used to search the *ifa_ list in_device* instance of the network device.

Here the scope plays an important role in selecting the source IP address. This function selects an ingress address with a scope the same as or smaller than the scope of the destination address. If the scope of the ingress address is greater than the scope of the destination address, we skip that address and continue the search at line 732. Another option is to search all interfaces for an address with an appropriate scope at line 758.

14.12.7   *ROUTE_SCOPES*

The scope of a route is used to find out much precisely the route for a given destination. fields *fn→fn_scope* and *key→scope* are compared in *fn_hash_lookup()* to check if an entry found satisfies the scope criteria. For higher values of scope, we need to find a more specific route for the destination. For lower values of scope, the routes belong to a destination network.

The scopes are listed in cs 14.77.

RT_SCOPE_HOST indicates that the destination address is for the local
host.

RT_SCOPE_LINK indicates that the destination address is for the local
network.

```
include/linux/rtnetlink.h
    155 enum rt_scope_t
    156 {
    157      RT_SCOPE_UNIVERSE=0,
    158 /* User defined values  */
    159      RT_SCOPE_SITE=200,
    160      RT_SCOPE_LINK=253,
    161      RT_SCOPE_HOST=254,
    162      RT_SCOPE_NOWHERE=255
    163 };
```

cs 14.77. *rt_scope_t.*

RT_SCOPE_NOWHERE indicates that there is no route to the destination address.

RT_SCOPE_SITE indicates an interior route within the site.

RT_SCOPE_UNIVERSE indicates that the destination address is not directly connected and it is more than one hop away.

Important Routing Control Flags

RTCF_LOCAL is an indication that the route is specific to the local IP address. For the routes that are destined to originate from one of local interfaces, routes have *RTCF_LOCAL* bit set.

RTCF_MULTICAST is an indication that the route is to the multicast address.

RTCF_BROADCAST is an indication that the route is to the broadcast address.

RTCF_ONLINK is an indication for a locally rechable destination.

Important Routing Types

RTN_UNICAST: Route is a gateway or direct route.

RTN_LOCAL: Route is a local address.

RTN_BROADCAST: Accepts packets locally as broadcast, send packet as broadcast.

RTN_MULTICAST: Indicates that this is a multicast route.

14.12.8   fib_lookup()

There are two versions of *fib_lookup ( )*:

1. If policy routing is not enabled, then the following version of *fib_lookup ( )* gets invoked. The *fib_lookup()* function gets *struct rt_key* and *fib_result* as input parameters. It calls the function pointer *tb_lookup* for both local and main table at lines 157 and 158 to find the destination match entry either in the local table or in the main table. This *tb_lookup* function pointer is resolved to *fn_hash_lookup()* function. This *fn_hash_lookup_function()* returns 0 on success and nonzero on failure. The lookup returns network unreachable error at line 159 only when didn't

```
nclude/net/ip_fib.h
155 static inline int fib_lookup(const struct rt_key *key, struct fib_result *res)
156 {
157     if (local_table->tb_lookup(local_table, key, res) &&
158        main_table->tb_lookup(main_table, key, res))
159           return -ENETUNREACH;
160     return 0;
161 }
```

CS 14.78. *fib_lookup ().*

```
net/ipv4/fib_rules.c
310 int fib_lookup(const struct rt_key *key, struct fib_result *res)
311 {
312      int err;
313      struct fib_rule *r, *policy;
314      struct fib_table *tb;
315
316      u32 daddr = key->dst;
317      u32 saddr = key->src;
318
      . . . .
321      read_lock(&fib_rules_lock);
322      for (r = fib_rules; r; r=r->r_next) {
323           if (((saddr^r->r_src) & r->r_srcmask) ||
324               ((daddr^r->r_dst) & r->r_dstmask) ||
325 #ifdef CONFIG_IP_ROUTE_TOS
326               (r->r_tos && r->r_tos != key->tos) ||
327 #endif
328 #ifdef CONFIG_IP_ROUTE_FWMARK
329               (r->r_fwmark && r->r_fwmark != key->fwmark) ||
330 #endif
331               (r->r_ifindex && r->r_ifindex != key->iif))
332                continue;
                                              cont . . .
```

cs 14.79. fib_lookup ().

get any match from either of the tables. The local table has precedence over the main table.

The lookup here consists of only two tables, namely, local and main tables. If policy routing is defined in the kernel, several routing tables can be configured.

2. If policy routing (*CONFIG_IP_MULTIPLE_TABLES*) is defined in the kernel, then the version of *fib_lookup* shown in cs 14.79 gets invoked.

In the case of policy routing (for detailed information see Section 14.2), several routing tables are configured and we can define a rule to select a particular routing table based on the packet routing requirement.

What Is This Rule?

In the case of nornal routing for a single routing table, the routing decisions are based on the destination address. With policy routing configured, including destination address, we can also use the source address, tos field, and iptables marking (fwmark) as parameters to define a rule for packet. This rule based on these parameters is used to select the routing table. Each rule has a unique priority, and this priority rules list is searched for the given rule. The rules list is sorted in increasing order based on the priority.

There are three default rules in the system without any configuration added by the user:

1. *local_rule*
2. *main_rule*
3. *default_rule*

```
net/ipv4/fib_rules.c
fib_lookup () cont . . .
335              switch (r->r_action) {
336              case RTN_UNICAST:
337              case RTN_NAT:
338                  policy = r;
339                  break;
340              case RTN_UNREACHABLE:
341                  read_unlock(&fib_rules_lock);
342                  return -ENETUNREACH;
343              default:
344              case RTN_BLACKHOLE:
345                  read_unlock(&fib_rules_lock);
346                  return -EINVAL;
347              case RTN_PROHIBIT:
348                  read_unlock(&fib_rules_lock);
349                  return -EACCES;
350              }
cont . . .
```

cs 14.80. *fib_lookup () (continued).*

local_rule: The priority of this rule is 0 and it is the highest priority. Whenever the rules list is searched to match the given rule, this rule always matches for any rule and it does lookup in the local routing table. So if there are any packets for a local system, it doesn't require any further routing decisions. The local table is maintained by the kernel for local and broadcast addresses.

main_rule: The priority of this rule is 32766, and this is the main routing table in the system and it always matches and searches the route.

default_rule: The priority of this rule is 32767, and this rule is at the end of the rules list.

Any user added rule is inserted between the local and main rule.

The global variable *fib_rules* points to the rules list in the system. Before searching this rules list, we need acquire a '*fib_rules_lock*' at line 321, which is an rwlock and protects the *fib_rules* list of *fib_rule* data structures. Then the for loop is used to search the given rule of the packet from the rules list; and if there is a match for the given rule of the packet, we can continue to find the routing table based on the policy action defined in the matched rule; otherwise, if there is no match, continue the search in the rules list (cs 14.80).

Once a matching rule for the packet is found from the *fib_rules* list, the matching rule (*fib_rule* struct) has the policy action field; based on this action, we decide the policy type.

There are five policy types:

1. *RTN_UNICAST:* Based on the rule, a specific routing table lookup is done to find the route for the packet.
2. *RTN_BLACKHOLE:* The packet is discarded and no feedback is given.
3. *RTN_UNREACHABLE:* The packet is discarded and the destination network is unreachable.

```
net/ipv4/fib_rules.c
fib_lookup () cont...
    352              if ((tb = fib_get_table(r->r_table)) == NULL)
    353                  continue;
    354          err = tb->tb_lookup(tb, key, res);
    355          if (err == 0) {
    356              res->r = policy;
    357              if (policy)
    358                  atomic_inc(&policy->r_clntref);
    359              read_unlock(&fib_rules_lock);
    360              return 0;
    361          }
    362          if (err < 0 && err != -EAGAIN) {
    363              read_unlock(&fib_rules_lock);
    364              return err;
    365          }
    366      }
    367 FRprintk("FAILURE\n");
    368      read_unlock(&fib_rules_lock);
    369      return -ENETUNREACH;
    370 }


                              cont...
```

cs 14.81. *fib_lookup ()* (continued).

4. *RTN_PROHIBIT:* The packet is discarded and the communication is not allowed.

5. *RTN_NAT:* This is used for status network address translation (NAT).

If the policy type is *RTN_UNICAST*, then find the routing table based on the table id (*r→r_table*) from the matched rule (*fib_rule*) by calling the function *fib_table_get ( )* at line 352 (cs 14.81); lookup is done for that table to find the route. Other policy types lead to error.

The lookup function here is the *fn_hash_lookup ( )*. This function is a registered handler to the *tb_lookup* function pointer, and this is done in the function *fib_hash_init ( )*. If the lookup is successful, then we initialize the *res→r* (*fib_rule* of *fib-result struct*) to the policy (matched rule from the fib rules list) and then increment the count to keep track of the number of refrences to the *fib_rule* struct (matched rule) at line 358. Finally release the *fib_rules_lock* at line 359 and return 0 to the caller function.

14.12.8.1 fn_hash_lookup ( ). The *fn_hash_lookup( )* function is used for routing table lookup, to match and find a destination route for the packet. The main function does the lookup in a single routing table at a time by acquiring the proper locks to read the table information.

Input parameters to this function are as follows:

tb: routing table to search for finding the destination route for the packet.

key: search key used for lookup in the table.

res: route lookup is successful and then *res* is intialized to route information.

```
net/ipv4/fib_hash.c
268 static int
269 fn_hash_lookup(struct fib_table *tb, const struct rt_key *key, struct fib_result *res)
270 {
271     int err;
272     struct fn_zone *fz;
273     struct fn_hash *t = (struct fn_hash*)tb->tb_data;
274
275     read_lock(&fib_hash_lock);
276     for (fz = t->fn_zone_list; fz; fz = fz->fz_next) {
277         struct fib_node *f;
278         fn_key_t k = fz_key(key->dst, fz);
279
280         for (f = fz_chain(k, fz); f; f = f->fn_next) {
281             if (!fn_key_eq(k, f->fn_key)) {
282                 if (fn_key_leq(k, f->fn_key))
283                     break;
284                 else
285                     continue;
286             }
        cont . . .
```

cs 14.82. fib_hash_lookup ().

tb→tb_data pointer at line 273 (cs 14.82) is a pointer to the associated FIB hash table (*fn_hash*) of the routing table (*fib_table*). Before doing any lookup operation in the routing table, we need to acquire a '*fn_hash_lock*' lock in shared mode at line 275. '*fn_hash_lock*' is a read–write spin lock (*rwlock*).

The lookup algorithm is based on the LPM (Longest Prefix Match) algorithm. This algorithm is used to find the most specific route for the destination. Each routing table (*fib_table*) contains a associated pointer to FIB hash table (*fn_hash*), and this FIB hash table contains a array of fib zones (*fz_zone*) and a pointer to the fib zones list (*fn_zone_list*). Based on the netmask (prefix) length which is 32 bits, for each bit of the netmask there is a zone associated with it; this is the reason why *fz_zones[33]* is defined in *fn_hash* struct. Each element of this zones array represents a single zone. The *fn_zone_list* pointer points to the longest netmask zone. Hence the LPM algorithm starts the search with the longest netmask zone to find the more specific route for the packet (closer to the final destination).

Why LPM Algorithm for Routing Table Lookup?

IP performs the steps in the following order to find the destination route in its routing table:

- Searches for a matching host address (IP address)
- Searches for a matching network address
- Searches for a default entry (the default entry is a network address with 0)

A matching host address (host's IP address) is always used before matching a network address. If both host address and network address are not matched, then we use the default entry (default route), which is a network address with ID 0 for which a default gateway address is defined in the routing table.

```
net/ipv4/fib_hash.c
123 static __inline__ fn_key_t fz_key(u32 dst, struct fn_zone *fz)
124 {
125     fn_key_t k;
126     k.datum = dst & FZ_MASK(fz);
127     return k;
128 }
```

cs 14.83. fz_key().

```
net/ipv4/fib_hash.c
135 static __inline__ struct fib_node * fz_chain(fn_key_t key, struct fn_zone *fz)
136 {
137     return fz->fz_hash[fn_hash(key, fz).datum];
138 }
```

cs 14.84. fz_chain ().

fn_zone[0] represents the default entry (default route).

fn_zone[32] represents the more specific route.

This is achieved by using the for loop at line 276, which loops over the zones list starting with the longest netmask to find the more specific route. Before starting the search into the zone, using the search key's destination, a test key is built by AND'ing the destination address with the zone's netmask. This is done by calling the function *fz_key( )* at line 278. This test key is used for the lookup into the *fib_node* chain (cs 14.83).

Each zone has a pointer to the hash table (*fz_hash*). This hash table's each bucket points to the *fib_node* list. To calculate which bucket of the hash table to be searched *fz_chain( )* function is called at line 280. This is again a one more for loop to traverse through the *fib_mode* list based on the bucket returned by the *fz_chain ( )* function (cs 14.84).

The *fz_chain( )* function calculates the the hashing value to get the hash table bucket for accessing the *fib_node* list by calling the function *fn_hash( )*.

The *fn_hash( )* function calculates the hash value by AND'ing the ket.datum (after performaing the shift operations) value with the *fz_hashmask* (0xf) to get a hash table bucket. The hash table consists of the 16 buckets, and that's the reason why the *fz_hashmask* value is always 0xf(15) (cs 14.85).

On returning to the *fn_hash_lookup( )*, the first step in the inner loop after getting the *fib_node* list to traverse is to compare the test key built by the *fz_key ( )* function with the key (f→fn_key, which is an address) from the *fib_node* list. This is done by calling the function *fn_key_eq( )* at line 281 (see cs 14.86).

If the *fn_key_eq( )* function returns true—that is, the key value are matching—then we continue to check whether the matched *fib_node* is a valid one; if the *fn_*

```
net/ipv4/fib_hash.c
110 static __inline__ fn_hash_idx_t fn_hash(fn_key_t key, struct fn_zone *fz)
111 {
112     u32 h = ntohl(key.datum)>>(32 - fz->fz_order);
113     h ^= (h>>20);
114     h ^= (h>>10);
115     h ^= (h>>5);
116     h &= FZ_HASHMASK(fz);
117     return *(fn_hash_idx_t*)&h;
118 }
```

cs 14.85. fn_hash().

```
net/ipv4/fib_hash.c
140 extern __inline__ int fn_key_eq(fn_key_t a, fn_key_t b)
141 {
142     return a.datum == b.datum;
143 }
```

cs 14.86. fn_key_eq ().

key_eq( ) function returns false—that is, the keys are matching—then the function fn_leq_key( ) is called at line 282 to check whether the test key value is greater than that of the key value from the fib_node; if it is, we continue to search the next fib_node—otherwise we come out of the inner for loop. This is because the fib_nodes on the list are sorted in decreasing order by prefix.

If the control reaches at line 287 and if the CONFIG_IP_TOS is defined in the kernel and if the tos value of the fib_node is not equal to the tos value of the key, the match is discarded and the search continues. fib_node state information is checked for ACCESSED or ZOMBIE.

ZOMBIE nodes are currently not in use and related to deleted routes or dead interfaces. If the state is ZOMBIE at line 293, then we discard the search and continue. The fib_node scope should be at least equal to or greater than the key node scope; if it is less than the key scope, then the match is discarded at line 296 and the search continues.

The fib_semantic_match( ) is called at line 298 is to check the usability of the matched fib_node. It represents an acceptable route, the next hop is alive or not, and the output interface mentioned in the search key is the same as the one associated with the next hop. If any of these are not correct fib_semantic_match( ), then return error. If there are no errors, then we initialize the fib_result struct (res) with the fn_type, fn_scope, and fz→fz_order and then jump to the label out at line 303 and release the fib_hash_lock before returning the err at line 312 (cs 14.87, Fig. 14.18).

```
net/ipv4/fib_hash.c
fn_hash_lookup () cont . . .

287 #ifdef CONFIG_IP_ROUTE_TOS
288             if (f->fn_tos && f->fn_tos != key->tos)
289                 continue;
290 #endif
291             f->fn_state |= FN_S_ACCESSED;
292
293             if (f->fn_state&FN_S_ZOMBIE)
294                 continue;
295             if (f->fn_scope < key->scope)
296                 continue;
297
298             err = fib_semantic_match(f->fn_type, FIB_INFO(f), key, res);
299             if (err == 0) {
300                 res->type = f->fn_type;
301                 res->scope = f->fn_scope;
302                 res->prefixlen = fz->fz_order;
303                 goto out;
304             }
305             if (err < 0)
306                 goto out;
307         }
308     }
309     err = 1;
310 out:
311     read_unlock(&fib_hash_lock);
312     return err;
313 }
```

cs 14.87. fib_hash_lookup () (continued).

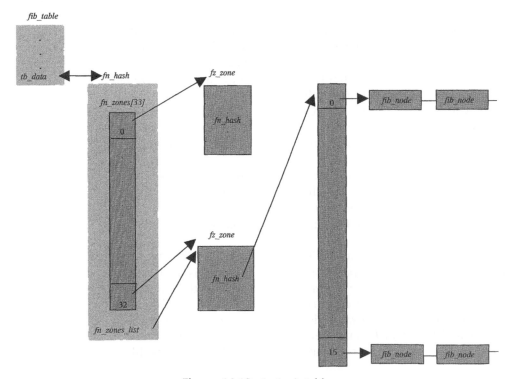

Figure 14.18. fn_hash table.

14.13 SUMMARY

IP routing decides the best possible route for a packet transfer between computers.

The IP layer handles the routing between computers.

The two main functionality of the IP routing are:

1. Forwarding of the IP packets in routers.
2. Identifying the best possible routes for transport of each packet between networks.

Linux uses the following tables for routing:

1. Forwarding Information Base (FIB): contains and keep tracks of every known route.
2. Routing cache: faster cache for destinations that are currently in use.
3. Neighbor table: keeps track of computers that are physically connected to a host.

Different types of routing supported in Linux are: policy-based routing, multipath routing, source routing, and record routing.

15

IP QUALITY OF SERVICE IN LINUX (IP QoS)

In this chapter we are going to discuss the *pfifo_fast* and cbq queueing disciplines; *pfifo_fast* is the default qdisc for the linux and is classless queueing discipline, whereas the cbq qdisc is not the default qdisc for linux, needs to configured by user, and is a class-based queueing discipline. We explain in detail the data structures for Qdisc (Queueing Discipline) and then the implementation details of *pfifo_fast* qdisc and the CBQ qdisc. Also we will see in detail how to configure CBQ—that is, overriding default qdisc, configuring CBQ classes for handling traffic, and creating filters for the classes. In addition to this, we will also see types of filters configurable for classes and discuss implementation details of u32 and route filters. Finally, we will look at the details of how *cbq_enqueue* and *cbq_dequeue* are implemented.

15.1 INTRODUCTION

The basic functionality of quality of service (Queueing Discipline) in Linux is to decide how the input network packets will be accepted in order and what bandwidth rate and make a decision on when and how the output network packet is arranged in queues and transmitted at allocated bandwidth rate. It basically administers the bandwidth based on the application requirements.

In Linux, a "qdisc" represents a queueing discipline. The default qdisc attached to the network interface for linux is *"pfifo_fast_qdisc"*; this qdisc can be replaced based on the requirement for other types of queueing discipline.

TCP/IP Architecture, Design, and Implementation in Linux. By S. Seth and M. A. Venkatesulu
Copyright © 2008 the IEEE Computer Society

Following are the types of the queueing discipline supported in Linux:

1. First In, First Out (FIFO)
2. Priority FIFO (PFIFO)
3. Token Bucket Flow (TBF)
4. Asynchronous Transfer Mode (ATM)
5. Random Early Detection (RED)
6. Stochastic Fair Queueing (SFQ)
7. Class-Based Queueing Discipline (CBQ)
8. Generalized RED (GED)
9. Diff-Serv Marker (DS_MARK)
10. Clark–Shenker–Zhang (CSZ)

15.2 BASIC COMPONENTS OF LINUX TRAFFIC CONTROL

- Queueing Discipline
- Classes
- Filters/Classifiers
- Policing

Queueing Discipline. Each network device on Linux has a queueing discipline, which controls how the network packets are enqueued and dequeued before transmission (Figs. 15.1– 15.3).

Classes. Classes are supported by only class-based queueing discipline. We can divide the network traffic based on filters (IP address, TCP/IP port, etc.) for classification into different classes before transmission, and each class will be scheduled for dequeuing a packet based on the priority.

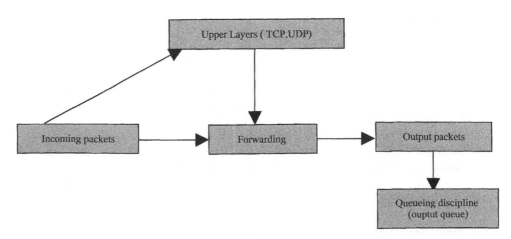

Figure 15.1. Block diagram of Linux traffic control.

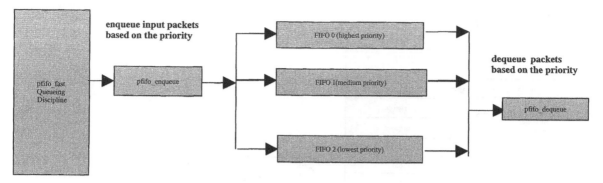

Figure 15.2. pfifo_fast queueing discipline in Linux (default queueing discilpline in Linux).

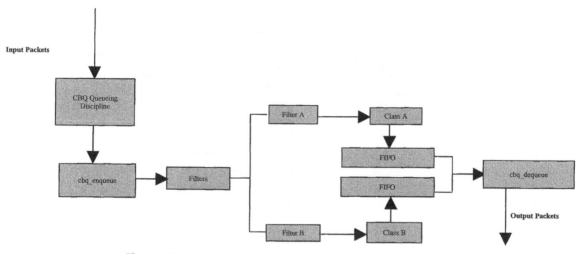

Figure 15.3. Cbq queueing discipline in Linux.

Filters. Filter organize the packets into different classes based on the certain parameters (IP addr, TCP/IP port, etc.).

Policing. After the enqueueing of the network packets, the packets can be policed for letting the packets go, dropping of the packets and the packets can go but mark them.

15.3 LINUX IMPLEMENTATION OF *pfifo_fast qdisc*

pfifo_fast qdisc is the default qdisc for all the network interfaces on the Linux system. *pfifo_fast* queueing discipline can be replaced by any other queueing discipline for the Linux system (Fig. 15.4).

pfifo_fast contains three different FIFO queues (different bands) for enqueueing of the packets based on the priority. The highest-priority packet goes into FIFO 0, and this highest packet is dequeued first before handling any packets in FIFO 1 and FIFO 2. Similarly, packets in FIFO 1 are considered first before any packets handling in FIFO 2.

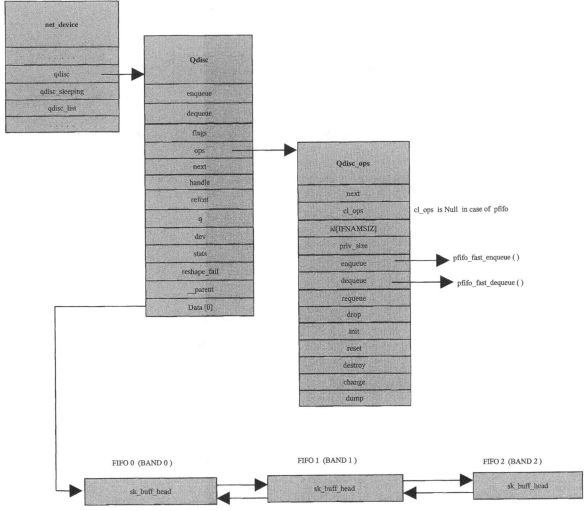

Figure 15.4. *pfifo_fast* qdisc implementation overview.

pfifo_fast is not user-configurable because it it hardwired by default. The packet priorities are assigned by the kernel and mapped to the appropriate band (FIFO) based on the TOS octet of the packet (priomap) (Fig. 15.5).

For packets enqueueing and dequeueing, the *pfifo_fast* qdisc uses the *pfifo_fast_enqueue()* and *pfifo_fast_dequeue()* functions.

The four TOS bits are defined as follows:

Binary	Decimal	Meanings
1000	8	Minimize delay
0100	4	Maximize throughput
0010	2	Maximize realiability
0001	1	Minimize monetary cost
0000	0	Normal service

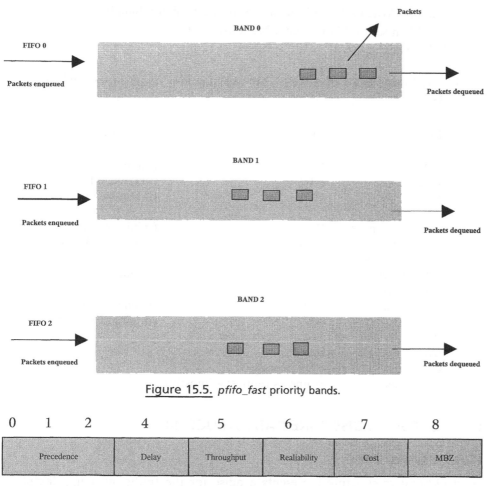

Figure 15.5. *pfifo_fast* priority bands.

0	1	2	4	5	6	7	8
Precedence			Delay	Throughput	Realiability	Cost	MBZ

Figure 15.6. TOS field.

Figure 15.6 illustrates the TOS field in detail:
The precedence bits and their possible values are as follows:

000 (0): Routine
001 (1): Priority
010 (2): Immediate
011 (3): Flash
100 (4): Flash override
101 (5): Critical
110 (6): Internetwork control
111 (7): Network control

Now the TOS bits:

Delay: When set to '1,' the packet requests low delay.
Throughout: When set to '1,' the packet requests high throughput.

Reliability: When set to '1,' the packet requests high reliability.

Cost: When set to '1,' the packet has a low cost.

MBZ: Checking bit.

This following table from RFC 1349 explains how applications might use the TOS bits:

TELNET	1000	(minimize delay)
FTP		
Control	1000	(minimize delay)
Data	0100	(maximize throughput)
TFTP	1000	(minimize delay)
SMTP		
Command phase	1000	(minimize delay)
DATA phase	0100	(maximize throughput)
Domain Name Service		
UDP Query	1000	(minimize delay)
TCP Query	0000	
Zone Transfer	0100	(maximize throughput)
NNTP	0001	(minimize monetary cost)
ICMP		
Errors	0000	
Requests	0000 (mostly)	
Responses	<same as request> (mostly)	

15.4 QUEUEING DISCIPLINE DATA STRUCTURE

15.4.1 *struct Qdisc*

struct Qdisc data structure represents a qdisc for the traffic queueing discipline and is attached to the net device (cs 15.1). This qdisc is responsible for the traffic control (packets queueing) before sending to the network interface of the Linux system.

enqueue: Function pointer pointing to the enqueuing function of the queuing discipline. The default function is *pfifo_fast_enqueue()* if no other queueing discipline is configured. The main purpose of the enqueue function is to enqueue an *sk_buff* in the proper queue of the scheduler.

dequeue: Function pointer pointing to the dequeuing function of the queueing discipline. The default function is *pfifo_fast_dequeue()*. The main purpose is to dequeue the packet from the highest-priority non–empty queue.

ops: Each queueing discipline has a set of functions to control its operation, and the *Qdisc_ops* data structure contains all these control functions.

next: The Linux net device structure maintains the *qdisc_list* to link all the queueing disciplines which are used for the device's queueing. Here the next pointer is pointing to the next queuing discipline supported by the device.

handle: There are more than one instance of queueing disciplines in the kernel, and each instance of queuing discipline is identified by the 32-bit number.

```
include/net/pkt_sched.h
 74 struct Qdisc
 75 {
 76     int              (*enqueue)(struct sk_buff *skb, struct Qdisc *dev);
 77     struct sk_buff *   (*dequeue)(struct Qdisc *dev);
 78     unsigned          flags;
        . . .
 82     struct Qdisc_ops    *ops;
 83     struct Qdisc       *next;
 84     u32              handle;
 85     atomic_t          refcnt;
 86     struct sk_buff_head   q;
 87     struct net_device    *dev;
 88
 89     struct tc_stats      stats;
 90     int              (*reshape_fail)(struct sk_buff *skb, struct Qdisc *q);
 91
        . . .
 95     struct Qdisc      * __parent;
 96
 97     char             data[0];
 98 };
```

cs 15.1. *Qdisc* data structure.

handle represents this 32-bit number (consists of major and minor number, minor number is always zero) .

q: Represents the head of the queue.

dev: Points to the net device.

stats: Represents the statistics—that is, number of enqueued bytes and packets, packets dropped, and so on.

data: This is a place holder. In the case of default *pfifo_fast*, this points to an array of *sk_buff_head* structures; for CBQ, this points to the *cbq_sched_data* data structure which contains classes for different queues.

15.4.2 struct Qdisc_ops

struct Qdisc_ops data structure provides the set of control functions for various operations to be performed on the queueing discipline.

next: points to next *Qdisc_ops* to link all the queuing discipline operation that has registered in the kernel.

cl_ops: This is a class operation data structure *Qdisc_class_ops* which provides a set of functions for a particular class.

id: Char array contains the identity of the queueing discipline (e.g., pfifo, cbq, etc.).

The function pointers to the queueing discipline are as follows:

enqueue(): Function pointer pointing to the enqueueing function of the queueing discipline.

```
include/net/pkt_sched.h
  52 struct Qdisc_ops
  53 {
  54      struct Qdisc_ops        *next;
  55      struct Qdisc_class_ops *cl_ops;
  56      char            id[IFNAMSIZ];
  57      int             priv_size;
  58
  59      int             (*enqueue)(struct sk_buff *, struct Qdisc *);
  60      struct sk_buff *     (*dequeue)(struct Qdisc *);
  61      int             (*requeue)(struct sk_buff *, struct Qdisc *);
  62      int             (*drop)(struct Qdisc *);
  63
  64      int             (*init)(struct Qdisc *, struct rtattr *arg);
  65      void            (*reset)(struct Qdisc *);
  66      void            (*destroy)(struct Qdisc *);
  67      int             (*change)(struct Qdisc *, struct rtattr *arg);
  68
  69      int             (*dump)(struct Qdisc *, struct sk_buff *);
  70 };
```

<u>cs 15.2.</u> *Qdisc_ops* data structure.

dequeue(): Function pointer pointing to the dequeuing function of the queue-ing discipline.

requeue(): If the packet was dequeued to send but it fails for unknown reason, then the requeue function puts back the packet back to the queue at the same place whereit had been before.

drop(): Removes the packet from the queue and drops it.

reset(): Resets the queueing discipline back to the initial state.

init(): Initialize new queueing discipline.

destroy(): Destroys the resources used during initialization of the queuing discipline.

change(): Changes values of the parameters of a queueing discipline.

dump(): Shows the statistics of the queueing discipline.

15.4.3   struct Qdisc_class_ops

This is a class operation data structure that provides a set of control functions for a particular class (cs 15.3).

graft: Functionality is to attach a new queueing discipline to a class and return the previously attached queueing discipline.

leaf: Returns a pointer to the queueing discipline of class.

get: Returns the internal ID of the class.

put: Invoked when a class returned by the get is dereferenced.

change: Changes the properties of the class, also used for creating new classes.

delete: Deletes a class.

```
include/net/pkt_sched.h
  30 struct Qdisc_class_ops
  31 {
    . . .
  33      int              (*graft)(struct Qdisc *, unsigned long cl, struct Qdisc *, struct Qdisc **);
  34      struct Qdisc *     (*leaf)(struct Qdisc *, unsigned long cl);
  35
    . . .
  37      unsigned long       (*get)(struct Qdisc *, u32 classid);
  38      void              (*put)(struct Qdisc *, unsigned long);
  39      int              (*change)(struct Qdisc *, u32, u32, struct rtattr **, unsigned long *);
  40      int              (*delete)(struct Qdisc *, unsigned long);
  41      void              (*walk)(struct Qdisc *, struct qdisc_walker * arg);
  42
    . . .
  44      struct tcf_proto **   (*tcf_chain)(struct Qdisc *, unsigned long);
  45      unsigned long        (*bind_tcf)(struct Qdisc *, unsigned long, u32 classid);
  46      void              (*unbind_tcf)(struct Qdisc *, unsigned long);
    . . .
  49      int              (*dump)(struct Qdisc *, unsigned long, struct sk_buff *skb, struct tcmsg*);
  50 };
```

cs 15.3. *Qdisc_class_ops* data.

walk: Iterated over all classes of a queueing discipline, used to obtain diagnostic data for all classes.

tcf_chain: Returns a pointer to the list of filters for a class, used to manipulate the filter list.

bind_tcf: Binds an instance of a filter to the class.

unbind_tcf: Removes an instance of a filter from the class.

dump_class: Returns stats for a class.

15.4.4 *struct cbq_class*

struct cbq_class data structure represents a traffic class for the cbq queueing discipline for scheduling a packet based on the bandwidth allocated for the class (cs 15.4).

```
net/sched/sch_cbq.c

  91 struct cbq_class
  92 {
  93      struct cbq_class     *next;
  94      struct cbq_class     *next_alive;
    . . .
  97      u32               classid;
  98      unsigned char        priority;
  99      unsigned char        priority2;
 100      unsigned char        ewma_log;
                        cont . . .
```

cs 15.4. *cbq_class* data structure.

```
net/sched/sch_cbq.c
struct  cbq_class cont ...

    120     long            allot;
    121     long            quantum;
    122     long            weight;
                            cont ...
```

cs 15.5. *cbq_class* data structure (*continued*).

```
net/sched/sch_cbq.c
    struct  cbq_class cont ...

    127     struct cbq_class    *tparent;
    128     struct cbq_class    *borrow;
    129
    130     struct cbq_class    *sibling;
    131     struct cbq_class    *children;
                                cont ...
```

cs 15.6. *cbq_class* data structure (*continued*).

Here we will discuss important fields of the *cbq_class*:

next: Points to the next class in the class tree (hash table link).

next_alive: cbq scheduling algorithm maintains a list of active traffic classes for scheduling the class based on the priority. This field will point to the next class with backlog of packets from the list of active classes.

classid: Every class in the cbq queueing discipline is represented by an id. This field contains a unique id for a cbq class.

priority: This field contains the class priority which is used in scheduling a cbq class.

priority2: This field contains the class priority to be used after the overlimit. A cbq class is of three types: overlimit, underlimit, and at limit. Depending on the usage of the class in cbq scheduling function, a class is classed overlimit, underlimit, and at limit based on the allocated bandwidth.

ewma_log: The field is used for calculating the idle time calculation required in cbq scheduling function.

allot: Specifies how many bytes a qdisc can dequeue during each round. This is reconfigurable and depends on the weight field of the *cbq_class* struct (cs 15.5).

quantum: Specifies the allotment per weighted round robin based on the bandwidth assigned for the class.

weight: If the *cbq_class* has more bandwidth than other classes in the queue, then the weight field is used for the high-bandwidth class to send more data in one round than the others.

tparent: points to the parent of the *cbq_class* tree (cs 15.6).

```
net/sched/sch_cbq.c
    struct  cbq_class cont . . .

    139     unsigned char       level;
                . . . .
    147     long                deficit;
```

cs 15.7. cbq_class data structure (continued).

borrow: This field indicates if the child class can borrow the bandwidth from the parent class. If it is NULL, then class is bandwidth-limited and not able to borrow bandwidth from parent class.

siblings: Points to the siblings class.

children: Points to the children class.

level: Level of the class in the class tree (cs 15.7).

deficit: This field is used in the round-robin process of the scheduling. This field contains a saved deficit value if the allocated bytes are not sent in the same round, and this deficit value will be used for the next round.

15.5   tc USER PROGRAM AND KERNEL IMPLEMENTATION DETAILS

The tc is a user program which overrides and updates the default queueing discipline in Linux. It uses a netlink as communication channel for interaction between user space and kernel. It adds the new queuing discipline, traffic classes, filters, and so on.

Here we will discuss the CBQ queueing discipline.

How is tc used?

From command prompt:

> # tc qdisc add dev eth1 root handle 1: cbq bandwidth
> 10 Mbit cell 8 avpkt 1000 mpu 64

The above tc command adds the new cbq queueing discipline.

For more details on tc command flow and how the doit function pointer is invoked, see Chapter 13.

The doit function pointer points to *tc_modify_qdisc()* in the case of adding *qdisc* to queueing discipline (cs 15.8).

15.5.1   *tc_modify_qdisc()*

This function first calls the *dev_get_by_index()* function to find out the network interface device at line 604. The argument to the *dev_get_by_index()* is *tcm→tcm_ifindex*, which is specified at the command prompt.

dev_get_by_index(), based on the argument (ifindex), searches for an interface and returns the pointer to the device.

```
net/sched/sch_api.c
594 static int tc_modify_qdisc(struct sk_buff *skb, struct nlmsghdr *n, void *arg)
595 {
    . . .
604     if ((dev = __dev_get_by_index(tcm->tcm_ifindex)) == NULL)
605         return -ENODEV;
606
607     if (clid) {
608         if (clid != TC_H_ROOT) {
609             if (clid != TC_H_INGRESS) {
610                 if ((p = qdisc_lookup(dev, TC_H_MAJ(clid))) == NULL)
611                     return -ENOENT;
612                 q = qdisc_leaf(p, clid);
613             } else { /*ingress */
614                 q = dev->qdisc_ingress;
615             }
616         } else {
617             q = dev->qdisc_sleeping;
618         }
619
                                                              cont . . .
```

cs 15.8. tc_modify_qdisc().

Then *tc_modify_qdisc()* checks for the *tcm→tcm_parent* value at line 607. If it's not equal to *TC_H_ROOT*, it calls the functions *qdisc_lookup()* and *qdisc_leaf()* at lines 610 and 612 for finding out the parent qdisc and band qdisc. If *tcm→tcm_parent* is equal to the *TC_H_ROOT*, then the band qdisc points to the device's *qdisc_sleeping* at line 614.

After this, *tc_modify_qdisc()* checks for the *tcm→tcm_handle* value at line 624. If it is not empty, then it calls the function *qdsic_lookup()* at line 630 to search for the band qdisc q with dev and *tcm→tcm_handle* as the arguments (cs 15.9). If it doesn't find the band qdisc, then it jumps to *create_n_graft* label at line 631; otherwise, it jumps to the label graft at line 640.

At *create_n_graft* label line 690 the kernel first checks for the *nlmsghdr→ nlmsg_flags* has its *NLM_F_CREATE* bit set to 1 (cs 15.10). If it is set to 1, then it checks for INGRESS or EGRESS before calling the *qdisc_create()* at lines 694 or 696 which allocates and initializes the new qdisc.

Again at graft label line 700, the *qdisc_graft()* function is called at line 703; it sets the dev's *qdisc_sleeping* to the new queueing discipline and sets *dev→qdisc* to *noop_qdisc*, and it reactivates the device at the end and returns the old queueing discipline oqdisc.

If there is no error, the graft finally calls *qdisc_notify()* function at line 712 and sends the message(skb) to the user space.

15.5.2 *qdisc_create()*

Based on the kind of qdisc by looking at the TCA_KIND-1 entry in the argument tca at line 390, it searches for the queueing discipline by name by calls the function *qdisc_lookup_ops()* (cs 15.11). Then it allocates space for the queuing discipline

```
net/sched/sch_api.c
tc_modify_qdisc()
cont . . .

624            if (!q || !tcm->tcm_handle || q->handle != tcm->tcm_handle) {

630                    if ((q = qdisc_lookup(dev, tcm->tcm_handle)) == NULL)
631                        goto create_n_graft;

640                    goto graft;
641            } else {
642                    if (q == NULL)
643                        goto create_n_graft;

664                    if ((n->nlmsg_flags&NLM_F_CREATE) &&
665                        (n->nlmsg_flags&NLM_F_REPLACE) &&
666                        ((n->nlmsg_flags&NLM_F_EXCL) ||
667                        (tca[TCA_KIND-1] &&
668                        rtattr_strcmp(tca[TCA_KIND-1], q->ops->id))))
669                        goto create_n_graft;
670                    }
671            }
672       } else {
          . . .
```

cs 15.9. *tc_modify_qdisc()* (continued).

```
net/sched/sch_api.c
tc_modify_qdisc()
cont . . .
690 create_n_graft:
691        if (!(n->nlmsg_flags&NLM_F_CREATE))
692            return -ENOENT;
693        if (clid == TC_H_INGRESS)
694            q = qdisc_create(dev, tcm->tcm_parent, tca, &err);
695        else
696            q = qdisc_create(dev, tcm->tcm_handle, tca, &err);
697        if (q == NULL)
698            return err;
699
700 graft:
701        if (1) {
702            struct Qdisc *old_q = NULL;
703            err = qdisc_graft(dev, p, clid, q, &old_q);
          . . .
710                return err;
711            }
712            qdisc_notify(skb, n, clid, old_q, q);
          . . .
720 }
```

cs 15.10. *tc_modify_qdisc()* (continued).

```
net/sched/sch_api.c
  386 static struct Qdisc *
  387 qdisc_create(struct net_device *dev, u32 handle, struct rtattr **tca, int *errp)
  388 {
    .  .  .
  390    struct rtattr *kind = tca[TCA_KIND-1];.
  391    struct Qdisc *sch = NULL;
  392    struct Qdisc_ops *ops;
    .  .  .
  395    ops = qdisc_lookup_ops(kind);
    .  .  .
  412    size = sizeof(*sch) + ops->priv_size;
  413
  414    sch = kmalloc(size, GFP_KERNEL);
    .  .
  421    err = -EINVAL;
    .  .  .
  425    memset(sch, 0, size);
  426
  427    skb_queue_head_init(&sch->q);
    .  .  .  .
                                                                      cont . . .
```

cs 15.11. *qdisc_create()*.

qdisc where size is equal to the size of Qdisc with additional space for the Qdisc private data structure and finally initializes the Qdisc queue by calling the function *skb_queue_head()* at line 427.

At line 432, it initializes the Qdisc operational (*sch→ops*) pointer which sets up queueing discipline operations such as enqueue, dequeue, and device at lines 433,434, and 435 (cs 15.12). Finally, it calls the *ops→init* function pointer and in this case it is pointing to *cbq_init()* function.

15.5.3 *cbq_init()*

This function is responsible for initializing the cbq queueing discipline. It sets up the classid of class at line 1422 (cs 15.13), priority at line 1427, siblings link at line 1421, and so on, and then creates a default qdisc for the queueing discipline by calling the function *qdisc_create_dflt()*. By default, the type of qdisc is pfifo.

15.5.4 *qdisc_graft()*

The arguments to the *qdisc_graft()* are dev, p, clid, q & old, where p is the parent queueing discipline, clid is the class ID, q is the band queueing discipline, and old_q is the old queueing and is set to NULL.

The basic functionality of the *qdisc_graft()* is to graft qdisc "new" to class "classid" of qdisc "parent" or to device "dev." *qdisc_graft()* first checks whether the parent queueing discipline p is empty or not at line 358 and then it calls the function *dev_graft_qdisc()* at line 360 or 362 based on the EGRESS and INGRESS; otherwise it calls the *get()* from the parent queueing discipline's class operation set at line 370 (cs 15.14).

```
net/sched/sch_api.c
qdisc_create ()
cont . . .
    . . .
    432      sch->ops = ops;
    433      sch->enqueue = ops->enqueue;
    434      sch->dequeue = ops->dequeue;
    435      sch->dev = dev;
    436      atomic_set(&sch->refcnt, 1);
    437      sch->stats.lock = &dev->queue_lock;

    . . .
    450      if (!ops->init || (err = ops->init(sch, tca[TCA_OPTIONS-1])) == 0) {
    451          write_lock(&qdisc_tree_lock);
    452          sch->next = dev->qdisc_list;
    453          dev->qdisc_list = sch;
    454          write_unlock(&qdisc_tree_lock);

    . . .
    459          return sch;
    460      }

    . . .
    467 }
```

<u>cs 15.12.</u> *qdisc_create()* (continued).

```
net/sched/sch_cbq.c
    1420     q->link.refcnt = 1;
    1421     q->link.sibling = &q->link;
    1422     q->link.classid = sch->handle;
    1423     q->link.qdisc = sch;
    1424     if (!(q->link.q = qdisc_create_dflt(sch->dev, &pfifo_qdisc_ops)))
    1425         q->link.q = &noop_qdisc;
    1426
    1427     q->link.priority = TC_CBQ_MAXPRIO-1;
```

<u>cs 15.13.</u> *cbq_init()*.

15.5.5 *dev_graft_qdisc()*

This first deactivates the device by calling the *dev_deactivate()* function at line 305, and then it checks for the INGRESS or EGRESS (cs 15.15). If it is EGRESS, then set the old *qdisc_sleeping* to an oqdisc variable. Then it checks whether the supplied new queueing discipline is empty or not. If it is empty, set the new queueing discipline to *noop_qdisc*. Then it sets the dev's *qdisc_sleeping* to the new queueing discipline and set *dev→qdisc* to *noop_qdisc* and reactivate the device at the end and return the old queueing discipline oqdisc.

15.6 THE tc COMMANDS FOR CREATING CLASS HIERARCHY FOR CBQ

tc class add dev eth0 parent 1:0 classid 1:1 cbq bandwidth 10 Mbit rate 10 Mbit
    allot 1514 cell 8 weight 1 Mbit prio 8 maxburst 20 avpkt 1000

net/sched/sch_api.c

```
351 int qdisc_graft(struct net_device *dev, struct Qdisc *parent, u32 classid,
352          struct Qdisc *new, struct Qdisc **old)
353 {
354     int err = 0;
355     struct Qdisc *q = *old;
356
357
358     if (parent == NULL) {
359         if (q && q->flags&TCQ_F_INGRES) {
360             *old = dev_graft_qdisc(dev, q);
361         } else {
362             *old = dev_graft_qdisc(dev, new);
363         }
364     } else {
365         struct Qdisc_class_ops *cops = parent->ops->cl_ops;
366
367         err = -EINVAL;
368
369         if (cops) {
370             unsigned long cl = cops->get(parent, classid);
371             if (cl) {
372                 err = cops->graft(parent, cl, new, old);
373                 cops->put(parent, cl);
374             }
375         }
376     }
377     return err;
378 }
```

cs 15.14. qdisc_graft().

net/sched/sch_api.c

```
299 static struct Qdisc *
300 dev_graft_qdisc(struct net_device *dev, struct Qdisc *qdisc)
301 {
302     struct Qdisc *oqdisc;
303
304     if (dev->flags & IFF_UP)
305         dev_deactivate(dev);
306

309     if (qdisc && qdisc->flags&TCQ_F_INGRES) {

316         } else { /* new */
317             dev->qdisc_ingress = qdisc;
318         }
319
320     } else {
321
322         oqdisc = dev->qdisc_sleeping;
323

328         /* ... and graft new one */
329         if (qdisc == NULL)
330             qdisc = &noop_qdisc;
331         dev->qdisc_sleeping = qdisc;
332         dev->qdisc = &noop_qdisc;
333     }

338     if (dev->flags & IFF_UP)
339         dev_activate(dev);
340
341     return oqdisc;
342 }
```

cs 15.15. dev_graft_qdisc().

tc class add dev eth0 parent 1:1 classid 1:2 cbq bandwidth 10 Mbit rate 3 Mbit
   allot 1514 cell 8 weight 100 Kbit prio 3 maxburst 20 avpkt 1000 split 1:0

tc class add dev eth0 parent 1:1 classid 1:3 cbq bandwidth 10 Mbit rate 7 Mbit
   allot 1514 cell 8 weight 800 Kbit prio 7 maxburst 20 avpkt 1000 split 1:0

In this case the doit function pointer (more details on how it is assigned are given above) from *rtnetlink_rcv_msg()* would point to *tc_ctl_tclass()*, and this function gets invoked when the tc command for creating class is executed.

For more details on tc command flow & how the doit function pointer invoked, see Chapter 13.

15.6.1   *tc_ctl_tclass()*

This function first calls the *dev_get_by_index()* function to find out the network interface device at line 852 (cs 15.16). The argument to the *dev_get_by_index()* is *tcm→tcm_ifindex*, which is specified at the command *prompt..dev_get_by_index()* based on the argument (ifindex) searches for an interface and returns a pointer to the device.

dev_get_by_index() based on the argument (ifindex) searches for an interface and returns a pointer to the device.

Then based on the *tcm→tcm_parent* value, it determines whether the class is root (which has no parent) or the class is node in hierarchy and locates the qdisc by calling the function *qdisc_lookup()* at line 895 and then checks whether it supports a class or not at line 899.

If yes, it then checks for the classid at line 904 based on the value set at the command prompt. If the classid is zero and equal *TC_H_ROOT*, then it is a parent class; otherwise, it's a child class.

Next it calls the function *cbq_get()* at line 911 which tries to get the class by calling the function *cbq_class_lookup()*, which checks if class already exists with the same classid or not; if yes, it returns the class or the returns NULL.

tc_ctl_tclass() calls the function *cbq_change_class* (*cops→change*) at line 939. Finally, the *tc_ctl_tclass()* calls the *tclass_notify()* function and sends the message (skb) to the user space. Fig. 15.8 shows the flow diagram for *tc_ctl_tclass()*.

15.6.2   *cbq_change_class()*

The main functionality of this function is to

- Allocate memory for the *cbq_class* data struct.
- Initialize all the class elements based on the arguments.
- Link the class in the hierarchy by calling the function *cbq_link_class*.

The memory for the new class is allocated and initialized at line 1914s and 191 and then creates a default qdisc for this class by calling the function at line 1921 (cs 15.17). It sets up the classid of class at line 1923, class parent at line 1924, and qdisc at line 1925. The allot and quantum values of the class are set at lines 1926 and 1927, which are used in *cbq_dequeue()* function for scheduling this class and the siblings link at line 1932.

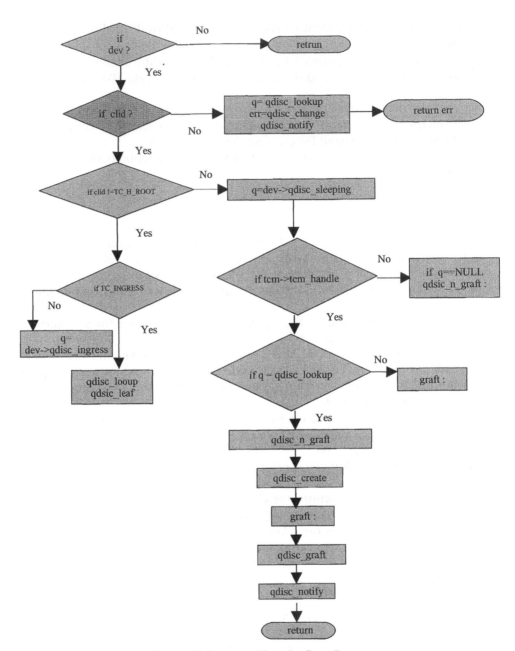

Figure 15.7. *tc_modify_qdisc* flow diagram.

```
net/sched/sch_api.c
838 static int tc_ctl_tclass(struct sk_buff *skb, struct nlmsghdr *n, void *arg)
839 {

852     if ((dev = __dev_get_by_index(tcm->tcm_ifindex)) == NULL)
853         return -ENODEV;

895     if ((q = qdisc_lookup(dev, qid)) == NULL)
896         return -ENOENT;

899     cops = q->ops->cl_ops;

904     if (clid == 0) {
905         if (pid == TC_H_ROOT)
906             clid = qid;
907     } else
908         clid = TC_H_MAKE(qid, clid);
909
910     if (clid)
911         cl = cops->get(q, clid);

938     new_cl = cl;
939     err = cops->change(q, clid, pid, tca, &new_cl);
940     if (err == 0)
941         tclass_notify(skb, n, q, new_cl, RTM_NEWTCLASS);

947     return err;
948 }
```

cs 15.16. tc_ctl_tclass().

```
net/sched/sch_cbq.c
1773 static int
1774 cbq_change_class(struct Qdisc *sch, u32 classid, u32 parentid, struct rtattr **tca,
1775         unsigned long *arg)
1776 {

1779     struct cbq_class *cl = (struct cbq_class*)*arg;

1914     cl = kmalloc(sizeof(*cl), GFP_KERNEL);

1917     memset(cl, 0, sizeof(*cl));

1921     if (!(cl->q = qdisc_create_dflt(sch->dev, &pfifo_qdisc_ops)))
1922         cl->q = &noop_qdisc;
1923     cl->classid = classid;
1924     cl->tparent = parent;
1925     cl->qdisc = sch;
1926     cl->allot = parent->allot;
1927     cl->quantum = cl->allot;
1928     cl->weight = cl->R_tab->rate.rate;

1932     cbq_link_class(cl);
1933     cl->borrow = cl->tparent;
1934     if (cl->tparent != &q->link)
1935         cl->share = cl->tparent;
1936     cbq_adjust_levels(parent);
1937     cl->minidle = -0x7FFFFFFF;
1938     cbq_set_lss(cl, RTA_DATA(tb[TCA_CBQ_LSSOPT-1]));
1939     cbq_set_wrr(cl, RTA_DATA(tb[TCA_CBQ_WRROPT-1]));
```

cs 15.17. cbq_change_class().

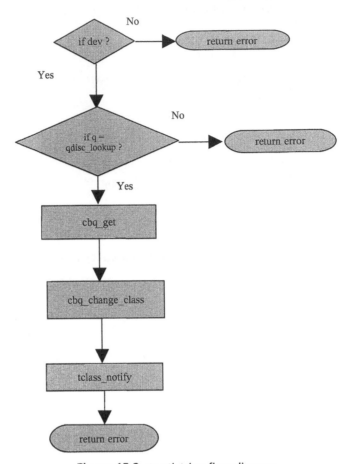

Figure 15.8. *tc_ctl_tclass* flow diagram.

15.7 FILTERS

The main function of filters is to assign the incoming packets to classes for a qdisc. The classification of packets are based on the IP address, port numbers, and so on.

Types of Filters

- RSVP
- U32
- Route
- Police
- Estimator
- Firewall-based

We will discuss only the U32 and route filters.
How do we set filters using route and U32?

tc filter add dev eth0 parent 1:0 protocol ip prio 100 route or
tc filter add dev eth0 parent 1:0 protocol ip prio 100 u32

In this case the doit function pointer (more details on how it is assigned are given above) from *rtnetlink_rcv_msg()* would point to *tc_ctl_tfilter()*, and this function gets invoked when the tc command for setting filters is executed.

For more details on tc command flow and how the doit function pointer is invoked, see Chapter 13.

15.7.1 *tc_ctl_tfilter()*

The main functionality of the *tc_ctl_tfilter()* is to add/delete/change/get the filter. The main message argument for the *tc_ctl_tfilter* is the struct *nlmsghdr*, which embeds another message struct *tcmsg* at line 121 (cs 15.18). The message provides the three important types of information (*tcm_info*): node's protocol (minor part of *tcm_info*), filter's node priority (major part of *tcm_info*), and the parent ID (*tcm_parent*).

tc_ctl_tfilter first identifies the device by calling the function *_dev_get_by_index()* using the *tcm_ifindex* value at line 146 (cs 15.19), and then we do the lookup for the qdisc by calling the function *qdisc_lookup()* for the queueing discipline using the parent ID (*tcm_parent*). Then using the *tcf_chain* of the queuing discipline class operation at line 168, we identify the queueing discipline filter list. After that we check for the filter by traversing the list using the loop at lines 174–183, if not found, then we create/allocate a new filter node.

After traversing the filter list, if the filter node is not found, then it creates/allocates a new filter node at line 199 and initializes the filter node operation structure *tp_ops* at line 201 by calling the *tcf_proto_lookup_ops()* function using the optional argument struct rtattr **tca (cs 15.20). Then using the filter node operation, struct values initialize the filter node from lines 220–226.

The main data structures initialized are *tcp_proto* and *tcf_proto_ops*.

- First, struct values initialize and assign the filter type to the new filter node operation pointer (*tcf_proto_ops* *ops) by calling the function *tcf_proto_lookup_ops()* whose functionality is to find a classifier type by string name.

```
net/sched/cls_api.c

118 static int tc_ctl_tfilter(struct sk_buff *skb, struct nlmsghdr *n, void *arg)
119 {
120     struct rtattr **tca = arg;
121     struct tcmsg *t = NLMSG_DATA(n);
122     u32 protocol = TC_H_MIN(t->tcm_info);
123     u32 prio = TC_H_MAJ(t->tcm_info);
       . . .
125     u32 parent = t->tcm_parent;
       . . .
129     struct tcf_proto *tp = NULL;
130     struct tcf_proto_ops *tp_ops;
131     struct Qdisc_class_ops *cops;

       . . . .
                                    cont. . .
```

cs 15.18. *tc_ctl_tfilter()*.

```
net/sched/cls_api.c
tc_ctl_tfilter() cont . . .

146    if ((dev = __dev_get_by_index(t->tcm_ifindex)) == NULL)
147        return -ENODEV;
        . . . .
150    if (!parent) {
151        q = dev->qdisc_sleeping;
152        parent = q->handle;
153    } else if ((q = qdisc_lookup(dev, TC_H_MAJ(t->tcm_parent))) == NULL)
154        return -EINVAL;
        . . . .
168    chain = cops->tcf_chain(q, cl);
        . . .
174    for (back = chain; (tp=*back) != NULL; back = &tp->next) {
175        if (tp->prio >= prio) {
176            if (tp->prio == prio) {
177                if (!nprio || (tp->protocol != protocol && protocol))
178                    goto errout;
179            } else
180                tp = NULL;
181            break;
182        }
183    }
                                                    cont . . .
```

cs 15.19. *tc_ctl_tfilter()* (continued).

```
net/sched/cls_api.c
tc_ctl_tfilter() cont . . .

185    if (tp == NULL) {
186        . . .
199        if ((tp = kmalloc(sizeof(*tp), GFP_KERNEL)) == NULL)
200            goto errout;
201        tp_ops = tcf_proto_lookup_ops(tca[TCA_KIND-1]);
           . . .
219        memset(tp, 0, sizeof(*tp));
220        tp->ops = tp_ops;
221        tp->protocol = protocol;
222        tp->prio = nprio ? : tcf_auto_prio(*back);
223        tp->q = q;
224        tp->classify = tp_ops->classify;
225        tp->classid = parent;
226        err = tp_ops->init(tp);
           . . . .
240    fh = tp->ops->get(tp, t->tcm_handle);
241

277
278    err = tp->ops->change(tp, cl, t->tcm_handle, tca, &fh);
279    if (err == 0)
280        tfilter_notify(skb, n, tp, fh, RTM_NEWTFILTER);
       . . . .
286 }
```

cs 15.20. *tc_ctl_tfilter()* (continued).

- The queuing discipline pointer points to the queueing discipline associated with this filter.
- The classifier function pointer points to the classify function in its filter operation.
- The classid is assigned to the ID of the queueing discipline.
- Then the classid calls the init function to initialize the rest of the filter structure.

And finally the classid calls the change function of filter either *u32_change* or *route4_change*. Fig 15.9 shows the flow diagram for *tc_ctl_tfilter()*.

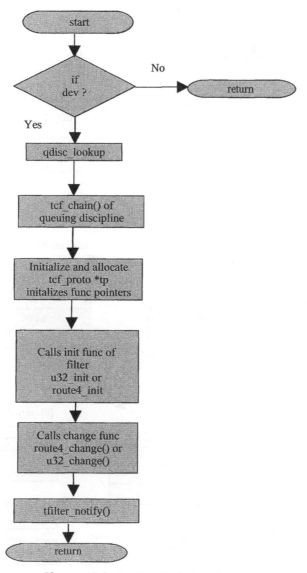

Figure 15.9. *tc_ctl_tfilter()* flow diagram.

15.8   u32 FILTER IMPLEMENTATION

In u32 filters the classification of packets is done based on the destination IP, destination TCP/IP port, source IP address, source TCP/IP port, TOS byte, and protocol
(Fig. 15.10).

Commands for Setting *u32_filter*

> /root/work/iproute/iproute2-ss050607/tc/tc filter add dev eth1 parent 1:0 proto-
> col ip prio 1 u32 match ip dst 192.168.2.101 match ip sport 23 0xfff flowid
> 1:2

> /root/work/iproute/iproute2-ss050607/tc/tc filter add dev eth1 parent 1:0 proto-
> col ip prio 1 u32 match ip dst 192.168.2.102 match ip sport 80 0xfff flowid
> 1:3

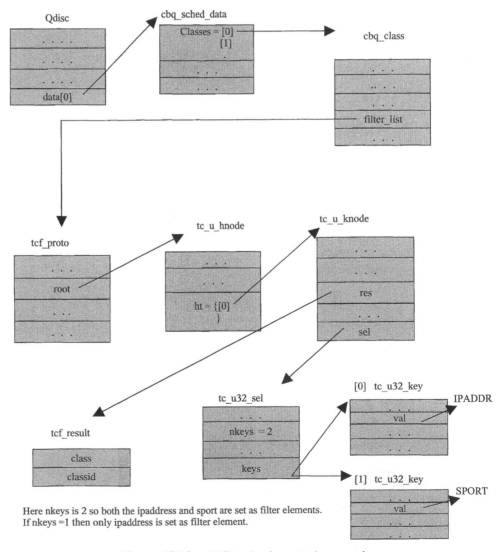

Here nkeys is 2 so both the ipaddress and sport are set as filter elements.
If nkeys =1 then only ipaddress is set as filter element.

Figure 15.10. u32 filter implementation overview.

15.8.1 *u32_change()*

The *u32_filters* are stored in hash tables, the data structure defined for the hash table is struct *tc_u_hnode* at line 502, and the key nodes for storing the information for filters are defined as struct *tc_u_knode* at line 503 (cs 15.21). Then define a key struct (i.e., struct *tc_u32_key*) at line 504 which is used to hold information about the filter type (i.e., IP address info, TCP/IP port, etc.).

The rtattr struct contains information about the tc command arguments for setting the filter parameters at lines 505–506, and the struct *tc_u_common* which holds a pointer for the queuing discipline type is defined at line 501.

The if condition at line 523 becomes true if a new hash node is required. Based on the divisor value at line 524, a new hash node for the struct *tc_u_hnode* is allocated at line 535 and initialized at line 538 (cs 15.22).

Then the new hash node's *tp_c* pointer is initialized at line 539 to point to the *tc_u_common tp_c* which contains information of the queuing discipline type and the ref count is set to 0 at line 540.

The divisor and the handle value is set at lines 541–542 based on the tc user arguments. Finally the hlist (hash list) of struct *tc_u_common* is updated with the new hash node at line 544.

The if condition at line 549 will be true if a new hash key node is required (cs 15.23). It starts with getting the value of ID of the *tc_u_hnode* for adding the new hash key node to the specific node of the hnode hash table. Then next it gets the information about the struct *tc_u32_sel* and its associated keys from the table entry *TCA_U32_SEL* at line 578.

Then u32_change() allocates the memory for the new hash key node at line 579. The memory space allocated depends on the number of keys specified in *tc_u32_key→nkeys* and initializes this memory at line 582. After the memory allocation, memcpy will be called at line 583 to copy the contents of *TCA_U32_SEL* to the keys of the new key node. Next the *tc_u_node* (ht) and the handle are assigned to the new key node at lines 584–585.

Finally the function *u32_set_params()* is called at line 586 to set the class-specific information inside the new key node.

```
net/sched/cls_u32.c
497 static int u32_change(struct tcf_proto *tp, unsigned long base, u32 handle,
498                       struct rtattr **tca,
499                       unsigned long *arg)
500 {
501     struct tc_u_common *tp_c = tp->data;
502     struct tc_u_hnode *ht;
503     struct tc_u_knode *n;
504     struct tc_u32_sel *s;
505     struct rtattr *opt = tca[TCA_OPTIONS-1];
506     struct rtattr *tb[TCA_U32_MAX];
507     u32 htid;
508     int err;
        . . .
                                              cont . . .
```

cs 15.21. *u32_change.*

```
net/sched/cls_u32.c
u32_change () cont...

523     if (tb[TCA_U32_DIVISOR-1]) {
524         unsigned divisor = *(unsigned*)RTA_DATA(tb[TCA_U32_DIVISOR-1]);
            . . .
530         if (handle == 0) {
531             handle = gen_new_htid(tp->data);
            . . .
534         }
535         ht = kmalloc(sizeof(*ht) + divisor*sizeof(void*), GFP_KERNEL);
            . . .
538         memset(ht, 0, sizeof(*ht) + divisor*sizeof(void*));
539         ht->tp_c = tp_c;
540         ht->refcnt = 0;
541         ht->divisor = divisor;
542         ht->handle = handle;
543         ht->next = tp_c->hlist;
544         tp_c->hlist = ht;
545         *arg = (unsigned long)ht;
546         return 0;
547     }
        . . .
                                                              cont . . .
```

cs 15.22. *u32_change()* (continued).

```
net/sched/cls_u32.c
 u32_change () cont...

549     if (tb[TCA_U32_HASH-1]) {
550         htid = *(unsigned*)RTA_DATA(tb[TCA_U32_HASH-1]);
        . . .
578     s = RTA_DATA(tb[TCA_U32_SEL-1]);
579     n = kmalloc(sizeof(*n) + s->nkeys*sizeof(struct tc_u32_key), GFP_KERNEL);
        . . .
582     memset(n, 0, sizeof(*n) + s->nkeys*sizeof(struct tc_u32_key));
583     memcpy(&n->sel, s, sizeof(*s) + s->nkeys*sizeof(struct tc_u32_key));
584     n->ht_up = ht;
585     n->handle = handle;
586     err = u32_set_parms(tp->q, base, ht, n, tb, tca[TCA_RATE-1]);
        . . .
598         return 0;
599     }
        . . .
```

cs 15.23. *u32_change()* (continued).

15.9 ROUTE FILTER IMPLEMENTATION

Here the classification of packets is based on the routing tables. Based on the information in the routing table, a route filter is set for a specific destination (Fig. 15.11).

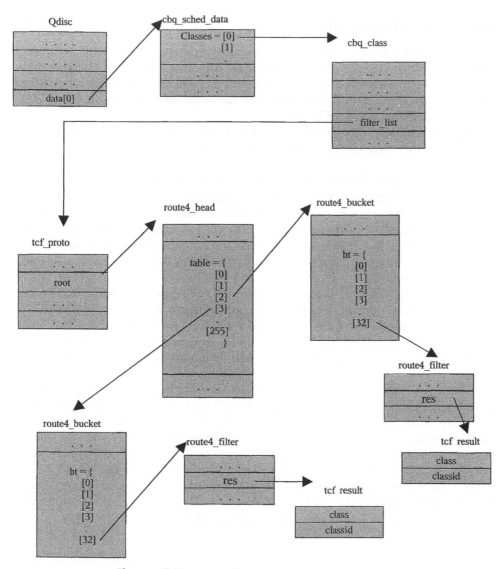

Figure 15.11. Route filter implementation overview.

Route Filter Commands

[root@localhost root]# ip route add 192.168.2.101 via 192.168.2.100 realm 2

[root@localhost root]# ip route add 192.168.2.102 via 192.168.2.100 realm 3

[root@localhost root]# tc filter add dev eth1 parent 1:0 protocol ip prio 100
    route to 3 flowid 1:3

[root@localhost root]# tc filter add dev eth1 parent 1:0 protocol ip prio 100
    route to 2 flowid 1:2

15.9.1 *route4_change()*

The struct rtattr at lines 373–374 contains the different types of command arguments (information) for setting the filter parameters for route (cs 15.24). The main data structure for the route filters is the struct *route4_head* at line 370, which is initialized to point to the queuing discipline type. Then the struct *route4_filter* and the *route4_bucket* are declared at lines 371–372.

The *route4_head* data structure contains the hash table of type struct *route4_bucket*, and this *route4_bucket* data structure again maintains a table for struct *route4_filter*.

The *rtattr_parse()* function at line 381 is called to sort out the arguments from the command arguments from *struct rtattr* and arrange this specific information in the form of a table. Then it checks for whether the struct *route4_head* is NULL; if sturct route4_head is NULL, then route4_change() allocates the memory space for the struct *route4_head* at line 414 and initializes this memory space at line 417 (cs 15.25). It also allocates the memory space for the struct *route4_filter* at line 424 and initializes it at line 428.

The *TCA_ROUTE4_TO* table entry of *struct rtattr* contains information for the realm id, and this is getting assigned to the (struct *route4_filter*) *f→id* at line 437 (cs 15.26). Then it checks for the classid entry in the arguments table; and if the classid entry available, the *TCA_ROUTE4_TO* entry assigns this classid to the *f→res. classid*, where *res* is of type struct *tcf_result* which contains information for the class.

Using the *f→handle* value, to_hash() calculates the index for the *route4_bucket* table by calling the function *to_hash()* at line 475 (cs 15.27). Then it checks whether the entry at the index it is NULL; if it is null, the *f→handle* value allocates the memory space for the struct *route4_bucket* and initializes at lines 478–481. Finally, it inserts the allocated *route4_bucket* entry into the table *head→table[h1]* at line 484. Again, *route4_change()* calculates the indexing value for the *route4_bucket* table by calling the function *from_hash()* at line 490. Using the index value returned by from_hash() route4_change() calculates the address of the *route4_bucket* table entry where the *route4_filter* gets assigned at line 506.

```
net/sched/cls_route.c
 365 static int route4_change(struct tcf_proto *tp, unsigned long base,
 366                 u32 handle,
 367                 struct rtattr **tca,
 368                 unsigned long *arg)
 369 {
 370     struct route4_head *head = tp->root;
 371     struct route4_filter *f, *f1, **ins_f;
 372     struct route4_bucket *b;
 373     struct rtattr *opt = tca[TCA_OPTIONS-1];
 374     struct rtattr *tb[TCA_ROUTE4_MAX];
 375     unsigned h1, h2;
 376     int err;
         . . .
                                                   cont . . .
```

cs 15.24. *route_change()*.

```
net/sched/cls_route.c
route4_change () cont ...

381        if (rtattr_parse(tb, TCA_ROUTE4_MAX, RTA_DATA(opt), RTA_PAYLOAD(opt)) < 0)
382            return -EINVAL;
           . . .
413        if (head == NULL) {
414            head = kmalloc(sizeof(struct route4_head), GFP_KERNEL);
           . . .
417            memset(head, 0, sizeof(struct route4_head));
           . . .
424        f = kmalloc(sizeof(struct route4_filter), GFP_KERNEL);
           . . .
428        memset(f, 0, sizeof(*f));
           . . .
431        f->handle = 0x8000;
           . . .
                                                              cont ...
```

cs 15.25. route_change() (continued).

```
net/sched/cls_route.c
route4_change () cont ...
432        if (tb[TCA_ROUTE4_TO-1]) {
           . . .
437            f->id = *(u32*)RTA_DATA(tb[TCA_ROUTE4_TO-1]);
           . . .
440            f->handle = f->id;
441        }
           . . .
469        if (tb[TCA_ROUTE4_CLASSID-1]) {
           . . .
472            f->res.classid = *(u32*)RTA_DATA(tb[TCA_ROUTE4_CLASSID-1]);
473        }
           . . .
                                                              cont ...
```

cs 15.26. route4_change() (continued).

15.10 ENQUEUE

The enqueue function enqueues a packet (*sk_buff*) in the scheduling queue of the queuing discipline.

When the enqueue function is called, the *dev_queue_xmit()* function from the IP layer calls the enqueue function at line 1028 (cs 15.28) of the queuing discipline. The default function is called *pfifo_fast_enqueue()* if the default queuing discipline is not overridden by another queuing discipline.

Here we are discussing the *cbq_enqueue()* function for the CBQ queuing discipline.

```
net/sched/cls_route.c
route4_change () cont...
475     h1 = to_hash(f->handle);
476     if ((b = head->table[h1]) == NULL) {
477         err = -ENOBUFS;
478         b = kmalloc(sizeof(struct route4_bucket), GFP_KERNEL);
        . . .
481         memset(b, 0, sizeof(*b));
482
483         tcf_tree_lock(tp);
484         head->table[h1] = b;
485         tcf_tree_unlock(tp);
486     }
487     f->bkt = b;

490     h2 = from_hash(f->handle>>16);
491     for (ins_f = &b->ht[h2]; (f1=*ins_f) != NULL; ins_f = &f1->next) {
492         if (f->handle < f1->handle)
493             break;
494         if (f1->handle == f->handle)
495             goto errout;
496     }
497
498     cls_set_class(tp, &f->res.class, tp->q->ops->cl_ops->bind_tcf(tp->q, base, f->res.classid));
        . . .
504     f->next = f1;
505     tcf_tree_lock(tp);
506     *ins_f = f;
507     tcf_tree_unlock(tp);
509     route4_reset_fastmap(tp->q->dev, head, f->id);
510     *arg = (unsigned long)f;
511     return 0;
        . . .
```

cs 15.27. route4_change().

```
net/core/dev.c
991 int dev_queue_xmit(struct sk_buff *skb)
992 {
        . . .
1027    q = dev->qdisc;
1028    if (q->enqueue) {
1029        int ret = q->enqueue(skb, q);
        . . .
```

cs 15.28. dev_queue_xmit().

15.10.1 cbq_enqueue()

The arguments passed to the *cbq_enqueue()* function are *struct sk_buff* (packet to be queued) and the *struct Qdisc* (device qdisc). The kernel represents each class by a unique internal classid for identifying the classes. The *cbq_enqueue()* function first calls the *cbq_classify()* function at line 397 with a buffer skb and a pointer to Qdisc (scheduler) as arguments (cs 15.29). The *cbq_classify()* function's main purpose is

```
net/sched/sch_cbq.c
  393 static int
  394 cbq_enqueue(struct sk_buff *skb, struct Qdisc *sch)
  395 {
  396     struct cbq_sched_data *q = (struct cbq_sched_data *)sch->data;
  397     struct cbq_class *cl = cbq_classify(skb, sch);
      . . .
  404     if (cl) {
      . . .
  408         if ((ret = cl->q->enqueue(skb, cl->q)) == 0) {
  409             sch->q.qlen++;
  410             sch->stats.packets++;
  411             sch->stats.bytes+=len;
  412             cbq_mark_toplevel(q, cl);
  413             if (!cl->next_alive)
  414                 cbq_activate_class(cl);
  415             return 0;
  416         }
  417     }
      . . .
  427 }
```

cs 15.29. *cbq_enqueue()*.

to identify the class by applying the filters that are already set for enqueuing the packets in proper identified queue; and if the filter matching is successful, the *cbq_classify()* returns the class for enqueuing the packets. Then it checks for the class at line 404 and calls the enqueue function of the queueing discipline owned by that class at line 408; and if the enqueuing of the packet is successful, then it updates the queue length at line 409, updates the packet statistics at lines 410 and 411, and marks the top level of the class tree by calling the function *cbq_mark_toplevel()* at line 412. Finally, it activates the class for scheduling purpose at line 414 by calling the function *cbq_activate_class()*.

15.10.2 *cbq_classify()*

The *cbq_classify()* function first checks if *skb→priority* (prio) points to one of the classes at lines 253 and 254 and calls the function *cbq_class_lookup()* (cs 15.30). If it is pointing to one of the classes, then it returns a class to the calling enqueue function.

If class is not found based on the *skb→priority*, then *cbq_classify()* checks for the *filter_list* and calls the *tc_classify()* function at line 265 for finding the class-based on the filter parameter (IP addr, TCP/IP source port, etc.). The *tc_classify* is a function pointer that points to the classify function of the filter based on the filter type (e.g., *u32_classify()* in the case of u32 filters, *route4_classify()* in the case of route filters, ets.).

15.10.3 Overview of *cbq_enqueue()*

Figure 15.12 shows *cbq_enqueue()* flow diagram.

```
net/sched/sch_cbq.c
 240 static struct cbq_class *
 241 cbq_classify(struct sk_buff *skb, struct Qdisc *sch)
 242 {
       . . .
 253    if (TC_H_MAJ(prio^sch->handle) == 0 &&
 254      (cl = cbq_class_lookup(q, prio)) != NULL)
 255            return cl;
 256
 257    for (;;) {
          . . .
 265        if (!head->filter_list || (result = tc_classify(skb, head->filter_list, &res)) < 0)
 266            goto fallback;
          . . .
 288        if (cl->level == 0)
 289            return cl;
          . . .
 296        head = cl;
 297    }
 298
 299 fallback:
 300    cl = head;
          . . .
 305    if (TC_H_MAJ(prio) == 0 &&
 306      !(cl = head->defaults[prio&TC_PRIO_MAX]) &&
 307      !(cl = head->defaults[TC_PRIO_BESTEFFORT]))
 308        return head;
 309
 310    return cl;
 311 }
```

cs 15.30. cbq_clasify().

15.11   OVERVIEW OF LINUX IMPLEMENTATION OF CBQ

Fig 15.13 is an overview of CBQ implementation in Linux.

15.12   cbq_dequeue()

The Class-based Queueing (CBQ) mechanism divides the network link's bandwidth within different multiple classes and provides a link-sharing approach by using the same physical (network) link. The traffic classes within the CBQ mechanism has different priorities; and based on the priority, each class within the CBQ framework is scheduled for packet transmission.

The main blocks for the CBQ dequeueing mechanism are shown in Fig. 15.14. The mechanism consists of

1. General scheduler
2. Link–sharing scheduler
3. Estimator

The classifier part in Fig. 15.14 for each arriving packet provides a classification based on the IP addr, source, or destination port, and so on, and puts the arriving packet into the appropriate class using the cbq enqueue mechanism.

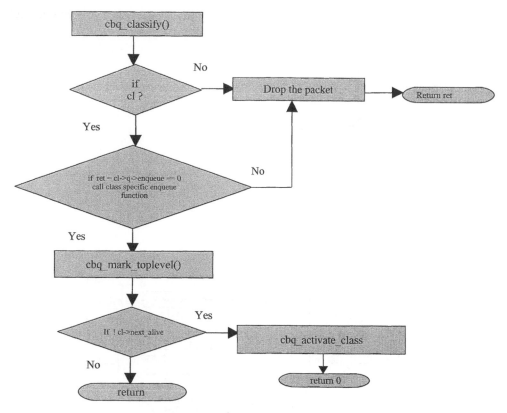

Figure 15.12. *cbq_enqueue()* flow diagram.

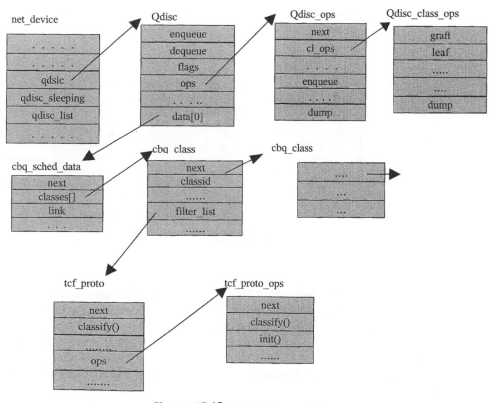

Figure 15.13. CBQ implementation.

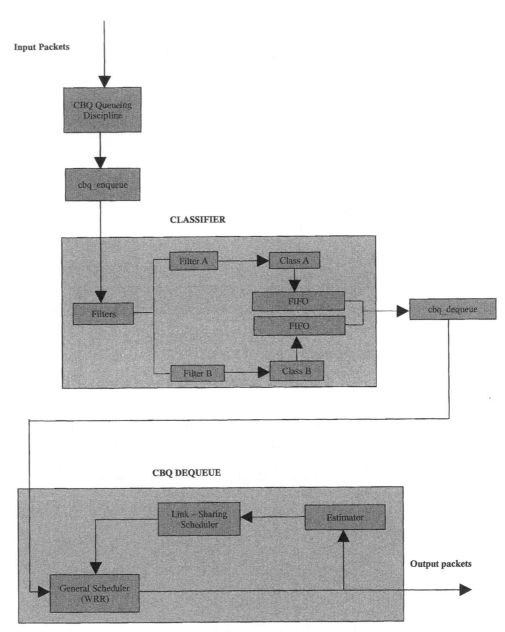

Figure 15.14. CBQ block diagram.

General Scheduler. The CBQ general scheduler uses a modified weighted round-robin (WRR) scheduling algorithm. CBQ maintains a circularly linked list of active classes and, based on the priority the WRR schedules a class for packet transmission. A class is active only if it has packets for transmission. Each class is allocated a quantum of bytes for one round. After the class has transmitted the allocated bytes, it then moves on to the next active class in the circularly linked list.

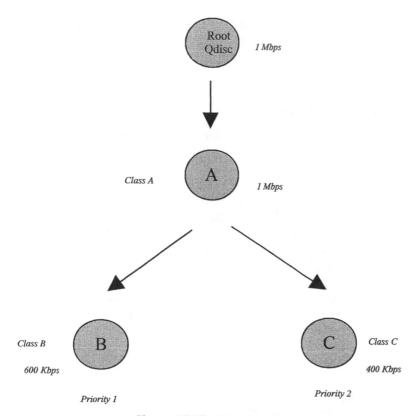

Figure 15.15. CBQ example.

Link–Sharing Scheduler. The link-sharing algorithm's main functionality is to check the status of each class and distribute the excess bandwidth based on the class's idle time.

Estimator. The estimator is used to measure the bandwidth used by the class. For this it uses certain parameters of the class to determine the bandwidth consumed. It used the idle and avgidle parameters of the class. Where the idle parameter is the interpacket time (gap between two packets) and the avgidle parameter value determines whether the class is overlimit, underlimet, and at limit. This value is calculated using the Exponential Weighted Moving Average (EWMA) function.

1. A class is overlimit when it uses more than its allocated bandwidth.
2. A class is underlimit when it uses less than its allocated bandwidth.
3. A class is at limit when it uses equal to its allocated bandwidth.

Class-based queueing is arranged in a hierarchical manner (Fig. 15.15). The top of the hierarchy is the root qdisc class that defines the total bandwidth for the entire hierarchy of the classes. This bandwidth is further divided into the hierarchy for the other classes.

CBQ assigns priority for the each class in the hierarchy; and based on the priority, a class will get a chance to send the packets to the interface. Also, a CBQ class can be configured to borrow bandwidth from its parent, if the parent has excess bandwidth.

15.12.1 From *net/dev/core.c*

Figure 15.16 shows a data flow diagram for CBQ enqueing and dequeing process.

15.12.2 *qdisc_run()*

After successfully enqueueing the packet in the appropriate class of the CBQ hierarchy, the function *dev_queue_xmit()* calls the *qdisc_run()* function.

The *qdisc_run()* function basically checks at lines 439–440 for *qdisc_restart(dev)* until there are no more packets in the output queue or until the network device does not accept any more packets—that is, *!netif_queue_stopped(dev)* (cs 15.31).

The *qdisc_restart(dev)* function is responsible for getting the next packet from the queue of network device, using qdisc of the device and sending it by calling the function *hard_start_xmit()*.

```
include/net/pkt_sched.h
   437 static inline void qdisc_run(struct net_device *dev)
   438 {
   439      while (!netif_queue_stopped(dev) &&
   440           qdisc_restart(dev)<0)
   441           /* NOTHING */;
   442 }
```

cs 15.31. *qdisc_run()*.

15.12.3 *qdisc_restart()*

This function is responsible for getting the next packet from the queue of network device using the qdisc of the network device. It starts with calling the dequeue function of the device at line 83, which is a function pointer, that is, $q \rightarrow$ *dequeue(q)*. In this case it is initialized to the *cbq_dequeue()* function and it gets called. This *cbq_dequeue()* function gets the next packet from the appropriate class. If the packet is successfully dequeued and to send this dequeued packet from the class to over the wire, the *cbq_dequeue()* function invokes the net device's *hard_start_xmit()* function. If the packet is transmitted successfully by the device's *hard_xmit()* function, then it returns –1 at line 100 to *qdisc_run()* and again the loop in *qdisc_run()* continues to dequeue the next packet from the class (cs 15.32). If the *hard_xmit()* fails or the dequeue function is failed, then in both the cases the packet is requeued in the queue and, using *NET_TX_SOFTIRQ*, is raised in *net_if_schedule()* at line 137 for transmission of the packet when *do_softirq()* function is invoked.

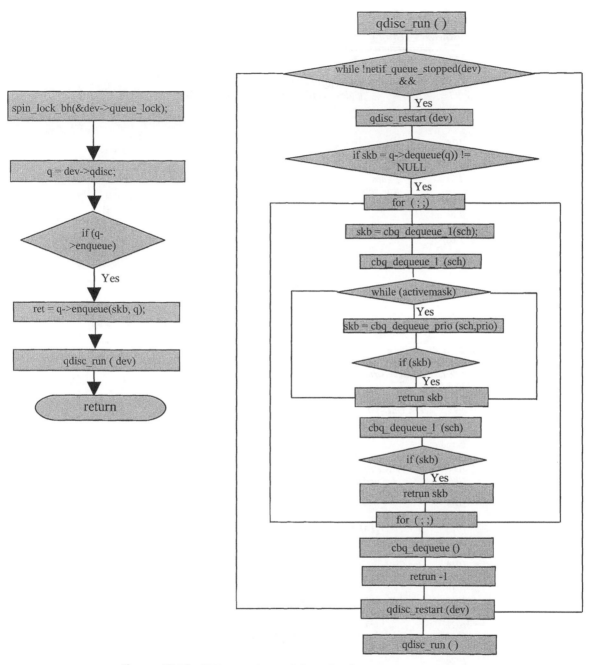

Figure 15.16. CBQ enqueing and dequeing flow.

15.12.4 *cbq_dequeue()*

The argument passed to the *cbq_dequeue()* function is the qdisc of the net device. When this function gets invoked for the first time before starting the dequeueing of packet from the queue, it gets the current (start) time using the macro *PSCHED_GET_TIME* at line 995 (cs 15.33). Then it checks to determine the transmitting class

```
net/sched/sch_generic.c
  77 int qdisc_restart(struct net_device *dev)
  78 {
            . . .
  83     if ((skb = q->dequeue(q)) != NULL) {
  95                 if (dev->hard_start_xmit(skb, dev) == 0) {
           . . .
  100                     return -1;
           . . .
  108             q = dev->qdisc;
  109         } else {
         . . .
  136         q->ops->requeue(skb, q);
  137         netif_schedule(dev);
  138         return 1;
  139     }
  140     return q->q.qlen;
  141 }
```

cs 15.32. qdisc_restart().

```
net/sched/sch_cbq.c
  987 static struct sk_buff *
  988 cbq_dequeue(struct Qdisc *sch)
  989 {
          . . .
  995     PSCHED_GET_TIME(now);
  998     if (q->tx_class) {
  999         psched_tdiff_t incr2;
          . . .
  1007        incr2 = L2T(&q->link, q->tx_len);
  1008        PSCHED_TADD(q->now, incr2);
  1009        cbq_update(q);
  1010        if ((incr -= incr2) < 0)
  1011            incr = 0;
  1012    }
  1013    PSCHED_TADD(q->now, incr);
  1014    q->now_rt = now;
  1015
  1016    for (;;) {
  1017        q->wd_expires = 0;
  1018
  1019        skb = cbq_dequeue_1(sch);
  1020        if (skb) {
  1021            sch->q.qlen--;
  1022            sch->flags &= ~TCQ_F_THROTTLED;
  1023            return skb;
  1024        }
cont...
```

cs 15.33. cbq_dequeue().

(i.e., $q{\rightarrow}tc\_class$); initially this condition at line 998 is false since this will be set in the *cbq_dequeue_prio()* function after selecting the transmitting class from the active classes list. If the transmitting class ($q{\rightarrow}tx\_class$) is set, then it invokes the function *cbq_update()*, which basically calculates the CBQ parameters (idle and avgidle) that will be used to identify whether the transmitting class is using the link for transmission based on the allocated bandwidth rate. It decides this based on factors such as whether the class is overlimit or underlimit or is at limit. The class is overlimit if it is transmitting the packets faster than the allocated bandwidth, it is at underlimit if it is transmitting slower than the allocated rate and has more backlog, and it is at limit if it is transmitting at the allocated rate.

Basically, *cbq_update()* does the following:

1. It calculates the interdeparture time (using the timer) between successive packets and subtracts from it the allocated interdeparture time for the class ($cl{\rightarrow}last$) to get the idle time. This idle time is defined as the difference between the desired time and the measured actual time between the most recent packet transmissions for the last two packets sent from this class.

2. Then it computes the avgidle time using the exponentially weighted moving average of idle, where the avidle is defined as average of the idle and where avgidle <0, $=0$, and >0 define whether the class is overlimit, at limit, and underlimit, respectively.

Based on this avgidle value, *cbq_update* decides whether the class is overlimit, underlimit, or at limit and checks whether class can borrow bandwidth from a parent or wait for a certain time before for transmitting a packet to achieve proper link sharing. Then the *cbq_dequeue* calls the function *cbq_dequeue_l()* for selecting the proper class from the active list at line 1019.

15.12.5   *cbq_dequeue_1()*

This function calculates the activemask value at line 976 based on the $q{\rightarrow}activemask$ value which is set in the function *cbq_activate class()* when the class is enqueued in *cbq_enqueue()* function. This value is required for getting the prio value at line 978 for indexing into the active classes queue list and calls the function *cbq_dequeue_l()* at line 980 function to schedule the class based on the prio value (cs 15.34).

```
net/sched/sch_cbq.c
 970 cbq_dequeue_1(struct Qdisc *sch)
 971 {
       . . .
 976     activemask = q->activemask&0xFF;
 977     while (activemask) {
 978         int prio = ffz(~activemask);
 979         activemask &= ~(1<<prio);
 980         skb = cbq_dequeue_prio(sch, prio);
 981         if (skb)
 982             return skb;
 983     }
 984     return NULL;
 985 }
```

cs 15.34. *cbq_dequeue_1().*

```
net/sched/sch_cbq.c

866 static __inline__ struct sk_buff *
867 cbq_dequeue_prio(struct Qdisc *sch, int prio)
868 {
        . . .
874     cl_tail = cl_prev = q->active[prio];
875     cl = cl_prev->next_alive;
                                        cont . . .
```

cs 15.35. cbq_dequeue_prio().

15.12.6   cbq_dequeue_prio()

This function is responsible for selecting the class from the active list and runs the class with allocated bytes. Based on the prio passed from the *cbq_dequeue_l()* function, it selects the class at lines 874–875 (cs 15.35).

The *cbq_dequeue_prio()* uses a weighted round robin for active classes where each class is allocated a quantum of bytes for one round. So under certain circumstances, a class may transmit more or less than its quantum in a round; we keep track of its deficit so that the allocation of that class in the next round could be adjusted accordingly.

The quantum required for every class is calculated in function *cbq_normalize_ quanta()* based on the class's weight, allot, and quanta which are set by the user arguments.

Before starting the round, check for whether the class is underlimit at line 885; if it is, then jump to label *skip_class* (cs 15.36). If not, check for the deficit value of the class; and if it is less than 0, then jump to label *next_class* at line 886; otherwise continue and call the dequeue function of the class's queueing discipline at line 897, which is by default the *pfifo_dequeue()* function. It checks whether the dequeue function of the class returns *sk_buff* or not at line 903. If *sk_buff* is returned, then it returns the skb to the calling function *cbq_dequeue_l()* at line 925; but before that, it again checks for the deficit value of the class at line 920.

The *skip_class* label basically checks for whether a class is empty or is penalized at line 928; if it is penalized, then it unlinks the class from the active list and returns NULL.

The *next_class* label changes the next round for the next class from the active list and if the while conditions at lines 961–962 fail, then it returns NULL to the calling function *cbq_dequeue_l()* and then *cbq_dequeue_l()* also returns NULL to the calling function *cbq_dequeue()* (cs 15.39).

If skb is not returned from *cbq_dequeue_l()*, then *cbq_dequeue()* checks whether the *q→toplevel* is equal to *TC_CBQ_MAXLEVEL* and also whether it is time for past perfect; if it is, then it comes out the infinite loop at line 1046; otherwise, it continues by setting the top level and the time. This happens when the class is overlimit or the top level class is inhibited from borrowing. If there are still packets in the scheduler at line 1055, then the watchdog timer is started for scheduling the packets and finally returns the NULL to the calling function *qdisc_restart()* (cs 15.40).

```
877    do {
878        deficit = 0;
    . . .
881        do {
882            struct cbq_class *borrow = cl;
883
884            if (cl->q->q.qlen &&
885                (borrow = cbq_under_limit(cl)) == NULL)
886                goto skip_class;
887
888            if (cl->deficit <= 0) {
    . . .
892                deficit = 1;
893                cl->deficit += cl->quantum;
894                goto next_class;
895            }
896
897            skb = cl->q->dequeue(cl->q);
                                        cont . . .
```

cs 15.36. *cbq_dequeue_prio() (continued).*

```
903            if (skb == NULL)
904                goto skip_class;
905
906            cl->deficit -= skb->len;
907            q->tx_class = cl;
    . . .
918            q->tx_len = skb->len;
919
920            if (cl->deficit <= 0) {
921                q->active[prio] = cl;
922                cl = cl->next_alive;
923                cl->deficit += cl->quantum;
924            }
925            return skb;
                            cont . . .
```

cs 15.37. *cbq_dequeue_prio() (continued).*

```
927 skip_class:
928            if (cl->q->q.qlen == 0 || prio != cl->cpriority) {
        . . .
943                q->active[prio] = NULL;
944                q->activemask &= ~(1<<prio);
                                        cont . . .
```

cs 15.38. *cbq_dequeue_prio() (continued).*

```
net/sched/sch_cbq.c
  cbq_dequeue_prio () cont...

958 next_class:
959                cl_prev = cl;
960                cl = cl->next_alive;
961          } while (cl_prev != cl_tail);
962      } while (deficit);
 . . .
966      return NULL;
967 }
```

cs 15.39. cbq_dequeue_prio() (continued).

```
net/sched/sch_cbq.c
cbq_dequeue () cont...

1044        if (q->toplevel == TC_CBQ_MAXLEVEL &&
1045            PSCHED_IS_PASTPERFECT(q->link.undertime))
1046            break;
1047
1048        q->toplevel = TC_CBQ_MAXLEVEL;
1049        PSCHED_SET_PASTPERFECT(q->link.undertime);
1050    }

1055    if (sch->q.qlen) {
1056        sch->stats.overlimits++;
1057        if (q->wd_expires && !netif_queue_stopped(sch->dev)) {
1058            long delay = PSCHED_US2JIFFIE(q->wd_expires);
1059            del_timer(&q->wd_timer);
 . . .
1062            q->wd_timer.expires = jiffies + delay;
1063            add_timer(&q->wd_timer);
1064            sch->flags |= TCQ_F_THROTTLED;
1065        }
1066    }
1067    return NULL;
1068 }
```

cs 15.40. cbq_dequeue() (continued).

The summary of the *cbq_dequeue* process is that each class is not allowed to send at length; they can only dequeue an allocated amount of data during each round. Using a weighted round robin, it decides which of its classes will be allowed to send. First it considers the highest-priority class for transmission of packets and will continue to do so until there are no more packets, and then it considers lower-priority classes. It also checks for the whether a class is overlimit,underlimit or is at limit and based on this schedules other classes.

15.13 SUMMARY

The basic principle of Qos is to decide at what rate input/output packets would be received/transmitted based on the available network speed. In Linux, the default qdisc attached to the network interface for Linux is "*pfifo_fast_qdisc*"; this qdisc can be replaced based on the requirement for other types of queueing discipline. The class-based queueing discipline allows us to shape the link speed between different types of subclasses to achieve the quality-based transmission and to make use of the allotted bandwidth for reception/transmission.

16

IP FILTER AND FIREWALL

In the age of computer networking and internetworking in a broader sense, the computer is exposed to all sorts of invasions. Private networks and individuals are connected to the public Internet for one or the other requirements. This kind of access invites malicious ideas for attacks for the sole purpose of intruding the computer or the network. The reason for intrusion may be anything from getting private information of the organization to just block the network. These will have a serious effect on the business. Attacks from outside the network were the cause of concern. There are other issues like providing access to a specific service to a known host when your services are known to many others. For example, when a machine is connected to the Internet, we get a public IP address. If I run a web site on a public machine and I need to update certain scripts on the server, only my machine should be given access to use telnet or ftp services and no others. Also within an organization if we want certain groups not to access the Internet, we should be allowed to do that. On the routers we would not like to pass certain types of traffic to be routed.

All the above situations are handled by firewall software that can be installed on a single point of entry/exit on the network. The firewall mainly works on the three directions of traffic movement:

- Incoming traffic
- Outgoing traffic
- Forwarded traffic

The firewall has a chain of rules to be applied for a specific traffic. It can be configured to accept/reject traffic to and from specific IP, as well as traffic bound to specific ports. The firewall can also be configured to block ICMP messages.

This kind of facility not only blocks traffic from an unwanted source to enter/exit the network but also restricts specific network services from limited/known hosts.

In this chapter we are not going to discuss any firewall configuration. We will have an overview of the firewall framework. We will see the point of entry into the firewall when a packet arrives and leaves the host. We will also cover two different implementations:

- ip chains
- ip tables

16.1 NETFILTER HOOK FRAMEWORK

Linux installs firewall check posts at various points in the packet traversal path in both directions. These check posts are known by the term netfilter hooks and is defined as a macro *NF_HOOK*. It checks if any firewall hook is registered for a specific check and the protocol family to which the packet belongs. If so, we need to go through all the firewall checks points registered by calling *nf_hook_slow()*. The routine makes a decision about what to do with the packet, depending on the firewall policy. It may accept the packet or reject it. In the case where there is no firewall registered for the HOOK type, we will call a callback routine *okfn* passed as a parameter to the macro that will take the packet forward for further processing (cs 16.1). The framework not only supports firewall check posts but can also be used to add features to the IP stack such as NAT/Masquerading, IP sec, and so on.

Global table *nf_hooks* is a two-dimensional array of list of registered firewall checks for each hook and protocol family (cs 16.2). NRPROTO is a protocol family and *NF_MAX_HOOKS* is the maximum hooks that each protocol family can have. We will restrict our discussion to the Internet protocol family *PF_INET*.

```
include/linux/netfilter.h

122 #define NF_HOOK(pf, hook, skb, indev, outdev, okfn)                    \
123 (list_empty(&nf_hooks[(pf)][(hook)])                                   \
124   ? (okfn)(skb)                                                        \
125   : nf_hook_slow((pf), (hook), (skb), (indev), (outdev), (okfn)))
```

cs 16.1. Macro that implements netfilter hooks.

```
net/core/netfilter.c

47 struct list_head nf_hooks[NPROTO][NF_MAX_HOOKS];
```

cs 16.2. Registered netfilter hooks are linked with *nf_hooks*.

```
net/core/netfilter.c

41 #define NF_IP_PRE_ROUTING     0
   ...
43 #define NF_IP_LOCAL_IN        1
   ...
45 #define NF_IP_FORWARD         2
   ...
47 #define NF_IP_LOCAL_OUT       3
   ...
49 #define NF_IP_POST_ROUTING    4
50 #define NF_IP_NUMHOOKS        5
```

cs 16.3. Netfilter hook numbers.

Each hook corresponds to a check post while the packet is traversing through the stack (cs 16.3).

NF_IP_PRE_ROUTING. This is a firewall hook applied for NAT/masquerading. Before incoming packets are routed, we need to alter the destination in the case where masquerading/NAT is applied to the connection; otherwise we may end up delivering the packets locally. If the rule does not allow us or we don't find any translation for the destination, we should drop the request. This is actually done for the very first packet, and the result is used for the rest of the connection. Not only NAT/Masquerading but also IPsec modules can have processing done here on this hook.

NF_IP_POST_ROUTING. This is a firewall hook applied for NAT/masquerading to alter the source of the packet. The NAT server needs to replace the source IP address of the originator with the IP address of the interface directly connected to the Internet and also the source port (to distinguish the connection). NAT may alter the source IP address only with the available public IP address. So, this firewall checks if we can do this and does the alteration if allowed; otherwise, it rejects the packet. This is done after routing decisions are made for the outgoing packet. Not only NAT/Masquerading but also IPsec modules can have processing done here on this hook.

NF_IP_LOCAL_IN. This is a firewall hook applied to the packets which are destined for us; that is, the packet needs to be delivered locally. We do this check after routing decisions are made that the packet needs to be delivered locally. The firewall checks if the packets needs to be received for specific port (network services) from a given source.

NF_IP_LOCAL_OUT. This is a firewall hook for all packets generated locally for transmission. The post is installed just after the routing is done for the packet.

NF_IP_FORWARD. This is a firewall hook for the packets that needs to be forwarded through different interface. This hook is installed for the packets that arrive at one interface and needs to be transmitted through different interface. The Linux machine should be acting as a router for this hook to be in place.

16.2 NETFILTER HOOKS ON IP STACK

In this section we will see where on the IP stack we have firewall check posts installed. First we will discuss the path for packets generated locally and then we will discuss the incoming packets. Netfilter posts on an IP stack are shown in Fig. 16.1. We will keep it very simple to just show a minimal number of netfilter entries.

16.2.1 Hooks for Outgoing Packets

After being processed by the higher protocol layers (TCP/UDP), packets need to find a route to the destination. A packet is sent to the IP layer, where a route is

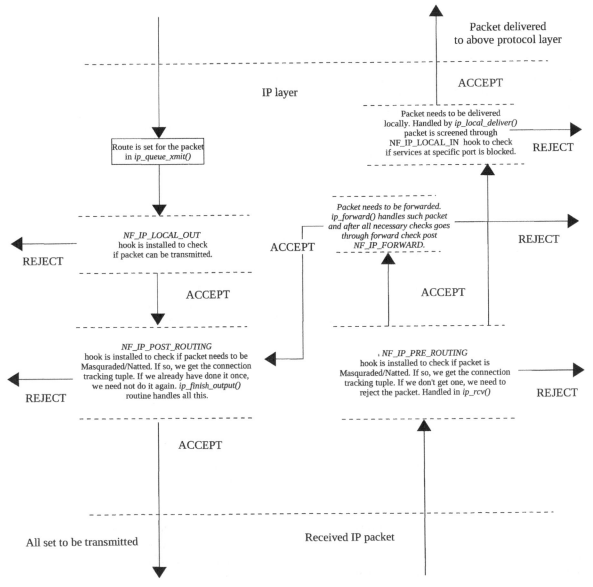

Figure 16.1. Firewall hooks installed on IP stack.

```
net/ipv4/ip_output.c

339 int ip_queue_xmit(struct sk_buff *skb)
340 {
341     struct sock *sk = skb->sk;
        ....
399
400     return NF_HOOK(PF_INET, NF_IP_LOCAL_OUT, skb, NULL, rt->u.dst.dev,
401              ip_queue_xmit2);
402
        ....
406     return -EHOSTUNREACH;
407 }
```

cs 16.4. *ip_queue_xmit()*.

```
net/ipv4/ip_output.c

184 __inline__ int ip_finish_output(struct sk_buff *skb)
185 {
186     struct net_device *dev = skb->dst->dev;
        ....
191     return NF_HOOK(PF_INET, NF_IP_POST_ROUTING, skb, NULL, dev,
192              ip_finish_output2);
193 }
```

cs 16.5. *ip_finish_output()*.

found for the packet and an IP header is built based on the routing information. This is done in *ip_queue_xmit()* (cs 16.4). Once a header for IP is built, the packet is screened by the firewall hook *NF_IP_LOCAL_OUT*. At this point in time, we need to check if the packet from source port/IP is allowed to be routed through the path. We also check whether we can send out packets to a given destination and also make a request for a service running on the specified destination. If the hook fails to acknowledge the packet, it is dropped.

If we are through with the first check post, we need to go through one more check post finally before putting the packet on the device queue for final transmission. This one is generally used for the NAT/Masquerading purpose but can also be used by IPsec modules to have their own hooks installed here. This check is done in *ip_finish_output()* (cs 16.5).

If the firewall policy allows, we finally transmit the segment. Otherwise we drop the segment at this level.

16.2.2 Hooks for Incoming Packets

Once the packet is received and is identified as IP datagram, the *ip_rcv()* routine handles this (cs 16.6). It does all the sanity checks on the IP header and finally sends the packet through the very first firewall hook *NF_IP_PRE_ROUTING*. Here we can perform NAT/Masquerading-related demultiplexing. Also, this can be used to implement IP sec.

Once we are through with the hook, the next step is to check if the packet needs to be delivered locally or it needs to be forwarded. If the packet belongs to the local process, it needs to go through another hook *NF_IP_LOCAL_IN* that is installed

```
net/ipv4/ip_input.c

379 int ip_rcv(struct sk_buff *skb, struct net_device *dev, struct packet_type *380 {
381      struct iphdr *iph;
              ....
437      return NF_HOOK(PF_INET, NF_IP_PRE_ROUTING, skb, dev, NULL,
438              ip_rcv_finish);
              ....
446 }
```

cs 16.6. ip_rcv().

```
net/ipv4/ip_input.c

290 int ip_local_deliver(struct sk_buff *skb)
291 {
              ....
302      return NF_HOOK(PF_INET, NF_IP_LOCAL_IN, skb, skb->dev, NULL,
303              ip_local_deliver_finish);
304 }
```

cs 16.7. ip_local_deliver().

```
net/ipv4/ip_forward.c

 73 int ip_forward(struct sk_buff *skb)
 74 {
 75      struct net_device *dev2;      /* Output device */
              ....
145      return NF_HOOK(PF_INET, NF_IP_FORWARD, skb, skb->dev, dev2,
146              ip_forward_finish);
              ....
163 drop:
164      kfree_skb(skb);
165      return NET_RX_DROP;
166 }
```

cs 16.8. ip_forward().

in *ip_local_deliver()* (cs 16.7). Here we may have firewall filters based on source and destination IP/port.

In case the received packet needs to be forwarded, the situation is handled by *ip_forward()* (cs 16.8). Here IP firewall rules will be installed to check if the packet is allowed to be routed. If allowed, it needs to go through one more hook *NF_IP_POST_ROUTING*. We treat forwarded packets as if they are generated locally before transmitting it over the wire. This is required because the packet may require NATing/Masquerading. Also, if all the packets being forwarded through this router needs to be encrypted, we take care of it in the *NF_IP_POST_ROUTING* hook.

16.3   OVERVIEW OF NETFILTER HOOKS ON LINUX TCP-IP STACK

16.4   REGISTRATION OF NETFILTER HOOKS

Until now we have seen how netfilter hooks are installed on the IP stack. We need to know how these firewall hooks work. These hooks are first registered from the

```
net/core/netfilter.c

60 int nf_register_hook(struct nf_hook_ops *reg)
61 {
62     struct list_head *i;
63
64     br_write_lock_bh(BR_NETPROTO_LOCK);
65     for (i = nf_hooks[reg->pf][reg->hooknum].next;
66         i != &nf_hooks[reg->pf][reg->hooknum];
67         i = i->next) {
68             if (reg->priority < ((struct nf_hook_ops *)i)->priority)
69                     break;
70     }
71     list_add(&reg->list, i->prev);
72     br_write_unlock_bh(BR_NETPROTO_LOCK);
73     return 0;
74 }
```

cs 16.9. nf_register_hook().

```
include/linux/netfilter_ipv4.h

52 enum nf_ip_hook_priorities {
53     NF_IP_PRI_FIRST = INT_MIN,
54     NF_IP_PRI_CONNTRACK = -200,
55     NF_IP_PRI_MANGLE = -150,
56     NF_IP_PRI_NAT_DST = -100,
57     NF_IP_PRI_FILTER = 0,
58     NF_IP_PRI_NAT_SRC = 100,
59     NF_IP_PRI_LAST = INT_MAX,
60 };
```

cs 16.10. Netfilter hook priorities.

modules that implement them. The interface to register hooks is *nf_register_ hook()*(cs 16.9). We need to hold *BR_NETPROTO_LOCK* write lock to register the hook. As discussed in Section 16.1, *nf_hooks* is a global table that registers hooks for a different protocol family.

We need to register object *nf_hook_ops* as a netfilter hook. We will look at the structure later, but first we will see what the registration routine does. Object *list_ head* is embedded in *nf_hook_ops* object. We have more than one netfilter hook registerd for a given hook type and protocol family. These hooks are linked through the chain *nf_hooks[pf][hooknum]*, where *pf* is the protocol family and *hooknum* is the hook type that we will discuss in Section 16.5.3 for IP. We insert a hook in the chain according to the hook priority defined by the *priority* field of object *nf_hook_ ops*. We loop through each entry in the chain; and once we find a hook with priority higher than the priority of the hook being registered (line 68, cs 16.9), we insert the hook prior to that hook in the list. Lower value of *priority* means higher priority, line 71 (cs 16.9).

The hooks are arranged in the chain according to their priority. Packets are passed through each hook in the order that they are arranged in the chain, which means that packet is passed through the highest-priority hook first and then pass through lower-priority hooks. The reason for this is the order in which certain tasks need to be performed. It is not necessary that hooks with all the priority mentioned in cs- 16.10 is part of same hook type. But hooks with priorities *NF_IP_PRI_CONN-*

TRACK and *NF_IP_PRI_NAT_DST* can be registered for the same hook number and protocol family, which means that they can exist in the same chain arranged according to their priority. The hook with priority *NF_IP_PRI_CONNTRACK* will be the first to be processed because it tracks the connection for the NAT packet; and then the hook with priority *NF_IP_PRI_NAT_DST* (cs- 16.10) is processed, which modifies the destination of IP datagram for NAT.

16.5   PROCESSING OF NETFILTER HOOKS

In Section 16.1 we discussed the macro NF_HOOK. Macro acts as entry point to netfilter hook processing for a packet. We check if the entry for a particular hook type and protocol family exists in the *nf_hooks* global table, and we go through each hook that is registered for the hook type by calling *nf_hook_slow()*.

16.5.1   *nf_hook_slow()*

In this routine we do some sanity check on the packet buffer *(sk_buff)* and IP header. We call *nf_iterate()* at line 483 (cs-16.11) to process the packet through all the registered hooks. The routine returns the verdict that indicates what do do with the packet. If the verdict is *NF_DROP*, it means that the packet was rejected by one of the hooks. So, we drop the packet. If the verdict is *NF_ACCEPT*, our packet

```
net/core/netfilter.c

449 int nf_hook_slow(int pf, unsigned int hook, struct sk_buff *skb,
450            struct net_device *indev,
451            struct net_device *outdev,
452            int (*okfn)(struct sk_buff *))
453 {
454     struct list_head *elem;
        ....
482     elem = &nf_hooks[pf][hook];
483     verdict = nf_iterate(&nf_hooks[pf][hook], &skb, hook, indev,
484             outdev, &elem, okfn);
485     if (verdict == NF_QUEUE) {
486         NFDEBUG("nf_hook: Verdict = QUEUE.\n");
487         nf_queue(skb, elem, pf, hook, indev, outdev, okfn);
488     }
489
490     switch (verdict) {
491     case NF_ACCEPT:
492         ret = okfn(skb);
493         break;
494
495     case NF_DROP:
496         kfree_skb(skb);
497         ret = -EPERM;
498         break;
499     }
500
501     br_read_unlock_bh(BR_NETPROTO_LOCK);
502     return ret;
503 }
```

cs 16.11. *nf_hook_slow()*.

is accepted by all the hooks registered and we need to proceed further by making a call to the callback routine *okfn* at line 492.

16.5.2 *nf_iterate()*

This routine processes the packet through all the registered hooks, lines 347–372. In each iteration, the callback routine for the hook is used to process the packet, line 349 (cs 16.12). The *hook* field of the object *nf_hook_ops* points to the callback routine. The result of the hook processing is the verdict that decides what action needs to be taken next. If the verdict at any stage is *NF_QUEUE, NF_STOLEN* or *NF_DROP*, we return with these values to the caller, which means that the decision of higher-priority hooks will be considered final.

> *NF_QUEUE* means that the hook wants the packet to be queued for asynchronous processing later.
> *NF_STOLEN* means that the hook has already processed the packet and it need not go through rest of the hooks.
> *NF_DROP* means that hook has rejected the packet.

The processing is aborted as soon as we need to drop the packet as it is rejected by high-priority hook. We continue to process the hooks, if hooks in each iteration

```
net/core/netfilter.c

339  static unsigned int nf_iterate(struct list_head *head,
340                       struct sk_buff **skb,
341                       int hook,
342                       const struct net_device *indev,
343                       const struct net_device *outdev,
344                       struct list_head **i,
345                       int (*okfn)(struct sk_buff *))
346  {
347      for (*i = (*i)->next; *i != head; *i = (*i)->next) {
348          struct nf_hook_ops *elem = (struct nf_hook_ops *)*i;
349          switch (elem->hook(hook, skb, indev, outdev, okfn)) {
350          case NF_QUEUE:
351              return NF_QUEUE;
352
353          case NF_STOLEN:
354              return NF_STOLEN;
355
356          case NF_DROP:
357              return NF_DROP;
358
359          case NF_REPEAT:
360              *i = (*i)->prev;
361              break;
362
              ....
371          }
372      }
373      return NF_ACCEPT;
374  }
```

cs 16.12. *nf_iterate()*.

```
include/linux/netfilter.h

44 struct nf_hook_ops
45 {
46        struct list_head list;
              ....
49        nf_hookfn *hook;
50        int pf;
51        int hooknum;
52        /* Hooks are ordered in ascending priority. */
53        int priority;
54 };
```

cs 16.13. netfilter hook operations registered with netfilter framework.

keeps accepting the packet. If the verdict is NF_REPEAT, we need to repeat processing the packet through the same hook.

16.5.3 *struct nf_hook_ops*

This structure defines the netfilter hook (cs 16.13).

> *list* is the embedded structure that links the hook to the chain of hooks registered for same protocol family and hook type in global array *nf_hooks*.
>
> *pf* is the protocol family for which the hook should be applied.
>
> *hooknum* is the type of hook—for example, *NF_IP_POST_ROUTING*.
>
> *priority* is the priority associated with the hook. It decides the position of the hook in the chain and the order in which the hook will be processed in the chain.

16.6 COMPATIBILITY FRAMEWORK

Ipchains is an old-style firewall that works with a compatibility framework which allows only a single firewall installed using this framework. The framework is called compatibility. It requires a compat module to be installed on the system. The compatibility framework requires a firewall to register itself by calling *register_firewall()* (cs 16.14).

The object of type *firewall_ops* needs to be registered with the compat framework. The global variable fwops is made to point to the the registered firewall *firewall_ops* object at line 62 (cs 16.14). The check at line 57 (cs 16.14) makes sure that only a single firewall can be registered with the framework. *firewall_ops* has pointers to set of callback routines that implement firewall check posts for minimum entry, exit, and forwarding points.

The compat framework registers a single set of hooks for any firewall registered with it. *NF_IP_PRE_ROUTING, NF_IP_POST_ROUTING*, and *NF_IP_FORWARD* are processed using a single point of entry, *fw_in()*. They all have the same priority, that is, NF_IP_PRI_FILTER. The required functionality for each of these hooks is separately handled in *fw_in()*, depending on the hook type. The *NF_IP_LOCAL_IN* hook is handled separately by *fw_confirm()*. *fw_confirm()* is used to track connections for the received in the case of masqueraded packets.

```
net/ipv4/netfilter/ip_fw_compat.c

51 int register_firewall(int pf, struct firewall_ops *fw)
52 {
          ....
57      if (fwops) {
58          printk("Attempt to register multiple firewall modules.\n");
59          return -EBUSY;
60      }
61
62      fwops = fw;
63      return 0;
64 }
```

cs 16.14. register_firewall().

```
net/ipv4/netfilter/ip_fw_compat.c

223 static struct nf_hook_ops preroute_ops
224 = { { NULL, NULL }, fw_in, PF_INET, NF_IP_PRE_ROUTING, NF_IP_PRI_FILTER };
225
226 static struct nf_hook_ops postroute_ops
227 = { { NULL, NULL }, fw_in, PF_INET, NF_IP_POST_ROUTING, NF_IP_PRI_FILTER };
228
229 static struct nf_hook_ops forward_ops
230 = { { NULL, NULL }, fw_in, PF_INET, NF_IP_FORWARD, NF_IP_PRI_FILTER };
231
232 static struct nf_hook_ops local_in_ops
233 = { { NULL, NULL }, fw_confirm, PF_INET, NF_IP_LOCAL_IN, NF_IP_PRI_LAST - 1 };
```

cs 16.15. Compat netfilter hooks.

Later we will see in $fw\_in()$ that $NF\_IP\_PRE\_ROUTING$ maps to an incoming check post, $NF\_IP\_POST\_ROUTING$ maps to an outgoing check post, and forwarding is as usual. According to current netfilter hook arrangements on the IP stack, $NF\_IP\_PRE\_ROUTING$ is the first check post for the packets entering the system and $NF\_IP\_POST\_ROUTING$ is the final check post for the packets leaving the system. (cs-16.15)

If hooks only from compat framework are installed, we will have all the filtering done for incoming packets before routing decisions are taken and for the outgoing packets after routing is done, whereas we see that the filtering of packets is done at a much different stage, with the latest hooks depending on whether it needs to be delivered locally or needs to be forwarded.

16.6.1 *fw_in()* (see cs 16.16 unless mentioned)

This is a callback routine to execute netfilter hooks registered with a compat firewall framework. This is a common routine for incoming, outgoing, and forwarding hooks. Depending on the hook type, firewall-specific input, output, and forwarding routines are called to execute the hook. If we are processing an $NF\_IP\_PRE\_ROUTING$ hook for the registered firewall, then the $fwops{\rightarrow}fw\_input$ input callback routine is used to process the hook (line 111, cs 16.16). For an $NF\_IP\_POST\_ROUTING$ hook, an $fwops{\rightarrow}$ an fw_output output callback routine is used to process the hook (line 126). For an $NF\_IP\_FORWARD$ hook, an $fwops{\rightarrow}fw\_forward$ forward callback routine is used to process the hook (line 120).

```
net/ipv4/netfilter/ip_fw_compat.c
72 static unsigned int
73 fw_in(unsigned int hooknum,
74    struct sk_buff **pskb,
75    const struct net_device *in,
76    const struct net_device *out,
77    int (*okfn)(struct sk_buff *))
78 {
79    int ret = FW_BLOCK;
      ....
97    switch (hooknum) {
98    case NF_IP_PRE_ROUTING:
          ....
111       ret = fwops->fw_input(fwops, PF_INET, (struct net_device *)in,
112                   (*pskb)->nh.raw, &redirpt, pskb);
113       break;
114
115   case NF_IP_FORWARD:
          ....
118       if ((*pskb)->nfct)
119           ret = FW_ACCEPT;
120       else ret = fwops->fw_forward(fwops, PF_INET,
121                   (struct net_device *)out,
122                   (*pskb)->nh.raw, &redirpt, pskb);
123       break;
124
125   case NF_IP_POST_ROUTING:
126       ret = fwops->fw_output(fwops, PF_INET,
127                   (struct net_device *)out,
128                   (*pskb)->nh.raw, &redirpt, pskb);
129       if (ret == FW_ACCEPT || ret == FW_SKIP) {
130           if (fwops->fw_acct_out)
131               fwops->fw_acct_out(fwops, PF_INET,
132                       (struct net_device *)out,
133                       (*pskb)->nh.raw, &redirpt,
134                       pskb);
          ....
137           if (ip_conntrack_confirm(*pskb) == NF_DROP)
138               ret = FW_BLOCK;
139       }
140       break;
141   }
142
143   switch (ret) {
144   case FW_REJECT: {
          ....
150       struct iphdr *iph = (*pskb)->nh.iph;
151
152       if ((*pskb)->dst != NULL
153           || ip_route_input(*pskb, iph->daddr, iph->saddr, iph->tos,
154               (struct net_device *)in) == 0)
155           icmp_send(*pskb, ICMP_DEST_UNREACH, ICMP_PORT_UNREACH,
156               0);
157       return NF_DROP;
158   }
159
160   case FW_ACCEPT:
161   case FW_SKIP:
162       if (hooknum == NF_IP_PRE_ROUTING) {
163           check_for_demasq(pskb);
164           check_for_redirect(*pskb);
165       } else if (hooknum == NF_IP_POST_ROUTING) {
166           check_for_unredirect(*pskb);
167           /* Handle ICMP errors from client here */
168           if ((*pskb)->nh.iph->protocol == IPPROTO_ICMP
169               && (*pskb)->nfct)
170               check_for_masq_error(*pskb);
171       }
172       return NF_ACCEPT;
173
174   case FW_MASQUERADE:
175       if (hooknum == NF_IP_FORWARD)
176           return do_masquerade(pskb, out);
177       else return NF_ACCEPT;
178
179   case FW_REDIRECT:
180       if (hooknum == NF_IP_PRE_ROUTING)
181           return do_redirect(*pskb, in, redirpt);
182       else return NF_ACCEPT;
183
184   default:
185       /* FW_BLOCK */
186       return NF_DROP;
187   }
188 }
```

cs 16.16. *fw_in()*.

These routines will return the final verdict as to what action should be taken on the packet after the packet is screened through the filters. The verdict is also known as a target for the filters. Let's see how verdicts are processed.

FW_REJECT. This verdict is set when the packet is rejected by the firewall policy. This verdict is similar to a drop where the packet is dropped except we try to send out an ICMP error message if the route for the source of the packet is known, line 155. If the route is not set for the packet, we try to get a route by calling *ip_route_input()* at line 153.

FW_ACCEPT and FW_SKIP. These verdicts are interpreted in the same way. *FW_SKIP* means that we should move to the next rule. Sometimes a hook may return this verdict. In this case, we need to perform some more tasks. If the hook for which we came here is *NF_IP_PRE_ROUTING*, we have received a packet and may need to demasquerade before we can send this to IP layer for routing by calling *check_for_demasq()* at line 163. We also need to check if the connection was redirected by calling *check_for_redirect()* at line 164. For redirected connections we maintain a table of all the connection that maps original tuple source IP/source port/destination port/ destination IP with new source IP/port. For the received we check if it belonged to a redirected connection by checking the entry in the table. If so, we need to change the destination port/IP before we go for routing for the incoming packet for this redirected connection.

In case we are processing an *NF_IP_POST_ROUTING* hook, we need to do the reverse of what we did for hook *NF_IP_POST_ROUTING*. If the packet belongs to a redirected connection, the source IP/port needs to be changed in the IP/TCP headers with the new values by calling *check_for_unredirect()*.

FW_MASQUERADE. Linux implements masquerading through a netfilter because it is an extended feature of an IP stack. The filter may require packets going through a certain interface to be masqueraded. So, we masquerade the connection here by calling *do_masquerade()* at line 176 only if the we are processing an *NF_IP_FORWARD* hook. The routine checks if we are already part of the connection or we need to create a new masqueraded connection. It would return its own verdict for the packet.

FW_REDIRECT. Once again redirection of connections is also done using a netfilter framework. For a compat framework, we need to redirect a connection if the policy for the rule is set to *FW_REDIRECT*.

The default case is to drop the packet.

16.7 IP CHAINS

Ipchains is a firewall implementation that works with a compat framework. The scope of the discussion is limited to design and implementation of ip chains. We won't discuss how rules are set by the user land. A firewall is registered with the compat framework when an ipchains module is initialized by calling *register_firewall()* at line 1740 (cs 16.17).

```
net/ipv4/netfilter/ipchains_core.c

1722 int ipfw_init_or_cleanup(int init)
1723 {
          ....
1740      ret = register_firewall(PF_INET, &ipfw_ops);
          ....
1780      return ret;
1781 }
```

<u>cs 16.17.</u> *ipfw_init_or_cleanup()*.

```
net/ipv4/netfilter/ipchains_core.c

1712 struct firewall_ops ipfw_ops=
1713 {
1714      NULL,
1715      ipfw_forward_check,
1716      ipfw_input_check,
1717      ipfw_output_check,
1718      NULL,
1719      NULL
1720 };
```

<u>cs 16.18.</u> Firewall operations registered with a compat framework.

ipfw_ops is an object that implements an ip chain firewall. There are three routines registered for ipchain (cs 16.18):

- *ipfw_forward_check()* implements a forward hook.
- *ipfw_input_check()* implements a hook for incoming traffic.
- *ipfw_output_check()* implements a hook for outgoing traffic.

ip_fw_check() is a common routine called from all these registered routines with specific netfilter hook numbers.

16.7.1   Filtering with Ipchains

The way ipchains works is that it has a chain of filter rules that is traversed for the packet. If the packet matches any of these rules, it may require the packet to be passed through a different chain of rules as specified by the target for that rule. Once the packet has passed through the entire chain of rules in the branched chain, it needs to continue with the first chain of rules from where it branched.

Let's take an example of how rules are traversed and how we reach the final target for an IP packet. Suppose we get a TCP packet with destination port X2 and destination IP a.b.c.d and we need to process it through the firewall rule as shown in Fig. 16.2. The packet enters chain C0 for screening. It doesn't match rule 1. It is screened through rule 2. Since this is a TCP packet, R2 matches. The target for this rule is chain C1. We need to be screened through each rule in the chain C1. The first rule of C1 does not match, so we move down to the next rule R2 in same chain. Rule R2 also does not match, so we need to jump to chain C0 back and start our

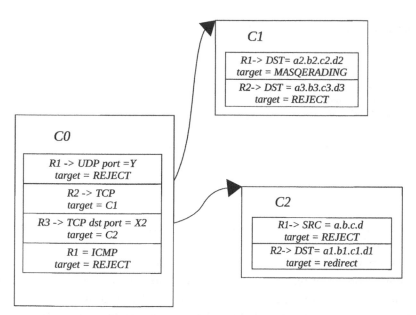

Figure 16.2. Ipchains rules and target.

```
net/ipv4/netfilter/ipchains_core.c

265 static struct ip_chain *ip_fw_chains;
266
267 #define IP_FW_INPUT_CHAIN ip_fw_chains
268 #define IP_FW_FORWARD_CHAIN (ip_fw_chains->next)
269 #define IP_FW_OUTPUT_CHAIN (ip_fw_chains->next->next)
```

cs 16.19. Firewall chains for ipchain framework.

screening from R3. R3 matches because we are a TCP packet with destination port X2. The target for this rule is chain C2. We need to screen the packet through rules in chain C2. The first rule in C2 matches the packet, and the target for this is REJECT. So, further screening of the packet is stopped and we reject the packet outrightly.

16.7.2 Ipchain Chain of Rules

ip_fw_chains points to the head of the list for different ipchain firewall hooks. The ipchain firewall chain of rules is defined as *struct ip_chain*. There are three different chains for each firewall hook. These are defined as *IP_FW_INPUT_CHAIN* for incoming packets, *IP_FW_FORWARD_CHAIN* for forwarded packets, and *IP_FW_OUTPUT_CHAIN* for outgoing packets (cs 16.19). Only input chain points to the head of the list rest can be accessed by *next* field of object *ip_chain*. Implementation of *ipchain* rules and chains is shown in Fig. 16.3.

16.7.3 *struct ip_chain*

This is the main table that defines filter rules for a specific hook (cs 16.20). Each firewall hook will have one *ip_chain* object. It has following fields:

```
net/ipv4/netfilter/ipchains_core.c

234 struct ip_chain
235 {
236      ip_chainlabel label;
237      struct ip_chain *next;
238      struct ip_fwkernel *chain;
239      __u32 refcount;
240      int policy;
241
242      struct ip_reent reent[0];
243 };
```

cs 16.20. Ipchain main table.

label is the name of the hook to which this object belongs. Rule for any table is modified by using this label.

next is a pointer to the table for next firewall hook.

chain is an object of type *ip_fwkernel*. This object defines rules for the hook.

refcount is the reference counter for the hook. Each hook is registered individully and may be referred in many places. So, we need to keep track of the references for the object so that we unregister only when reference count drops down to 0.

policy is the default policy for the hook.

recent points to the end of the object *ip_chain*. An object of type *ip_reent* is attached to the end of this structure. There one *ip_reent* object per CPU.

16.7.4 struct ip_fwkernel

This object defines packet filter rules (cs 16.21). There is a chain of such rules for a hook linked by the *next* field of the structure.

ipfw is the object of type *ip_fw*. This structure contains the information about the filter rule.

branch is a pointer to an object *ip_chain*. Whenever a rule matches, this field decides about the next rule for the packet.

simplebranch just tells what to do in case the branch is not set and we match the rule. The value indicates either to branch off the chain or proceed with the next rule in the chain.

```
net/ipv4/netfilter/ipchains_core.c

216 struct ip_fwkernel
217 {
218      struct ip_fw ipfw;
219      struct ip_fwkernel *next;
220
221      struct ip_chain *branch;
222
223      int simplebranch;
224      struct ip_counters counters[0];
225 };
```

cs 16.21. Ipchain filter rule.

```
net/ipv4/netfilter/ipchains_core.c

227 struct ip_reent
228 {
229      struct ip_chain *prevchain;
230      struct ip_fwkernel *prevrule;
231      struct ip_counters counters;
232 };
```

cs 16.22. Back pointer management for ipchains.

```
include/linux/netfilter_ipv4/ipchains_core.h

35 struct ip_fw
36 {
37      struct in_addr fw_src, fw_dst;
38      struct in_addr fw_smsk, fw_dmsk;
39      __u32 fw_mark;
40      __u16 fw_proto;
41      __u16 fw_flg;
42      __u16 fw_invflg;
43      __u16 fw_spts[2];
44      __u16 fw_dpts[2];
45      __u16 fw_redirpt;
46      __u16 fw_outputsize;
47
48      char      fw_vianame[IFNAMSIZ];
49      __u8      fw_tosand, fw_tosxor;
50 };
```

cs 16.23. Packet match for rule.

ip_counters points to the end of the object *ip_fwkernel*. At the end of this structure we have storage for an *ip_counters* object.

This is one per CPU for better cache locality. The object keeps account of the number of packets filtered and the number of bytes in each IP datagram.

16.7.5 *struct ip_reent*

This structure keeps the back pointer to the chain and the rule whenever we branch off from the current chain (cs 16.22). Ths is required to jump back to the previous chain once all the filter rules are covered in the branched chain. This object is stored at the end of the object *ip_chain*, and it exists per CPU for cache locality purpose.

prevchain is the back pointer to the chain from where we have branched.

prevrule is the pointer to the next rule that needs to be accessed on the chain from where we have branched after we jump back to that chain.

16.7.6 *struct ip_fw*

This structure keeps all the required information for the filter rule to be matched (cs 16.23).

fw_dst & *fw_src* are destination and source IP addresses.

fw_smsk & *fw_dmsk* netmask for source and destination IP addresses.

fw_proto is the protocol field in the IP header, that is, TCP/UDP.

fw_spts is the range of source port addresses to match.

fw_dpts is the range of destination port addresses to match.

fw_redirect is the port to which the packet is redirected in case it is required.

fw_vianame is the name of the interface to be matched for the firewall rule.

fw_invflg is the flag per match entities that inverse the match rule. For example, if the match rule says anything other than source IP, a.b.c.d will have the flag on for source ip.

fw_flg is the flag to indicate special match entities that are not mentioned in the structure, such as match SYN packet, rule for fragment, and so on.

16.7.7 Organization of Tables in Ipchains

Figure 16.3 represent kernel data structures that are linked together to implement ip chains filters.

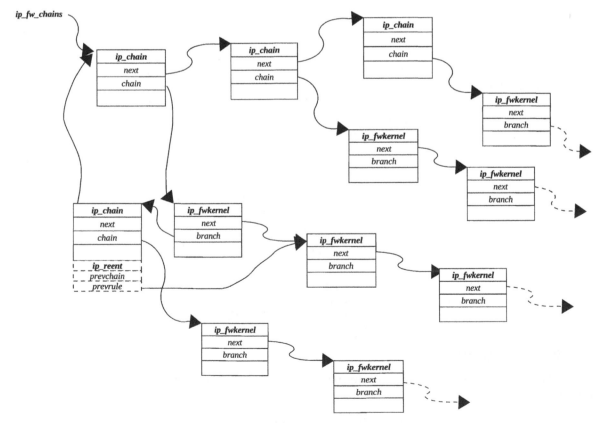

Figure 16.3. Ipchains filter rules and chains.

16.8 HOW IS THE PACKET FILTERED WITH IPCHAINS

In Section 16.7.2 we saw that there are three netfilter hooks registered by ip chains to filter incoming, outgoing, and forwarded packets. A common routine that handles filtering in all three cases is *ip_fw_check()*. This is the place where the packet is passed through all the filters, and the fate of the packet is decided. Let's see how this is done.

16.8.1 *ip_fw_check()*

We have a packet to be filtered and the hook-specific filter chain passed to this routine. We need to keep a scanning packet until we find a target for the filter rule or we have ended scanning all the rules. We access the filter rule chain at line 713 (cs 16.24). There are two loops.

- The outer loop keeps us iterating (line 714–787) until we find the final target or we have completed the entire search and no target is found, condition at line 787.
- The inner loop loops through the filter rule chain and comes out only if we have found a matching rule or no matching rule is found and we have completed scanning through all the rules, lines 716–731.

Before processing the chain of rules, we need to do some groundwork like extracting IP address, port numbers, flag fragments, SYN segments, and so on.

Processing in Inner Loop. We traverse through the filer rules in the current chain. In each iteration, we match filter rules by calling *ip_rule_match()* at line 718. If we don't match the rule, we move on to the next rule in the chain by accessing *next* field of the object *ip_fwkernel*. We come out of the loop only if we have covered the entire chain or we matched the rule.

If we have come out of the loop because we have been scanned through the entire chain of rules and we didn't match any of the rules, then we need to check if the chain we are processing is the one we have branched to. In case this is a branched chain, the *prevchain* field of *reent* object for current CPU must hold a valid back pointer to the chain from where we jumped (line 772). We need to jump back to the previous chain (line 775) and start from the rule next to the one where we left the chain (line 774). We reset the pointer to the previous chain in this case at line 776. Now we continue traversing the chain of rules from the previous chain as usual in the inner loop. In the case where the pointer to previous chain is not set, we are in the root chain. In this case, we take the default policy set for the chain as the final verdict, line 779. We account for the packet count and length of IP datagram scanned through the chain, lines 781–782. We come out of the outer loop after complete scanning.

In case we have come out of the loop because we found matching rule for the packet, we need to find target for the the rule for further processing. If a *branch* field is set, we need to jump to that chain for further processing (line 756). The next rule to be scanned on the chain is taken from the branched chain (line 757). We also need to store the back pointer to the current chain and next rule to be scanned on the current chain in the *reent* object of the branched chain, lines 752–754. We do

```
net/ipv4/netfilter/ipchains_core.c
573 static int
574 ip_fw_check(struct iphdr *ip,
575         const char *rif,
576         __u16 *redirport,
577         struct ip_chain *chain,
578         struct sk_buff *skb,
579         unsigned int slot,
580         int testing)
581 {
        ....
713     f = chain->chain;
714     do {
715         count = 0;
716         for (; f; f = f->next) {
717             count++;
718             if (ip_rule_match(f,rif,ip,
719                         tcpsyn,src_port,dst_port,offset)) {
                    ....
729                 break;
730             }
731         }
732         if (f) {
733             if (f->branch) {
                    ....
737                 if (f->branch->reent[slot].prevchain) {
738                     if (!testing) {
                            ....
744                         cleanup(chain, 1, slot);
745                         ret = FW_BLOCK;
746                     } else {
747                         cleanup(chain, 0, slot);
748                         ret = FW_SKIP+1;
749                     }
750                 }
751                 else {
752                     f->branch->reent[slot].prevchain
753                         = chain;
754                     f->branch->reent[slot].prevrule
755                         = f->next;
756                     chain = f->branch;
757                     f = chain->chain;
758                 }
759             }
760             else if (f->simplebranch == FW_SKIP)
761                 f = f->next;
762             else if (f->simplebranch == FW_SKIP+1) {
763                 /* Just like falling off the chain */
764                 goto fall_off_chain;
765             } else {
766                 cleanup(chain, 0, slot);
767                 ret = f->simplebranch;
768             }
769         } /* f == NULL */
770         else {
771         fall_off_chain:
772             if (chain->reent[slot].prevchain) {
773                 struct ip_chain *tmp = chain;
774                 f = chain->reent[slot].prevrule;
775                 chain = chain->reent[slot].prevchain;
776                 tmp->reent[slot].prevchain = NULL;
777             }
778             else {
779                 ret = chain->policy;
780                 if (!testing) {
781                     chain->reent[slot].counters.pcnt++;
782                     chain->reent[slot].counters.bcnt
783                         += ntohs(ip->tot_len);
784                 }
785             }
786         }
787     } while (ret == FW_SKIP+2);
788
789 out:
790     if (!testing) FWC_READ_UNLOCK(&ip_fw_lock);
        ...
811     return ret;
        ...
813 }
```

cs 16.24. ip_fw_check().

this so that if none of the rules match in the branched chain, we need to return to the chain from where we branched off and start scanning the next rule in the chain from where we left. In case *branch* is not set, we check from the *simplebranch* field what to do next. If this field is set to *FW_SKIP*, we may need to skip to the next filter rule in the chain. If the value is set to *FW_SKIP+1*, we need to branch off from the current chain at line 764, which means that we should stop scanning the current list so either we branch or stop scanning further. For any other value, we just need to check if we need to exit further scanning. We clear back pointer information for the CPU slot from the current chain at line 766.

16.8.2 *ip_rule_match()*

The rule matching is done here (cs 16.25). Object *ip_fwkernel* is the rule structure containing all the rules to be matched. Macro FWINV is one smart way to handle inverse rules. The inverse rules signifies *anything other than the match*. The *fw_invflag* field of object *ip_fwkernel* has one bit for each inverse rule entity. FWINV does both inverse and simple matching. The result of match is passed to the macro which is XORed with the inverse bit for the entity. If the inverse flag for that bit for the entity is set, the result of the match is inversed; otherwise it remains the same. If any of the rule doesn't match, we return.

First we start with matching source and destination IP/network IDs at line 295. If the mask is set to all 1s, we are exactly matching the IP address, otherwise we compare the network IDs. Next we do wild matching for the interface name whose packet is used only if the wild card flag (*IP_FW_F_WILDIF*) is set for the match at line 313. If the flag is not set, we do exact matching of the interface name at line 322. If the rule is set for the fragment (*IP_FW_F_FRAG* flags is set), we return if the packet is not fragmented at line 339. If the rule is set to test SYN packet (*IP_FW_F_TCPSYN* flag is set), we test it only if the packet is not fragmented, line 344. If the rule is set to filter a higher-layer protocol (*fw_proto* is set), we need to check the port against the port range set for TCP/UDP. *port_match()* matches the port only if the packet is not fragmented because only the first fragment contains the protocol header while the rest will contain only data. Otherwise, protocol port is matched against the port range specified in *fw_dpts* and *fw_spts* fields of object *ip_fwkernel*.

16.9 IPTABLES

Iptables is designed keeping in mind many of the shortcomings of ipchains. The scope of the discussion is limited to design and implementation of ipchains. We won't discuss how rules are set by the user land. We won't discuss here all those features but look at the design and implementation of iptables in the kernel.

1. The current design of ip tables is independent of any compat framework, which means that it doesn't need to be registered with the compatibility framework.
2. Memory management of the iptables is much better than those of ipchains.
3. Filter rules are traversed in a much more efficient way than ipchains.

```
net/ipv4/netfilter/ipchains_core.c
 281 static int ip_rule_match(struct ip_fwkernel *f,
 282                const char *ifname,
 283                struct iphdr *ip,
 284                char tcpsyn,
 285                __u16 src_port, __u16 dst_port,
 286                char isfrag)
 287 {
 288 #define FWINV(bool,invflg) ((bool) ^ !!(f->ipfw.fw_invflg & invflg))
     ....
 295     if (FWINV((ip->saddr&f->ipfw.fw_smsk.s_addr) != f->ipfw.fw_src.s_addr,
 296         IP_FW_INV_SRCIP)
 297       || FWINV((ip->daddr&f->ipfw.fw_dmsk.s_addr)!=f->ipfw.fw_dst.s_addr,
 298           IP_FW_INV_DSTIP)) {
     ....
 307       return 0;
 308     }
     ....
 313     if (f->ipfw.fw_flg & IP_FW_F_WILDIF) {
 314       if (FWINV(strncmp(ifname, f->ipfw.fw_vianame,
 315             strlen(f->ipfw.fw_vianame)) != 0,
 316           IP_FW_INV_VIA)) {
     ....
 319         return 0;      /* Mismatch */
 320       }
 321     }
 322     else if (FWINV(strcmp(ifname, f->ipfw.fw_vianame) != 0,
 323           IP_FW_INV_VIA)) {
     ....
 327       return 0;   /* Mismatch */
 328     }
     ....
 336     if (FWINV((f->ipfw.fw_flg&IP_FW_F_FRAG) && !isfrag, IP_FW_INV_FRAG)) {
     ....
 339       return 0;
 340     }
     ....
 343     if (FWINV((f->ipfw.fw_flg&IP_FW_F_TCPSYN) && !tcpsyn, IP_FW_INV_SYN)
 344       || (isfrag && (f->ipfw.fw_flg&IP_FW_F_TCPSYN))) {
     ....
 347       return 0;
 348     }
 349
 350     if (f->ipfw.fw_proto) {
     ....
 356         if (FWINV(ip->protocol!=f->ipfw.fw_proto, IP_FW_INV_PROTO)) {
     ....
 360           return 0;
 361         }
     ....
 364         if (!port_match(f->ipfw.fw_spts[0],
 365               f->ipfw.fw_spts[1],
 366               src_port, isfrag,
 367               !!(f->ipfw.fw_invflg&IP_FW_INV_SRCPT))
 368           || !port_match(f->ipfw.fw_dpts[0],
 369                 f->ipfw.fw_dpts[1],
 370                 dst_port, isfrag,
 371                 !!(f->ipfw.fw_invflg
 372                   &IP_FW_INV_DSTPT))) {
     ....
 374           return 0;
 375         }
 376     }
     ....
 379     return 1;
 380 }
```

cs 16.25. ip_rule_match().

4. Per CPU filter tables have better cache locality and hence faster memory access, leading to faster processing.

16.9.1 Registration of Iptables Hooks

Iptables directly registers its default hooks and need not register itself with the compat framework. By default, it registers three hooks for local delivery, locally generated traffic, and forwarded traffic. *ipt_ops* array lists these hooks. *ipt_hook()* is a common hook callback routine for both locally delivered and locally generated outgoing traffic. The callback routine for forwarding a hook is *ipt_local_out_hook()* (cs 16.26). When we look at these routines, a common routine used to filter the traffic is *ipt_do_table()*.

These hooks are registered when the *iptables* module is initialized by calling *nf_register_hook()*. Each table associated with the iptables is registered with the iptables framework using *ipt_register_table()*. *ipt_tables* is the list head for all the tables registered with the iptables, which means that we can have different modules register their tables with iptable framework. It looks like management of filter tables for all those modules compatible with iptables is centralized and becomes simpler. *packet_filter* is a master table used to traverse through the filter rule.

16.10 IPTABLES FILTER RULES AND TARGET ORGANIZATION

A complete overview of iptables table organization is shown in Fig. 16.4.

```
net/ipv4/netfilter/iptable_filter.c

117 static struct nf_hook_ops ipt_ops[]
118 = { { { NULL, NULL }, ipt_hook, PF_INET, NF_IP_LOCAL_IN, NF_IP_PRI_FILTER },
119     { { NULL, NULL }, ipt_hook, PF_INET, NF_IP_FORWARD, NF_IP_PRI_FILTER },
120     { { NULL, NULL }, ipt_local_out_hook, PF_INET, NF_IP_LOCAL_OUT,
121          NF_IP_PRI_FILTER }
122 };
```

cs 16.26. Netfilter hooks for iptables.

```
net/ipv4/netfilter/iptable_filter.c

128 static int __init init(void)
129 {
130     int ret;
        ....
141     ret = ipt_register_table(&packet_filter);
        ....
146     ret = nf_register_hook(&ipt_ops[0]);
        ...
150     ret = nf_register_hook(&ipt_ops[1]);
        ...
154     ret = nf_register_hook(&ipt_ops[2]);
        ....
167     return ret;
168 }
```

cs 16.27. *init()* routine for iptables module.

```
include/linux/netfilter_ipv4/ip_tables.h

413 struct ipt_table
414 {
415        struct list_head list;
           ...
418        char name[IPT_TABLE_MAXNAMELEN];
           ...
421        struct ipt_replace *table;
           ...
424        unsigned int valid_hooks;
           ...
427        rwlock_t lock;
           ...
430        struct ipt_table_info *private;
           ....
433        struct module *me;
434 };
```

cs 16.28. Main table for iptable framework.

16.10.1 *struct ipt_table*

This is the table header that keeps pointers to the tables and gives an identity to the table. This is the structure that is registered with the iptable framework and is linked into *ipt_tables* (cs 16.28).

> *list* links the table with *ipt_tables* list.
>
> *name* is the name of the table.
>
> *table* is a pointer to the object that keeps complete information about the table and hook entries. The table is built from the information available in this object. Table is built in *ipt_register_table()*.
>
> *valid_hooks* is a field holds bits corresponding to the hooks supported by the table.
>
> *lock* is a read–writer spin lock held when we are accessing the table. For filtering we hold reader lock. While modifying we need to hold writers lock.
>
> *private* is a pointer to object *ipt_table_info* that keeps complete information about the hook entry tables.
>
> *me* points to the module to which the table belongs; otherwise this is NULL.

16.10.2 *struct ipt_table_info*

This structure keeps complete information about the table (cs 16.29). Tables are appended to the end of the object, and the table is replicated one per CPU for better cache locality. Then it has pointers to traverse the filter chain and manipulate the jumps.

> *size* is the size of the table. Since there is one copy of table per CPU, the size of each table should be the same.
>
> *number* is the total number of ipt rule entries in the table.
>
> *initial_entries* is the total number of entries at the time of initializing the table.

```
net/ipv4/netfilter/ip_tables.c

87 struct ipt_table_info
88 {
       ...
90     unsigned int size;
       ...
92     unsigned int number;
       ...
94     unsigned int initial_entries;
       ....
97     unsigned int hook_entry[NF_IP_NUMHOOKS];
98     unsigned int underflow[NF_IP_NUMHOOKS];
       ....
101    char entries[0] ____cacheline_aligned;
102 };
```

cs 16.29. Table information for iptable chains.

```
net/ipv4/netfilter/ip_tables.c

1380 int ipt_register_table(struct ipt_table *table)
1381 {
       ....
1388     newinfo = vmalloc(sizeof(struct ipt_table_info
1389               + SMP_ALIGN(table->table->size) * smp_num_cpus);
       ....
1395     memcpy(newinfo->entries, table->table->entries, table->table->size);
       ...
1433     list_prepend(&ipt_tables, table);
       ....
1443 }
```

cs 16.30. ipt_register_table().

hook_entry has an offset for each hook entry in the table. This is initialized at the time of registering the table in *translate_table()* by calling *check_entry_size_and_hooks()*.

underflow is the base entry points for each hook that contains standard targets. If all the rules are scanned through and no target is found, we come back to the base hook entry point for a standard target.

entries is the base of per CPU tables. When a new table is registered, the space for a hook entry table is allocated at the end of this object. If it is an SMP machine, the total space allocated is the *size of the table* times the number of CPUs (see Fig. 16.4).

cs 16.30 shows total space allocated at the time of registering new table is for object *ipt_table_info* + *size of the table* times number of CPUs at line 1388. So, object *ipt_table_info* and entry tables are at contiguous memory location. Entry table is copied at the end of the object *ipt_table_info* (line 1395), and later it will be replicated for each CPU. The new table is inserted in the list *ipt_tables* at line 1433.

cs 16.31 shows the table being replicated for each CPU in the loop 869–873. *translate_table()* is called from *ipt_register_table()*. We already have one copy of the table at the base of the table (*newinfo->entries*) before being called. So, we start

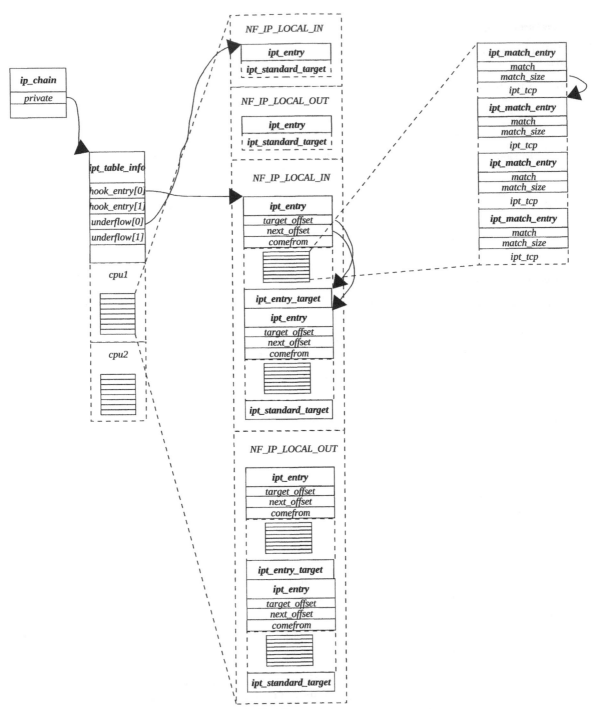

Figure 16.4. Iptables filter rules and chains.

replicating the table from *newinfo→entries* to the location that is a multiple of size
of the table from the base of the table for each CPU (line 870). The size of the table
is an SMP cache aligned at a 128-byte boundary for fast access of the table entry
points.

```
net/ipv4/netfilter/ip_tables.c

798 static int
799 translate_table(const char *name,
        ....
806 {
        ....
869     for (i = 1; i < smp_num_cpus; i++) {
870         memcpy(newinfo->entries + SMP_ALIGN(newinfo->size)*i,
871             newinfo->entries,
872             SMP_ALIGN(newinfo->size));
873     }
        ....
875     return ret;
876 }
```

cs 16.31. translate_table().

```
net/ipv4/netfilter/ip_tables.c

733 static inline int
734 check_entry_size_and_hooks(struct ipt_entry *e,
        ....
741 {
742     unsigned int h;
        ....
758     for (h = 0; h < NF_IP_NUMHOOKS; h++) {
759         if ((unsigned char *)e - base == hook_entries[h])
760             newinfo->hook_entry[h] = hook_entries[h];
761         if ((unsigned char *)e - base == underflows[h])
762             newinfo->underflow[h] = underflows[h];
763     }
        ....
773     return 0;
774 }
```

cs 16.32. check_entry_size_and_hooks().

cs 16.32 shows the way that *hook_entries* and underflows array are initialized. The creater of the table knows how the rules entry are organized for each hook. So, it supplies the offset for each hook entry points and also the offset for the standard target entry points for each hook. From *translate_table()* a macro *IPT_ENTRY_ ITERATE* is used to traverse through the entire table entries. For each entry, *check_entry_size_and_hooks()* is called to check if the user supplied values for entry points are correct (lines 759 and 761). If they are correct, we store the value in the table information base (line 760 and 762). Each time we are called, we have a pointer to the next entry in the table. The difference of the table base and the entry point is the offset of the entry from the table base.

16.10.3 *struct ipt_entry*

This is the entry point for the rule chain (cs 16.33). It contains a series of match rules objects of type *ipt_entry_match* at the end of the object *ipt_entry* to be matched. If we find the packet that matches the rule for the *ipt_entry* object, then we traverse through specific filter rules attached to the end of the *ipt_entry*. Finally we have a target at the end of the *ipt_entry* object as a whole (*ipt_entry*, including all the filter rules) (see Fig. 16.4).

```
include/linux/netfilter_ipv4/ip_tables.h

122 struct ipt_entry
123 {
124        struct ipt_ip ip;
              ....
127        unsigned int nfcache;
              ....
130        u_int16_t target_offset;
              ...
132        u_int16_t next_offset;
              .....
135        unsigned int comefrom;
              .....
138        struct ipt_counters counters;
              .....
141        unsigned char elems[0];
142 };
```

cs 16.33. Chain entry point for rules.

ipt_ip contains all the general information about the packet we are interested in. It keeps all the information about the packet we are interested in, along with data on interfaces, protocol, flags, and so on, in the same way object *ip_ fw* for ipchains. We have much better control on the interface wildcard check here using outiface_mask/iniface_mask fields, check *ip_packet_match()*. Once we find the packet of interest, we can proceed with more specific filter rules at the end of the *ipt_entry* object.

nfcache is the cache flags used for tracking connections and also for fragmented packets.

target_offset is the offset for the target object, *ipt_entry_target*, for the rule chain from the beginning of the *ipt_entry* object. This object is located at the end of the *ipt_entry* object. Since the size of the ipt_entry object is not known because of the number of filter rules of type *ipt_entry_match* attached to its tail, we need to have this offset to reach the target.

next_offset is the offset of the next table entry with respect to the current entry where the next rule chain is located. The reason is that *ipt_entry* has variable length because of its variable tail length.

comefrom stores the back pointer to the chain from where we branched off.

counters is used to keep account of the byte count and number of packets filtered.

elems is the head of the specific rule chain for the match entry. We add filter rules—that is, objects of type *ipt_entry_match* at the tail of *ipt_entry* object that can be accessed using *elems* field.

16.10.4 *struct ipt_entry_match*

This object contains information about protocol-specific matches (cs 16.34). It is divided into three parts:

1. The user part that contains the name of the match such as 'TCP,' 'UDP,' and 'ICMP.' Then it contains the length of the match size. The match size is the

```
include/linux/netfilter_ipv4/ip_tables.h

48 struct ipt_entry_match
49 {
50      union {
51          struct {
52              u_int16_t match_size;
            ....
55              char name[IPT_FUNCTION_MAXNAMELEN];
56          } user;
57          struct {
58              u_int16_t match_size;
            ....
61              struct ipt_match *match;
62          } kernel;
            ....
65          u_int16_t match_size;
66      } u;
67
68      unsigned char data[0];
69 };
```

cs 16.34. Match information for rule.

size of the object that defines the match for the match name. This is required when the user wants to add a protocol specific rule for a specific match name such as tcp, udp, and so on.

2. Kernel part, which contains size of the match which is same as the one for the user part and the pointer to the object. *ipt_match* contains a pointer to callback routines to process the match for the rule and to check the validity of the rule when the new rule is added. For each match name, its corresponding *ipt_match* object should be registered with the iptable framework. *ipt_match* maintains a list where each registered entry gets linked.

3. Data that contains a user-specified rule to be matched. This is appended at the tail of the object *ipt_entry_match*. For example for TCP, data should point to an object of type *ipt_tcp*. Similarly, for udp and icmp the matching object is *ipt_udp* and *ipt_icmp*, respectively.

16.10.5 *struct ipt_tcp* (cs 16.35)

The object contains information about the entities to be matched for TCP-specific filters.

spts is the source port range to be matched against source port in the TCP header.

dpts is the destination port range to be matched against destination port in the TCP header.

option is a field checks for any TCP options that are present in the TCP header such as SACK, timestamp, and so on.

flg_mask & *flg_cmp* are related to TCP flags in the header.

invflags is used to inverse the search pattern. Check *tcp_match()* for more details (cs 16.35).

```
include/linux/netfilter_ipv4/ip_tables.h

165 struct ipt_tcp
166 {
167        u_int16_t spts[2];
168        u_int16_t dpts[2];
169        u_int8_t option;
170        u_int8_t flg_mask;
171        u_int8_t flg_cmp;
172        u_int8_t invflags;
173 };
```

cs 16.35. Match for TCP-specific rule.

```
include/linux/netfilter_ipv4/ip_tables.h

94 struct ipt_standard_target
95 {
96        struct ipt_entry_target target;
97        int verdict;
98 };
```

cs 16.36. *standard target for chain.*

16.10.6   *struct ipt_entry_target*

This is the same as *ipt_entry_match* the only difference is that this object contains all the information specific to the target for the match rule.

16.10.7   *struct ipt_standard_target*

This structure is used as a standard target by the search rule. It is used either to jump to different chain of rules or when we encounter the end of the search. If the *verdict* field is *IPT_RETURN*, we need to go back from the inbuilt chain to the standard targets. If the verdict field is some positive nonzero number, it means that we need to branch to a new chain for the next filter chain screening.

16.11   ORGANIZATION OF FILTER RULES AND TARGET FOR IPTABLES

Figure 16.4 shows kernel data structures that implement ip table filters. Filter tables are replicated pes CPU for performance guin.

16.12   FILTERING PACKETS WITH IPTABLES

As discussed in Section 16.9.1, we have three basic filter hooks for incoming, outgoing, and forwarded packets. Callback routines that do filter processing in all three cases internally call *ipt_do_table()*, which implements filtering logic. In this section we will discuss filtering logic implemented by iptables.

16.12.1   *ipt_do_table()* (see cs 16.38a and cs 16.38b
unless mentioned)

This filters the packet through all the possible rules for the hook. Once we find an entry for the packet, we do more specific filtering at the protocol level if required.

```
net/ipv4/netfilter/ip_tables.c

110 #define TABLE_OFFSET(t,p) (SMP_ALIGN((t)->size)*(p))
```

cs 16.37. Offset used to access per CPU table.

Once the packet matches all the set rules, we find out the target for the filter rule. The target may be another entry for rule matching, in which case we remember the back pointer to the current chain of entries in case we need to return to the current chain. If the target provides us with a final verdict, we stop further filtering and return with the verdict. In the case, where we don't find any rule for the packet, standard targets will return appropriate verdicts. The last chain entry for the hook should contain a wild card match that should accept any packet; otherwise we won't be able to come out of the loop. We reach the end chain only if the packet did not match any of the entry-level filtering rule.

We hold the table read lock before we start the filtering process at line 289. Hook entry tables are based at the end of the object *ipt_table_info*. Since this table is replicated for each CPU, we need to access the base of the table for our CPU slot (cs 16.37). *cpu_number_map()* gets us our CPU number. Since the size of each table is the same (stored in *size* field of object *ipt_table_info*), the offset of the table base for current CPU can be accessed from macro *TABLE_OFFSET*.

Adding the offset of the table base for current CPU with location of the table base for the table will yield the location of the table base for current CPU, line 291 (cs 16.38a). Next is to find out entry point for the hook in the table. The offset for each hook entry is provided in the *hook_entry* field of the object *ipt_table_info*. This hook entry offset is with respect to the current CPU's table base at line 294. Offset for standard targets for the hooks can be accessed by using *underflow* field of object *ipt_table_info*. It contains an offset for standard targets for each hook from the table base. We keep record of standard target entry (line 310) so that we can jump to this entry when required. Now we are all set to start the filtering process for our packet.

We iterate in a loop (line 312–397) until we get the final verdict. The verdict may be from standard targets or target set for the rule chain. In the loop we first try to find if the packet is the one we are interested in by the first round of screening *ip_packet_match()*. This has a rule to match IP address, network IDs, incoming/outgoing interface, fragments, and upper layer protocol for the packet. The rule is accessed from the *ip* field of the entry object (*it_entry*). If our packet didn't match the current rule, we check with the next chain rule for the hook that can be accessed from the *next_offset* field of current *ipt_entry* object (line 395, cs 16.38b).

In the case where we match the entry, the packet needs to be scanned through more specific filters for this entry using macro *IPT_MATCH_ITERATE*. These filters are the objects of type *ipt_entry_match* containing filter rule and are located at the end of the object *ipt_entry*. These filters contain a match specific to an upper layer protocol such as TCP/UDP/ICMP. If we are able to match all the filter rules, we need to find the target for the rule. Otherwise we move on to the next entry that can be accessed by the *next_offset* field (line 395).

If all the filter rules match, we need to find the target for the match entry by calling *ipt_get_target()* at line 327. The *target_offset* field is offset to the target for the entry with respect to entry object (cs 16.39). From the target pointer, we access

```
net/ipv4/netfilter/ip_tables.c

255 unsigned int
256 ipt_do_table(struct sk_buff **pskb,
            ....
262 {
            ....

289     read_lock_bh(&table->lock);
290     IP_NF_ASSERT(table->valid_hooks & (1 << hook));
291     table_base = (void *)table->private->entries
292             + TABLE_OFFSET(table->private,
293                     cpu_number_map(smp_processor_id()));
294     e = get_entry(table_base, table->private->hook_entry[hook]);
            ....
310     back = get_entry(table_base, table->private->underflow[hook]);
311
312     do {
313         IP_NF_ASSERT(e);
314         IP_NF_ASSERT(back);
315         (*pskb)->nfcache |= e->nfcache;
316         if (ip_packet_match(ip, indev, outdev, &e->ip, offset)) {
317             struct ipt_entry_target *t;
318
319             if (IPT_MATCH_ITERATE(e, do_match,
320                             *pskb, in, out,
321                             offset, protohdr,
322                             datalen, &hotdrop) != 0)
323                 goto no_match;
                    ....
327             t = ipt_get_target(e);
                    ....
330             if (!t->u.kernel.target->target) {
331                 int v;
332
333                 v = ((struct ipt_standard_target *)t)->verdict;
334                 if (v < 0) {
335                     /* Pop from stack? */
336                     if (v != IPT_RETURN) {
337                         verdict = (unsigned)(-v) - 1;
338                         break;
339                     }
340                     e = back;
341                     back = get_entry(table_base,
342                             back->comefrom);
343                     continue;
344                 }
345                 if (table_base + v
346                     != (void *)e + e->next_offset) {
                        ....
348                     struct ipt_entry *next
349                         = (void *)e + e->next_offset;
350                     next->comefrom
351                         = (void *)back - table_base;
                        ....
353                     back = next;
354                 }
355
356                 e = get_entry(table_base, v);
357             } else {
                    ....
364                 verdict = t->u.kernel.target->target(pskb,
365                                 hook,
366                                 in, out,
367                                 t->data,
368                                 userdata);
                    ....
382                 ip = (*pskb)->nh.iph;
383                 protohdr = (u_int32_t *)ip + ip->ihl;
384                 datalen = (*pskb)->len - ip->ihl * 4;
385
386                 if (verdict == IPT_CONTINUE)
387                     e = (void *)e + e->next_offset;
388                 else
389                     /* Verdict */
390                     break;
391             }
```

cs 16.38a. *ipt_do_table().*

```
net/ipv4/netfilter/ip_tables.c  ipt_do_table() contd ....

392            } else {
393
394        no_match:
395            e = (void *)e + e->next_offset;
396        }
397    } while (!hotdrop);
        ....
402    read_unlock_bh(&table->lock);
        ....
407    if (hotdrop)
408        return NF_DROP;
409    else return verdict;
        ....
411 }
```

cs 16.38b. *ipt_do_table() (continued).*

```
include/linux/netfilter_ipv4/ip_tables.h

292 static __inline__ struct ipt_entry_target *
293 ipt_get_target(struct ipt_entry *e)
294 {
295     return (void *)e + e->target_offset;
296 }
```

cs 16.39. *ipt_get_target().*

a target that may be a specific target for the rule or standard target. We need standard targets in case none of the rule match or we need to branch to some different chain for filter. Standard targets will have *verdict* field in addition to target object (*ipt_entry_target*). One more thing, standard targets will not have *target* callback routine initialised for its *ipt_target* object. We check iftarget for the match is standard target at line 330. If so, we need to work upon the *verdict* field for the standard target for next course of action. If the verdict is a negative value, there can be two possibilities:

1. We got final verdict.
2. The verdict is *IPT_RETURN*.

In the former case, we return with this final verdict. In the latter case, we need to get back to the standard target by back jumping to the standard target for the hook entry. We traverse the back path by having one *back* pointer that keeps the pointer to the location where we branched last. The next back pointer for the next level of back jump is stored in the *comeback* field of the *back* entry. In this case, we jump to entry pointed to by *back* at line 340 and store the back pointer to the next back jump using the offset stored in the *comeback* field of the current *back* pointer.

In the case where the verdict is a positive nonzero value, it means that we may be asked to branch off from the current chain to the different entry point or to the next entry in the current chain. In the former case, we simply use *next_offset* field of the object to locate the next entry. In the latter case, we need to store the pointer

```
include/linux/netfilter_ipv4/ip_tables.h

299 #define IPT_MATCH_ITERATE(e, fn, args...)      \
300 ({                                             \
301      unsigned int __i;                         \
302      int __ret = 0;                            \
303      struct ipt_entry_match *__match;          \
304                                                \
305      for (__i = sizeof(struct ipt_entry);      \
306          __i < (e)->target_offset;             \
307          __i += __match->u.match_size) {       \
308          __match = (void *)(e) + __i;          \
309                                                \
310          __ret = fn(__match , ## args);        \
311          if (__ret != 0)                       \
312              break;                            \
313      }                                         \
314      __ret;                                    \
315 })
```

cs 16.40. *IPT_MATCH_ITERATE()*.

to the next entry in the current chain in the back pointer before we branch off (line 353). This is required in the case where none of the rules match in the branched chain, in which case we need to start matching from the next entry in the current chain. Also we need to store the current back pointers' offset for the current chain in *comefrom* field of the next entry (line 350) as *back* pointer is modified now. We start traversing the new branched-off chain.

In the case where the target is nonstandard, we have a target callback routine set for the target that we call at line 364. The return value of the target will return either the final verdict or *IPT_CONTINUE*. In the former case, we return with the routine with the verdict. Otherwise we continue with the next entry in the chain.

16.12.2 *IPT_MATCH_ITERATE*

This macro takes us through the list of protocol-specific rules for the hook entry. These match rules are located at the end of the object *ipt_entry*. A target is located at the end of list of protocol-specific rules. We start accessing first rule at an offset—that is, size of the object *ipt_entry*, line 305 (cs 16.40). In each iteration we calculate offset for the next rule entry by adding size of the current rule, line 307. We iterate in the loop until we reach the start of the target for the hook entry, line 306. For each rule, we use a function pointer to process the filter rule at line 310. If we match the current rule, we continue to match the next rule; otherwise we return on the first mismatch (line 311).

16.13 SUMMARY

In the above discussion we saw that a netfilter framework is used to implement firewall in Linux. We use not only firewall but also netfilter hooks to implement any extension to the IP stack such as IP sec, connection tracking, IP masquerading, NAT, redirection, and so on.

An entry point to the netfilter hooks is NF_HOOK macro. The TCP/IP stack for Linux 2.4 kernel implements the netfilter hook entries for both the up and down stacks. The two hooks for outgoing packets are as follows:

NF_IP_LOCAL_OUT applies filter rules for outgoing packets.
NF_IP_POST_ROUTING implements IP masquerading, IP Sec, and so on.

The two hooks for incoming packets are as follows:

NF_IP_LOCAL_IN applies filter rules for incoming packets, and this hook is applied after the kernel has routed the packet for local delivery.
NF_IP_PRE_ROUTING is a hook that is applied prior to routing as soon as packet enters IP layer. It may be required by IP Sec, IP Masquerading, NAT, and so on.

Compat provides a netfilter framework with which only one firewall can be registered with the kernel. The object of type *firewall_ops* is registered using a *register_firewall()* using compat framework. Ipchain is designed to work with compat framework.

Iptables is not compatible with compat framework. Netfilter hooks are registered using *nf_register_hook()*. It registers an object of type *nf_hook_ops* for a specific hook type. Registered hooks are linked in global hash table *nf_hooks*.

To register an Ipchain table, an *ipt_register_table()* interface is provided. It registers an object of type *ipt_table* with global list *ipt_tables*.

Iptable is much faster as and has many advanced features as compared to Ipchains. Iptables maintains per CPU filter tables that get a much better performance because of cache locality.

17

NET SoftIRQ

Interrupts processing is divided into two parts. The minor part is done in the interrupt handler, and the major part or lower half is deferred further to be processed at safe time with minimum possible delay. This is done to avoid longer interrupt latency. The Interrupt is disabled, while the interrupt handler is in action. Once the interrupt processing is over, the interrupt is enabled. If we take a long time in the interrupt handler, interrupt latency will be high.

Earlier Linux kernel versions 2.2 and below implemented the bottom-half framework to handle a major portion of interrupt handling. It used to work well with a single CPU machine because it would hold the big bottom-half lock to the execute the bottom half. With SMP machines, this framework would give serialized access to the execute bottom half on each CPU because we need to hold lock to execute bottom halves. The framework could not scale on SMP machines.

To improve scalability of bottom-half execution, the framework is modified to scale better on SMP machines. The new framework is called softIRQ. SoftIRQs are designed to run parallelly on more than one CPU. Also, the same softIRQ can run parallelly on different CPUs at the same time. SoftIRQs can be raised independently on each CPU because data on which they operate are also maintained per CPU.

Each interrupt event does not have a separate softIRQ. There are two network softIRQs, one each for Tx and Rx interrupts. Other interrupt events register their bottom-halves as either high-priority or low-priority tasklets. There are two softIRQs for high priority and low priority, one for each tasklet. A tasklet has the characteristic of being executed only on one CPU at a time, which means that a

TCP/IP Architecture, Design, and Implementation in Linux. By S. Seth and M. A. Venkatesulu

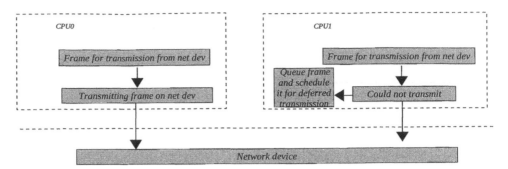

Figure 17.1. Tx net softIRQ.

specific tasklet can run on one CPU at a time. In the current chapter, we will learn more about softIRQs and their execution.

17.1 WHY NET SoftIRQs, AND HOW DO WE RAISE THEM?

Once a packet needs to be transmitted or received, how will that be done? Let's take the cases one-by-one. First we take the case of transmission on an SMP machine with two CPUs.

17.1.1 Transmission

Two frames need to be transmitted parallelly from the same interface. One kernel control path gets the device lock and comeback after transmitting the frame. In the meantime, the other kernel control that also has to transmit a frame on the same outgoing interface can either wait or loop until it gets the device lock. This brings in performance issues. If the kernel returns because some other CPU is transmitting the frame, it drops the packet and goes away, in which case the higher layer once again has to build the entire packet and then retransmit it. If the other kernel control path waits for the device lock to be freed in a loop, this again will waste CPU cycles on the other CPU. On SMP architecture, this kind of arrangement will heavily penalize the system and will certainly slow down the system at medium outgoing network traffic. What if we can queue-up the frames to be transmitted in some queue and defer the processing of the frame transmission for some later point of time in the near future as shown in Fig. 17.1?

17.1.2 Reception

In the case of reception, we take an example where we have a single interface. We receive one frame. In the interrupt handler we need to do a lot of jobs such as pulling out a frame from a device DMA buffer, finding out the next protocol layer, processing the packet at each protocol layer, and finally delivering data or control message to the socket layer. All this takes a lot of time. We can't spend a long time in the interrupt handler because it increases the latency of the network interface. In this duration, whatever frames we receive over the interface are dropped. So, the interrupt handler should be as fast as possible doing a minimum amount of work. What

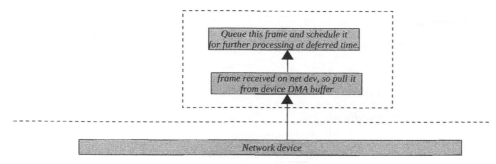

Figure 17.2. Rx net softIRQ.

```
include/linux/interrupt.h

56  enum
57  {
58      HI_SOFTIRQ=0,
59      NET_TX_SOFTIRQ,
60      NET_RX_SOFTIRQ,
61      TASKLET_SOFTIRQ
62  };
```

cs 17.1. SoftIRQ supported by 2.4 kernel.

if we can just pull out the frame in the kernel buffer from device DMA buffer and queue it for later processing? The received frame can be scheduled for later processing by the protocol layers, and we can return from the interrupt quickly as shown in Fig. 17.2.

In our last discussion we saw the need for deferred processing of frames in the case of both reception and transmission. This deferred processing is done by scheduling the packets to be processed by raising net softIRQs. For reception and transmission we have separate IRQs that are mutually exclusive. The concept is the same as that of the bottom half until kernel 2.2. The disadvantage with the bottom half was that the bottom-half execution was serialized across CPUs. One bottom half could be executed on only one CPU. With softIRQs, that limitation has gone and now we can run the same bottom half on multiple CPUs and there need not be any global lock acquired for doing that, which means that any softIRQ can run parallelly on different CPUs. With this design of concurrency in running net softIRQs on different CPUs, great network performance is gained on SMP architectures.

Net softIRQs can be raised for transmit or receive by a call to *raise_softirq()*. For each softIRQ registered with the system, we have a bit assigned to it. For transmit softIRQ we have *NET_TX_SOFTIRQ*, and for receive softIRQ we have *NET_RX_SOFTIRQ* bits, respectively (see cs 17.1). SoftIRQs are per CPU. Different softIRQs can be scheduled on different CPUs independent of each other.

We call *raise_softirq()* with the corresponding bit for the softIRQ. We need to raise IRQ for current CPU so we call *cpu_raise_softirq()* (see cs 17.2). *cpu_raise_softirq()* actually raises softIRQ with the help of macro __cpu_raise_softirq() (see cs 17.3). This sets the bit in the CPU-specific structure field corresponding to the softIRQ. We access a CPU-specific field by calling *softirq_pending()* for the CPU (see cs 17.4). *softirq_pending()* accesses *__softirq_pending* field of cpu-specific

```
kernel/softirq.c

131  void raise_softirq(unsigned int nr)
132  {
133       unsigned long flags;
134
135       local_irq_save(flags);
136       cpu_raise_softirq(smp_processor_id(), nr);
137       local_irq_restore(flags);
138  }
```

cs 17.2. *raise_softirq().*

```
include/linux/interrupt.h

77  #define __cpu_raise_softirq(cpu, nr) do { softirq_pending(cpu) |= 1UL << (nr); } while (0)
```

cs 17.3. *__cpu_raise_softirq().*

```
include/linux/irq_cpustat.h

29  #define softirq_pending(cpu)    __IRQ_STAT((cpu), __softirq_pending)
```

cs 17.4. *softirq_pending().*

```
include/linux/irq_cpustat.h

22  #ifdef CONFIG_SMP
23  #define __IRQ_STAT(cpu, member) (irq_stat[cpu].member)
24  #else
25  #define __IRQ_STAT(cpu, member) ((void)(cpu), irq_stat[0].member)
26  #endif
```

cs 17.5. *__IRQ_STAT().*

```
include/asm-x86_64/hardirq.h

 8  typedef struct {
 9       unsigned long __softirq_pending;
10       unsigned int __local_irq_count;
11       unsigned int __local_bh_count;
12       unsigned int __syscall_count;
13       struct task_struct * __ksoftirqd_task;
14  } ____cacheline_aligned irq_cpustat_t;
```

cs 17.6. *irq_cpustat_t.*

structure *irq_cpustat_t* (see cs 17.6) with the help of macro *__IRQ_STAT()* (see cs 17.5). We have an array of structure *irq_cpustat_t* one element per CPU (see cs 17.6).

Finally we can say that we set bit corresponding to the softIRQ in *__softirq_pending* field of structure *irq_cpustat_t* corresponding to the current CPU (nothing but *irq_stat[CPU].__softirq_pending*). *irq_stat* is an array of type *irq_cpustat_t* one per CPU (cs 17.7).

```
kernel/softirq.c

43  irq_cpustat_t irq_stat[NR_CPUS] ____cacheline_aligned;
```

cs 17.7. *irq_stat.*

```
kernel/softirq.c

114  inline void cpu_raise_softirq(unsigned int cpu, unsigned int nr)
115  {
116      __cpu_raise_softirq(cpu, nr);
         ...
127      if (!(local_irq_count(cpu) | local_bh_count(cpu)))
128          wakeup_softirqd(cpu);
129  }
```

cs 17.8. *cpu_raise_softirq().*

irq_cpustat_t. This structure keeps status information and does accounting for any CPU. It keeps account of an event that occurred on the CPU at any given point of time, and at the same time it keeps a pointer to the kernel thread that is responsible for processing softIRQs on the CPU. Let's look at the fields of this structure (see cs 17.6):

- *__softirq_pending:* This field keeps information about any pending softIRQs on the current CPU. Each bit in this field corresponds to a specific IRQ. If the field assumes a positive value, some softIRQ is pending to be processed. Thereafter we need to check the bit field.
- *__local_irq_count:* This keeps the number of IRQs raised on this CPU.
- *__local_bh_count:* This keeps the number of times that bottom halves were executed.
- *__syscall_count:* The keeps the number of system calls that were made on the CPU.
- *__ksoftirqd_task:* This keeps the pointer to the *ksoftirqd* daemon's *task_struct* structure responsible for processing softIRQ on the current CPU.

If we are raising softIRQ from interrupt or bottom half, we need not wakeup daemon processing softIRQ for the CPU. Otherwise we should wake it up in *cpu_raise_softirq()* (see lines 127–128 in cs 17.8). We will see the reason for this conditional waking up of the daemon in the next section.

17.2   HOW ARE SoftIRQs PROCESSED, AND WHEN?

SoftIRQ is processed in function *do_softirq()*. This function is called from many places in the kernel. This function returns if we are calling it from interrupt mode (cs 17.9, lines 68–69). Somebody may accidently call *do_softirq()* from an interrupt handler or a bottom half. If it is called from an interrupt handler, the whole purpose of having deferred processing via softIRQ is defeated because an interrupt handler

```
kernel/softirq.c

61  asmlinkage void do_softirq()
62  {
        ....
68      if (in_interrupt())
69          return;
70
71      local_irq_save(flags);
72
73      pending = softirq_pending(cpu);
74
75      if (pending) {
            ...
78          mask = ~pending;
79          local_bh_disable();
80  restart:
81          /* Reset the pending bitmask before enabling irqs */
82          softirq_pending(cpu) = 0;
83
84          local_irq_enable();
85
86          h = softirq_vec;
87
88          do {
89              if (pending & 1)
90                  h->action(h);
91              h++;
92              pending >>= 1;
93          } while (pending);
94
95          local_irq_disable();
96
97          pending = softirq_pending(cpu);
98          if (pending & mask) {
99              mask &= ~pending;
100             goto restart;
101         }
102         __local_bh_enable();
103
104         if (pending)
105             wakeup_softirqd(cpu);
106     }
107
108     local_irq_restore(flags);
109 }
```

cs 17.9. do_softirq().

will take a lot of time and latency again will be too high. In the case where it is
called from a bottom-half handler, it will become recursive and may overflow the
kernel stack. It uses macro *softirq_pending()* to check if any softIRQ is pending on
the CPU (see cs 17.9, line 73). If softIRQ is pending, we duplicate the bits corresponding to the active softIRQs locally and start processing them one-by-one (cs
17.9, lines 88–93). After processing all the active softIRQs, we check if any softIRQs
(other than just processed) was raised in the meantime when the active softIRQs
were being processed (cs 17.9, lines 97–101). If yes, we process them once again. If
the same softIRQs were raised which are already being processed, we schedule them
to be processed by *softirqd* daemon at some later point of time because we don't

want to be stuck here long while depriving other kernel paths and application of CPU resources (cs 17.9, lines 104–105).

Let's see how this is implemented. There are two local variables that will be used:

Pending
Mask

Pending stores the bit pattern for all the softIRQs that are currently active, and *mask* is just a complement of *pending*. Now before starting to execute softIRQ handler for the raised softIRQs, we have *pending and mask* variables initialized to appropriate values and *irq_stat[cpu]. __softirq_pending* is set to zero. We check all the bits in *pending*, until it has processed all the active softIRQs. We do this by left-shifting *pending* by 1 in each iteration (cs 17.9, line 92). We continue looping, until *pending* in nonzero.

Once we have processed all the active softIRQs, we again check if any softIRQs was raised in the meantime (cs 17.9, line 97). We need to check if the new softIRQ raised is one of those that are not processed just now. Since *mask* has all the bits reset corresponding to the softIRQs that are just handled. If we AND mask with *pending*, now it gives us positive number only if any softIRQs is raised which is surely not being processed currently (cs 17.9, lines 88–93). In this case, we once again go through the loop cs 17.9, lines 88–93. Otherwise if we have IRQs pending (*pending* > 0), it is one of those which are just processed. In this case we wake up *softirqd* for this CPU to process these softIRQs at later point of time. This is done in order to provide proper CPU share to user land applications because kernel is not preemptible. SoftIRQs take longer to complete than IRQ. If the interrupts are coming at higher rate, we will be spending more time in softIRQs handling.

We manipulate *irq_stat[cpu].__softirq_pending* by disabling IRQ on the local CPU by calling *local_irq_save()* and *local_irq_disable()* (see lines 71 and 95 on cs 17.9). After we have manipulated, we enable IRQs on the local CPU by calling *local_irq_enable()* and *local_irq_restore()* (see cs 17.9, lines 84 and 108). We do this because *irq_stat[cpu].__softirq_pending* is modified in the interrupt handler.

We process softIRQ with bottom half disabled by calling *local_bh_disable()* (see cs 17.9, line 79). This increments *irq_stat[cpu].__local_bh_count* by one. We do this because other kernel control paths on this CPU should not be able to process softIRQ. There is one way this could happen. For example, one kernel control path is executing *do_softirq()*, and an interrupt is raised. Interrupt is handled and while returning from interrupt in *do_IRQ()*, we may call *do_softirq()* if any soft IRQ is pending (refer cs 17.10, lines 654 and 655).

If we disable the bottom half while processing softIRQs in *do_softirq()*, we are making sure that it won't be executed while returning from *do_IRQ()*. Even if it enters *do_softirq()* while returning from *do_IRQ()*, it won't proceed further because *in_interrupt()* will always return a positive value.

do_softirq() is called when we

- Return from interrupt in *do_IRQ()* (cs 17.10). We have just returned from an interrupt routine, and there is a chance that some softIRQ is raised as most of the interrupt work is done in bottom half now implemented as softIRQ. That is the reason why we check here. There may be a chance that softIRQ

```
arch/i386/kernel/irq.c

563 asmlinkage unsigned int do_IRQ(struct pt_regs regs)
 564 {
          ....
 654       if (softirq_pending(cpu))
 655           do_softirq();
 656       return 1;
 657 }
```

<u>cs 17.10.</u> *do_IRQ()*.

on the local CPU is disabled because of any valid reason. In this case, any softIRQ will not be processed even if raised.

• Enable local bottom halves locally by calling *local_bh_enable()*. There are many situations where softIRQs need to be disabled locally because we are manipulating some data that are being accessed in softIRQ without disabling IRQ. We just increment local bottom-half counters when we disable softIRQ, which means that interrupts are allowed on local CPU. If this is not done, we may get an interrupt that executes softIRQ on return from interrupt and we are gone. This disabling of softIRQ avoids dead locks on SMP architecture and freezing single CPU machine because there may be a situation where the same lock needs to be acquired by kernel path and softIRQ. If we don't disable softIRQ and interrupt happens when some kernel control path is holding a lock, which is showed with softIRQ that gets processed as a result of interrupt, we end up in a deadlock. With SMP architecture, we are not avoiding softIRQ to run on some other CPU which is OK as far as deadlock is concerned. Once we are done with the execution of a critical code in the kernel, we enable the bottom half. Here we decrement the local bottom-half count; and if it has become zero, we execute softIRQ by calling *do_softirq()*. This way we can have nested disabling of bottom half. The outermost enabling of softIRQ will cause the processing of pending softIRQ. One small example is that we lock a socket with the bottom half-disabled, referred to as *lock_sock()*. This is required because tcp handler *tcp_v4_rcv()* is run in the bottom half that also wants to acquire a socket lock (bh_lock_sock()).

17.3 REGISTRATION OF SoftIRQs

Each softIRQ is associated with specific bit in *irq_stat[cpu].__softirq_pending*. In our current discussion design, we have *struct softirq_action* that represents softIRQ. *softirq_action* has two fields, *action* and *data* (see cs 17.11). *Action* is the function pointer to the soft IRQ handler, and *data* holds the argument to the handler *action*. We have an array of *struct softirq_action*, named *softirq_vec* (see cs 17.12). Each element in the array corresponds to one softIRQ. As of kernel 2.4.20, we have only four softIRQ as shown in cs 17.1. Array index in *softirq_vec* corresponds to bit number associated with each softIRQ. For example, *TASKLET_SOFTIRQ* is assigned a third bit and it has a fourth element in *softirq_vec* associated with it. With this design, we need not do searching for a softIRQ handler while processing soft-IRQs. We just traverse through all the bits in the 32-bit variable *pending*. In each iteration we move one bit toward MSB and check if the bit is set. If the bit is set, it

```
include/linux/interrupt.h

68  struct softirq_action
69  {
70      void  (*action)(struct softirq_action *);
71      void  *data;
72  };
```

cs 17.11. *softirq_action.*

```
include/linux/interrupt.h

45  static struct softirq_action softirq_vec[32] __cacheline_aligned;
```

cs 17.12. *softirq_vec.*

```
kernel/softirq.c

140  void open_softirq(int nr, void (*action)(struct softirq_action*), void *data)
141  {
142      softirq_vec[nr].data = data;
143      softirq_vec[nr].action = action;
144  }
```

cs 17.13. *open_softirq().*

```
net/core/dev.c

2665  int __init net_dev_init(void)
2666  {
          ....
2789      open_softirq(NET_TX_SOFTIRQ, net_tx_action, NULL);
2790      open_softirq(NET_RX_SOFTIRQ, net_rx_action, NULL);
          ....
2805  }
```

cs 17.14. *net_dev_init().*

means that the softIRQ corresponding to this bit number is raised and needs to be processed. So, we call a softIRQ handler corresponding to softIRQ from *softirq_vec*, which is *softirq_vec[iteration].action()*. *Iteration* is nothing but the number of times we have traversed in the loop to find this bit set.

We register softIRQ handler by calling *open_softirq()*. It makes entry for the softirq handler in *softirq_vec[32]* corresponding to the soft IRQ bit (see cs 17.12).

We register net soft IRQs for Rx and Tx in *net_dev_init()* by calling *open_softirq()* (see cs 17.13 and cs 17.14).

17.4 PACKET RECEPTION AND DELAYED PROCESSING BY Rx SoftIRQ

When a frame is completely received at the network interface in its DMA buffer, Rx interrupt for the device is raised. It is the job of the Rx handler to pull the frame out of the Rx DMA buffer and send it to the upper layer for processing. The Rx

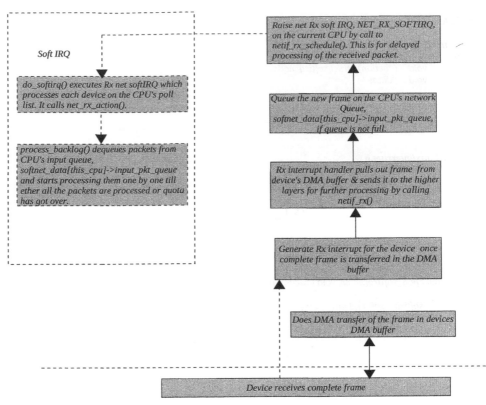

Figure 17.3. Processing of packets with softIRQ framework.

handler should not take much time for processing the packet. So, it just queues it on the CPU specific *soft_net*'s input queue *softnet_data[this_cpu]→input_pkt_queue* (by calling *netif_rx()*) and schedules the device associated with current CPU's soft net queue (*softnet_data[this_cpu]→blog_dev*) for later processing by calling *netif_rx_schedule()*. This raises net Rx softIRQ, *NET_RX_SOFTIRQ* on the CPU that will process the received packet at later point in time. The complete process of packet reception and scheduling it for delayed processing is shown in Fig. 17.3. *do_softirq()* is the function that is called to process all the raised softIRQ. It may be called when we return from interrupts or is called from *softirqd* daemon.

Let's see what does *netif_rx_schedule()* do. It calls *netif_rx_schedule_prep()* to check if the device is already scheduled or is off (see cs 17.15). Here we check if device is in running state (dev→state should be set to __LINK_STATE_START) and it is already not scheduled (dev→state should not be set to __LINK_STATE_RX_SCHED). If both are true, *netif_rx_schedule_prep()* returns true (see cs 17.16). There is only one net device per CPU which is scheduled to process received packet. This is a special and hypothetical device *softnet_data[this_cpu]→blog_dev*.

If the device *softnet_data[this_cpu]→blog_dev* is already scheduled, we don't schedule it once again and then we return. Otherwise we need to schedule it by calling __*netif_rx_schedule()*.

__*netif_rx_schedule()* finds the current CPU ID (refer cs 17.17, line 729). It adds the net device, passed as an argument to the function (*softnet_data[this_cpu]→ blog_dev*), to the CPU's soft net poll list (*softnet_data[cpu].poll_list*) (see cs 17.17,

```
include/linux/netdevice.h

744  static inline void netif_rx_schedule(struct net_device *dev)
745  {
746       if (netif_rx_schedule_prep(dev))
747           __netif_rx_schedule(dev);
748  }
```

cs 17.15. *netif_rx_schedule()*.

```
include/linux/netdevice.h

716  static inline int netif_rx_schedule_prep(struct net_device *dev)
717  {
718       return netif_running(dev) &&
719            !test_and_set_bit(__LINK_STATE_RX_SCHED, &dev->state);
720  }
```

cs 17.16. *netif_rx_schedule_prep()*.

```
include/linux/netdevice.h

726  static inline void __netif_rx_schedule(struct net_device *dev)
727  {
         ...
729       int cpu = smp_processor_id();
         ...
733       list_add_tail(&dev->poll_list, &softnet_data[cpu].poll_list);
734       if (dev->quota < 0)
735            dev->quota += dev->weight;
736       else
737            dev->quota = dev->weight;
738       __cpu_raise_softirq(cpu, NET_RX_SOFTIRQ);
         ...
740  }
```

cs 17.17. *__netif_rx_schedule()*.

line 733). If the device's quota is consumed (cs 17.17, line 734), we increment the existing quota by default (*dev→weight*). Otherwise we reinitialize the device quota to default. The device quota limits the number of packets that a Rx softIRQ can process on a given CPU in one go. We will see how the device quota plays a role when we discuss *net_rx_action()* later. Finally we raise net Rx softIRQ on the CPU by calling *__cpu_raise_softirq()*. On a single CPU machine with multiple network interfaces, all the incoming packets on different devices are queued up on the same CPU's *softnet_data[this_cpu]→ input_pkt_*queue. Whatever be the case, there is only one poll device per CPU (*softnet_data[cpu].poll_list*), which is on the CPU's poll list no matter which interface has received the packet. The picture looks very similar to what is shown in Fig. 17.4.

On SMP machines, there is a per CPU device poll list, and packets from same device may be queued up on different CPU's *softnet_data* input queue; or if there are more than one network device, the packets from different devices may be queued up on different CPU's *softnet_data* input queues as they appear on the interface. This is shown in Fig. 17.5.

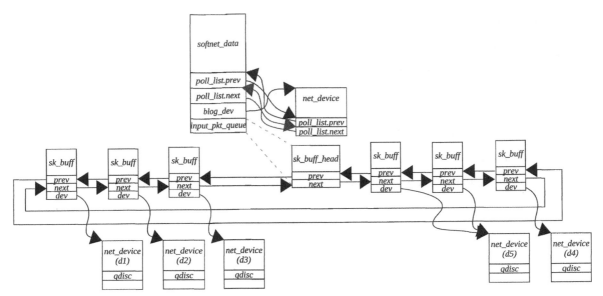

Figure 17.4. Packets being queued on CPU input queue.

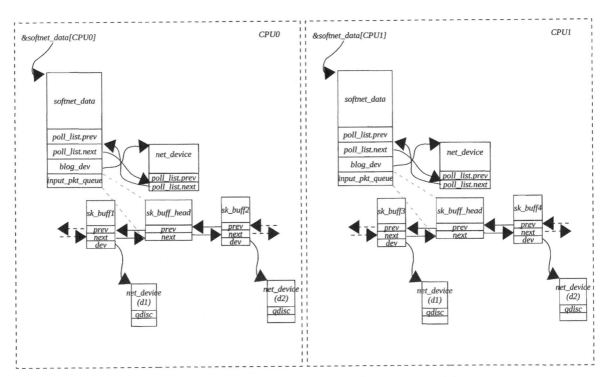

Figure 17.5. Packets being queued on per CPU input queue.

17.5 PROCESSING OF NET Rx SoftIRQ

Net Rx softIRQ is processed in *do_softirq()*. Handler for net Rx softIRQ is *net_rx_ action()*. Let's see how *net_rx_action()* works. The main job of this routine is to pull the device from soft net poll list and start processing the packets one-by-one on the

```
net/core/dev.c

1558  static void net_rx_action(struct softirq_action *h)
1559  {
1560        int this_cpu = smp_processor_id();
1561        struct softnet_data *queue = &softnet_data[this_cpu];
1562        unsigned long start_time = jiffies;
1563        int budget = netdev_max_backlog;
             ....

1566        local_irq_disable();
1567
1568        while (!list_empty(&queue->poll_list)) {
1569              struct net_device *dev;
                 ....
1571              if (budget <= 0 || jiffies - start_time > 1)
1572                    goto softnet_break;
                    ....
1574              local_irq_enable();
1575
1576              dev = list_entry(queue->poll_list.next, struct net_device, poll_list);
1577
1578              if (dev->quota <= 0 || dev->poll(dev, &budget)) {
1579                    local_irq_disable();
1580                    list_del(&dev->poll_list);
1581                    list_add_tail(&dev->poll_list, &queue->poll_list);
1582                    if (dev->quota < 0)
1583                          dev->quota += dev->weight;
1584                    else
1585                          dev->quota = dev->weight;
1586              } else {
1587                    dev_put(dev);
1588                    local_irq_disable();
1589              }
1590        }
1591
1592        local_irq_enable();
1593        br_read_unlock(BR_NETPROTO_LOCK);
1594        return;
1595
1596  softnet_break:
1597        netdev_rx_stat[this_cpu].time_squeeze++;
1598        __cpu_raise_softirq(this_cpu, NET_RX_SOFTIRQ);
1599
1600        local_irq_enable();
1601        br_read_unlock(BR_NETPROTO_LOCK);
1602  }
```

cs 17.18. *net_rx_action()*.

CPU's soft net input queue until we have exhausted our quota of time or number of packets processed.

We need to get CPU ID (cs 17.18, line 1560). The next step is to get the *softnet_data* array element for the CPU (cs 17.18, line 1561). We initialize other variables related to quota. Budget is initialized to *netdev_max_backlog*. *netdev_max_backlog* is a global variable initialized to 300 (see cs 17.19). *start_time* is initilaized to current CPU's *jiffies* (cs 17.18, line 1562). We disable IRQs on the local CPU before accessing the poll list and jiffies (cs 17.18, lines 1566–1574). Interrupts are disabled because *jiffies* is modified in timer interrupt, and the poll list is modified in the Rx interrupt for the NIC. We check if we have exhausted the budget allocated for processing Rx softIRQ (cs 17.18, line 1571). If yes, we still have some more devices in the poll list

```
net/core/dev.c

1089  int netdev_max_backlog = 300;
```

cs 17.19. Maximum packets that can be queued on CPU input queue before throttling.

to be processed. We reschedule the device to be processed at a later time by raising softIRQ, enabling local IRQs, and returning (cs 17.18, line 1596–1600).

We access the next device from the poll list after enabling IRQ on the local CPU (cs 17.18, line 1576). We check the quota for the device. If we have exhausted the quota, we disable interrupts on the local CPU, remove the device from the poll list, add it to the end of the poll list, manipulate the device quota (see cs 17.18, lines 1578–1585), and start all over again with the next device in the poll list (see cs 17.18, line 1568). If we have not exhausted our quota ($dev \rightarrow quota > 0$), call $dev \rightarrow poll()$. This points to *process_backlog()* by default and we are going to discuss it in the next section. If $dev \rightarrow poll()$ returns 0, we move on to the next device in the poll list; otherwise we once again repeat cs 17.18, lines 1578–1585.

We have exhausted all the devices on the poll list, enabled local IRQs, and returned (see cs 17.18, lines 1592–1594).

process_backlog() is routine called to process the queued packets on the CPU's *softnet_data* input queue. This is called when net softIRQ for Rx is processed in *net_rx_action()*. We pass net device queued up in the softnet_data's poll list for the CPU. The idea is to process as many packets queued up at the softnet_data *input_pkt_queue* as permitted by time or the quota. We calculate the quota for the packet processing as minimum of the budget passed and the device's quota (see cs 17.20, line 1499). We get hold of the *softnet_data* queue to be processed for the current CPU (see cs 17.20, lines 1500–1501). We store the current value of jiffies in local variable (see cs 17.20, line 1502) for further calculating time spent.

Now we are all set to process packets one-by-one from the CPU's backlog queue *softnet_data[this_cpu]→input_pkt_queue*. First we disable IRQs on the local CPU and try to pull out the next packet to be processed (see cs 17.20, lines 1508–1509). We disable IRQ before accessing *softnet_data[this_cpu]→input_pkt_queue* for the CPU because this queue is accessed from the Rx interrupt handler for the device. If no packets are there in the backlog queue for processing, we need to pack up (see cs 17.20, lines 1510–1511). If we need to pack up, which means we have consumed all the packets in the backlog queue on the CPU, device's quota and *budget* (passed as an argument to the routine) are decremented by number of packets processed (see cs 17.20, lines 1541–1542). We now delete the device from the CPU's poll list and clear the schedule bit for the device (refer cs 17.20, lines 1544–1545). We clear it because it has been removed from the CPU's poll list. Next time a packet arrives and IRQ is raised on this CPU, we once again schedule the device on the CPU's poll list and set *__LINK_STATE_RX_SCHED* bit for the device.

If we still have packets in the backlog queue, we dequeue it from the *softnet_data[this_cpu]→ input_pkt_queue* queue with IRQ disabled. We enable local IRQ and send the packet for further processing by calling *netif_receive_skb()* (see cs 17.20, lines 1512–1516). *netif_receive_skb()* actually processes the packet until the end of the last protocol before returning. For example, if this is a data packet for some TCP connection, it needs to be processed by an IP layer and then a TCP layer

```
net/core/dev.c

1496  static int process_backlog(struct net_device *blog_dev, int *budget)
1497  {
1498        int work = 0;
1499        int quota = min(blog_dev->quota, *budget);
1500        int this_cpu = smp_processor_id();
1501        struct softnet_data *queue = &softnet_data[this_cpu];
1502        unsigned long start_time = jiffies;
1503
1504        for (;;) {
              ....
1508              local_irq_disable();
1509              skb = __skb_dequeue(&queue->input_pkt_queue);
1510              if (skb == NULL)
1511                  goto job_done;
1512              local_irq_enable();
1513
1514              dev = skb->dev;
1515
1516              netif_receive_skb(skb);
1517
1518              dev_put(dev);
1519
1520              work++;
1521
1522              if (work >= quota || jiffies - start_time > 1)
1523                  break;
              ....
1534        }
1535
1536        blog_dev->quota -= work;
1537        *budget -= work;
1538        return -1;
1539
1540  job_done:
1541        blog_dev->quota -= work;
1542        *budget -= work;
1543
1544        list_del(&blog_dev->poll_list);
1545        clear_bit(__LINK_STATE_RX_SCHED, &blog_dev->state);
1546
1547        if (queue->throttle) {
1548            queue->throttle = 0;
              ....
1553        }
1554        local_irq_enable();
1555        return 0;
1556  }
```

cs 17.20. *process_backlog()*.

and finally return. We increment the local variable *work*, which indicates the number
of packets processed inside this function at any given point of time (see cs 17.20,
line 1520). Now we check if we have already exhausted the quota or time allocated
for processing backlog packets (see cs 17.20, line 1522). *Work* indicates the number
of packets just processed, and *quota* is the maximum number of packets that can
be processed; if *work* has exceeded *quota* or if *jiffies-start_time* is more than 1, it is
time to just return. *jiffies-start_time* gives us an indication of how much time is spent
processing the backlog queue; this value more than 1 means we are at least allowed
to process the backlog packets for at least 1 *jiffies*, which means until the time

another time interrupt is raised. In case we have exhausted our quota or time, we will not remove the device from the CPU's poll list and will not reset the schedule flag for the device; we just update devices quota (*dev→quota*) and the *budget* and return –1. This is required because if we have other devices in the CPU's poll list to be processed and we have quota left for backlog processing on the CPU, *net_rx_action()* the calling function will know it with the help of *budget* argument passed to this routine. *budget* is a global quota whereas *dev→quota* is quota per device, which means that if there are many devices queued up in the CPU's poll list, each device will be allowed to process packets as per each device quota because we are taking a minimum of the device's quota and the global quota (cs 17.20, line 1499). Each time we call *process_backlog()*, we may or may not consume the current device's quota but we return with global quota decremented by the number of packets it has processed until now in *net_rx_action()*. If for the current device we have not processed all the packets in *process_backlog()*, we just requeue this device at the end of the poll list; otherwise it is removed from the poll list (cs 17.18, lines 1578–1581).

To *summarize*, we will continue to process backlog packets in *net_rx_action()* until either *we have consumed global quota* or the *next timer interrupt has occurred*. In *process_backlog()*, we continue to process packets until we have consumed the *global quota or the device's quota, whichever is smaller*, or until the *next timer interrupt has occurred*. This way, *net_rx_action()* works together with *process_backlog()* to process backlog packets. Thus with the help of global and device quota, we are able to give enough time for net Rx softIRQ to process backlog queues without completely hogging CPUs at heavy network traffic. The quota system doesn't keep the system busy processing backlog queue even if the backlog queue keeps on growing on a given CPU while we are still processing it in *net_rx_action()*. The current design of backlog queues per CPU allows us to get network packets for the same device being queued on different CPU's backlog queues and to get processed by respective CPU's net Rx softIRQs as shown in Fig. 17.6.

17.6 PACKET TRANSMISSION AND SOFTIRQ

- We need to explain the need for Tx net softIRQ.
- Explain the queuing of packet for transmission.
- Flow of packet transmission.
- Tx net softIRQ.

In this section we will study how the complete packet is queued up for transmission on the device queue, and finally they are dequeued and actually transmitted over the wire. Why do we need softIRQ in the case of transmission? The answer is that we cannot always ensure that a device is ready for transmitting a packet over the wire. The same device cannot be accessed by two or more CPUs to transmit frames simultaneously. The hardware needs to be accessed serially for transmitting frames. On SMP machines, if each CPU is running the same driver code to access the hardware device to transmit frame, other CPUs either will need to wait or will need to return back with the indication that the packet could not be transmitted. This will hit the performance badly. So, in order to solve this issue on SMP machines, we just requeue the frame on the device's queue, schedule the device on CPU's

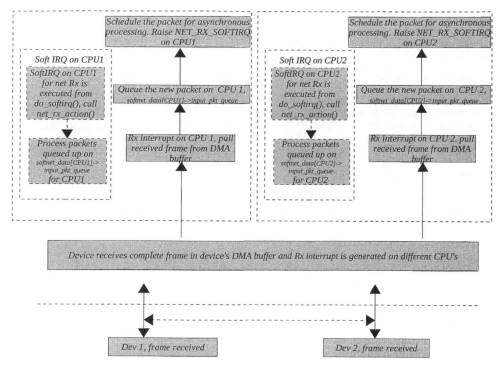

Figure 17.6. Two packets from the different devices being received on different CPUs.

output queue, and raise Tx IRQ on the CPU for later processing of the frames as shown in Fig. 17.1 (Section 17.1.1). The same device may be queued on different CPUs to be processed by Tx softIRQs raised on each of those CPU. The design of Tx softIRQ makes sure that only one CPU will be allowed to process one device's queue at any given point of time. We will see later in this chapter how we achieve this.

We will start our discussion for packet transmission at the level where a complete packet is formed and is ready for transmission. This packet is first queued with the device's queue, and then the device queue is processed one-by-one for final transmission. In our discussion we will also see how we take the path of Tx softIRQ for delayed processing of the device output queue. We will start from *dev_queue_ xmit()*. A complete frame is received by this routine. This frame is queued onto a device's queue by using device queuing routines specified in structure Qdisc (*dev→ qdisc*). Queue manipulation routines are initialized in a Qdisc structure for the device.

We need to hold a queue lock for the device (see cs 17.21, line 1026) with the bottom half disabled for an enqueuing packet on the device queue. This is done because the device queue is accessed from a Tx softIRQ that we will see in a short while from now. Now we call an *enqueue* function specific to the algorithm used for the outgoing packet (*dev→qdisc→enqueue()*). Here, we have queued the packet for transmission and we are not discussing algorithm for queuing, and this will be discussed in Chapter 15. The next step is to dequeue the packet from the device queue one-by-one and process them on this CPU. We call *qdisc_run()* to process the packets queued on the device queue (see cs 17.21, line 1031). This is done with queue

```
net/core/dev.c

 991  int dev_queue_xmit(struct sk_buff *skb)
 992  {
 993       struct net_device *dev = skb->dev;
 994       struct Qdisc  *q;
      ....
1025      /* Grab device queue */
1026      spin_lock_bh(&dev->queue_lock);
1027      q = dev->qdisc;
1028      if (q->enqueue) {
1029           int ret = q->enqueue(skb, q);
1030
1031           qdisc_run(dev);
1032
1033           spin_unlock_bh(&dev->queue_lock);
1034           return ret == NET_XMIT_BYPASS ? NET_XMIT_SUCCESS : ret;
1035      }
      ....
1078      spin_unlock_bh(&dev->queue_lock);
1079
1080      kfree_skb(skb);
1081      return -ENETDOWN;
1082  }
```

cs 17.21. *dev_queue_xmit().*

```
include/net/pkt_sched.h

 437  static inline void qdisc_run(struct net_device *dev)
 438  {
 439       while (!netif_queue_stopped(dev) &&
 440           qdisc_restart(dev)<0)
 441           /* NOTHING */;
 442  }
```

cs 17.22. *qdisc_run().*

lock held so that no two CPUs should start processing the same device parallely. We just unlock the device queue after return after from qdisc_run() and return from *qdisc_run()*. We need to know how *qdisc_run()* works.

In *qdisc_run()* we continue to loop until the device is not closed (cs 17.22, line 439) and we can process some more packets in the device's queue (cs 17.22, line 440). Let's see how exactly *qdisc_restart()* works to process the packets on the device queue. Get the pointer to the Qdisc structure for the device (cs 17.23, line 79). This can be accessed as *dev→qdisc*. Use a dequeue function specific to the queuing algorithm selected for the outgoing packet by calling *q→dequeue()* (cs 17.23, line 83) to get the next packet out of the queue. If we have processed all the packets, we return with the queue length (cs 17.23, line 140). Otherwise we have to process the next packet pulled from the device queue for transmission. The first step is to grab a device transmit lock (cs 17.23, line 84). At this point in time, we already have a device queue lock held so now we release the queue lock as we already have a packet from the device queue (cs 17.23, line 89). The next step is to check if the device is put off (cs 17.23, line 91). In the case where it is not put off, we call a device transmit routine specific to hardware to start packet transmission (cs 17.23, line 95). If we are able to transmit the packet successfully, we enter the block (cs 17.23, lines

```
net/sched/sch_generic.c

 77  int qdisc_restart(struct net_device *dev)
 78  {
 79      struct Qdisc *q = dev->qdisc;
         ....
 83      if ((skb = q->dequeue(q)) != NULL) {
 84          if (spin_trylock(&dev->xmit_lock)) {
 85              /* Remember that the driver is grabbed by us. */
 86              dev->xmit_lock_owner = smp_processor_id();
 87
 88              /* And release queue */
 89              spin_unlock(&dev->queue_lock);
 90
 91              if (!netif_queue_stopped(dev)) {
                     ....
 95                  if (dev->hard_start_xmit(skb, dev) == 0) {
 96                      dev->xmit_lock_owner = -1;
 97                      spin_unlock(&dev->xmit_lock);
 98
 99                      spin_lock(&dev->queue_lock);
100                      return -1;
101                  }
102              }
103
104              /* Release the driver */
105              dev->xmit_lock_owner = -1;
106              spin_unlock(&dev->xmit_lock);
107              spin_lock(&dev->queue_lock);
108              q = dev->qdisc;
109          } else {
                 ....
117              if (dev->xmit_lock_owner == smp_processor_id()) {
118                  kfree_skb(skb);
                     ....
121                  return -1;
122              }
123              netdev_rx_stat[smp_processor_id()].cpu_collision++;
124          }
                 ....
136          q->ops->requeue(skb, q);
137          netif_schedule(dev);
138          return 1;
139      }
140      return q->q.qlen;
141  }
```

cs 17.23. qdisc_restart().

96–100). Here, we set the lock owner to –1 (cs 17.23, line 96) because it is always set to a valid CPU ID that has held the lock (cs 17.23, line 86). We need to set this field in order to track if the buggy driver is trying to hold the device transmit lock twice on the same CPU. Next we release the device transmit lock (cs 17.23, line 97), hold the device queue lock, and finally return –1. This returns to *qdisc_run()*, where it once again calls *qdisc_restart()* because of the condition.

There may be error conditions such as the following:

- We could not get the device transmit lock because some other CPU already has it.
- We are not able to transmit the packet.

```
include/linux/netdevice.h

528  static inline void netif_schedule(struct net_device *dev)
529  {
530      if (!test_bit(__LINK_STATE_XOFF, &dev->state))
531          __netif_schedule(dev);
532  }
```

cs 17.24. netif_schedule().

```
include/linux/netdevice.h

514  static inline void __netif_schedule(struct net_device *dev)
515  {
516      if (!test_and_set_bit(__LINK_STATE_SCHED, &dev->state)) {
517          unsigned long flags;
518          int cpu = smp_processor_id();
519
520          local_irq_save(flags);
521          dev->next_sched = softnet_data[cpu].output_queue;
522          softnet_data[cpu].output_queue = dev;
523          cpu_raise_softirq(cpu, NET_TX_SOFTIRQ);
524          local_irq_restore(flags);
525      }
526  }
```

cs 17.25. __netif_schedule().

In both the cases we will stop the processing of transmission on the device and schedule the device for later processing on the CPU by raising net Tx softIRQ. In the latter case we need to reset the lock owner to nobody (−1), release the device transmit lock, and hold the device queue lock (cs 17.23, lines 105–107). In case we are not able to get the device transmit lock, we check if the lock is held by the same CPU on which the driver is being executed currently (cs 17.23, line 117). If that is the case, we release the *sk_buff* and return −1 so that we can continue processing the next packet in the queue. If this is not the case, we need to requeue the packet on the device queue, schedule the device for later processing by raising net Tx softIRQ on the CPU, and return 1 (cs 17.23, lines 136–138). This time we return 1 so that *qdisc_run()* should break from the loop and return, because we have already scheduled the device for later processing that will take care of all the packets queued up on the device when softIRQ for Tx is executed.

Let's see how do we schedule device for later processing in *netif_schedule()*. It checks if the device is still on. If it is on, it calls *__netif_schedule()* to actually schedule the device for later processing (cs 17.24, lines 530–531). The complete flow of the packet transmission process is shown in Fig. 17.7.

In *__netif_schedule()* first we check if the device is already scheduled on any CPU (cs 17.25, line 516). If already scheduled, don't do anything and just return because we have already queued the packet on the device queue which is already being run on this or any other CPU and will process our packet. If the device is not already scheduled, we find out the CPU on which we are running, disable local IRQs (cs 17.25, lines 518–520) and proceed further. Queue the device on the CPU's output queue linked through *dev→next_sched* (cs 17.25, lines 521–522). Now we raise net Tx softIRQ on local CPU to process the packets (*sk_buff*) queued on this device

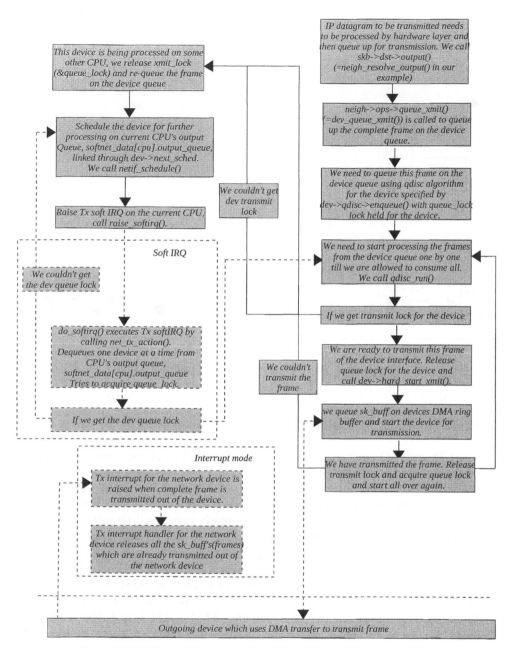

Figure 17.7. Packets being transmitted using Tx softIRQ framework.

(cs 17.25, line 523). Enable interrupts on the local CPU. We disable interrupts on local CPU to access *softnet_data[cpu].output_queue* because the device may be scheduled from from Tx interrupts also (see e100tx_interrupt() in arch/cris/drivers/ethernet.c). Our job is done here, and we have already scheduled the device to process our packet sooner in the future and we return from here. Let's wait for Tx net softIRQ to start processing the device queue. The outgoing packet (*sk_buff*) is queued on the device queue, and this device is queued on CPU's output queue for

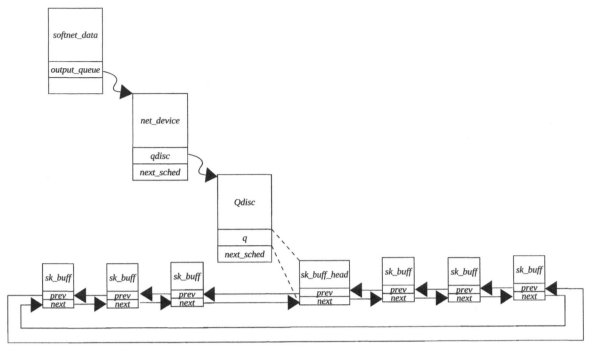

Figure 17.8. Packets queued on device transmit queue.

deferred processing by softIRQ; the entire arrangement looks as shown in Fig. 17.8.

Net Tx softIRQ callback routine is *net_tx_action()*. Let's see what this routine does. We will always process *output_queue* of the CPU on which soft IRQ is raised. The first thing it does is to get the CPU ID (cs 17.26, line 1337). The next thing we check is the completion queue, *softnet_data[cpu].completion_queue*. This queue has a list of all the packets (*sk_buffs*) that are already processed (transmitted). Once the packet is transmitted, *sk_buff* corresponding to the packet is queued in this *completion_queue* on the CPU (for example, look at *e100tx_interrupt()* in arch/cris/drivers/ethernet.c). If there are any *sk_buff's* on the *completion_queue* of the CPU, we dequeue them and free them one-by-one (cs 17.26, lines 1347–1353). One thing worth noticing here is that the *completion_queue* is detached from the CPU with IRQ disabled on the local CPU (cs 17.26, lines 1342–1345). Local IRQ is disabled because the list is modified inside the Tx interrupt handler (look at the same example *e100tx_interrupt()*). The next step is to process the *output_queue* on the CPU, *softnet_data[cpu].output_queue*. If there are devices to be processed on the *softnet_data[cpu].output_queue*, we will start processing them one-by-one (cs 17.26, lines 1356–1378). The first thing that we do here is detach the device list from the CPU's *output_queue* with local IRQs disabled (cs 17.26, lines 1359–1362). The reason for disabling the IRQ's on local CPU is already explained above. Now we start processing each device on the *output_queue* one-by-one (cs 17.26, lines 1364–1378). For each device on the list, we will repeat steps as explained ahead. We clear the schedule status for the device as it is being processed (cs 17.26, line 1369). This is

```
net/core/dev.c

1335  static void net_tx_action(struct softirq_action *h)
1336  {
1337      int cpu = smp_processor_id();
1338
1339      if (softnet_data[cpu].completion_queue) {
1340          struct sk_buff *clist;
1341
1342          local_irq_disable();
1343          clist = softnet_data[cpu].completion_queue;
1344          softnet_data[cpu].completion_queue = NULL;
1345          local_irq_enable();
1346
1347          while (clist != NULL) {
1348              struct sk_buff *skb = clist;
1349              clist = clist->next;
1350
1351              BUG_TRAP(atomic_read(&skb->users) == 0);
1352              __kfree_skb(skb);
1353          }
1354      }
1355
1356      if (softnet_data[cpu].output_queue) {
1357          struct net_device *head;
1358
1359          local_irq_disable();
1360          head = softnet_data[cpu].output_queue;
1361          softnet_data[cpu].output_queue = NULL;
1362          local_irq_enable();
1363
1364          while (head != NULL) {
1365              struct net_device *dev = head;
1366              head = head->next_sched;
1367
1368              smp_mb__before_clear_bit();
1369              clear_bit(__LINK_STATE_SCHED, &dev->state);
1370
1371              if (spin_trylock(&dev->queue_lock)) {
1372                  qdisc_run(dev);
1373                  spin_unlock(&dev->queue_lock);
1374              } else {
1375                  netif_schedule(dev);
1376              }
1377          }
1378      }
1379  }
```

cs 17.26. net_tx_action().

done so that if any packet arrives for transmission on some other CPU, it can be queued on the device queue and the device can be scheduled for processing on that CPU. This way we can have the same device being processed on different CPUs, whichever has the slightest chance of running it. At the same time, the same device cannot be processed on the different CPUs parallelly as *dev→xmit_lock* takes care of this. The entire arrangement of the devices being queued on different CPU's output queue on the SMP machine is shown in Fig. 17.9. We try to get the device's queue lock before calling *qdisc_run()* on the device. This is because other CPUs may also be trying to access the same device for processing or adding *sk_buffs* on

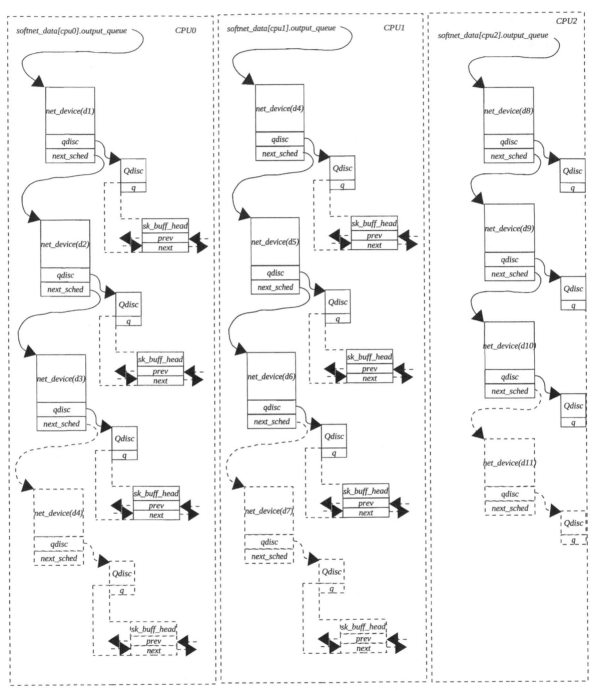

Figure 17.9. Packets being transmitted from different devices using Tx softIRQ framework on SMP machine.

the device queue, and only one CPU may get access to device queue. The device queue lock will be released in *qdisc_restart()* after dequeuing the first packet for transmission. So, if we get the queue lock, we call *qdisc_restart()* to process the next packet (*sk_buff*) on the device queue (cs 17.26, lines 1371–1373). Otherwise we schedule the device for later processing by raising softIRQ on this CPU (cs 17.26, line 1375). A block diagram for the transmission process on SMP machines is shown in Fig. 17.10.

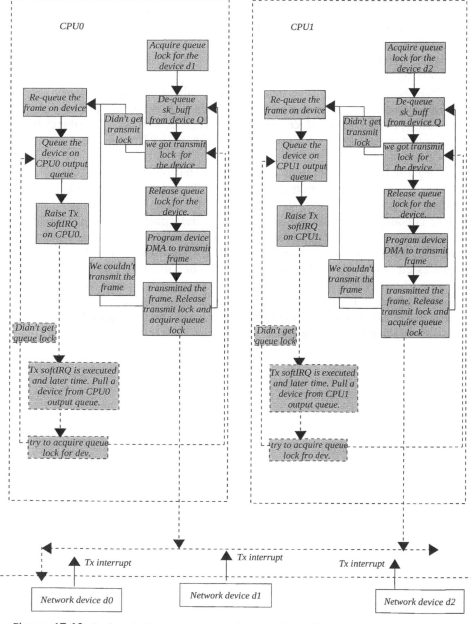

Figure 17.10. Packets being transmitted using Tx softIRQ framework on SMP machine.

17.7 SUMMARY

Linux kernel 2.4 supports four inbuilt softIRQs:

- *HI_SOFTIRQ*, for high-priority tasks (e.g., timer tasklet).
- *NET_TX_SOFTIRQ*, for network transmit interrupt.
- *NET_RX_SOFTIRQ*, for network Rx interrupt.
- *TASKLET_SOFTIRQ*, for low-priority tasks.

SoftIRQs can be scheduled and run parallelly on different CPUs.

SoftIRQs are executed on return from interrupt in *do_IRQ()*.

SoftIRQs can be disabled locally by calling *local_bh_disable()*. Interrupts may occur while softIRQs are being disabled on the CPU. These softIRQs are executed when softIRQs are enabled in *local_bh_enable()*.

SoftIRQs are designed to be disabled and enabled in nested fashion.

raise_softirq() is an interface provided to schedule softIRQ on current CPU.

softirq_open() is an interface provided to register softIRQ. An object of type *softirq_action* needs to be provided along with a softIRQ number to register softIRQ.

softirq_vec is an array of type *softirq_action* that registers softIRQ.

There is one kernel daemon running per CPU to execute softIRQ.

After all is said and done, there seems to be a small issue as far as network softIRQ is concerned. If two consecutive TCP data packets are received for the same connection but interrupted different CPUs, we are not very sure which packet will be processed first with the current softIRQ. If the order in which these packets are processed is reverse of the order in which they are transmitted, to TCP they have arrived out-of-order. This penalizes the TCP performance because ACK is generated immediately on reception of an out-of-order segment. In a more adverse situation, more than three packets may get reordered and may cause false entry into a fast-recovery and fast retransmission state.

18

TRANSMISSION AND RECEPTION OF PACKETS

We will discuss the reception and transmission of packets on the network cards that are DMA-capable. The intent is not to discuss hardware functioning; we will just see how DMA descriptors are initialized and designed to receive and transmit network packets. In our discussion we will take an example of an ether network driver that has DMA capability and then discuss the topic. We will study the design of network *DMA ring buffers* that are programmed for a network card for the reception and transmission of packets. We will discuss the interrupt handlers for the reception and transmission of packets where the ring buffers Rx and Tx are manipulated. In the case of reception, the packet is pulled out of the next DMA buffer marked for reception and sent to the next protocol layer for processing, and the next DMA descriptor pointer is advanced in DMA ring buffer for next reception. In the case of transmission, the functionality is slightly different. Tx interrupt is generated after the complete packet is transmitted and we release *sk_buff* in Tx handler. Let's see how it all happens.

Network adapters that don't have DMA capability work on the simple principle of frame transmission and reception. Once a complete frame is received in the device's Rx buffer, it generates an Rx interrupt. The interrupt handler routine takes the packet out of the device queue and copies it to the network buffer. This network buffer is then passed to higher protocol layers for further processing raising the net Rx softIRQ. On the transmit side, we copy a complete frame in device Tx buffer which is then programmed to start transmission if it is not already started. Once a complete frame is transmitted, a Tx interrupt is generated which would then free the buffer.

TCP/IP Architecture, Design, and Implementation in Linux. By S. Seth and M. A. Venkatesulu
Copyright © 2008 the IEEE Computer Society

18.1 DMA RING BUFFERS FOR TRANSMISSION AND RECEPTION OF PACKETS

DMA buffer descriptors for the network device are initialized at the time of device initialization when the driver module is loaded. For receiving, DMA buffer descriptors are initialized with DMA buffer allocated for each DMA descriptor. For transmission, only DMA buffer descriptors are initialized without a DMA buffer allocated for a DMA buffer descriptor. Now the device registers are programmed to use the initialized DMA buffer descriptors for Rx and Tx DMA buffers. Each DMA buffer descriptor has the physical address of the DMA buffer (where the network packets are actually stored) and certain control flags. A DMA buffer descriptor also has physical address of the next DMA buffer descriptor. We always use a physical address when doing DMA transfer because it doesn't know anything about the kernel virtual addresses. It does a frame transfer from the device to the DMA memory without interference of CPU.

18.2 PACKET RECEPTION PROCESS

On a DMA-capable network card, we program Rx DMA descriptors for network device. These descriptors are used by the device to store frames received on a network card by using DMA transfer. When a complete frame is received in the kernel memory, it is stored in the device's Rx DMA buffer pointed to by the next available DMA buffer descriptor. Once a complete frame is received using a device DMA transfer in the DMA buffer, the device raises the Rx interrupt for the device. Rx interrupt pulls out the frame from the DMA Rx ring buffer and advances the next pointer to point to buffer in the next descriptor from where next frame is to be read. In the next section we will see how the interrupt handler knows which DMA buffer in the Rx ring needs to be pulled out (see Fig. 18.1).

An Rx interrupt handler queues the packet on an element of array *softnet_data* corresponding to the CPU (*queue→input_pkt_queue*) on which interrupt has occurred by a call to *netif_rx()*. The device on which the packet is received is also queued up on a current CPU's *softnet_data* poll list (*softnet_data[cpu].poll_list*). A network Rx soft interrupt is raised on the current CPU. This soft interrupt will be processed on the same CPU. Any packet is queued on any single CPU's *softnet_data* array element corresponding to the current CPU (*softnet_data[current_cpu]→ input_pkt_queue*), and there is no chance of two CPUs processing the same packet. Even though the same device may be queued on different CPU's softnet queues, there won't be any synchronization required to process these devices on different CPUs via Rx softIRQ.

18.2.1 Flow of Packet Reception with DMA

Figure 18.1 illustrates the process of reception of packet from network interface into DMA ring buffer. Complete process is explained in Section 18.2.

18.2.2 Reception Ring Buffer

On complete reception of the frame in the DMA buffer, an Rx interrupt for device is raised. Received frames will be queued up in the next available DMA ring buffer:

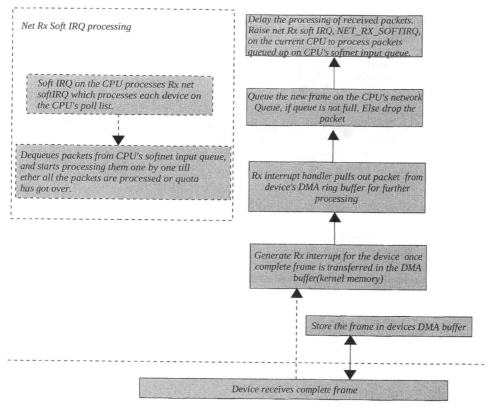

Figure 18.1. Network frame is received into kernel memory and processed further.

- An interrupt is already being processed at the time when the complete frame is received in the DMA buffer.
- A device is programmed to generate an interrupt on reception of more than one complete frames.

Let's look at it with the help of an example. Ring buffer for Rx is initialized as shown in Fig. 18.2. No packet is received at this point of time. Three pointers are initialized by the driver to keep track of where in the ring buffer the next frame should be taken off and also to track the end of the ring. *next* points to the DMA descriptor from where next frame to be received, *prev* points to the DMA descriptor from where frame was last received, and *last* points to the end of the ring buffer.

Figure 18.3 represents a scenario of Rx ring buffer when two frames are received but interrupt is not generated. *next* has moved clockwise by two descriptors. There is a difference between the *next* pointer and the location where the next frame is received by NIC. *next* is the location from where the next frame is to be processed by the Rx interrupt. The latter is advanced by the DMA engine logic to point to the next buffer in the ring once it has received a full frame.

Figure 18.4 represents a scenario where Rx interrupt is generated and the first frame is processed from the Rx ring buffer. *next* and *prev* pointers move by one unit in an anti-clockwise direction. The position of *last* will remain unchanged. The position of *last* changes only when we have processed half of the ring buffer with respect to the *last* pointer. We will see this later. On the same Rx interrupt event,

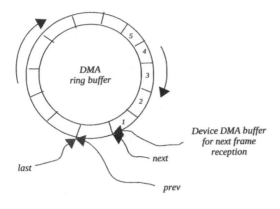

Figure 18.2. DMA Rx descriptors initialized and no packet is received.

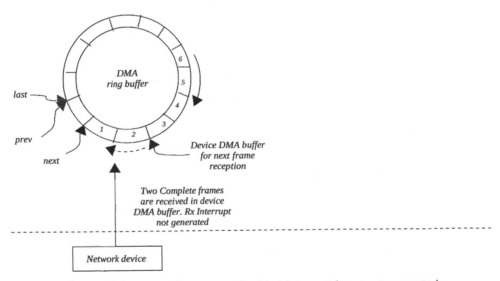

Figure 18.3. Two packets are received but interrupt is not yet generated.

all the frames in the Rx ring buffer will be processed. So, both of the frames are processed by one interrupt event, and the final scenario after the interrupt handler returns is shown in Fig. 18.5. It looks like the Rx ring buffer has moved two units in a clockwise direction, with *last* pointing to the end of the ring buffer.

18.3 PACKET TRANSMISSION PROCESS

We start our discussion from the point in the stack where IP datagram is ready to be transmitted. The outgoing device for the datagram is known, and it is queued on a devices queue. The device is scheduled to transmit a packet on its queue. The packet scheduler for the device removes a packet from the device queue one-by-one

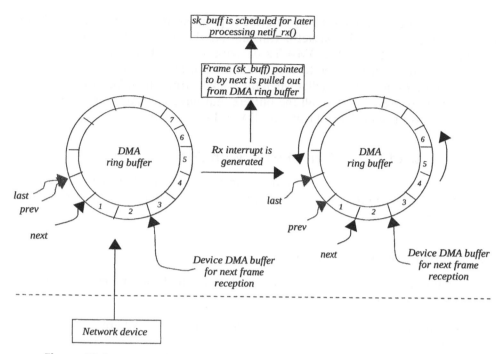

Figure 18.4. Interrupt is generated and first packet from ring buffer is processed.

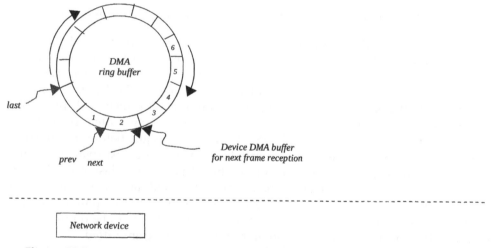

Figure 18.5. Both the packets in the ring buffer are processed on one interrupt event.

and tries to transmit them by making a call to a device-specific hardware transmit routine. The hardware transmit routine builds a link layer header to the IP datagram and programs the next available DMA Tx ring buffer to point to the frame to be transmitted. If no error occurs in the hardware transmit process until now, the packet will be transmitted. Once the packet is transmitted, the device's DMA controller generates an interrupt to let the kernel know the status of the frame transmission. In the Tx interrupt handler, we will free the buffer just transmitted and also adjust the pointer to the first descriptor in the Tx ring that needs to be transmitted next (see Fig. 18.6).

The packet that needs to be transmitted is pointed to by the next available Tx DMA descriptor. Once the packet is transmitted, the next descriptor is advanced to point to the next available DMA Tx descriptor. If the DMA Tx ring buffer is full, we stop the device to stop further scheduling of packets. The device queue is enabled in the Tx interrupt handler when the packets from the DMA Tx ring buffer are transmitted. We try to free all the buffers that have been transmitted successfully but not yet been removed from the DMA Tx ring buffer.

18.3.1 Flow of Packet Transmission with DMA

Figure 18.6 illustrates process involved in transmission of packet by programming transmit DMA ring buffer for the interface card. Complete process is explained in Section 18.3.

18.3.2 Transmission Ring Buffer

Tx ring buffers are initialized at the time of device initialization. The device keeps three pointers to manage the Tx ring buffer:

- *next* points to the DMA descriptor in the Tx ring buffer where next frame for transmission should go.
- *first* points to the DMA descriptor in the Tx ring buffer which is first to be transmitted.
- *last* is the last descriptor in the DMA Tx ring buffer to be transmitted.

The left side of the ring in Fig. 18.7 represents a situation when the Tx ring buffer is initialized. One frame is queued to the controller's Tx ring buffer, and *next* is modified to point to the next buffer in the Tx ring where the next frame for transmission should go (see right side of the ring in Fig. 18.7). The frame is just queued up in the device's transmit ring buffer and not yet transmitted. Two more frames are queued up in Tx ring buffer before they all are transmitted. The left side of the Tx ring buffer as shown in Fig. 18.8 is the scenario just before transmission of the frame starts. *next* points to the fourth buffer where the next frame for transmission should be queued. *last* points to the third frame that is last in the Tx ring buffer to be transmitted. A single frame is transmitted and the scenario of the ring buffer is shown in the right side of Fig. 18.8. *first* has moved three positions clockwise, whereas *next* points to the location where the next frame to be transmitted is pointing. This means that there are no more frames to be transmitted.

The next step is to generate a Tx interrupt once frames are transmitted. Here we try to free the buffer's queue up in the Tx DMA buffer. We start freeing buffers from the location pointed to by *first* and traverse the ring buffer until we reach the *next* pointer or the device pointer (pointing to the next buffer to be transmitted), whichever comes first. The DMA controller Tx pointer advances itself by one unit in an anti-clockwise direction to point to next frame to be transmitted in the ring buffer on transmission of the frame. The right ring in Fig. 18.9 shows that scenario when two buffers from Tx ring buffers are freed, and Fig. 18.10 shows the final position of buffer pointers after all the buffers in Tx ring buffer are freed on the same interrupt event.

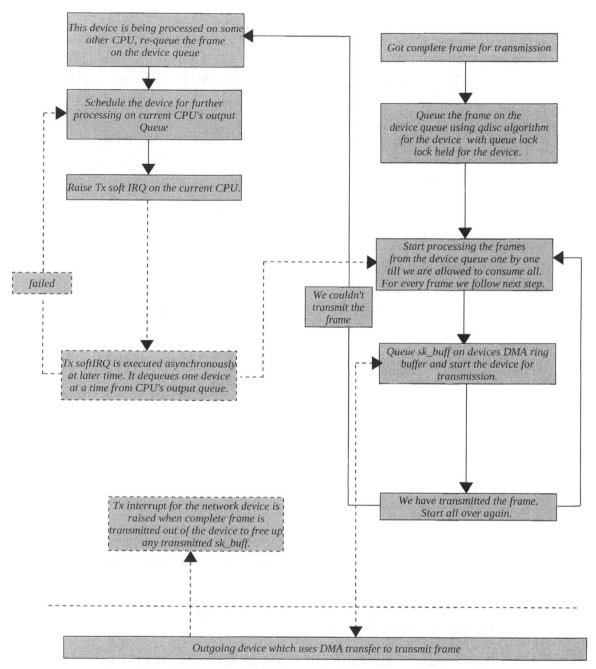

Figure 18.6. Process of packet transmission.

18.3.3 Transmission Ring Buffer

Figure 18.7 to Figure 18.10 illustrates processing of packets in transmit DMA ring buffers for transmission. We can see the status of DMA ring buffers after packet transmission. Complete process is explained in Section 18.3.1.

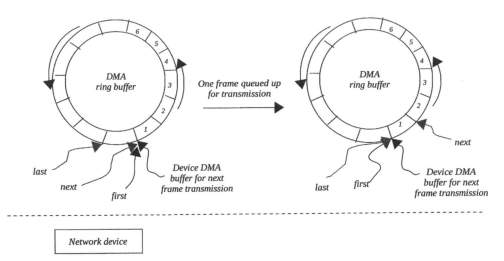

Figure 18.7. Single frame queued to a network controller that is not yet transmitted.

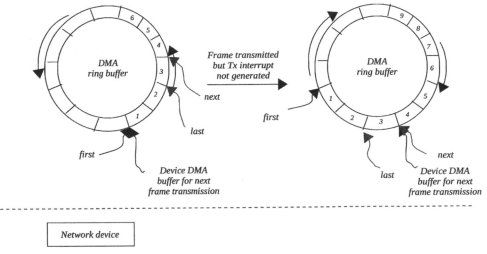

Figure 18.8. All three frames queued on a Tx ring buffer are transmitted using DMA engine but interrupt not yet generated.

18.4 IMPLEMENTATION OF RECEPTION AND TRANSMISSION OF PACKETS

We will take an example of an ETRAX network controller to explain DAM ring buffers and frame reception and transmission process. From cs 18.5, we can see that at the time of device initialization, we initialize Tx and Rx ring buffers. These buffers are actually queues used by the device to buffer packets to transmit and receive. There may always be a chance that the rate at which packets are being received is less than the rate at which they are pushed to the higher layers for processing. On the other hand, many connections may be sending packets for transmission. If there is no concept of device transmit buffers, we may end up dropping packets when the outgoing traffic is too high over a given device. These Tx and Rx

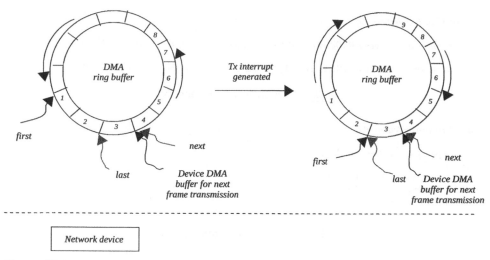

Figure 18.9. Tx interrupt generated and two buffers in the Tx ring buffer and freed from the ring.

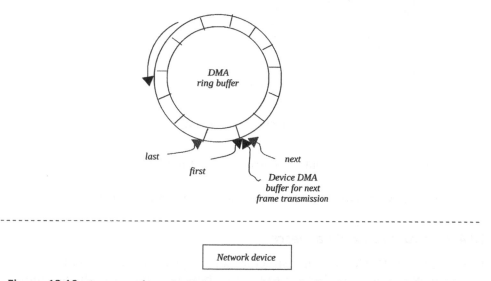

Figure 18.10. On return from the Tx interrupt, all three buffers in Tx ring buffer are freed.

buffer descriptors are of type *etrax_dma_descr* as shown in cs 18.1. The DMA transmit ring buffer is named as *TxDescList* of size *NBR_OF_TX_DESC*. Similarly, we have receive DMA ring buffer named as *RxDescList* of size *NBR_OF_RX_ DESC*. We will see in the later section how these tables are used to implement ring buffer.

18.4.1   *struct etrax_eth_descr*

This object is used by the driver to implement DMA ring buffers (cs 18.2). It has two parts:

```
arch/cris/drivers/ethernet.c

277  static etrax_eth_descr RxDescList[NBR_OF_RX_DESC] __attribute__ ((aligned(32)));
...
282  static etrax_eth_descr TxDescList[NBR_OF_TX_DESC] __attribute__ ((aligned(32)));
```

cs 18.1. Ring buffers for Rx and Tx.

```
arch/cris/drivers/ethernet.c

196  typedef struct etrax_eth_descr
197  {
198       etrax_dma_descr descr;
199       struct sk_buff* skb;
200  } etrax_eth_descr;
```

cs 18.2. DMA buffer descriptor for driver.

```
include/asm-cris/svinto.h

30  typedef struct etrax_dma_descr {
31       unsigned short sw_len;        /* 0-1 */
32       unsigned short ctrl;          /* 2-3 */
33       unsigned long  next;          /* 4-7 */
34       unsigned long  buf;           /* 8-11 */
35       unsigned short hw_len;        /* 12-13 */
36       unsigned char  status;        /* 14 */
37       unsigned char  fifo_len;      /* 15 */
38  } etrax_dma_descr;
```

cs 18.3. DMA buffer descriptor for network controller.

descr object is a DMA controller structure that implements a rig buffer on the hardware.

skb is a network buffer that has a pointer to the complete frame.

18.4.2 *struct etrax_dma_descr*

This object is a DMA controller structure and implements a ring buffer on the hardware. We program a DMA controller ring buffer for the Tx/Rx by just initializing this object. The descriptor contains DMA status and control flags along with the fields that manage the DMA buffer (cs 18.3).

sw_len. This is the length of the DMA buffer (containing data) that is pointed to by this DMA desctiptor (*buf* field).

ctrl. This fields contains the control information (flags) for the DMA channel. These control flags are specified in cs 18.4. We will discuss them as and when they are referred.

next. This field points to the next descriptor in the DMA ring buffer list. cs 18.5 explains how a ring buffer is created.

buf. This field points to the start of the DMA buffer for this descriptor. This field points to the DMA location where data for transmission to device or reception from device is actually located.

```
include/asm-cris/svinto.h

10  enum {                        /* Available in: */
11       d_eol    = (1 << 0), /* flags        */
12       d_eop    = (1 << 1), /* flags & status */
13       d_wait   = (1 << 2), /* flags        */
14       d_int    = (1 << 3), /* flags        */
15       d_txerr  = (1 << 4), /* flags        */
16       d_stop   = (1 << 4), /*         status */
17       d_ecp    = (1 << 4), /* flags & status */
18       d_pri    = (1 << 5), /* flags & status */
19       d_alignerr = (1 << 6), /*       status */
20       d_crcerr = (1 << 7)  /*        status */
21  };
```

cs 18.4. DMA buffer descriptor control/status flags for network controller.

hw_len. This field contains hardware length for the DMA data. This is different from *sw_len* as because it may contain some hardware control bytes also indicating the end of a frame.

status. This field contains the status/control flags for the DMA descriptor on the controller. For example, the status may be set to *d_eop*, which indicates that the descriptor is pointing to the DMA buffer that is the last packet package in the case where a large packet is divided into many small packages. cs 18.4 shows the bits that are used as status/control flags.

18.4.3 Initialization of Device

At the time of module initialization for the Ethernet device, we do certain initializations, some of which are generic to an Ethernet protocol in general while others are specific to the network controller type. *etrax_ethernet_init()* is a routine called to initialize the device. *ether_setup()* is called to initialize very generic callback routines and flags related to the Ethernet protocol. These routines are related to caching and building of an Ethernet header.

Next we initialize receive and transmit ring buffers from DMA descriptors. A ring buffer in the hardware is implemented by programing a DMA controller represented by *struct etrax_dma_descr*. We build the entire chain of DMA descriptor linked with the next field of the DMA descriptor (*etrax_dma_descr* object). *etrax_dma_descr* is a DMA controller structure. The very first descriptor is written into a hardware-controller-specific location that implements the ring buffer. Once the first DMA descriptor is processed, the controller loads the next descriptor from the *next* field of the structure and moves ahead in the ring buffer. So, we just need to build Rx and Tx DMA descriptor chain and write the head of the chain in the hardware logic that implements the ring buffer. Flags of the DMA descriptor take care of the rest.

18.4.5 Initialization of DMA Transmit Ring Buffers

From the example of the Ethernet driver (cs 18.5, lines 418–426), we see that Tx DMA descriptors are initialized when the module is initialized. This is an array of *TxDescList* of type *etrax_eth_descr* of size NBR_OF_TX_DESC. These descriptors implement Tx DMA ring buffers for transmission of network packets. We see that consecutive elements of the array are linked together by a *descr* field (of type

```
arch/cris/drivers/ethernet.c

345  static int __init
346  etrax_ethernet_init(struct net_device *dev)
347  {
        ...
368      ether_setup(dev);
        ....
384      dev->open          = e100_open;
385      dev->hard_start_xmit = e100_send_packet;
386      dev->stop          = e100_close;
387      dev->get_stats     = e100_get_stats;
        ....
401      for (i = 0; i < NBR_OF_RX_DESC; i++) {
402          RxDescList[i].skb = dev_alloc_skb(MAX_MEDIA_DATA_SIZE);
403          RxDescList[i].descr.ctrl   = 0;
404          RxDescList[i].descr.sw_len = MAX_MEDIA_DATA_SIZE;
405          RxDescList[i].descr.next   = virt_to_phys(&RxDescList[i + 1]);
406          RxDescList[i].descr.buf    = virt_to_phys(RxDescList[i].skb->data);
407          RxDescList[i].descr.status = 0;
408          RxDescList[i].descr.hw_len = 0;
409
410          prepare_rx_descriptor(&RxDescList[i].descr);
411      }
412
413      RxDescList[NBR_OF_RX_DESC - 1].descr.ctrl  = d_eol;
414      RxDescList[NBR_OF_RX_DESC - 1].descr.next  = virt_to_phys(&RxDescList[0]);
415      rx_queue_len = 0;
417      /* Initialize transmit descriptors */
418      for (i = 0; i < NBR_OF_TX_DESC; i++) {
419          TxDescList[i].descr.ctrl   = 0;
420          TxDescList[i].descr.sw_len = 0;
421          TxDescList[i].descr.next   = virt_to_phys(&TxDescList[i + 1].descr);
422          TxDescList[i].descr.buf    = 0;
423          TxDescList[i].descr.status = 0;
424          TxDescList[i].descr.hw_len = 0;
425          TxDescList[i].skb = 0;
426      }
        ....
433      myNextRxDesc = &RxDescList[0];
434      myLastRxDesc = &RxDescList[NBR_OF_RX_DESC - 1];
435      myPrevRxDesc = &RxDescList[NBR_OF_RX_DESC - 1];
436      myFirstTxDesc = &TxDescList[0];
437      myNextTxDesc  = &TxDescList[0];
438      myLastTxDesc  = &TxDescList[NBR_OF_TX_DESC - 1];
        ....
456      return 0;
457  }
```

cs 18.5. *etrax_ethernet_init()*.

etrax_dma_descr) using its *next* field. This arrangement makes the array *TxDescList* look like a singly linked circular link list. None of the fields of the DMA descriptor and object *etrax_dma_descr are* initialized in the case of Tx because they are initialized when the frame needs to be transmitted.

The last thing that we need to do is to initialize the variables *myNextTxDesc*, *myLastTxDesc*, and *myFirstTxDesc* for the device (cs 18.6). *MyNextTxDesc* points to the descriptor where the next frame for transmission needs to go. The next complete frame from the higher protocol layer will be pointed to by the *MyNextTxDesc*. *MyLastTxDesc* is the last descriptor in the DMA descriptor ring buffer that points to a frame transmitted last. The *d_eol* control bit is always set for this descriptor

```
arch/cris/drivers/ethernet.c


279  static etrax_eth_descr* myFirstTxDesc;
280  static etrax_eth_descr* myLastTxDesc;
281  static etrax_eth_descr* myNextTxDesc;
```

<u>cs 18.6.</u> Buffer pointers for Tx ring buffers.

```
arch/cris/drivers/ethernet.c


272  static etrax_eth_descr *myNextRxDesc;
          ....
274  static etrax_eth_descr *myLastRxDesc;
275  static etrax_eth_descr *myPrevRxDesc;
```

<u>cs 18.7.</u> Buffer pointers for Rx ring buffers.

($myLastTxDesc{\rightarrow}descr.ctrl$). *MyFirstTxDesc* points to the first packet that needs to be transmitted. So, finally after the Tx descriptor is initialized, it will be arranged as shown in Fig. 18.14.

18.4.6 Initialization of DMA Receive Ring Buffers

Once again from the example of Ethernet driver (cs 18.5, lines 401–411), we see that Rx descriptors are initialized at the time of module initialization. This is an array of *RxDescList* of type *etrax_eth_descr of length NBR_OF_RX_DESC*. These descriptors manage DMA storage for the reception of network packets. We see that consecutive elements of the array are linked together by *next* field of the *descr* field (of type *etrax_dma_descr*) of each array element. We initialize *skb* field of each descriptor to point to *sk_buff* of buffer size *MAX_MEDIA_DATA_SIZE*. Network buffers are initialized for receive DMA descriptors because the received frames are directly DMAed in these buffers.

This arrangement makes the array *RxDescList* look like singly linked circular link list. This way we have built a DMA ring buffer for the reception of packets. The last thing that we need to do is to initialize the variables *myNextRxDesc*, *myLastRxDesc*, and *myPrevRxDesc* for the device (cs 18.7). *MyNextRxDesc* points to the next descriptor from where the next frame is read by the interrupt handler, which means that it points to the next packet that is received and is yet to be taken off the device's DMA queue for processing. *MyLastRxDesc* is the last descriptor in the DMA ring buffer. The *d_eol* control bit is always set for this descriptor ($myLastRxDesc{\rightarrow}descr.ctrl$). *MyPrevRxDesc* always points to the descriptor that is processed last, which means that it marks the end of the descriptor in the ring buffer. Finally, after the Rx descriptor is initialized, it will be arranged as shown in Fig. 18.11.

18.5 Rx INTERRUPT FOR RECEPTION OF PACKETS

e100rx_interrupt() is the interrupt handler for the reception of packets. This interrupt comes when we have completely received one frame in the device's DMA ring

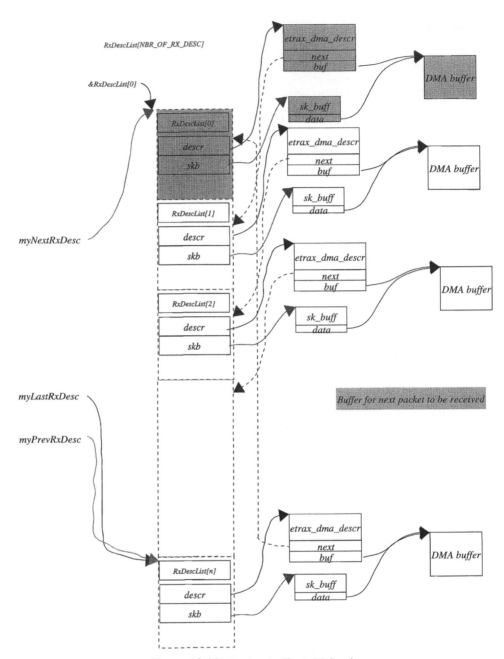

Figure 18.11. Rx ring buffer initialized.

buffer managed by a DMA descriptor for Rx as shown in Fig. 18.11. We need to get this packet out of the DMA buffer and process it further. To receive the frame in the DMA ring buffer, we need to program the device DMA to tell it the location of the Rx DMA descriptor. We do this while opening the device in *e100_open()* (cs 18.8). *R_DMA_CH1_FIRST* is made to point to location of the next Rx DMA descriptor initialized to *myNextRxDesc*. When a complete frame is received in the DMA Rx buffer, the frame is stored in the buffer pointed to by *R_DMA_CH1_FIRST*. After the reception of a packet, the DMA engine advances *R_DMA_CH1_*

```
arch/cris/drivers/ethernet.c

505 static int
506 e100_open(struct net_device *dev)
507 {
          ....
633       *R_DMA_CH1_FIRST = virt_to_phys(myNextRxDesc);
634       *R_DMA_CH1_CMD = IO_STATE(R_DMA_CH1_CMD, cmd, start);
          .....
638       *R_DMA_CH0_FIRST = 0;
639       *R_DMA_CH0_DESCR = virt_to_phys(myLastTxDesc);
          .....
660 }
```

cs 18.8. e100_open().

```
arch/cris/drivers/ethernet.c

987 static void
988 e100rx_interrupt(int irq, void *dev_id, struct pt_regs * regs)
989 {
990      struct net_device *dev = (struct net_device *)dev_id;
991      unsigned long irqbits = *R_IRQ_MASK2_RD;
992
993      if (irqbits & IO_STATE(R_IRQ_MASK2_RD, dma1_eop, active)) {
          ....
996          *R_DMA_CH1_CLR_INTR = IO_STATE(R_DMA_CH1_CLR_INTR, clr_eop, do);
          .....
1000         while (*R_DMA_CH1_FIRST != virt_to_phys(myNextRxDesc)) {
             ....
1004             e100_rx(dev);
             .....
1015         }
1016     }
1017 }
```

cs 18.9. e100rx_interrupt().

FIRST to point to the next Rx DMA descriptor in the Rx ring buffer pointed to by *myNextRxDesc→descr.next* as *R_DMA_CH1_FIRST* stores the physical address of the location where *myNextRxDesc* points to. We first check if *R_DMA_CH1_FIRST* is the same as *myNextRxDesc*. If that is the case, we have should stop processing as there is nothing left in the Rx ring buffer. If they are not same, we have something and we proceed ahead to get the frame out of the Rx DMA buffer by calling *e100_rx()* (cs 18.9, line 1004). We continue to check if we have another packet to process in the while loop lines 1000–1015. Each frame in the Rx ring buffer is processed here.

18.5.1   Rx DMA Buffer Initialized

Figure 18.11 illustrates how device DMA structures implementing Rx DMA ring buffer are linked on initialization. Section 18.5 explains the process in detail.

18.5.2   e100_rx()

This routine is called to pull off the next received frame from Rx DMA buffer pointed to by *myNextRxDesc*. We read the frame length from *myNextRxDesc→ descr.hw_len*. If the frame length is more than a certain threshold, *RX_COPY-*

```
arch/cris/drivers/ethernet.c


1086  static void
1087  e100_rx(struct net_device *dev)
1088  {
1089      struct sk_buff *skb;
1090      int length = 0;
          ....
1107      length = myNextRxDesc->descr.hw_len - 4;
          ....
1122      if (length < RX_COPYBREAK) {
1123          /* Small packet, copy data */
1124          skb = dev_alloc_skb(length - ETHER_HEAD_LEN);
              ....
1131          skb_put(skb, length - ETHER_HEAD_LEN);
1132          skb_data_ptr = skb_push(skb, ETHER_HEAD_LEN);
              ....
1140          memcpy(skb_data_ptr, phys_to_virt(myNextRxDesc->descr.buf), length);
1141      }
1142      else {
1144          skb = myNextRxDesc->skb;
1145          skb_put(skb, length);
1146          myNextRxDesc->skb = dev_alloc_skb(MAX_MEDIA_DATA_SIZE);
1147          myNextRxDesc->descr.buf = virt_to_phys(myNextRxDesc->skb->data);
1148      }
          ....
1151      skb->protocol = eth_type_trans(skb, dev);
          ....
1154      netif_rx(skb);
          ....
1157      myNextRxDesc->descr.status = 0;
1158      myPrevRxDesc = myNextRxDesc;
1159      myNextRxDesc = phys_to_virt(myNextRxDesc->descr.next);
          ....
1161      rx_queue_len++;
          ....
1164      if (rx_queue_len == RX_QUEUE_THRESHOLD) {
1165          flush_etrax_cache();
1166          myPrevRxDesc->descr.ctrl |= d_eol;
1167          myLastRxDesc->descr.ctrl &= ~d_eol;
1168          myLastRxDesc = myPrevRxDesc;
1169          rx_queue_len = 0;
1170      }
1171  }
```

cs 18.10. e100_rx().

BREAK, we pull off sk_buff from DMA ring buffer to the upper protocol layers for processing. We allocate a new network buffer to replace the old buffer in the DMA ring buffer and initialize a DMA descriptor at lines 1146–1147 (cs 18.10). Otherwise we make a copy of the sk_buff from DMA descriptor (myNextRxDesc→ skb) and pass a new network buffer to the upper layer for processing at line 1140. In the former case, we are reducing the burden of copying a large datagram, hence saving some CPU cycles in processing the frames. In the latter case, we are saving the allocation of DMA buffers, which is expensive in terms of both size of the buffer and size of the DMA tag.

We fill dev and proto fields of sk_buff to indicate the next protocol layer to which the packet belongs by calling eth_type_trans(). Send the packet to upper layers for further processing by calling netif_rx(). We discuss more about it later.

Lastly, myPrevRxDesc is made to point to *myNextRxDesc,* and *myNextRxDesc* is advanced to point to the next descriptor in the Rx DMA ring buffer, *myNextRx-Desc→descr.next* (lines 1158–1159). If we had three packets already queued on the DMA ring buffer before an Rx interrupt was generated in Fig. 18.12, the final picture of the Rx DMA descriptors after the first packet is processed will be as shown in Fig. 18.13 when the frame pointed to by *myNextRxDesc* is taken out of the Rx descriptor list for further processing by the higher-layer protocols.

If we have processed *RX_QUEUE_THRESHOLD* number of frames so far with respect to the current last descriptor pointed to by *myLastRxDesc*, we need to release the ring buffers. By releasing ring buffers, it means that new frames should be allowed to be stored in DMA ring buffers beyond the last descriptor because they are no longer in use. Every time a new frame is processed from the DMA ring buffer, the descriptor previous (myPrevRxDesc) is made to point to the processed descriptor. So, the previous descriptor should be marked as the end of the ring buffer by setting *d_eol* flag for this descriptor, lines 1164–1170.

18.5.3 Rx Descriptors After Reception of Three Packets in DMA Buffer Before Rx Interrupt Being Raised

Figure 18.12 illustrates the state of Rx DMA ring buffer after the reception of three packets. These packets will be processed from ring buffer only when Rx interrupt is generated. MyNextRxDesc and myPrevRxDesc are pointing to element in the Rx Ring buffer that needs to be processed first more is discussed in Section 18.5.2.

18.5.4 Rx Descriptors After First Packet Is Pulled Out of DMA Buffer and Given to OS in Rx Interrupt Handler

Figure 18.13 illustrates the shapshot of Rx DMA ring buffer when first packet is pulled out of the Rx DMA ring buffer for processing in Rx interrupt handler. MyNextRxDesc points to the next descriptor to be processed. MyPrevRxDesc still points to first descriptor because discuss need to free processed buffers tasting from here. See Section 18.5.2 for details.

18.6 TRANSMISSION OF PACKETS

18.6.1 *e100_send_packet()*

e100_send_packet() is the interface routine registered for sending a frame over the wire. This is the final step in packet transmission down the stack. This routine programs the device's DMA channel to point to the packet frame to be transmitted and then start the channel. So, make the next available DMA descriptor in the Tx ring buffer, *MyNextTxDesc*, point to the network buffer just poured in from the network stack (cs 18.11, line 946). Call *e100_hardware_send_packet()* to initialize the rest of the fields of *MyNextTxDesc* descriptor and start DMA channel. Now we advance next descriptor in the Tx ring buffer to point to the next descriptor in the ring buffer (line 952). Figure 18.15 represents the scenario where two packets are queued up in the DMA channel to be transmitted. *MyFirstTxDesc* points to the first

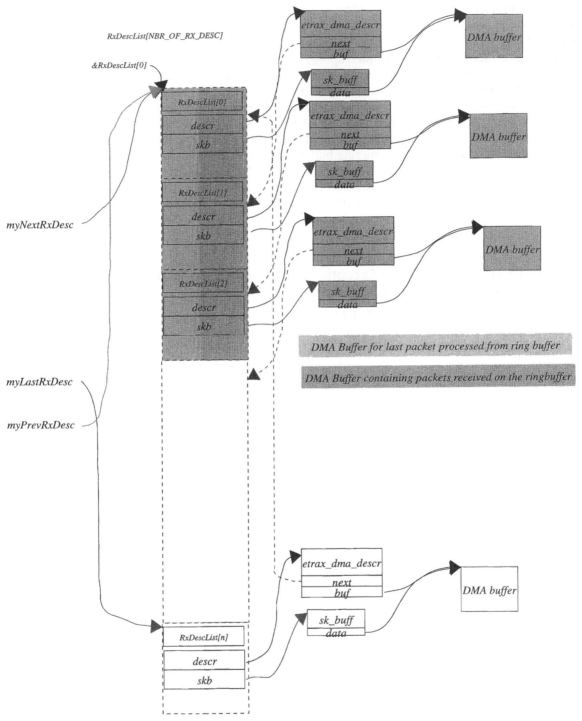

Figure 18.12. Three packets already queued on Rx ring buffer.

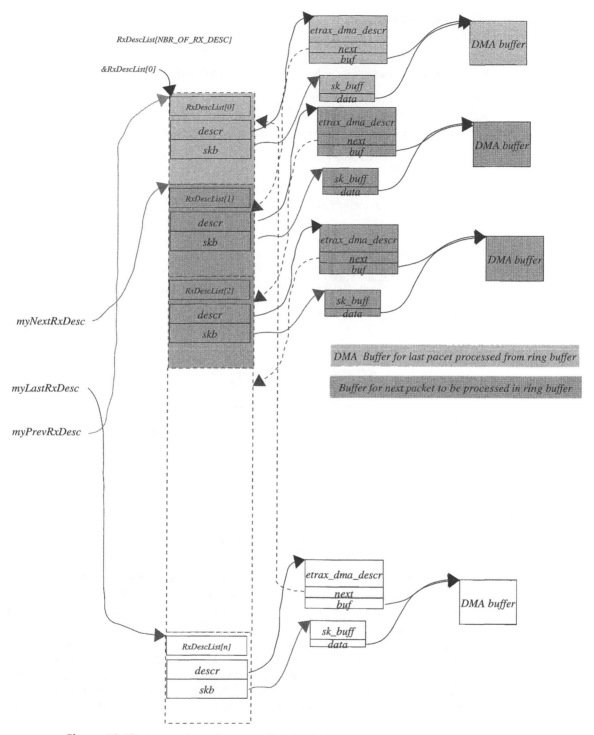

Figure 18.13. One packet taken out of Rx ring buffer for processing.

```
arch/cris/drivers/ethernet.c


934  static int
935  e100_send_packet(struct sk_buff *skb, struct net_device *dev)
936  {
         ....
939      unsigned char *buf = skb->data;
         ....
944      spin_lock_irq(&np->lock);  /* protect from tx_interrupt and ourself */
945
946      myNextTxDesc->skb = skb;
947
948      dev->trans_start = jiffies;
949
950      e100_hardware_send_packet(buf, length);
951
952      myNextTxDesc = phys_to_virt(myNextTxDesc->descr.next);
953
954      /* Stop queue if full */
955      if (myNextTxDesc == myFirstTxDesc) {
956          /* Enable transmit interrupt to wake up queue */
957          *R_DMA_CH0_CLR_INTR = IO_STATE(R_DMA_CH0_CLR_INTR, clr_eop, do);
958          *R_IRQ_MASK2_SET = IO_STATE(R_IRQ_MASK2_SET, dma0_eop, set);
959          netif_stop_queue(dev);
960      }
961      else {
962      /* Report any packets that have been sent */
963          while (myFirstTxDesc != phys_to_virt(*R_DMA_CH0_FIRST) &&
964              myFirstTxDesc != myNextTxDesc)
965          {
                 ....
971              dev_kfree_skb(myFirstTxDesc->skb);
972              myFirstTxDesc->skb = 0;
973              myFirstTxDesc = phys_to_virt(myFirstTxDesc->descr.next);
974          }
975      }
976
977      spin_unlock_irq(&np->lock);
978
979      return 0;
980  }
```

cs 18.11. *e100_send_packet().*

DMA descriptor which is yet to be processed, *myLastTxDesc* points to the last DMA descriptor that is the last in the Tx ring buffer that needs to be transmitted, and *MyNextTxDesc* points to next DMA descriptor that is unused and can be used for queuing the next packet that needs to be transmitted.

We check if the DMA ring buffer is full at line 955. *MyNextTxDesc* points to the first frame to be processed, and *MyNextTxDesc* is the descriptor that is used to queue the next frame to be transmitted; and if both of them point to the same location, it means that the device queue is full. In this case, we put off the device by calling *netif_stop_queue()* at line 959 so that no more frames should be accepted by the device. We see in a later section that once the frames are transmitted, the Tx interrupt wakes up the device queue to start accepting more packets from the upper layer for transmission. Otherwise we check if we need to do the cleanup operation on the DMA ring buffer that is already processed. This may be required if Tx interrupt is not yet generated after frames in the Tx ring buffer are actually transmitted.

```
arch/cris/drivers/ethernet.c

1375 void
 1376 e100_hardware_send_packet(char *buf, int length)
 1377 {
            ....
 1391        myNextTxDesc->descr.sw_len = length;
 1392        myNextTxDesc->descr.ctrl = d_eop | d_eol | d_wait;
 1393        myNextTxDesc->descr.buf = virt_to_phys(buf);
            ....
 1396        myLastTxDesc->descr.ctrl &= ~d_eol;
 1397        myLastTxDesc = myNextTxDesc;
            ....
 1400        *R_DMA_CH0_CMD = IO_STATE(R_DMA_CH0_CMD, cmd, restart);
 1401 }
```

<u>cs 18.12.</u> *e100_hardware_send_packet()*.

The *R_DMA_CH0_FIRST* macro points to the descriptor that is yet to be processed in the ring buffer. So we will always know which DMA descriptor is being processed currently and will not free the *sk_buff* associated with this DMA descriptor and beyond this descriptor. We traverse through the Tx DMA ring buffers until the end and check if the frame pointed to by the DMA is already processed, line 963. If it being processed, we just free the *sk_buff* associated with the DMA descriptor.

myFirstTxDesc is advanced to point to the next descriptor in the ring buffer.

18.6.2 Tx DMA Ring Buffer Descriptor After Initialization

Figure 18.14 illustrates the snapshot of transmit DMA ring buffer just after it is initialized details are coversed in Section 18.6.1.

18.6.3 *e100_hardware_send_packet()*

The *e100_hardware_send_packet()* routine is called from *e100_send_packet()* to initialize some of the fields of the *MyNextTxDesc* descriptor and start the DMA channel to trigger transmission. We initialize the length and frame to be transmitted for the current DMA descriptor (pointed to by *MyNextTxDesc*), line 1391 (cs 18.12). Mark this descriptor as the last descriptor in the Tx ring buffer for transmission; the *d_eol* control bit is set for this descriptor at line 1392. Provide the physical address of the frame buffer to be transmitted to the current descriptor at line 1391. We do this because the DMA engine doesn't go through the kernel VM subsystem. The control bit of the last descriptor is modified to indicate that it is not the last descriptor in the Tx ring buffer, line 1396. The last descriptor pointer, *myLastTx-Desc*, is made to point to the current descriptor (line 1397) because this points to the last buffer in the TX ring buffer to be transmitted. Restart the DMA channel to start transmission at line 1400.

18.6.4 There Are Two Packets in Device's DMA Tx Ring Buffer to Be Transmitted

Figure 18.15 illustrates the snapshot of the transmit DMA ring buffer when two packets are queued in the ring buffer for transmission. These packets are yet to be

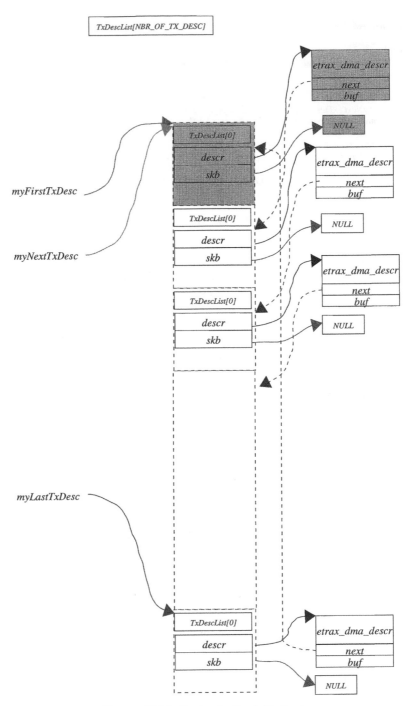

Figure 18.14. Tx ring buffer initialized.

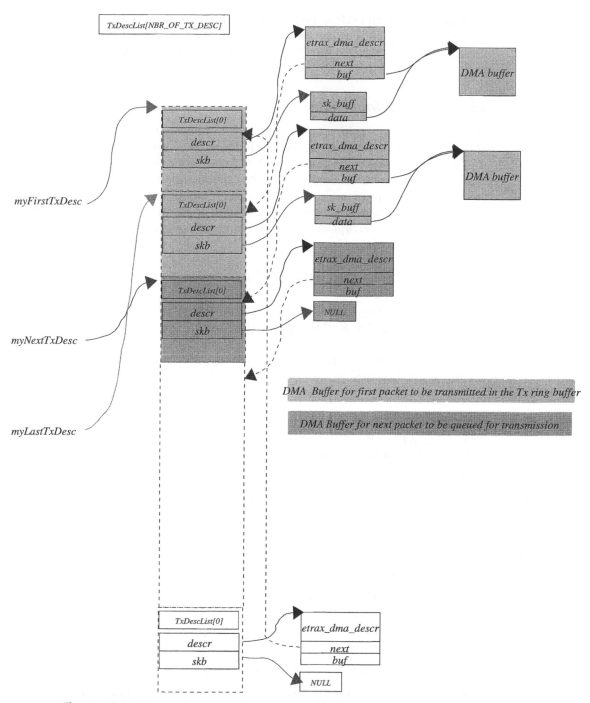

Figure 18.15. Two packets queued on Tx ring buffer for transmission.

transmitted. MyFirstTxDesc points to the first descriptor to be processed and MyLastTxDesc points to the last description to be processed in the ring buffer. These are used by the driver to know start and end of the descriptor to be processed in the ring buffer.

18.6.5 e100tx_interrupt()

e100_send_packet() queues up the frame for transmission, and it programs the DMA channel to start transmission of the frame. We have registered the Tx interrupt handler for the device which will be executed at the time when complete DMA transfer for one frame is completed. In the Tx interrupt handler we will check how many DMA descriptors are already processed (number of frames already transmitted). The *e100tx_interrupt()* routine is registered as an interrupt handler for Tx. We acknowledge the interrupt at line 1037. We iterate between lines 1035–1053 until either of the following occurs:

- We have reached the end of the list. In this case, *myFirstTxDesc* is the same as *myNextTxDesc*.
- We are pointing to the DMA descriptor that is being currently processed by the DMA engine *R_DMA_CH0_FIRST*.

In each iteration we advance *myFirstTxDesc* to point to the next descriptor in the Tx ring buffer, line 1052 (cs 18.13). In each iteration, we free the *sk_buff* associated

```
arch/cris/drivers/ethernet.c

1025 static void
1026 e100tx_interrupt(int irq, void *dev_id, struct pt_regs * regs)
1027 {
1028     struct net_device *dev = (struct net_device *)dev_id;
1029     unsigned long irqbits = *R_IRQ_MASK2_RD;
1030     struct net_local *np = (struct net_local *)dev->priv;
         ....
1033     if (irqbits & IO_STATE(R_IRQ_MASK2_RD, dma0_eop, active)) {
1034         /* Report all sent packets */
1035         do {
                 ....
1037             *R_DMA_CH0_CLR_INTR = IO_STATE(R_DMA_CH0_CLR_INTR, clr_eop, do);
1038
1039             np->stats.tx_bytes += myFirstTxDesc->skb->len;
1040             np->stats.tx_packets++;
                 ....
1044             dev_kfree_skb_irq(myFirstTxDesc->skb);
1045             myFirstTxDesc->skb = 0;
1046
1047             if (netif_queue_stopped(dev)) {
                     ....
1049                 *R_IRQ_MASK2_CLR = IO_STATE(R_IRQ_MASK2_CLR, dma0_eop, clr);
1050                 netif_wake_queue(dev);
1051             }
1052             myFirstTxDesc = phys_to_virt(myFirstTxDesc->descr.next);
1053         } while (myFirstTxDesc != phys_to_virt(*R_DMA_CH0_FIRST) &&
1054                  myFirstTxDesc != myNextTxDesc);
1055     }
1056 }
```

cs 18.13. *e100tx_interrupt()*.

with the DMA descriptor. The scenario looks very much like Fig. 18.16 after the
first frame is transmitted and the Tx interrupt is generated. We also take care of
the device that is stopped because the DMA ring buffer is full. Since we are releasing processed buffers in the Tx interrupt, we check if the device needs to be started
by calling *netif_queue_stopped()* at line 1047. In case we find that the device is
stopped, try to wake up the device to accept more packets for transmission by calling
netif_wake_queue() at line 1050.

18.6.6 First Packet from the DMA Queue Is Transmitted and Second One Is yet to Be Transmitted; After Interrupt Is Generated, Transmitted Buffer Is Freed

Figure 18.16 illustrates snapshot of the transmit DMA ring buffer when first DMA
descriptor is processed. The transmitted buffer is freed in the Tx interrupt handler.
MyFirstTxDesc and myLastTxDesc point to same descriptor that is the only one to
be processed in the ring buffer. Details are covered in Section 18.6.5.

18.7 SUMMARY

Each network interface is defined by *struct net_device*. This structure has callback
routines specific to hardware such as transmission building headers. When the
module is installed for the network card, the *net_device* object is initialized with
device-specific callback routines and certain parameters in the init routine. Tx and
Rx DMA ring buffers for the network controller are also initialized. When the
device is opened, DMA memory allocation, IRQ number, and interrupt handlers
are registered with the kernel.

In this chapter we learned about Rx and Tx ring buffer design and functioning.
The DMA ring buffers logic is implemented on the DMA-capable NIC. We just
program it to point to the first DMA descriptor in the DMA descriptor ring. The
DMA buffer for an Rx ring is preallocated, and its length is the maximum frame
length that we can receive on the interface.

In the above discussion we learned the process of reception and transmission
of packets over the Ethernet interface. The packet is received in a DMA buffer
registered for reception, and the interrupt handler for the receive pulls out a frame
from the Rx ring and is queued on a per CPU input queue and the softIRQ is raised
by calling *netif_rx()*. The Rx softIRQ pulls out a packet from the CPU input queue
and gives it to the upper layer for further processing. The DMA controller can be
programmed to generate an interrupt on reception of more than one frame.

Packet transmission takes a simple path. An IP datagram is queued on the
device queue and then the device scheduler is run to dequeue the device. Packets
are then processed by a device-specific hard transmit routine where a link layer
header is added to the IP datagram and a frame is added to the DMA Tx ring buffer.
A DMA controller is then programmed to start the transmission. Once the packet
is transmitted, a Tx interrupt is generated. A single Tx interrupt can be generated
for multiple transmissions.

An added functionality that the DMA-enabled NIC provides helps in enhancing I/O performance. For example, an Rx interrupt is generated when the frame is
completely received in the kernel memory with a DMA-enabled NIC. Otherwise,
we need to copy a frame from the device queue into kernel memory in the interrupt

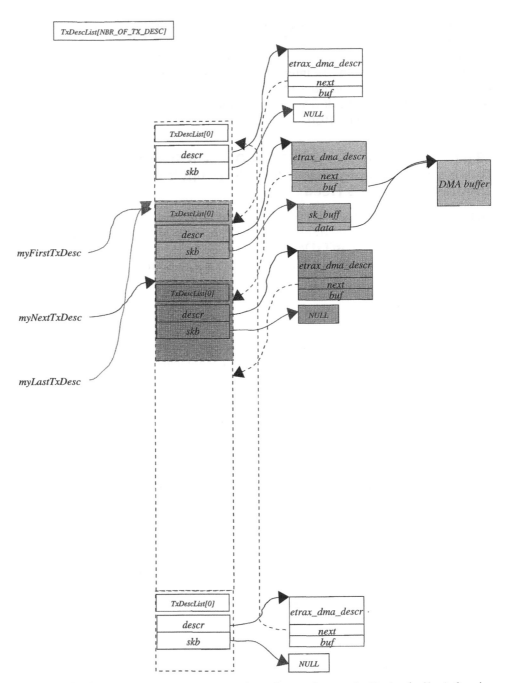

Figure 18.16. Tx interrupt is generated and the first packet on the Tx ring buffer is freed.

handler. This saves us a huge number of CPU cycles. While transmitting, we need not copy the frame to the device queue. With an DMA-enabled NIC, transmission is simplified and once again saves us CPU cycles. We program NIC DMA with the address of the network buffer, and the rest is taken care of by the DMA engine itself.

19

lkcd AND DEBUGGING TCP/IP STACK

There are different debuggers available to debug a Linux kernel such as *kdb, gdb, lkcd,* and so on. *lkcd* is a Linux kernel crash dump analyzer. This tool can generate kernel crash dumps and can save it on the specified location, and the crash can be used to analyze the cause of kernel crash. We can't do much as far as step debugging on a live system is concerned, for which *kdb* or *gdb* can be used. But *lkcd* can be used on the live kernel memory to analyze kernel data structures.

In this chapter an attempt is made to familiarize the reader with lkcd and how it can be used to peep through the kernel data structures related to TCP/IP stack. We take small examples related to TCP connections, add a new route (QOS), and try to peep through the related data structures to see how changes are taking place. Because of lack of resources and time, performance-related tests and tools could not be illustrated. But one can get an idea and feel of various aspects of TCP/IP stack debugging after the discussion.

I'd say that the best way to debug is to build a kernel module that records the statistics for a given connection, route, interrupt, or any subsystem and report it whenever requested. For example, I may need to analyze the complete history related to reception and transmission of packets for a given connection by a TCP state machine. I may write a kernel module to record certain TCP state machine variables such as congestion window, slow-start threshold, receive and send buffer space, timestamp, send window, rto, and so on, for each packet that is transmitted and received. This statistics can be collected at the end of the connection for analysis. Many such ideas can be implemented to make life easier to test and analyze the behavior of TCP/IP protocol and related framework in different situations.

TCP/IP Architecture, Design, and Implementation in Linux. By S. Seth and M. A. Venkatesulu
Copyright © 2008 the IEEE Computer Society

We won't discuss configuration and features of *lkcd* in our current discussion but will discuss only the relevant stuff related to the topic. This will be peeping into different kernel data structures and some analysis. The rest is left to the practice and imagination of the reader.

19.1 *lkcd* SOURCE AND PATCHES

We can get an *lkcd* source from sourceforge.net. *kerntypes* is a database of kernel data structures which is generated when lkcd is built. The path of *kerntypes* and a system map file are arguments to the *lcrash*. The following command can start the lcrash program on the kernel crash dump:

   lcrash *kerntypes core-file system.map*

lcrash can also be used on the live system by running the following command:

   lcrash *kerntypes /dev/mem system.map*

kerntypes generated by default may not contain stub for all the kernel subsystems data structures. SG has developed a tool to generate a stub for all kernel data types. We need to build a kernel in the debug mode and run *dwarfextract* binary to build a kerntypes file in the following way:

   dwarfextract-p vmlinux kerntypes

Type in the modules you will need to add to the *kerntypes* with *dwarfextract*-c or -C.
   kerntypes comes with the 7.0.1-27 version of *lkcdutils* and is found under lkcdutils/dwarf/dwarfdump directory.
   All this is for *lkcd* utilities. We also need to configure a kernel with frame pointer options and build a kernel with an *lkcd* patch. For kernel 2.4 a patch can be found at

   http://lkcd.sourceforge.net/

User documentation for an lcrash can be found at

*lkcd.sourceforge.net/doc/**lcrash**.pdf*

Complete information about lcrash can be found at

   http://www.faqs.org/docs/Linux-HOWTO/Linux-Crash-HOWTO.html

19.2 TOUCHING THE SOCKET

In this section, we will see how we can access a socket structure inside the kernel when an application opens a TCP socket. In Chapter 3 we have discussed about

```
2    lcrash>  ps | grep client
3    > c579c000    0   2906   2703 0x01 0x00000000  341:78   client_do_nothing
4    >
5    > print (*(struct task_struct * )c579c000)->files
6    > (struct files_struct *) 0xc66bdbf0

8    > print *(struct files_struct *) 0xc66bdbf0
9    >struct files_struct {
        ....
17      -next_fd = 4
18       fd = 0xc484fc00
22      ....
23 }
```

Figure 19.1. Accessing process file table.

```
26    lcrash > dump -x 0xc484fc00 10
27    > 0xc484fc00: c7806c80 c7806c80 c7806c80 c5e7cd60 : .l...l...l. ...
28      0xc484fc10: 00000000 00000000 00000000 00000000 : ..............
29      0xc484fc20: 00000000 00000000                    : ........
```

Figure 19.2. Dump of pointers to file objects corresponding to open files for the process.

how kernel data structures are linked through VFS layer to get to reach socket. Just to refresh our memories, a socket is treated just like any other file, and an application can access a socket using file descriptors. An entry goes in the process file table when we open a socket. Let's first see how can we access a process file table (Fig. 19.1). *lcrash* is run on live memory (*/dev/mem*), and a simple application is run that opens a TCP socket (*INET_STREAM*).

We start an *lcrash* program as mentioned in Section 19.1. The socket program for which we need to find socket in the kernel is *client_do_nothing*. First we find out the *task_struct* object for the process associated with our program *client_do_ nothing*. We run *ps* command at *lcrash* command line interface at line 2 in Fig. 19.1 to identify our process inside the kernel. The next step is to find the file table for the process. *files* field of the *task_struct* object points to the file table, which is object of type *files_struct*. Using a print command at line 5, we get the address of the file table. Now we dump *files_struct* object with the given address at line 8. The *fd* field of the *files_struct* is an array of pointer to a *file* object, one for each open file for the process. We found the file table, and the next step is to identify our socket file descriptor from the file table.

We dump 10 words (32-bit) from the address of *fd* at line 26 as shown in Fig. 19.2. The first three entries point to standard input, standard output, and standard error. The third entry points to the file opened by the process. Since our program has opened only one socket, the fourth entry should correspond to the socket. Let's examine this.

We will examine the fourth entry in the open file descriptor table. The fourth entry is pointer to *file* object. We want to get to the *inode* object for this file. First we access *dentry* object for the file that is pointed to by *f_dentry* field of the *file* object at line 32, Fig. 19.3. *inode* object is pointed to by the *d_inode* field of the *dentry* object at line 35. We have the address of the *inode* object for the fourth entry

```
32    >> print (*(struct file *)c5e7cd60)->f_dentry
33      (struct dentry *) 0xc75b5e40
34
35    >> print (*(struct dentry *) 0xc75b5e40)->d_inode
36      (struct inode *) 0xc72d4740
37
38    >> print (*(struct inode *) 0xc72d4740)->i_sock
39      '\001'
```

Figure 19.3. Reaching inode entry from file object.

```
41 >> print (*(struct inode *) 0xc72d4740)->u.socket_i
42      struct socket {
43        state = (SS_CONNECTED=3)
44        flags = 0
45        ops = 0xc0295a40
46        inode = 0xc72d4740
          ....
48        file = 0xc5e7cd60
49        sk = 0xc41e4540
          ....
60 }
```

Figure 19.4. Accessing socket object from inode.

in the process file table at line 36. First we check whether the *inode* corresponds to the socket from the *i_sock* field. Since this field is set, we are sure that the fourth entry corresponds to the open socket.

The next step is to find the socket object corresponding to the inode. Since the inode is a common interface provided by VFS for any type of file, *u* is the union of all types of file-specific objects supported by Linux. For the socket *inode*, there is a socket object as part of the *inode* union *u*. This object is pointed to by the *socket_i* field of the *inode* union in Fig. 19.4, and we dump socket object at line 41. The state of the socket is connected, as is obvious from line 43. The socket has a back pointer to the *inode* object at line 46 and to the *file* object at line 48, which are very much tallying.

We have come to the BSD socket object. The *sk* field of the BSD socket object points to protocol-specific socket. In the next section we are going to examine a TCP socket object. The BSD socket keeps account of the connection and links the protocol-specific socket with the VFS and the process. The protocol-specific socket, pointed to by *sk*, is actually responsible for doing protocol-specific operations and for managing the protocol-specific state and the data for the connection.

19.3 LOOKING INTO THE RECEIVE SOCKET BUFFER

From the previous section, we extend our discussion to one step ahead. The application is receiving data in chunks of 18 bytes, and the data is '*I got your message.*' This application has not issued any *recv()* syscall to read data from the socket's receive buffer. So, we get a chance to peep through the socket's receive buffer dumped in Fig. 19.5.

```
62 >> print (*(struct sock*)0xc41e4540)->receive_queue
63     struct sk_buff_head {
64         next = 0xc4e1e970
65         prev = 0xc4e88710
66         qlen = 48
67         lock = spinlock_t {
68         }
69 }
```

Figure 19.5. Socket receive buffer.

```
72 >> print (*(struct sk_buff*)0xc4e1e970)->data
73  0xc40ea914
74
75 >> dump -c 0xc40ea914 18
76 0xc40ea914: 6f6720496f7920746d20727561737365: I got your messa
77 0xc40ea924: 000065670000000000000000000000001: ge...........
78 ....
```

Figure 19.6. Network buffer (*sk_buff*) content.

Since the application is not reading data over the socket, all the socket buffers will get piled up on the socket receive queue. So, we can see 48 socket buffers queued up at a receive queue at line 66 in Fig. 19.5. These buffers are linked by *next* and *prev* field of the *sk_buff_head* object. We pick up the first buffer from the receive queue and see what's is in it from Fig. 19.6.

When the buffer is queued on the sockets' receive queue, the protocol headers are already stripped. So, the *data* field of the buffer (*sk_buff*) will be pointing to the TCP payload. The pointer to the *data* field is accessed at line 72. We dump 18 bytes from the location pointed to by the *data* field at line 75. We can see that the buffer contains same data—'I got the message'—at lines 76–77.

19.3.1 Route Information in *sk_buff*

Each network buffer that traverses up the stack contains route information once it is routed. This will contain all relevant information about the route. The incoming packet may need to be forwarded. In this case, all the information about the outgoing interface, along with other information about the route, is cached with the buffer itself. The information is available with a *dst* field of *sk_buff* which is of type *dst_entry*. We get the address of cached route information in *sk_buff* at line 82 in Fig. 19.7. This has a pointer to *net_device* object pointing to an outgoing interface pointed to by *dev* field. We get a pointer to an outgoing interface at line 85. Next I cross-checked whether the interface is reported correctly by printing the name of the interface at line 87. The interface reported was correct, that is, eth0.

19.4 PEEP INTO SEND SOCKET BUFFER

Whenever we write data over the socket, it first goes into the socket send buffer and is then transmitted from the send buffer. This is required for so many reasons, such as we may want to queue data for the socket even if we are not able to transmit

```
81 >> print (*(struct sk_buff*)0xc4e1e970)->dst
82 (struct dst_entry *) 0xc6d3b490
83
84 >> print (*(struct dst_entry *) 0xc6d3b490)->dev
85 (struct net_device *) 0xc79f0800
86
87 >> print (*(struct net_device*)0xc79f0800)->name
88 "eth0"
```

Figure 19.7. Route information for network buffer, *sk_buff*.

```
355 >> ps | grep client
356    c193c000    0    2891    2700 0x01 0x00000000  341:78   client_do_nothing
357 >> print (*(struct task_struct*)c193c000)->files
358    (struct files_struct *) 0xc27b7d90
359
360 >> print (*(struct files_struct *) 0xc27b7d90)->fd
361    (struct file **) 0xc71fe000
362
363 >> dump -x 0xc51cbc00 10
364    0xc51cbc00: c777eeb0 c777eeb0 c777eeb0 c4301c10 : ..w...w...w...0.
365    0xc51cbc10: 00000000 00000000 00000000 00000000 : ..............
366    0xc51cbc20: 00000000 00000000                   : ........
367
368 >> print (*(struct file*)c4301c10)->f_dentry->d_inode
369    (struct inode *) 0xc78f6900
       ....
374 >> print (*(struct inode *) 0xc78f6900)->i_sock
375    '\001'
376
377 >> print (*(struct inode *) 0xc78f6900)->u.socket_i
378    struct socket {
379        state = (SS_CONNECTED=3)
           ....
385        sk = 0xc77e09f0
           ....
396    }
       ....
398 >> print (*(struct sock*)0xc77e09f0)->write_queue
399 struct sk_buff_head {
400        next = 0xc4d15c00
401        prev = 0xc5b6cac0
402        qlen = 2
403        lock = spinlock_t {
404        }
405 }
```

Figure 19.8. Access socket send buffer.

it at once. Then we need to queue the transmitted segment until it is ACKed. The data are removed from the send socket buffer as soon as data are ACKed. We learned in Section 7.1 that the data from the application are broken into smaller segments before transmission. So, we will examine the send buffer of the socket where the application wrote data in small chunks of 1 mss size so that data are not overlapping. In every write, the application fills the buffer of 1 mss with the next alphabet. Let's examine these buffers.

Figure 19.8 shows the complete path for reaching a socket's send buffer (*sk→write_queue*). The experiment is very simple where client and server programs

```
407 >> print (*(struct sock*)0xc77e09f0)->tp_pinfo.af_tcp->send_head
408    0xc5b6cac0

       ....
414 >> print (*(struct sock*)0xc77e09f0)->write_queue
415    struct sk_buff_head {
416        next = 0xc77e0a48
417        prev = 0xc77e0a48
418        qlen = 0

       .....
421 }
```

Figure 19.9. Send head pointing to next segment to send.

are running on two different hosts within LAN. We will be examining the socket's send buffer and the send head (*tp→send_head*). Since there is no congestion and data are transmitted at high rate in LAN, packets are transmitted as soon as they are queued on the socket's send queue. The data segments on the socket's send queue are removed as soon as they are ACKed. Data are ACKed so fast in the LAN environment that however fast we examine the send buffer, there won't be anything there to be examined. For the same reason, we tried a trick of unplugging the receiving end from the network for some time. In this duration, packets won't be ACKed and we can easily examine the socket send buffer.

We find a socket for the connection at line 377 in Fig. 19.8 for which an explanation is already provided in Section 19.2. Next we dump the send queue (*sk→write_queue*) for the buffer at line 398. We can see that two packets are queued on the send queue at line 402. At this point, the send head points to the next packet to be transmitted. This should point to the segment pointed to by *prev* in the *sk→write_queue* because the first segment pointed to by the *next* field of *sk→write_queue* is already transmitted; and because the retransmit timer fired, it has already been retransmitted. This is clear from lines 407–408 in Fig. 19.9. Just after examining the socket's send buffer, the receiver was plugged once again and all the data in the send queue were transmitted and ACK. So, a snapshot of the socket's send queue dumped at line 414 shows that there is no segment in the queue for transmission in Fig. 19.9. In this case, the send head points to NULL, which is not shown here.

Once again, the same step is repeated and the receiver is unplugged from the network. We find there are two segments in socket's send buffer in Fig. 19.10 at line 427. We examine the contents of these segments. The *data* field of the buffer points to the start of the data because no header is built at this point. Since the application is writing data in chunks of 1 mss, we don't see any overlapping of data in the segments. The first segment contains all *k*'s dumped at line 436, and second segment contains all *j*'s dumped at line 443.

19.5 TCP SEGMENTATION UNIT

In this section we will see how a segmentation unit tries to make a full-length segment in the case where an application sends data for transmission and there exists a partial segment at the tail of the send queue. By full segment we mean 1 mss segment. The experiment is the same as explained in Section 19.4. The only difference is that instead of the application sending data in chunks of 1 mss, it is

```
423 >> print (*(struct sock*)0xc77e09f0)->write_queue
424    struct sk_buff_head {
425            next = 0xc763c170
426            prev = 0xc4d15980
427            qlen = 2
428            lock = spinlock_t {
429            }
430    }
431
432 >> print (*(struct sk_buff *)0xc4d15980)->data
433    0xc388a110
434
435 >> dump -x 0xc388a110 10
436    0xc388a110: 6b6b6b6b 6b6b6b6b 6b6b6b6b 6b6b6b6b : kkkkkkkkkkkkkkkk
437    0xc388a120: 6b6b6b6b 6b6b6b6b 6b6b6b6b 6b6b6b6b : kkkkkkkkkkkkkkkk
438    0xc388a130: 6b6b6b6b 6b6b6b6b               : kkkkkkkk
439
440 >> print (*(struct sk_buff *)0xc763c170)->data
441    0xc6f9b910
442
443 >> dump -x 0xc6f9b910 10
444    0xc6f9b910: 6a6a6a6a 6a6a6a6a 6a6a6a6a 6a6a6a6a : jjjjjjjjjjjjjjjj
445    0xc6f9b920: 6a6a6a6a 6a6a6a6a 6a6a6a6a 6a6a6a6a : jjjjjjjjjjjjjjjj
446    0xc6f9b930: 6a6a6a6a 6a6a6a6a               : jjjjjjjj
```

Figure 19.10. Examining data in the socket send buffers.

sending data in much smaller chunks. The application writes 18 bytes of data each time the receiver is unplugged from the network.

The process to find a socket is the same as discussed in Section 19.2. We find a socket for our connection at line 123 in Fig. 19.11. We can see that there are two segments in the send queue at line 158. The first segment pointed to by the *next* field of *sk→write_queue* is already transmitted; and because of timing out, it is retransmitted as well. So, this segment contains only 18 bytes of data indicated by the *len* field of *sk_buff* dumped at line 154. The length of the next buffer in the send queue is dumped at line 165 and shows 342. On examining data in the buffers, it is found that the first one contains '*I got the message*' data (line 159) and the second buffer has the same data appended many times (line 168). Since the application is writing 18 bytes of data ('*I got the message*') each time, TCP's segmentation unit appends data to the buffer at the tail of the send queue since it is partial and is not creating new segment for each write. Once the other end is connected to the network, we can see that these two segments are transmitted and all the subsequent segments contain only 18 bytes of data because they are transmitted because soon as they are queued.

19.6 SEND CONGESTION WINDOW AND *ssthresh*

In this section we will see how a congestion window changes with ACKs received when we send data in bulk. A simple experiment is carried out to check this behavior. First we sent out one data segment at an interval of 1 second; in another program, 20 full-sized segment were sent out in the burst, and this is repeated at an interval of 10 seconds. The socket for the connection is accessed at line 620 in Fig. 19.12. The send congestion window (*snd_cwnd*) and the send slow-start

```
101 >> ps | grep client
102    c5694000    0   2963   2832 0x01 0x00000000  341:78   client_do_nothi
103 >> print (*(struct task_struct*)c5694000)->files
104    (struct files_struct *) 0xc6ba6dc0
105
106 >> print (*(struct files_struct *)0xc6ba6dc0)->fd
107 (struct file **) 0xc7bd0000
108
109 >> dump -x 0xc7bd0000 10
110    0xc7bd0000: c5900190 c5900190 c5900190 c5cfc580 : ...............
111    0xc7bd0010: 00000000 00000000 00000000 00000000 : ...............
112    0xc7bd0020: 00000000 00000000                :  ........
113
114 >> print (*(struct file*)c5cfc580)->f_dentry->d_inode
118    (struct inode *) 0xc45ab900
119
120 >> print (*(struct inode *) 0xc45ab900)->i_sock
121    '\001'
122
123 >> print (*(struct inode *) 0xc45ab900)->u.socket_i
124    struct socket {
125        state = (SS_CONNECTED=3)
           ....
131        sk = 0xc34655a0
           ....
142    }
144 >> print (*(struct sock*)0xc34655a0)->write_queue
145 struct sk_buff_head {
146        next = 0xc55faa20
147        prev = 0xc550c350
148        qlen = 2
149        lock = spinlock_t {
150        }
151 }
154 >> print (*(struct sk_buff*)0xc55faa20)->len
155    18
156
157 >> print (*(struct sk_buff*)0xc55faa20)->data
158    0xc6dff910
159 >> dump -c 0xc6dff910 100
160 0xc6dff910: 6f6720496f7920746d20727561737365: I got your messa
161 0xc6dff920: 1dde65671dde1dde1dde1dde1dde1dde: ge..............
162
163
164 >> print (*(struct sk_buff*)0xc550c350)->len
165    342
166 >> print (*(struct sk_buff*)0xc550c350)->data
167    0xc7261110
168 >> dump -c 0xc7261110 200
169    0xc7261110: 6f6720496f7920746d20727561737365: I got your messa
170    0xc7261120: 2049656720746f6772756f7973656d20: geI got your mes
171    0xc7261130: 656761736f6720496f7920746d207275: sageI got your m
172    0xc7261140: 61737365204965672074066772756f79: essageI got your
173    0xc7261150: 73656d2065676173666f6720496f7920: messageI got yo
174    0xc7261160: 6d20727561737365204965672074066f: ur messageI got
       .....
```

Figure 19.11. Filling of partial segments to make it complete by segmentation unit.

```
604 >> print (*(struct task_struct*)c12da000)->files
605    (struct files_struct *) 0xc2e4aa50
606 >> print (*(struct files_struct *) 0xc2e4aa50)->fd
607    (struct file **) 0xc7ee9800
608 >> dump -x 0xc7ee9800 10
609    0xc7ee9800: c5fe4f20 c5fe4f20 c5fe4f20 c2fec7b0 : O.. O.. O.....
        ....
613 >> print (*(struct file*)c2fec7b0)->f_dentry
614    (struct dentry *) 0xc1b32c10
615 >> print (*(struct dentry *) 0xc1b32c10)->d_inode
616    (struct inode *) 0xc425f040
617 >> print (*(struct inode *) 0xc425f040)->i_sock
618    '\001'
620 >> print (*(struct inode *) 0xc425f040)->u.socket_i
621    struct socket {
622         state = (SS_CONNECTED=3)
            ....
628         sk = 0xc510aaf0
            ....
639    }
        ....
653 >> print (*(struct sock*)0xc510aaf0)->tp_pinfo.af_tcp->snd_cwnd
654    2
655 >> print (*(struct sock*)0xc510aaf0)->tp_pinfo.af_tcp->snd_ssthresh
656    2147483647
```

Figure 19.12. *snd_cwnd & snd_ssthresh.*

threshold (*snd_ssthresh*) are state variables for TCP, as part of the *tcp_opt* object. The initial value of the congestion window is set to two (line 653), and the slow-start threshold is set to a very large value (line 655).

In the first experiment where an application was sending 1 mss of data at an interval of 1 second, it was observed that the congestion window remained constant at two. The reason for this observation is that the congestion window is increased only if we are using a network at full capacity offered at any point in time. In this case the application sends out the next chunk of data only after ACK for the first chunk of data is received. So, we are not saturating the network enough with our data transmission rate.

In the second experiment, an application is sending data in a burst of 20 full-sized segments. The application is stuffing in enough data to the TCP socket buffer so that next the data are ready by the time ACK for the first data segment is received. In this case we can expect an exponential rise in the congestion window. Since the application is sending data in bursts, we can't guarantee all the data from an application to be sent to the socket before it is scheduled out. Let's see whether there is an exponential rise in the congestion window. Two snapshots are taken after the application sends out a burst of 20 full data chunks in 20 writes in Fig. 19.13.

After the first burst is sent out, the congestion window is incremented to 8 where we are expecting some higher value. The reason for this is cumulative ACKs. The receiver is sending cumulative ACKs for 4, 3, and 2 data segments, which is not certain. Then we may not have data ready in the socket's send queue at the time when ACKs arrive because the application may have scheduled out without sending out a complete burst of 20 full-sized data chunks in 20 writes. One can try out a small program that sends out a big data chunk of 20 mss in one write. Probably this may give us some higher value of congestion window at the end of full transmission of data.

```
829 >> print (*(struct sock*)0xc510aaf0)->tp_pinfo.af_tcp->snd_ssthresh
830    2147483647
831 >>print (*(struct sock*)0xc510aaf0)->tp_pinfo.af_tcp->snd_cwnd
832    8
833 >> print (*(struct sock*)0xc510aaf0)->tp_pinfo.af_tcp->snd_nxt
834    603230558
835 >> print (*(struct sock*)0xc510aaf0)->tp_pinfo.af_tcp->snd_una
836    603230558
```

Figure 19.13. snd_cwnd & snd_ssthresh.

```
901 >> print (*(struct sock*)0xc510aaf0)->tp_pinfo.af_tcp->retransmits
902    '\010' = '\b'
       ....
910 >> print (*(struct sock*)0xc510aaf0)->dst_cache
911    (struct dst_entry *) 0x0
```

Figure 19.14. Number of retransmissions and routing information.

19.7   RETRANSMISSIONS AND ROUTE

A simple experiment was conducted to check how a number of retransmissions and routing information for the connection are related. Normal TCP connection is established and the peer is unplugged from the network. The application continues to send out data. Since we are on LAN, RTO will be much less. By the time we check the probe using lcrash, the number of retransmissions reaches 10 as shown in Fig. 19.14, line 901. In this case, we have already retransmitted a segment 10 times and are still not able to get an ACK. The route for the connection has vanished for the socket, line 910. In the retransmit timer callback routine, we call *tcp_write_timeout()* to check whether it is time to check the route for the connection. First we check whether the number of retransmits has exceeded *sysctl_tcp_retries1*. If so, we need to check the route for the connection if it is valid. Here we call *dst_negative_advice()*, which will update the route for the connection (*sk→dst_cache*). If the number of retransmits has exceeded *sysctl_tcp_retries2*, we need to close the connection. The values of these two control parameters are checked out by using *fsyms lcrash* command as shown in Fig. 19.15. We have exceeded *sysctl_tcp_retries1* which is 3, we check route for the connection. The route is found to be invalid because the destination is unreachable since the peer is not in the network. So, the socket's route cache is made NULL by call to *ipv4_negative_advice()*.

19.8   PEEPING INTO CONNECTION QUEUES AND SYN QUEUES

In this section we will see how connections are accepted and queued on the different queues for a listening socket. The listening socket has two queues which is discussed in great detail in Section (4.4). These queues are accept queue and SYN queue. New requests are queued on the SYN queue; and once they are established, it is dequeued from the SYN queue and are queued on the accept queue. The number of requests that can be queued on the accept queue is defined by backlog parameter to the *listen()* system call, and by default it is 5.

```
913 >> fsym sysctl_tcp_retries1
914   ADDR  OFFSET SECTION    NAME            TYPE
915   ===============================================
916   0xc0294e04   0 GLOBAL_DATA sysctl_tcp_retries1 (unknown)
917   ===============================================
918   1 symbol found
919
920 >> dump -x 0xc0294e04
921   0xc0294e04: 00000003


923 >> fsym sysctl_tcp_retries2
924   ADDR  OFFSET SECTION    NAME            TYPE
925   ===============================================
926   0xc0294e08   0 GLOBAL_DATA sysctl_tcp_retries2 (unknown)
927   ===============================================
928   1 symbol found
929
930 >> dump -x 0xc0294e08 1
931   0xc0294e08: 0000000f
```

Figure 19.15. Retransmissions tries control parameters.

A simple server program is written which is run on the machine on which *lcrash* is run to examine connection queues for the listening socket. The length of the accept queue is set to 1 from application using *listen()* syscall. From the other machine in the network, a number of connection requests are sent for this listen socket. We will examine both the accept queue and the SYN queue for this scenario.

An accept queue for the listening socket is pointed to by *accept_queue* field of *tcp_opt* object. SYN queue queues all the open requests and is pointed to by the *syn_table* field of the *tcp_listen_opt* object. The server program is running as *server_ do_nothing*, and it doesn't issue accept syscall. We get hold of the listening socket at line 231 in Fig. 19.16. The state of the socket is unconnected, line 233.

Since the socket is in the listening state, 11 connection requests are issued for the listening socket. We examine the *tcp_listen_opt* object for the listening socket pointed to by the *listen_opt* field of the *tcp_opt* object. We get hold of *tcp_listen_opt* object at line 281 in Fig. 19.17. It has queue management parameters and the SYN queue has table *syn_table* of type *open_request*. The new connection request goes in this table first. Once the three-way hand shake is over, a new socket is created for the connection request and the request is moved to the accept queue. If the accept queue is full, the connection request may be retained by the SYN queue so that later when connections are accepted from the accept queue, the established connections can make their way into the accept queue.

A snapshot of the connection requests shown in Fig. 19.17 indicates that there are a total of nine requests queued up in the SYN queue (line 287). None of these requests are young (line 288), which means that all the requests in the SYN queue have retransmitted SYN-ACK at least once. This may happen in two cases:

- SYN-ACK is not getting ACKed.
- The accept queue is full with Partial Connections (three-way TCP handshake not yet over).

```
208 >> ps | grep server
209    c1412000    0   3609   2832 0x01 0x00000000  341:78   server_do_nothing
210
211 >> print (*(struct task_struct *)c1412000)->files
212    (struct files_struct *) 0xc6ba6c20
213
214 >> print (*(struct files_struct *) 0xc6ba6c20)->fd
215 (struct file **) 0xc25db800
216
217 >> dump -x 0xc25db800 10
218 0xc25db800: c5900190 c5900190 c5900190 c50403c0 : ..............
219 0xc25db810: 00000000 00000000 00000000 00000000 : ..............
220 0xc25db820: 00000000 00000000            : .......
221
222 >> print (*(struct file*)c50403c0)->f_dentry->d_inode
226 (struct inode *) 0xc72ffac0
228 >> print (*(struct inode *) 0xc72ffac0)->i_sock
229 '\001'
230
231 >> print (*(struct inode *) 0xc72ffac0)->u.socket_i
232 struct socket {
233      state = (SS_UNCONNECTED=1)
         ....
239      sk = 0xc53010c0
         ....
250 }
```

Figure 19.16. Reaching listening socket.

The timer is set to expire periodically once there is any connection request in the SYN queue. It removes old entries from the SYN queue once the entry has expired. *syn_table* is the actual SYN queue of *open_request*. We can see all nine entries in the SYN queue. Let's examine one of these in Fig. 19.18. The *open_request* object contains all the information for the connection request that is contained in the SYN segment. These will be TCP options, initial sequence number of both the ends, window size, and so on; the *acked* field at line 341 indicates that the request has not yet received the final ACK for the SYN sent. If this field is set and the request is still on the SYN queue, it means that we accept that the queue is full, because of which we are here.

Let's see the status of the accept queue. We set the accept queue length to 1, and for that reason the maximum number of requests that can be queued on the accept queue is 2. The first request on the queue is examined at line 256. The *dl_next* field is non-null, which means that there is one more request queued on the accept queue. The *dl_next* field of the next request is NULL, which we have not shown here. The *Sk* field points to the socket created for this request because the three-way handshake for the connection is over and the connection is in an established state.

19.9 ROUTING AND IP Qos lcrash STEPS

19.9.1 lcrash Steps for Default Queueing Discipline in Linux *(pfifo_fast)*

In this section we will see the data structures for the queueing discipline, as well as how the default Linux queueing discipline is set up. Linux uses *pfifo_fast* as the

```
281 >> print (*(struct sock*)0xc53010c0)->tp_pinfo.af_tcp->listen_opt
282    (struct tcp_listen_opt *) 0xc3dca000
283
284 >> print *((struct tcp_listen_opt *) 0xc3dca000) | more
285    struct tcp_listen_opt {
286          max_qlen_log = '\010' = '\b'
287          qlen = 9
288          qlen_young = 0
289          clock_hand = 492
290          syn_table = {
291              [0] (nil)
292              [1] (nil)
293              ...
295              [244] (nil)
296              [245] 0xc5b96390
297              [246] (nil)
298              [247] 0xc5b963f0
299              [248] (nil)
300              [249] 0xc5b96210
301              [250] (nil)
302              [251] 0xc5b96450
303              [252] (nil)
304              ...
306              [496] 0xc5b964b0
                 .....
309              [499] (nil)
310              [500] 0xc5b962d0
311              [501] (nil)
312              [502] 0xc5b96330
313              [503] (nil)
314              [504] 0xc5b961b0
315              [505] (nil)
316              [506] 0xc5b96270
                 .....
322          }
323    }
```

Figure 19.17. *SYN Queue table.*

```
326 >> print (*(struct open_request*)0xc5b964b0) | more
327    struct open_request {
328          dl_next = 0x0
329          rcv_isn = 1594224023
330          snt_isn = 1593662849
              ....
341          acked = 0
              ....
345          expires = 1285790

348          ...
349    }
```

Figure 19.18. Open request entry in the SYN queue.

```
253 >> print (*(struct sock*)0xc53010c0)->tp_pinfo.af_tcp->accept_queue
254     (struct open_request *) 0xc5b960f0
255
256     struct open_request {
257         dl_next = 0xc5b96150
258         rcv_isn = 2925901706
259         snt_isn = 311737211
260         rmt_port = 4737
            ....
270         acked = 0
            ....
276         sk = 0xc3465a60
278         ...
279     }
```

Figure 19.19. Established connection in the accept queue.

```
14 >> fsym dev_base
15     ADDR  OFFSET SECTION   NAME          TYPE
16 ========================================================
17 0xc02808d8    0 GLOBAL_DATA dev_base     (unknown)
18 ========================================================
19 1 symbol found
20 >> print -x (*(int *)0xc02808d8)
21 0xc0280780
22 >> print -x (*(struct net_device *)0xc0280780)->next
23 (struct net_device *) 0xc02aa7e0
24 >> print -x (*(struct net_device *)0xc02aa7e0)->next
25 (struct net_device *) 0xceec3000
26 >> print -x (*(struct net_device *)0xceec3000)->next
27 (struct net_device *) 0xceec3800
28 >> print -x (*(struct net_device *)0xceec3800)
29 struct net_device {
30     name = "eth1"
       . . . .
184    qdisc = 0xced1a88c

       . . . . .
224 }
```

Figure 19.20. Examine net_device objects in the system.

default queueing discipline for enqueueing the packets before transmitting them to the interface.

First we can find out the *net_device* structure for the interface from Fig. 19.20. For this, we get the address of the *dev_base* list using the fsym command in lcrash at line 14 where the *dev_base* symbol is a list that contains the *net_device* for each network interface in the system. Then we can walk through the *dev_base* list to find out the required *net_device* struct. In our case we are looking for eth1 network device, so we walk through the device list. We can see this from lines 20–27, and

```
226 >> print -x (*(Qdisc *)0xced1a88c)
227 struct Qdisc {


228       enqueue = 0xc01e0878
229       dequeue = 0xc01e08e4


          . . .
258       data = ""
259 }


261 >> fsym 0xc01e0878


262    ADDR OFFSET SECTION    NAME            TYPE
263 ==================================================
264 0xc01e0878   0 LOCAL_TEXT  pfifo_fast_enqueue  (unknown)
265 ==================================================
```

Figure 19.21. Examine enqueue and dequeue call back routine for Qdisc.

finally we print the *net_device* struct for the required device at line 28. Basically we are looking for the qdisc data structure address from the *net_device* struct, which is at line 184. The qdisc data structure of the *net_device* represents the queueing discipline for that network interface.

Using the qdisc object address from the *net_device* struct here, we are checking the enqueue field, which is a function pointer, this got initialized to the *pfifo_fast_enqueue( )* function when the Linux system booted up. This function gets called for enqueueing the packets. From Fig. 19.21 we access the qdisc object and then check the value for the enqueue field at line 228. Then, using this address of the enqueue field, we check for which function is pointing to the enqueue field at line 261.

The data field from the qdisc object in Fig. 19.21 is an anonymous pointer which is a place holder for the private data structures of the queueing discilpline. In the case of default *pfifo_fast* queueing discipline, this data field points to the array of *sk_buff_head* structures. Basically, this contains the three different FIFO queues (different bands) for enqueueing the packets based on the priority: FIFO 0, FIFO 1, and FIFO 2. In the next section, we will see how we can access these FIFOs.

For accessing the array of the *sk_buff_head* objects for qdisc from Fig. 19.22, we first get the size of Qdisc struct at line 268 which is 0x5c bytes. The data field of the qdisc object contains the private data structures of the queueing discilpline, in this case it is an array of three *sk_buff_head* data structures. To access the first element of the array, we use the sizeof value of the qdisc object (i.e., 0x5c) as an offset from the base address of the qdisc object. After adding this offset value to the base address of the qdisc object at line 278, we can acccess the first *sk_buff* head struct (FIFO 0) for the *pfifo_fast* queueing discilpline.

For accessing the next element of the array, we calculate the size of the *sk_buff_head* struct, which is 0x0c bytes. By adding this value to the base address of the *sk_buff_head* array, we get the second the *sk_buff_head* structure (FIFO 1) at line 297. Then again adding the size two *sk_buff_head* structures to the base address of the *sk_buff_head* array, we get the third *sk_buff_head* structure (FIFO 2) at line 306 from Fig. 19.23.

```
268 size of "Qdisc": 92 bytes
269 >> base 92
270
271 ---------------------------------------------
272   hex: 0x5c
273 decimal: 92
274   octal: 0134
275   binary: 0b1011100
276 ---------------------------------------------
277 >>
278 >> print -x (*(struct sk_buff_head *)(0xced1a88c + 0x5c))
279 struct sk_buff_head {
280      next = 0xced1a8e8
281      prev = 0xced1a8e8
282      qlen = 0x0
283      lock = spinlock_t {
284      }
285 }
```

Figure 19.22. Examine sk_buff's queued on Qdisc.

19.10   CBQ (CLASS-BASED) QUEUEING DISCIPLINE lcrash STEPS

In this section we are going to see the data structures for the CBQ queueing discipline in lcrash.

Commands for Setting Up CBQ Queueing Discipline

   # tc qdisc add dev eth1 root handle 1: cbq bandwidth 10 Mbit cell 8 avpkt 1000 mpu 64

   # tc class add dev eth1 parent 1:0 classid 1:1 cbq bandwidth 10 Mbit rate 10 Mbit allot 1514 cell 8 weight 1 Mbit prio 8 maxburst 20 avpkt 1000

   # tc class add dev eth1 parent 1:1 classid 1:2 cbq bandwidth 10 Mbit rate 2 Mbit allot 1514 cell 8 weight 100 Kbit prio 3 maxburst 20 avpkt 1000

   # tc class add dev eth1 parent 1:1 classid 1:3 cbq bandwidth 10 Mbit rate 8 Mbit allot 1514 cell 8 weight 800 Kbit prio 5 maxburst 20 avpkt 1000

We will check the CBQ configuration for u32 and route filters separately. The next section starts with how u32 filters are configured. (see Figure 19.24)

19.11   U32 FILTERS

Commands for Setting Up u32 Filters

   # /root/work/iproute/iproute2-ss050607/tc/tc filter add dev eth1 parent 1:0 protocol ip prio 1 u32 match ip dst 192.168.2.101 match ip sport 23 0xfff flowid 1:2

```
288 Size of "sk_buff_head": 12 bytes
289 >> base 12
290
291 ------------------------------------------------
292   hex: 0xc
293 decimal: 12
294   octal: 014
295   binary: 0b1100
296 ------------------------------------------------
297 >> print -x (*(struct sk_buff_head *)(0xced1a88c + 0x5c + 0x0c))
298 struct sk_buff_head {
299     next = 0xced1a8f4
300     prev = 0xced1a8f4
301     qlen = 0x0
302     lock = spinlock_t {
303     }
304 }
305
306 >> print -x (*(struct sk_buff_head *)(0xced1a88c + 0x5c + 0x0c + 0x0c))
307 struct sk_buff_head {
308     next = 0xced1a900
309     prev = 0xced1a900
310     qlen = 0x0
311     lock = spinlock_t {
312     }
313 }
```

Figure 19.23. Examine sk_buff's Queued on Qdisc (contd.).

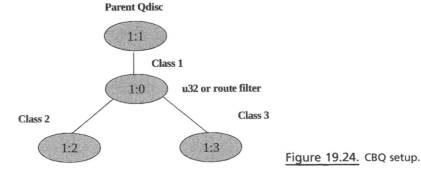

Figure 19.24. CBQ setup.

/root/work/iproute/iproute2-ss050607/tc/tc filter add dev eth1 parent 1:0 protocol ip prio 1 u32 match ip dst 192.168.2.102 match ip sport 80 0xfff flowid 1:3

Here the filter is set up for traffic classes—that is, class 2 and class 3.

If the destination is IP 192.168.2.101 and the source port is 23, then the packet that matches this specification must be queued in class 2.

```
53 >> fsym dev_base
54    ADDR  OFFSET SECTION    NAME            TYPE
55 ================================================
56 0xc02804d8    0 GLOBAL_DATA  dev_base       (unknown)
57 ================================================
58 1 symbol found

59 >> print -x (*(int *)0xc02804d8)
60 0xc0280380
61 >> print -x (*(net_device *)0xc0280380)->next
62 (struct net_device *) 0xc02aa3e0
63 >> print -x (*(net_device *)0xc02aa3e0)->next
64 (struct net_device *) 0xcee2c000
65 >> print -x (*(net_device *)0xcee2c000)->next
66 (struct net_device *) 0xcee2c800

67 >> print -x (*(net_device *)0xcee2c800)
68 struct net_device {
69    name = "eth1"

      . . .
223    qdisc = 0xc2da5800
      . . .
263 }
```

Figure 19.25. Access qdisc field for net_device object.

If the destination is IP 192.168.2.102 and the source port is 80, then the packet that matches this specification must be queued in class 3.

First we can find out the *net_device* structure for the interface from Fig. 19.25. For this, we get the address of the *dev_base* list using the fsym command in lcrash at line 53, where *dev_base* symbol is a list that contains the *net_device* for each network interface in the system. Then we can walk through the *dev_base* list to find out the required *net_device* struct. In our case we are looking for eth1 network device, so we walk through the device list. We can see this from lines 59–65, and finally we print the *net_device* struct for the required device at line 67. Basically we are looking for the qdisc data structure address from the *net_device* struct, which is at line 223. The qdisc data structure of the *net_device* represents the queueing discipline for that network interface. In this case it is the CBQ queueing discipline.

Using the qdisc object address from the *net_device* struct here, we are checking the enqueue field, which is a function pointer; this got initialized to the *cbq_enqueue ( )* function when the Linux system booted up. This function gets called for enqueueing the packets. From Fig. 19.26 we access the qdisc object and then check the value for the enqueue field at line 267. Then using this address of the enqueue field, we check for which function is pointing to the enqueue field at line 300.

The data field from the qdisc object in Fig. 19.26 is an anonymous pointer which is a place holder for the private data strucutures of the queueing discilpline. In the case of CBQ queueing discipline, this data field points to the *cbq_sched_data*

```
265 >> print -x (*(Qdisc *)0xc2da5800)
266 struct Qdisc {
267      enqueue = 0xc01e4494
268      dequeue = 0xc01e4d0c
         . . .


297      data = ""
298 }
299
300 >> fsym 0xc01e4494
301     ADDR  OFFSET SECTION    NAME           TYPE
302 ==========================================
303 0xc01e4494    0 LOCAL_TEXT  cbq_enqueue    (unknown)
304 ==========================================
305 1 symbol found
```

Figure 19.26. Examine enqueue routine for Q discipline.

```
306 >> print -x (*(cbq_sched_data *)(0xc2da5800 + 0x5c))
307 struct cbq_sched_data {
308      classes = {
309          [0] 0xc2da58e4     --------> class 1:0
310          [1] 0xcf72f200     --------> class 1:1
311          [2] 0xcf72f600     --------> class 1:2
312          [3] 0xcf72fc00     --------> class 1:3


         . . .
401          filter_list = 0xc5d21bfc
         . . .
470 }
```

Figure 19.27. Access list of classes for cbq queueing discipline.

structure. Basically, the *cbq_sched_data* struct contains the information about the classes setup, *filter_list* configured for the classes, and so on.

The *cbq_sched_data* struct contains the information about the classes in CBQ. We can see from Fig. 19.27 that it contains an array of classes (*cbq_class* struct) which are configured for CBQ queueing discipline. In this case we configured a parent qdisc class 1:0 at line 309; this parent qdisc class has a child class 1:1 at line 310, and this child class has again two child classes 1:2 and 1:3 at lines 311 and 312. The basic structure for this hierarchy is shown in Fig. 19.24.

Then we can see the filter is set for this class hierarchy. At line 401 the *filter_list* field of *cbq_sched_data* struct contains the address of the root data structure of the u32 filter.

To see the information in the *cbq_class* structure, we just checked the parent qdisc class information in Fig. 19.28. We can see the classid of the class at line 476 and

```
472 >> print -x (*(cbq_class *)0xc2da58e4)    ----------> class 1:0 parent
473 struct cbq_class {

    . . .

476     classid = 0x10000
477     priority = 0x7

    . . .

499     children = 0xcf72f200
500     q = 0xc5ee8bbc

    . . .

526     filter_list = 0xc5d21bfc ---------------> filter

    . . .

547 }
```

Figure 19.28. Examine cbq-class object.

then the priority of the class at line 477; and we can also see if this class has any children or not at line 499, qdisc for the class at line 500, and finally the *filter_list* at line 526.

Using the *filter_list* address from the parent qdisc class, we check the root data structure for filter which is *tcf_proto* structure in Fig. 19.29.

This structure contains the information about which type of filter is configured. In this case it is u32 filter. This we have verified by checking the function pointer classify at line 553 and then checking the symbol at this address, which is *u32_classify()* function at line 562. Then using the root field value, we check the *tc_u_hnode* structure at line 571 which maintains a table of *tc_u_knode* structure at line 578 for each u32 filter.

Using the address of the first entry from the ht[ ] table of the *tc_u_hnode* struct, we check the *tc_u_knode* struct at line 595 in Fig. 19.30. This tc_u_knode struct contains the address of next knode struct at line 597. The struct *tcf_result* at line 601 contains the information about the class for which the filter is set. The struct *tc_u32_sel* at line 606 contains the information about the number of filters set at line 609 and about the *tc_u32_key* struct for each filter at line 615.

Using the sizeof value for struct *tc_u_knode.sel* (exact offset of struct *tc_u32_sel* in struct *tc_u_knode*) and the sizeof value for struct *tc_u32_sel*, we check the exact values of keys array of struct *tc_u_knode*. nkeys from Fig. 19.30 represents the number of elements for keys array. In this case, one for IP addr and the other for sport. So we check the first element of keys array, which is a struct *tc_u32_key* at line 673 for IP addr and then again at line 681 for sport in Fig. 19.31.

We repeated the same procedure as above for checking the u32 filter data structure for class 1:3 in Figs. 19.32 and 19.33.

19.12 ROUTE FILTERS

Commands for Setting Up the Route Filter

```
[root@localhost root]# ip route add 192.168.2.101 via 192.168.2.100 realm 2
[root@localhost root]# ip route add 192.168.2.102 via 192.168.2.100 realm 3
```

```
549 >> print -x (*(tcf_proto *)0xc5d21bfc)
550 struct tcf_proto {

      . . .
552     root = 0xc629070c
553     classify = 0xc01f08c0

      . . .
556     classid = 0x10000

      . . .
560 }
561
562 >> fsym 0xc01f08c0
563    ADDR  OFFSET SECTION    NAME              TYPE
564 ============================================
565 0xc01f08c0    0 LOCAL_TEXT u32_classify     (unknown)
566 ============================================
567 1 symbol found
568
569
570 >> print -x (*(tc_u_hnode *)0xc629070c)
571 struct tc_u_hnode {

      . . .
578     ht = {
579           [0] 0xc5ee8ddc
580     }
581 }
```

Figure 19.29. Access tc_u_hnode object from tcf_proto pointer.

[root@localhost root]# tc filter add dev eth1 parent 1:0 protocol ip prio 100
    route to 3 flowid 1:3
[root@localhost root]# tc filter add dev eth1 parent 1:0 protocol ip prio 100
    route to 2 flowid 1:2

Here we are setting up the route filter based on the destination IP addresses 192.168.2.101 and 192.168.2.102. If the destination of the packet is 192.168.2.101, then this packet is enqueued in class 2. If the destination of the packet is 192.168.2.102, then this packet is enqueued in class 3.

We are using the ip and tc commands for setting up the route-based filter for each class.

The ip command will update the forwarding information base (FIB) database with the realm setting for the class.

The tc command will update the route filter data structure with the classid for the particular realm.

```
595 >> print -x (*(tc_u_knode *)0xc5ee8ddc)
596 struct tc_u_knode {
597        next = 0xc91e0094

        . . .

601        res = struct tcf_result {
602               class = 0xcf72f600
603               classid = 0x10002   -----------> class 1:2
604        }

        . . .

606        sel = struct tc_u32_sel {

               . . .

609               nkeys = 0x2

               . . .

615               keys = {
616                      [0] struct tc_u32_key {

                          . . .

621                      }
622               }
623        }
624 }
```

Figure 19.30. Access filter key for class 1:2.

19.13   FIB TABLE lcrash OUTPUT FOR SETTING UP THE REALM USING ip COMMAND

From Fig. 19.34, first we find out the address of the *fib_tables* global variable, which is defined as an array of *fib_table* struct. Using the fsym command at line 48, we get the address of *fib_tables*. Then using this address, we dump the 255 words (32-bit) to get the address of *fib_table*, which is a default routing table when the system comes up. At location 255 from the dumped output, we get the address of *fib_table* at line 118. Using print command at line 119, we print the contents of the *fib_table*. We can see the table id at line 121, and then we can see the insert function pointer pointing to function address at line 124; in this case it is pointing to fn_hash_insert() function this we can see at lines 133–136. The data pointer of fib_table struct at lines 130 is a place holder for private data structures of FIB database. This data pointer is pointing to the fn_hash struct of the FIB database which contains information about the different zones.

Using the size of the struct *fib_table*, which is 0×24 bytes, we print the contents of *fn_hash* structure (data field of *fib_table* struct) at line 139 in Fig. 19.35. *fn_hash* struct contains array of *fn_zone* structures and the *fn_zone_list*. Each element in the *fn_zones* array represents each bit in the netmask (32-bit) field. We added the realms using 32-bit netmask values, so the 32nd element of the *fn_zones* array contains the address of *fn_zone* structure for this entry of the routing table at line 174.

```
627 >> sizeof -o tc_u_knode.sel
628 Offset: 28 bytes.
629 >> base 28
631 -------------------------------------------
632    hex: 0x1c
633 decimal: 28
634   octal: 034
635  binary: 0b11100
636 -------------------------------------------
663 >> sizeof tc_u32_sel
664 Size of "tc_u32_sel": 16 bytes
665 >> base 16
667 -------------------------------------------
668    hex: 0x10
669 decimal: 16
670   octal: 020
671  binary: 0b10000
672 -------------------------------------------
673 >> print -x (*(tc_u32_key *)(0xc5ee8ddc + 0x1c + 0x10))
674 struct tc_u32_key {
675      mask = 0xffffffff
676      val = 0x6502a8c0      ------------> ipaddr
677      off = 0x10
678      offmask = 0x0
679 }
680
681 >> print -x (*(tc_u32_key *)(0xc5ee8ddc + 0x1c + 0x10 + 0x10))
682 struct tc_u32_key {
683      mask = 0xff0f
684      val = 0x1700 --------------> sport
685      off = 0x14
686      offmask = 0x0
687 }
```

Figure 19.31. Examining filter keys for class 1:2.

Next we print the contents of fn_zone struct at line 179 in Fig. 36. The *fn_zone* struct contains a pointer to the hash table at line 182, a hash table divisor value at line 184, a hashmask for the hash table indexing at line 185, an order of the hash table at line 186, and the netmask of the zone at line 187.

Then using the pointer address of the *fib_node* hash table, we dump the 16 words (32-bit) to get the address for the *fib_node* struct, which contains the *fn_info* struct that represents the routing table entries. Here the array of *fib_node* is initialized and contains the *fib_node* addresses at 12th and 15th index of the array. We

```
689 >> print -x (*(tc_u_knode *)0xc91e0094)
690 struct tc_u_knode {
691     next = 0x0
        . . .
695     res = struct tcf_result {
696         class = 0xcf72fc00
697         classid = 0x10003        ---------> class 1:3
698     }
        . . .
700     sel = struct tc_u32_sel {
        . . .
703         nkeys = 0x2
        . . .
709         keys = {
710             [0] struct tc_u32_key {
            . . . .
715             }
716         }
717     }
718 }
```

Figure 19.32. Access filter key for class 1:3.

```
740 >> print -x (*(tc_u32_key *)(0xc91e0094 + 0x1c + 0x10))
741 struct tc_u32_key {
742     mask = 0xffffffff
743     val = 0x6602a8c0 ----------> ipaddr
744     off = 0x10
745     offmask = 0x0
746 }
748 >> print -x (*(tc_u32_key *)(0xc91e0094 + 0x1c + 0x10 + 0x10))
749 struct tc_u32_key {
750     mask = 0xff0f
751     val = 0x5000 ----------> sport
752     off = 0x14
753     offmask = 0x0
```

Figure 19.33. Examining filter keys for class 1:3.

start with the first *fib_node* address from the array at line 195. The *fib_node* struct contains the address of *fn_info* struct at line 198. Then the key value is the destination address at line 200. Also we can find the values of tos, type, scope, and state at lines 202–205.

```
48 >> fsym fib_tables
49    ADDR OFFSET SECTION   NAME            TYPE
50 ==================================================
51 0xc03096c0   0 GLOBAL_DATA fib_tables      (unknown)
52 ==================================================
53 1 symbol found
54 >> dump 0xc03096c0 255
55 0xc03096c0: 00000000 00000000 00000000 00000000 : ...............
. . . . . .
118 0xc0309ab0: 00000000 00000000 cee79074       : .........t...
119 >> print -x (*(fib_table *)cee79074)
120 struct fib_table {
121     tb_id = 0xfe
   . . .
124     tb_insert = 0xc02203c8
   . . .
130     tb_data = ""
131 }
132
133 >> fsym 0xc02203c8
134    ADDR OFFSET SECTION   NAME            TYPE
135 ==================================================
136 0xc02203c8   0 LOCAL_TEXT fn_hash_insert   (unknown)
137 ==================================================
138 1 symbol found
```

Figure 19.34. Examining fib_tables.

```
139 >> print -x (*(fn_hash *)(0xcee79074 + 0x24))
140 struct fn_hash {
141     fn_zones = {
142         [0] 0xced302fc
       . . .
150         [8] 0xcf53ff2c
       . . .
158         [16] 0xcf53ff54
       . . .
166         [24] 0xced302d4
       . . .
174         [32] 0xc5e04bbc    ----------------> added realm 2 & 3
175     }
176     fn_zone_list = 0xc5e04bbc
177 }
```

Figure 19.35. Examining fn_hash object from fib_table.

```
179 >> print -x (*(fn_zone *)0xc5e04bbc)
180 struct fn_zone {
181      fz_next = 0xced302d4
182      fz_hash = 0xc5d43614   ------------> pointer to pointer of type fib_node
183      fz_nent = 0x2
184      fz_divisor = 0x10
185      fz_hashmask = 0xf
186      fz_order = 0x20
187      fz_mask = 0xffffffff
188 }
190 >> dump 0xc5d43614 16     --------------------> fib_node*[16]
191 0xc5d43614: 00000000 00000000 00000000 00000000 : ...............
       . . . .
194 0xc5d43644: cefa63e4 00000000 00000000 cefa63cc : .c...........c..
195 >> print -x (*(fib_node *)cefa63e4)
196 struct fib_node {
197      fn_next = 0x0
198      fn_info = 0xcee4566c
199      fn_key = fn_key_t {
200           datum = 0x6602a8c0
201      }
202      fn_tos = 0x0

203      fn_type = 0x1
204      fn_scope = 0x0
205      fn_state = 0x0
206 }
```

Figure 19.36. Examining fib_node object from fn_zone.

Then using the *fn_info* address from the *fib_node* struct in Fig. 19.37 at line 208, we print the contents of the *fn_info* struct. The *fn_info* struct contains another data structure *fib_nh* at line 235, which has the routing table entries, and the field *fn_nhs* value at line 232 informs about how may *fib_nh* struct entries are present in the array of *fib_nh* table at line 234.

And finally we print the contents of the *fib_nh* struct from the array of *fib_nh* table at line 248 using the sizeof value of *fib_info* struct to get the exact offset from the base address of *fib_info* struct. The *fib_nh* struct contains the information for the *net_device* at line 250 and contains flags, scope, weight, and power at lines 251–254.

The realm value that we set from the command line is at line 255, and the gateway address is at line 257.

To check the realm value for class 2 again, the same procedure as above is followed. We can the see Fig. 19.38 to check the realm value for class 2.

19.14 lcrash OUTPUT FOR SETTING UP ROUTE FILTER USING tc COMMAND

First we can find out the *net_device* structure for the interface from Fig. 19.39. For this, we get the address of the *dev_base* list using the fsym command in lcrash at line 63, where *dev_base* symbol is a list that contains the *net_device* for each network interface in the system. Then we can walk through the *dev_base* list to find out the required *net_device* struct. In our case we are looking for the eth1 network device, so we walk through the device list. We can see this from lines 69–76, and finally we

```
208 >> print -x (*(fib_info *)0xcee4566c)
209 struct fib_info {
210      fib_next = 0xcee45e64

      . . .

218      fib_protocol = 0x3

      . . .

232      fib_nhs = 0x1

      . . .

234      fib_nh = {
235          [0] struct fib_nh {

          . . .

244          }
245      }
246 }
248 >> print -x (*(fib_nh *)(0xcee4566c + 0x50))    ------------> (addr of fib_info) + sizeof (fib_info)
249 struct fib_nh {
250      nh_dev = 0xcee2b800
251      nh_flags = 0x0
252      nh_scope = 0xfe
253      nh_weight = 0x1
254      nh_power = 0x0
255      nh_tclassid = 0x3 -----------------> realm 3
256      nh_oif = 0x4
257      nh_gw = 0x6402a8c0
258 }
```

Figure 19.37. Accessing fib_nh object from fib_info for realm 3.

print the *net_device* struct for the required device at line 77. Basically, we are looking for the qdisc data structure address from the *net_device* struct, which is at line 233. The qdisc data structure of the *net_device* represents the queueing discipline for that network interface.

Using the qdisc object address from the *net_device* struct in Fig. 19.40, we are checking the enqueue field, which is a function pointer; this got initialized to the *cbq_enqueue( )* function when the Linux system booted up. This function gets called for enqueueing the packets. From Fig. 19.39 we access the qdisc object and then check the value for the enqueue field at line 277. Then using this address of the enqueue field, we check for which function is pointing to the enqueue field at line 310.

The data field from the qdisc object in Fig. 19.40 is an anonymous pointer which is a place holder for the private data strucutures of the queueing discilpline. In the case of CBQ queueing discipline, this data field points to the *cbq_sched_data* structure. Basically, the *cbq_sched_data* struct contains the information about the classes setup, *filter_list* configured for the classes, and so on.

```
260 >> print -x (*(fib_node *)cefa63cc)
  261 struct fib_node {
  262      fn_next = 0x0
  263      fn_info = 0xcee45e64
  264      fn_key = fn_key_t {
  265          datum = 0x6502a8c0
  266      }
  267      fn_tos = 0x0
  268      fn_type = 0x1
  269      fn_scope = 0x0
  270      fn_state = 0x0
  271 }
  273 >> print -x (*(fib_info *)0xcee45e64)
  274 struct fib_info {
           . . .
  283      fib_protocol = 0x3
           . . .
  297      fib_nhs = 0x1
  299      fib_nh = {
  300          [0] struct fib_nh {
           . . .
  309          }
  310      }
  311 }
  313 >> print -x (*(fib_nh *)(0xcee45e64 + 0x50)) ------------> (addr of fib_info) + sizeof (fib_info)
  314 struct fib_nh {
  315      nh_dev = 0xcee2b800
  316      nh_flags = 0x0
  317      nh_scope = 0xfe
  318      nh_weight = 0x1
  319      nh_power = 0x0
  320      nh_tclassid = 0x2 ----------------> realm 2
  321      nh_oif = 0x4
  322      nh_gw = 0x6402a8c0
  323 }
```

Figure 19.38. Accessing fib_nh object from fib_info for realm 2.

The cbq_sched_data struct contains the information about the classes in CBQ. We can see from Fig. 19.40 that it contains an array of classes (*cbq_class* struct) which are configured for CBQ queueing discipline. In this case we configured a parent qdisc class 1:0 at line 319; this parent qdisc class has a child class 1:1 at line 320, and this child class has again two child classes 1:2 and 1:3 at lines 321 and 322. The basic structure for this hierarchy is shown in Fig. 19.24.

```
63 >> fsym dev_base
64    ADDR OFFSET SECTION   NAME          TYPE
65 ==========================================
66 0xc02803d8   0 GLOBAL_DATA  dev_base      (unknown)
67 ==========================================
68 1 symbol found
69 >> print -x (*(int *)0xc02803d8)
70 0xc0280280
71 >> print -x (*(net_device *)0xc0280280)->next
72 (struct net_device *) 0xc02aa2e0
73 >> print -x (*(net_device *)0xc02aa2e0)->next
74 (struct net_device *) 0xcee25000
75 >> print -x (*(net_device *)0xcee25000)->next
76 (struct net_device *) 0xcee25800
77 >> print -x (*(net_device *)0xcee25800)
78 struct net_device {
79     name = "eth1"
       . . .
233    qdisc = 0xca2b7c00

       . . .
273 }
```

Figure 19.39. Access qdisc object for net_device.

```
275 >> print -x (*(Qdisc *)0xca2b7c00)
276 struct Qdisc {
277    enqueue = 0xc01e4494
278    dequeue = 0xc01e4d0c

       . . .
307    data = ""
308 }
310 >> fsym 0xc01e4494
311    ADDR  OFFSET SECTION   NAME          TYPE
312 ==========================================
313 0xc01e4494   0 LOCAL_TEXT  cbq_enqueue     (unknown)
314 ==========================================
315 1 symbol found
316 >> print -x (*(cbq_sched_data *)(0xca2b7c00 + 0x5c))
317 struct cbq_sched_data {
318    classes = {
319        [0] 0xca2b7ce4     ----------> 1:0
320        [1] 0xcfdfd600     ----------> 1:1
321        [2] 0xcfdfdc00     ----------> 1:2
322        [3] 0xcfdfd200     ----------> 1:3

       . . .
480 }
```

Figure 19.40. Accessing cbq_class objects for queue discipline.

```
482 >> print -x (*(cbq_class *)0xca2b7ce4)      ---------> 1:0
483 struct cbq_class {
484      next = (nil)
485      next_alive = 0x0
486      classid = 0x10000
487      priority = 0x7
           . . .
509      children = 0xcfdfd600
510      q = 0xcef86eec
           . . .
536      filter_list = 0xc60a89bc     ---------------> route classifier filter
           . . .
557 }
558
559 >> print -x (*(tcf_proto *)0xc60a89bc) -------------> filter_list from 1:0
560 struct tcf_proto {
           . . .
562      root = 0xc715f800
563      classify = 0xc01f36dc
           . . .
566      classid = 0x10000
           . . .
570 }
573 >> fsym 0xc01f36dc
574     ADDR  OFFSET SECTION    NAME           TYPE
575 ============================================
576 0xc01f36dc    0 LOCAL_TEXT  route4_classify   (unknown)
577 ============================================
578 1 symbol found
```

Figure 19.41. Examining tcf_proto object for class1:0.

To see the information in the *cbq_class* struct, we just examined the parent qdisc class information in Fig. 19.41. We can see (a) the classid of the class at line 486, (b) the priority of the class at line 487, and (c) whether this class has any children or not at line 509, (d) the qdisc for the class at line 510, and (e) the *filter_list* at line 536.

Using the *filter_list* address from the parent qdisc class, we check the root data structure for the filter, which is *tcf_proto* struct in Fig. 19.41.

This structure contains the information about which type of filter is configured. In this case, it is route filter. We have verified this by checking the function pointer classify at line 563 and then checking the symbol at this address, which is *route4_classify()* function at line 573.

The *route4_head* data structure contains the hash table of type struct *route4_bucket*, and this *route4_bucket* data structure again maintains a table for *route4_filter*.

```
579 >> print -x (*(route4_head *)0xc715f800) ------------> root from tcf_proto of 1:0
580 struct route4_head {
           . . .
663      table = {
              . . .
666           [2] 0xcccb28b4        ---------> realm 2 flowid 1:2
667           [3] 0xcccb2284        ---------> realm 3 flowid 1:3
              . . .
921      }
922 }
924 >> print -x (*(route4_bucket *)0xcccb28b4)    ------------> realm 2
925 struct route4_bucket {
926      ht = {
              . . .
959           [32] 0xccbc52fc
960      }
961 }
963 >> print -x (*(route4_filter *)0xccbc52fc)
964 struct route4_filter {
965      next = 0x0
966      id = 0x2
967      iif = 0x0
968      res = struct tcf_result {
969           class = 0xcfdfdc00
970           classid = 0x10002         ---------> class 1:2
971      }
972      police = 0x0
973      handle = 0xffff0002
974      bkt = 0xcccb28b4
975 }
```

Figure 19.42. Examining route4_filter for class 1:2.

Using the root field value from *tcf_proto* struct, we can see the contents of *route4_head* data structure at line 579 in Fig. 19.42. This *route4_head* data structure maintains a hash table. From lines 666–667 we can see the values for new *route4_bucket* structure for class 2 and class 3.

Based on the address at line 666, we can see the contents of *route4_bucket* struct at line 924 which again maintains a table of *route4_filter* struct. This *route4_filter* struct contains the information about the class. The *tcf_result* struct contains the information about the class address and the class id at lines 969 and 970.

Figure 19.43 shows the lcrash output for the class 3 route filter; again the same procedure as explained above is followed.

```
977 >> print -x (*(route4_bucket *)0xcccb2284)      ---------> realm 3
978 struct route4_bucket {
979     ht = {
                . . .
1012          [32] 0xccbc51bc
1013      }
1014 }
1015
1016 >> print -x (*(route4_filter *)0xccbc51bc)
1017 struct route4_filter {
1018     next = 0x0
1019     id = 0x3
1020     iif = 0x0
1021     res = struct tcf_result {
1022          class = 0xcfdfd200
1023          classid = 0x10003      ---------> class 1:3
1024      }
1025     police = 0x0
1026     handle = 0xffff0003
1027     bkt = 0xcccb2284
1028 }
```

Figure 19.43. Examining route4_filter for class 1:3.

19.15 NETLINK DATA STRUCTURE

19.15.1 *nl_table*

nl_table is an array of pointers to sock structure. Each element of *nl_table* array represents a NETLINK protocol family—for example, *NETLINK_ROUTE, NETLINK_FIREWALL*, and so on. From Fig. 19.44 we can see how we got the pointer address to the *nl_table* lines 42–45. Then by derefrencing the pointer address we get the first sock element of the *nl_table*. Here we are just checking the sock structure for the *data_ready* function pointers and to which function it is pointing.

19.15.2 *rtnetlink_link*

rtnetlink_links is defined as an array of pointers to *rtnetlink_link* data structure. Each *rtnetlink_link* data structure corresponds to a rtnetlink command—for example, RTM_NEWQDISC, which is a command for adding new qdisc. Figure 19.45 shows the lcrash steps for accessing the *rtnetlink_links* table.

```
42 >> whatis nl_table
43    ADDR SECTION    NAME            TYPE
44 ======================================
45 0xc0308560 LOCAL_DATA   nl_table         (unknown)
46 ======================================
47 >> print -x (*(int *)0xc0308560)
48 0xc12d7030
49 >> print -x (*(sock *)0xc12d7030)
50 struct sock {
       .....
587     protinfo = union {
         ....
2301        af_netlink = 0xcfff9334
         ....
2322     data_ready = 0xc01f62f4
         ....
2327 }
         ....
2329 >> fsym 0xc01f62f4
2330    ADDR OFFSET SECTION    NAME            TYPE
2331 =================================================================
2332 0xc01f62f4    0 GLOBAL_TEXT netlink_data_ready  (unknown)
2333 =================================================================
2334 1 symbol found
2335 >> print -x (*(netlink_opt *)0xcfff9334) ----> address of af_netlink from protinfo union
2336 struct netlink_opt {
         ....
2354     data_ready = 0xc01dc9e4
2355 }
2356
2357 >> fsym 0xc01dc9e4
2358    ADDR OFFSET SECTION    NAME            TYPE
2359 =======================================
2360 0xc01dc9e4    0 LOCAL_TEXT  rtnetlink_rcv    (unknown)
2361 =======================================
2362 1 symbol found
```

Figure 19.44. Examine nl_table.

```
42 >> whatis rtnetlink_links
43    ADDR SECTION    NAME          TYPE
44 ============================================================
45 0xc03079c0 GLOBAL_DATA  rtnetlink_links    (unknown)
46 ============================================================
48 >> print -x (*(int *)0xc03079c0)
49 0xc02aab60
51 >> print -x (*(rtnetlink_link *)(0xc02aab60 + 0xa0))
52 struct rtnetlink_link {
53     doit = 0xc01e17fc
54     dumpit = 0x0
55 }
57 >> fsym 0xc01e17fc
58    ADDR  OFFSET SECTION    NAME          TYPE
59 ============================================================
60 0xc01e17fc   0 LOCAL_TEXT  tc_modify_qdisc   (unknown)
61 ============================================================
62 1 symbol found
65 In above print statement,i.e
67 (0xc02aab60 + 0xa0)) -------> How we got the offset 0xa0 ?
69 In rtnetlink_rcv_msg(), link = &rtnetlink_links[type];
71 In this case "type" is 0x14 i.e 20 which is the value of RTM_NEWQDISC ( from tc user code) and
72 in kernel this value is assined as i.e type = nlh->nlmsg_type in rtnetlink_rcv_msg().
74 so here the address of rtnetlink_links is 0xc03079c0 and after derefrencing this address we get the
75 first element of rtnetlink_links[NPROTO] as 0xc02aab60 (pointer to the struct rtnetlink_link).
77 struct rtnetlink_link * rtnetlink_links[NPROTO];
79 The sizeof rtnetlink_link is 8 bytes.
81 0x14 * 8 = 0xa0
```

Figure 19.45. Examine &rt_netlinkLinks.

19.16 SUMMARY

lcrash is a very powerful tool to analyze Linux crash dumps.

dwarfextract is lcrash utility to generate kerntypes for the complete set of kernel datatypes. This comes with the 7.0.1-27 version of *lkcdutils*.

fsyms command can be used to get the address for kernel global symbols.

Double pointers can be dereferenced by using the *dump* command as is shown in Fig. 19.2, where a file table is dumped.

Kernel data structures are complex in nature and they need to be very clearly traversed in small steps as is illustrated in different sections.

20

NEXT EDITION

KERNEL 2.6 DESCRIPTION

This chapter discusses TCP/IP implementation on kernel 2.6. There are not many changes as far as basic framework and design are concerned. TCP/IP stack implementation has evolved over the period and with every release. These changes will be with respect to the performance enhancement or introduction of new features or congestion control algorithms. For example, in 2.6 there is a new feature added from 2.6.18 onward to DMA TCP data to the user buffer (*CONFIG_NET_DMA*). This is also called receive offloading, where copying of socket data from the kernel to the user buffer is done by programing the DMA channel, hence saving a lot of CPU cycles by offloading the job to the DMA engine; this is also known as I/OAT DMA. This feature requires some modifications to the device layer, the TCP layer, and the socket layer, which will be discussed in detail.

Kernel is preemptive though not completely preemptive. There are preemption points within the kernel where high-priority tasks can cause the kernel to preempt. When we enter a critical region within the kernel, we disable preemption; and while exiting, we enable kernel preemption. While enabling preemption, we check whether rescheduling is required. If so, a scheduler is called. The scheduler checks whether the preempting thread has higher priority than the currently running thread. If so, it preempts the kernel; otherwise, not. This topic is discussed in detail.

UDP

We have not discussed UDP sockets from the point of view of application and kernel implementation. We will see how basic UDP client and server program is written. Since UDP is a connectionless protocol, it does not need to initiate and close connection for every interaction between the two ends. The client just needs to know the port number and the IP address of the server to which it sends a message, and that is it. The life cycle of the UDP connection involves just sending a message to the server, and the server needs to take action. The UDP echo client–server application requires two packets to be exchanged between the client and the server. One UDP packet is sent from the client to the server, and the other packet is an echo message back from the server to the client. If it were TCP, three packets are required to initiate the connection, minimum three packets for closing the connection and 2 packets for echo request and response. So, a total of minimum eight packets are required in the case of TCP to complete an echo request and a response connection life cycle. But UDP is an unreliable protocol unlike TCP, which keeps account of each byte received at the other end. In all, UDP is a lightweight protocol and is used for a very different type of communication.

In the next revision we will discuss different aspects related to the UDP protocol and will also discuss kernel implementation of UDP sockets. We will see how UDP packets are handled by the kernel. Then we will see how a socket is recognized corresponding to the UDP packet—that is, what hash tables are looked up for UDP connections.

MULTICASTING AND BROADCASTING

Until now we have seen connections that send and receive packet to and from a single host. There are different applications that have the requirement of sending a message from one point to many hosts in or even outside the network. For example, when a diskless client is booting, it needs to know about its own IP address. In such cases, it sends out a broadcast RARP message to all the hosts in the subnet. The machine that knows its IP address will respond and sends back a unicast reply to the originator of the machine. There are many different applications that require messages to be sent out to multiple hosts, and this is possible because of the broadcasting technique. The UDP protocol supports the broadcasting of messages while TCP doesn't.

In the similar way, there are requirements that require sending messages to multiple hosts but not all hosts in the subnet. This is also possible with the help of the multicasting technique. This requires multicast message receivers to register themselves with the kernel to receive multicast messages destined for specific multicast addresses. The biggest example is the SAP or routing daemons. Once again, UDP supports multicasting and TCP doesn't because the latter is a connection-oriented protocol, which means that the two ends are fixed.

We will discuss broadcast and multicasting on UDP protocol, how Ethernet addresses are mapped to multicast addresses, and how applications register with the kernel to receive messages destined for specific multicast address.

FRAGMENTATION AND REASSEMBLY

We have already discussed fragmentation and reassembly in this version of the book but not in much detail. In the next version we will see complete implementation of fragmentation and reassembly unit.

IP FORWARDING

Forwarding is functionality implemented at the router. Linux can act as a fully functional router. Link layer header modifications may be required before forwarding a frame to the outgoing interface. In the next version we will see at what point we come to know that the packet needs to be forwarded, and we will learn how to handle those packets.

ADDING NEW INTERFACE

We will learn how *ifconfig* works within the kernel and how to interact with the network devices. We will also learn how to configure virtual interfaces for the single physical network interface.

Ipv6

Ipv6 will be explained in complete totality, and its implementation in the kernel will be covered comprehensively.

BIBLIOGRAPHY

Maurice J. Bach, *Design of the UNIX Operating System*, Prentice-Hall ECS Professional, Englewood Cliffs, NJ, 1986.

Christian Benvenuti, *Understanding Linux Internals*, O'Reilly, 2005.

Daniel P. Bovet and Marco Cesati, *Understanding the Linux Kernel*, Second Edition, O'Reilly, 2003.

Intel® 64 and IA-32, *Architectures Software Developer's Manual*, Vol. 3A: *System Programming Guide*.

Mike Fisk and Wu-chun Feng, *Dynamic Adjustment of TCP Window Sizes*, Los Alamos Unclassified Report LA-UR 00-3321, 2000.

Matthew Mathis et al., *Forward Acknowledgment: Refining TCP Congestion Control*, Pittsburgh Supercomputing Center, ACM, 1996.

W. Richard Stevens, *TCP/IP Illustrated*, Vol. 1: The Protocols, Addison-Wesley, Reading, MA, 1994.

W. Richard Stevens, *Advanced Programming in the UNIX Environment*, Addison-Wesley, Reading, MA, 1992.

Richard Stevens, Bill Fenner, and Andrew M. Rudoff, *Unix Network Programming*, Vol. I, Prentice-Hall, India, 2005.

Richard Stevens, *Unix Network Programming*, Vol. II, Prentice-Hall, India, 2002.

RFC 1388: G. Malken et al., RIP version 2 Carrying Additional Information, 1993.

RFC 1247: J. May et al., OSPF version 2, 1991.

RFC 1349: P. Almquist, Type of Service in the Internet Protocol Suite, 1992.

RFC 1122: R. Braden, Requirement for Internet Hosts—Communication Layer, 1989.

RFC 2018: M. Mathis et al., TCP Selective Acknowledgement Options, 1996.

RFC 1323: V. Jacobson et al., *TCP Extensions for High Performance*, 1992.

RFC 2581: M. Allman et al., *TCP Congestion Control*, 1999.

RFC 2582: S. Floyd et al., *The NewReno Modification to TCP's Fast Recovery Algorithm*, 1999.

RFC 2883: S. Floyd et al., *An Extension to the Selective Acknowledgement (SACK) Option for TCP*, 2000.

RFC 2988: V. Paxson et al., *Computing TCP's Retransmission Timer*, 2000.

RFC 4138: P. Sarolahti et al., *Forward RTO-Recovery (F-RTO)*, 1995.

RFC 3522: Reiner Ludwig et al., *The Eifel Detection Algorithm for TCP*, 2003.

RFC 791: *Internet Protocol*, 1981.

RFC 793: Transmission control protocol, 1981.

Pasi Sarolahti et al., FRTO—A New Recovery Algorithm for TCP Re-transmission Timeouts, University of Helsinki, 7C-2002-07, 2003.

WEBSITES

Werner Almesberger, Linux Network Trac Control | Implementation Overview, www.simpleweb.org/bibliography/articles/general/alm9904.pdf.

Differentiated Services on Linux, http://diffserv.sourceforge.net/.

S. Floyd and V. Jacobson, References On CBQ (Class-Based Queueing), http://ftp.ee.lbl.gov/floyd/cbq.html.

Netlink Sockets Tour, http://www.skyfree.org/linux/kernel_network/netlink.html.

Kernel Korner—Why and How to Use Netlink Socket, http://www.linuxjournal.com/article/7356.

tc-cbq-details(8) Linux man page, http://linux.die.net/man/8/tc-cbq-details.

Linux 2.4 Advanced Routing HOWTO, http://www.linuxdocs.org/HOWTOs/Adv-Routing-HOWTO.html#toc8.

Lcrash Howto, http://lkcd.sourceforge.net/.

http://devresources.linux-foundation.org/dev/iproute2/download/, iproute2 (tc) source.

http://lxr.linux.no/, Linux source.

http://www.kerne.l.org/, download Linux source.

http://lkcd.sourceforge.net/, lcrash.

INDEX

Page numbers followed by *f* indicate figures

Printed and bound by CPI Group (UK) Ltd, Croydon, CR0 4YY

Printed and bound by CPI Group (UK) Ltd, Croydon, CR0 4YY

27/10/2024